Mass Media and Mass Communications in Society

Frederick C. Whitney
California State University
San Diego

Mass Media and Mass Communications in Society

wcb

Wm. C. Brown Company Publishers
Dubuque, Iowa

Copyright © 1975 by Wm. C. Brown Company Publishers

Library of Congress Catalog Card Number: 74-82045

ISBN 0-697-04302-9

All rights reserved. No part of this publication may be reproduced, stored in a retrieval system, or transmitted, in any form or by any means, electronic, mechanical, photocopying, recording, or otherwise, without the prior written permission of the copyright owner.

Second Printing, 1975

Printed in the United States of America

for

my father

in loving memory

CONTENTS

preface xi

overview

1	Communication		3
2	Functions		18
3	Development		31
4	Theory		49

the continua

5	Media Continuum		69
6	Audience Continuum		84

ethics and controls

7	Controls		105
8	Ethics		125

print media

9	Books		142
10	Newspapers		158
11	Magazines		178

electromedia

12	Film		202
13	Radio and Recordings		222
14	Network Television		243
15	TV's Progeny		267

indirect media

16	News Services and Sources		289
17	Advertising		310
18	Public Relations		333

integration and conclusion

19	Personal Media		359
20	The Arts and Cultural Transmission		383
21	Public Opinion and Polls		408
22	Crossroads		429

selected readings 455

index 459

PREFACE

Mass communications has been called the central nervous system of society. This is a good analogy, hinting at deep, complex interrelationships, and emphasizing the living, growing, changing quality of the system through forces only vaguely understood. Contemporary American society is probably more self-consciously aware of its mass communications system than any other in history in what could be characterized, in extending the analogy, as a sort of social hypochondria. For all this preoccupation, Americans seem to be remarkably naive about the scope, nature, and operation of their mass communications network.

Mass communications has often been damned on the one hand as another pollutant, filling heads with specious trivia, beclouding perception, and feeding confusion in the ranks through its rising decibels of noise. Some have already tuned it out.

It has been heralded on the other hand as a catalyst of the social structure offering constantly ever-changing, ever-multiplying views of both fantasy and reality, which by their very diversity enrich one's life and bring him to the brink of truth.

Mass communications is regarded both as the guardian of the status quo and as the radical vehicle of change. It can't be both—but it obviously is.

It is the purpose of this work to explore this and other paradoxes surrounding mass communications, and to try to put them in a perspective that will expose some of the myths surrounding mass media and open avenues to understanding.

In a complex, institutionalized society, one thing is certain — the mass media vicariously provide access to the world. Local, national, and global reality are what is only indirectly perceived through these media. The better their form and nature are understood, the more clearly the world is seen. This is the principal objective herein: to instill a working knowledge of the vast and complex mass communications network so that the student will have the life-long tools with which to gauge the merit of the views it shows him.

There are a number of explanations of media paradoxes in the shape of communication theories. Some theories attack them broadly, some narrowly. Some show a sociological perspective; others take their orientation from journalism; others yet from mathematics. Some are concerned with the channels of communication—the media; others with purpose; others still with audiences. Major communications theories will be explored to see where they lead. These are the approaches that other knowledgeable students have used.

There is some agreement among theories, some disparity. One should be aware of this. All offer something—a probing of the problem. This inventory of varying views becomes a part of the tool kit the student can use as he himself is increasingly exposed to mass communications each succeeding year.

There is no single approach to mass communications—no school answer. In so sweeping a field, one's reaction will depend on one's orientation, one's perspective. The social psychologist will see a different vista than the advertising man; the journalist will have a different frame of reference than the politician. Eschewing these disciplinary approaches, it is the intention of the following chapters to take a more phenomenological approach, to get the big picture, to see the interrelationships of the multiple paths winding through the maze.

It should be apparent that the study of mass communications is truly interdisciplinary. This has been one of the problems in its scrutiny; it has not fit happily into any one academic pigeonhole. It cuts across journalism with its information content and the media. Sociology and social psychology are concerned with audiences large and small, while psychology studies the effect on the individual who composes both. Advertising provides a commercial base and combines with political science and public relations in the crucial question of persuasion—dollars and votes. Economics plays its role in the relative affluence without which mass communications could not exist and in the expanding technology responsible for its development. Most recently, mathematics and engineering have entered media and communications, not only through the computer, but in such things as channel capacity and noise, as well as cybernetics and the feedback phenomenon.

The following will be an integrated approach to mass communications, a distillation from many disciplines of their pertinent contributions into some sort of balanced overview from which the student, according to his bent, can reach some conclusions of his own.

As an aid, a pair of twin continua have been developed, a mass media continuum and continuum of audiences. This device arose from the fact that one of the problems in investigating so dynamic a field as mass communications is that a static matrix on the state of the subject tends to get frozen between the hard covers of a book while the subject matter marches on.

The continua provide for movement, regarding contemporary mass communications less as the culmination of all that has gone before than as a moving point in a logical progression stretching back into the fogs of antiquity and forward toward an only dimly perceived horizon. Such movement can be predictive, if not of the exact future course of mass communications in our society, at least in indicating certain preferred options.

Mass media have always been characterized by twin drives for ever greater speed and ever greater numbers of audience; so has Western society. The continua reflect this. The media continuum and that of audiences are parallel, almost like railroad tracks, to the point where it is pointless to consider one without the other. One, in fact, by itself is useless.

Each of the mass media will be examined in the light of the continuum: its historical development, relationship to other media, and its effect on the audience continuum, which is in a larger sense society. Media are also discussed in terms of their broad social functions and their individual characteristics, which are surprisingly complementary.

This is to say that these discrete media will be viewed not as separate phenomena like caged animals in the zoo, without relationship to one another or to their environment. This will be more a wild-animal-park-of-a-book in which each species is studied in relationship to the rest as well as to the social milieu of which it is, of course, a part.

When one thinks of mass communications, the tendency is to think in terms of its information function. Journalists, whose province this is, were early in the field, and little can be added to their efforts and analyses. However, the emphasis on information has equally tended to shy attention away from such crucial factors as entertainment, advertising, and economic factors; the role of persuasion is frequently downplayed and the whole vague, broad realm of mass communications as a carrier of the culture is generally omitted completely.

The concern herein with mass media will be as a vehicle to gauge their effect. Effect, of course, is effect on people, the individuals who collectively compose the audiences that are media targets. Thus, this is less a book about things than one about people within a certain context, and their paramount role as prime movers within the system.

Effect, of course, implies purpose. Mass communication or any communication does not exist in a vacuum. Some attention will be paid to purpose in mass communications, and also persuasion.

Since this is a book about people, there will be a minimal amount of the sort of statistical data and historical dates one usually encounters; enough only to provide milestones along the path of development.

Finally, since the focus herein is on the exquisite interrelationship of mass communications and society, discussion will be restricted to mass communications in the contemporary United States. This should not prevent American students of the late twentieth century (at whom the book is basically aimed) from enhancing their understanding of their world whether they ever enter any of the mass communications disciplines or not.

ACKNOWLEDGMENTS

Any book in our contemporary society is a joint venture. I have noted this in the chapter on books. However, until I wrote one I had no idea just how extensive the partnership was. Author and publisher are recognized on the cover, but there is also a sizeable platoon without whose unique and knowledgeable contributions the work would never take place.

In this instance, I owe a debt to many scholars of mass communication and its included disciplines whose work I respectfully and gratefully acknowledge in the suggested readings and footnotes.

I want also to express gratitude to my colleagues, the journalism faculty of San Diego State University, whose prolonged understanding has helped immeasurably.

A particular tribute is due Richard C. Crews, Executive Editor, Wm. C. Brown Company Publishers, without whose relentless encouragement and faith this effort would never have been completed.

I also owe a continuing debt to Prof. Robert H. Farson of the School of Journalism, Pennsylvania State University, and to Prof. Richard E. Pavlik, chairman of the mass communications department, Southern Colorado State College, for their meticulous reviewing of this manuscript in all stages for well over a year. Their perceptive suggestions so generously offered have made it a better book by far.

It would not be appropriate to omit Linda Jones Maneen, my production editor, who has become a close friend in a few short months, and whom I hope to meet one day, for it was she who resolutely sanded the edges and buffed the surface of this manuscript, and above all, who coordinated the many painstaking details of publication to bring it out on schedule.

To Jo Gifford, who has a remarkable talent for detail, and to Pat Summers, who typed this manuscript through three years and three drafts, I also want to express deep appreciation for help and loyalty.

Finally, to my students and my family—thank you.

Part I

OVERVIEW

The four chapters of this introductory section will be engaged in defining and establishing the parameters of mass communications in society, which is, after all, simply communication extended to a grand scale. Mass communications differs not only quantitatively, but qualitatively from the basic person-to-person involvement which started in man's cradle, or long before that, when man's forerunners grunted in the gloom of the cave. Even so, there remain significant personal relationships in the operation of mass communications as the central nervous system of society. The interplay of these factors is a fascinating study, for no matter how "mass" society becomes, most relevant communication is still direct and interpersonal.

In this respect, one must think of himself, and his time, and how time-consuming mass media are. Man is essentially time-limited, each person cramming the business of living (of which mass communications is only a part) into a mere twenty-four hours each day. Man is not indiscriminate, but rather, selective in his media choice; this is key to understanding mass communications, because others, called gatekeepers, are forever second-guessing the public's aggregate selectivity.

The functions of mass communications are, broadly, what they do, and more specifically, what they are used for. These functions are four: information, entertainment, persuasion (which in contemporary society has acquired important commercial overtones), and a vague general function of carrying the culture. These functions are seldom performed singly, but in varying combinations. Their interplay with individual characteristics of the various media, which in themselves differ widely, shall be examined. No single medium is all things to all people, and out of this pervasity and diversity of function and characteristics emerges in different degrees a wondrous battleground for attention, and a curious balance that stretches on imperfectly self-correcting—like society.

Nature's history is one of stability and change. That nature is inherently conservative, but contains the seeds of change is axiomatic. From this it is but a short leap to note that society, composed of human organisms within an environment, reflects both conservatism and progressive change. Mass communications, the central nervous system of society, will parallel and reflect that course. But how?

The history of mass communications in the Western world, and particularly on American shores, where it has attained its greatest growth, is a study of the interrelationships of social institutions and technological progress. It is in the development of mass communications that one will note that some of the communications miracles and social change witnessed were less miraculous than inevitable.

The interdisciplinary nature of mass communications will be met head on.

Mass communications theories are a tangled thicket of often conflicting views, but there is a pattern to them, and all show some element of truth. It is the balance of these different truths that will be sought. Avoiding polarization, extractions that shed the greatest light will be made from each. The myth of "the power of the press" will be explored, as will its update, "mass man"; the role that people play in the mass communications process will also be examined, and an attempt made to determine if the mass media have an effect of their own, or perhaps a side effect, apart from the news or entertainment or advertising that they carry. McLuhan contends that they probably do, and sets forth his case in *Understanding Media* (see "Suggested Readings," p. 457).

1

COMMUNICATION

THE BASIC INGREDIENTS

Before moving into mass communications, it seems worthwhile to spend a little time with the communication process. Some have defined it in simplest terms as s-r, stimulus-response, and while this may be an oversimplification, it is a reasonable beginning. Communication takes at least two entities: an event outside the individual and the individual himself reacting. Thunder and lightning striking fear in a child constitutes communication. They are outside him and fear is his reaction. From this simplest example, another factor in the communication process can be inferred. The child is changed. The thunder and lightning have been programmed into his mental computer and will remain there as a part of his experience. This is the effect of communication, and all communication has some effect, if only of total boredom.

The two principal factors in the communication process are a *source* and a *receiver*. Communication requires both. A thunderstorm in the wilderness out of sight and earshot constitutes no communication—there is no receiver, no human effect—and communication is a uniquely human phenomenon.

Further, this simple s-r model points up that all communication is an individual, even a personal process. Thunder and lightning over the city strike fear into many little hearts, but into each one separately, without reference to any other. Each little child will react differently—sobbing, crying, cowering, or sturdily fighting back the tears—according to his bent. In this sense the thunderstorm becomes a form of mass communication.

Different persons react differently to different stimuli. The fire alarm means different things to the fireman and the theatergoer. "Women's lib" evokes different reactions from Gloria Steinem and Norman Mailer. Man-made communication involves a *message*—fire or women's lib—that is carried over a *channel,* whether alarm bell or magazine article. Man-made communication has a purpose. It does not rise out of thin air. In these instances the purpose was of communication to call attention to a fire (information) or to voice an opinion on a controversial topic (persuasion). That these messages were received differently is the crux of communication. Reception and, consequently, reaction and effect will differ according to each individual's orientation. Orientation, in turn, will depend on many factors, which can be reduced to the individual's experience—that is, the sum total of all that has gone before. Since a good deal of that experience has been communication, the complexities of the process and its circularity become apparent.

THE COMMUNICATION MODEL

Emerging from all this is a model of the communication process, which consists of a source sending a message over a channel to a receiver. Communication shorthand for this is:

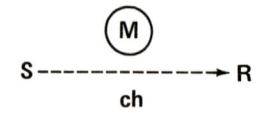

$$S \xrightarrow[\text{ch}]{\text{M}} R$$

The source implies purpose. There is an effect on the receiver that results in a response or reaction if communication has really taken place. This reaction is called *feedback* and constitutes another element in the basic communication model, which now appears as follows:

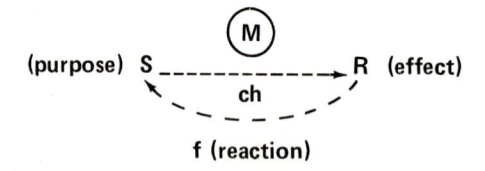

$$(\text{purpose})\ S \xrightarrow[\text{ch}]{\text{M}} R\ (\text{effect})$$
$$f\ (\text{reaction})$$

The simplest illustration, of course, is an ordinary conversation. One man says "Good morning." He is the source; his purpose is to establish contact. The message is "Good morning," the channel is speech, and another individual is the receiver. This may seem a bit complicated for such a simple transaction, but if the sequence and ingredients of communication are understood at the outset, it will enormously simplify the investigation of mass communications.

A second person hears the greeting. Communication has taken place; the effect is one of warmth and reciprocity, and he responds, smiling and saying "How are you?" This is his reaction; it constitutes feedback to the first man, and the communication process is completed.

FEEDBACK

Note, however, that both the smile and response of the second man were a part of the feedback. Note further that in replying he became a secondary sender and the first man a receiver; thus, the mod-

Overview

el reverses itself with his reply. Note finally that the second man's answer partially determines what the first will say next. "How are you?" demands an answer: "Fine, thank you," or "Terrible." The principle here is that feedback conditions the course of future communication between the men by limiting the options available to them.

This feedback principle demonstrates again the circularity of the communication process and introduces the matter of *cybernetics*. Cybernetics, a term coined by Norbert Weiner, is the adaptation of an engineering principle to the communication process.[1] Weiner, who played a considerable role in the perfection of antiaircraft artillery during World War II, points out that radar tracks enemy bombers while computers determine, from course, speed, and altitude, what the bombers' future position will be when the shells arrive; the guns are aimed at that future point. In the same fashion in mass communications, Weiner says, do mass audience reactions, measured by increasingly sophisticated devices and interpreted through computers, dictate what future messages will be sent.

1. Norbert Weiner, *Cybernetics*, 2d ed. (Cambridge, Mass.: The M. I. T. Press, 1969).

INTERFERENCE

There remains one more element in the basic communication process—interference. The technical term for interference is *noise*, and it consists of two types: channel noise and semantic noise. Channel noise is interference within the channel or medium, or exterior to it. If, for instance, the gentleman was seized with a fit of coughing when he said "Good morning," the receiver would have difficulty in understanding him. The first man might have to repeat; in any event, there was channel interference in his speech. Alternately, if he said "Good morning" in a New York subway during rush hour, it is doubtful that anything could be heard.

Channel noise can be corrected in two ways: first, the gentleman may try not to cough or sneeze, to use clear enunciation, and to speak loudly enough for the other to hear; in short, by perfecting the channel—speech. The other means is by repetition; if the receiver didn't hear the first time, he may the second or the third.

Semantic noise, on the other hand, is more complex; it is interference within the communication process itself. If the first man was Chinese and greeted the other in a Chinese dialect, he would not be understood, though heard. This language barrier is the simplest example of semantic noise, but there are more prevalent and subtle forms indicated by differences in education, socioeconomic status, residency, occupation, age, experience, and interest.

Often one hears another say "I simply can't talk to him"—this is an example of semantic noise. These two individuals may be poles apart in their orientation, interests, backgrounds, and habits. "The generation gap" is a glib description of semantic noise provoked by age differences.

The solutions to semantic noise, as in the case of channel noise, are incumbent upon the source or sender. It is, after all, his purpose originally to communicate. One solution consists of trying to communicate on the level of the receiver. The kindergarten teacher uses simple words, short sentences, and brief lessons because she knows her students' vocabularies are as tiny as they are and their spans of attention short. She is trying to eliminate semantic noise. In briefest summary, the solution to semantic noise is to appeal in terms of the receiver's interest.

Recognizing the semantic problems that can arise in person-to-person encounters, and the degree of interference that surrounds the simplest conversation, the scope of interference that is inevitable when situations are multiplied by many in mass communications becomes apparent. In fact, it is safe to say that mass communications exists in a cloud of noise, interferences, and distractions. This is one of the principal problems in mass communications, one to which frantic attention is paid to try to reduce mass noise. But this geometric expansion of noise is but one of the differences between mass communications and the simpler face-to-face encounter.

MASS COMMUNICATIONS DIFFERENCES

Basically, differences between one-to-one and mass communications are quantitative, but the discrepancy is so vast between the single one-to-one situation and contemporary mass communications, often involving tens of millions of receivers, that the numerical differences become differences in kind. Further, these differences stretch across the entire model, showing various changes in source and channel, receiver and in feedback, as well as in noise.

The main difference between mass communications and the elemental model is, of course, the matter of multiple receivers, sometimes receiving simultaneously, immediately, as in network television, other times receiving individually over longer periods as with a movie, or even over centuries, as with the Bible or the Pyramids.

To make this distinction in the communication model, the sender is called the *source*, and the multiple receivers, the *audience*. The channels, whether they be television, radio, newspapers, magazines, books, movies, or even such long-term phenomena as the antic and static arts (drama, ballet, galleries, football games, paintings, poetry, culture, or architecture) are known as *media*.

AUDIENCES EXPAND

It should be obvious that audiences come in different sizes, from the 40 million or so of network television, to the several thousands of an average book, to the few hundreds of a scholarly journal. Regardless of size, it is crucial to remember that each audience is composed of that many individual persons, each one a separate thinking-machine reacting to the medium's message in a different fashion, viewing the message through his own separate lens ground from his own experience and orientation. This individuality of audiences belies the concept of a single mass reacting as so many automatons.

Multiple receivers of a mass medium will also react with one an-

Overview

other. One comments on a television show with his family. Scholars discuss articles from academic journals. Did you see...? Have you read...? The papers said.... Have you heard...? They say...: The contents of mass media constantly become topics of conversation within man's daily life, and thus media influence is extended; indirect or secondary audiences may, in many cases, be far larger than the original receivers.

Thus, it appears that the effect of mass communications reaches far beyond the initial audience. This is a significant point, for it illustrates the catalytic nature of mass communications in triggering individual reactions. This fact led Paul Lazarsfeld to develop his two-step or indirect theory of communication.[2] For the meantime, it is enough to adapt the basic communication model to accommodate these additional factors:

2. Paul F. Lazarsfeld et al., *People's Choice: How the Voter Makes up His Mind in a Presidential Election,* 3rd ed. (New York: Columbia University Press, 1969).

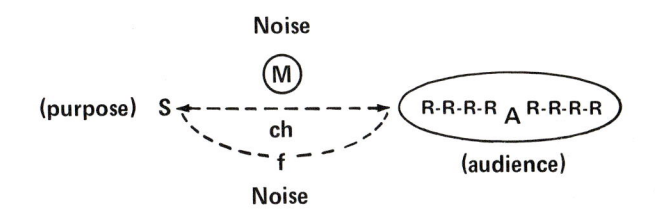

Noise

(purpose) S ← — — Ⓜ — — → R-R-R-R A R-R-R-R
         ch
         f   (audience)
Noise

INDIRECT FEEDBACK

The new model indicates also some subtle changes. First, feedback in mass communications is rarely instantaneous and direct, as it is in face-to-face conversation. Rather, feedback becomes an aggregate ingredient reflected back to the source after a considerable lag in time, often from great distance, and frequently in a different nature. Feedback from a political campaign's issues and rhetoric will only be reflected, often many weeks later, at the ballot box on election day. The appeal of a television commercial or a magazine advertisement will be known at the sponsor's cash register. A movie's popularity can only be measured in dollars at the box office, and a book's success generally in over-the-counter sales, both of which may involve a wait of more than a year. Delayed and indirect feedback are indigenous to mass communications.

This delay has led over the last couple of decades, as a result of technological advances in computerization (note the interrelationship with technology), to the development of some forms of ersatz feedback. In political campaigns, often costing millions of dollars, it is tactically unwise to await the verdict at the polls, by which time strategies cannot be corrected. Public opinion polling has proven able to offer an indication of election day results to perceptive candidates as a guide in their campaigns.

Similarly, when advertisers spend up to $140 thousand a minute for prime-time television commercials, they need to know far in advance whether this kind of investment will pay off at the cash register. This need has led to television and radio ratings. There is an empirical correlation between audience size and the subsequent sales of consumer products. Consequently, the audience size of television shows, as reflected in ratings, gives a reasonable clue to the relative success of the programs and commercials.

Public opinion polling as a feedback device has another use too. By indicating what is acceptable and unacceptable to different audiences, polls tend to condition the kind of campaign or the kinds of programs that will be offered in the future. The candidate who finds his corruption-at-city-hall issue falling flat will abandon it. The advertiser who finds a science fiction TV series of less appeal than a western will switch to the horse opera. These examples point out the circularity of the mass communications process and the role of audiences as a partial source in society. Since in either example the purpose of communication is to get elected or to sell soap, it is incumbent upon the source to devise that vehicle or message which the audience will accept in the greatest numbers—the appeal must be made to audience interest in order to accomplish purpose.

These examples indicate the recent significance of cybernetic feedback in the mass communications system, and position public opinion polling itself as a major ingredient of mass communications. Today, in fact, in a commercially oriented society a major portion of mass communications research is devoted to trying to perfect the cybernetic cycle.

CHANNEL NOISE

Noise in mass communications is a mammoth aggravation of the forms noted. Within the media, channel noise consists of such things as typographical errors, misspellings, scrambled words, or omitted paragraphs in the newspaper; it is the fuzzy picture on the tube, static on the radio, missing pages in a magazine. It is also a broken television set, a dead battery in the transistor radio, the Sunday paper in a mud puddle outside the door, or the magazine subscription that doesn't arrive. Obviously, the more technologically complex society becomes, the greater opportunity there is for this kind of channel noise. As both the numbers, varieties, and complexities of media increase, the more chance there is that one will be exposed to mounting noise.

Since channel noise also includes outside interference, it will perforce encompass such things as kids fighting during a television program, a thunderstorm at the football game, visitors interrupting one's reading, or an overflowing sink while one looks at the paper. At the same time such interferences may also be the persistent telephone as one watches television, a youngster's hi-fi at full volume while his parents are trying to read, or even competing programs to watch, magazines to read, and media from which to choose. From these examples it is evident that in many cases the media interfere with one another and constitute a considerable part of their own

Intermedia channel noise.

noise. As more media develop and become available, the problem must exacerbate.

REPETITION

One of the solutions for channel noise is repetition, and it is in use constantly in mass communications. Disc jockeys repeat phone numbers; television commercials reappear during a program. Department stores advertise daily with multiple pages in both morning and evening papers. Repetition employs the law of averages to work on the source's behalf. If the message was interrupted the first time—by doorbell or conversation—chances are it won't be the second or third. Repetition in broadcast media offers an opportunity to reach those who tuned in late. However, repetition operates on a law of diminishing return. There comes a point in repetition where the receiver, as an individual, will tune it out. When multiplied by many individuals, the message is lost. Repetition must be used with discretion.

It is significant that the greatest portion of repetition employed in mass communications serves the advertising or commercial function. The other functions, information and entertainment, are generally on a one-time-only basis, which indicates the commercial significance of the mass communications network and suggests that the other functions, information and entertainment, may indeed be only vehicles for advertising.

PERFECTING THE CHANNEL

Another cure for channel noise is perfecting the channel performance. This includes avoiding static on the radio, prolonging the life of a transistor's batteries, proofing the typos and scrambled paragraphs in the newspaper, and cleaning up the fuzzy picture on the tube. These are rather obvious solutions, but accomplishing them leads in several directions.

Removing static on the radio, for instance, may require increasing the wattage of the station, which calls for FCC approval and demands considerable capital investment. The long-life transistor

Communication

battery stems directly from improved technology, a constant probing of new frontiers. Such technology already has developed transistors themselves (in lieu of bulky vacuum tubes), printed circuits, and miniaturization, making the radio a personal, portable mass communications tool.

A fuzzy picture may demand a new picture tube at the owner's expense, but it also may require new cameras at the studio or a new control console or better engineers. Perfecting the channel on television can run all the way from improving the transmitter's output via intricate engineering through the quality of engineers, the talent of directors, and the diction of the announcer. It goes on to include the ability of the advertising salesmen about whom all revolves, the efficiency of the overall organization, and the imagination of management. All this is required to bring the audience what it wants to watch in a form that can be watched. Any breach in any of these functions spells disaster, for the audience has too many options available to waste precious time with a medium that is less than satisfying.

It is interesting to note that Community Antenna Television, CATV, was originally developed to correct channel noise by bringing a clearer signal to communities on the perimeter of a television station's signal or otherwise out of reach of television's line-of-sight signal. However, the fact that cable TV has two-way capacity, like telephone lines, the fact that homes are physically connected to the station, the fact that the station can itself originate programming over the cable, the fact that computers can be linked to the system and demographics fed into them has opened up possibilities the scope of which cannot yet be determined. This illustrates how a relatively simple attempt to correct television channel noise technologically has introduced radical changes of a kind that some say will revolutionize the entire mass communications network.

The typos and misspellings in the newspaper demand better proofreaders, of course, but they may also demand better linotype operators, or more efficient presses, or updated typesetting machines, or better-trained personnel. But these mechanical improvements are useless unless the money is there to finance them, and that will depend on advertising and circulation, which demand a large readership, which, in turn, will depend on the quality of reporting and features, which relies on talented editors directed by a wise publisher adhering to an appropriate editorial policy. Further in the archaic distribution system employed by newspapers, a part of channel noise will depend on the working condition of the newsboy's bicycle. Again, so interrelated and complex is the mass communications system, even within a single medium, that a change in any element—such as correcting typos or misspellings—affects in some degree all other aspects of that medium.

Overview

SEMANTIC NOISE

Semantic noise in mass communications also differs both quantitatively and qualitatively from interpersonal communication. With so many people composing a mass audience, it is impossible to pinpoint a message toward any individual's personal interest. However, mass media do try. Two of the techniques most frequently employed are simplicity and commonality.

Journalese, the style in which the daily newspaper is written, is an example of the former technique. The most significant facts, the most captivating, are placed in the lead at the top of the story as attention getters. The "who, what, when, and where" are answered early in the story so a time-pressed reader can skim without missing the really pertinent data. The balance of the article is composed of additional data in order of decreasing significance. The words used are simple, denotative, the sentence structure uncomplicated, the paragraphs brief. A simple style aimed at a mass audience is designed to convey maximum information requiring minimal reader effort.

Journalese, by definition, is applied to the news. There are other techniques of commonality designed to reach the mass audience. The clearest example is seen on network television, although it is by no means restricted to this medium. This is the lowest common denominator (lcd), wherein television's programming content is theoretically aimed at that audience intelligence or interest level that will attract and hold the greatest number of viewers. Much of the criticism aimed at television programming is directed toward a bland and sometimes mindless array of private eyes, situation comedies, and celebrity specials, all interspersed with simplistic, catchy commercials. Whether this diet is all that bad is speculatory, but it certainly is an example of purposeful appeal to the presumed lcd of a vast and invisible audience in an attempt to overcome semantic noise.

COMPETITION FOR ATTENTION

Earlier examples of media interfering with one another were noted in which media constituted a part of their own noise, a problem which seriously compounds as mass media proliferate in society. But the problem is broader than that. In a sense, with their persistent messages, the mass media are in competition with everything man does for his attention, not merely with one another. This competition for attention is the single most significant problem in the operation of a free mass communications network as the central nervous system of a highly competitive and technologically expanding society. It was noted earlier that no communication can take place without a receiver. Translated into contemporary mass communications terms, this means that the attention of the audience and the individual receivers within it must be focused on a medium and its message. If they are not, then the communication is taking place in a vacuum. It is not sufficient merely to print or to broadcast or to exhibit; there must be an effect on people. If they are too busy to pay attention, there is no mass communication; there is, in fact, no communication at all.

A half-dozen television channels are not only in competition with each other, but with a couple of daily newspapers, several weeklies, a couple of dozen AM and FM radio stations, up to ten or so magazines, and a couple of dozen current movie options. In addition, these mass media are in competition with jobs, eating, sleeping, playing, lovemaking, a social life, zoos, reading, writing, sailing, skiing, dune buggying, beach time, bowling leagues, and golf courses. The list is not exhaustive. The more things there are to do, the greater the competition for attention, and the more thinly man must slice his time. It is this matter of time that is at the base of the problem, for no matter how much society expands nor how much our media proliferate, man is still a severely time-limited person who must somehow cram all of these mounting activities into a rigidly inflexible twenty-four hours a day.

SELECTIVITY

That the mass media are time-consuming is obvious, so obvious that this fact is often overlooked. It takes an hour and a half to see a movie; there are two to three hours consumed in an evening's television watching, another half-hour in reading a daily paper. Media consumption mounts up to great blocks of time that have to come from something else.

An answer to this problem of time has been one of increasing selectivity on the part of individuals. A man does not read everything, watch everything, or do everything. Rather, from the smorgasbord of availabilities necessities are selected first: eating, sleeping, working; then preferences.

That individuals are selective has not gone unnoticed by the profit-conscious mass media, which introduces the final factors in this introductory chapter—the mass media themselves as channels.

MERGING SOURCE AND CHANNEL

If there is a single preeminent distinction between mass communications and the simpler person-to-person model, it probably lies in the fact that in contemporary mass communications there is a blending of source and channel to the point where they become all but indistinguishable. A newspaper is a corporate production in which many authors, reporters whose work is modified and edited by multiple editors and copyreaders, all meld together to create a joint product specifically designed to catch the fancy of that newspaper's particular readership.

A television station carries a menu of offerings that are the aggregate work of many writers, programmers, actors, directors, and producers, not forgetting musicians, conductors, engineers, lighting, and sound men. Depending on what is being watched, the picture that is seen on television has had anywhere from a dozen to a hundred hands involved. The channel is the source, and the source is the channel. Even such a relatively simple medium as a book is a

Overview

joint venture between publisher, editor, and author at the very least, with the publisher generally holding the whip hand. It is no longer a question of an author with a message finding a publisher as a vehicle. Rather, the corporate publisher seeks those specific authors who he believes can best fill the gaps in his inventory of titles.

Contemporary mass media have become highly organized, institutionalized entities whose basic purpose, paralleling that of the society they serve, is essentially commercially oriented—therefore, intensely competitive—and rigidly controlled in an economic sense.

Source has purpose. A marriage of source and channel transfers purpose to the channel, and the corporate purpose of contemporary mass media is to survive. Survival in a competitive free enterprise economy means showing a profit. That is the media's basic purpose, toward which all other functions either contribute or are subordinated.

The economic reasons for considering the audience's selectivity places a high premium on identifying audiences' interests and tailoring the corporate product to meeting those interests. Thus, audience selectivity generated out of a competition for attention has a companion effect in the media's selectivity of content.

COMMERCIAL LIMITATIONS

3. Ben H. Bagdikian, *Information Machines: Their Impact on Men & the Media* (New York: Harper & Row, Publishers, 1971).

The daily newspaper is an example of commercial limitation. There is generally about ten times more news available on any given day than the newspaper has room to print.[3] The number of pages in the daily newspaper is determined by the number of pages of advertising committed for that day, generally on a 60–40 ratio. If there are 60 pages of advertising sold, the newspaper will have 100 total pages. A large metropolitan daily will have around forty reporters covering events and beats, from Rotary luncheons to city hall. There will be a half-dozen wire services, at least, and batteries of teletypes spewing out great yellow reams on events from all over the world; there will be foreign correspondents filing stories from trouble spots, and a handful of bureaus in Washington and state and major foreign capitals with their own contributions. There will be a host of specialized editors, feature writers, and syndicated columnists. From all of this, a series of editors—city editor, managing editor, wire editor, photo editor, and departmental editors—must make up a budget of news and features to offer the citizens of the city, and only about 10 percent of this news makes print.

GATEKEEPERS

The editors are the gatekeepers of the newspaper. They determine what the public reads, or at least what is available to read. What they bypass, the 90 percent or so, are events that never happened as far as the public is concerned. In the gatekeeper's hands is society's exposure to the day's reality and fantasy. Theirs is a prime responsibility.

As with journalese, gatekeeping has generally been associated with the news, specifically with newspapers. However, an under-

Communication

standing of its role in mass communications demands an extension of this definition.

An editor constantly has his eye on audience as he sorts through the day's events. He tends to place emphasis on the unusual, the sensational, the spectacular, not to say the criminal and deviant. These types of stories historically make good reading; subscribers like them. Within the severe space limitation in which an editor operates, he sometimes finds he must forego a story on zoning controls in favor of a gory three-car accident, or pass up a scientific breakthrough for an axe murder.

Before an editor got the story, the reporter exercised a form of gatekeeping in his selection and presentation of the facts. No matter how objective the reporter tried to be, something of himself and his orientation crept into the story. No two reporters will write the same story; more broadly, no two observers will see the same thing. Thus, the public's view of an event will be colored to a degree by the kind of fact-finding glasses the reporter wore.

CORPORATE GATEKEEPING

Editorial policy is also a form of gatekeeping. Different newspapers have different values. Two examples that come readily to mind are the *New York Times* and the *New York Daily News*. The *New York Times*—"All the News That's Fit to Print"—prides itself on completeness and detail in its substantive reporting. It plays down the sensational and deviant in the interest of propriety and taste. On the other hand, the *New York Daily News,* as a matter of policy, emphasizes the sensational, the odd, the different, downplaying the substantive as of little interest to its readership. Both approaches constitute forms of gatekeeping. Both deprive the audience of something, but from the two there is achieved for the residents of New York a kind of imperfect balance.

MEDIA SPECIALIZATION

The degree of audience appeal that enters into a mass medium's consideration begins to become apparent. Magazines and radio stations further emphasize this principle. Each has developed a format of appeal to a specific audience, and audiences differ. Some stations play rock 'n' roll, some classical music, some "oldies but goodies." These stations are not free to depart from their format, except at the risk of losing their established audiences.

Among magazines there are equally well-defined formats to appeal to specific audiences: *Vogue* for the fashion-conscious, *Field and Stream* for the outdoor buff, *Cosmopolitan* for the unmarried working girl. Such audiences have grown to expect a certain diet from these periodicals, and editors screen and prune all the available material to come up with the exact menu their readerships expect. There are no articles on fly-fishing in *Mademoiselle*, no economic forecasts in *Popular Mechanics*. Magazines and radio are as selective in what they present as the selective audiences they serve, and this is a form of gatekeeping.

Overview

Television news is even more condensed than the newspaper, cramming into thirty minutes synopses of world events of the past twenty-four hours. The result is a highly fragmentary mosaic allowing little time for more than headline news representing perhaps no more than 2 or 3 percent of the total news of the day.

Among the three major networks programmers of prime-time shows wrestle with what to air and what kind of a balance to strive for. From hundreds of potential shows—serials, specials, westerns, situation comedies, police shows, mysteries, and international intrigue shows—they must screen out no more than a dozen each for evening viewing.

Even book publishers and movie producers who cater to a self-selective, numerically unpredictable audience have their gatekeeping problems. From hundreds of manuscripts, screenplays, and scenarios that come to their attention from authors and agents, solicited and unsolicited, they must select those to be published or produced. The public will never know of the remaining hundreds, the thousands in a year, that failed to be approved. For audiences they have ceased to exist, dying before birth.

From all this two things become apparent concerning the gatekeeping function. First, it is limiting in that it restricts what the public is exposed to as an audience, whether in news, television programs, movies, books, or radio. Due to the marvelous diversity of the media, however, there is in the aggregate a certain balance of exposure achieved from so many media catering to so many different audiences. Second, the gatekeeping function is subjective, personal. It is another's surrogate judgment substituted for that of the audience, and is basically a professionally educated guess as to what the public will like and react to.

CIRCULATORY OF MASS COMMUNICATIONS

Finally, institutionalized mass media are organized to perform their gatekeeping function as efficiently as possible, for in their success in serving the exact meal expected by their respective audiences hangs their survival in the competitive mass communications field.

The mass media are specialized to anticipate their various audiences' selective expectations, from the lowest common denominator of the "massest" mass to the most esoteric taste. Where there's an audience, there's a medium.

The merger of source and channel in the corporate world of contemporary American mass communications has been noted; that institutionalized media cater to the known or presumed preferences of its specific audience should also be recognized. To paraphrase a concept from industry, the consumer as producer translates in mass communications terms into the audience as source. In a highly competitive free enterprise society of many different modes, this simply means that, spurred on by increasing competition for attention and regulated by sophisticated institutionalized feedback, the mass media offer by and large what their audiences expect of them.

Communication

Therefore, there is in mass communications not merely a blending of source and channel, but of audience as well, into an integrated, circular whole, no element of which is entirely free of the others, but in which under threat of boycott the fickle audience, composed of so many autonomous individuals, has the upper hand.

These are the same individuals who together compose our society. Their geographical, political, socioeconomic, ethnic, religious, age, and interest differences create the movement of public opinion and change. It is these social tides that mass communications serves and reflects in reciprocal action.

SUMMARY

Mass communications is an extension of the basic communication process. As such it is always individual—that is, individually received. The classic communication model requires a source, a message, a channel, and a receiver. To these four basic elements must be added the element of feedback, which constantly alters or refines the message in a continuing communications situation.

Communication is purposeful, it originates for a reason; consequently, there is always an effect upon the receiver. It is this matter of effect which is too often overlooked in the study of mass communications.

Mass communications takes place in a cloud of noise which interferes with the receipt of the message. Noise may be channel noise, contained within the channel or medium, or, equally, external to it in the form of outside disturbance. There may also be semantic noise, which is internal to the communication process: an interference between the source and the receiver in how they communicate. A language difference is the best example of semantic noise, but more often semantic noise is found in terms of orientation or interest.

In a complex society, conflicting media often interfere with one another, constituting a part of their own channel noise. This occurs in their competition for audience attention. One solution to channel noise is to have the channel itself in as perfect an operating condition as possible; another is repetition. Cures for semantic noise include extreme simplicity, leading to the concept of the lowest common denominator (lcd), or a conscious effort to pinpoint the message toward the receivers' interest.

In mass communications, there are multiple receivers, generally referred to as audiences. There is interchange between these individual receivers in an audience and mass communications messages are often relayed between individuals in an indirect process. In mass communications, also, feedback is indirect and delayed, requiring at times contrived forms of feedback such as public opinion polling and ratings.

In the sophisticated, institutionalized mass communications network of the United States there is merging of source and channel, which requires the intervention of gatekeepers in various mass media. Gatekeepers are surrogates who select from the diversity of possible news, entertainment, and other availabilities what they think their audiences will respond to. Thus, the responsibility of the gatekeeper is heavy, as reality is, in a vicarious world, generally what the mass media say reality is.

2 FUNCTIONS

WHAT MASS COMMUNICATIONS DOES

What does mass communications do in society? It informs, it keeps one up-to-date. It educates, broadens, and deepens one's perspectives. It persuades, it sells goods and services and candidates and opinions. It entertains, it creates laughter, it fills a void. It costs money and it makes money.

This list can be boiled down to four functions common to all communication: information, persuasion, entertainment, and transmission of the culture, in that mass communications is the pipeline of social heredity from history to posterity.

In the person-to-person mode these functions of communication are also present. Someone tells a joke to a friend. An acquaintance is urged to vote for "Whoozis." One gives the time to a stranger. The importance of honesty is explained to a child. These are simplistic examples of entertainment, persuasion, information, and transmission of the culture.

But the friend may repeat the joke; in a very limited sense, a contribution has been made to the transmission of the culture—contemporary humor. The acquaintance learned something about "Whoozis'" record—information. The stranger became a friend, so there must have been an element of persuasion present. The child learned integrity, which is information. The functions of communication are not discrete. They do not exist by themselves, singly, but rather in consort, in varying combinations and often all together.

In mass communications also the functions are there generally in some combination. Often, in fact, the differentiations are all but indistinguishably blurred.

In ancient times the Roman circuses were patently spectacles for entertainment, but actually they were pure persuasion, planned by the Caesars as an integral part of a propaganda campaign, that of "bread and circuses," designed

impios hominū. Vnū vero hoc non
lateat vos carissimi: qa unus dies a-
pud dnm sicut mille anni: et mille anni
sicut dies unus. Non tardat dns pro-
missi: sed patienter agit propter vos:
nolens aliquos perire sed oēs ad pe-
nitentiam reverti. Adveniet aūt dies do-
mini ut fur: quo celi magno impetu
transient: elementa vero calore solventur. Cū hec igit oīa dissolvenda sunt:
quales oportet vos esse in sanctis conver-
sationibus et pietatibus expectantes et proper-
antes in adventū diei dni: p que celi arden-
tes solventur et elementa ignis ardore tabes-
cent. Novos vero celos et novam ter-
ram p missa ipsius expectamus: in quibus
iustitia habitat. Propter qd carissimi
hec expectantes - satagite immaculati
et inviolati ei inveniri in pace: et dni nri
longanimitate salutē arbitramini: sicut et carissimus frater noster paulus secū-
dū datā sibi sapientiā scripsit vobis: sicut et in omnibus epistolis loquens in eis de his:
in quibus sunt quedā difficilia intellectu: que
indocti et instabiles depravant: sicut et ce-
teras scripturas: ad suā ipsorum perditionē.
Vos igitur fratres prescientes custodite ne insi-
pientium errore traducti excidatis a propria
firmitate: crescite vero in gratia et in cogni-
tione dni nri et salvatoris ihesu xpi.
Ipsi gloria et nunc et in diē eternitatis amē.

*Explicit epistola beati petri apostoli secūda.
Incipit argumentum in epistolam beati
iohannis apostoli prima.*

Rationem verbi - et qd de ipso
sit caritas manifestat : et
susurrones fratrum nec deum
scire - nec pios esse posse
eo usq disserat ut esse comprobet ho-
micidas : eo qd odiū sit interfectionis
occasio. *Explicit argumenti. Incipit
epistola beati iohannis apostoli prima.*

uod fuit ab initio:
quod audivimus.
quod vidimus ocu-
lis nostris: qd perspe-
ximus. et manus nre
scrutate sunt de ver-
bo vite: et vita manifesta est: et vidimus et te-
stamur et annunciamus vobis vitam eter-
nam: que erat apud patrem et apparuit
nobis. Quod vidimus et audivimus
annunciamus vobis: ut et vos societatē
habeatis nobiscum: et societas nostra sit
cum patre et cum filio eius ihesu xpo. Et hec
scribimus vobis: ut gaudeatis et gaudi-
um vestrum sit plenum. Et hec est annunciatio
quam audivimus ab eo : et annunciamus
vobis: quoniam deus lux est: et tenebre in eo
non sunt ulle. Si dixerimus quoniam societa-
tem habemus cum eo et in tenebris ambulamus: mentimur: et veritatem non facimus.
Si aūt in luce ambulamus sicut et ipse est in
luce societatē habemus ad invicem: et san-
guis ihesu filii eius mundat nos ab omni
peccato. Si dixerimus quoniam peccatum non
habemus ipsi nos seducimus: et veritas in
nobis non est. Si confiteamur peccata
nostra: fidelis est et iustus ut remittat nobis peccata nostra: et emundet nos ab omni
iniquitate. Si dixerimus quoniam non pecca-
vimus: mendacem facimus eum :
et verbum eius non est in nobis.

Filioli mei: hec scribo vobis ut non
peccetis. Sed et si quis peccaver-
it: advocatum habemus apud patrem ihe-
sum xpm iustum. Et ipse est propitiatio pro
peccatis nostris: non pro nostris autem tan-
tum: sed etiam pro totius mundi. Et in hoc
scimus quoniam cognovimus eum: si mandata
eius observemus. Qui dicit se nosse eum
et mandata eius non custodit mendax est:
et in hoc veritas non est. Qui autem servat
verbum eius: vere in hoc caritas dei perfecta

1. Scott M. Cutlip and Allen H. Center, *Effective Public Relations,* 4th ed. (Englewood, N. J.: Prentice-Hall, Inc., 1971).

2. Alexander Hamilton et al., *Federalist Papers,* ed. Clinton Rossiter (New York: Mentor Books, 1961).

THE FUNCTIONAL MIX

PROFIT MOTIVE

to keep the people's minds off the excesses of corruption and poverty.[1]

From our own history, Alexander Hamilton's *Federalist Papers,* written as a series of newspaper articles, is generally believed to have been a persuasive attempt to bolster the concept of strong federal government.[2] Yet contained therein is voluminous information pertaining to democratic government.

The raucous political rallies—torchlight parades, marching bands, dancing, slogans, free rum and beer—from the boisterous earlier days of the Republic were clearly persuasive in their search for votes, but they were also riotous entertainment.

Gutenberg's first Bible, the early forerunner of mass communications, was certainly informative. It also served to persuasively reinforce the religious mode of the times, and in a limited society probably provided the basis for whatever entertainment existed: religious drawings, playlets and the like.

These examples of early mass communications, using whatever media were at hand to accomplish a purpose, all indicate the multiplicity of functions present and the difficulty sometimes of distinguishing between them. Nor is it important to do so; it is sufficient that one realizes that there is more than one function present, often more than one purpose served.

These historical examples further show a common thread of cultural transmission; they would not otherwise be sufficiently familiar to serve as examples. This thread of cultural transmission, both long-term and short-term, runs through all mass communications. It is particularly evident, of course, in education and closely allied to the information function. But it is also inescapable in all of mass communications, which transmits the differing values of the social order in fulfilling its role as the central nervous system of society.

Contemporary American mass communications differs in one important degree from the person-to-person variety of individual communication, from earlier forms of mass communications, and, for that matter, from mass communications in a good part of the rest of the world. This is in the matter of its economic base—specifically, profit.

It was inevitable that a highly industrialized, competitive free enterprise system should be reflected in mass communications. Mass communications in this society is another institution, competitive and organized to show a profit.

In other parts of the world, lacking a free enterprise economy and its communication counterpart, a free press, profit is less a consideration. The essential purpose of mass communications in such countries is one of propaganda, persuasion in its broadest sense, serving the nation's objectives. To this purpose all mass media are bent; in fact, they are generally instruments of a government that

Functions

has merged source and channel for persuasive purposes as the U. S. has for economic; merging of source and channel is not merely a variant, but one of the distinctions of mass communications in a complex society. Two things are apparent: first, the universal role of mass communications as the central nervous system of any society; second, the uniquely American concentration on profit in mass communications.

Consequently, as mass communications in the latter quarter of the twentieth-century United States are observed, not only the intertwining operation of the four communication functions, but also the overriding effect of profit concern will be apparent.

FUNCTIONAL THRUST OF MASS MEDIA

In individual communication functional gears can be constantly changed at will: one pleads, asserts, instructs, jokes, asks—moving rapidly from one mode to another as situation and inclination demand. In mass communications it is more difficult, if not impossible, to alter the basic functional thrust of a medium. This is so because the highly organized, institutionalized nature of the mass media creates a ponderous inertia resistant to change. Media are organized with a primary intent; to do anything else belies their purpose.

Audiences have grown to expect one format or a certain combination of formats from each medium, and a departure deceives audience expectations and threatens profit. The thrust of the *New York Daily News* is basically entertainment: sensation, spice, and violence. The concern of the *New York Times* is information, to be "the newspaper of record."

The *New York Daily News* could not one day appear in the *New York Times'* format with an analysis of international monetary policy. First, editorial expertise to produce such an analysis would be lacking. Second, the tabloid presses could not possibly accommodate the *New York Times'* full-page format, and finally, and most significantly, the readership would be appalled. Nor could the *New York Times* issue sensational headlines of sex and disaster. Their reporters are otherwise oriented, and they do not write in that style; but most importantly, readers would desert and advertisers cancel.

JOURNALISM'S INFLUENCE

When one thinks of the various functions of mass communications, it is generally information that comes to mind first. Information is the easiest of the functions to identify since it comprises a part of each. For example, a good deal of persuasion, particularly propaganda, is disguised as information.

Journalism's influence has been particularly strong in mass communications. Journalism was the first of the social sciences to investigate in any depth the phenomenon of mass communications, and journalism's preoccupation with news is a heritage still dominating the discipline. This news emphasis has camouflaged the fact that 60 percent of the average newspaper is advertising, and that a considerable portion of what is left is entertainment of one sort or another, starting with the comics, ranging through selected features and columnists (Art Buchwald, for example), to a wide range of sensational and human interest stories. However, the basic thrust of the newspaper remains informational. That is what its audience expect of it. The *New York Daily News* satisfies its information function, for example, by finding a high quotient of sensational material, such as violence and sex, and masquerading it as news, with proper news leads, written in punchy journalese.

This news fetish has carried over into television, and much has been made by the networks of their news and public affairs programming. This ignores the fact that viewers must pass over hours of entertainment and commercials to get at a marginal half-hour of news, which, with its personality cult and visual emphasis, is a good part show-biz anyway.

This is not to downgrade the significance of the information function or of news, but rather to place both in perspective. News is only one aspect of a broader information picture as far as functions are concerned, and information is but one leg of the mass communications table—one, of course, without which it would not stand.

EDUCATION

Education is the institution in society which utilizes information in its purest form. That it is also the principal bridge in the transmission of the culture from one generation to the next and from the past to the future points up the close relationship of these two functions.

From a mass communications viewpoint, it is significant that there is a good half of all book publishing—textbook publishing—that is designed to serve the educational institution. Textbooks, by and large, are pure information. Also, their voluntary readership is slight; they are generally read under duress at a professor's direction. Thus, their captive audience is offered little entertainment.

However, it isn't merely book publishing that serves education. The existence of a large, national captive audience spelled profit to many other mass media forms. There has been an increasing use of films, closed-circuit television, educational television, tapes, cassettes and recordings, and a wide variety of graphic training aids, all of which are focused on the information function.

The other branches of book publishing—trade books, fiction and nonfiction—are freer to depart from pure information as their thrust, but their information function is still relatively high, covering a wide variety of topics from which one selects and chooses at his own discretion. While there are exceptions—comic books and the sex-and-violence formula novels of Harold Robbins and Ian Fleming—there is in the overall little attempt to market most hardcover books to a mass audience. Even so, who is to say that someone hasn't learned something about baccarat strategy from Fleming's 007 or picked up a fantasied version of jet-set life from Harold Robbins...and the admixture of functions is again present.

Among the other mass media the wire services, particularly the

Associated Press (AP) and United Press International (UPI), have the highest information content. Their business is selling information, specifically news of current events gathered worldwide. Further, their customers or clients, the newspapers, television networks, and individual television and radio stations across the nation, represent such a broad spectrum of approaches, interests, formats, and editorial policies that the wire services must rely on a straight-news, objective, unadulterated informational approach, eschewing any attempt to color the news. The wire services leave it to their clients to choose specific items from those offered and to season those items as they see fit. This concentration on objective and typically comprehensive information is what wire service clients expect of them. Profit demands they offer nothing different. Indeed, they are the media's medium.

NEWSPAPER—INFORMATION

The newspaper remains the source of most daily information. Some is indirectly gathered through the wire services; some is directly reported from the community. There is a division in a newspaper within the information function—local news and other. A newspaper's basic allegiance is to the local community, and its concentration perforce must be on the local news, which by and large is that which is of the most immediate interest to the lives of its geographically circumscribed audience.

Even in the contemporary era of instantaneous news from radio and television, it is to the newspaper that one turns for a rounding out of the major stories. The newspaper can provide a depth of information on items that the broadcast media can merely make one aware of in their critically time-limited format.

Important to an understanding of the function of information in its relationship to news is the fact that all news is not information, and all information is not news in its journalistic sense: a good deal of television news has heavy overtones of entertainment.

ADVERTISING AS INFORMATION

Sixty percent of a newspaper is advertising. On first consideration one might label all advertising as commercial persuasion. But this is not actually the case. There are two kinds of advertising in a newspaper: local (or retail) and national. Local advertising is essentially informational and is read as such. Local advertising generally calls attention to goods and services available: where, when, and in the case of sales, and at what price. The big Thursday morning market ads are read by the housewife as pure information. There is little persuasion to them. She knows she is going to buy food, and they simply tell her where she can buy it most economically. Movie and theater ads are of the same genre; they inform one what is playing at the local theaters. Local advertising is a community bargain counter over which consumers hover to pick out what they want.

Overview

Local information.

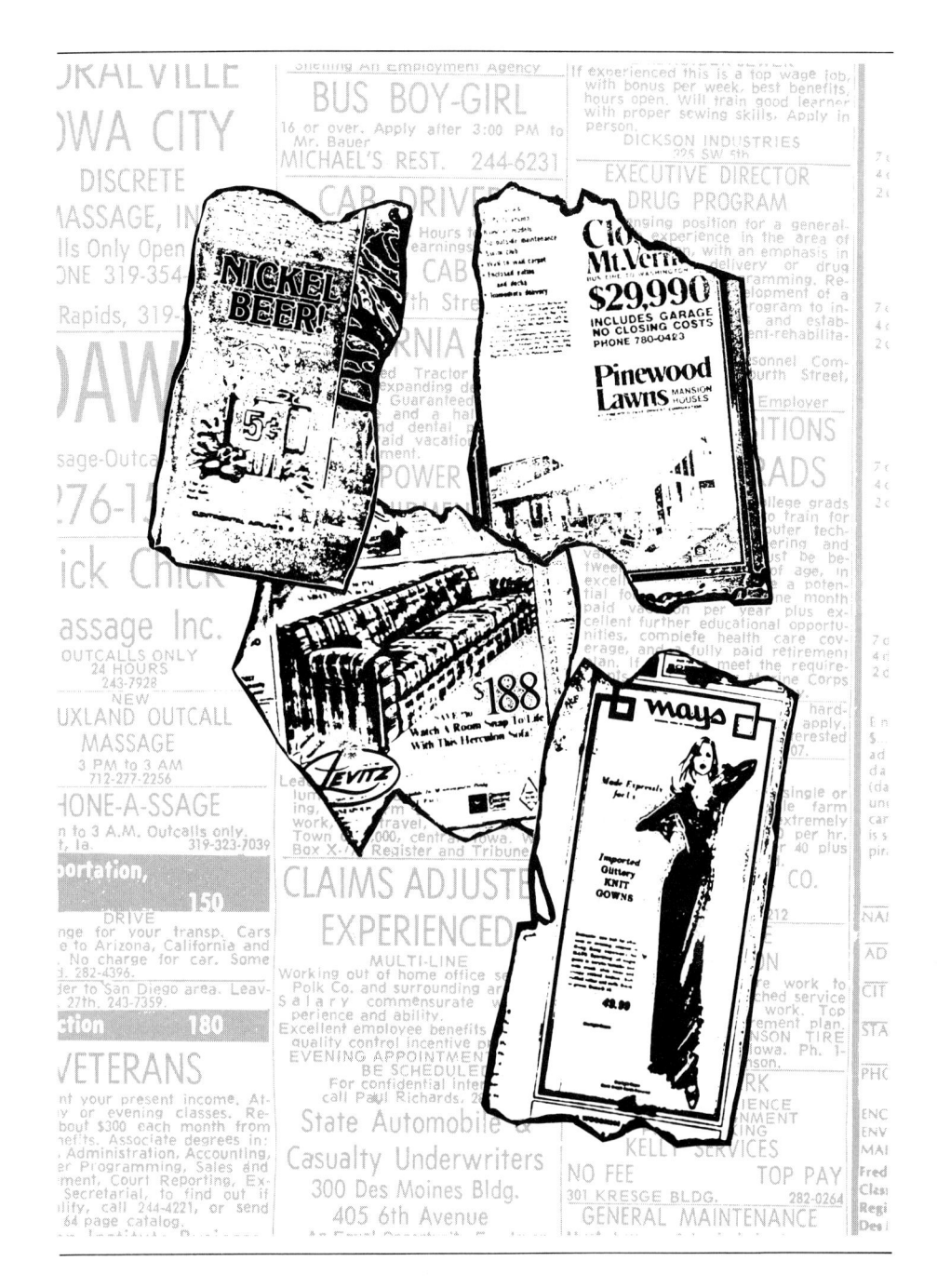

The classifieds, too, are almost pure information. Often they are used for personal messages. In the aggregate they comprise a community bulletin board.

National advertising differs from local advertising. Here the goods and services are not immediately available. The seeds of desire

Functions

Mass medium—the event: "The Battle of the Sexes." Saturated media coverage reflected all four functions of communication.

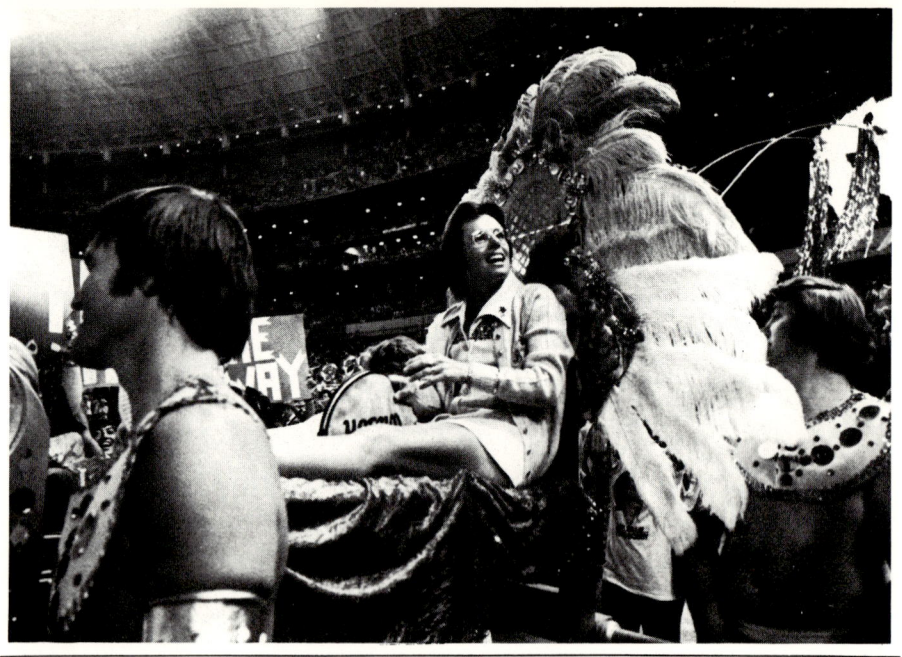

UPI

are sown, a desire for a future purchase is created. This is persuasion. The line, of course, is hard to draw, but the principle remains that much of newspaper advertising is basically information.

Considered previously has been news that is also entertainment, some of it rather gruesome in the same sense that horror movies are entertainment. Stories of epic disasters, of children lost in the wilds, of bridal dismemberment, evoke a vicarious thrill, and create within the public a catharsis in the Aristotlean sense, a real sense of horror and attendant relief.

This budget of information, entertainment, and persuasion, no matter how disguised, is the newspaper's stock-in-trade—and it is what the public expects. If there are certain concessions to entertainment to liven its pages and to commercial persuasion for profit, it is still essentially an information medium in which the other functions are necessary adjuncts to its basic thrust.

MAGAZINES

3. John Hohenberg, *The News Media: A Journalist Looks at His Profession* (New York: Holt, Rinehart and Winston, 1968).

Magazines are subtly different than newspapers. In general a higher proportion of their content is advertising, sometimes as much as three quarters, and nearly all of this advertising, because of its national nature, is persuasive. John Hohenberg, citing fashion and travel magazines as examples, states that a good deal of the editorial matter—which should be information—is instead persuasion in support of the advertising.[3] Be this as it may, persuasion, whether commercially paid for or injected gratis and masquerading as information, still provides a considerable level of entertainment.

Overview
24

However, the increasingly specialized nature of magazines, sometimes to the point of esotericism, demands that magazines contain a high quotient of information of a specialized nature. Such titles in many instances speak for themselves: *Gun Collector, Field and Stream, Popular Mechanics, Yachting, Consumer Reports, Psychology Today,* and so on. Specialized though their information be, it is still information. This is their stock-in-trade, what their audiences expect, and from this format magazines can depart only at their profit's peril.

Taken in the aggregate, the print media as a whole have a basic information thrust. The relative proportions of information, entertainment, and persuasion will vary widely, of course, not only from medium to medium, but within each medium itself: *New York Daily News* vs. *New York Times, Rise and Fall of the Third Reich* vs. *Portnoy's Complaint, Atlantic Monthly* vs. *Mad,* but, on balance, print's emphasis is informational. Not so the broadcast media, which, while showing a similar admixture of functions, has entertainment at its base.

BROADCAST—ENTERTAINMENT

The broadcast media—radio, television, and film—have a basic although by no means exclusive entertainment thrust. Film is included in this category because, although there are differences, film is such a large part of contemporary television that one cannot realistically be considered without the other.

That the broadcast media are intensely, purposefully, and enthusiastically entertainment oriented is obvious to any observer. Anyone who has had the misfortune to be hospitalized for a week or so can testify to the unremitting and highly imaginative diet of entertainment fare that TV offers. Daytime television, with its fantasies of soap operas, game shows, old movies, and reruns, is simply the beginning. Prime time, the evening hours, is a wonderland of scheduled westerns, hospitals, private eyes, police situations, situation comedies, personalities, serials, and premier movies that move inexorably in the direction of sex and deviance.

That television is not all entertainment is also obvious. The schedule is regularly interspersed during day and evening with a mosaic of commercials touting used cars, beer, cosmetics, household sprays, utility rationales, major appliances, and ball point pens. Some of the commercials, one might note, are better than the surrounding programming. That advertising should conform to the format of the medium is not surprising at all.

In fact, a good case can be made that the role of advertising agencies in mass communications is to inject entertainment into commercial persuasion, lest the public's attention, subjected to unrelenting exposure to so many sales pitches, begins to pall and thus defeat the advertiser's purpose. In any event, it becomes apparent that the purpose of television programming is to provide a vehicle for the commercials.

Functions

TELEVISION'S INFORMATION

The information content of television, however, is considerable. There are regularly scheduled newscasts. These, as noted, tend to take on entertainment overtones. News commentators are not so much in competition with each other as they are with other prime-time personalities. Their formats are doctored to move quickly and dramatically regardless of informative significance.

There are also the self-conscious documentaries. Here, again, they take on a dramatic quality and sometimes, not always, develop a point of view which: (a) is designed to appeal to the presumed taste of their massive audience; and (b) is not, consequently, entirely objective in its analysis.

Television cannot be entirely blamed for this cursory treatment of serious topics. Profit is the motivating force. Television's ratings indicate massive, regular departures of audience whenever a documentary appears, and the news itself suffers a 40 percent decline in audience. To save what they can of audience numbers, television is forced to make its information as close to entertainment as possible.

The Public Broadcasting System, PBS, is sad confirmation of broadcast's necessary entertainment thrust. The PBS, which is publicly supported, has no commercial requirements to make money or show a profit. It is enjoined from carrying advertising. Devoid of these commercial pressures, it is also free to offer programs of consequence (culture, education, documentaries) and it does so before no audience at all to speak of. There is little incentive either to produce or to watch a public medium in a commercial society.

RADIO: MORE OF THE SAME

The largest portion of radio is the same mixture of entertainment and commercials that television has shown. Lacking television's video quality, radio must concentrate on what it does best—appeal to the ear—and this generally means music. The spectrum of music offered by radio is impressive. Station by station, radio has selectively carved out a segment of audience to appeal to. Station by station it continues to move the goods to these audiences: components to hi-fi enthusiasts, blemish ointment to teenagers, annuities to the affluent. Radio's audiences are far more diversified than television's, and its costs of production far less. This permits it to specialize toward selective audiences, neglecting the lcd. Some radio stations have found their niche in broadcasting a series of constantly updated news bulletins. They are the exceptions, of course, to the general entertainment thrust of broadcast media, the exception that proves the rule.

FILM: A HYBRID

Film is hybrid. A little-considered but highly profitable aspect of filmmaking is concerned with persuasion and information. This is the area of training, educational, and institutional films: travelogues, driver-training films, how-to-do-its, sales orientations, and such. Like textbooks, these films have limited appeals and are shown for specific reasons before captive audiences. They constitute a large portion

Overview

of filmmaking, probably the greatest number of new films each year. But they lack the public exposure of either paid-admission films or television's "nights at the movies."

Film has shown a gradual metamorphosis in recent years. What was in its heyday during the thirties and early forties an essentially mass entertainment medium, playing in baroque palaces to large audiences, has moved under television's competitive pressure to be a far more expressive medium, freed from the tyranny of appealing to the lowest common denominator of taste.

Film today shows considerable persuasive and informational content. It begins to lay serious claim also as a prime medium of cultural transmission, recording and playing for inspection the triumphs, failures, and foibles of society. A good deal of social concern has proven profitable, and movies appear to be a medium that has capitalized on this.

Thus, while most of film still has a basic entertainment thrust, particularly that portion which serves the television industry, two other facets of filmmaking are evident: a distinctly persuasive-informative orientation in industrial or commercial films, and a self-conscious role of social critic emerging in the so-called popular movies, which typically play to smaller, more selective audiences, and which cost proportionately less than did the mass-appeal extravaganzas of yesteryear.

While the broadcast media and film have been identified as the basic purveyors of entertainment, this function is always intermixed with others. There is a high degree of entertainment in all mass communication; often entertainment is the vehicle for more serious functions.

ENTERTAINMENT, ADVERTISING, AND AFFLUENCE

One comment remains in connection with media's entertainment function. It requires an extraordinarily affluent society to support the level of entertainment inherent in American mass communications. Mass communications is time-consuming, and when a substantial portion is pure entertainment, as evidenced in television, one becomes aware of the leisure and prerequisite affluence of a society that enables so many of its members to spend so much of their time unproductively.

Equally significant in contemporary society is the persuasive function of the media. Advertising, of course, is its most apparent form, but there are other, more subtle manifestations of persuasion that bid fair to have lasting effects on the future of mass communications.

Most of American mass media are supported by advertising in one way or another; commercial radio and television are 100 percent so. Newspapers and magazines in varying degrees rely heavily upon advertising revenues. The price of a newspaper does little more than cover the cost of distribution, leaving all editorial costs, all production costs, and all profit to be borne by paid advertising. Magazines vary widely, but generally at least half their revenue, and hence, all their profit comes from advertising. Consequently, the persuasive content influenced by advertising in most regularly scheduled mass media is enormous.

It is also significant that, although only 10 percent or less of the available information or news can pass the gatekeeping test, 100 percent of the available advertising (with only minor exceptions) is published or broadcast. This offers a commentary on the relative values placed on advertising and information in a commercial society.

PERSUASION AND NEWS—PROPAGANDA

A good deal of the persuasion in mass communications is concealed. Any public relations man can testify that a considerable portion of what passes for news in the media has a persuasive origin and an ulterior purpose. Much of what the public reads, hears, or watches in all the media is designed to influence in one way or another.

Political campaigns, which periodically command vast attention in the mass media, are almost pure persuasion. Much of governmental news at all levels has a propaganda base as government seeks to promulgate or justify its actions in a democratic society. A good part of business and financial news is advocacy. Increasingly in today's environmental and consumer-conscious society business is under attack and seeks to utilize the mass media in defense.

The doses of persuasion masquerading as information in mass communications are huge, and inevitably the functions have tended to merge, obliterating distinctions. This then leads to a credibility gap. As what appears to be bona fide news repeatedly turns out to be political or commercial advocacy, one begins to hear more and more of newspaper bias or television distortion.

A viewpoint is a factor that mass media must possess in their constant search for audiences, and viewpoint will inevitably appear in the course of their operations. Viewpoint is persuasion, and persuasion is inevitable in the peculiar operation of a free press within a competitive, free enterprise economy. This is simply another example of how mass communications is responsive to the social structure.

COMMUNICATION AS PERSUASION

Melvin De Fleur contends that all communication is persuasive at base.[4] His case is strong, particularly in American mass communications, considering the corporate structure of the mass media and the profit incentive of the entire society.

Such commercial and political persuasion may not be entirely bad. Because persuasion is a reality, one should look at it to see if there is not considerable information intermixed; there surely is. A political campaign is a good example: from the cries of conflicting advocacy, the voting public gains understanding of the candidates and their respective issues. From the contrast of competing products, the consumer derives information on which to base his choice. In a politically competitive democracy and a commercially competitive free en-

4. Melvin DeFleur, *Theories of Mass Communications* (New York: David McKay Co., Inc., 1966).

Overview

terprise system mass communications functions through providing the competitive arena in which the advocates of all do battle. It is in the incredibly wide diversity of the mass communications network as a whole that an imperfect balance of viewpoints is achieved. Persuasion per se is not abhorrent; it is unbalanced advocacy that threatens.

Finally, of course, it is commercial persuasion evidenced through advertising that makes the breadth, depth, and diversity of the mass communications possible, and which permits an incomprehensible balance which does, in fact, reflect society and its viewpoints.

CULTURAL TRANSMISSION

All mass communications are inescapably transmitters of the culture as they discover, feed, and record the variations of popular taste. Television, for instance, in its empirically demonstrated appeal to the lowest common denominator, is a mirror of the times. Further, as television programs and original movies move increasingly to show previously taboo themes such as homosexuality and unwed parenthood, they reflect a growing permissiveness within the social structure. The market ads and white goods sales of the daily newspapers are pretty good indices of contemporary living standards; so, of course, is the proliferation of media. Media write a current history not only of current events but of how the public reacts to them in the aggregate, and of the public's tastes and values as a society. The multiplicity of media catering to different audiences of varying sizes is also indicative of the tides and currents within the body politic. Never before has any nation had so clear and comprehensive a record written of its growth, structure, and movement.

THE ARTS

It is the arts, of course, that have traditionally been the accepted barometers of cultural transmission. Painting and sculpture have brought a timelessness, a sense of permanence to transitory life. They make the past apparent. They are the vehicles of history. Dance and music, ballet and drama fulfill essentially the same functions, and the arenas in which these arts are available—museums and galleries and theaters of all kinds—constitute a kind of media of their own. The stadia should not be overlooked, as even from ancient times they have been the amphitheaters of popular culture. Professional football is an American version of the Greek games and the Roman circuses.

All this is living culture, and it is also mass communications for two reasons. In a contemporary sense, the numbers of audience who annually patronize galleries, museums, attractions of all sorts, and a wide variety of indoor and outdoor stadia, including but not limited to the professional golf tours, the Newport Races, Forest Hills, the NBA, the Indy 500, etc., is huge. In living bodies these attractions match all but television in audience mass. Further, they are widely reported and broadcast as news events, geometrically expanding their audiences.

Functions

In a longer range, the fine arts, over decades, centuries, and millenia, have developed huge audiences of succeeding generations. The Mona Lisa still lives for countless future millions, while yesterday's television special is forgotten.

But despite the fact that their most apparent role is that of a cultural pipeline, one cannot forget that the arts have other functions, other values. They are information, historical information. They are entertainment, they are persuasion, each in its own way to each individual. Like books and movies, the nonscheduled media, they are self-selective, each individual choosing what he wants and taking from it what he wishes.

In the final analysis, the functions of mass communications will boil down to individuals as receivers, regardless of audience size. Some will read information from the newspapers; others will see only persuasion. Some will be entertained by television; others will be sold a car; perhaps both will occur simultaneously.

Despite the functional thrust of a given medium, so intermixed are all that finally each individual himself will take that particular combination which best suits him, determining himself what is preeminent and to what degree. Out of all of it he will see his world, by and large, as he wants to, selecting not only those media that best conform to his particular vision, but within those media discriminating those functions that best fit his perspective.

There are those who bewail the credibility gap born of unmitigated persuasion, and those who decry the high entertainment quotient of the mass media, which, they say, saps public strength. There are others who claim, with some justification, that the commercial emphasis of mass communications has made Americans acquisitive, even greedy, and that the volume of ulterior persuasion has made the public generally distrustful. This may be, but it places too much credit for credibility on the power of the media and the power of the press, and too little acknowledgement of individuals as functioning human beings. It also overlooks the fact of mass communications as the central nervous system of society, and if it is ulterior and acquisitive, that is because society is.

SUMMARY

In summary, then, the four functions of mass communications each have a role: entertainment provides the vehicle, and information the sense of most mass communications. Persuasion of one sort or another is its purpose, with profit as the overriding motivation, and through it all, cultural transmission is the inevitable result. One may weigh these functions individually, but it will not alter either their ubiquity or, in the aggregate, their social balance.

3 DEVELOPMENT

EVERYDAY MIRACLES

Society takes its mass communications too much for granted. An individual becomes so accustomed to them that he is only dimly aware of the daily miracles that surround him: the newspaper at the door represents tens of thousands of technical and creative man-hours crammed into less than twenty-four hours and reaching from the far corners of the earth. The instantaneousness of television's performance on a typical evening represents a couple of million dollars at least of entertainment and advertising at no cost to the viewer. The ubiquity and variety of magazines and the cinema go unnoticed, a part of life; neither is one ever alone unless he wishes to be. Radio is a constant companion, capable of changing its moods to suit one's own simply by the touch of a button. Nor in contemporary living does one often think of the many ways to occupy his leisure: of the recordings, cassettes, museums, galleries, libraries, and theaters available to him; the spectator sports directly or vicariously participated in. Nor does one heed the hundreds of thousands of book titles begging to be read, ready to take him from the deepest crannies of gothic terror to the stars or the depths and to everything in between, the end product of human imagination and study, reflecting man's glory and his depths of depravity, there for the asking. This is the world of mass communications. A person can speak with a friend oceans away or just down the block, or send a few thoughts and some money to an absent child with the assurance he will receive them in a day or two. This is the diverse world of mass communications, sophisticated, ubiquitous, clamoring for attention.

Mass communications did not spring into being overnight. While accidents of invention and discovery played their roles, the evolution of mass communications was no accident. It was, rather, the emergent result of the interplay of social, geographical, political, technological, and even philosophical forces at work in the sometimes chaotic development of Western society, particularly on American shores.

There must be a starting point to mass communications; most often recognized as such is Johann Gutenberg's invention of movable type circa 1440. Gutenberg's converted winepress ushered in the era of print; this was the beginning of mass communications. Print meant the theoretically endless, repetitive, and almost silmultaneous production of identical symbols—the mass production of meaning. In this, as Marshall McLuhan points out, Gutenberg was also the early ancestor of the assembly line.[1] The industrial revolution, he noted, was the outgrowth of print technology, linear and sequential, differing only in being the mass production of things instead of meaning.

1. Marshall McLuhan, *The Gutenberg Galaxy* (Toronto, Canada: University of Toronto Press, 1967).

Washington handpress.

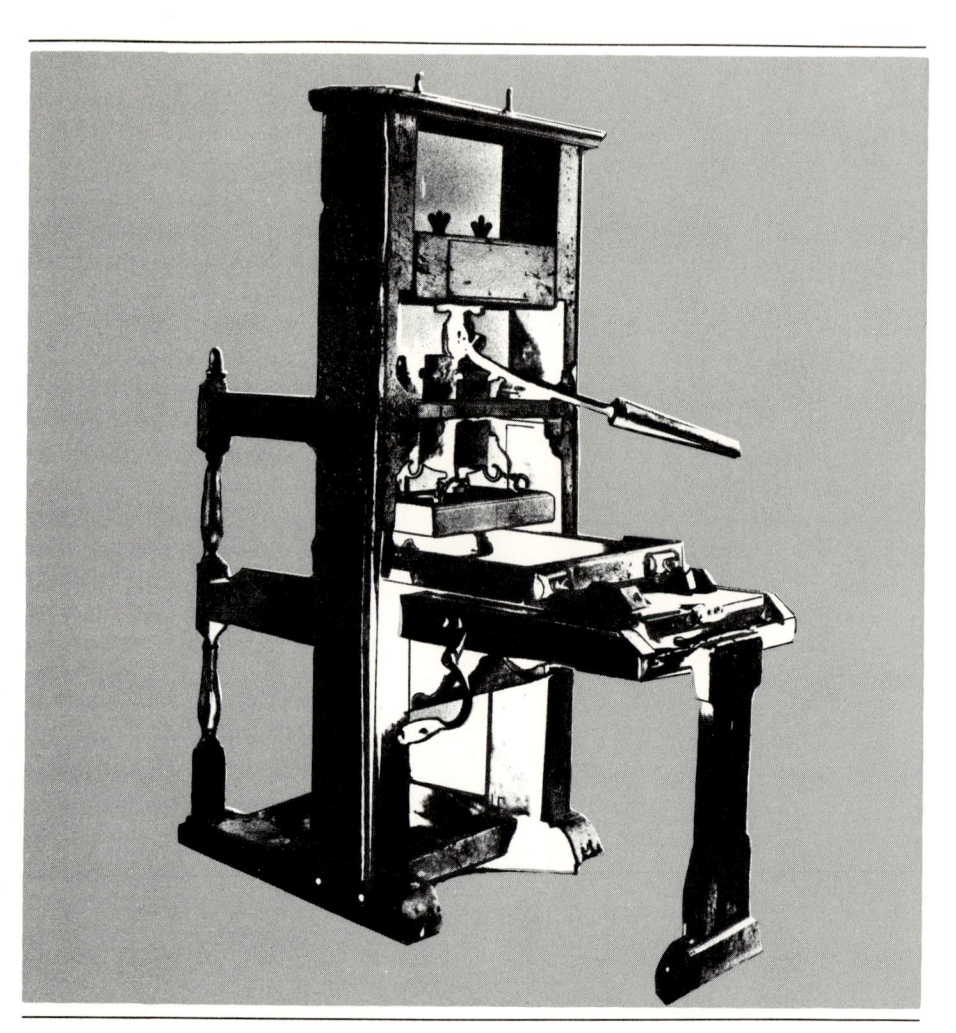

Overview

DAWN OF MASS COMMUNICATIONS

That there had been some form of mass communications before Gutenberg is, of course, apparent. Books were not unknown. But their readership was restricted by almost total illiteracy.

Another form of early mass communication utilized the poem. Poetry, with its structured rhyme and meter, lent itself to memorization, and thus assured that it would pass from person to person, and from generation to generation, relatively unchanged. To change the words and hence the meaning demanded changing both the rhyme and meter. The early historians relied on the poetic form, as in Homer's *Iliad* and *Odyssey*. Early persuaders took to poetry, such as Virgil's *Georgics*, to relieve the population pressure in Rome's urban sprawl; *Le Chanson de Roland* and the Cid were both panegyrics to folk heroes. In ancient Greece, Simonides of Ceos and Pindar made a gracious living writing odes of praise for the ambitious.

Printing was more efficient than other communication forms—quicker, more exact, and private—but printing did not take the world by storm overnight. There was a lag before its full effect on society could be realized, a ponderous inertia to be overcome. The widespread use of books had to await increased literacy, which, in a circular process, depended on the increased distribution of books as the principal tools of literacy. Thus, the direct relationship between mass communications, particularly books, and education was established early.

However, there were side effects to printing unforeseen at the outset. Printing was a private medium; it still is, the results of which are to be consumed at leisure and subject to each individual's interpretation. This thinking in private contravened the authoritative, hierarchical order of earlier society, injecting new viewpoints into the consensus. It encouraged specialization and ultimately the fragmentation of a cohesive society.

UNFORESEEN EFFECTS

Gutenberg's first book was the Bible. Prior to print, in an era of illiteracy, man's view of the Gospel was taken hierarchically from the priesthood, which with rare exception had sole access to books through the privilege of literacy. With printing, man's opportunity to become literate was enormously enhanced. A man could sequester himself with his Bible, reading and making his own interpretations of Gospel—interpretations which were sometimes at variance with Church dogma. As more men did this, formulating new opinions, winning converts and writing their own interpretations, it led to schism within the Church, to fragmentation into different denominations. Both Martin Luther's reform and the establishment of the Anglican Church by Henry VIII—in fact, the entire concept of Protestantism—seems to have had its basis in this process.

In other fields, too, specialization was a product of print. The sciences, medicine, and the law flourished as more scholars personally interested in these fields concentrated their efforts there and, in

Development

turn, contributed new knowledge to print for others to read. This process accelerated, spreading in its wake new currents of individualism and freedom.

Henry the VIII of England saw all too clearly the threat to established order that the new medium represented, and undertook to control it. The principal device he used was the royal licensing of printers; that is, only printers whose loyalty to the crown was unquestioned could receive a license to print. Those who printed without a license were summarily tried and often executed by the court of star chamber. In this fashion were the first controls on mass communications instituted; in this process was the necessarily adversary relationship between government and the press first demonstrated.

THE BOOK IS TOO SLOW

The book was too slow—too slow in production and too slow in consumption—and too costly. Even today as much as a year or more will elapse between an author's finishing touches and publication. Also, a book requires hours of lonely concentration to transfer its message.

The development of society itself, and hence of mass communications, has always been characterized by twin drives for ever greater speed and ever greater numbers. Once the technique of printing had been gradually perfected, it was a simple matter for printers to start issuing tracts and pamphlets, embryonic newspapers and the forerunners of magazines. This proliferation of print, produced in days and sometimes hours for only a few pence, vastly expanded the scope of the print medium, bringing it within reach of whole new audiences in terms of cost and current interest. It further encouraged literacy and accelerated the dissemination of news.

From this expanding interest in current events, backed up by increasing knowledge, grew a new concept of media freedom called *libertarianism*. John Milton, the poet, was its first formal exponent. Libertarianism held that the free and uninhibited expression of thought—traditional or radical, fact or fantasy, true or false—created a marketplace of ideas from which individuals could pick and choose. It further held that mankind was essentially rational and would unerringly, in the aggregate, choose the good and true over the false and evil. The Age of Reason was born, the philosophies of which placed an enormous confidence in the essential wisdom of the people.

This essentially philosophical credo was translated into political terms on American shores following the Revolution and the founding of the first of the Western democracies. This faith in common man, or the body politic, is written into the Constitution politically, and from a mass communications standpoint is reflected in the First Amendment, which guarantees freedom of speech, press, and peaceable assembly.

From a political standpoint the First Amendment protects the adversary relationship between government and the press and constitutes a part of the democratic checks and balances by setting up the press as the watchdog of government. Despite this guarantee, there have been repeated efforts, beginning at the dawn of the Republic and still continuing, to control the press—to muzzle the watchdog.

FACTORS IN AMERICA

With print well established as a medium for over two centuries, showing an imaginative diversity of topical forms as well as daily, weekly, fortnightly, and monthly publications in addition to books, the second phase of medium development evolved as print crossed the Atlantic with the first rebellious settlers.

From the time of the Pilgrims until the winning of the West, and residually since then, the geography of the continent played a significant role not only in social evolution but in its mass communications counterpart.

Life was hard in the wilderness, permitting little leisure. The settling and subduing of a vast continent whose boundaries were unknown at the outset left little time for reading. While the first settlers had an advantage in that they were, for the most part, somewhat literate, they were forced to acquire their news and information on the run, as it were. As a result, books have never been an essentially American medium in the sense that they were in the Old World. America seized upon and developed the newspaper. These newspapers, beginning with the mercantile press of Colonial times, have always patterned their content to suit their audience demand, something that the self-selective book as an author's creation does less well.

There were other factors of geography that played a part in the development of American print media. The early settlements were isolated, far apart, with few interconnections, and only a tenuous sea link to the Old World. Even as transportation grew, it was slow. This factor placed a premium on self-reliance, which fitted nicely into the independent spirit of the settlers. Thus was fostered the spirit of local autonomy, which would be one of the guiding principles of the nation's overall growth. Home rule, states' rights, parochial education, and the local emphasis of the press were to be manifestations of this local autonomy. Even today, with burgeoning federal and state governments, Americans cling to this concept.

Geography played another, more subtle role in mass communications development. A whole continent and its abundant resources lay for the taking. The self-reliance and the aggressive nature of the settlers led them to constantly expand their wealth. They sought and acquired more land at first, then mining, manufacturing, and transportation riches. In this historic expansion lies the reason for America's emphasis on growth. More had always been there for the taking. This concept was fed by the rugged individualism of the American

Development

2. Richard Hofstadter, *Social Darwinism in American Thought* (Boston, Mass.: Beacon Press, 1955).

breed, rebels at heart, and fostered by the spirit of the survival of the fittest—social Darwinism—rampant during the decades of greatest expansion following the Civil War.[2]

LOCAL EMPHASIS OF THE MEDIA

In America the press is locally oriented, owing its basic allegiance to the community in which it lives. As the wagon trains and later the railroads established new communities along the frontier, they brought printers and their Washington handpresses with them to found new newspapers serving the unique demands of each separate community. Even when in the last quarter of the nineteenth century the nations' newspapers were linked together by the telegraph and wire services, they retained their local character.

So strong was the tradition of local autonomy that when the broadcast media burst forth in the 1920s, it was the local stations that were licensed by the federal government to operate "in the public interest, convenience, and necessity" in their own communities. Today, with the dominance of national network television, it is still the individual local stations that are licensed and held responsible for their programming by the Federal Communications Commission.

Everywhere, in American schools, in governmental structure, in election process, in churches and in media, one sees the residual evidence of this local emphasis that began in the lonely, scattered settlements along the Atlantic seaboard almost 400 years ago.

THE TRADITION OF GROWTH

The emphasis on growth as a part of our tradition is reflected in mass communications in three ways. First, it led to the corporate nature of the mass media. As populations and technology grew, the personal newspaper of the individual printer was no longer sufficient. Newspapers, then magazines, radio, and television, became big business. As they did, their purpose subtly changed. They became preoccupied with the balance sheet and with audience size, often measured by extremely sophisticated tools such as television ratings. As they did this, a corporate concept of press freedom evolved, one which was no longer the libertarian concept of an individual's access to expression that the founding fathers had visualized. Press freedom came to mean the institutionalized right of a major corporation to express itself however it pleased.

The framers of the Constitution had no such thought of corporate press freedom in mind. They had no knowledge of contemporary mass media. The Colonial press that they knew was a tiny, personal expression to which most citizens had access. There is little such personal access today to the mass media. The corporate gatekeepers are in control, and press freedom is an institutionalized entity. Public access is difficult, if not impossible.

THE ROLE OF AFFLUENCE

Another of the ramifications of expansion was the accumulation of wealth, individually and in the aggregate, to an extent impossible in the already matured Old World. This composite wealth would result, in time, in the world's highest standard of living, reflected in gross national product. It would also lead to the sizable personal affluence and leisure that are required to support the mass communications of today.

Mass communications is costly in money and in time: the cost of a color television set, maybe several, and of antenna; of radios and transistors, at home and in automobiles; of tape decks and hi-fi; of books; of subscriptions to newspapers and magazines; of payments and interest on such purchases; of movie-going; of attending theaters, concerts, galleries, and shows. All this represents enormous personal outlay, reflective of tremendous affluence. No other nation can directly support mass media as America can. Additionally, they are supported indirectly in the purchase of advertised goods and services.

Mass communications involves another cost, also—the cost of time. It takes a great deal of time to consume mass media on the scale in which Americans do. It takes time to watch television, to read papers and magazines and books, to listen to the radio, to go to the movies and concerts and galleries. Perhaps as much as a quarter of the public's time is given to mass media. It is an affluent people who can afford that degree of nonproductive time from their lives.

This personal and social affluence goes back to the boundless wealth of a great continent there for the taking. No other people has ever had such wealth shoved at them. As the continent now stabilizes, the question arises, "Can we in the future expect the same kind of economic growth that has brought us to the present?"

THE PRESS IN AMERICA

In the New England colonies the press kept track of shipping news, on which the economy depended, plus some modicum of local "ockurrences." In pre-Revolutionary times the Colonial newspapers played a considerable role in advocating independence and nurturing the seeds of revolution. Later, with the founding of the Republic, the press took on a partisan hue and was, by and large, supported by the political parties. In this fashion the kept press, closely paralleling the democratic experiment, played its part in polarizing the body politic into the two-party system. In this it was protected by the guarantees of the First Amendment. Later, in the 1830s, following the populist movement, the press cut its ties to the respective political parties and sought a constituency of its own in the crowded cities. Although it retained its political advocacy, even to the present, the press discovered mass audiences and began to cater to them.

From that day until now there has taken place a seesaw battle between the press' temptation to appeal in terms of sensationalism and its sense of responsibility to inform. Sometimes the former has held sway, such as in the Gay Nineties days of yellow journalism—originated by Pulitzer and Hearst—and in the irresponsible jazz journalism of the 1920s. At other times responsibility has come to the fore, such as during the muckraking crusade of the first decade of this century, and in contemporary times, when the press as a whole, deeply introspective, searches its conscience for a social role.

THE INDUSTRIAL REVOLUTION

The third result of growth emphasis was the competitive free enterprise system characteristic of the American economic structure. As the country moved from the rural agricultural society under which it was founded to an urban, industrialized society under the pressure of the industrial revolution, sweeping changes were wrought. The mass production of goods was, at first, concentrated in the northeast. As factories grew, they soon overflowed their local markets and sought wider distribution. In this they were assisted by the railroads, themselves a product of the industrial revolution. These were the same railroads that concentrated populations at their railheads and interconnections across the expanding nation, uniting, in a sense, press and factory.

These new markets, at great distance from the source of goods, demanded a sales tool and advertising was the answer. Advertising is a sort of automated selling, bearing the same relationship to distribution that the machine does to production.

After the Civil War, it was perhaps inevitable that the nation's growing newspapers, turning out thousands of identical copies daily, each one demanding a reader, and the nation's factories, turning out thousands of identical products, each one demanding a consumer, would find common cause.

Under technological pressure, the costs of newspaper production rose in mid-century; publishers discovered that a few pennies a copy could no longer cover their costs and that advertising could make up the deficit.

In the latter quarter of the century another factor was added to a complex production distribution system—the department store, which offered a showcase, a sales counter, and a warehouse for the products of many manufacturers, thus simplifying the system. Department stores also provided a local source of national advertising that tied in well with the newspaper's local emphasis. Marking this trend, the nation's first advertising agency, N. W. Ayer & Son, opened its doors in 1869.

Thus, the motivating force behind most of our mass media began gradually. Economic pressure gave birth to a commercial circularity that still dominates the mass media. Newspapers, which had already discovered mass audiences in the growing cities and the economics of popular appeal, came under new incentives to cater to even larger audiences, to attract more advertising, to gain greater revenues, to

Overview

provide more capital investment in plant, more efficient production, and better editorial staff to appeal to more readers, and thus attract more advertising. It is the natural process of economic expansion under which the nation has grown that reflected mass communications in the newspapers first, and later in the broadcast media.

EFFECTS OF THE EDUCATIONAL PANACEA

Education also had a part in the development of mass communications. The first settlers were, for the most part, literate, establishing a tradition of education. Harvard College was founded in 1638, less than twenty years after Plymouth Rock. As the industrial revolution began to concentrate populations in the cities with their attendant social problems, the concept of compulsory, universal public education began to take hold. It was felt that only a literate, educated people could achieve the nation's manifest destiny. Consequently, public education created new mass audiences for the nation's newspapers.

As the nation moved into the twentieth century and literacy and education did, in fact, become almost universal, the goal of universal wealth and happiness fell short of the dream. The answer appeared to be more education, first high school, then college. And as college graduates experienced difficulty in finding work commensurate with their education, more and more—again a product of affluence and leisure—sought advanced degrees.

From this unforeseen spiral results began to shape. Up through high school, most education was common. Students were exposed to more or less the same curricula: reading, writing, and 'rithmetic. But at the college level, and particularly in postgraduate work, students began to specialize in fields of their own interest. Gradually, this kind of specialization had a mass communications effect in creating numerous small, specialized audiences that were increasingly catered to by a wide range of "new media"—highly specialized radio, a large assortment of magazines of limited appeal, concerts, movies, and a renaissance of the arts. The case appears sound that this continuing upgrading of the educational level had a direct effect on the specialization of society and the attendant fragmenting of the mass media, resulting in the incredible diversity that contemporary mass communications shows.

TECHNOLOGICAL FACTORS

The wizardry of today's mass communications is overpowering. Millions of identical newspapers land on millions of doorsteps and tens of millions of avid watchers are glued to full-color presentations costing sometimes millions of dollars. Satellites bounce mass messages and individual conversations simultaneously, and computers summarize the collective opinions of nearly a quarter-billion people in an hour or two.

The first channels of communications in the early colonies, following the seventeenth-century European model, were the coffee-

Colonial exchange of information.

houses and taverns where citizens gathered to exchange information and gossip. Some of the proprietors, seeking competitive advantage in the news, sent boats to meet incoming vessels, and began publishing bulletins of ship movements and commodity prices. The seaports where the population concentrated were trade connections between the Old World and new. Gradually, an embryonic press emerged, regularly issued and sold on subscription, concentrating on mercantile news. As these newspapers supplemented the coffeehouses as media, they too organized chains of boats and couriers to meet ships from Europe and be first with the news from abroad. Pooling arrangements developed as the costs of such services increased. These consortiums were the forerunners of the wire services of a century or so later.

The Colonial press flexed its muscles in the cause of independence under the stirring of Samuel Adams, architect of the Revolution. As much as anything, this demonstrated the persuasive effect of mass communications.

Following the Revolution the political identity of the press was

Overview

"Extra! Extra!" After radio, a vanished scene.

THE BETTMANN ARCHIVE

encouraged by the feuding political parties through direct subsidy. This trend was enhanced during the westward movement as printers became United States postmasters, which both facilitated their access to government news sources, assured their loyalty (shades of Henry VIII), and reduced their distribution costs through use of the franking privilege.

But the steam that drove the cotton mills was harnessed to the presses, and the industrial revolution found its mass communications application in 1811. Closer to mid-century, the paper pulp process made cheap paper—newsprint—and thus mass circulation feasible just in time to reach the swelling populations of the industrialized cities. The invention of the rotary press transformed this potential into reality.

In the middle of the Civil War, introduction of the web press doubled production by permitting printing on both sides of the paper at once. Twenty years later the linotype cut makeup time in half, further speeding the dissemination of news and making possible multiple editions and "extras," which were common until the instantaneousness of broadcast media made them obsolete.

Meanwhile, Samuel Morse's telegraph was prophetic in its first message—"What God hath wrought..."—and it ushered in the electric age and the communications revolution in 1844, connecting Balti-

Development

more and Washington. The earlier pooling arrangements of the New York newspapers were organized into the Associated Press, which began to distribute national news via the telegraph, eroding the provincialism of the press; two decades later the trans-Atlantic cable added international news. Alexander Graham Bell's telephone, in 1876, facilitated the gathering of news.

Marconi's wireless at the turn of the century freed information dissemination from its physical net, and opened the door to the broadcast era. Lee De Forest, five years later, perfected the process with the vacuum tube and voice transmission in the ether and radio was born; the electronic age had dawned.

ANOTHER SOURCE: PHOTOGRAPHY

The photograph was perfected by 1839 and began to bring a new dimension of selective reality to graphics. Forty years later the halftone engraving gave greater flexibility of illustration to the nation's presses. Newspapers were further enhanced with the addition of color printing in 1893.

Photography also took another fork, as psychology's contribution in 1822 showed that the eye retains an image fleetingly after the image is gone. This principle, on which the movie is based, was tested a half-century later when twenty-four synchronized cameras photographed a horse race to create the illusion that horses were running. Edison's electric light provided a power source. Then, in quick succession, roll film and sprocket feed for it made the movie possible, and the first halting kinetoscopes appeared in 1895 just in time to entertain the illiterate millions who poured into the United States from southern and eastern Europe.

The electric light also extended the day, fostered the evening paper, and increased considerably the scope of education by means of night schools and the like.

SOCIAL DARWINISM AND LAISSEZ-FAIRE

Meanwhile, other forces were at work. The uninhibited development following the Civil War and the winning of the West were the result of the socioeconomic application of social Darwinism and the political doctrine of laissez-faire, no interference by government. The temper of the times was best summed up in William Henry Vanderbilt's famous quotation, "The public be damned."

However, decades of business excesses by the robber barons and government collusion resulted in reaction by the turn of the century. Socially conscious journalists, editors, and authors (who as a group became known as the muckrakers) utilized all the existent mass communications, newspapers, magazines, and books to expose these excesses and corruption. Their campaign, although national, was uncoordinated; nonetheless, it struck a popular chord and ushered in the first halting pieces of social legislation and control, which, from that time on, would have as much effect on mass communications as it would on the social structure itself.

Overview

Waves of immigrants at the turn of the century affected the direction the media were to take.

Upton Sinclair with his son in 1905, when **The Jungle** was written.

Development

Business under attack fought back, borrowing weapons from theatrical press-agentry, and the practice of public relations as an adjunct to the mass media began. Ivy Lee, known as the "father of public relations," opened his shop in 1906. Public relations was to grow under the impetus of two world wars and the Great Depression. A number of presidents added their unique contributions; business and industry perfected their techniques. Public relations was to become a mainstay of governmental policy, closely allied to politics; a great number of agencies, labor unions, welfare groups, and women's clubs also employed its practitioners.

Public relations became a partner in the news and an ally of advertising, sometimes indistinguishable from either—a situation that would in time create credibility gaps. Today there is, as a result, an inherent and widespread distrust of news sources reaching a climax, reflected in widespread distrust of both government and the news media. It is this sort of situation that can lead to a deterioration of mass communications, to increasing governmental controls, to the rise of demagogues, or to all three.

BROADCAST

After De Forest's vacuum tube, the United States was technologically ready for radio. Its development was held up by World War I, but it burst rapidly upon the nation in the early 1920s. From the beginning radio was basically an entertainment medium, to which advertising was a natural corollary.

Radio also followed the local pattern already well established by the newspapers from Colonial times. It grew up in cities and its early range was short. Pittsburgh was first on the scene with radio in 1919. A year later Pittsburgh and New York were linked in a crude network using telephone lines, and the considerable role that the Bell system would play in broadcast development, both of radio and later, television, was begun. Such early networking established considerable savings in programming costs.

By 1922 radio stations were selling advertising and the commercial influence on mass media made itself felt. It is interesting to note that department stores were among the early owners of radio stations. This liaison with the world of advertising and its considerable revenues caused the emnity of the nation's well-entrenched newspapers. They fought the new medium, clearly seeing its considerable advantage in being first with the news. For a time, through their control of the wire services, newspapers were able to prevent radio from receiving any news from that source. Later, considerable restrictions were placed on wire service material, and it was not until 1936 that radio could obtain the entire daily budget of wire service releases.

But radio was more than a newspaper of the air. It required no physical distribution. It crossed municipal boundaries and state lines indiscriminately, particularly on the crowded East Coast where it was born.

The National Broadcasting Company arrived in 1926 out of a consortium of radio manufacturers seeking to market their product. The Columbia Broadcasting System followed a year later. A year after that the proliferation of radio stations in the eastern cities created an intolerable situation. There were so many operating so close together on the band that none could be received clearly. Radio was destroying itself.

REGULATION BEGINS

When the radio industry itself finally sought regulation, the federal government was the only logical agency to do so, as cities and states could regulate only within their own jurisdictions, and radio signals in the ether carried over political boundaries.

The Federal Radio Commission (FRC) came into being in 1928 to assign frequencies to stations. There were those in government and out who felt that broadcast had a public significance surmounting commercial considerations. They argued for public broadcasting such as England had with the British Broadcasting Corporation (BBC). However, the commercial precedent for radio was already a half-dozen years old; the battle of commercial dominance of the mass media had already been fought and won in the newspapers; and the clear statement of the First Amendment was difficult to circumvent—if radio was a form of the press, and it apparently was.

As a partial salve to the proponents of public radio, the Federal Radio Commission made the requirement that the individual stations must operate in the "public interest, convenience, and necessity" of their own communities. This was a principle to be continued by a successor agency, the Federal Communications Commission (FCC), in 1934. It is to be noted that the individual local stations were licensed by both the FRC and later the FCC, thus perpetuating the local tradition into an era of national media.

As radio gained a foothold newspaper publishers showed interest and began to acquire stations. Theirs was a natural media partnership, one that sought to preserve advertising contacts and increase existing influence. This cross-media ownership would subsequently extend to television.

The Great Depression of the 1930s gave an unforeseen boost to radio. In a time of poverty, radio was free. Radio became America's home entertainment, establishing and solidifying a pattern that would be inherited intact by television. President Franklin D. Roosevelt also clearly saw that the broadcast media went into America's homes directly and without the interpretation and gatekeeping of the press. FDR made radio his own political instrument as he reached into America's living rooms quietly to reassure the people through his fireside chats, a device that he parlayed into four terms in office and

Development

that set the pace for the political use of broadcast media in the future.

ENTER TELEVISION

Surprisingly, the iconoscope and the kinescope, nephews of the vacuum tube and essential ingredients of television, had made their appearance by 1923, and the first experimental television station was on the air in Schenectady, New York, five years later. But social and political forces were to delay television development, first in the form of the Great Depression, and, second, by the demands of World War II. After the war, television was to take the nation by storm, and in a short quarter-century achieve an effect on and penetration into American life unequalled by any medium.

Radio had laid a groundwork for television, establishing the commercial, entertainment, and information mix, creating the networks and their nationwide linkage, and organizing the basis for an ever more complex system of controls through the FCC.

The impact of television radically altered the practice of politics and the operation of government; it fostered the spectacular growth

Antennae of modern man.

Overview

of both advertising and public relations; it brought new vistas of mass entertainment; it took away newspapers' currency, radio's prime time, national magazines' advertising, and the movies' audiences, and, in addition, created a whole new multibillion-dollar industry within a decade. More than any medium, television became a part of daily life—constant and demanding.

THE ELECTRONIC REVOLUTION

In the decades since World War II an accelerating series of technological miracles compounded, giving the name "the electronic revolution" to the era. Battery packs and transistors offered miniaturization to radio, freeing it from a permanent power source and allowing it to be taken anywhere as constant companion, particularly to youth. The FM radio, with its higher clarity and shorter range, opened the door for marriage with the recording industry, and introduced radio's own personality cult with the appearance of DJs, as well as giving radio a new local dimension.

Television was vastly expanded by the UHF band, making a potential of eighty-four channels theoretically possible. Also, CATV opened undreamed-of doors, prophesying a wired nation and instantaneous feedback.

Four generations of computers invaded all facets of society, but particularly in the mass communications field, and heralded a new era of automated information processing, storage, and retrieval. The coaxial cable, microwave relay, laser, and satellite in rapid succession sped increasing quantities of data around the world. Offset printing, facsimile reproduction, color processing, and three-dimensional experimentation brought new aspects to print. In fact, three-dimensionalism was reflected in film, print, and holography, suggesting a new reality around the corner. Electronic instruments and stereophonic sound merging with flashing colored lights added a multimedia effect to concert halls. Advertising and public relations probed the psychological basis of man's motivation, and incredibly accurate sampling techniques became predictive of the future.

Under the influence of television, politics, like the news, also became increasingly reliant on advertising and public relations.

SUMMARY

The phenomena of media change has a cause-and-effect relationship with society as the old dies hard and the new matures slowly.

The development of mass communications, like society itself, has been characterized by twin drives for ever greater speed and ever greater numbers.

In contemporary times the instantaneousness of electronic media indicates that the ultimate in speed has been achieved. Also, since approximately 98 percent of American homes receive television, total saturation has been almost achieved. Today the pinnacle has been reached toward which mass communications has strived since Gutenberg's first laborious Bible.

Development

Despite the near achievement of these original goals, this is not the end; society and mass communications will continue to develop. This is a point in a progression, not the ultimate peak of some communications mountain. What the future holds will be determined in part by the patterns established in the past. From them one may be able to make some educated guesses as to what lies ahead and, at the very least, perceive the kinds of options open.

4 THEORY

TENTATIVE EXPLANATIONS

In any field that cuts across so many aspects of human endeavor, and particularly one that is so closely interwoven with the entire fabric of the social structure as mass communications, it is inevitable that a great many tentative explanations of its operation and effects should be advanced.

Some of these explanations arise out of folk myth. Others are the product of occasional intuitive insights by students and scholars. Others yet are the product of organized research. Some have a long history and the credibility of traditional acceptance. Others have sprung lately to attention. Some are limited in their scope, focusing on a single aspect of the phenomenon of mass communications. Others are so sweeping that their parameters are only vaguely known and they take on the scope of a philosophy.

All share two traits: all have a point of view and an approach dependent on the author's orientation. Thus, they tend to emphasize a single discipline. All lack a complete explanation because of this initial limitation.

One's knowledge of some of the major historical theories of mass communications and some of the contemporary explanations will not only round out a knowledge of the field's complexities, but also provide an inventory from which one can select those items that, in the light of his own knowledge and orientation, best seem to fit the field as he sees it. However, even as none of these theories are the complete explanation, neither are any entirely false; all contain some elements of truth, although some more so than others.

The interdisciplinary nature of mass communications has been noted. Over centuries of development new knowledge has been gained and new theories advanced. There has been a modification of older theories and, more significantly, a cross-fertilization between various explanations. Presently the study of mass communications is becoming increasingly a gestalt in which scholars of many disciplines, freed from the perceptual blinders of the past, have been able to work with each other's tools.

Earliest of the mass communications theories was the *authoritarian*.[1] Henry VIII recognized the inherent threat that uncontrolled printing posed to royal authority, and took steps to control it. His was an entirely pragmatic approach to the problem, which is essentially what the authoritarian theory is. The means of control chosen by Henry VIII was the granting of a license to those of proven loyalty coupled with severe penalties for infraction. To this he added a specific prohibition of certain titles and some instances of precensorship. Thus, less than a hundred years after the invention of mass communications, almost the whole arsenal of communication controls was introduced. These controls were subsequently refined in succeeding centuries to meet different social situations.

1. Fred S. Siebert et al., *Four Theories of the Press* (Urbana, Ill.: University of Illinois Press, 1963).

AUTHORITARIANISM

The authoritarian theory recognizes the adversary relationship between government and the mass media. It seeks to provide some semblance of free expression, so long as this expression is not at odds with government purpose. It also seeks an expression in the mass media favorable to governmental policy. It was this positive aspect of the authoritarian form that Henry VIII sought to encourage by licensing loyal printers whose work, therefore, could be presumed as favorable. Authoritarian theory places great confidence in the power of the press, and little confidence in the individual's ability to select for himself in rational fashion.

LIBERTARIANISM

The opposite of the authoritarian theory was philosophical in base, stemming from the Age of Reason (or Enlightenment) in the seventeenth century. This was an age, born in print, of unparalleled medical and scientific discovery. Scholars perceived an order to the universe and ascribed to man a rational sense. So closely intertwined are communications and the social order that it was inevitable that this Age of Reason should find its communications counterpart in the *libertarian* theory. It was under this theory of completely uninhibited expression that this nation was founded, with a guarantee in the First Amendment to the Constitution. Libertarian theory is a prerequisite to political democracy. Both have their bases in the belief of man's inherent ability to choose correctly, and both hold that multiple choices in the marketplace of ideas increase man's opportunities.

No nation enjoys total freedom of either expression or mass communications. Some controls in the public interest have always been necessary. However, very few nations have total control, finding that some freedom of expression both injects new vitality and provides a public safety valve. This mix of authoritarianism and libertarianism in mass communications, of control and freedom, varies widely in different nations, always stemming from a nation's particular social concepts, traditions, and beliefs. Controls are very much part and parcel of the mass communications system and, thus, will reflect any society's basic economic, philosophical, and political thrust. The United States enjoys a degree of press freedom and communications expression found nowhere else in the world. This is surprising considering the complexity of the American network, which reciprocally probably could not have been developed to the degree it has been without freedom from constraint, either from political sources or economic limitations.

SOCIAL RESPONSIBILITY

2. Ibid.

New legislation, both to control mass communications' effect and protect its freedom, is constantly advocated under social pressure. Into this milieu a new theory of *social responsibility* has recently been advanced.[2]

Essentially, the theory of social responsibility is an extension of libertarianism in that it seeks to protect free expression. Social responsibility places a burden on the mass media to adequately represent all hues of the social spectrum. It seeks to make the mass media responsible for the quality of their offerings, print or broadcast. It seeks to inject truth in advertising and remove the concept of caveat emptor, which, in the uncontrolled commercial world, has seriously eroded a part of media credibility. Social responsibility charges the mass media with the development of and enforcement of ethics in the public interest.

However, any restriction on mass communications, self-imposed or not, is still an erosion of the libertarian concept. And as much as social responsibility anticipates governmental interference and future control and seeks to avoid it through self-policing, a part of the media's total freedom is still destroyed. Self-legislation to forestall governmental legislation is still a form of state control.

Also to be noted is that social responsibility theory is a formal recognition of the corporate organization and institutionalized nature of mass media.

That self-examination and social concern is meritorious on the part of the media is not questioned. Nevertheless, it is an erosion of freedom of speech. In mass communications, freedom and social responsibility, while related, are not synonymous. Further, the concept of social responsibility arose out of social forces: a growing distrust of big business, of which the major mass media was obviously a part; a growing philosophical skepticism that questioned the basic assumptions of the Age of Reason about man; and the infiltration of the media by a growing number of educated professionals (of whom the muckrackers were the first) who sought to right perceived wrongs. In this they were essentially elitist, but they reflected a growing trend in government and many other fields.

Social responsibility continues to be reflected in media reaction

Theory

to social forces abounding in the land. If the press concerns itself and controls itself, it does so as a reflection of popular mood, and because it is good business to do so. Consequently, the self-balancing concept of mass communications as the central nervous system of society still applies. A free press is free to be unfree in response to popular demand.

SOVIET APPLICATION

The *Soviet-Communist* theory of the press, logically, is an extension of authoritarianism, with one important exception. Authoritarian theory holds the need to control dear, but still recognizes the press as an entity outside government. In Soviet-Communist theory, the press is the state; it is a part of the state; it does not exist outside the state. Consequently, all media reflect the national policy or the party line, and all media efforts are pointed toward furthering the state's aim. There can be no repression of the press, for the press is the state.

Soviet-Communist theory, more than any other, emphasizes the corporate, institutionalized nature of mass communications. It is further more sophisticated in its treatment of mass communications than the Western democracies in that it recognizes the arts, drama, architecture, and dance as tools of mass communications in that they have an effect on audience.

The single shortcoming of the theories examined thus far has been their emphasis on the media. Some are mutually contradictory, and others are modifications reflecting an evolutionary process of

The People's Republic of China carefully orchestrates all mass communications.

Overview

change. They are really theories of the press, as Siebert, Peterson, and Schramm so entitled their book, rather than theories of mass communications, for they omit a number of aspects of the mass communications process.

PROFIT THEORY

3. Jack Haberstroh, "Should Fourth Press Theory Really Be Called 'Make-A-Buck'?" *Journalism Educator* 27 (1): 1972.

Another theory is the "make-a-buck" theory of the press, or that of give-'em-what-they-want. Despite its irreverent title, it acknowledges the circularity of the communications process in American society and its commercial influence.[3] It points out that the most successful of mass media in terms of audience and profit are those that cater directly to their specific audiences. The *profit* theory is the expression of the concept of consumer as producer—a concept from which the media depart only at their peril. Such a theory applies not only to the advertising-supported mass media, but to any medium that, if it fails to satisfy its particular audience, will lose that audience. A book becomes a best-seller or a film a box office success as it strikes a chord of appeal in mass audiences.

STIMULUS-RESPONSE: POWER OF THE PRESS

Perhaps most prevalent of the mass communications theories is that best identified as *stimulus-response* and best known as the *power of the press*. The concept behind this theory was born in the last decade or so of the nineteenth century, and was conceived through essentially two factors. In a new psychology, Pavlov's experiments with dogs had captured the public imagination in much the same fashion as Darwin's theory of natural selection, popularized as the survival of the fittest, had captured the American mind a generation earlier and lent philosophical justification to rampant exploitation and laissez-faire economics.

Pavlov popularized the idea of stimulus-response (ring a bell, the dog salivates). It was one short step to apply this principle to the rapidly growing press empires across the nation. Pulitzer, Hearst, Scripps, and others provided a kind of social stimulus, and the public did their bidding. This concept was assisted by Hearst's alleged wire to artist Frederic Remington in Cuba on the eve of the Spanish-American War: "You furnish the pictures, I'll provide the war." The public felt, and wanted to feel, that the power of the press was so great that it could bend America's will around its headlines.

Additional fodder for the power of the press theory was provided forty years later through Dr. Goebbels' propaganda machine during Hitler's Third Reich; his propaganda fanned Hitler's concept of a master race into worldwide conflagration.

The case for stimulus-response as a mass communications theory is strong, but later evidence and research tends to disprove the power of the press as a motivating factor. First, the concept conceives of a single, vast, homogenous public simply awaiting the media's bidding. Recent research indicates that there is not a single public, but many publics of differing views and interests, publics that do not re-

Nowhere is the case disproving a homogeneous public more strong than in attitudes toward sex and censorship.

UPI

spond monolithically. Second, social psychologists have evidence that it is difficult if not impossible to make an individual do anything that he does not already have a predisposition, albeit subconscious, toward doing. As it is the individual that comprises the basic building block of mass communications, these facts seem to cloud the concept of the power of the press.

STIMULUS-RESPONSE CRITIQUE

Although the media have real power, that power is not total. Nor is it likely to be effective unless the media purposefully, or even accidentally, strike a popular chord—that is to say, unless the temper of society at the time is reflected.

In both the Spanish-American War and the Third Reich, such seems to have been the case. Hearst hit upon a popular nerve of Manifest Destiny and American Empire. The country was spoiling for a war to flex its international muscles, and the Spanish-American was a fun war, the last of them. Intuitively, perhaps, Hearst sensed the public mood. America did not salivate because the newspaper empires rang a bell; it was drooling already.

In the instance of the Third Reich, Hitler seems to have sensed the confusion and disappointment in Germany following its defeat in World War I. He felt it crying for leadership and gave it that. In both instances, mass communications seemed to follow rather than lead.

Mass communications is unexcelled at making people aware of products, issues, candidates, and events. It appears to have considerable influence in trivial matters, but far less in matters perceived as substantive.

Contemporary history is replete with examples of political candidates who placed supreme confidence in the power of the press and

Overview

Dr. Joseph Goebels, German Propaganda Minister, 1939.

UPI

were defeated. Most simply stated, the public does not react unless it wishes to.

Among the reasons for the growth of the power of the press theory and the fact that it lingers on despite evidence to the contrary is that it is simplistic, a blanket excuse for many of the irrational acts performed by society. It also generates a certain amount of self-satisfaction in the communications industry. The media and their partners—advertising and public relations—found it in their interest to perpetuate this myth. Much of it, however, seems to be crumbling under both government and social pressure. The prize may no longer be worth the cost.

MASS SOCIETY CONCEPT

An extension of the stimulus-response theory that was popular in the fifties and sixties is the *mass society* theory. Social scientists surveying their world saw increasing violence, social inequity, racial and sexual bias, and what they felt was an appallingly low level of popular culture.

Looking at the candid appeal to the lowest common denominator offered by television and the increasing centralization of media control, they inferred a conspiracy. They felt that the grossness they saw in society was the product of the mass media, and that the mass media purposely fed this base appetite.[4]

They neglected to note that there exists not one big undifferentiated audience, but many intermingling, reflecting all shades of the spectrum of opinion that composes society. Such social scientists were elitist in that they sought to impose their own views of justice

4. Alan Casty, *Mass Media and Mass Man* (New York: Holt, Rinehart and Winston, 1968).

Theory

and culture upon an entire people (whom they largely disdained). They did not observe that when programs of a cultural or educational nature were offered, audiences were small. Finally, they imputed all of society's woes to the mass media. It was easy to find a scapegoat, harder to find an explanation. They neglected the evidence indicating that the mass media were more reflective of society than society was of the media. They credited the common man with little ability to think for himself, to properly judge. In this they were righteously arrogant, with little patience for human foibles. Entertainment, on which a good deal of mass communications was built, was wrong, they felt, because it served no useful social purpose.

Mass society theory verged closely toward the Soviet-Communist theory in its insistence that all mass communications serve a social purpose. While the theory was loose and aloof, it focused attention on many of the shortcomings of the mass media. It held them up to valid criticism, and it hastened social responsibility as a viable alternative to the make-a-buck practice.

THE TWO-STEP THEORY OF COMMUNICATIONS

A theory that places emphasis on the role of the individual in mass communications rather than on the media is that advanced by Lazarsfeld and Berelson. Based on massive studies during the 1940 and 1948 presidential elections, they put forth a *two-step* theory of communications. Two-step is probably better stated as an *indirect* theory of communications; it holds that the effect of the mass media on society is more indirect, filtered through other individuals, than it is direct on the individual himself.

In effect, Lazarsfeld and Berelson emphasize word-of-mouth and interpersonal contact as the bases of public opinion formation and change. Their concentration is less on the tools and techniques of mass communications than on its social effect.

In the course of their studies, they identified opinion leaders appearing horizontally through all levels of society whose views and opinions had great weight with their peers. These opinion leaders further were far greater than average consumers of the mass media. They read more newspapers more thoroughly, they subscribed to more magazines, they read more books, and they listened to more radio (television had not yet appeared on the scene).

Substance is lent to this indirect theory, for common sense and history indicate that public opinion formation and change existed as a major social and political factor long before mass communications. Mass communications has accelerated the process, but it surely did not originate it.

TWO-STEP CRITIQUE

The greatest shortcoming of the two-step theory appears to be that if pursued too diligently, it discredits the considerable original, direct influence of mass communications. While the dimensions of this influence are not entirely known, it is safest to hypothesize that the real function of mass media in the molding of opinion lies in some combination of the stimulus-response and two-step theories.

There are other shortcomings to the indirect theory. It evolved from the political realm, which, because of its polarized nature in society, is relatively easy to study. Consequently, it omits many of the factors of confusion and overlap extant in a broader arena. Because the studies used were concerned with presidential elections, they were necessarily concentrated in time. Public opinion formation is not so restricted. They were also conducted much more than a quarter-century ago and have not been significantly updated. Finally, they were conducted in an atmosphere devoid of television, a media whose full impact, while unknown, is nonetheless enormous.

However, one's own experience can illustrate instances of the two-step theory in action. One tends to defer to significant others in the formation of views. An individual tends to acquiesce to peer group modes and to hereditary examples, which, again, are interpersonal influences. These experiential, traditional, and sociopsychological factors were the fundamentals of Lazarsfeld and Berelson's studies.[5] Their researchers adequately confirmed them and pointed the way toward the interplay of mass communications in the process.

5. Bernard Berelson et al., *Voting: A Study of Opinion Formation in a Presidential Campaign* (Chicago: University of Chicago Press, 1954).

Opinions do not rise out of thin air; they originate with people. In a mass society it is mass communications that speeds and facilitates the dissemination of these opinions and provides at least the stage on which they can perform as society, the actors, gives them life and meaning. In a mass society, the mass media are the interconnections between individuals.

The two-step theory goes a long way toward explaining the spasmodic nature of mass media's effects by injecting individual filtration between the media and consensus. It confirms the expanding effect of mass communications noted in the mass communications model in chapter one. It also seems to place a special significance on the role of the individual in audiences in recognition of the fact that communication is always an individual process.

In expansion of this theory, an individual will receive and interpret mass communications messages according to his own special orientation, regardless of the media used. That individuals do not all perceive stimuli as the same is well recognized. The indirect theory makes allowance for this and further grants the weighted effect of other's opinions. People are simply not all equal in influence.

Opinion leaders take cognizance of this, but theirs is a label easily misunderstood. Opinion leaders are not necessarily, Lazarsfeld and Berelson found, city councilmen, bank chairmen, chamber of commerce presidents, labor leaders, and the like. They exist everywhere, in the classroom, in the shop, on the assembly line, in the ranks. They are those to whom others defer, possibly because of perceived expertise, certainly because of a confidence in them. They may be only vaguely recognized as opinion leaders. Lazarsfeld and Berelson cite the example of a cafe waitress who accepted an unknown customer's opinion overheard in a conversation because "he looked like he knew what he was talking about." Thus, it is perceived expertise that matters. With reference to civic leaders and the like, whose prestige is great and whose opinions are sought, it is more likely that they hold their positions of prestige because they are, in effect, natural opinion leaders by Lazarsfeld and Berelson's definition rather than the reverse. This concept also goes a long way toward explaining the popular appeal of certain charismatic leaders, to whom others defer in business, government, in society as a whole, and at the ballot box because "they act like they know what they're doing."

The two-step theory desperately needs updating and testing in a different social context. It suffers from specialization and time lag, but as a hypothesis of mass communications' effect, it satisfactorily explains known phenomena while still allowing for other views.

THE MEDIUM IS THE MESSAGE

6. Marshall McLuhan, *Understanding Media* (New York: Signet Books, 1966); *Gutenberg Galaxy* (Toronto, Canada: University of Toronto Press, 1967).

A new concept of mass communication that has generated considerable controversy because of its looseness and highly intuitive, even mystical, origin is that of Marshall McLuhan.[6] Wordily outlined in his popular *Understanding Media*, but more concretely defined in his lesser-known *The Gutenberg Galaxy*. McLuhan's concept can be summarized in the familiar phrase, "The medium is the message."

McLuhan embarked on a study of mass media, including advertising, with emphasis on television. He reasoned that mass media reflects society. His studies revealed that it also affects society, but in a far broader, more evolutionary sense than others previously had suggested. McLuhan borrowed a good deal of his initial insight from Norbert Weiner's concept of cybernetics and firmly, though roughly, detailed the two-way-street relationship between mass communications and society, which makes it the central nervous system that it is.[7]

7. Norbert Weiner, *Cybernetics,* 2d ed. (Cambridge, Mass.: The M.I.T. Press, 1969).

Some scholars have misinterpreted "the medium as the message" to mean that the messages that media carry are insignificant. This, of course, is patent nonsense. One ignores the flood warning only at one's peril. One ignores the movie advertisement at the cost of missing the show. Mass media carry messages in terms of information, entertainment, and persuasion; they are significant and important to individuals in varying degrees. McLuhan focuses on the mass media as cultural carriers and sometimes dramatizes their reciprocal effect on social development.

PRINT'S SOCIAL INFLUENCE

In *The Gutenberg Galaxy*, with reference to print, McLuhan points out that as literacy spread, mankind became increasingly accustomed to the literate, linear, sequential, specialized nature of print. Print popularized the logic of symbolic construction wherein isolated characters—letters—were arranged into words of limited meaning, whose connotations were then expanded in sentences,

Overview

strung together in paragraphs of arranged thoughts, organized into chapters for convenience, and finally emerged as a book, a comprehensive examination of a viewpoint.

This logic and discipline evolved into a way of thinking. Increasing specialization led men to expertise, a limited rather than general expertise, which as it grew had the effect of fragmenting society.

McLuhan also describes print as the lineal forebear of the assembly line, in which the mass production of things followed the same logical patterns as the mass production of meaning. From the assembly line the industrial revolution, in combination with specialization, hastened technological advance. Technological acceleration led, in turn, to the communications or electronic revolution into which McLuhan sees society entering now, a revolution that will again alter man's relationship to his world as drastically as print did.

"The medium is the message" means in the largest sense that all forms of media in all ages contain messages for both their present generations and for posterity. McLuhan sees society now at the interface of two cultures—print and the electronic—trying to treat new and radical developments with old tools and print technology: "looking forward through a rearview mirror."

TELEVISION EFFECTS

Narrowing down from his almost cosmic view of long-term media effect, McLuhan concentrates on the electronic media: television, radio, and computers. McLuhan is to be credited for his insight that computers are indeed in the vanguard of the new communications revolution. That they store and process information is well known. It is not generally as well known, however, the degree to which computers communicate with computers—machines talk to machines, enormously shortcutting many of the steps in the communications process, compressing it in time. So independent have computers become in the performance of their functions that McLuhan visualizes man entering a period where he will become little more than the servomechanism of his machines, their sexual organs. He will create them and keep them running; they will do the rest. It is this kind of displaced humanity that McLuhan visualizes as an end product of the electronic revolution.

But the electronic media are already having a potent effect on thought patterns. McLuhan focuses on the phenomenon of television, noting its dominance of lives, and particularly its sweeping influence on youth, whose time it commands from early childhood to puberty. The phrase "electronic babysitter" indicates some of the significance of this influence. McLuhan sees television as transferring more information haphazardly, even indiscriminately, to little brains during their most impressionable years than parental influence, peers, and schooling put together.

But the phenomenon of television is too new to effectively gauge its results. Research has tended to concentrate on the presumed ef-

Theory

Electronic babysitter.

H. ARMSTRONG ROBERTS

fect of television's violence on children while overlooking other questions. What of the sense of impatience and frustration engendered in the young? After a childhood with television, where mammoth problems are capable of solution within thirty, sixty, or ninety minutes, what of a child's ability to cope with the real world, many of whose problems continue for years, if indeed they are capable of solution at all? What long-range effect will this have on the society that the young will dominate in the future?

Television brings a whole world into a person's life. The young travel vicariously to the far corners of the earth. They observe situations known only vaguely to their predecessors. They are participants in complex social situations. This seems to have bred a surface sophistication unparalleled in history; youth know so much. But there is equally a cost; knowing so much, so broadly, the young have little depth. They do not know much deeply; they have had no time to pursue an interest in depth, perhaps not even to develop one. Again, what will the effect of such scattered interest be on society? Will there be leaders capable of devoting intensive time to society's growing problems, or will the job be turned over to machines?

HOT AND COOL MEDIA

These are some of the questions McLuhan raises in regard to the media. Perhaps the most controversial of McLuhan's theories is his widely misinterpreted theory of *hot and cool media*. Hot and cool are relative terms. A hot medium is one whose message is clear and apparent without particular effort or participation on the part of the receiver. A photograph, clear and full color in a slick magazine, is hot. The screen is fine, the colors true, and it is a realistic representation of an actual scene.

Overview
60

Conversely, a cool medium is one whose message requires participation, involvement on the part of a receiver. For example, a cool medium is a cartoon where minimal information is projected, the situation only sketched in a line drawing with a short punch line, requiring the receiver to bring his own experience to bear to find the humor.

Television, McLuhan finds, is cool, demanding active participation from the viewer. First, in a complex physiological sense, the viewer must mentally fill in the blank spaces in television's coarse photographic screen. He must be physically present, and he must draw on his own experience to bring meaning to the screen. Further, the message is continually interrupted by unrelated commercials, which present a mosaic pattern demanding intense concentration and frequent, although subconscious, changing of mental gears. Television is involving, McLuhan points out; it transports one to its origin and his mind is the screen rather than the tube.

There appears to be some evidence in support of participative viewing. One notes the enormous incidence of travel, coincident with the television era. As one is transported on the tube to the far corners of the world, he discovers the urge to go himself. Travel appears so very simple as one sees others like himself in St. Peter's Square or the Ginza. The same is true of skiing, of golf, of a wide variety of other activities, even, surprisingly, professional football and reading. Television's popularization of professional football has brought fans to the stadia in droves despite the fact that, ironically, it can be seen and followed better on the video screen. Further, whenever an author appears on a television talk show to plug his book, the bookstores sell out of that title the next day, and libraries put all their copies out on loan. The involvement aspects of television are little understood, but nonetheless extraordinary. This is one of the principal highlights of McLuhan's media theories, which, while much criticized for their lack of rigor and their intuitive rather than empirical basis, do still point a way that shows some promise of greater communications understanding in the future.

MATHEMATICAL THEORY: CHANNEL CAPACITY

8. Claude E. Shannon and Warren Weaver, *Mathematical Theory of Communication,* 4th ed. (Urbana, Ill.: University of Illinois Press, 1969).

Another approach to mass communications is Shannon and Weaver's *mathematical* theory of communications.[8] Essentially, this is a theory of channel capacity developed for the Bell System by whom they were both employed. As the name suggests, their theory is heavily involved with the mathematical and engineering aspects of communications, and less so with either effect or the semantic questions of transferral of meaning. However, as Weaver points out, the communications process is so tightly interwoven that matters pertinent to channel capacity, particularly encoding and decoding techniques, cannot help but have an effect on the larger questions.

Most significant among Shannon and Weaver's tools was the use of the *bit* of information. The word *bit* is an abbreviated form meaning binary digit, where "0" stands for "yes" and "1" for "no." A simple electrical relay in closed position, current flowing, is 1—that is, no, and in open position, with no current flowing, is 0—yes. Theoretically, 0 and 1 can stand for anything, the King James Version of the Bible or the Gettysburg Address; it is simply a matter of encoding and decoding. Since binary digits are the language of computers, Shannon and Weaver have cleared a trail for a new understanding of their roles in computer communications.

Studying the term *entropy* from thermodynamics, Shannon and Weaver found evidence of the existence of this phenomenon in communications. Entropy is the tendency for any system to run down, to resolve in chaos. That this should be true as the limits of channel capacity in communications are mathematically extended brings an exciting relationship with the physical sciences into the heretofore essentially social science world of mass communications.

On another front, Shannon and Weaver, looking at Norbert Weiner's work in cybernetics, found considerable evidence that freedom of choice in communications on the sender's part is limited by different feedback. In one instance the syntax of the language itself is limiting. For example, the probability in a telegram that u will follow q is very high. Similarly, the probability that the word following the word "inasmuch" is "as" is correspondingly high. Continuing this thought, one finds instances of communication limitation as a conversation progresses, that is, as mutual feedback progresses. It was noted in chapter one that when a person says "Good morning, how are you," he has effectively limited another's choice of replies. This continuing limitation of choice and tendency for entropy is known as a Markov chain.

The investigations of Shannon and Weaver into encoding and decoding devices is valuable as society continues to place additional emphasis on the computer. Computer breakdown is almost always an encoding or decoding failure. One often hears of the computer making a mistake. Actually the computer does not make mistakes; the computer does exactly what it is told to do. It cannot do otherwise, so any mistake of the computer must go back to inadequate instructions—an encoding failure, human error. As these electronic devices become more sophisticated, furthermore, the opportunity for failure increases.

Noise, which was also discussed briefly in chapter one, can also be traced to encoding failure. The blurred picture on a television screen can mean that the encoding device transforming an actual scene into electrical impulses is not performing correctly, or a bad connection on the telephone can mean that the encoding device transforming voices into electric impulses is malfunctioning. Shannon and Weaver's encoding and decoding devices are purely physical, electrical or mechanical, and have no relationship to the semantic encoding and decoding devices between sender and receiver. However, as their research indicates that some noise—channel noise—is the result of encoding failure, so they open the door to the concept that there is a close relationship between channel noise and semantic noise, which has been recognized for some time as encoding or decoding failure on the part of individuals. It was this type of correlation that Weaver had in mind when he hinted at the direct, although to date unseen relationship between their work in channel capacity and the larger questions of meaning and effect.

LUDENIC THEORY: PLAY

9. William Stephenson, *The Play Theory of Mass Communication* (Chicago: University of Chicago Press, 1967).

The last theory with which we shall be concerned is also the most recent: William Stephenson's *ludenic* theory, or the play theory of communication.[9] Stephenson's work is significant for several reasons. Working from a complex Q-sort methodology, he offers empirical evidence of the relationship between the mass media, mass audiences, and the entertainment function. In doing so, he gives firm support to the notion of consumer as producer: "In my view, mass communications is better understood as being manipulated subjectively by its audiences who thoroughly enjoy what they are being offered for the first time in man's history."

Stephenson also bears down on the consideration that in an emerging postindustrial society, where the total of man's efforts need to be devoted neither to production nor to survival, relative affluence is the key factor not only in permitting the mass media explosion, but in permitting persons to devote so much of their time to nonproductive activities—to leisure. Consequently, Stephenson makes a distinction between work and play: work is serious, gainful, hard; play is fun, relaxing, leisurely.

A considerable portion of mass communication is work, concentrating on the information function. But a lot more of it, in fact most of it in contemporary American society, is play—nonproductive entertainment. Stephenson makes the point that in a less leisurely era, in the formative phases of American society during the last century, a far greater portion of mass communications was work, purposeful information. He also notes that there was always injected a fill of play, of entertainment, as a relief or contrast or balance to an unrelenting diet of purposeful information. He sees this true even in the Soviet Union today. In the USSR, where all mass communications serves the purpose of the state, Russian radio still provides hours of music as a break or fill for the purposeful propaganda that it carries.

In his treatment of the relative affluence that permits Americans to indulge in leisure, Stephenson makes room for the wide assortment of esoteric mass media which are gradually achieving unprecedented popularity in American society. These cultural carriers have been previously noted: theater, art, museums, ballet, drama, poetry, music, symphony, multimedia rock shows, sculpture, and the like. They are media in terms of audience effect, as he demonstrates through his methodology, thus tying in the vague function of cultur-

Theory

al transmission more closely to the study of mass communications, and identifying them at the same time as a part of the play tendency now achieving ascendency in the mass media.

Nowhere but in ludenic theory is there so close an association between entertainment and affluence, and, by inference, the advertising that pursues affluence.

CONVERGENT SELECTIVITY

Perhaps Stephenson's greatest contribution, however, is the distinction, hinted at by others, of two different forms of persuasion, one of which he identifies, perhaps poorly in a semantic sense, as "social control." This is the kind of persuasion, associated with politics and public opinion change, that has its basis in one's deepest beliefs and attitudes, which are very difficult to change. The other form of persuasion Stephenson calls "convergent selectivity" on the part of audiences or, rather, the individuals within them. Convergent selectivity is the perception of persuasive messages; an individual perceives that nothing of substance is at stake. It perceives some messages as inconsequential in terms of attitudes, trivial—purposeless. Thus, since no basic principles are involved, the members of audiences are free to indulge themselves. To this Stephenson attributes the observable success of modern advertising in selling consumer goods and its sometimes spectacular failures in changing attitudes or electing candidates. This phenomenon has been observed by others, such as J.A.C. Brown, but not previously placed within a theoretical framework where it could be examined.[10]

Stephenson's play theory of communication is an integrating theory. It suffers from wide gaps and from too little evidence, but it does go a long way toward establishing the close relationship between mass media usage and the values of society. As it does this, substance is added to the analogy of mass communications as the central nervous system of society, alternately reflecting and modifying that society.

Stephenson's theory is also at odds with some of the classic theories of mass communications developed by early journalists, first in the field with their emphasis on information. If there is a glaring weakness in Stephenson's theory, it is the partial exclusion of information as a major factor in mass communications. As all communication is at base information exchange, this down-playing of the information function (work) is a penalty. In the mass media, the production of television, newspapers, magazines, books, and movies are for some hard work; these media have a purpose, a basic economic purpose. However, recognizing this shortcoming, one can still credit ludenic theory with a great step forward toward explaining signs of the times wherein there is more play and less work in society and more entertainment and less information in mass communications.

There is talk of a four-day workweek. Recreation departments in colleges and universities are overflowing; there is more and more lei-

10. J.A.C. Brown, *Techniques of Persuasion* (Baltimore, Md.: Penguin Books Inc., 1963).

sure and travel and theater-going, second homes and longer vacations. Ludenic theory unites these social phenomena with mass communications.

SUMMARY

There have been a number of tentative explanations of mass communications phenomena, each varying widely according to the discipline of the theorist. None is totally correct, nor totally in error. A knowledge of each is essential to an understanding of mass communications.

The authoritarian theory is the oldest. It recognizes the adversary relationship between authority and the media, and seeks to control the media by various means. It recognizes the effect of mass communications on audiences.

The libertarian concept, under which the United States was founded, developed in reaction to authoritarianism. It holds that in a free marketplace of ideas man can and will make correct judgments, that truth will out. It places a premium on man's inherent good judgment.

A melding of these two concepts is the social responsibility theory, which places a burden on the media to serve a public responsibility. Problems arise in defining social responsibility, and also in the fact that the media may only undertake this burden to avoid more stringent controls.

The Soviet-Communist theory makes no distinction between media and state; they are one whose purpose is to foster the aims of the state.

The theory of the power of the press grew out of the stimulus-response (s-r) theory, which holds that massive exposure of any concept in the mass media inevitably results in desired public reaction. Despite the fact that this concept has been largely disproven, there remains considerable lingering influence.

A recent addition to communication theory is the profit theory, which simply holds that the mass media will offer their audiences whatever is profitable for them to offer. It is difficult to refute this theory in a highly commercialized society.

The mass society concept is an offshoot of the s-r theory; it holds that mass media are denigrating mankind, molding it into a sameness of mediocrity. Although there is some evidence to support this theory, it does not take into consideration the diversity and multiplicity of the mass media themselves nor their audiences.

Marshall McLuhan's controversial theories are based in the electronic revolution. He maintains that the form of the media themselves has greater effect on society than the messages it contains. This is not to discount the effect of the content, but rather to emphasize the effect of the long-term and often overlooked media forms.

The mathematical theory of communication is a theory of channel capacity developed for the Bell System. It is based on *bits* of information that have their origin in binary theory. It particularly lends itself to computerization.

The ludenic or play theory is an integrating theory that quite successfully seeks to pull together many of the loose ends of communication theory. It is the communication counterpart of the theory of cognitive dissonance.

Finally, there is Lazarsfeld and Berelson's two-step theory of communication, which grew out of massive empirical studies. It points out with considerable evidence that the effects of mass communications are less direct than indirect, filtered through other people.

Part II

THE CONTINUA

In considering mass communications as a social institution, one must perforce talk about people, living entities. It is this aspect of mass communications that has been too often overlooked. The reasons are unimportant, but evidence seems to point toward the fact that the mass media themselves are easier to isolate and to treat; they are tangible, audible, visible. This media emphasis does a disservice to communications, first, by treating only a part of the process, but more significantly, by discounting people as a part of the process.

One of the miracles of mass communications, unlike other social institutions, has been that its various forms have continued to survive, even to thrive, after they have been replaced by more efficient forms. To coin a phrase, in mass communications obsolescence seems to be the gateway to prosperity. One notes, for example, how television replaced radio as the primary national mass medium, usurping networks, audiences, and prime time. Radio should have died. It didn't and it exists today more proliferate and more profitable than it ever was in its heyday in the twenties and thirties. Why? Because more people turn it on, of course. Why?

Mass communications, like all society, has been attuned to progress. This has meant a historical striving on the part of the mass media for ever greater speed and ever greater numbers of audience. Today society is on the brink of the ultimate in both these categories, with the instantaneousness of the electronic media and the almost total saturation of American homes represented by television—98 percent or so. With ultimate goals nearly reached, where does communications go from here? Mass communications, as the central nervous system of society, is dynamic; it keeps moving. But where does it move when it has reached its destination? These are key questions to be asked as one considers mass communications.

The device used to assess this process of progress is a pair of twin continua—one of mass media and one of audiences—that parallel one another like railroad tracks. This analogy is fair in that without both tracks, no train can run; without both media and audiences, there is no mass communications.

The continua are models of reality, and like all models they are imperfect, but they go a long way toward integrating the tangible properties of media with the intangible qualities of people, both as individuals and in larger aggregations. Further, they permit a certain flow to the communications process that involves both, permitting one to see at what junctures the two continua involve each other.

Followed along the path of their development, the continua, which are spectra of people and of organizations, also show a certain vague predictability of the future course that mass communications may take in the United States. These predictions, while not absolute, are at least indicative of what the future options may be.

Taken in their entirety, too, the continua offer some explanations for recent social phenomena, namely, the increasing selectivity and individuality accompanying increasing uniformity, and the intense competition for the time-limited individual's attention, not merely by the deafening noise of accelerating mass communications, but by the increasing pace of life, of which, of course, mass communications is an integral and significant part.

Finally, the continua, if nothing more, place the emphasis in mass communications on the individual who is a member of every audience, large and small, every group and public, every crowd, and of whom the ratings are but a sterile and demeaning, although remarkably accurate, representation.

The continua show mass communications as a moving, changing force acting on and acted upon by its audiences.

5 MEDIA CONTINUUM

SPEED AND NUMBERS

The evolution of mass communications has always been marked by the twin drives for ever greater speed and ever greater numbers of audience. Speed and size have been its goals. Consequently, mass communications has always taken advantage of developing technology and paralleled the course of other social institutions.

But, uniquely among social institutions, mass communications has been characterized by the fact that as older and slower forms of mass media have been supplanted by newer and more efficient forms, the older ones have nonetheless continued to exist, and to thrive.

Within a generation the horse and buggy faded into oblivion before the onslaught of the automobile. Yet in the realm of mass media, books and periodicals, movies and newspapers, radio and telegraph all continue to coexist alongside predominant television.

The answer to this paradox seems to lie in the fact that the mass media are not separate and discrete, but are rather part and parcel of a single continuum, united by the factor of effect upon the people who individually and collectively, in different groups and in the broadest mass, comprise their respective audiences.

A historical examination of such a media continuum will reveal that each of these media was, in its own time, the preeminent mass medium. That is, each medium occupied a point in history when it served and catered to the largest possible audience. It is significant, for example, that Gutenberg's first effort was the Bible, for the literate of the time who composed his only audience were mostly clerics. The influence of the church was predominant, and the prevailing cultural interest was religious in 1440. Gutenberg, father of mass communications, catered to the largest audience capable of receiving.

The book was a social revolution opening the doorway to ever-expanding literacy and knowledge. It piqued a public curiosity, which, once aroused, demanded more. This snowballing effect of print, combined with the constant pressure for greater speed and numbers, quite early led to not only more books but different forms of print in tracts and flyers. These new forms offered a more immediate, if cursory, overview of contemporary events at a much cheaper cost, sacrificing as they did so the book's elegance, permanence, and depth.

Marshall McLuhan points out that each new medium grows out of an earlier form and evolves into something totally different. As this process compounds, it forms the basis of the media continuum. The media represent an incomplete spectrum along which at present society occupies a moving and an accelerating point leading rapidly to media forms only guessed at or even unknown yet.

THE INSTITUTIONALIZING PROCESS

The book yielded to the tract, capable of reaching more people more quickly; yet the book remained, for, unlike the tract, its permanence and depth suited it to the scholar and the specialist. No longer beamed to the cleric nor bound to religious themes, it became the reservoir of knowledge and discovered a new freedom of expression, ideas, and a new market—the individual. This is still its basic appeal. The book is self-selective, like fashions in a boutique, purchased by individuals for their own consumption.

With growth, there is a certain institutionalizing effect as society seeks to order its creations. This happened to the little tract. Discovering a popular market and with an eye for commerce, the early printers sought to capitalize their advantage. They began to publish regularly and discovered that they could count on roughly the same numbers of customers for each issue. The concept of circulation was born—the formal, quantitative expression of audience numbers. Such a profitable concept encouraged schemes of increment. One method was to step up the frequency of publication from monthly to fortnightly to weekly and eventually to daily as technology improved, yielding factors 2x, 4x, and 30x to circulation. The tract evolved into a periodical, which was, of course, the early ancestor of both newspapers and magazines.

One of the offshoots of circulation was a certain predictability of audience and hence of revenue, which led, in turn, to an opportunity for planning, both of investment and technology. This was a giant step forward for the little tract, and it found itself becoming highly organized and institutionalized, ever paralleling the course of a more complex society.

ADVERTISING

With regular publication and predictability of audience, another factor was injected into printing. Dealing basically in information, this factor turned to a different sort of information: the availability of goods and services. Thus, an early form of advertising entered the picture. The early printers often included announcements in their

The Continua

tracts of other titles in their inventory. It was but a small step to make such announcements available to others—the butcher, the baker, and the candlestick maker—at a price.

As the mass media evolution took place, preoccupation with audience size led to fairly sophisticated circulation predictability, which paved the way for more and more publishing costs to be borne by advertising and less and less by the item itself.

Along the media continuum, the early book evolved into the tract, the periodical, and finally, the daily newspaper in its search for greater speed, numbers and, incidentally, profit.

As books and daily newspapers grew, they created a vacuum in the continuum, and nature abhors a vacuum. There was a wide gap between the slow, ponderous and self-selective book and the frenetic newspaper chattering away at presold urban audiences. The gap cried for occupancy, and magazines were the answer. They found a willing market in national audiences on two counts: they had a freedom from the newspaper's geographical circumscription, and from the newspaper's preoccupation with the immediate. The magazine had a little time to digest and reflect and offer a more rounded version of news. Its slightly slower pace also accommodated it to mail distribution, for which the U.S. Post Office granted it special rates. It also drew willing support from national advertisers whose goods were just beginning to move across the entire continent.

ELECTRIC IMPACT

With the coming of the telegraph in 1844 the electronic age dawned and no one knew it.

From the perspective of the continuum, the telegraph permitted newspapers to compete in the national marketplace with magazines and to do it quicker. The telegraph heralded the age of the great newspaper empires of Joseph Pulitzer, William Randolph Hearst, and E. W. Scripps in making possible centralized control, simultaneous national advertising on short schedule, and the rapid dissemination of national news. Born in the Gay Nineties, and although still focused on the population centers, the wire-service-linked newspaper empires, in terms of overall breadth and aggregate circulation, became the nation's first mass medium in the modern sense. Magazines and books continued their supplementary roles.

The miracle of electricity grew apace, compressing space and extending time, heralding a revolution the dimensions of which are not yet known. After the telegraph came the transoceanic cable, adding international news to the daily fare and foreshortening the world. The wireless was only a step beyond, the forerunner of radio and eventually television.

Versatile electric energy lit the night, increasing literacy, education, and knowledge, extending the day and filling the hours, creating in its wake an ever-increasing demand for more and more media. One of its spin-offs was the cinema, which rose rapidly as a mass medium, but because of certain inherent limitations was destined to remain in a supplemental role.

RADIO: A NEW MEDIUM

Newspapers peaked as the country's preeminent mass medium in the late 1920s. This is considered their peak in that after this period they were no longer the only mass medium capable of reaching the vast majority of the people. Radio became a competitor. Not only could radio disseminate information (and entertainment) faster, but radio could reach with equal speed into the nooks and crannies of rural America as well as its urban centers, greatly increasing audience and, incidentally, attracting advertisers.

Radio also made a unique contribution to the media continuum. It was the first of the mass media to be supported exclusively by advertising, in which the product was in effect, a giveaway. As an essentially commercial medium as none before had ever been, radio placed a new premium on entertainment to attract and to hold audiences.

This factor, quite apparent on the continuum, forces the inescapable conclusion that the entertainment and commercial functions of mass media positively correlate and exist to the greatest degree in the presence of the "massest" audience. These functions decline and the information function rises as audiences grow smaller and more selective, the information function attaining its zenith among the relatively tiny audiences of the self-selective book.

While newspapers recognized radio's competition for their audience and advertising dollars and feared it, they found they could live with it by altering their operations. The advent of radio as a serious medium was the beginning of the end of the helter-skelter proliferation of newspapers. There were other factors involved in the demise of newspaper primacy, of course: rising costs of operations, the enormity of investment. But essentially, the competition that radio offered in the field of information, plus the radically expanded entertainment feature, forced a retrenchment and consolidation on the part of the nation's metropolitan newspapers. There began a trend toward fewer newspapers, and they began to concentrate to a greater degree on their information function, offering more news in depth, which is what they could do best; gradually the totally flamboyant and ultrasensational, which characterized the eras of yellow journalism and jazz journalism and carried forward well into the third decade of the twentieth century, was forsaken. In short, instead of being in competition with each other, newspapers found themselves in competition with radio, not so much in the realm of news as for audiences and, hence, advertisers. They began to specialize in what they could do best, rather than catering to the entire broad spectrum of human appeal. It was a slow change; newspapers are still changing.

Then came television.

Radio, the first of the broadcast media, had no sooner begun to mature than its giant rival was born. Delayed by World War II, television came into its own in the postwar years. A stirring infant in 1949, it had taken its first steps by 1952, reached puberty by 1955, and fully matured a decade later.

Individual consumption of the printed word.

COMPLEMENTARY CHARACTERISTICS

At this point in the continuum of media development, it is useful to compare the characteristics of those two media at the poles of the continuum, the oldest and the newest forms, the book and television. It will be evident that the constant striving for speed and numbers, which has by now nearly achieved the ultimate, with instantaneous transmission into approximately 98 percent of American homes, has not been accomplished without some cost.

The ancient book was slow both in production and in consumption. This is not congruent to today's pace. The book is difficult to obtain and expensive to purchase. Trade books range upward from five dollars, and bookstores are remote and generally restricted to the larger cities. In order to obtain a book an individual must be willing to invest some time and money to do so. In this books are unlike most other media. But the book's liabilities are also its strengths in today's society. It is permanent, a ready reference. It adds an element of stability and a link to the past in a too rapidly changing world. Of all media, its information content is the highest. Its length and the slowness of its consumption permit it to explore a single topic in considerable detail. It is specific; it caters generally not to a mass audience but to an individual taste. It is in this sense self-selective. Finally, the book pays its own way; it has no advertising support whatever because its potential audience size is unknown.

Media Continuum

At the other end of the continuum, national network television appears to be the diametric opposite of the book in every aspect. Far from slow, it is instantaneous. Its availability is constant, and reception is free (although its indirect costs are considerable). These are its great advantages, but here too there are concessions. Television can give only the most cursory overview of events. It is severely time-limited, presenting tiny fragments of topics in a haphazard mosaic. Far from a single topic, it skips and jumps, demanding a constant changing of mental gears from program to commercial, from documentary to cartoon to news. Television is, in every sense, a "now" medium.

Furthermore, because it is apparently free, it is totally supported by advertising and, consequently, must cater to the largest possible audience with programming to attract the common interest—the lowest common denominator of appeal.

As the book was high in information, television minimizes this function, restricting its news coverage to marginal hours on the fringes of prime time.

While entertainment, to a degree, is a function of all mass communication, television raised it to the place of honor as bait for audience, which, in turn, was bait for advertisers who paid the bills.

Thus, from the point of view of freedom of expression, the expansive book, with no predetermined audience and no advertisers to worry about, is freest of all to offer what it wishes for whomever wishes to buy. Network television, under the tyranny of ratings, is forced to program "proven" material that will appeal to the forty million homes tuned to prime time.

Thus, each medium, as it appears along the contemporary continuum, forms a part of a mass communications whole. The separate media complement one another in fulfilling the functions of mass communications. Where one is low in entertainment, another is high; conversely, where one is low in information, another is high. Where the audiences are largest, approaching totality, advertising and entertainment are highest too, but at a cost in depth and information, which is still necessary in society. This information function is admirably filled by the smaller and more specialized media such as the self-selective book. Thus, each succeeding mass medium has continued to survive and to prosper, even after it was replaced along the continuum in the course of events by a more efficient medium.

Toward what is this efficiency directed? The sole goal of mass communications is not to achieve greater speed and numbers; too often such has been believed. The goal is rather to fulfill the mass media functions in their totality. If television best serves the commercial and entertainment functions, the book best serves the information function; at least half of all books are textbooks. The other media respectively find fulfillment in differing combinations and weightings of functions somewhere between these extreme poles.

The Continua

SPECIALIZATION

Media have survived by specializing, by fragmenting, by seeking smaller and more specific audiences that they can serve, parts of the mass. The classic example of this specialization is that of radio, which, by all rights, should have died when television was born. It did not, and it survives today in far healthier and wealthier condition in the aggregate than it ever enjoyed when it was America's preeminent mass medium during the depression and World War II.

Television took radio's evening prime time. Television usurped radio's national advertisers and network operation. Television communicated better with sound and pictures and motion, instead of the little black sound box. Radio should be dead.

Radio found a new prime time that television couldn't match, in the driving time when America goes to work and back. Radio put itself in automobiles. Radio found new local markets; it also found music and teenagers and fed one to the other. Under technological pressure radio pioneered miniaturization and battery packs, freeing it from a power source. Its new mobility took it places where television couldn't follow: to the beach, to the country, to the stadium, to the picnic. Radio went local; it perfected the disc jockey as a personality; it diversified, with each station picking a segment of the total audience for its own. It fragmented, concentrated, specialized, and in so doing built up new audiences with transistors to their ears.

In instance after instance, this specialization under pressure has restored obsolescent media as they concentrate on that unique combination of media functions that they can perform best. In the gestalt of American society each media form finds its own place where its particular formula of characteristics ideally suits it to a particular grouping of people—its audience.

THE INDIVIDUAL AND THE AUDIENCE

It is important to note that audiences are not discrete, that ordinarily they ebb and flow, always changing as individuals move in and out of them. It is the individual, each member of society, who comprises audiences. Membership in these audiences is voluntary for the most part, and one joins these different media audiences as the mood strikes. Audiences have a random composition.

Society comprises the "massest" audiences for network television; individuals within this society are also the self-selective consumers of a book that strikes the fancy. Some are the esoteric audience for a magazine on dry fly fishing, as well as the urban audience for a metropolitan newspaper, and the audience for radio's rock 'n' roll. Society is comprised of separate individuals who move in and out of these media audiences in accordance with how best each fits the changing moods and needs of any given moment. These separate media continue to thrive because there are so very many individuals, and they are collectively so affluent.

John Merrill and Ralph Lowenstein point out in *Media, Messages and Men* that the media cannot be separated from one another.[1] This

1. John Merrill and Ralph Lowenstein, *Media, Messages and Men* (New York: David McKay Co., Inc., 1971).

Media Continuum

is true, and this is a part of the significance of the continuum that is a whole, an expanding whole, along which each medium can be imperfectly observed—imperfectly because more than anything, it is a part of mass communications while an entity in itself. Also, even as it is observed, each medium becomes something somewhat different. The media are the central nervous system of society, an analogy that describes their basic activity and emphasizes their inseparability, their "part and parcelness" of contemporary American society. No other society has this particular mass communications network; no other society could have it because no other society is identical.

Further, in performing their various functions, the media feed one another's audiences in their changing roles, in the same general sense that the big chain department stores and speciality shops and boutiques in a giant shopping center feed one another customers. The late news on television arouses curiosity about an event that is partially satisfied by the morning paper and more fully satiated in *Newsweek*. A novel read constitutes an invitation to the movie based upon it. Radio disc jockeys and their wares excite audiences for rock group concerts. A collection of old masters in a museum leads an individual to books on Renaissance painting. There is a circularity to the various media appeals that correlates closely with the interests of society.

Marshall McLuhan has noted that each new medium grows out of an older form. In fact, the older medium becomes the content of the new—as speech became the content of print, and print the content of the book, and the book the content of the movie, and the movie the content of television.

HYBRID FORMS OF MEDIA

In this interrelationship of the various media forms, McLuhan failed to note a certain bridging action as the various media seek to fill the gaps, the vacuums, in the continuum. This action seems to be a direct function of commercial pressure, a constant seeking of new markets. The proprietors of the various media, since they are all in the communications business, look with envy at the markets of their competitors. The corporate structure of the mass communications network is manifest by implication on the media continuum in the interesting variety of hybrid media that appear along the spectrum as the corporate media proprietors seek to adapt each other's business for profit. Nor is it surprising that in a highly organized, institutionalized, corporate, contemporary society that the mass media should themselves be highly organized, institutionalized, and corporate.

Book publishing, for example, which is always a chancy game, has led publishers to look for wider markets and greater security. One approach in diversity has been the paperback, which sought to combine book publishing with the widened consignment distribution system used by magazines. The smaller size and cheaper price of the paperback lent itself to this kind of distribution through drug stores, liquor stores, supermarkets, newsstands, and terminals, where display racks provided a showcase.

At the same time, innovative book publishers took to prepublication serialization of forthcoming titles in consumer magazines for both additional exposure and revenue.

Nor is it unknown in the magazine field for publishers to go to hardcover in search of additional, more prestigious, and presumably more affluent audiences. The *American Heritage*, for example, is this kind of quarterly hardcover magazine.

The newspapers eye the magazine field within their own publications in the form of Sunday supplements. The *Los Angeles Times'* "Home" section, as an example, is a weekly magazine in direct competition for both audience and advertising revenue with *Sunset*.

The *Wall Street Journal* and *Women's Wear Daily* in view of their specific interest concentration on the business and clothing worlds, are both daily magazines in newspaper format; *Time* and *Newsweek* can be considered weekly newspapers in the light of their general, departmentalized interest and their attempt to capitalize on the newspaper's basic strength of timely information.

The movie studios make movies and serials for television, while television movies find secondary outlets in theaters. Book publishers sell movie and magazine rights as a part of their package.

These hybrid media forms narrow the gaps in the media spectrum, blending the communication colors ever closer.

CORPORATE INTER-RELATIONSHIPS

From the corporate standpoint, the interrelationship of the various media proprietors is even closer. Magazine publishers have bought both book-publishing houses and television outlets. Newspapers own magazines and radio and television channels. Both newspapers and magazines are heavily involved in cable television (CATV).

These sometimes complex interrelationships, both of media forms and corporate ownerships, give eloquent testimony to the overall unity of the mass media as a social institution, the parts of which can be separated long enough for scrutiny but which, insofar as their effect on people in their changing role as audiences is concerned, are in reality an integrated whole.

In fact, one might say that the media's genius for subdividing itself is matched only by society's ability to fragment itself, a process in which the mass media merely follow suit. And yet, society remains, for all its complexity, a single entity of many parts.

STABILITY AND CHANGE

2. Sandman et al., *Media* (Englewood Cliffs, N. J.: Prentice-Hall, Inc., 1972).

Peter Sandman and others in *Media* point to a lag in the media's treatment of social and moral issues.[2] They point to television's and the press' coverage of the racial riots of the late sixties as events rather than as explorations of underlying causes. Also for consideration is television's ten-year lag in the recognition of anything more than black tokenism in programming. There are, however, contrary examples. John Kenneth Gailbraith's *The Affluent Society* and some

Media Continuum

3. Vance Packard, *The Hidden Persuaders* (New York: David McKay Co., Inc., 1969).

of Vance Packard's work, as well as Rachel Carson's *Silent Spring* in the early sixties, foretold concern over consumerism and the environment long before they became public issues in the early seventies.[3]

Whether the media lead or follow the social structure seems to be a function of audience size. The "massest" media tend to mirror society in their concern with maximum appeal. The media with smaller audiences and particularly those without advertising support are freer for self-expression.

The point can be made that the mass media, therefore, represent both stability and change; that they are both conservators of the status quo and the vehicles of radical change. In this they adequately mirror society itself, which, like the human organisms that compose it, is both inherently conservative and containing the seeds of change. The media with the smaller audiences can, with apparent impunity, suggest new themes, explore radical thought—introduce and innovate. This, to a degree, is what is expected of them. Following this lead, there is typically a period of social digestion after which the "massest" media mirror these matured concepts back to the society from which they sprang, because that too is what is expected of them.

MEDIA FEED EACH OTHER

Not only do the various media feed one another audiences, but they feed one another content in a disorderly sort of two-way exchange. It is well known that many successful books become movies, of which *Gone With the Wind* is the classic example, topping both the best-seller lists and box office records. In fact, many publishers look to movie rights as a considerable part of their revenue.

In less obvious fashion the thread of a theme espoused by some of the smaller media (books, highly specialized magazines, or the underground press) may strike a responsive chord in underlying public sentiment and gradually snowball its way to popular acclaim and effusive treatment in the "massest" media. One thinks of Ralph Nader's *Unsafe at Any Speed* as a good example. More particularly, there is the example of the tenacious drumbeat for peace in Viet Nam, starting in the underground press in the mid-sixties and gradually echoing and reechoing through the more liberal magazines until the rhythm caught on and the popular consumer magazines joined the melody; eventually, the metropolitan press and network television completed the orchestration in a deafening finale. As this process of popularization takes place, the compelling attention paid to a theme by the "massest" media more or less forces the smaller media not originally involved in the theme's development to join the chorus in economic self-protection.

A reverse example of this process is the improbable attention paid to the hippy movement in the mid-sixties as it centered around San Francisco's Haight-Ashbury district. The flower children were picturesque, bizarre in their life-style, clothing, and hairdos. Their very visualness lent itself to television exploitation, and with such

The Continua

national exposure, other media felt the need to join in. For a time magazine editors and staff feature writers, illustrators and photographic teams, free lancers, wire service reporters, movie producers, camera crews, and authors congregated in Haight-Ashbury in such packs that they almost outnumbered the flower children. There exists a certain faddishness to media coverage that seems to parallel public sentiment. In any event, the mass media feed one another, either laboriously as a theme grows in audience acceptance, or in full-blown enthusiasm as they seek to keep au courant, or in both processes combined in a cycle. This media exchange also lends substance to the tight interrelationship and unity of the media continuum.

Media coverage drew hundreds of youngsters to Haight-Ashbury.

EMERGING CHANGE

Returning to the media continuum, which represents the flow of social evolution, it was noted earlier that this was an incomplete spectrum, ever merging into new colors, some of which haven't been discovered yet. The media are on the verge of such discovery.

Marshall McLuhan noted that while each new medium grew out of an older form, it became something entirely different in its effect on society. As the horseless carriage grew out of the horse and bug-

Media Continuum

gy, it performed essentially the same function in carrying the country doctor on his rounds or the farmer to market. But the contemporary automobile is a different thing. It is responsible for the growth of suburbia, American mobility, the deterioration of the central city, air pollution, and more deaths annually than all American wars. It is responsible for thousands of square miles of paving all across the nation, acres of valuable property dedicated to the dead storage of metal; it is the reason for Detroit, mainstay of the insurance, construction, and steel industries, as well as the backbone of the American economy with all its affluence.

Such has also been the effect of CATV. It grew out of airwave broadcast as a correction for channel noise, intended for the eradication of blurred pictures by atmospheric interference, the introduction of broadcast to valley communities that television's line-of-sight signal couldn't reach, and the extension of a station's effective range.

But CATV is becoming something totally different. Cable opens up the full range of both UHF and VHF channels on each set to a theoretically possible total of eighty-four over-the-air channels. In actuality this number will probably be restricted to somewhere around forty. Forty channels available to the viewer cannot help but mean a fragmentation of television's audiences. Cable is two-way; thus, the viewer can talk back to the broadcaster, opening up new vistas. Cable, because it is individually wired rather than broadcast, also permits sophisticated usage in both demographics and their hardware companion, the computer, in the preselection of audiences and appropriate messages.

This much is clear from the continuum; the media move inexorably on. New media forms are coming across the horizon: CATV in all its forms, pay TV (which is free from advertisers), and satellite television, which spells geographic freedom from local stations. These are all new media forms that will all alter the present socio-media gestalt—how, one cannot exactly tell.

One thing is certain: the principle of fragmentation—which all media to date have followed in order to survive before the onslaught of more efficient forms—is being followed again. Television is already fragmenting; following past patterns it will continue fragmenting to serve ever more selective audiences with topical matters of their interest. It is possible that the days of mass media as one now knows it are numbered. Professor Maxwell McCombs thinks so.[4]

Some credence is given this view by the fact that television has apparently peaked as the preeminent mass medium. Still overwhelming in comparison to the other media, it nonetheless is attracting proportionately smaller audiences for shorter periods than it did in 1966. At that time 40 million American homes, on the average, tuned in to prime time, and the average American family watched television for six hours daily. In 1972 there were still 40 million homes tuned in to national network television in prime time—which, in view of the

4. Maxwell McCombs, "Mass Media in the Marketplace," *Monographs* (24): April, 1972.

The Continua

population increase, represents a net decline. Furthermore, in 1972 average watching had gone down to four and one-half hours daily, representing a 25 percent reduction in overall exposure. Television has passed its zenith. It is literally deteriorating before one's eyes; its audience is fragmenting to other media, other activities, other pastimes. It is this factor of audience fragmentation and the paralleling media fragmentation with which this discussion is principally concerned.

In CATV, television may have spawned a child that will destroy it as it is now known. This is a future option indicated by the media continuum. However, one cannot be certain that this will happen, because the continuum has revealed other factors. Unity is one of these factors, one which indicates a place for each medium based on its unique formula of characteristics. Network television has proven itself to be the most efficient means of reaching almost the entire nation instantly. It is not difficult to imagine the circumstances where this is of overpowering significance. One remembers the assassinations of the Kennedy brothers and the funeral of JFK. As the world grows smaller and man becomes more intimately involved with others' affairs, as McLuhan suggests in his concept of the global village, society may easily demand the availability of such instantaneous data.

ACCELERATION

A final factor in the media continuum is its accelerating pace, which is difficult to show in a static model. However, a comparison of the rates of growth of the principal media is significant in several ways. It dramatically illustrates the acceleration of contemporary living in which the media are only a part, and it drives home the matter of media saturation to which present-day Americans are uniquely subjected.

From Gutenberg's first printing press to the time that newspapers in the United States reached their zenith as the preeminent mass medium nearly 500 years passed. From the time that the first jumpy kinescopes found a ready market at the turn of this century to the high point of the movie's popularity during World War II a little less than a half-century elapsed. From radio's chaotic beginnings in the early twenties to the peak of its career as America's number one mass medium was only thirty years. It took television only half that time, a mere fifteen years, to attain almost total saturation of the population, around 98 percent of American homes. Today, new forms of media appear on the horizon and rise steadily in perspective.

This incredible acceleration of the newer mass media forms, in their role as the central nervous system of society, places extraordinary pressure on society and particularly the individual to merely keep up. Such is the theme of Alvin Toffler's *Future Shock*.[5] The individual is capable neither psychologically nor physiologically of withstanding the accelerating rate of technological increase.

5. Alvin Toffler, *Future Shock* (New York: Random House, Inc., 1970).

It is the mass media that reflect this technological trauma to the components of society, from the individual to the greatest mass, and it may well be that it is in the mass media that society first registers its rejection by tuning down the volume. This may be a partial explanation for the fading incidence of television viewing.

ECONOMIC FACTORS

Another factor related to this matter of acceleration is an economic one. The tight relationship of economic affluence to technological expansion and resultant progress was explored earlier (see chapter three). If unforeseen developments should slow the rate of economic growth, if society should reorder its priorities to no longer place total emphasis on quantitative growth, then an accompanying slowdown of the economy, technology, and acceleration of the media may be expected. This, too, is a thesis of Professor McCombs, an imponderable thesis at this point, but clearly one of a number of future options.

Related to this concept is the fact that all earlier media have continued to survive and to thrive in survival. Not only is the massiveness of television and exotic new forms approaching, but newspapers, movies, magazines, and books are present still, plus an imaginative array of hybrid media also demanding attention. Contemporary American society is inundated with media; it is patently impossible for the individual to keep up with all—to see every movie, read every magazine, buy every book, watch every television program, listen to every radio station, and scan every newspaper, even those of his own geographical area. He must be selective, and selectivity breeds specialization and the fragmentation of society into ever smaller enclaves of interest.

ORAL REEMPHASIS

One additional thread running through all media, from pre-Gutenberg, even preliterate times, to the present, is the substance of speech. Speech was preeminent before Gutenberg as a quasi mass medium even though limited to the range of the human voice.

Although print altered its form, speech remained an indirect content of books and all the subsequent silent media, as well as retaining its earlier function of audible information exchange between men. It, too, specialized under printed pressure.

In the present century, with the advent of the electric media—movies, radio, and television—speech, the audible form, became an increasingly larger proportion of the content of the newer media. So all-encompassing have these audible and oral media become that their adverse effect on literacy may be substantial and may already be evident on current generations. Movies, radio, and television deal in the spoken word, and to the extent that they attract audiences, they deemphasize the need for the written word as a communications medium.

There are parts of the world (for example, the United Arab Republic) where radio particularly has abruptly plunged illiterate soci-

The Continua

AUDIENCE

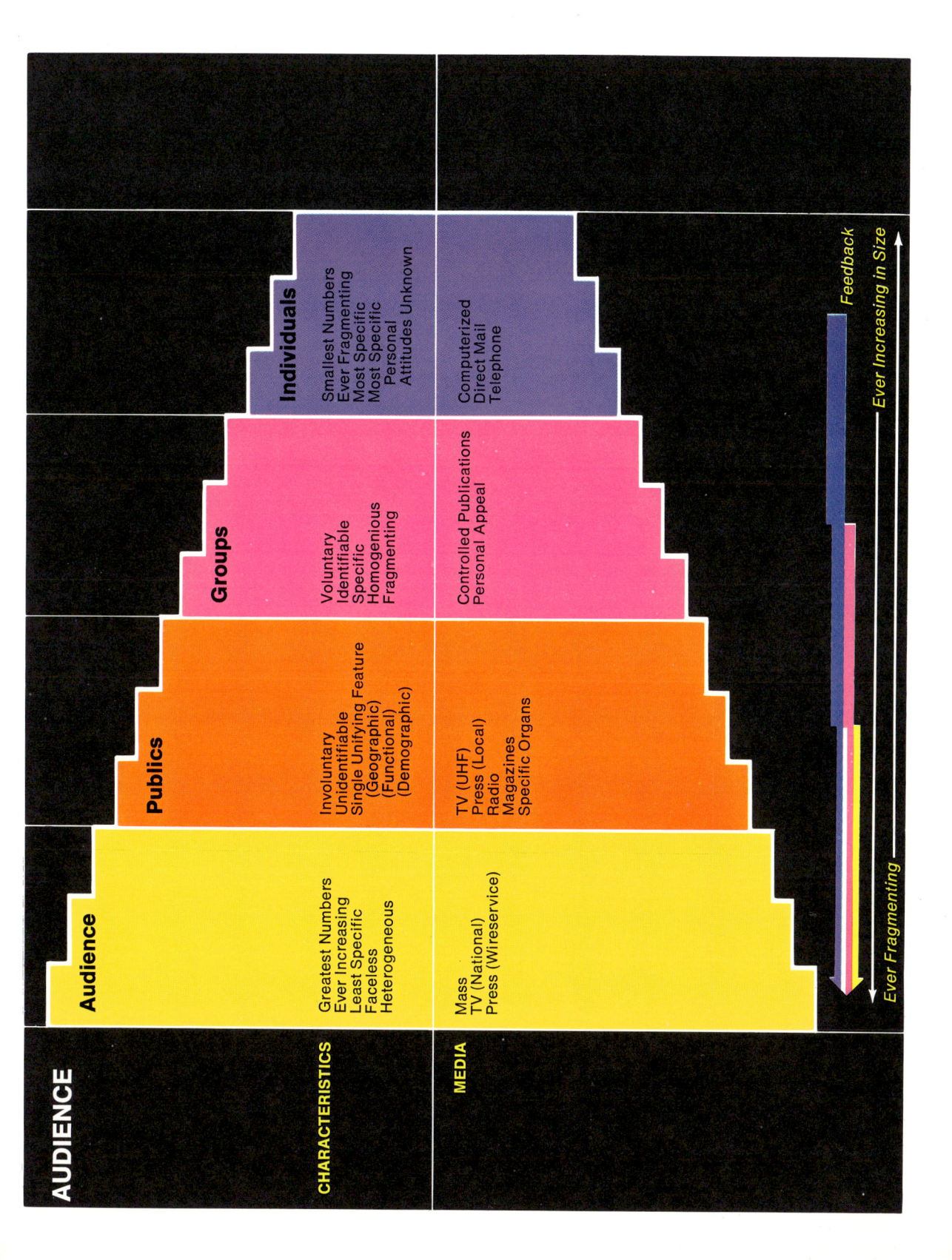

Audience
CHARACTERISTICS:
Greatest Numbers
Ever Increasing
Least Specific
Faceless
Heterogeneous

MEDIA:
Mass
TV (National)
Press (Wireservice)

Publics
Involuntary
Unidentifiable
Single Unifying Feature
(Geographic)
(Functional)
(Demographic)

TV (UHF)
Press (Local)
Radio
Magazines
Specific Organs

Groups
Voluntary
Identifiable
Specific
Homogenious
Fragmenting

Controlled Publications
Personal Appeal

Individuals
Smallest Numbers
Ever Fragmenting
Most Specific
Most Specific Personal
Attitudes Unknown

Computerized
Direct Mail
Telephone

Feedback
Ever Increasing in Size
Ever Fragmenting

MEDIA

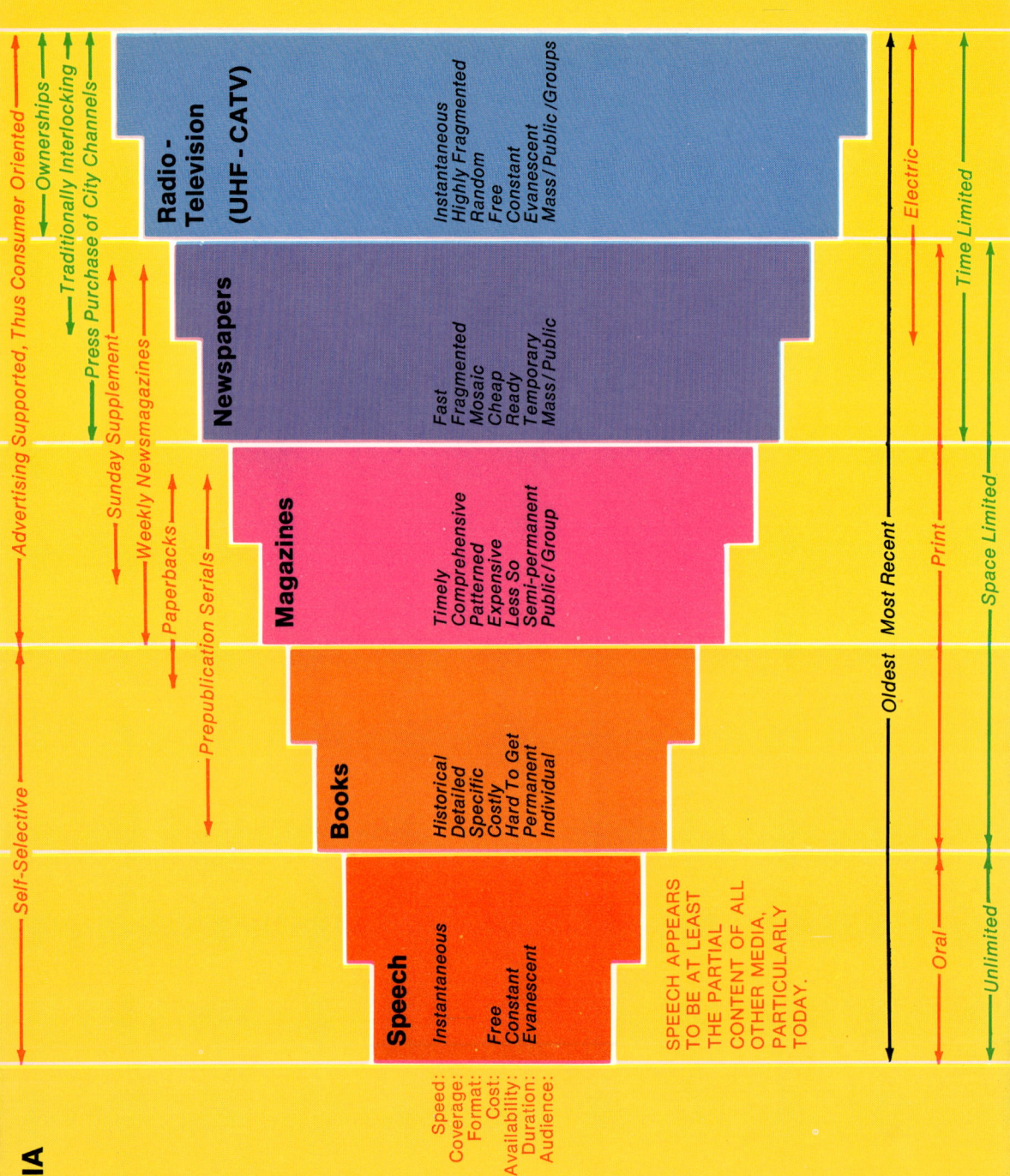

Radio-Television (UHF - CATV)
- Instantaneous
- Highly Fragmented
- Random
- Free
- Constant
- Evanescent
- Mass/Public/Groups

Newspapers
- Fast
- Fragmented
- Mosaic
- Cheap
- Ready
- Temporary
- Mass/Public

Magazines
- Timely
- Comprehensive
- Patterned
- Expensive
- Less So
- Semi-permanent
- Public/Group

Books
- Historical
- Detailed
- Specific
- Costly
- Hard To Get
- Permanent
- Individual

Speech
- Instantaneous
- Free
- Constant
- Evanescent

SPEECH APPEARS TO BE AT LEAST THE PARTIAL CONTENT OF ALL OTHER MEDIA, PARTICULARLY TODAY.

Speed:
Coverage:
Format:
Cost:
Availability:
Duration:
Audience:

- Self-Selective
- Prepublication Serials
- Paperbacks
- Weekly Newsmagazines
- Sunday Supplement
- Press Purchase of City Channels
- Traditionally Interlocking Ownerships
- Advertising Supported, Thus Consumer Oriented

Oldest ←→ Most Recent

Oral — Print — Electric

Unlimited — Space Limited — Time Limited

eties into the era of instantaneous mass communications. Such societies may bypass the literate period completely, walking directly from the sixteenth into the twentieth century.

In American society this reconcentration on the oral forms may signal a retreat from literacy and an outmoding of the printed forms, with the specializing qualities of CATV providing the breadth and depth of mass media and relegating print to those remoter areas outside the reach of the cable.

SUMMARY

This analysis of the media continuum has partially explained the ability of each succeeding medium to continue to survive after it has been overtaken by a more efficient form capable of reaching larger numbers of audience more quickly. The various media have survived by specializing in their appeal to ever more selective audiences.

This survival has demonstrated the unity of the mass media and has illustrated how they serve the total demands of society. Most succinctly, media are the mirror image of a changing society, and their fragmentation is actually society's fragmentation made visible and audible.

Also apparent in the media continuum is the phenomenon of advertising support as the media reflection of society's commercial emphasis. The overwhelming role of advertising in the "massest" of the media has led directly to a concentration on numbers of audience, wherein the content of the media has played a role principally as bait for audiences. Thus, advertising plays an almost tyrannical role in dictating the approach and content of the media for which it is significant. The nonadvertising-supported media are freer to explore.

Implicit in the media continuum is the matter of media acceleration. A half-millenium was required for print to mature, but, within this century alone, movies, radios, and television matured at an ever-accelerating pace.

Finally, the media continuum shows a certain predictability. There exists both a fragmenting effect (already applicable to television) and an overall unity. Moreover, the continuum demonstrates some of the social danger inherent in unrestrained technological acceleration (as it applies to media, at least).

Obviously, media are a social institution with people—audiences—at their base. The following chapter will explore the relationships between media and audiences in twin, paralleling continua.

Media Continuum

6 AUDIENCE CONTINUUM

AUDIENCE DE-EMPHASIZED

1. John Merrill and Ralph Lowenstein, *Media, Messages and Men* (New York: David McKay Co., Inc., 1971).

In many discussions of mass communications, as Merrill and Lowenstein point out in *Media, Messages and Men*, scant attention is paid to the audiences of the mass media except to acknowledge their presence.[1] The mass media are tangible, audible, visible, and treatable—the institutionalized product of a corporate society. Consequently, it has been far easier to examine them in operational terms than it has been to probe audiences in terms of reaction and effect. Audiences are vague will-o'-the-wisp conglomerates composed of differing individuals whose membership in them is indeterminate. As Merrill and Lowenstein put it, "The mass audience is a distributed entity without real structure."

As the various mass media can be located along a moving continuum to illustrate their changing nature and their interrelationship both with each other and the structure of society, so do the elements of that society itself take their places along a parallel continuum. These elements of society comprise the audience continuum, which is no more than a model of the social structure itself, oriented toward communication. On the audience continuum the human building blocks of society range from the theoretical "massest" mass of everyone in these United States down through publics and groups and corporations and institutions and associations and crowds to the individual himself.

The best way to visualize the audience continuum is as a giant funnel with the "massest" audience at one end of it. This huge audience is served best, although not completely, by national network television. The funnel narrows as it includes various publics and groups and associations until it culminates at the individual. This "single" audience is, of course, served by telephone and the mails and, most importantly, by face-to-face encounters with other individuals.

As the media continuum represented a historical development, so does the audience continuum—in media terms. The "massest" audience has only existed in mass communications for little more than a half-century. Prior to the perfection of network radio in the 1920s, mass audiences were geographically circumscribed and limited. In a nation far more rural than today, there were large segments of the population that were not served efficiently by any scheduled mass medium.

HISTORICAL PROGRESSION

Moving back along the continuum to its genesis in Gutenberg's time, one can see that the growth of the mass audience was inhibited first by the problem of illiteracy and later by the predominantly rural nature of the nation. Print media is tied to physical distribution, and the growth of print has paralleled urban growth. Only when the electronic media freed mass communications from this physical distribution was the theoretically total audience possible. Today all the previous audiences are historically developed, and some uniquely modern refinements of them, plus the "massest" mass. The significant thing to remember is that where there is an audience, an aggregate of persons of any number, there will be a medium to serve it, perhaps several.

Another key point of peculiar significance to the audience continuum is that audiences, regardless of size, are not simply passive receivers of media, but rather active participants in the dynamic process called mass communications.

IMPORTANCE OF THE INDIVIDUAL

It is the individual, with all his differences, in different arrangements, for different periods of time, and often simultaneously, who composes different audiences. It is this single individual, not a crowd or a group, who casts his ballot in the sanctity of the polling place, passes his dollars across the counter, buys an admission to the stadium or the theater, and who holds opinions and attitudes that, in an aggregate with others, will be translated into some sort of temporary and incomplete consensus called public opinion. Further, it is the individual who subscribes to a newspaper, buys a magazine, reads a book, laughs at a TV comic, or listens to the news on the way to work. In this technological age and with a social emphasis on size and quantitative measurement, attention has been too preoccupied with mass audiences.

By and large, audiences get what they want from the mass media serving them. Their interests are catered to. However, the formulation of those interests do not arise out of thin air, but rather from a complex and continuing series of interpersonal contacts, beginning with the family, continuing through school, peer group associations, influences on the job, and new family relationships. The influence of individuals on each other is enormous, and it is from this process that communities of interest are formed.

Audience Continuum

INDIVIDUAL INFLUENCE

Looking at the model of the audience continuum for a moment, it is evident that the influence of the individual is greatest on his immediate or primary group. He may belong to several primary groups simultaneously. Group influences, in turn, bear heavily on larger publics, and these publics play substantial roles in the formulation of a consensus shared by the "massest" mass. But influence is a two-way street. The influence of the mass interpreted through the mass media bears strongest on the various publics. These publics, in turn, influence the smaller and smaller groupings within them until the process finally filters down to the individual at the base of the funnel, modifying, in some respect, his viewpoint. Such is the interaction of mass media at every level and in every society. However, this is not a chain-of-command situation; the individual is a member of all groups and all publics and of the mass as well. He both receives from and contributes to the content of all the mass media serving the entire spectrum or continuum.

As one observes the continuum, it becomes evident that there are dual drives in action in contemporary America: one is the traditional drive toward greater speed and numbers. Man seeks to enlarge the "massest" audience to make the theoretical totality a reality. He seeks to extend the range of television to reach farther and farther into the hinterlands. Huge antennae dot the plains to blanket the wheat belt, and CATV reaches into hidden crannies of the population; satellites bring worldwide information to worldwide audiences instead of merely national ones. The mass end of the continuum continues to grow—not merely by population pressure, but through conscious effort.

Simultaneously, a diametrically opposed trend is taking place on the audience continuum as mass media seek to reach ever closer to the individual himself. Media attempt to isolate ever smaller groups where the influence is greatest on the "prime moving" individual. They seek to appeal to these smaller groupings in terms of presumed interest. Finally, and increasingly, media are finding ways to approach the individual himself as an individual with an appeal designed specifically, if artificially, for him as consumer, voter, or opinion holder.

SEEKING SMALLER AUDIENCES

A part of this trend toward reaching the individual has been due to a disappointment with the "massest" media to deliver the goods as it were—or the votes. Massive media campaigns have failed to sell the Edsel, to elect Goldwater, to modify opinion. In a commercial society the failure of vast sums to deliver the goods has forced a reappraisal of the traditionally presumed homogenous effects of the mass media on mass audiences.

The rising incidence of "boiler shop" telephoning is an example of appeal to the individual; so is the increasing volume of direct mail, particularly computerized direct mail. Advertising agencies, in reaching the mass audiences of network television, are positioning their advertisements to appeal to specific individuals or groupings within the mass. In political campaigns discrete audiences and publics are sought and appealed to in terms of their own interests; issues of the campaign are explained in audience frames of reference. More and more candidates are finding that the door-to-door approach pays off, particularly in local elections. The thrust of this new media trend is an emphasis on the individual as a building block of society, coupled with the attempt to reach him where he lives or in groups to which he belongs.

Nowhere is this trend better exemplified than in the case of computerized direct mail. Demographic factors pertaining to individuals or households are gathered and paragraphs in letters are carefully constructed to appeal to these separate characteristics or traits. The accommodating computer then can match these paragraphs with each individual on a list and send an ersatz personal letter to him couched exclusively in terms of that individual's presumed interests. Given the accelerating sophistication of computers and the developing technology of cassettes and videotape, it is not hard to imagine a synthetic personal visit of the politician or salesman on CATV screens.

CONTRADICTORY FORCES AT WORK

These companion drives to extend the range of the continuum on either end seem to pose something of a paradox. Two different forces of the mass media appear to be at work. At the one end, appeals toward an ever "masser massest mass" must rely on the lowest common denominator of that mass audience, which embraces all other audiences and all individuals within society. At the other end, ever more specific appeals are directed toward ever smaller audiences based on their real or demographically determined presumed interests.

This is not such a paradox as one might think. In the past, the prevailing attitude was that the effect of mass media on audiences was single and direct. This is a hangover from the stimulus-response, or "power of the press," theory.

In some respects the Soviet attitude is more sophisticated. Within their vocabulary are two words, *agitator* and *propagandist.* If one can separate himself from the general connotations of these words, their differences become apparent. An agitator is one who is charged with acquainting a mass audience with a single thought or doctrine. He makes his audience aware, and he utilizes special techniques to do so, including slogans, simplistic statements, posters, and mottos. The propagandist, on the other hand, has a more sophisticated task. He must *persuade* different groups within a mass of the practicality and wisdom of a doctrine, always in terms of their own understanding and interests. He is the salesman.

2. J. A. C. Brown, *Techniques of Persuasion* (Baltimore, Md.: Penguin Books Inc., 1963).

A point of the same nature is made by J.A.C. Brown and others and implied in Stephenson's play theory of communication.[2] This is that the entertainment-oriented "massest" media excel in calling at-

The American stereotypic connotations of "agitator." Note text discussion of the role of the agitator.

THE BETTMANN ARCHIVE

tention to things, trivial things, matters of inconsequence. They make the public aware. A change in attitude, however, is a far more difficult undertaking, altering stored and treasured beliefs. Such a change requires a more intensive and more personal approach and is more easily resolved on the basis of group or individual interests.

Thus, the appeals of mass media to American society are actually of two types: a broad, simplistic appeal aimed at the lowest common denominator of the "massest" audiences, and a pinpointed, specific appeal made to individuals. All along the continuum between these two poles are audiences of various sizes and compositions, responding to varying degrees of these two approaches in different combinations.

PUBLICS DEFINED

The audience continuum moves from the mass to publics, to groups, to associations, and, finally, to the individual. The totality of the mass is easy to recognize; so is the individual. In between, in the intermediate divisions, the distinctions are blurred. While the difference between publics and groups is essentially quantitative in that publics are generally larger than groups, this is not always the case.

Publics are vague, general entities—conglomerates of individuals who generally share a single trait. Membership in publics is scarcely voluntary, although this is not absolute. Members are characterized by what they are or what they do or where they live. Broadly, publics can be defined as geographic or functional bodies. The geographic breakdown is easiest to understand. There are southerners, New Englanders, and midwesterners—but there are also New Yorkers,

The Continua
88

The role of the propagandist is one of persuasion.

Georgians, Hoosiers, and Texans. There are San Franciscans and Bostonians. There are also urban dwellers, rural dwellers, and inhabitants of suburbia. Regardless of the size of the geographic audience, there is some medium to serve it, from state and regional radio and television networks, huge metropolitan daily newspapers, rural weeklies, and suburban dailies.

From a functional standpoint there are even greater possibilities of diversification. There are men and women, Protestants, Catholics, Jews, and agnostics; there are Democrats, Republicans, and Independents; there are blacks, whites, yellows, reds, and browns; there are young and old; there are blue-collar and white-collar workers—and so on, ad infinitum. There is generally a medium, perhaps several, to serve each. There is a wide range of women's magazines, *Redbook*, *Ms.*, and *Vogue*; for men, *Sports Illustrated*, *Playboy*, and *Esquire*. There is black radio; there is Spanish television in Los Angeles, New York, and Texas, where large Latin-American populations are concentrated. There is *New Republic* for liberals and *U.S. News and World Report* for conservatives. *Fortune* serves executives

Audience Continuum

and the *Labor Leader* speaks for itself. There's Saturday morning television for tots, daytime television for housewives, and Sunday sports programs for men.

DEMOGRAPHIC PUBLICS

A newer variation of these functional publics is that of demographic publics, identifiable through the computer. In these contrived publics, more than one characteristic is identified in a sort of communications "twenty questions" game. A given geographical public, for instance, California, is given the limitation "male" and the population thereby cut in half; "college graduate" cuts the remainder by two-thirds; "lawyer" further reduces this number; successively, "Catholic," "golfer," "father of two," and "over fifty" will continuously refine the number of individuals meeting the specific requirements of this public until an extremely small segment of the overall population is reached. Applying these demographic factors across the board with the speed and efficiency of the computer permits the computer to select an almost infinite number of small, discrete publics. Demography isolates people so that they can be found and persuaded.

One thing that should be noted about demographics is that the publics isolated may not exist at all. The *New York Times*, in conducting a readership survey, found that it could isolate the numbers of "divorced young women with two children between the ages of two and five living in garden apartments in suburban New York who visited mid-Manhattan at least once a month to shop for paper clothing with an American Express card." It may easily be that such an esoteric public might not be a public at all, but a single individual artificially identified, and further may not even exist at all.

The significant point about publics, of whatever origin, is not so much the single characteristic that they share as that this characteristic represents certain attitudes or interests to which appeals can be directed. Southerners are not as significant because they live among the magnolia blossoms as they are for the fact that they share a certain traditionally conservative attitude, and this has been the political import of the solid South. Blacks are not as significant for the pigment of their skin as they are for the commonality of their views of the predominately white world. Youth are not important in point of years alone as they are for their peer-influenced life-style, while the elderly count less for their age than for their inherently traditional viewpoint.

Within these broad groupings there are exceptions, to be sure, but in the institutionalized world of mass communications, with its commercial emphasis, it is the consensus found within these publics, the averages as it were, that are important. Such broad groups of shared interests make for more efficient appeal. They minimize overkill and its attendant costs by reducing the level of semantic noise, but only for the average.

The Continua

GROUPS

Groups on the audience continuum generally are smaller and share a more specific interest than publics, interests such as bowling, dry fly fishing, or antiques. Groups are not merely subdivisions of publics, as neurosurgeons are of the medical profession, although they may be. Groups can be formed and identified without relationship to any larger public. An interest in astrology, for instance, to which several media cater, does not suggest a larger entity. Groups in general are voluntary in nature. People belong because they want to, because they see or have an advantage in doing so, or because they have an interest in the group's purposes and activities. People belong to such groups because of a shared commonality. They may never meet; they may never know one another, but the interest is there, and there will be a medium to serve it. Those interested in dry fly fishing, for example, are a scattered audience, spread in tiny numbers across the length and breadth of the nation and united only by their subscription to *Fly Fisherman*.

ASSOCIATIONS: FORMAL GROUPS

Associations are formalized groups. Their activities are regulated by codes; they are identifiable; rosters are kept. Associations are formal audiences, reflections of society's corporate structure. So defined, associations include the entire spectrum of American business and social life.

Across the entire spread, large and small, there are media to serve those audiences identified on the organizational or association rosters. Such media include company bulletins, employee newsletters, stockholder reports, trade associations magazines, house organs, corporate annual reports, billing inserts, professional and scholarly journals, bulletin board notices and posters and, in some instances, sales promotional and training films and closed circuit television. Whatever the form and the purpose, these media are directed to a specific audience in terms of that audience's interests or livelihood, which frequently coincide.

As with publics and groups, it is the composition of these associations and their purpose that will determine specific media content, and this content will change as the interests and orientation of that membership changes.

CROWDS

Crowds are an entity that does not fit readily into the continuum; nonetheless, they constitute a real audience for mass communications. The crowd is a happenstance audience. Its shared characteristic is simply being in one place at one time and often for a purpose: to watch pro football, hear a rock concert, or attend a religious revival. Such an event, as well as supplying the audience, constitutes a medium of its own, of which the audience is a part of the content.

Generally, such events are free of all but peripheral advertising because of the relative lack of cohesiveness, of size predictability, and the sometimes nature of the crowd. Crowds are a one-shot audi-

Audience Continuum

Woodstock, 1969: the event, the crowd. The vibrations of Woodstock engulfed a generation, affected a nation.

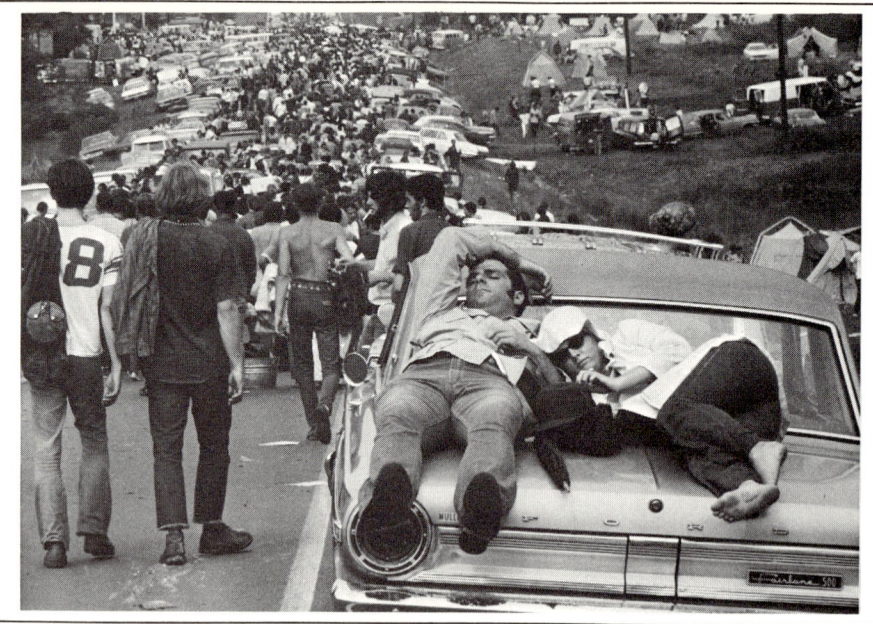

UPI

The event as a mass medium: Winter Olympics.

UPI

The Continua

ence that will never come together again in exactly the same fashion, thus affording little opportunity for repeatability. But the size of the event crowd alone is enough to demand attention for that event as a mass medium. Fifty thousand people in a stadium on a Sunday afternoon are enough to make a book a best-seller. A quarter-million people listening to Billy Graham and a half-million at Woodstock are equal to the circulation of all but the largest newspapers.

These events and crowds are significant mass media in themselves. Further, their increasing frequency as a social phenomenon demands attention for their effect on other mass media from which they, to a degree, detract. From the standpoint of media functions these events are, of course, high in entertainment. As transmitters of the culture, such events represent a resurgence of historical phenomena stretching back to the circuses of the Caesars and the Sermon on the Mount. Perhaps from their spontaneity, they best reflect contemporary society in terms that no contrived medium can. Crowds, as Merrill and Lowenstein point out in *Media, Messages and Men*, have a collective hypnotic quality born of deep, intimate human association, where the audience interacts not only with the medium but with each other. To speculate for a moment, there is an emotional quality generated by physical presence which individuals find of value. Why else would they pay admission to the stadium when they can watch the game free and better at home—with instant replay? Why Woodstock when any hi-fi can give far better clarity and better acoustics, except as a shared rhythmic orgy?

These are media and audience phenomena that cannot be visualized along static continua but that, nonetheless, exert a very real influence on attitudes. Their meaning to the individual personally may be far greater than that of the more institutionalized, indirect, and partially sterile mass media to which Americans have become accustomed.

Further, the rising popularity of such direct contact media, including theater, symphony, museums, Disneyland and Disney World—the entire renaissance of the antic and static arts—seems to sustain the thought of the unity of the media, how they balance each other, and how, in this era of increased impersonality, of commercially oriented, assembly-line mass media, there arises a public and an individual need for personal participation.

It should be noted that, like a movie or a book, such events are self-selective. The audiences are not preselected; they are, as noted, more unpredictable than not. If a movie is an electric book, then an event is a living book.

Crowds are unique as audiences in that they are the only audience form that is visible, tangible, and physically present. That is to say, they are the only audience that is alive and cohesively human, and not a separated quantitative approximation or a demographic abstraction. They are the only real audience (and the origin of the term) and as such share a moment of reality. There is a humanness in crowds found only in personal contact, and they are, for purposes herein, a form of mass personal contact—the most dynamic, if the most limited and unpredictable, of the mass media.

LONGEVITY AS A FACTOR

Audiences vary also in their longevity or duration. The crowd at the pro football game lasts about two and one-half hours. Television's prime-time audience on any given evening will come and go over a three-hour period, while the audience for any given program will last only an hour or so. But a popular movie may take a year to fulfill its audience in thousands of theaters throughout the land. A best-seller may take a couple of years or more to reach its quota. The Bible is still going strong after nearly two millenia; Shakespeare draws new readers annually after 400 years. The longer the duration of an audience, the more concrete the effect of the medium seems. The media continuum reflects this durability or permanence of some of the more individualized media, such as movies or books, in comparison to the evanescent qualities of radio and television, whose individual programs die aborning and whose individual, specific effect perforce is generally short-lived.

Now that the progression of audiences of varying sizes and compositions have been noted along the continuum, attention is directed to a dynamic factor that, again, the model cannot show—that is, the fragmentation of audiences in this society. This fragmentation occurs as a result of several factors: specialization due to an increase in knowledge; an increase in interests born both of affluence and greater education; and a markedly increased mobility.

The doctor of old, the general practitioner, is almost a thing of the past. His place has been taken by numbers of specialists unheard of a generation or so ago: neurosurgeons, radiologists, ophthalmologists, gynecologists, and so on. Likewise, lawyers are now criminal lawyers, probate lawyers, corporation lawyers, and specialists in forensics. Through profession after profession, there is increasing specialization to meet society's demands. As these professions specialize, they tend to develop languages of their own, techniques, and an increasing body of specialized knowledge that not only demands their attention but requires media to feed it.

SPECIALIZATION

Increasing leisure has permitted increasing numbers of people to pursue hobbies and interests as laymen: some go in for cabinetmaking; amateur yachtsmen fill the marinas; stamp, coin, and art collecting become more prevalent; model railroading enjoys a new popularity. These diverse activities are fragmenting as people pursue their own interests, do their own thing, and a rash of magazines and occasional programs meet these needs.

The postwar concentration on higher education and the proliferation of advanced degrees has had a further fragmenting effect on society. First, more specialists are created. Second, an increasing percentage of the population is discovering interests and activities of which they would have been deprived a mere generation ago. Relieved of survival pressure, people take interests in matters of the mind. The magazine *Psychology Today* caters less to the professional than to an audience of upper-middle-class, educated young liberals who have discovered fascination in the world of human behavior.

As personal mobility through the automobile made surburbia possible, it also focused interest in suburban affairs. This inevitably led to a dramatic increase in the number of suburban newspapers, and even encouraged the establishment of some purely suburban or community FM radio stations. In both instances the rationale was the same: a local interest was there. The huge metropolitan dailies lacked the resources, manpower, and space to adequately cover the civic, social, and governmental affairs of perhaps a dozen subcommunities on their periphery. Nor could local merchants afford the space and time rates for the larger metropolitan media, rates that were based on large, wide-area audiences, only a tiny fraction of which a local merchant could ever hope to serve. The answer from both an information and advertising standpoint was smaller, fragmented, pinpointed, local media serving just a specific suburb.

On a wider scale, growing affluence and jet aircraft whisked people across the world and encouraged an interest in travel undreamed of in the past. As this occurred, newspaper travel sections and travel magazines sprang up to feed the public interest and to accommodate a host of airlines, hotel, travel agency, steamship, and resort advertising.

Increased specialization and fragmentation within society is reflected on the audience continuum, and groups break into subgroups as publics deteriorate from large, monolithic groupings to more specialized subdivisions. To say that one is a Republican is no longer descriptive enough: there is an Eastern liberal wing and a conservative wing; there are moderates and members of the John Birch Society. The subdivisions of the Democratic party are also well known. The previously cohesive women's audience has been broken into that of the traditional housewife, the young working girl, the professional, and the feminist. Again, there are media to serve all.

PROCESS OF FRAGMENTATION

All across the audience continuum broad publics break up into smaller subdivisions of common interest stemming from the original thread of unity. As these subdivisions develop in significant numbers and become cohesive, media of varying kinds develop to serve their interests. As all this happens and the smaller, more specialized media develop to serve fragmented audiences, the larger public sometimes disintegrates and the media that had served it disappear. Nowhere is this trend more noticeable than in the magazine-publishing field as huge, general magazines of broad appeal close their doors and smaller, specialized magazines proliferate. Similarly, groups splinter into subgroups, refining their basic interest, and as this trend intensifies, mini mass media develop to serve them. The *Journal of the American Medical Association* is now supplemented with dozens of professional journals covering various specialties within the medical profession. Academia is rife with scores of scholarly publications.

This trend, of course, has infected the airways as radio stations multiply to cater to almost every conceivable brand of musical taste. As the television band expands through UHF, a smattering of new stations begins to specialize in sports, in cultural offerings, and drama, and under pressure from the FCC, in public access channels and local government channels.

INDIVIDUAL MEDIA

At the level of the individual himself, there are also an increasing number of media wares awaiting his selection. Principally, these are books and film, although increasingly they include the wide range of attractions available in sports, the antic and static arts, historical restorations, and the like. This phenomenon is greatly enhanced by individual personal mobility and relative affluence.

In comparing these media to those commercially supported one may liken them to a meal. From a huge, diversified menu, the individual selects what he really wants. No one is planning a dinner for him; he is free to select. These individual media are freer in the content they can offer than the mass, scheduled media, whether advertising-supported or dictated by purpose; the latter must plan a meal for maximum appeal, recognizing that some of the courses will be distasteful to some of the diners.

In comparing the media and the audience continua, one should note that these are models of reality. Also, there is an essential distinction between them. Audiences are alike; they are people reacting, thinking. No matter how synthetically contrived, they still represent human beings. Mass media are things: rolls of newsprint and huge presses, a bewildering complexity of electronic gadgetry and cameras, whirring computers and giant antennae. The mass media are perfectly capable of pouring out tons of gibberish and acres of nonsense. To bridge the space between the mass media and their respective audiences sit the gatekeepers.

The print media are space-limited, and the broadcast media are even more severely time-limited. Somehow, into each medium across the broad spectrum, the significant content for its particular audience must be crammed. Furthermore, the proper balance of information, entertainment, and advertising for that medium's specific audience must be achieved. This is the considerable role of the gatekeeper wherever he is found.

REALITY IS:

In a very real sense in the impersonal world in which Americans live vicariously, reality is what the mass media say reality is. The reality to which an individual is exposed in any given medium is that which a particular gatekeeper chose to expose. These gatekeepers, of course, are the various publishers and editors of the nation's newspapers and the news directors and commentators of radio and

The Continua

television, but they are not alone, for one must also consider the programmers who determine the entertainment mix. These gatekeepers include the publishers and editors of magazines and books, as well as the producers and directors of movies of all kinds. Also included are producers, musical directors, art directors, and a wide range of promoters who sponsor the antic and static arts (museums, theater, and the like) as well as the multiple attractions to which individuals are exposed.

These gatekeepers are surrogates, choosing for others what they will experience, for as society grows more complex and the world expands, direct experience of the world, already small, grows smaller.

The critical factor in this gatekeeping is that it is only a fraction of the events of the world, of the potential knowledge, of the available entertainment to which others are exposed, no matter how broad and sweeping or how esoterically refined the medium. There simply is neither the time nor the space for consistently comprehensive media coverage. For example, even the largest newspaper, on the average, contains only about 10 percent of the available news material on any given day. This figure is not nearly so significant, however, as the 90 percent of available and presumably interesting material that will never see print and thus, as far as readers are concerned, never took place. The gatekeeper's responsibility is awesome.

CONSUMER AS PRODUCER

How does the gatekeeper make his selection? He makes it on the basis of maximum appeal. He delivers that daily diet of hard news, human interest, sports, pure entertainment, humor, tragedy, and crime that his experience has shown readers will appreciate sufficiently to buy and read the newspaper and to keep on doing so. When his feedback, either intuitively achieved or empirically demonstrated through circulation, indicates that interest lags, then something must change.

In this simplistic instance, it is clear that although it is the gatekeeper who is the bridge between the medium and the audience it serves, it is that audience in the final analysis who will direct his judgment through its feedback at the cash register. In simplest terms the audience gets what it wants, and in the proportions it wants, from each medium, whether it is entertainment or information, folklore or pornography.

In the other mass media the situation is the same. Magazines must publish what their particular audiences desire. *Fortune* cannot publish articles on child care, nor is *Cosmopolitan*, catering to the unmarried working girl, able to offer articles on hot rod racing. Each must choose from among an incredible potpourri of material on business and finance on the one hand and sexuality and mod fashion on the other to find what is most timely, appealing, current, and provoking for its readership.

In book publishing and filmmaking, the situation is slightly different. Here, from a wide variety of manuscripts and screenplays and conversions from other media, the publisher or producer must make a selection of what he thinks will appeal to the greatest number of the potential audience selected for a particular film or book. Not too often do they try to reach everyone. As with Broadway producers, book publishers and film producers are severely limited by their own time, and even the largest publishing house can produce only a tiny fraction of the hundreds of manuscripts, both solicited and "over-the-transom," that are submitted to it. This judgment by the gatekeepers will be a subjective one to be sure, but one nonetheless guided by their belief of what the audience wants to read or see. Although less so than in the scheduled media, films and books are still extremely sensitive to box office and sales, and do whatever they can to assure maximum potential.

BROADCAST GATEKEEPERS

Radio and television are time-limited. Their situation is no different than that of other media; rather, it is intensified. Network television tries to appeal to everyone in terms of the lowest common denominator. This has demanded a very high entertainment content that, in view of constantly changing public tastes, places an enormous burden on the programmers in trying to second-guess a vast and diversified audience, guided only by their own intuition and the cold numbers of a few hundred families who constitute a statistical population for the ratings. Sometimes these programmers are way out in front of public acceptance; sometimes the lag is embarrassing. The key point, however, is that more than in any other medium they must cater to mass whimsy daily with tens of millions of dollars riding on their judgment. A flicker in the ratings can kill a show; the graveyard of dead programs is scattered with impressive headstones: "Playhouse 90," a live drama; "The Ed Sullivan Show," with vaudeville restored; "Have Gun, Will Travel," a sophisticated western; and "The Lawrence Welk Show," featuring geriatric music. It is not that these shows didn't have merit; they just didn't have enough.

The television programmer or gatekeeper's task is complicated by the fact that he is in direct, daily, murderous competition with two other networks, all reaching toward exactly the same mass audience at the same time—weekday prime time. Independent television gatekeepers are hard-pressed to hold on to the dregs of mass audience that the networks leave. Often independents tend to concentrate on local news or on a sports format, and many feed on the nostalgia of old and great television programs or movies now abandoned by the networks in their own frantic struggle to keep up.

Radio has specialized, largely in musical terms. Here, again, stations have preselected the audiences that they are striving to reach, and they must feed them. A rock 'n' roll station cannot play "Aida," nor is it likely that one will find Mick Jagger on a pops or classical station. An all-news station doesn't go in for music at all, nor will there be much soap opera on the recent phenomenon of the radio sex/talk shows.

AUDIENCE EXPECTATIONS

As one notes the activities of the media's gatekeepers, it becomes evident that they are operating in the light of the medium's policy, a predetermined share of the overall audience market, and that they are carrying out this policy by devising those programs, that content mix, or that specific title, which, in their professional judgment, will best appeal to the largest numbers of the particular audience they have come to think of as their own, ruthlessly abandoning all others. This places an enormous emphasis on audience expectations. Translated, this means that in the final analysis, it is each medium's audience that dictates what it will receive. Thus, "consumer as producer" applies to mass communications also.

Each audience determines within certain limitations exactly what kind of material it will consume. It does this in mass communications just as it does in selecting the clothes it will wear, the cars it will drive, the homes it will live in, and the style of furniture it will put in them. A tour of shopping centers will confirm the rigorous specificity of clothing, furniture, and housewares bound together by a thread of twentieth-century commonality. The mass media are both the giant shopping centers and the tiny boutiques on the mall of mass communications, each one catering to certain specific customers in both large and small groupings, customers who wander in and out of both the enormous chain stores and the tiny specialty shops more or less as the mood strikes them. As are mass communications, shopping centers are social institutions whose gatekeepers are called buyers and who are guided by management policy as to what public they will cater to, and by that public as to what they will buy.

Media consumerism results in an arithmetic expansion of mass media, all of which are aimed at the individual who regularly becomes a member of new audiences, publics, groups, and crowds without ceding his membership in any of the original audiences. The individual is repeatedly exposed to more and more media, media which are more often than not literally seeking him out where he lives. This is media's competition for attention.

TIME-LIMITED INDIVIDUALS

The individual is time-limited. He has but twenty-four hours a day in which to crowd an increasingly more eventful life: more media, more things to do and see and play, more people to encounter, more crowds, more shopping centers, more worlds to go to. Mass media and their persistent commercials are in competition with everything the individual does: eating, sleeping, lovemaking, bowling, golf, studying, family, friends, job, and traveling.

The mass media are not merely in competition with each other for attention but with all facets of an individual's life also. Nor are they the exclusive influences upon an individual. Despite the overwhelming volume and diversity of mass communications, the bigger portion of one's life is still devoted to other things, mostly to other people with whom he comes in contact and shares a moment of reality: friends and acquaintances, families, co-workers, classmates, fra-

Audience Continuum

ternity brothers; teachers and bosses, ministers and politicians; fellow theater audiences; filling station attendants, bank tellers, parking attendants, shopkeepers, market checkers, and casual acquaintances—the list is as endless as mankind. These people may have only a passing influence, but the encounter is real, a part of experience, and not a fleeting cerebral relationship such as one has with the mass media.

It is this factor of direct personal experience, its volume and its relationship to reality, that Lazarsfeld and Berelson saw in their two-step theory of communications.

It is due to this factor that the content of mass communications, regardless of source, is filtered through other people, a process that diminishes the direct effect of mass communications upon individuals. It is this indirect effect of the mass media, not so much upon its respective audiences but upon each societal member as an individual, that will be of critical importance when each of the separate mass media are subsequently considered.

However, media volume is nonetheless horrendous. Americans are constantly bombarded on every side by a barrage of mass media of all kinds, big cannon and tiny pistols and a bow and arrow or two, seeking to sell, to educate, to change in some way, to motivate. The media intrude on leisure, and sometimes interfere with working, sleeping, and eating. They assail people on the way to work, both inside and outside the car; they follow to the beach and command the sky above it. They are ubiquitous and omnipresent and frequently interfere with each other, constituting each other's channel noise. And the din rises.

COMPETITION FOR ATTENTION

3. Alvin Toffler, *Future Shock* (New York: Random House, Inc., 1970).

This barrage is compounded by the acceleration of the mass media; they press against the limits of human tolerance, a factor noted by Alvin Toffler in *Future Shock*, and pose a threat, he says, to society's future.[3]

The individual who is the end recipient of this barrage can assimilate just so much. Earlier writers have noted this factor. C. Wright Mills speaks of "psychological illiteracy," the result of media overdose wherein the individual simply turns away from this saturation, this credibility assault, repudiating it and withdrawing.

In this accelerated society, the media more and more are encroaching on the individual's time, taking proportionately more and more of it as he seeks to keep up, not to miss anything. As media do this, they remove the individual more and more from reality and direct experience. His becomes a filtered role wherein the various gatekeepers at whatever level are the prime movers of his experience. Such a world borders on fantasy and tends to substitute myth for fact and stereotypes for people. Although such is not the case yet, it is clearly one of the options for the future.

Society is saved, perhaps, by an increasing selectivity on the part of individuals, wherein they more frequently choose only that which is appealing to them, that which has some relationship to their par-

The Continua

ticular orientation. But this trend is in itself narrowing as people more and more withdraw into their own particular psychic enclaves, limiting their experience and exposure.

Society is also saved perhaps by the very diversity of so many media serving so many audiences; in so doing, they offer an imperfect balance. People cannot specialize without abandoning a broader existence.

The audience continuum shows the individual lying at the focal point of an enormous funnel bearing the cumulative weight, geometrically increasing, of all the audiences of which he is even a happenstance member, and of all of those media serving those audiences. He bears an onerous burden, but one of his own making. Society grows more complex and fragments itself. Because of the tight circularity of the communications process, that of interaction between audiences and the mass media, mass communications is the means by which society inevitably interprets itself to the individual and he, through feedback mechanisms, to it.

SUMMARY

The audience continuum parallels the media continuum because in reality they are part of the same process. Mass audiences have been painstakingly slow in developing. They were first held up by the restriction of literacy, later by a lack of technology and affluence. Today, however, society stands on the threshold of total instant reception.

The mass media have always had to cater to popular taste in terms of the lowest common denominator, avoiding controversy and complication. This situation is no different with television than it has been in the past with other forms, a sort of "communications populism."

Beginning with television's "massest" mass, audiences fragment into smaller groupings called, for convenience, publics and groups, on down to the individual who is a part of all audiences—the mass and the individual and of everything in between.

The individual is time-limited, having to cram his lifetime, including mass communications, into a mere twenty-four hours a day. This has led to an increasing competition for attention among the various mass media, all of whom compete in different ways, but most commonly by seeking to appeal to the presumed interests of those specialized audiences they have chosen to be their own.

Within this framework, the gatekeepers of the respective media are actually the surrogates of their audiences, seeking to second-guess them as to what they want. The penalties for failure are high; media fail on the judgment of their gatekeepers.

Thus, in a very real sense, the ultimate decision as to media content lies not with the medium itself but rather with its particular audience, who will, in the long run, buy what it wants from the mass media menu. The theory of "consumer as producer," or audience as source, is as applicable to mass communications as it is to automobiles, houses, or food.

Part III

ETHICS AND CONTROLS

Ethics and controls are of the same breed. Actually, they form a progression inhibiting the independent exercise of pure libertarianism. This is not to say that ethics and controls are necessarily undesirable, but merely to put them in perspective by recognizing that they are disturbing influences on the free operation of the mass communications process. To the degree that they are effective, they subvert the socially self-righting process envisioned by libertarians.

This places ethics and controls more in the column of authoritarianism, which, in reality, is increasingly the case. In fact, Petersen and others advance a theory of social responsibility in *Four Theories of the Press* that is a compromise between a socially obsolescent libertarianism and the more stringent controls of authoritariansim. Even the casual observer can see that mass communications in the United States today is moving increasingly in this direction.

A large, diverse, and complex society does not offer the social sanctions that traditionally controlled human behavior and its outward manifestations in mass communications. In the past, close, tightly knit, and separated communities adhered to their own informal and unwritten codes; these were generally sufficient. But a helter-skelter national society with competing interests has increasingly found it necessary to bridle several activities in the interest of social functioning.

Two things seem to be involved here. Ethics at base is an individual affair. At one time this was sufficient, but as society grew larger and the mass media became corporate institutions, these individual ethics also became organized into media and functional groupings. As these ethics became organized, they also became codified.

One problem with codes is that they write man's conscience down, and once it is in print, exceptions can be found. A written code no longer possesses the moral constraints that an individual conscience does: that which is legal, rather than moral, becomes the criterion. To compound the problem, the various codes were purposely loosely drawn to avoid extensive soul-searching on the part of their adherents. It is not entirely surprising, then, that more formal means of restraining unbridled mass media operations should be sought in law and enforced through the courts and governmental agencies, many of them organized for the specific purpose of media control.

These controls serve different interests and purposes. Some are technological in origin; others are economic sanctions. Some are demanded by social adjustment; some are utilized by government for its own protection in recognition of an adversary relationship. Yet others are deemed necessary in the fulfillment of justice. Some are purely selfish, even whimsical. Some are sound and others misguided.

The various controls, formal and otherwise, that operate within the American system are frequently at odds. Yet, despite the imperfect functioning of separate controls, there does arise a dynamic tension resulting, again, in a sort of imperfect balance. As Sandman and others point out (see "Suggested Readings," p. 457), government alone is big enough to thwart the television networks or major conglomerates interested in the mass communications business. On the other hand, these same networks and conglomerates alone have the resources to stand up to government and maintain the principle of press freedom. So diverse and far-reaching are the mass media that none of these controls can exist without the tacit approval of the public, and many of the controls, for better or for worse, are the direct result of social pressure expressed through these same mass media.

The greatest control of all is that which is exerted by the body politic in the formation of that vague reality called public opinion. Media simply are not free to print or broadcast or produce anything that comes into their heads. They must conform to the expectations of their respective and often highly selective audiences.

Controls are paramount in an understanding of mass communications, while ethics by and large, except for individual instances, have evolved and been formalized in the hope of averting the direct intercession of government.

Controls and ethics seem to center about two main functional problems; one is the confusion of information with persuasion. Too often the considerable power of the press to inform has been distorted for devious purposes, often with the knowledge and assistance of the press itself. The other functional problem concerns excesses. Both obscenity and sensationalism come in here: the exploitation of private lives for a cheap headline, the manufacturing of news to meet popular criteria, or the overemphasis of the visual, active, and sensational are techniques employed. Since information is such a subjective commodity and since the mass communications process is so sensitively balanced, media lend themselves to such distortion and, sometimes defenseless against it, invite regulation.

CONTROLS

AUTHORITARIAN CONTROL

In the investigations of mass communication in this society there has been a tendency to regard the process as a more or less steady flow subject only to the interference of noise. In reality the process is far more complicated than that because, as a social institution, mass communications is interrupted by controls of various kinds. An early example of such control has already been mentioned: the royal licensing of printers by Henry VIII in recognition of the adversary relationship between government and the mass media.

As with this sixteenth-century example, when people think of controls they tend to think of authoritarian controls, ex parte to the communications process, imposed from above. However, there is a wide range of controls: social, legal, political, economic, religious, and technological; all affect the communications process. Far from being entirely authoritarian, many of them exist within the communications process itself, at the source, channel, and audience levels.

BALANCE OF CONTROLS

Whatever their origin, controls have this in common: they disturb the free operation of the mass communications process. In so doing, they have often surprising, unpredictable, and sometimes contrary effects to their original purpose. These side effects of controls in this sophisticated age are becoming an increasing problem.

One thing to remember is that controls are imposed by society and inevitably have an effect on society. They stem from people and affect people. Thus, all controls are not the same. They exist for different purposes, serving different ends, and are, therefore, often in conflict with one another. From all this arises a kind of dynamic tension that results in a certain pragmatic balance.

Since a discussion of controls necessarily focuses on restrictions, it is important to remember that the contemporary American mass communications system is far and away the freest from overt control that exists in the world today. The following discussion is less directed critically than in an attempt to understand additional forces that affect the operation of that system.

To define the premise herein, controls are held to be forces that inhibit in any fashion the total freedom of any medium to print, broadcast, or produce anything in the entire world for any purpose, even as individuals are more or less free to say anything that comes into their heads. Within this definition, one can see that feedback constitutes a form of media control, particularly in network television.

Within this context one should also remember that, as with all social institutions, there has been an evolutionary pattern to controls; since they are in conflict with each other, this means that some ebb as others flow, always in response to social direction. For example, in the laissez-faire period during the last century, government control of newspapers was negligible and public control almost nonexistent; however, owner, advertiser, and monopoly controls were prevalent. Today government control is increasingly felt, public or audience control is predominant, and owner, advertiser, and monopoly controls are waning. At the same time, another control arises, which is institutional control. As mass communications becomes more institutionalized, like all institutions its operation becomes ponderous, filled with an inertia that inhibits experimentation and discourages innovation, particularly among the "massest" media.

THE FIRST AMENDMENT

In the examination of controls, a logical starting point is with the information function, which is, after all, basic to all communications. The First Amendment to the Constitution guarantees the freedom of speech, press, and peaceable assembly. It is significant that these three freedoms are contained in the same amendment, even the same sentence. Those who drew up this amendment, men steeped in libertarian theory, were not thinking of massive institutions but of people, of individuals. Specifically, they were thinking of individual access to the press and to the public forum, rights to print a pamphlet, expound radical ideas in a coffeehouse or tavern, or grab a tree stump on the common—such were the media of the time.

The founding fathers had no knowledge of mass media. Had they known what was ahead they would have been staggered. They had no concept of the huge, expensive, institutionalized plants that today deliver information, entertainment, and persuasion in massive daily doses. They saw only an embryonic Colonial press, isolated, and of extremely limited circulation, concerned with information. Although this was the simple context within which the First Amendment was written as an individual guarantee of access. it has progressed and been interpreted under technological, economic, and social forces, as discussed in chapter two, to become an institutional guarantee to the mass media as corporate entities, with an entirely different connotation, one which de-emphasizes the individual. This is illustrative of social evolution in action.

At base in considering press freedom is the principle of truth established in the 1735 trial of Peter Zenger even before the nation was founded. This is the case that established truth in some circumstances as a defense against libel. It might be noted that even truth as a qualification is a contradiction of libertarianism and that, in view of the abstract nature of what truth is, it poses considerable problems in interpretation.

Obviously, from an information standpoint, the mass media cannot stand on so abstract a qualification, and could not perform their function if they published and broadcast in constant fear of libel suits. The fact that most mass media retain counsel to review controversial matters is testimony to this fact.

LIBEL AND PRIVILEGE

The media are aided in defining libel by the doctrines of *privilege* and *fair comment*. Absolute privilege is an individual right accorded to members of Congress on their respective floors, exempting them from libel for any statements made. By interpretation it has been extended to state and local officials and to the news media. In this case it is known as *qualified privilege* and exempts the news media from libel in reporting the official acts of any government official at any level in reference to acts performed or statements made in the line of duty. This assures that the news media can report government business without threat of damage suits.

Fair comment is a related concept that holds that a reporter or medium in performance of the job is on safe ground if he accurately and fairly reports facts. A drama critic can harshly judge an actress' performance with impunity, but not her home life. A sportswriter can criticize Joe Namath's passing, but not his morals. That the concepts of privilege and fair comment are in constant use in the news or information media is an indication of the kind of clarification and complexity that arises once any criterion, even so obvious a one as truth, is made a condition of mass communications.

A related doctrine is that of *privacy*, the right of an individual to avoid exposure. Gradually, this concept has been eroded by the courts to exclude public officials and ultimately almost anyone in the public eye on the grounds that their business is public if they are a part of the news that is public, or on the basis that by becoming public figures, they forfeit the right to privacy. These controls, such as they are, are attempts to keep open the channels of communication.

THE ADVERSARY RELATIONSHIP

By the nature of the adversary relationship, there is always a temptation on the part of authority to exercise its power to muzzle the press. It didn't take Congress long to succumb to this temptation; a short eight years after the Bill of Rights, it passed the Alien and Sedition laws aimed principally at muzzling the critically rampaging press. The act was short-lived and inimical to the concept of freedom, but it served early notice of government's role in the adversary relationship.

Once abandoned by government the matter of direct censorship of the press did not appreciably rise again. In fact, even in its major wars, the United States has relied on voluntary censorship in the national interest by the press itself. It should be noted that voluntary censorship, backed by the very real power of the government to apply more stringent controls, involves control by implication. However, this should not detract from the fact that the meticulous observation of this voluntary agreement by the nation's press in wartime constitutes a commendation to the press' responsibility here as in no other nation. Even in the Viet Nam war, despite an increasingly hostile press from the mid-sixties on, a press that seriously questioned the conduct and purposes of the war, the federal government did not apply direct censorship. There were, of course, isolated examples of constraint by local commanders in the field, but it was nowhere a part of federal policy.

CLASSIFICATION

In today's sophisticated climate government relies on subtle controls in its adversary relationship with the press. Instead of trying to control the press, which is an obvious technique, it seeks to manipulate or outmaneuver it. Most frequently at the federal level this takes the form of classification.

Certain kinds of information deemed in the national interest are labeled as secret or top secret and withheld from the press. Dissemination of such material is punishable by law. No one reasonably questions the right or wisdom of government to withhold certain information from the public view that would seriously jeopardize the nation's position in its sensitive and sometimes perilous international dealings. However, in reality this practice works differently. Classification is an invitation to government authorities to hide their shortcomings, errors, duplicity, and poor judgment in the guise of national security.

But the mass media are nearly as institutionalized as government itself. They are not entirely powerless in the situation of classified materials. The adversary relationship demands that they continue to seek, to probe, and to uncover; their interest lies in the sensational, the scandalous—material that has a high audience rating. Media may sometimes cloak their investigations with pious phrases about the public's right to know, but in essence they're looking for the kind of spicy news that will attract audiences in droves.

Ethics and Controls

A corps of newsmen inhabit the capital—columnists and commentators, a dozen or so wire services, bureaus of major newspapers, magazines, and the television networks—and make a daily living out of probing disguised and secret items. These newsmen are assisted in their probes by the nature of the bureaucratic hierarchy. Federal agencies are in constant competition with each other; so are the legislative and executive branches and the courts. Departments are often at odds with the executive staff. Jealousies arise; the competition for preferment and advancement is intense. The major political parties are at war with each other. Lobbyists scurry back and forth bearing tidings from one faction to another. The Congress disagrees, House and Senate, and is composed of individuals seeking widely different goals for hundreds of constituencies, interests, and personal ambitions.

In such a grand arena there are ample opportunities for the probing press to encounter the ambitious or disgruntled who are anxious to serve their own devious ends. This makes it almost impossible to keep a secret or a top secret for very long without the voluntary cooperation of the press. The greater the competition, the better the balance. If government were more forthright, the press would be less diligent; if the press were less alert, the government would be more secretive. From this dynamic tension comes an informal system of checks and balances resulting in the pragmatic balance mentioned earlier.

There is no better example of this balance than the incident of *The Pentagon Papers*, top-secret documents stolen from government

The adversary relationship between government and press.

Controls

files by a disillusioned employee and offered to the *New York Times*, which printed them to the considerable embarrassment of at least three administrations and dozens of officials.

NEWS MANAGEMENT

There are also a number of refined techniques at work that subtly pervert the information function to one of persuasion. Such techniques come under the general heading of "news management." They are not ex parte controls imposed from above; they are, rather, source controls.

One of these techniques most utilized by government is that of backgrounders. The theory of backgrounding is commendable; it is to provide newsmen with a depth of perspective in sensitive situations with which they can better interpret the events they report. As some of the background data may be classified, newsmen are asked not to reveal it.

In practice, however, this technique has frequently acted as either a kind of gag on newsmen or as a perversion of its purpose. Backgrounders are of two types: some are "off the record," others, "not for attribution." In an off-the-record statement or interview, an official talks quite candidly about a whole range of highly classified material. The press is free to listen but not to report. There is an informal honor system to this, for if an off-the-record statement is reported, the newsman's sources of information dry up. No one will talk to him again, not even to say good morning. Nor are reporters free to use the material from an off-the-record statement even if they get it from another source; they are effectively muzzled on that topic.

One needs little imagination to see how a backgrounder can be used to gag the press. If an official suspects that an embarrassing matter may be made public from another source, he has merely to call a press conference and discuss the matter openly, off the record; this effectively silences the press. This technique is used sufficiently often that some reporters and media have refused to participate in backgrounders lest they cut themselves off from future news sources.

A second type of backgrounder involves not-for-attribution statements. Here, the press is quite free to use the background material as it sees fit, but it may not quote the source nor attribute to him statements made. Not-for-attributions are responsible for those phrases so often encountered in the news: "a generally reliable administration source disclosed today..." or "a high Pentagon official announced today...."

The not-for-attribution backgrounder is often used as a trial balloon. A projected government policy is released not-for-attribution, and public reaction to it is assessed. If public reaction is favorable, an appropriate spokesman confirms the policy on record, taking due credit. If public reaction is unfavorable, there is no one to blame. Another variation on this theme is that of the sacrificial goat. Here, a

Ethics and Controls

minor official is used as a quotable spokesman. Favorable public reaction leads to confirmation by his superiors; unfavorable public reaction leads to his sacrifice—transfer, firing, or whatever.

Further, the not-for-attribution statement invites investigation; it propels the press to seek a quotable source. This technique is used to call attention to an opponent's errors, to invite investigations of other agencies' activities. It can be venomously self-serving.

These practices are tolerated because backgrounders often do what they set out to do—provide a realistic framework for interpretation. Furthermore, out of the entire specious operation some scraps of significant information do come to the experienced player, information that is probably not obtainable in any other way.

The smoke screen is another government news management technique. It capitalizes on the press' well-known preoccupation with the sensational, the different, the odd, and it seeks to substitute glamor for substance, to divert attention away from an embarrassing or undesirable topic.

PERSONAL RELATIONSHIPS

Since mass communications is composed of individuals, it isn't surprising that personal relationships between potential sources of news and the newsmen themselves are going to have some effect on the process. In government these relationships generally constitute some distortion of the adversary relationship.

For example, the reporters from all the information media who comprise the Washington press corps have, for the most part, been on the job a long time—an average of around five years. It takes that long in the arena to learn the ropes and more significantly to develop trusted contacts or sources. People being what they are, it is inevitable that a certain rapport will develop between contact and reporter as the result of long exposure.

From both practical and personal standpoints, there is a natural inclination to protect one's source and friend if he should err. It is relatively easy to overlook a friend's indiscretion or to give him the benefit of the doubt when the alternative is the loss of a valuable source painstakingly developed.

Nor are officials above exploiting their media contacts. In Washington officials from the presidency down make a practice of entertaining the press personally. Newsmen are valuable contacts in providing an access to news, a bit of one-upmanship in the game of practical politics.

There are bolder attempts in governmental news management. Government is not without influence in the media. Sometimes it has been possible to silence a press critic by a word to his employer, particularly when there are mutual interests involved. Sometimes, too, it has been possible to have a press critic transferred or fired, although these are drastic resorts. Often the solution to an obstreperous critic is to hire him—in effect, to buy his loyalty.

These, then, comprise an inventory of some of the informal controls that are employed in the communications process, with particular emphasis on its news or information function. Such controls do tend to distort the picture of reality that the public receives; on the other hand, they do much to facilitate the complex operations of government, as much by making the press a part of it as in any other way. Finally, they open up bits of significant information and avenues of investigation that would have been otherwise impossible.

OWNERS AND ADVERTISERS

Another series of controls that are unrelated to government but still pertinent to the information function are advertiser, owner, and monopoly controls. There are many who, looking at the enormous corporate power of the mass media and their commercial advertisers, fear misuse. A case might well be made, however, that there are practical reasons why these fears are overemphasized.

As the mass media grow larger, more pervasive, and more expensive to maintain, they find themselves constantly in keener competition with one another for a declining profit margin. Their only hope of meeting this competition is to keep their respective audiences satisfied, to continually fulfill their expectations. In this sort of a commercially competitive situation, it does not make economic sense for the media to indulge in personal whims or political philosophy that is contrary to its audience's demands. Media owners, whether corporate monopoly barons controlling chains of media or single individuals, are primarily businessmen whose concern for the profit and loss statement is far greater than for their personal ideologies.

By the same token, advertisers no longer hold a threat over the media's heads. The mass media themselves are greater and more powerful than their advertisers. They do not need to jeopardize their audience position to satisfy advertisers anymore. Whereas advertisers once enforced their will by threatening to withhold or cancel their advertising, they can no longer do so. The truth is that they need the media to market their goods as much as the media need them for fiscal support. To cancel advertising is self-defeating.

Of course, there are still examples of owners indulging their whims and of advertisers exerting pressure, but these instances are not nearly so prevalent nor are advertisers as influential as they were in an earlier time when the competition for attention was less strenuous and the mechanics of audience control less clearly understood. For example, NBC news programs simply cannot be the publicity arm for RCA's corporate empire without sacrificing competitive advantage to CBS or ABC news, which is not in RCA's overall economic interest.

The courts have been a part of the mass information picture from the beginning. They defined truth and circumscribed libel; they created and enforced a possible if not optimum atmosphere in which the news could circulate. But the courts themselves pose problems as one social institution impinges on another.

RESTRAINT OF TRADE

There is an area of corporate control that is worth examining briefly. With the turn of the century and the apparent excesses developing in a corporate society, the federal government found it necessary to regulate in restraint of trade for the protection of competition as a leveling force in a commercial society. Today, among other legal devices, such regulation often takes the form of antitrust suits prosecuted by the Justice Department.

Originally, federal legislation was aimed at major manufacturers. As the twentieth century developed and the economy became more and more service-oriented, inevitably the mass communications industry reached a size and influence that called for its regulation. It was actually a latecomer to the industrial scene.

One of the first instances of mass media application occurred in 1941, when the FCC, in a surprising show of strength, ordered the National Broadcasting Company, which was operating two radio networks, the Red and the Blue, to divest itself of one of them. Such concentration, the FCC felt, was not in the public interest. As a result, NBC sold the Blue network, which became the American Broadcasting Company (ABC).

Since that time the FCC and other federal agencies have shown concern over cross-media ownership, particularly in the same community. Shortly after the Blue network case, the FCC handed down its duopoly ruling, which precluded any licensee from owning two or more stations of the same kind in the same market. It then went on to expound its rule of seven, which put a national limit on the numbers and kinds of stations that a single licensee could own: seven AM radio stations, seven FM, or seven television stations, provided no more than five of these were VHF.

There elapsed a quarter-century hiatus while the FCC turned its attention to other matters. Then again in 1970 it came out with new proposals: (a) no newspaper owner could own a broadcast medium of any kind in the same city; (b) no television station could own a radio station in the same city; and (c) no broadcaster could own a newspaper in the same market. At present, these are still proposals, but ones that are fraught with much contention. Many newspapers (*Los Angeles Times, Long Beach Press Telegram*) are acquiring CATV franchises in their conviction that tomorrow's newspaper will be delivered via television.

The antitrust division of the Justice Department has also turned its attention to the print media, an area wherein the FCC lacks jurisdiction. Again, its concern has been less with size and growth as it has been with geographic domination. In 1968 the Department of Justice demanded that the *Los Angeles Times* sell the *San Bernardi-*

Controls

no *Sun and Telegram*, which it had recently acquired. (San Bernardino is on the outskirts of the Los Angeles metropolitan area.) Two years later, however, it approved the *Los Angeles Times'* acquisition of *Newsday* on Long Island, outside New York; it has never questioned the *Times'* ownership of the *Dallas Times Herald* in Texas.

GEOGRAPHIC FACTORS

In both FCC rulings and Justice Department considerations it is less overall size as concentration or market domination that is compelling. This is in recognition of the considerable role that geography still plays in audience makeup despite the national character of much of the mass media. In recent years the Justice Department and the FCC have formed an alliance, with Justice providing the legal rationale for the FCC to move against cross-media ownerships and encouraging it to prosecute.

Many media critics have deplored the decline of the numbers of independent or competitive newspapers, alleging an information monopoly. However, the situation is not entirely one-sided. Chain newspapers are generally more financially solvent and, therefore, less prone to either advertising or political pressure. Furthermore, newspapers seem to be adequately serving their markets (there is a practical limit to how many newspapers a time-limited twentieth-century urbanite can profitably absorb). Whatever lack of divergent viewpoint occurs as a result of the newspaper's supposed decline is more than made up by the proliferation of VHF and UHF television stations, AM and FM radio stations, and specialized magazines. In the aggregate there is no lack of diversity; the mass communications network must be considered as a whole in regard to its effect.

CONFLICT: FIRST AND SIXTH AMENDMENTS

A basic controversy arises out of the conflict between the First and Sixth Amendments to the Constitution. The First Amendment guarantees press freedom—the public's right to know. As applied by the courts it upholds the common-law principle of a public trial in which the press is the public's surrogate. The Sixth Amendment guarantees an individual a fair and speedy trial. A conflict arises when the press' preoccupation with the sensational and its diligence in seeking it results in a trial by press wherein often defendants are found guilty in public opinion before their judicial trial is even concluded. For example, in the trial of Dr. Samuel Sheppard, an accused wife killer, the press cried "Hang Sheppard!" in headlines even before the jury went out. It is apparent that such instances make it increasingly difficult to form panels of objective jurors, particularly in sensational cases. This was also an issue in choosing a jury for Jack Ruby after he shot Lee Harvey Oswald on national TV.

But which prevails—the spirit of justice or the spirit of truth? Increasingly, judges across the land are restricting what the press may report concerning a trial. Traditionally, photographers and television crews have been barred from the courtroom lest they disturb its or-

Dr. Sam Sheppard: media trial.

UPI

derly proceedings or lest the participants in the case play to the cameras and the court become a stage.

While justice itself is the worthiest of goals, it is necessary to point out that sometimes its execution constitutes a deprivation of another freedom—freedom of the press or the public's right to know. Neither is this dilemma particularly helped by the sometimes carefully developed relationships between reporters and counsel, who utilize each other to their own advantage in exactly the same fashion as do politicians and newsmen.

**CONFIDEN-
TIALITY AS
AN ISSUE**

Recently another point of contention between the law and the news has come to the fore—the question of confidentiality, or reporters' shield laws. It revolves around whether a reporter can be forced by a grand jury or a court or by Congress itself to reveal his sources of information. There are those who hold that such confidentiality or protection of source is essential to press freedom. How else, they ask, could a reporter acquire privileged and sometimes dangerous information. They maintain that the reporter-source relationship enjoys the same privilege in law as does that of the doctor-patient, lawyer-client, or priest-confessor. The argument may be specious, for the lat-

Controls

ter relationships are patently privy at base, while the reporter-source relationship is public by nature. The source communicates for the purpose of mass dissemination.

There are others who hold that the blanket shielding of sources lends itself to distortion and even fabrication by unscrupulous reporters and sources alike. Forced to choose between the press and the courts, the adherents of this view are opposed to shield laws and choose the courts because they at least are nonprofit, removed from economic incentive, and because justice has a higher value than sensation.

OBSCENITY AND PORNOGRAPHY

There is an additional area of mass communications in which controversy rages, an area specifically dealing with media's entertainment function rather than that of information. This is the matter of obscenity and pornography as suitable content in the mass media. Here the question may well revolve around audience size and duration. *Tropic of Cancer*, once held obscene, was unquestioned while restricted to the relatively small audience to which a hardcover book appeals. It ran into trouble, however, once it was published in paperback and made available to far wider audiences. A range of specifically erotic movies playing to tiny audiences goes unchallenged, as does a considerable roster of girlie, stag, foreign, transvestite, and homosexual magazines of limited circulation. But these themes do not appear on national television, in the *Reader's Digest*, or the daily newspaper.

One cannot help but note an increasing liberalism toward erotic themes in society as a whole. This is an evolutionary process in which media treatment has closely paralleled social acceptance.

However, the strain of puritanism that characterized the original settlements has shown remarkable tenacity, descending in only a modified form until recently. This strain has been reflected both in law and social acceptance, constituting a sort of dual control over the media.

From the standpoint of law, the *Esquire* case in the years following World War II opened the doors for an increasing flow of questionable material. The postmaster general had cancelled the magazine's second-class mailing privilege on the grounds of obscene content. This would have cost the publishers an additional half-million dollars a year in postage. The courts, however, held that although the material appeared obscene, such a judgment should not rest with a single postal official; they restored the magazine's postal permit.

In 1957 the Supreme Court set aside for all intents and purposes the issue of obscenity as a legal control in its *Roth* decision, which held that the test for obscenity should be "whether to the *average* person, applying *contemporary community* standards, the *dominant* theme of the material *taken as a whole* appeals to prurient interest" (italics added). The definition, as one can see, is loaded with qualifi-

Ethics and Controls

cation. Extensions of the definition subsequently added that the material must be "utterly without redeeming social value." There is at least one instance of a successful defense in an obscenity trial being that the material had redeeming social value if only as an example of that which was utterly without redeeming social value.

Since Supreme Court decisions are the law of the land, they have successfully preempted state and local regulations of obscenity in the media, leaving only social control, translated in terms of audience acceptance, as the principal restraint upon obscenity and pornography in the mass media. Such social controls, while a form of restriction, generally work fairly well in removing prurient material from the mainstream while permitting its availability to the smaller audiences who actively seek it.

BROADCAST REGULATION

There is another area in which government has stepped in to regulate the mass media, not so much in protection of its own power, but as a result of technological forces. This is in reference to the broadcast media, radio and television. Such regulation is not only a stringent control on the mass media but also undoubtedly an abridgement of the First Amendment's guarantees of press freedom. Ironically, such regulation arose at the request of the media themselves.

In chapter two the proliferation of uncontrolled radio broadcasting in the 1920s was discussed, and how it led first to an industry request for federal allocation of frequencies and then to the establishment of the Federal Radio Commission (FRC). Operation "in the public interest, convenience, and necessity" by the license holders later became a criterion for relicensing. Such a criterion is an infringement of the broadcast media's freedom in that it demands that they: (a) program a certain amount of certain kinds of material; and (b) not program certain other kinds. Further, though unstated in the law, the number of commercials that they may offer in any given time slot is restricted. This is not only a programming control, but a restriction of their economic rights in a free enterprise system. This is in contrast, for instance, with the print media, where the volume of advertising is totally unrestricted in any legal sense, and audience acceptance is the sole criterion.

The rationale for such regulation lies in the fact that the air and the airwaves are free and belong to the public; they must, therefore, be used on the public's behalf. These regulations were continued by the FCC, successor to the FRC, in 1934.

While both establishing acts specifically precluded the commissions from exerting any control over programming, it is obvious that the relicensing criteria of public interest, convenience, and necessity do, in fact, constitute a form of program control by describing the boundaries within which a station may program if it expects its license to be renewed every three years.

EQUAL TIME

The greatest abridgement of broadcast freedom has resulted from the application of two interrelated and sometimes confusing doctrines: those of *equal time* and *fairness*.

Section 315 of the Federal Communications Act of 1933 establishes the principle of equal time. This concept applies only to candidates for political office and provides that all candidates for a given office must be accorded the same amount of time on the same terms. Thus, if one mayoral candidate in a large race is given an opportunity to air his views, all twelve or fifteen of his opponents must be given the same amount of comparable time. This can become expensive for a station, so ordinarily they strenuously avoid free time for political candidates. Further, if one candidate with a well-financed campaign buys a considerable amount of television time early, the station must clear similar time for his opponents at the same price, no matter how late they may request it and without regard to whether the station's program log is completely booked or not. This means that in the midst of heated political campaigns, stations may have to preempt their regular programs and advertisers to make room for political programs and spots—often in prime time. The forced cancellation of regular programs and customers is certainly an abridgement of press freedom; again controversy revolves around the larger and unreconciled question of which freedom is paramount. The injection of any regulation in the mass communications process disturbs and sometimes perverts it.

Since section 315 is a part of an act of Congress, it took an act of Congress in 1960 suspending the equal-time requirement to permit the famous Kennedy-Nixon debates to take place. Otherwise, nearly

The Kennedy-Nixon debates.

UPI

Ethics and Controls

a half-dozen minor candidates for the presidency would have had to participate in the debates or at the very least been accorded comparable prime time; few viewers would have watched and such an arrangement would have cost the networks millions of dollars in lost revenue.

THE FAIRNESS DOCTRINE

The fairness doctrine is the creature of the FCC, gradually evolving over the years in answer to specific problems. The fairness doctrine applies not to people or politicians but to items of controversy. In 1929 the FRC revoked a license because the station had not presented both sides of a controversial issue. That a station may not be an advocate became the theme of the FRC. The effect, of course, of such a doctrine was that radio stations across the land avoided controversy in any form; not only didn't they advocate anything, but they refused to editorialize on significant community issues, and they avoided any programming that might have even bestirred differences of opinion. This was the source of broadcast's blandness and scarcely a fulfillment of the charge to operate "in the public interest, convenience, and necessity."

In 1949 the FCC had second thoughts on this issue and encouraged the airing of divergent viewpoints. The fairness doctrine as it now stands states that stations must devote a reasonable amount of time to controversial public issues and that in so doing, they must actively encourage the presentation of all viewpoints. They are similarly encouraged to editorialize on community issues, to make their station position known, provided they accord a balance of viewpoints. In the course of editorializing, if someone is attacked, whether individual or organization, they must be offered comparable free time in which to reply. News is exempt from all the foregoing.

While the ground rules are now a little clearer, fairness is still a complex doctrine, subject to many strange innovations. The net result, far from encouraging broadcasters, still tends to discourage them from active participation in controversy.

For example, the fairness doctrine was extended in 1967 to include broadcast advertising. Cigarette smoking was held to be a controversial issue, and stations were required by the FCC to give free time to smoking opponents to answer the barrage of cigarette commercials on the air. Such remedial advertising can be an expensive burden on a station. Although Congress subsequently resolved the problem by banning cigarette commercials entirely, the question of fairness in advertising is one of considerable intricacies.

From its inception until quite recently, the FCC has been a lackadaisical agency, understaffed and underfunded, that regarded its principal mission as technical and operated on a case-by-case basis. Often it appeared hesitant that its rulings might be found in contradiction of the First Amendment, and its rulings have been consistently vague. Such an atmosphere offered considerable leeway, both

1. Newton N. Minow, former chairman, Federal Communications Commission, speech before the National Association of Broadcasters, 9 May 1961.

to its individual licensees and particularly to the networks with their powerful economic, political, and legal resources. Individual commissioners such as Newton Minow, who called television programming a "vast wasteland," and Nicholas Johnson have shown some verve, but they were generally powerless against the lassitude and uncertainty of the commission as a whole.[1]

PROGRAMMING INROADS

In the late sixties, under the chairmanship of Dean Burch, a reconstituted FCC began to flex its muscles.

The FCC entered the programming area, not so much as with regard to content, but in recognition that audience size varies with the time of day and that prime time, the hours from seven until eleven weekday evenings, develops massive audiences and ratings. It was into this mass audience that the FCC sought to inject a greater variety of programming by prohibiting its individual local licensees from exclusively "carrying the net." Network news was exempt from the ruling.

The results have been somewhat contrary to FCC intentions. Instead of developing local programming focused on the communities they serve or airing programs of discussion or high cultural content, some individual stations have simply foresworn the networks during this time slot and have gone to a series of reruns, old movies, or prepackaged shows of dubious quality by independent producers and sometimes even advertisers. No one, neither individual stations nor the networks, is particularly happy with this arrangement. Both are losing audiences during prime time, and the public finds second-rate, sometimes amateurish programs substituted for first-run features. Local stations simply lack the network's resources for Grade A programming. Furthermore, the FCC granted an exception to its own ruling in permitting ABC to carry the Monday night pro football game in this time slot. This is a prime example of the sort of complexity and contradiction that arises when any facet of the delicately balanced mass communications process is artificially disturbed.

It should be reemphasized here that although television networks are the predominant factor in commercial television, the FCC has no direct jurisdiction or control over their operations whatever. It cannot regulate the networks except indirectly through their individually affiliated or wholly owned stations. It is ironic that the agency appointed to regulate broadcasting has no authority over the largest segment of that industry.

Belatedly, the FCC took jurisdiction over Community Antenna Television (CATV). Originally, it had held that since CATV did not operate on an interstate basis that it had no jurisdiction. More recently it recognized that CATV deals in interstate signals. It has precluded CATV stations from duplicating network or local programming within three days of origin either way, and has required CATV stations with more than 3,500 subscribers to originate a certain amount of its own programming, presumably in the public interest.

Ethics and Controls

The FCC has required that, in the largest cities, certain channels be reserved for public access, a sort of soapbox of the air, and for the use of local governments to instruct the citizens. How all this will work is yet to be seen, but it is a fascinating concept and, while well intended, still constitutes a considerable abridgement on press freedom, namely, the requirement of having to broadcast certain kinds of material.

FUTURE CONTROL

A related topic is the carrot-and-stick legislation proposed by the White House Office of Telecommunications as a form of thinly disguised control. This proposal sought to make the nation's 600 affiliated stations responsible for correcting the imbalance of opinion that the Nixon administration felt was contained in the "ideological plugola" of network news commentary. This proposal capitalized on the uneasy relationship that exists between the television networks and their affiliates. In return for enforcing a balance of viewpoint, the individual stations would be offered incentives. Their relicensing period would be extended from three to five years; new applications for an existing license would be considered by the FCC only after it had determined to cancel or not to renew the existing license; and the proportion formulae for "public interest, convenience, and necessity," the unprofitable span of the programming spectrum, would disappear, to be replaced by a vague generality of "attunement to community needs."

This kind of subtlety could be expected to serve notice on the networks to unbias their news treatment, at least in the government's eyes, at the risk of losing their affiliates. Further, it would place the individual station that complied in a more secure relicensing position.

TRUTH IN ADVERTISING

There is another area of control, one that involves the Federal Trade Commission (FTC). Like the FCC, the FTC has had a long and sleepy history. However, the rise of consumerism as a public philosophy and disenchantment with the earlier precept of caveat emptor have demanded new force in the agency. Congress has been more generous of recent years in the FTC's budget allocation, permitting it to fulfill and expand its role of public protector. Following successful campaigns for truth in packaging and truth in lending, the FTC has recently turned its attention to truth in advertising.

Truth in advertising presents a slightly different problem from earlier campaigns in that another element is introduced. Campaigns in packaging and lending involved only the FTC and the individual offender, whether manufacturer or financial institution. Truth in advertising involves both the offending source of the advertising and the mass media that carry it. Thus, truth in advertising by the FTC will affect all mass media, print and broadcast alike, and not merely the broadcast media falling under the jurisdiction of the FCC. Since advertising comprises the largest revenue portion of most of the mass media, a strengthened FTC cannot help but have significant repercussions on most of mass communications.

As an example, the American Dairy Association ran a series of television commercials consisting of celebrity monologues on milk and winding up with the semipun, "Every*body* needs milk—even Pat Boone's." On complaint the FTC demanded the commercial be changed, as doctors indicated that milk is indeed harmful to some people. The amended commercial said, "Milk has something for every*body*—even Pat Boone's." Milk may be bad for an individual, but it has something. Again, one returns to the abstract nature of truth, which is bound to haunt the truth-in-advertising plans of the FTC.

Truth in advertising, the American Dairy Association, and the FTC.

Milk has something for every body.

©FOSTER AND KLEISER CO.

DOCUMEN-TATION

One of the tactics taken by the FTC is to require advertisers to fully document the claims made in their advertising. This has taken the form of submitting huge dossiers of statistics and scientific tests to the commission. While the intent of the regulation is certainly sound, one of its side effects has been to obviate Brand X advertising.

Brand X advertising is a technique whereby a manufacturer compares his product with another (unnamed) competitors' product, pointing out the merits of his own to the detriment of theirs. Brand X advertising was popular because manufacturers and advertisers were loathe to get into a pitched battle in the industry, the outcome of which would have been uncertain. However, with the FTC requirement of full documentation of claims, advertisers have been encouraged to name their competitors' products; the FTC contends that the public is entitled to know to which products another is superior. The public shouldn't have to guess what Brand X is—or even if Brand X exists, the FTC says. Obviously, this tactic will open up full-scale warfare in the intensely competitive consumer industries.

These actions are not dreamt up by an idle bureaucracy; they emerge as a result of popular demand stirred by increasing knowledge and sophistication, increased sensitivity and concern, and a rising sense of populist power.

Ethics and Controls

REMEDIAL ADVERTISING

The basic weapon of the FTC has been an imaginative extension of the FCC's fairness doctrine. It has taken the form of threatened remedial advertising. In this doctrine an advertiser found to have employed false advertising is required to use a certain percentage of his future advertising to acknowledge his misrepresentation, to confess his sins as it were. The percentage devoted to admitting guilt is generally thought to be around 25 percent. However, the FTC has often been content with consent decrees obtained in the cases it has prosecuted. A consent decree issued by the hearing officer is an agreement by the plaintiff or advertiser to perform or abstain from certain actions in the future without admitting guilt as the price of the FTC not prosecuting. A consent decree, therefore, constitutes a kind of probation.

In another vein, the FTC issued a complaint against Wonder Bread, which had been advertising the vitamin and nutrient content of its bread. Wonder Bread could fully document its claims; it was actually as healthy and nutritious as it said it was. This was not the basis for the FTC complaint. Rather, the FTC said, the volume of Wonder Bread's advertising created the false impression that other brands lacked these same nutritious qualities. The FTC wanted Wonder Bread to make a series of remedial advertisements explaining that its competitors had these same qualities. This is tantamount to requiring General Motors to advertise Fiat because Fiat can't afford to advertise itself. While the issue is dormant for the present, it will rise again and surely set new precedents in America's unique advertising-supported mass communications net.

Other weapons in the FTC's armory consist of cease and desist orders, which are enforceable under the threat of prosecution for noncompliance and publicity. Publicity is an informal weapon, but does serve public notice on an advertiser's shortcomings. In the competitive economic climate in which advertisers operate, it is a weapon of great potency and, as it circumvents the hearing process, is one which probably should be used sparingly.

SUMMARY

In summary, then, controls on the mass media stem from three basic sources: from government itself, in its anxiety to protect itself from the prying eyes of the press; from the technological necessities of newer media; and from public pressure as represented in obscenity and consumerism legislation. To these are added relatively minor controls represented by individual owner, advertiser, or even gatekeeper bias, controls that tend to be self-correcting in the economics of the marketplace.

Any controls represent an abridgement of pure libertarian theory—of total press freedom. Some controls, of course, are necessary in a social sense, but their multiplication and compounding makes more complex an already complex interrelationship, and seems to mark a trend away from the basic tenet of libertarianism: that the individual is rational and capable of judging for himself.

By and large, government for its own part has foresworn the direct controls of censorship, and resorted rather to a series of subtle source controls that manipulate instead of directing the press. Broadcast media, particularly because of the impact of television, have required some more elaborate controls of a basically technical nature. Finally, advertiser control cuts across the whole band of the scheduled media, striking at its economic heart.

The controls discussed are both source and channel controls in recognition of the institutionalized nature of the mass media. It is an interesting point that America has survived as a nation without resorting to censorship in the national interest but is finding it necessary to resort to it in the consumer interest.

Controls have matured and grown following society's dictates. They have changed from the blatant injunctions of sedition laws to more subtle and sophisticated forms.

Controls, whether imposed ex parte or not, are inevitably a part of mass communications as an institution of society. Thus, they will be responsive to the ebbing and flowing of social demand, reflecting for the present at once a more liberal and at the same time a more restrictive spirit in recognition of the kinds of contradictory forces that are always at work in the social structure.

Ethics and Controls

8 ETHICS

ETHICS: PUBLIC AND PRIVATE

The question of ethics in the mass media seems to break into two parts: personal damage to an individual and affronts to the public—that is, to the separate audiences of each medium. As discussed, media vary widely in the size and composition of their individual audiences. A more widely damaging social affront will be committed in the massest of the media, and a less damaging one to the audiences of the smaller, more specialized audiences. Thus, the question of ethics also closely follows the parallel continua of media and audiences, and the results of ethics or their lack will be measured in terms of audience effect.

As in anything else, ethics in the mass media are concerned with integrity and values. These are subjective, judgmental qualities difficult to assess, but significant in that they are translated into media credibility, which, in light of media's role as the central nervous system of society, is a precious commodity indeed.

The known instances of lack of ethics in mass communications are rife. As they are only the tip of the iceberg that shows above the sea, one wonders what the full extent of such unethical conduct in the mass media really is.

During the Chicago riots at the 1968 Democratic National Convention, there were documented incidents where television camera crews faked scenes. In one case they bandaged a perfectly healthy couple, asked them to groan, and interviewed them about police brutality. In other cases they paid participants to scream "Don't beat me!" This makes good copy, but it is a patent misrepresentation. Yet, there are no laws against this, and the damage done to a presidential candidacy, to law enforcement, and to the cause of legitimate protest, not to mention the tenets of factual reporting and the effect on public credibility, is incalculable.

On a different level, some years ago protesters of the Viet Nam War were picketing the Oakland Induction Station. A peaceable eight hours of orderly sign-carrying passed—except for an approximate two-minute interlude in the early afternoon when one of the pickets slugged a cop, was slugged back with a billy club and hustled off in the paddy wagon. What was the scene on national network news that evening? That single two-minute incident in its entirety, to the total exclusion of seven hours and fifty-eight minutes of peaceable demonstration. This reporting created an unrealistic impression across the nation—but it was visual; it did happen, and it fully met television's criterion for action in the news. Photos of the incident appeared in the nation's newspapers. Since the mass media are in intense competition, the newspapers could not afford to ignore a dramatic incident already aired on television.

Ethics, in the final analysis, are moral guidelines for difficult dilemmas. However, there are other conflicting guidelines, economic and political ones, for example. Put to a pragmatic test, too often ethical standards fall back in a fanfare of rationalization.

Fact and fiction in Chicago, 1968. This scene is genuine; however, **staged** portrayals did little for the credibility of the press.

UPI

PAYOLA

At one time there was a great network scandal about "The $64,000 Question." Glued to its television chairs, America rooted week after week for the young father with the fantastic memory. Would he win the $64,000? Then, disillusion came. The public learned that he had been coached by the network.

Ethics and Controls

Payola to disc jockeys used to be prevalent. Record companies quite openly put disc jockeys on the payroll to play their records on the air. Such exposure from a popular personality often guaranteed sales. Many DJs were making more from payola than from their salaries. Some of the most popular personalities refused to play anything without payola. Certainly, such conduct inhibits the process of independent selection.

There was a reporter once in Philadelphia who made a practice of muckraking. Through diligent research he uncovered compromising data about a corporation. He then wrote his story and took it to the corporate president, with the suggestion that he be retained as their public relations counsel—the price of not printing the story. There are several elements at work here: conflict of interest, blackmail, and withholding of the news—all unethical, if not outright illegal.

There was a managing editor once who unearthed some most unflattering material about a prominent family—proprietors of a major retail outlet. He had the story set in type and took it to the family with the demand that they switch their advertising from the competition newspaper to his. They did.

COMMERCIAL INFLUENCES

Magazine editors, particularly in the fields of fashion and travel, are often prone to trade a certain amount of editorial coverage in return for significant volumes of advertising. Thus, an advertiser can, in effect, double or sometimes triple his exposure in a single issue at the same cost.[1]

There seems to be a kind of double damage here. Not only are the magazine's subscribers reading puffery, which they assume is fact, but preferential treatment is being shown to certain advertisers who are acquiring greater space at lesser cost. Other advertisers, ignorant of or unable to take advantage of such arrangements, have legitimate cause for complaint. While this practice is dubious, little actual harm is done. The puffery may easily be interesting, valid material fully competitive with other content. Further, there are strong factors for self-correction at work, for the practice protracted over a very long period will inevitably arouse general advertiser dissatisfaction, audience disenchantment, or both—a high price to pay for temporary advantage. The pragmatic forces at work for at least minimal ethics in the mass media are strong.

The travel sections of newspapers are in a similar predicament. Often their editorial content is simply an excuse for the advertising volume—filler material to meet the 60–40 ratio. More often than not, this filler material is supplied by publicists, travel agents, resorts, and airlines—by the advertisers themselves.

Junketing is allied to travel. Editors and reporters are taken on trips to faraway and exotic lands, wined and dined and billeted in regal spendor in the hope that they will write glowing articles. The hope is often fulfilled.

---

[1] John Hohenberg, *The News Media: A Journalist Looks at His Profession* (New York: Holt, Rinehart and Winston, 1968).

To a lesser degree theater critics, entertainment editors, and sportswriters get their share of free tickets and press invitations. It is difficult to be dispassionate in writing about one's host.

There is a balance to this, however; many newspapers cannot afford to buy all the tickets involved, so the alternatives are either freebies or no coverage at all. The solution to this problem is not easy.

Many major media pay their own way to everything. Even so, there is the possibility that their specialists may not be immune to the personal blandishments of long friendship and acquaintance. Sportswriters are exposed to managers constantly, critics to producers; it is quite likely that they may develop a community of interest and enduring friendships.

PERIPHERAL DEPARTMENTS

One sports editor refers to his desk as the toy department of the newspaper. The description is facile; however, the fact remains that sports, fashion, entertainment, and travel are peripheral departments in a newspaper. The entertainment function is basically their game, and different rules generally apply to entertainment than to hard news or information. When distortions creep over into the news sections, greater values are involved.

A good many columnists supplement their incomes by including favorable (and sometimes unfavorable) mention for pay. Financial editors are often in a position to glean inside knowledge of proposed transactions. These financial editors have a double-barreled opportunity. They can enhance a financial situation (or detract from it) through mention in their pages, and they are in a position to personally profit from privy information by speculation. Because of the sensitivity of financial transactions, distorted news read as fact can adversely affect readers where it hurts, in their pocketbooks.

Real estate editors have a similar opportunity. Through exposure they can greatly assist developers and profit either directly or indirectly. Making options available to financial and real estate editors is not unknown and tends to marry them to speculators for the duration of their tenure. Their personal profit will be in direct proportion to the publicity they can generate.

The facts are that wherever public exposure can show a profit in a commercial society, there are those who will exploit the opportunity. The concern here, however, is less with business ethics than with media ethics, although obviously the two are closely related. The dealings of public relations people, advertisers, etc., are with the gatekeepers of the media—those surrogates who select the small percentage of available news the public will see, read, and hear.

The point is not so much the damage done society by such personal exploitation, but rather in the light of competition for attention the numerous items of legitimate news that are crowded out of the media to make way for self-serving pieces. In fairness, it is conceiv-

Ethics and Controls

able that canned or publicity material may meet the test of merit alongside other contenders, but one should be aware that such usage is still ethically questionable, although not the kind of thing that should be legislated, lest the principle of press freedom be further eroded.

ETHICAL EVOLUTION

There is an ideological twist to the issue of ethics, which, in the evolution of American mass media, has shown an odd metamorphosis. After the founding of the Republic, for a half-century or so the nation's newspapers were openly partisan, sometimes vindictively so. Many, in fact, were subsidized by the political parties as mouthpieces. Any information contained in this press was purely incidental to its basic purpose of propaganda.

Such was the purpose of early press advocacy; this was what people expected of it. But times and the nation changed as publishers discovered first the magic of the penny press and popular appeal and, second, advertising as a more lucrative source of revenue than subsidy. Political opinion was gradually relegated to the editorial page.

The public temper today eschews the expression of personal opinion by the media, and thus what was completely ethical in the early days of the nation is now regarded as being questionable ethics at best, and certainly worthy of criticism. Ethics thus appears to be not only an individual subject, but also a relative one.

In at least two periods of the recent past, the nation's newspapers distinguished themselves by crass distortion of fact in search for readership. These were the eras of yellow journalism in the 1890s and of jazz journalism in the 1920s. Both, it might be pointed out, were in response to social demand. In the 1890s Hearst, Pulitzer, Scripps, and the vast newspaper empires they controlled were catering to a new readership, recently literate, uneducated, derived from the flooding immigration from southern and eastern Europe. This ethnic public fed on sensation, and the press barons served it to them. Ethics notwithstanding, this was what the public wanted.

Disillusioned by World War I, the Lost Generation of the 1920s, composed of swelling numbers of the recently educated, demanded spice in their lives—speakeasies, the Charleston, and a flamboyant press. Editors often invented headlines; they carried front-page photographs of electric chair executions. They probed private lives for scandal and debauchery.

Unethical by today's standards, these practices were then common. America's conscience was dormant. It has been only in recent times that a rising popular swell of public concern in many areas— consumerism, the environment, social justice, racism, sexism, etc.— has had a companion effect among the nation's mass media. There is a present outcry against mass communications' excess in many areas. Responsibility, constraint, and social concern are public watchwords, and the press is responding.

ETHICS OF THE MARKETPLACE

Ethics of the marketplace in a commercial society, and the controls that grow out of their disregard, are in themselves social institutions. Thus, they are relative to society's temper at any time, responsive to it. They are less absolute than they are the manifestation of the current state of the body politic's conscience. Nowhere, perhaps, is the role of mass communications as the central nervous system of society more evident than in its flexibility toward ethics. Communications will serve society as society as a whole wants to be served.

Mass media ethics in the decades following the Civil War were, for all intents and purposes, nonexistent. They closely followed the spirit of the time, subscribed to by the public in the freewheeling days of national expansion, the winning of the West, and social Darwinism, and best expressed by William Henry Vanderbilt in his famous "the public be damned" statement.[2]

2. William Henry Vanderbilt, Chicago press conference, October 8, 1882.

This climate lasted until the turn of the century when the muckrakers, individual journalists, discovered their considerable influence and touched a public nerve with their crusade against business corruption and government collusion. Through books, magazines, and newspapers for ten years they attacked social injustice in all the mass media of the time. To date this period may have been the highwater mark of journalistic ethics. It had a certain social currency, which both sustains the point of media responsiveness to the public temper and emphasizes the facility with which the mass media will conform.

Society and the media are now apparently entering upon another period of social concern. Practices long condoned or ignored are being questioned on many sides.

MEDIA CODES

Social responsibility as a press theory probably goes back to the Canons of Journalism adopted by the American Society of Newspaper Editors in 1923. It should be observed that members of the society were the working press, not the publishers, and that their doctrine of press responsibility to the public was adopted in the heyday of jazz journalism. In essence, they reflected their own individual repugnancies and consciences.

Other codes followed, but they differed markedly. The Code of the Motion Picture Industry, adopted in 1930, was a patent effort to forestall government regulation in an era of encroaching film obscenity. The codes of the radio industry (1937) and of its successor, television (1952), are the codes of the National Association of Broadcasters. All three are essentially entertainment-oriented, and tend to view responsibility in negative terms—"Thou shalt not"—rather than by positively stating the scope of responsibility to the various publics that support them.

The media industry codes have certain elements in common. They have no teeth. They are incumbent upon members only, and the only sanction that can be applied against a member is expulsion from membership, a small penalty. There are many instances of media resigning from their professional association, or welcoming expulsion as more profitable than obeying the code. Furthermore, the codes are bland, both unenforced and unenforceable. The codes have this further in common: they were drawn up in response to public disenchantment with media operations. At best, they are a stopgap of semiserious self-regulation in the hope that somehow their platitudes will both satisfy public critics and government's temptation to regulate.

The codes illustrate an additional common trait. By their existence, they are an attempt to organize, to standardize, and to codify ethics. This is a large order and, in the complexity of institutionalized mass media, comprises really only a halfway house toward the regulation that media are trying to avoid. Codes are caught between two irreconcilable forces: they arise in response to public demand, but they are framed to cause the least commotion. Laxity in enforcement further frustrates the public conscience, while codification opens loopholes and invites exception. In a real sense, codes may hasten controls.

COMMISSION ON FREEDOM OF THE PRESS

3. Commission on the Freedom of the Press, *A Free and Responsive Press* (Chicago: University of Chicago Press, 1947).

The next step in the institutionalizing of ethics was a positive one. The Commission on Freedom of the Press, a sort of blue-ribbon, self-appointed, postwar public conscience issued its report in 1947.[3] Recognizing the ineffectuality, negativism, and separateness of the various codes, it sought to integrate the mass media into a more positive approach. It, too, was basically information-oriented, which, of course, meant that it overlooked vast areas of mass media operation. Its report was sanctimonious, but was still the foundation of the social responsibility theory. It called for the press to express truth, to be a public forum of expression. It visualized the press as painting a current and continuing picture of society, even while serving as a showcase for social goals and values, and urged a full coverage of the world's activities—a large order.

In light of the intense competition for space and air time and in light of the commercial realities of audience expectations, the commission's report, although well intended, seems unrealistic in application as well as elitist in concept. It further ignored the specialization of many of the mass media apparently serving useful social functions that had no bearing whatever on the commission's goals. Despite its faults, the commission was sincere and, although perhaps a little impressed with itself, was trying to give expression to a vague undercurrent of public disillusion and to do it positively; this was a starting point.

One of the means suggested to expedite the commission's recommendations was the establishment of a press council on a local level and conceivably on a national level, such as exists in the United Kingdom. A press council is a quasi-official group, composed of both media members and public members, which acts as a watchdog on

Ethics

press activities, and to which the public may appeal, both individually and presumably in class action, against alleged instances of press mistreatment, discrimination, and distortion. To date, the concept of press councils has not met with widespread acclaim in the United States. They seem a further encroachment on press freedom; their constitutionality is questionable and they most assuredly would be challenged on this ground. Press councils would lend themselves particularly to manipulation by dissidents, and on the surface they appear quite contrary to the commercial orientation of the mass media in the United States.

Although press councils have worked satisfactorily in the United Kingdom, the situation is a bit different there. While their newspapers and magazines are commercially oriented, their broadcast media are publicly owned and operated for the most part, and the tradition of press freedom as a whole is not nearly as expanded as it is in the United States. The Official Secrets Act comes close to real censorship, and press coverage of the courts is severely limited.

SOCIAL RESPONSIBILITY THEORY

4. Fred S. Siebert et al., *Four Theories of the Press* (Urbana, Ill.: University of Illinois Press, 1963).

In essence the social responsibility theory of the press, as propounded by Theodore Peterson, is an attempt to explain in contemporary terms some of the undercurrents of public sentiment about the mass media that increasingly rise to the surface.[4] It is obviously a modification of the purely libertarian concept under which the nation was founded. Libertarianism views man as mature and self-sufficient. Social responsibility theory regards him as lethargic, and this may be today a social reality. Social responsibility is the most recent link in a chain of social concern that began with the muckrakers at the turn of the century, moved through the Canons of Journalism in the 1920s, resurrected with the Commission on Freedom of the Press in the postwar years, and now emerges coherently as a theory—guidelines to operations in an accelerating and uncertain future. It also has two glaring shortcomings in that it does not really recognize the historical entertainment function and that it wishfully underestimates the extent of commercial support in the mass media.

A part of its existence lies in the fact of education. The new breed of the nation's reporters and editors, producers, commentators, programmers, directors—gatekeepers—are college-educated; they are increasingly holding advanced degrees. They are young and steeped in social concern. The business of media itself attracts the intellectual and the liberal and these are the qualities brought to the job. Further, there is growing professionalism among newsmen, a rising independence from editors, and policy and source reliance. Some of this can be seen in the so-called new journalism. The new breed gradually remakes the media in its own image, although not entirely. There is still an audience accustomed to older modes and resistant to change; there are still grave economic factors bound up with advertising and audience expectation. But change is in the wind.

Ethics and Controls

Social responsibility theory notes the fact that freedom carries a concomitant responsibility and that press freedom is not the freedom to loot under constitutional protection, but is a freedom to inform that, if not met, may be revoked. Social responsibility theory, recognizing the fact that the press is the watchdog of government, suggests that perhaps the watchdog needs watching—that it has grown fat and lazy and doesn't bark and snarl as much as it should or even as much as it used to.

A good part of the societal demand for such responsibility in its institutions arises from the social confusion engendered by massive overdoses of propaganda and rank exploitation in the mass media. The manipulative techniques used to control the press have fostered a public suspicion. The unbridled effects of political campaigning have further taken their toll; charges and countercharges, mudslinging and vitriol have characterized national campaigns for the highest offices, degrading the concept of democracy and arousing a sense of widespread repugnance. The machinations that some of the nation's biggest institutions have conducted in the public arena—institutions of industry, labor, the professions (i.e., General Motors, ITT, the Teamsters, and the American Medical Association)—have called into question values of free enterprise previously regarded as sacrosanct. Again, the problem of reaction against excesses rises, which, in the case of the muckrakers, resulted in the hesitant beginnings of a now powerful inventory of social legislation. More is coming.

This time, however, the situation is changed somewhat, for it is the mass media themselves that are both the targets of disillusion as well as the means of correcting it and, more paradoxically, the principal critics are the criticized. Following historical precedent, however, it is safe to assume that public dissatisfaction will eventually be translated into more controls and that social responsibility will mature from theory into fiat.

POLITICS AND ADVERTISING

Realistically speaking, the collective ethics of the mass media in a competitive and commercial society are those of the marketplace. Economically, the mass media have little choice but to follow the lead of others. This contention is born out by the fact that some of the greatest perceived abuses of media ethics have been in the realms of advertising and political campaigning, two intensely lucrative sources of media income. Campaign expenditure limitations and full disclosure laws have already been written into the federal books and those of many states. Increasingly, cities and counties across the nation are contemplating similar laws.

A number of states and other legislative entities are considering licensing both advertising and the practice of public relations. Most already have lobbyist controls in the form of registration. It should be noted that the voters of California in June of 1974 overwhelmingly adopted an initiative measure, proposition nine, that placed the most stringent restrictions on lobbyists, campaign expenditures, and political advertising extant anywhere. These licensing provisions are a direct public reaction to the social ascendancy of consumerism. Such controls strike at the source, the monetary base of the mass communications process. It should be remembered that although it is the mass media that will be affected adversely, the mass media are little more than messengers in the political and commercial process—but they are such prominent messengers that inevitably they suffer from the social outcry.

In their own protection, therefore, some of the mass media are already applying belated measures of self-control. Many newspapers have an advertising review procedure to pass on the taste and truth of their political advertising. Many television stations are rejecting questionable material and refusing to accept political spot announcements of less than one minute on the theory that nothing substantive can be said in less time.

Belatedly, the advertising profession nationally, in collaboration with Better Business Bureaus, is establishing advertising review boards at several levels. The functions of these boards will be to investigate complaints by consumers against false advertising and to issue warnings. They will have little authority beyond the sanctions that their admonitions and attendant publicity can generate. They will also attempt to offer a prior service in checking proposed advertisements and commercials in advance to see if they are acceptable.

This is the same sort of approach that the movie industry has adopted in its rating system. The G, PG, R, and X alphabet is intended to guide parents as to what movies their children see: G, general audiences; PG, parental guidance; R, restricted, no one under seventeen admitted unless accompanied by an adult; and X, no one under eighteen admitted at all. However, the ratings also serve notice on children as to which are the most adult movies, and to the general public as to which are the most ridden with sex and violence. To the extent that they do this, they have a reverse effect in encouraging rather than discouraging attendance—often from the very groups they are seeking to discourage.

Many producers have purposely sought—fought for—X ratings because of the audiences they generate. Such a situation is comparable to a book being banned in Boston in the 1930s, a status eagerly solicited by publishers. *The Stewardesses,* a film that was a three-dimensional action inventory of erotic positions in living color, advertised itself as being "very, very X," which gives a clue to the efficacy of the film ratings.

A PRAGMATIC APPROACH

Meanwhile, the Public Relations Society of America (PRSA) is adopting perhaps a more realistic approach. Recognizing that most professional codes and self-controls have proven ineffectual and are little more than way stations along the road to controls, the PRSA is drafting model legislation for its chapters to advocate in their various states and communities when licensing appears imminent. Such draft legislation will be something that the PRSA can live with.

In the entire confusing question of corporate ethics and controls, the most promising approach in these times seems to be that in which the to-be-regulated body plays the role of counsel, at least in its own regulation. Not only is this approach pragmatic, but the expertise of the profession (or medium) is brought to bear. Its specialized and sometimes technical needs are considered.

Further, as most self-regulation is an attempt to forestall more formal regulation and control, the drafting of model legislation by the profession seems to be a more direct, more ethical approach.

OBJECTIVE VS. INTERPRETIVE REPORTING

To be considered also from an ethical standpoint is the entire controversy centering about the old and the new journalism. The ideal of the old journalism dealt in facts, straight facts. Opinion was anethema. Subject matter was treated objectively, sometimes to the point of mindlessness. The newspaper reader was left to draw his own conclusions, oftentimes an impossible task when he was not provided the framework within which an event took place.

For example, during the tyranny of the late Senator Joseph McCarthy in the early fifties, McCarthy would label prominent State Department officials as Communists and homosexuals. The press duly reported this factually—the fact of his utterance. They did not report that this was a familiar tactic of his, or that many such allegations in the past had proven erroneous. They did not report this because it would have been an expression of editorial opinion contrary to the accepted tenets of objective reporting.

The McCarthy hearings. Objective reporting did a disservice to both audience and subjects.

UPI

Ethics

Obviously, there is an ethical question here. The public should be provided sufficient data to reasonably make up its mind. There are situations in which the slavish dedication to facts alone constitutes an injustice.

Nor does it seem possible that complete objectivity can be achieved. A reporter, an editor, or a writer sees certain things. His vision is conditioned by his experience, upbringing, and values; these are subjective qualities. He may dutifully report factually what he sees, but what he sees may differ from what another reporter sees on the same scene. Each brings a different lens to the scene; each speaks to different witnesses; each approaches by a different route. Each story may be objective, factual, and entirely different, if not contradictory. Thus, the problem of what is objective is closely related to the abstract nature of truth.

There have also been instances of unscrupulous reporters, editors, and commentators who have used the connotations of words to convey a special meaning while remaining within a factual framework. "Radicals Demand Policy Veto" is a different headline than "Students Seek Curriculum Voice"; yet both are factual within word definitions and both refer to the same incident.

This is the same element of factual bias that Spiro Agnew had in mind when he referred to David Brinkley's lifted eyebrow. As long as journalistic practice demanded complete objectivity in reporting, there were also ways to utilize the connotations of words, emotional phrases, grimmaces, and gestures to circumvent the practice. This was both deceptive and ethically questionable and led to the new journalism.

THE NEW JOURNALISM

The new journalism takes interpretive reporting for its model. Interpretive reporting—the tell-it-like-it-is school—seeks to place an event within a meaningful framework. It tries to offer the audience a perspective with which to view the news. Certainly this, too, is a worthy goal, but again serious questions arise. Whose perspective? Whose framework? Whose interpretation and for what purpose? Interpretive reporting also seems to lend itself to abuses.

The television networks in their news treatment have been accused of using their forum to intermix a good deal of ideological liberalism with reporting the nation's affairs. Documentaries, in particular, have been singled out for their supposedly one-sided treatment. "The Selling of the Pentagon," CBS's 1972 documentary on Defense Department public relations, was criticized for statements taken out of context and for specious film editing, with which incidents widely separated in time were made to appear in sequence. It is held that this kind of reporting, while it does attract and hold audiences ("The Selling of the Pentagon" played several reruns, unheard of for a documentary) is audience-pandering at best, and a calculated attempt to denigrate one of the government's major executive departments at worst. Again, one can see the deliberate attempt to capitalize on assumed audience reaction playing its role in news judgment.

There are other instances of abuse. The Chicago camera crews who staged scenes to conform to some sort of personal scenario have previously been noted. This is a misuse of journalistic privilege, a distortion of facts, and a particular affront to audiences conditioned to believe that what they are receiving is factual information. It is not so much the injection of personal viewpoint or even the tampering with the facts that constitutes the affront as it is the betrayal of public confidence. The public indignation that such news meddling arouses is indicative of this betrayal. In an earlier libertarian day, when public expectations were geared to opinion and vitriol, slander and attack, no offense would have been taken. However, in today's climate of social consciousness and institutional suspicion, the entire question of ethics in mass communications gains new dimensions in its public sense.

VIOLENCE

There is another side to mass media ethics that reflects the effects of massive exposure. Following a hue and cry concerning the effects of violence on television, the networks sanctimoniously announced their intention to curtail violence in their "entertainment shows," particularly the serials and Saturday morning programs. But entertainment is generally perceived as fantasy; the public is capable of making the distinction. What does seem to have an effect is actual violence, as reflected in network coverage of the race riots in the mid-sixties. Some sociologists made a strong case for rioting being catching, like flu, with the mass media as the carriers. During the long, hot summers, scenes of burning, looting, and rioting in Detroit triggered riots in Washington and Milwaukee. Television seemed less the instigator of the rioting than a trigger to the latent violence of blacks in other cities with similar frustrations.

This is yet another area that needs exploration in a consideration of ethics. Ethics or their lack seem to revolve around two principal factors: deception and damage. While deception generally has an audience effect, straining credibility, damage generally has an individual effect. However, in the case of the Detroit riots, a coverage of real events, perceived reality, caused the public damage, to property and to life: looting and burning, arson and murder. There was no deception involved.

HIPPIES: HAIGHT-ASHBURY

The hippie phenomenon in the Haight-Ashbury section of San Francisco is another example of damage by the media. The press discovered hippies. They were colorful and different and dirty. They wore long hair and sandals, beads and beards. They lived in a make-believe slum and took drugs. They had a new and colorful life-style; the girls wore long dresses and no bras; all were opposed to both work and bathing. They played guitars, used a strange jargon, listened to wild music amid flickering colored lights, and artistically heralded a new renaissance.

They were manna for the media. They were colorful, visual, and different. Media coverage was good for tourism. Haight-Ashbury boomed, and the hippies became tour guides as travelers flocked from Minnesota and Kansas, from Connecticut and Ohio to cluck at the antics of the new, strange youth. The more enterprising hippies corrupted their own life-style by selling incense, posters, and the *Berkeley Barb*, all quite lucratively.

Unfortunately, there were other tourists, the romantic teens from the Midwest and Deep South who flocked to Haight-Ashbury to get caught up in drugs and prostitution and see their dreams burst. The question of media ethics in such a situation is controversial. America did have the right to see what was happening to a generation. The media had a responsibility to show realistically the dimension of alienation as a social phenomenon. But in so doing, an ethical question arises. Did the media overdose lure the unsuspecting into a ruined life? Was there a social penalty attached to actual reporting that might have been better avoided? Like most ethical questions, the case can be argued convincingly either way.

PRIVACY

Finally, the matter of privacy is also a consideration in media ethics. The individual, who is the basic building block of all mass communications, is private. Mass communications by its nature is public. Inevitably, there will arise conflict between the two. At one time invasion of privacy constituted a legal doctrine under which an individual might sue the mass media for unwarranted disclosures concerning his private life. The doctrine was vague at best and, as a result of successive court interpretations, has all but disappeared as a meaningful brake on media invasion, except in advertising. As a result of the doctrine of qualified privilege, which holds public officials publicly accountable for their public actions, the courts have repeatedly held that almost anyone who finds himself in the public eye, even accidentally, is a public figure and is news, thus forfeiting his right to privacy.

This places the onus for respecting personal privacy squarely on the backs of the media and, in essence, makes privacy an ethical question. Examples are rife of reporters rushing to the homes of murder and accident victims to interview the survivors, breaking the grisly news and duly recording all the shock and pathos on camera. Sandman and others note the case of a juror in a murder trial who had been arraigned on a homosexuality charge some eleven years earlier.[5] On a slow news day, the entire incident was publicly renewed and rehashed; reporters interviewed his wife. He resigned from the jury, eleven years of exemplary behavior needlessly sacrificed. This is an example of a cheap headline. but nonetheless news within the media definition. An overriding purpose does not seem to

5. Sandman et al., *Media* (Englewood Cliffs, N. J.: Prentice-Hall, Inc., 1972).

be served by such cruelty. The juror's eleven-year secret was not pertinent to the court trial. It is paradoxical that such examples are anachronistically protected by the truly libertarian sense of the First Amendment, while so much of what the First Amendment originally stood for has been eroded by progress and social custom.

In these delicate questions of private humanity, the ethical matter always boils down to the individual reporter, editor, or commentator. The question will finally be resolved in his judgment and taste. Yet he is under enormous pressure to come up with the moving, the sensational, the shocking, the different to feed a public hunger for pathos and cruelty and scandal. One wonders, therefore, about ethics on an individual level when they seem to be so lacking on a public level.

There are no answers in this chapter on ethics. There are merely questions, and perplexing ones at that, all of which point toward the individual nature of ethics and the difficulties it has in an arena oriented differently. However, the miracle is that there is a great deal of ethical conduct among the nation's media. It does not come to the fore because its practice is generally manifest in its absence, which is to say that ethical conduct doesn't make the news. What the public does see are the too frequent and deplorable examples of unethical conduct, which are almost guaranteed, by their nature, to make headlines.

SUMMARY

Ethical questions generally revolve around two separate, although related, factors: public deception and personal affront. The results of public deception are serious largely because of the vicarious nature of contemporary life. When the mass media betray their public trust and substitute fiction for fact they distort the public's view of the world. More significantly, they create a suspicion of the media and a credibility gap for the public they serve. The mass media are beginning to reap a harvest sown long ago, and their penalty is more controls.

The mass media are corporate and institutionalized. It is not surprising that there has arisen a form of corporate ethics reflected in the various media codes. These codes are, for the most part, innocuous statements of ideal conditions, unenforced and unenforceable, drafted by the accused as blandly as possible as a hopeful stopgap to regulation and control. Actually, controls appear inevitable once ethics have deteriorated to the point that codified guidance is demanded. The codes, therefore, of the newspaper, magazine, motion picture, advertising, public relations, radio, television, and even comic book industries are way stations on the road to controls. Most realistic is the PRSA's approach in drafting model legislation against the inevitable day that it will be necessary.

Morals and ethics are relative phenomenon in man's history. What in an era of social responsibility is now regarded as unethical was accepted as standard practice at a time in the not-to-distant past.

Peterson's theory of social responsibility is part and parcel of this relativity. It regards the mass media as a social institution and suggests that it assume a responsibility concomitant with the constitutional freedoms that it is accorded. While this is a worthy goal, it is also an excellent example of how far society has moved from the sense of independence and individual maturity that the self-righting concepts of the libertarian view expressed in the Constitution. Social responsibility is a protective doctrine regarding man as lethargic.

The question of mass media ethics circulates around the information function, for, in a substantive sense, it is information that will have the greatest bearing on mankind's future. There are, however, entertainment aspects to some media codes wherein the ethical question centers on the question of obscenity and its uses.

In the matter of privacy, incalculable harm can be done by the mass media in its relentless pursuit of headlines. Here the question of ethics revolves around the judgmental factors of the public's right to know balanced against an individual's rights and peace. The competitive situation in which the mass media find themselves mitigates against the individual. Yet, there are probably more ethics among the media than the public suspects, for one can never see, read, or hear about the cases where they were practiced.

Finally, ethics is an individual matter. Ethics is another word for morals, an intensely personal thing, almost impossible to legislate, differing from person to person and resisting codification.

Ethics in the mass media are those of the marketplace, engendered by the commercial base and the competitive nature of the institutionalized mass media, ameliorated occasionally by largely unknown instances of personal forebearance.

Part IV

PRINT MEDIA

The print media are the oldest forms of mass communications. They began essentially with Gutenberg's printing press and the mass-produced book. There was a spiralling process as books led to increased literacy, which created a demand for more books, and more education.

But the book was too slow both in production and consumption, which led in turn to development of other print forms: the tract, which led to newspapers on a regularly published basis, and then to magazines to fill an audience gap between the book and the newspaper.

Society to date has been basically print-oriented, and until very recently the mass communications network in the United States was exclusively print. As a result, the concepts of consumer as producer and of advertising support were well developed before the electric revolution took place.

The form of the electric revolution has had great effect on the print media. Newspapers no longer publish "extras" and national magazines have disappeared, even while a proliferation of smaller, more specific magazines has taken place. The book-publishing industry has turned toward paperbacks as a quicker and more inexpensive mode. Paperbacks are, in effect, a marriage of the book and magazine. There is additional evidence of such combination of forms, represented by Sunday supplements in newspapers, little magazines as it were, and the prepublication of books in serial form in magazines.

These all represent the strivings of the print form to seek its own level under the tremendous impact of the electric media, with its massive speed and numbers of audience.

Print is presently in flux.

9 BOOKS

HISTORICAL IMPACT

The impact of books is enormous. Someone once said that it takes a book to make a revolution, and when one considers the effect of Rousseau on the French Revolution, of Karl Marx' *Das Kapital,* Thomas Paine's booklet, *Common Sense,* or Hitler's *Mein Kampf,* the truth of this statement emerges. Books, some books at least, have a lasting power born of their durability and their repeatability in the sense that they can be read and reread on the reader's terms, their meaning uniquely becoming his, conditioned by him. The Bible is such a book.

As a pipeline of the culture in historical sense, books are paramount, bringing former eras to the present more or less intact; they represent the consciences of times and men gone by. They are private in a harrassed and public time. They are the deeper nerves in the central nervous system and less concerned with the agitated movements of daily living. This is their strength and their social force because of their intimacy with man, the person. Books have been described as old friends with some justification; a television serial or a magazine is no more than a passing acquaintance.

Books qualify as a mass medium on the basis of their aggregate audience, which is huge, rather than on the basis of the number of persons who might read any given title. The number of readers for a specific book, of course, will vary widely; this poses one of the major problems with book publishing as a business. In the media continuum, books lie close to the individual focus.

There is a distinction between trade books (those written for popular audiences) and textbooks in that they are different businesses, although the product may appear similar. Additionally, hardcover and paperback books differ in that they utilize different techniques of production and distribution, although some of the titles may be the same. These differences should be kept in mind.

FREEDOM OF CONTENT

Books traditionally have been characterized by a certain freedom of content, a freedom resulting from their smaller audiences. They are free to explore dimensions of radical politics or erotic interest that the "masser" or family media are not. Further, books are free to experiment with new language and techniques, new expression. In both cases, they are not tied to the tried and true because they can

Books are a mass medium maintaining a particularly private, one-to-one relationship with their audience.

exist on much smaller audiences and need not rely on the lcd of appeal. Charles Steinberg makes the point that the proportionately larger audiences that paperbacks attract show signs of eroding a part of this freedom.[1] The paperback industry demands a certain level of proved acceptance to bring a title into existence. He notes that *Catcher in the Rye* aroused no criticism for its questionable content while it was in hardcover, but a rash of public indignation burst forth as soon as it appeared in the more widely distributed paperback edition.

Book publishing did not grow rapidly in the centuries immediately following Gutenberg. Printing spread slowly from Germany to other nations, ironically assisted by political instability in fifteenth-century Germany that forced many printers to emigrate to other

1. Charles Steinberg, *The Communicative Arts* (New York: Hastings House Publishers, Inc., 1970).

Books

lands. Print's popularity depended on literacy. Even though print brought learning within the economic reach of the masses, there would still be a cultural lag of several generations before its social impact could be felt. Then, as literacy grew, human nature demanded more condensed packages than the unwieldy book. Thus, book-generated learning spawned the other, shorter forms of print, which, in turn, vastly increased literacy with an attendant yearning for more books.

This process was particularly evident in America. The first printing press was established at Harvard College in 1640, only twenty years after Plymouth Rock. However, the orientation of the colonists and their successor Americans was less toward the book than toward the shorter, more quickly digested forms of print. There was little leisure on the frontier; the settlers took their information on the run, as it were, and reading habits so inculcated have been lasting.

AMERICAN DEVELOPMENT

Emery contends that the newspaper is essentially the pinnacle achievement of print developed on American shores, a product of a collective personality, and that Americans are woefully behind in books. There are only around 800 bookstores in the entire United States. George Gallup points out that little Denmark, about the size of New Jersey, has 650 bookstores; proportionately, there ought to be 25,000 in the United States.[2] Further, the same survey revealed that England, with a much lower level of public education than in the U.S., consumes three times as many books per capita.

2. George Gallup, *The Sophisticated Poll-Watcher's Guide* (Princeton, N.J.: Princeton Opinion Press, 1972).

Up until the Civil War, most books in the United States were still imported from abroad; concentration was on the newspaper form of media. In 1850 both Harpers and Scribners began publishing both books and magazines. Paperbacks made their debut in the United States around 1885, and the establishment of public libraries in the same period further encouraged publishing. By this time also, the results of universal compulsory public education begun in the 1830s were beginning to show.

By the latter half of the century, the United States began to show a roster of extremely creditable native authors and a national literature was forming.

The scope of book publishing today, which Emery and others describe as a pygmy among industrial giants, is nonetheless impressive and growing at the rate of around 5 percent per annum.

THE PUBLISHING BUSINESS

At the latest reckoning, more than 1 billion hardcover books representing 50,000 new titles were being turned out annually by around 2,000 publishers. Of these, at least 90 percent are the product of no more than 300 publishers, with twenty-five of the top leaders accounting for two-thirds of the entire production. While this indicates a certain concentration in publishing, as elsewhere, it also indicates that there is room in the field for the small publisher with a specific interest.

Nearly half of the total books manufactured are textbooks, representing around $3 billion in sales. Of the trade titles, only about 3,000 are fiction; the balance—about 20,000—are nonfiction.

The hardcover trade books are distributed through some 10,000 retail outlets, including the 800 bookstores, as well as through seventy-five book-of-the-month clubs and 70,000 libraries, assisted by a corps of "travelers," the trade name for book salesmen. Most publishing is concentrated on the East Coast, primarily in New York, Boston, and Philadelphia, where its antecedents go back to the Revolution.

Perhaps no other medium of the American mass communications network is so hidebound and tradition-ridden as that of book publishing. But change is reaching into the ranks of publishers, particularly with the influence of paperback techniques.

Book publishing is an enormous gamble, which probably accounts for its relatively small size in the sprawling communications field. For instance, less than 5 percent of the 25,000 new trade titles each year sell as many as 5,000 copies. It takes a sale at least that large for a publisher to break even on his investment. This figure is particularly significant because it demonstrates that only a tiny fraction of books will be money-makers, and that, furthermore, this tiny fraction must show not only their own profit but also compensate for the 95 percent of the speculative titles that didn't make it at all. This is one of the reasons for the high price of books.

This has also led to some economizing in the industry and to a number of imaginative merchandizing techniques to reduce the gamble. For example, most publishers no longer operate their own printing plants. While certain savings accrued to in-house printing, the temptation to acquire and publish substandard titles in order to keep the presses rolling was strong and tended to offset the ruthless objectivity necessary in title selections.

Many publishers are also branching out away from the East Coast. There are certain travel economies to this. In the intensely competitive business of seeking authors, who are, after all, the raw material of books, publishers are trying to get closer to them, West Coast spin-offs of eastern publishing houses are becoming quite common. Prentice-Hall of Englewood Cliffs, New Jersey, is a leader in this field, due to other reasons than travel economics; for example, rising executives at Prentice-Hall find themselves plateaued with little opportunity for advancement in a relatively young management structure. Rather than lose such talent to competitors, Prentice-Hall finances them in their own publishing ventures in other areas, lending them the assistance of the parent house's in-depth staffing for distribution and promotion. In essence, these spin-offs act as subsidiaries of Prentice-Hall until their initial investment is repaid, after which the ties of familiarity and cooperation are still strong. This geographical decentralization is one of the more recent effects that economy has wrought on publishing.

Books

BOOK-OF-THE-MONTH CLUBS

Book-of-the-month clubs have proved a temptation as a marketing device. They offer, through membership rolls, an opportunity which publishers usually lack in being able to predict the approximate size of sales in the same way that magazines and newspapers can. A book-of-the-month club selection is a valuable publishing house asset, one that can be additionally merchandized in advertising and publicity. Publishers are eager to have their books so chosen. However, there are certain shortcomings to this particular system. Recognizing the leverage that they have on the publishers, the book clubs often beat the price down on titles they will accept to the point where there is little profit to the publisher beyond the exposure that a book-of-the-month club selection offers. This, in turn, has led many publishers to organize their own book-of-the-month clubs, with varying results. The odds are against their success because of the temptation to restrict themselves to their own inventory, and the lack of broad selection that this implies.

A variation on the club marketing technique has been the publication of specialized books by magazines, a technique introduced by *Life* in its Life Book series. There are two principal advantages to such publication. First, *Life* was able to take advantage of a good deal of material already accumulated by the magazine, paid for and depreciated. This considerably lowered the cost of production. Second, its own circulation list (at the time) provided a potential distribution list of individuals who had already demonstrated by their subscriptions a certain interest in this kind of material. *Psychology Today* has further perfected this technique, not so much in the double usage of material as in the double exposure of authors. Authors who have written acceptable articles for the magazine are paid flat fees or honoraria (in lieu of royalties) for contributing chapters to a book, the level of appeal of which is already established. Thus, a considerable portion of publishing's cost, continuing royalties, are avoided.

An essential ingredient of the book-of-the-month club operation is the so-called negative option. Book club operators doubt that the system would work without it. Under the negative option, a book-of-the-month club member receives his monthly selection unless he specifically declines it. He is advised each month of what the selection will be. He receives it (and is charged for it) unless he immediately returns a notice declining purchase. People being what they are, book-of-the-month club operators rely upon their members' lethargy not to decline the selection.

Recently, the negative option has come under fire by consumer lobbies and is being tested in the courts. An adverse decision would wipe out one of book publishing's most efficient distribution devices, and further deprive a considerable portion of the reading public the opportunity to read current material—more or less in spite of themselves.

FORMULA PUBLISHING

A time-honored technique in the publishing world has been the use of proven format or proven authors, or both if possible. Recognizing that publishing is a risk, the temptation is great to seize upon an established theme and exploit it. This alone accounts for the vast numbers of western, mystery, detective, and science fiction (sci-fi) titles that inhabit the bookshelves and particularly the paperback bookracks. It also accounts for the fabulous runs of Ian Fleming's series of James Bond international thrillers, where an established author, a popular fiction hero, and an exciting style united into an unbeatable combination which stretched out over more than a half-dozen best-selling novels until Fleming's death. The jet-set, sex, and violence novels of Harold Robbins are of the same ready-made genre, a kind of publisher's insurance policy. This is formula publishing.

PROMOTION TECHNIQUES

The final tool used by publishers to offset the tenuous nature of their business is promotion. Techniques have accelerated and been refined, but at base they include complimentary copies of new titles to reviewers, critics, and book editors of various publications in hopes of a review or mention. At the top of these desired lists is the *New York Times Book Review* section which is the bible of the publishing business. Here a review, even a bad one, is a treasured commodity assuring at least some sales. Competition for review by the *New York Times* is intense, and publishers spend much time and effort seeking it. Promotion also includes publicity techniques. Joe McGinnis wrote a number of newspaper and magazine articles about his writing of the *Selling of the President, 1968*, including one about the harrassed life of an author on the road drumming his book: the autograph parties in bookstores, literary luncheons, critics' cocktail parties, television talk show interviews, radio appearances, and the calls on newspaper critics, city after city, for days on end.[3]

3. Joe McGinniss, *The Selling of the President, 1968* (New York: Trident Press, 1969).

Another factor verging on the foregoing is the matter of the movies. For years Hollywood has capitalized on best-selling novels as the basis for films, figuring the exposure already achieved would pay off at the box office. Recently, a reversal of this technique has shown some promise. *Love Story* was both published as a book and released as a film simultaneously in order that each medium might feed upon the other's popularity. Further, the promotion expense of the title was amortized over two different media forms. There was no way, of course, of predicting the fantastic popularity of *Love Story,* but at least the promotional costs were minimized, and by virtue of the dual reinforcement probably both media got better promotion than either could have afforded individually.

This publicity and accompanying advertising is aimed not only at the critics, but also at the general public in order to create a demand, or at the least a little curiosity—enough to make persons seek a bookstore (which is not always easy), and spend their money (which is always hard). Once a fire is ignited, word of mouth does the rest.

Books

THE PUBLISHING MYTH

There is a myth about book publishing that tells of the young novelist completing his masterpiece after years of garret privation and finally, after heartbreak and disillusionment, finding a publisher who perceived the genius in his manuscript and brought out a bestseller. That is just not the way it is. Publication of the unsolicited or over-the-transom manuscript is virtually nonexistent and may easily have stopped with Margaret Mitchell's *Gone With the Wind* in the 1930s. The overwhelming number of published manuscripts are solicited, commissioned, or contracted. The idea for a book may arise with either author or publisher. When it originates with the author, he generally writes a relatively brief prospectus describing his idea, the approach, theme, and development. Generally, a couple of sample chapters to indicate style accompany it. It then goes through a successive and brutal screening process. "Readers," recent literature graduates, generally get the first opportunity to screen a manuscript. They can reject it out-of-hand and most often do so. Rejections usually consist of a curt form notice, with no personal letter from the reader or publisher; time and the quantity of rejections do not permit more. Most authors have impressive files of rejection slips, the number of which is a sort of badge of professionalism.

If a manuscript passes this test, it goes to an editor for consideration. If he should like the idea, he may send it out for evaluation by recognized authorities in the field. If it makes it this far, the manuscript then may go to an editorial board for final decision. The manuscript may be rejected anywhere along the line or the author may be asked to further elaborate his idea. From this description it should be obvious that an unsolicited manuscript stands little chance and that only a tiny percentage of the précis submitted survive to reach an editorial board decision. The competition for attention at the channel level in publishing is intense, and the gatekeeper's role more ruthless than even at a newspaper. The numbers involved are frightening: less than 2 percent of the prospecti submitted will ever see print, and less than 5 percent of those will attain enough exposure to pay expenses.

The other route a manuscript may take occurs when an idea originates with the publisher, whose business it is to keep his fingers on the public pulse, to know what people are reading, what kinds of books are selling, where the public interest lies. The process is somewhat simplified by the fact that many publishers tend to specialize in certain types of books—text or trade—and within these fields in certain concentrations: ficton or nonfiction, mysteries or westerns, international affairs or politics, and the like. Consequently, most publishers do not have to keep track of the entire market, but only their specialized fragment. If a publisher has an idea, he starts looking for the right person to write it. He does this either from his own knowledge of an author's prior work or from gleanings from magazines and newspapers. He may go to a literary agent to find the proper talent.

AGENTS

Agents play a significant role in book publishing. Each has a stable of significant authors whose work he sells. An agent maintains close contact with editors and publishers; he knows their inventories and the kinds of material that they are looking for. He also knows the market as well as the publishers do. Most agents have been in the business for years and have earned the confidence of the editors with whom they deal. An agent generally takes 10 percent of a book, both advance and royalties, and generally earns it by winning more sales and more generous advances for his authors than the authors could win for themselves. Agents have the time and contacts for this; authors do not.

Regardless of how a book gets started, the next step is the contract which specifies the author's advance, a flexible figure depending on the author's reputation for dependability, performance, and popularity. Successful authors obviously can command larger advances than beginning ones. An advance is a sum of money paid an author for writing the book; it is chargeable, for the most part, against his royalties when and if they develop. Generally, royalties are 15 percent of the list price of the book for every copy sold as it is sold—less the author's advances. If the book does not sell enough copies to return its investment, the author keeps his advance anyway. Thus, the larger the advance, the better the author is protected regardless of subsequent sales. Successful authors gamble little; beginning authors gamble their time along with the publisher's investment of money.

Thus far discussion has centered on hardcover trade books. Trade books are a one-shot phenomenon. They either make it or fail on their own merit, more or less immediately. The outcome of a book will be known within a relatively short time period; like a butterfly, a trade book has a short life span. There are exceptions, of course—the Bible and the works of Shakespeare—but these are scarcely trade books.

TEXTBOOKS

Textbooks are a different proposition than trade books, and an enticing one. Instead of passing fleetingly from the scene, a successful text keeps on living and earning for both author and publisher, year after year, as new classes of students and even new generations enter schools and universities. As a successful textbook becomes dated in four to six years, it is a relatively simple matter for the author, who is almost always a professor in the field, to update the material in the light of new knowledge, and the publisher to bring out a new edition trading on the text's already established reputation. It is not unusual for a successful text to run to six and eight editions.

A text also differs from a trade book in other ways. The author-source potential is smaller since texts are exclusively written by professors. Further, the market is smaller, restricted to those enrolled in school and college. However, the relative permanency of a long-term audience and the mandatory nature of sales more than compensate for these shortcomings.

It should be apparent that professors are not only the sources of text material but also the means of its distribution. College travelers from the publishing houses are well versed in academia and well acquainted with professors within their respective institutions and disciplines. It is the professors who order the texts for their classes; the campus bookstores merely stock them. In addition to their role as salesmen, college travelers are manuscript scouts for their publishers since they are dealing with the same people anyway.

PAPERBACKS

While most Americans have been conscious of the paperback phenomenon only since World War II or the depression years of the thirties at the earliest, paperbacks have a respectable history going back nearly a century and a half. As Germany was the home of the original book, so it was of the paperback. As early as 1837 Tauchnitz of Leipzig was publishing paperbacks in a library that eventually included nearly five thousand English titles.

In the United States, on a lesser scale, the Boston Society for the Diffusion of Knowledge, founded in 1827, began to publish in paperback for the American Library of Useful Knowledge in 1831. This was a technological by-product of cheap paper, mechanical typesetting, and rotary presses. Typical distribution was as unbound supplements in various magazines and newspapers, making them the early ancestors of both the Sunday supplements and of magazine distribution methods, a true hybrid. This form ended in 1843 when the post office began charging book postage instead of the lower newspaper rates.

The paperback technique was revived briefly in the post-Civil War explosion of cultural classicism by the *New York Tribune*, which proliferated culture in the form of newspaper extras selling at from five to fifteen cents a copy. While this was apparently a circulation device for the newspaper, nonetheless it made its contribution to popular education and the expanding culture. In fact, by 1885 about a third of the nearly five thousand titles published were in paperback.

Another innovation was Reclam's Universal Library, founded in Hamburg, Germany, in 1867. Reclam published ten titles per month to become the first book-of-the-month club without really knowing it.

Reclam also had a working arrangement with the Society for Popular Education which contributed enormously to its success. The society established 137,000 libraries with a total of more than four million volumes as well as operating nearly 25,000 traveling libraries with another million volumes. Reclam saw early the advantages of library distribution as an aspect of the business; in the United States libraries are generally restricted to hardcover books because of their permanency.

Whereas Tauchnitz had concentrated on classical titles, in 1932 Albatross Modern Continental Library in Hamburg began publishing contemporary works in paper. In 1935 the two merged; in that year Penguin Books also began operations in England with the basic paperback format familiar to everyone.

Penguin quickly penetrated the market in England and abroad. In the United States the success of a paper format was aided by the economic limitations of the Great Depression. People lacked money for entertainment. A twenty-five-cent movie was prohibitive; magazine subscriptions were a continuing cost or involved a heavy initial outlay. Paperbacks provided inexpensive and more or less permanent entertainment in that titles could be traded.

PAPERBACK MARKETING

The postwar paperback explosion was the publishing counterpart of a general communications explosion in the United States based on affluence, attendant leisure, and technology. In the paperback field technology produced the so-called perfect binding that didn't break, glossy and sometimes washable covers, high-speed presses, and offset printing from rubber mats.

Paperback distribution is a genuinely unique feature which accounts for nearly all the basic differences between paper and hardcover publishing. The smaller pocket size made paperbacks adaptable for retail locations where space was at a premium. The cheaper price tag permitted paperbacks to consort with sundries for the casual customer's dollar, and the lower production cost permitted returns to the publisher in which he did not have an enormous investment. In short, this was magazine distribution, utilizing basically the same

Contemporary bookstores often display more paperbacks than hardbound editions.

Books

distributors. Paperbacks are distributed through some eight hundred wholesalers across the country, or by the American News Company with its 350 distributors. Together, they serve around 100,000 retail outlets—cigar stores, drugstores, liquor stores, markets, shopping centers, airports, and the like—always locations where the casual traffic is high. Like magazines, paperbacks are displayed in racks which generally have about one hundred pockets holding three to five copies each. The racks occupy valuable floor space; however, there is a tremendous turnover in the paperbacks on display, with premium space going to the fast movers, while books which don't sell rapidly are returned, often after no more than a week. Paperbacks are fully returnable by the retailer for either cash or credit.

Essentially, on the retail floor paperbacks are in competition with magazines for the customer's purchase, and the paperback proliferation has further hurt the magazine industry by cutting into its casual or street sales. This is another of the contemporary media interrelationships arising out of competition for attention—and dollars. Lacking a conditioned acceptance, paperbacks need a longer display period than do transient magazines, and as they are generally not permitted it under competitive conditions, only the best-selling titles remain available on display.

While this system does not detract from paperback sales in the aggregate, it does tend to remove some of the "heavier" titles from circulation in favor of flamboyant fare represented by sex, western, mystery, detective, and sci-fi offerings. Experience has shown that classical reprints will move well if given long enough display time.

OVERLAP

Stores specializing in paperbacks have become popular in recent years. Also, paperbacks have found their way into bookstores and the book areas of department stores where previously they were anethema because it was believed that their cheaper cost would detract from the more profitable hardcover sales. This has not proven to be the case. They are, rather, traffic builders for these outlets, playing the same sales role that "loss leaders" do in markets. Publishers who have brought out both hardcover and paper editions of the same title have found that less than 10 percent of their readerships overlap. Surprisingly, although they are both books, the audiences for hardcover and paperback differ.

Sitting in racks in heavily trafficked areas, in competition with sundries and magazines, lacking magazine's conditioned appeal, tended by unknowledgeable sales persons, and without the hardcover's promotional efforts or even critical reviews, the little paperback generally has to make its way all by itself. There is little promotion that anyone can give, except perhaps a point of sale poster or display, or a better position on the rack. However, position comes at the expense of another title, and promotional efforts cut seriously into the slim profit margin of the paperback.

This margin is so slim that, where it required 5,000 copies of a hardcover to "make the nut," a sale of 200,000 is needed to pay off a paperback's investment. However, Kurt Enoch points out that 200,000 sales over 100,000 outlets at $.50–$1.00 is no harder than 5,000 sales at $7.00–$8.00 through 1,500 retailers.[4]

4. Kurt Enoch, "The Paper-Bound Book: Twentieth Century Publishing Phenomenon," *Library Quarterly* 24 (3): July, 1964.

Actually, paperback marketing is maturing. Distributors are separating their paperback and magazine divisions and employing personnel knowledgeable in the trade. Point of sale and other promotions are becoming prevalent. Some paperback publishers are issuing balanced monthly packages of ten to a dozen titles with the hope of selling all because the competition for one particular paperback title is intense. Also, some newspapers are beginning to run paperback review sections.

SOURCES FOR PAPERBACK

There are about a dozen major paperback publishers in the United States. Like their hardcover counterparts, each tends to specialize, some in entertainment, some in classics, some in significant reprints. Most try to achieve some sort of a balanced inventory of offerings, eating at all segments of the potential market from several directions. Publishing is one of the few fields where an operator can be in competition with himself by bringing out a number of competitive and even contradictory titles. His audiences, more than any other, are composed of individuals whose purchases need not be single, and whose interests are not mutually exclusive.

When one thinks of paperbacks, the cheaper editions of former hardcover best-sellers generally come to mind, and while this is certainly one practice, it is far from the entire story. There is a good deal of classical publishing in paperback for the simple reason that as the copyrights have expired; there are no royalties to be paid. Thus, with cheaper paperback publishing costs, profit can be shown on smaller sales. In this way, paperback publishers seek to tap the college and university market in the same fashion that hardcover publishers utilize texts.

There is also a substantial amount of original publishing in paperback. Author's royalties per copy are generally less and more flexible, hovering between 2 and 4 percent, but the greater projected sales more than compensate. Generally, these originals are concentrated in the entertainment field where their transiency is not significant, but occasionally a paperback original of considerable merit, such as J.A.C. Brown's *Techniques of Persuasion*, appears.

Few publishers attempt both hardcover and paperback work. While the profits from bringing out a paperback edition of a publisher's own best-seller are high, such occasions are limited. The temptation to build up one's own line of paperbacks from one's hardcover inventory is great, but not necessarily profitable. Also, the thought of turning over a valuable property to another publisher for paperback, when that same publisher may be in hardcover competition, is not generally attractive. The two forms of book publishing tend to remain separate for economic reasons, with hardcover publishers selling the reprint rights to paperback publishers on an advance and royalty basis, and paperback publishers making deals directly with authors for paperback originals.

Sometimes paperback publishers will pay more for a reprint title or an original than they can hope to make in profit. They do this looking at large anticipated sales with the thought that competitively they are enhancing their position with both their distributors and their retail outlets, as well as accruing certain prestige in the very limited paperback business. If they were not to acquire the rights, a competitor would, and sometimes a monetary loss on a best-seller is worth the less tangible advantages.

On the fringes of book publishing are a number of private publishers who specialize in individual works. Such publishers do not seek even the limited audiences that hardcover trade publishers need. They capitalize on the presumed status of books and the ambitions of authors who always wanted to see themselves in print. For a fee covering all costs and profit, they will bring out a specified number of copies of any length in any format for delivery to the author. Professors, corporation presidents, poets, and zealots comprise their market.

SERIALIZATION

A technique which has been used sparingly but with considerable success is the prepublication serialization of a book in magazines or newspapers. Both Truman Capote's successful *In Cold Blood*, which he described as a new art form, and William Manchester's *The Death of a President* were serialized in this fashion in *The New Yorker* and *Look* respectively. The case for prepublication serializing can be argued both ways. The additional revenue which comes to the publisher for the magazine rights offsets a considerable amount of his publication costs. On the other hand, serialization in a popular magazine may detract from the eventual audience. Naturally, the sophisticated readers of *The New Yorker*, for example, had to be subtracted from the eventual sales of *In Cold Blood*. On the other hand, the massive exposure accorded a title by magazine publication can precondition a responsive public for when the book does go on sale. The pro's and con's of serialization have not been resolved; like everything else in book publishing, serialization is a gamble.

CORPORATE STRUCTURE

From a corporate standpoint some of the gamble on a book's sales can be reduced fiscally. In 1959, Wall Street began to eye the traditionally ingrown and sole proprietorship book-publishing business and encouraged it to go public, to sell stock. Over the years, the result of this has been the corporate ownership and acquisition of many publishing houses that have become divisions of conglomerates or parts of horizontal communications empires. In such organizational settings, book publishing contributes a certain prestige and small profits—profits which are offset by the higher profits and more mundane divisions of the conglomerate. McGraw-Hill, for example, a book and magazine publisher, has recently gone into the network television business. Life Books is the only survivor, and a profitable one, of the national magazine, but it in turn is a part of Time Inc., and is broadly exposed in the magazine and CATV communications fields, and presently branching out into other areas. Also, CRM, which publishes *Psychology Today,* has entered the book field with a series of titles and interesting marketing concepts based on its magazine circulation lists, a factor that led to its acquisition by Random House in 1974. The television networks are acquiring publishing outlets as they seek diversification; the entire mass communications network becomes more interwoven.

Thus, under the impact of the communications explosion, even book publishing takes on corporate vestiture, decentralization, and promotional techniques. The entire industry, under the influence of the paperback, is radically altering. Marketing concepts edge to the fore, and the traditional book rapidly becomes less self-selective and independent than it once was—and at once more profitable. Book publishing still remains, with filmmaking, an essentially individualized mass medium, although this characteristic is gradually being eroded.

A part of the traditional independence of book publishing seems on shaky ground as a result of what Kurt Enoch calls vulgarization in paperbacks. He feels that, as outlets multiply and press runs grow, there is increasing pressure for uniformity in product and timidity in treatment, a catering to the lcd, a return to formula writing, and the avoidance of controversial themes. He still places great confidence in the integrity of paperback publishers and their dedication to their product, but this is an intangible facet of the business, difficult to document, and subject to severe pressure and attrition as the present generation of publishers fades and the business becomes more institutionalized, a process which seems inevitable.

THE BOOK AND WESTERN CIVILIZATION

Unquestionably, the book medium has had the greatest overall effect upon the development of Western society. More recent forms of media, the newspaper and broadcast, may have greater short-term impact on current generations, but it was the book which laid their groundwork and accumulated and ordered the thoughts of mankind in some sort of manageable form.

Books have a history going back five and a half millenia, always based on man's need to record and transmit his thoughts from generation to generation. Books, therefore, are responsible not only for man's cultural transmission from earliest time, but for the time-binding capacity itself, which makes man unique in his ability to build on what has gone before.

It was in ancient Egypt that the great library at Alexandria sought to accumulate and codify this knowledge of the ages in recognition of the book's role in cultural transmission. It is the Phoenicians who are credited with the first phonetic alphabet, which is based on man's ability to write as he speaks rather than in unwieldy pictographs or such abstract symbols as the wedge-shaped cuneiforms. Until the phonetic alphabet, literate man had essentially to learn two languages. Through the Greeks and the Romans, Western writing became more standardized, while the Christian influence made itself felt in keeping literacy alive during the centuries of the Dark Ages.

Meanwhile, writing materials became more portable, progressing from clay tablets to parchment, which was expensive but durable, and finally to paper, which arrived in time to accommodate the printing press.

Language and material and technology came together with Gutenberg's invention of print. This was the dawning of mass communications, the direct ancestor of all other print forms, and the indirect antecedent of the other mass media.

> "It is chiefly through books that we enjoy intercourse with superior minds. In the best books, great men talk to us, give us their most precious thoughts, and pour their souls into ours. God be thanked for books. They are the voices of the distant and the dead, and make us heirs of the spiritual life of past ages. Books are true levelers. They give to all, who will faithfully use them, the society, the spiritual presence, of the best and greatest of our race."
>
> William Ellery Channing, 1838

SUMMARY

The industrial revolution, which was itself responsible for most of the mass media's technological innovations, was the direct result of technical knowledge recorded and transmitted through print. The industrial revolution could not have occurred without the kind of technical knowledge which print made possible through its ability to record and transmit and augment what went before.

Books are the most individual of the mass media. They are not supported by advertising and must pay their own way. Thus, book publishing becomes a continuing gamble, for there is no way of predicting the potential audience, if any, of any given title.

Only about 5 percent of trade book titles sell as many as five thousand copies, the number necessary to recoup a publisher's investment. Thus, each book must not only pay its own way but compensate for around twenty unsuccessful efforts. This adds to the high costs of hardcover books and justifies the considerable promotional expense.

Books may be classified into trade books and texts, and further into hardcover and paperback. The peculiarities of each form are significant. Trade books are a one-shot undertaking having generally to achieve their sales within a short time period. Successful texts, on the other hand, keep on living year after year as new waves of students enter classes. Trade books are aimed toward the eventual buyer, while texts are pinpointed toward the teachers and professors who control their sale through classroom use.

Paperback publishing goes back nearly 150 years, and at present uses magazine distribution techniques through a hundred thousand retail outlets. Paperbacks require around two hundred thousand sales to break even. Paperback publishers not only reprint successful hardcover titles after they run their course, but also publish original titles. There is less than a 10 percent overlap between the potential audiences for hardcover and paperback.

Manuscripts go through a ruthless screening process, and most publication is on contract with a publisher, much of it solicited by him. The publication of an over-the-transom manuscript is rare. Authors are paid on an advance and royalty basis, with royalties being generally 15 percent of list on all sales.

There is a good deal of formula publication of tried and true authors, heroes, and plots, but most publication is aimed toward the indefinable interests of myriad individuals, interests which are not mutually exclusive. Thus, a publisher can successfully be in competition with himself for different audiences.

A recent trend has been the institutionalizing of book publishing as publishers are acquired by conglomerates or communications empires. Book publishing is less independent than it used to be, and shows signs particularly in paperback of catering to the lcd with uniform products and timid treatment.

10 NEWSPAPERS

**NEWSPAPERS:
THE PARENT
MEDIUM**

The newspaper, as Emery points out, is a uniquely American phenomenon representing the highest achievement of the print medium. Born overseas, it emigrated at an early age and, finding itself peculiarly suited to the rushed American temperament, matured and flourished on this continent in an extraordinary compatability with the society it served. It has demonstrated a remarkable adaptability to changing times, and even though it has been superceded in some respects by the broadcast media, it nonetheless provided the operational and even philosophical framework within which the broadcast media grew. Local emphasis, advertising support, and audience appeal were all lessons that broadcast learned from the press. Further, the fundamental concept of press freedom was a newspaper doctrine promulgated by the founding fathers and subsequently applied to all media. The American newspaper is the traditional base of a burgeoning mass communications network, a parent medium.

Despite the fact that there are more efficient electronic media today, reaching far wider audiences nationally in much less time, there is considerable evidence that most people still rely on the newspaper for most of their news, and that newspapers provide the largest local advertising showcase.

In a national survey Opinion Research of Princeton, New Jersey, found that 50 percent of the population rely on newspapers for their news; television was second with 46 percent.[1] Within this frame, those who relied on newspapers were the younger, the better educated, and the more affluent. With education on the rise nationally and a greater percentage of the population seeking advanced degrees, the data seem to indicate that newspapers will increase their preferred position as news source. The survey also noted that newspapers were the

---

1. Opinion Research Corporation (Princeton, N. J.), newspaper survey. Sample 2,023; individuals 18–50; completed April, 1972.

major source of advertising information and that the public regarded newspaper advertising as more trustworthy than that in other media. Such trust is most probably a product of the essentially local character of newspaper advertising, in that it can be readily checked and the advertiser held accountable at his own cash register. Newspaper advertisers live in their communities along with their readers.

LOCAL NATURE

A clue to the newspaper's strength lies in its local nature. The American newspaper has never been a truly mass medium. It is a local medium whose allegiance is exclusively to the geographic area it serves. Thus, it was always and still is geographically fragmented. With the advent of the telegraph and wire services, newspapers across the nation took on the illusion of a mass medium because it was theoretically possible to read the same wire service story verbatim in different corners of the nation. However, such national and international stories are a relatively small portion of the newspaper's daily budget. Newspapers cater to their communities, their merchants, and to local taste. They are and have always been mirrors of their communities. This local emphasis is the twentieth-century heritage from the early nation of isolated and widely separated communities along the Atlantic seaboard, self-reliant and served by a self-reliant press.

A newspaper is a geographically circumscribed print medium, regularly issued, serving the general interests of a specific community. This definition has nothing whatever to do with frequency of publication, size, or format. Newspapers can vary as widely as the multiple editions of the *New York Daily News,* reaching nearly four million people daily, to the little monthly *Borrego Sun,* serving the 440 residents of Borrego Springs, California. There are weekly newspapers and suburban dailies. Some do carry extensive regional, national, and international news, but most do not; all have in common a preoccupation with their own locale.

Thus, one should not confuse the *Wall Street Journal* or *Women's Wear Daily* with newspapers despite their newsprint format. They are really daily magazines serving specific interest groups nationally, the financial world and the fashion industry respectively.

NEWSPAPER EVOLUTION

A brief look at the history of newspapers will be revealing. Newspapers, of course, grew out of Gutenberg's print, but it was a hundred years after William Gaxton's first English printing press in 1476 before the first tracts containing news bulletins of topical interest appeared. By 1621 *corantos* were common. These were single sheets dealing basically with current foreign affairs of principal interest to the merchant classes who, by that time, might be presumed literate. Corantos were followed in 1641 by the diurnals, four-page bulletins of local news. Literacy was spreading and technology improving. The diurnals harkened back to the *Acta Diurna* of ancient

Rome, a daily publication of events posted in the forum. It was not until 1665, however, that the first regularly published newspaper, the *Oxford Gazette* (later the *London Gazette*) appeared, and not until the turn of the eighteenth century in 1702 that a daily newspaper came into being, the *Daily Courant*. Thus, it was around two hundred and fifty years from the printing press to the daily newspaper, a lag occupied by the battle for literacy and technological development.

America's first daily, the *Boston News Letter,* came two years later, published by the postmaster, John Campbell. The history of newspapers on American shores can be split into eight eras of varying lengths, each making its own contribution to the press. They are: the Colonial press, the Revolutionary press, the kept press, the penny press, the personal editors, yellow journalism, jazz journalism, and the present age of maturity and consolidation.

AMERICAN DEVELOPMENT

The Colonial press wasn't much by present standards, but it served a need. It grew out of the rumor mills in the coffeehouses and taverns which had provided the original communications net in the colonies. The Colonial press established the newspaper as a gossip machine, a tradition which has come down more or less intact. Its publishers were printers and often undereducated. They dealt in rumor and in shipping news which was crucial to the mercantile emphasis of the seaboard colonies.

Gradually, editors began to evolve out of printers, specialization took effect, and by 1746, three decades before the Revolution, a more educated and ideological man was in charge. The Revolutionary press established a role of advocacy and reflected the political stirrings of a restless country. Thomas Paine's *Crisis Papers* and later Alexander Hamilton's *Federalist Papers* were typical of the era which fostered the embryonic beginnings of public relations as an adjunct of the press.

After Independence, the press quite naturally evolved into its role as political advocate. The successful part that the press had played in keeping the fires of revolution fanned led to extreme factionalism as it divided itself in support of the two warring political parties. Not only did the press support political parties, but political parties supported it. This was the time of the kept press, with subsidies paid newspapers by political factions to act as their mouthpieces. Since this was also an era of expansion, new publishers moving westward tended to take their political allegiances along with them. Many were appointed postmasters, a kind of sinecure or political plum that permitted them to use the franking privilege and so distribute their papers through the mails at no cost. The official position further gave them access to privy data. From this era the American press' traditional political interest stemmed.

The nation was ripe for Benjamin H. Day's penny press by 1833. Day had the vision to see that there existed a backlog of the newly literate who, if the price were right, could become newspaper readers, and that they would require a diet of entertainment and human interest, of sensation and scandal. It was from his example that volume circulation based on sensational content grew.

JOURNALISM BEGINS

The penny press in time evolved into the era of the great personal editors. James Gordon Bennett's *New York Herald*, Horace Greeley's *New York Tribune*, and Henry J. Raymond's *New York Times* were all founded within a decade or so of mid-century. From these men stemmed some of the basic tenets of journalism as a discipline. They evidenced the first social concern in their newspapers. They established the newspaper in its role of public watchdog, and while they did not invent the adversary relationship, they brought it to a uniquely American fruition. They established crusading as a circulation device and began to adapt new techniques, the telegraph and high-speed presses, to their purpose, reaping the benefits of a new technology spawned in the industrial revolution. They opted for specialized coverage of finance, religion, society, and the arts, thus beginning the departmentalization of newspapers that is known today. And, most significantly, they discovered advertising. It was a golden age of newspapers, this age where it all came together, and the modern metropolitan press that of today first appeared, with wide coverage, an expertise, and a budget of varying appeals—something for everyone.

It was in this period, too, that newspapers began seriously to expand their coverage beyond the purely local and topical. Raymond, for example, organized relays of couriers stretching north to Newfoundland to meet incoming vessels from Europe so that his *New York Times* would be first with international news. He visited Europe himself to employ what were the first foreign correspondents to sniff out significant information exclusively for the *Times*. He personally accompanied presidential candidates on their campaign tours to give the *Times* firsthand political dispatches. His competitors soon followed suit, and news gathering became a specialized and, incidentally, an increasingly expensive function.

WIRE SERVICES AND JOURNALESE

The New York newspapers were the first to employ the telegraph after its invention in 1844. They banded together in 1848 into a consortium, which they called the Associated Press, to pool the expense of news gathering and, additionally, to defray a portion of their costs by selling this information on an exclusive basis to other newspapers in different geographical areas.

In the years of the Civil War, 1861–65, the telegraph method of news gathering was more or less perfected, and a new style of journalism made its appearance—journalese—which included "who, what, where, when, why, and how" in the lead or introductory paragraph of a story, and the inverted pyramid reporting form, in which successive paragraphs elaborated basic data in decreasing order of significance. The pragmatic reason behind this style was that the early telegraph was sufficiently unreliable that correspondents placed the most significant information first to assure that it got through.

The era of the personal editors was a bridge between the old press and the new. On the one hand they elaborated upon the principle of popular appeal; on the other they began a methodical organization of the press into a major social institution in which the interlocking demands of expensive technology, advertising support, and popular appeal created a cause and effect relationship which would characterize mass media from that time on. The press found it necessary to develop maximum circulation through sensational treatment in order to attract advertisers to provide the revenue with which to competitively offer more popular appeal that would attract greater audience, etc.

YELLOW JOURNALISM

Inevitably, this circular process, involving technological, sociological, and commercial factors, led to circulation wars in which the major newspaper publishers engaged in sometimes ruinous competition for audience. This was the age of the great newspaper empires of Hearst, Pulitzer, and Scripps, each of whom owned dozens of newspapers stretched out across the continent on which they sought to impose a centralized control via the telegraph. Both Hearst and Scripps formed their own wire services—International News Service (INS) and United Press (UP), respectively—to consolidate this control. The great westward push following the Civil War opened new territory and new population centers, a growing urbanization was born of the industrial revolution, and an influx of foreign immigrants further concentrated populations in the cities where the newspapers could reach them. The telegraph also assisted in dispensing national advertising attracted both by the population concentrations and by the press empires to serve many different geographical areas simply and simultaneously. Basically, the circulation wars were aimed at attempting to monopolize this growing volume of national advertising.

Advertising had become so significantly a part of the newspaper in this era that some realistic measure of circulation was required for both the newspapers' and the advertisers' protection. An advertiser in New York, buying space in dozens of newspapers across the country, had to be sure that he was getting the paid circulation that he thought he was buying. Paid circulation is a valid measure of a newspaper's readership. It demonstrates community interest in that the community is willing to purchase the news product. The Audit Bureau of Circulations (ABC) was founded in 1914 to give advertisers certified circulation figures for the nation's newspapers. The existence of this outside audit, in turn, led to numerous circulation devices—contests, prizes, and discount sales—all of which were newspaper-sponsored and all contingent upon buying or subscribing to the newspaper.

This was the era of yellow journalism. The name arose from the cartoon "The Yellow Kid," a simplistic, folksy philosopher in a yellow nightshirt. Hearst hired the artist from Pulitzer, who simply hired another artist to produce the same cartoon. America was treated to two yellow kids.

This was an era of flamboyant journalism with all the stops pulled; Hearst and Scripps, with an assist from Pulitzer, were accused of having started the Spanish-American War as a circulation device. The truth of this is highly questionable, but it does characterize an uninhibited era where editors invented incidents and headlines to go with them, and facts played a relatively small role in journalism. This was an era of excesses in journalism as elsewhere, the age of the robber barons (of whom the major publishers were simply the newspaper counterparts), an age of industrial giants who flexed their muscles in the invigorating climate of social Darwinism and laissez-faire government.

This era also saw an explosion of feature and nonnews content in the newspapers, of which the yellow kid was only a symbol. Comic strips and advice to the lovelorn, games and puzzles, features and columnists made their entrance, never to leave the stage again. Basically, yellow journalism was an appeal to the uneducated urban populations swelled by foreign immigration who demanded a substantial measure of entertainment in their press.

There had been a relatively high ratio of nonnews in the newspapers for some time. Throughout the century nearly a third of major newspapers' content was devoted to literary fare: Nathaniel Hawthorne, James Fenimore Cooper, Mark Twain, and the like. In the 1880s the Bok and McClure syndicates furnished syndicated literary material to the press. During the period of yellow journalism, this changed to material of appeal to the common man, and the comics, boiler plate, and popular columnists replaced serious authors as feature material.

Gradually, there was reaction to the press's excesses as there was elsewhere and, in a wave of social reform, the times were characterized by muckrakers and the press became more responsible.

It is interesting to note that it was in this period that the P.M. or afternoon paper made its appearance as a direct result of the electric light. Electricity extended the day and made it feasible to read an evening newspaper in the twilight hours. Further, afternoon newspapers were better able to keep up with a day's activities, while new press technology permitted more rapid dissemination of spot news. Rapidly, P.M.s captured a substantial portion of the market, and many of the newspaper barons rushed after the afternoon circulation, often with both A.M. and P.M. newspapers in the same city. Publishers discovered that they were appealing to essentially different audiences: the more educated and affluent tended to prefer the more reflective tone of the morning papers, while the workingman preferred the P.M.s' lighter treatment. In time this made for a distinct difference in

Newspapers

the content of the two papers, even if they were under the same management, and for a philosophical differentiation in which the A.M.S tended toward the conservative end of the spectrum, while the P.M.S were more liberal.

Jazz journalism made its debut during the roaring twenties, in the years of disillusionment following World War I. A demand for more sensation, more entertainment made itself felt. This was a time

THE ROARING TWENTIES

Walter Winchell, journalist and radio reporter.

Walter Winchell
Of New York

Sallies In Our Alley: A movieland ham checked his chappo at the Little Bohemia..."Cheez!" ejaculated a hatchickee, "lookit the pomade! Why don't he use greaseless stuff?"..."You crayzee?"... ha-ha'd another. "How would he get his hat awf?"...Hear about the real quickie producer? The plane (bringing his script) was grounded...

[...]

long"..."Really?" he countered. "I've been with Hearst 35 years. That long enough?"...The beginning of an exciting and profitable job for me and countless imitators.

Manhattan Murals: Sign in an Arthur Murray studio: "Wall-

UPI

Print Media
164

when editors did not permit the facts to stand in the way of a good story, and what might have happened was better copy than what really did. These were the glamorous years of journalism, with *Front Page* and a rash of other newspaper movies and the birth of the stereotyped reporter: tough, hard-drinking, fearless, sentimental; a man who spoke through a cigarette in the corner of his mouth, never took off his hat with the press pass in it; a man who solved crimes, cleaned up city hall, defeated dishonest politicians single-handedly, all in time for his deadline. This era was the age of the newspapers' glory, before inroads were made by radio, television, and the depression.

The Great Depression of the 1930s took its toll of marginal operators, and radio came into its own as a form of cheap entertainment. World War II forced the nation's press into a more responsible role, and the postwar years saw the radical effects of television on all media.

TELEVISION'S IMPACT

The birth of television heralded the age of maturity and consolidation for newspapers. Labor costs spiralled in both the shop and newsroom under trade unions and Newspaper Guild pressure. Costs of newsprint, of new technology to keep up, of distribution as circulation perimeters were extended, and of the presses themselves forced many marginal newspapers out of business.

In the early 1950s newspapers feared television as they had feared radio before it. In part, their fears were founded; it was a far better entertainment medium. So paranoid was the press about television that in this period many newspapers refused to mention television in their columns to the point of not publishing a television log. This is a far cry from today's pattern of special television editors on major metropolitan newspapers and the publishing of elaborate magazine-type television supplements in the Sunday papers to rival the *TV Guide*.

Actually, television helped the press in a sense. It forced them out of the popular entertainment business, reducing the quota of sensationalism. It also forced the press out of the spot-news field, which they were never fully equipped to handle under deadline pressure, into a more reflective role of interpreting the news and providing a rational framework within which the world's events took shape. It drove the "extra" off the streets. It further forced a concentration on local affairs which network television could not handle, and in that respect rendered a substantial public service to America's communities. An unexpected dividend accrued from all this. Far from sating America's appetite for news, television's treatment of it, typically fragmentary and mosaic, whetted the public appetite for more and they turned to their newspapers for explanation and elaboration.

It is significant that under the impact of television it was the flashy newspapers, those appealing to the lcd, that suffered the greatest circulation loss (except for the *New York Daily News*, which

Newspapers

is unique). The more reflective newspapers held their own.

Thus, television is more or less directly responsible for the coming of age of the nation's newspapers as they moved into local and topical fields that national television couldn't handle: food and fashion, travel, business and finance, opinion, criticism, recreation and leisure, youth, medicine and science, and international affairs. Today, in their depth of perspective, many of the nation's major newspapers are rivaling magazines. In fact, many of their Sunday supplements are weekly magazines, a dividend aimed at the same audiences and fully competitive with similar magazines.

MERGER AND CONSOLIDATION

2. Ben H. Bagdikian, *The Information Machines* (New York: Harper & Row, Publishers, 1971).

Economic pressures forced mergers and consolidations. There are fewer newspapers today than there were twenty years ago. In a ten-year period from the late fifties to the late sixties, newspaper costs rose an overall 85 percent, with a whopping 120 percent increase in editorial departments as more well-educated, better-trained, and hence, more expensive professionals began to take over newsrooms.[2] This same period showed a 30 percent increase in newspaper size, which also meant more pages to fill and more staff to employ; additional outlays offset any advertising revenue this increase represented.

The trend toward consolidation also brought group ownerships, which were attractive for certain inherent management economies. Top administrative expertise could be spread over a number of newspapers. Some functions could be advantageously centralized, such as bulk newsprint purchase. More flexible personnel utilization was possible. A more appealing package could be made available to national advertisers; syndicates, columns, and features were more or less standardized where appropriate. All this could happen without disturbing the basic local orientation of individual papers, nor the kind of service they could render independently both to their communities and their local advertisers. Group ownership presented the best of two worlds. Some of the major groups owning newspapers today are: Gannett, Scripps-Howard, Cowles, Newhouse, Thomson, Copley, Ridder, and McClatchey. In all, there are over one hundred and fifty groups in the United States owning nearly nine hundred dailies for an average of around six each. In fact, a good half of America's daily newspapers are in group ownerships.

Today one frequently finds single-newspaper cities where competition has disappeared. The case for decreased newspaper competition can be argued both ways. The absence of competition removes a balance of viewpoints—but actually the diversity of other media compensates. It also removes pressure for timeliness—the scoop. Additionally, a single newspaper is generally healthier financially, more stable, and less prone to either advertiser or political pressure. Although there are advantages to reduced competition, the tendency is always to view this situation with alarm.

ON BALANCE

Much has been made of the decline in the number of newspapers, but as in most things statistical, figures can sometimes be misleading. Metropolitan newspapers have declined both in number and overall circulation over the past couple of decades, from 79 in 1950 to 57 in 1968. Their respective circulation loss dropped from 23.5 million to 20.8 million. However, this loss was more than compensated by the growth of community or peripheral dailies, which over the same period increased by five to 310 and built their circulation from 6.2 million to 9.4 million. These figures simply reflect in newspaper terms the overall social movement away from the central cities to suburbia. It is significant that in this period, however, overall newspaper circulation has not kept pace with population growth, which means, of course, a net decline in readership and the effect of this medium.

To put the situation in perspective, these figures may merely reflect the addition of other media—radio, television, and the proliferation of magazines—wherein all are simply achieving their respective shares of the market in a competitive situation. The addition of a new medium, such as television, is bound to dilute the total media market.

NEWSPAPERS NOW

There was a certain striking drama to the closing of the prestigious *New York Herald Tribune* in 1970. It pointed up the fact that in twenty years New York declined from eight newspapers to three, Los Angeles from five to two, and Boston from seven to four. Paradoxically, the surviving newspapers in these major metropolitan areas continued to serve more people than did their multitudinous predecessors. Further, the number of cities getting daily newspaper service markedly rose in those same two decades. Newspaper publishing seems to have been—and still is—holding its own.

There are today around 1,750 daily newspapers in the United States, printing 63 million copies a day. At least half of these papers are small dailies with circulations of ten thousand or less. Only 125 of them have circulations of one hundred thousand or more; less than a handful exceed one million.

Although one generally tends to think of the more prestigious morning papers, the majority of papers are P.M.s: 1,440 as opposed to 330. Ironically, it is the P.M.s that have suffered most under television's impact, for fairly obvious reasons: the early news on television is in direct conflict with the P.M.

There are also about 9,500 weeklies in the United States, small operations serving the provincial interests of isolated communities or discrete suburbs. These are the real gossip sheets, concentrating on local news that is easy to acquire. Most have printing operations for independent jobs on the side and many are run by husband-and-wife teams. Still, they are newspapers and they serve both an information and a commercial purpose.

The last edition of the New York **Herald Tribune,** 1966.

UPI

The rationale for the increase in these smaller community newspapers in the outlying areas is directly related to American affluence. The major metropolitan press provides depth: national and interna-

Print Media

tional news, features of all kinds, the comics and entertainment, broad fare. Historical tradition, however, emphasizes the local community, the suburbs are where many people live, where they identify, belong. It is the local city councils and civic organizations that most directly touch residents' lives and the local school boards which educate their children. Further, it is generally in the regional shopping centers and from the local merchants that community members buy most of their goods. Suburban dwellers need information about their own communities, and local merchants need a vehicle in which to advertise their products and sales. These two needs meet in the community newspaper because the gross national product is large enough to provide sufficient disposable income to support the whole broad spectrum of media.

One point stands out, and that is the degree of affluence in America required to support both metropolitan and community newspapers, in addition to the diversity of other media extant, all competing for an individual's attention.

COMMUNITY NEWSPAPERS

Community newspapers fill a void that the big metropolitan dailies leave. No matter how large and wealthy, metropolitans lack the resources—time, money, and manpower—to adequately cover all the news of each community; there may be dozens of separate communities within their circulation area. They are not necessarily in competition with community newspapers; each fulfills essentially different roles. Even in their metropolitan editions, major newspapers cannot cover all the news of a dozen city councils and a half-dozen school boards, the speakers and activities of several hundred civic, women's, veterans, labor, cultural, or charitable organizations, and yet it is these very activities that are meaningful to suburban dwellers.

Similarly, local advertisers cannot afford the advertising rates of the metropolitan newspapers, which are based on overall circulations of several hundred thousand or more. They do not need all that exposure; they need simply to reach the 10 or 20 percent of that number who live in their trading area. The community newspaper provides local merchants an advertising showcase pinpointed toward the community they serve at prices proportionate to exposure.

There has been a trend toward the establishment of minigroups of several suburban newspapers under the same management, attempting to serve several adjacent communities. The major portion of the content of these newspapers is the same, little more than editorial filler to carry advertising. However, as a gesture to locality, they replate the front page, filling it with specific information about each separate community, and often publish under different mastheads to further the locality illusion. With rare exception, these minichains abdicate their basic responsibility to provide a full quota of local news and gossip and become little more than "shoppers," advertising throwaways.

THE VAN OF INNOVATION

Because they are smaller and more flexible than their metropolitan cousins and because they generally operate on a closer profit margin, the community dailies have been in the forefront of innovation. They were among the first to move toward offset printing, a cleaner operation which drastically cuts makeup time for the newspaper and reduces the amount of highly skilled, unionized "shop time" which goes into production. Relatively unskilled personnel can "paste up" full pages, which are then photographically transferred to thin metal plates ready for the presses. Another money-saving device is the teletypesetter (tts), through which punched tape is fed into the linotypes to produce hot type. It was inevitable technologically that the two techniques should merge to the point where now a number of systems, of which CompuScan is one, feed computer-produced punched tape into typesetting consoles which photographically spew out news stories fully justified and ready for paste-up. The advantages to such a system are several. It is a much cleaner operation. The scanners and consoles can handle twelve hundred words a minute in contrast to the fifty words per minute that a manual keyboard operator could produce, thus reducing lead time necessary in the newsroom for deadline.

In effect, these computerized innovations transfer a part of the composing room to the newsroom; editors and reporters become part-time compositors. Required are special electric typewriters which utilize a "golf ball" or type font. Copy is written on special paper which a scanner accepts. Copy corrections are made by different keyboard codes. Computerization has required the total retraining of reporters and editors, forcing them to write clean copy, to use electric typewriters with proper fonts on paper that the scanner can read, and to become familiar with computer codes.

OTHER ADVANTAGES

On the advertising end, production is similar to that described, except that a fully memorized computer can be used which more or less automatically spews out the day's quota of classified advertisements, remembering when to change them, cancel them, begin them again. Further, the advertising department can accept any camera-ready layout, copy, and artwork from advertisers; these are now furnished by advertising agencies in lieu of the former matrices. A considerable burden thus is placed on national agencies to provide both matrices to those newspapers still using letterpress and hot type, and to provide camera-ready ads to those which have converted to offset, or the cold type method; agencies must know which is which.

Other computerized offset systems use a closed-circuit television screen and computer, whereby the editor can call up any story from the computer's memory on his video screen and edit it with a special keyboard attached to the television computer circuit.

There are aesthetic advantages to the offset method. Offset makes for a better-looking paper, as photos and artwork reproduce with far greater clarity, utilizing a far finer screen than photoengrav-

Print Media

ing can. This has led the smaller papers to experimentation with different typestyles and different page formats, utilizing five and six columns instead of eight, and allowing wider margins, making a more readable and visually attractive product.

The larger metropolitan papers were shaken out of their lethargy by such innovations. The way was clear toward economies they could not ignore, despite the enormous capital investment required to transform huge plants and retrain hundreds of people. The *Sacramento Union*, a former Copley newspaper in the medium-metropolitan range, was the first in the nation to go fully offset in 1967. Success in Sacramento led the Copley people to convert their flagships, the *San Diego Union* and *Evening Tribune*, with a combined circulation of over a quarter of a million, to computerized offset as the nation's first major automated metropolitan newspaper plant in 1973.

ADVERTISING

Advertising, as previously discussed, is the principal content of all newspapers and, in many instances, is their entire raison d'être. Advertising generally provides at least 75 percent of newspaper revenue and occupies more than half the space. Advertising volume in the nation's newspapers amounted to well over five billion dollars annually at last count. By any yardstick, newspaper advertising is a significant function to both newspapers and the economy as a whole.

Newspaper advertising can be separated into two broad categories: display and classified. Displays are showcase advertisements occupying considerable space and distributed throughout the paper; they are generally measured and sold on a column-inch or lineage basis. They sell goods and services. Classifieds are notices, sometimes of sales, sometimes purely informational. They are concentrated into the classified sections of the newspaper; they carry no illustration, and are often read as news. Whereas display seeks the buyer, the buyer seeks the classifieds.

Display advertising can further be broken down into two less concrete subdivisions: retail and national. Retail advertising is local advertising. It sells at a lower rate than national advertising, and is aimed as a service to the local merchant. National advertising tends to be reinforcing or persuasive in nature. Retail advertising is a point of sale display. It is designed to promptly move goods and services which are presently in supply. Often it is read as news, pure information as in the case of the market ads, notice of weekend specials, theater and entertainment advertising, and notices of sales. The audience is presold by necessity or disposition and the retail advertisements are advices concerning where, when, and how much.

Newspaper advertising is sold off a rate card, a published schedule of prices for space and position in the paper. The rates are based on circulation, with larger circulation naturally demanding a higher rate. Recognizing the advantage that community newspapers have in soliciting advertisements of purely local merchants, some metropolitan papers have gone to zone advertising in an attempt to appeal to the merchants of local communities. Breaking their press runs down by different geographical areas of a metropolis, they sell advertising in the editions going to these areas alone at a far cheaper rate than the general metropolitan run. This technique has not proved too successful because metropolitan newspapers lack the other elements of community appeal—local news, gossip, and civic information.

The basic advertising rate is the open rate, a column-inch charge for display advertising on a one-shot basis. Since little advertising is placed on a one-shot basis, most advertisements are sold on contracts giving a considerable discount over the open rate. For example, a merchant would agree to buy one, five, or ten thousand column inches during a twelve-month period and receive a proportional reduction for doing so. The open rate is commissionable to advertising agencies; contract rates are not.

NEWSPAPER OPERATIONS

The circularity of a newspaper's basic operation has already been noted—how it must attract readers as an inducement for the advertisers who pay the bills and also show a profit to provide a better product to attract more circulation, etc. The organizational structure of a major metropolitan newspaper reflects this by being divided into five major divisions: (1) editorial, to produce the copy, to handle the news; (2) advertising, to solicit and to coordinate the basic revenue-producing activities; (3) production, which physically prints the newspaper, converting copy into editions; (4) circulation, which sells and distributes the finished product; and (5) administration, including purchasing, promotion, accounting, and the like, which coordinates the activities of the other four, whose basic departments are closely intertwined. As an example, a newspaper's deadlines for various editions, the last second that new copy can be accepted, are dependent upon circulation. Circulation schedules are based upon the farthest home on the farthest route of the newspaper's distribution area. A morning newspaper must be delivered by 6:00 A.M. to be useful, an afternoon paper by 5:00 P.M. These are the latest hours that the paper can reasonably be expected to arrive. After that, readership deteriorates and subscriptions slack off. It takes an hour for the newsboy to make his rounds and another half hour to fold his papers. It takes the delivery truck perhaps an hour to reach the farthest route, often longer. Thus, the papers must be loaded on the dock two and one-half hours before 6:00 A.M. (or 5:00 P.M., as the case may be). There is still press time and makeup time to be considered for the type to be cast and placed in form, the forms locked, flexible matrices impressed from the forms, curved metal stereotypes cast from the matrices, stereos locked on the presses, and the presses rolled. These are time-consuming processes which determine the last second that a city editor can take a new story from the reporter and send it down with the expectation that it will see print. The schedule is all but ironclad, and any supposition that people run about excitedly waving copy and shouting "Hold the presses!" is fantasy.

EDITIONS AND DEADLINES

Recognizing these severe time limitations while seeking to maximize their circulation by extending their area of penetration, most metropolitan newspapers publish a series of editions staggered in time. The metropolitan edition of a morning paper, for example, comes off the presses very early in order to reach far outlying areas, a hundred miles or more away, in time for breakfast. The home edition for the contiguous metropolitan area is printed next, possibly split into two runs according to the distances involved in distribution, with the final edition aimed basically at street sales. Obviously, because of the staggered deadlines for copy, the final edition will have the most up-to-date news, and the metropolitan the least. Nonetheless, the metropolitan edition does provide residents of isolated areas with a window to the world and nation, and a showcase for goods and services that they would not otherwise obtain. Afternoon newspapers work differently in that they bring out a "bulldog" edition to compete on the street in mid-morning with the A.M. paper, running through a series of "homes" and finally publishing a night final for street sale whose major contribution in new news is generally the stock market and racing results.

Another tactic to extend a metropolitan's circulation area is the establishment of branch printing plants on the periphery of the original area. The *Los Angeles Times* has such a plant in Orange County, California, about sixty miles south of the main plant, to tap the exploding market of the suburbs. Duplicate stereotypes of common pages are cast and rushed to the waiting Orange County presses where they are combined with other pages oriented toward the Orange County communities and run off for local delivery, saving a couple of hours in distribution time.

NEWSPAPER BUREAUCRACY

The ponderous organization and bureaucracy of contemporary metropolitan papers is the basis for the institutionalization of the press and its resultant massive inertia. In the final analysis, however, a bureaucracy is composed of people filling certain specified roles. At the top of the ladder in a major metropolitan newspaper is the publisher who has overall control. Answering to him are generally two people: a general manager in charge of administration, circulation, advertising, and production, and, in deference to the significance of news, an editor in command of the paper's editorial content.

Answering to the business manager are persons such as the controller, purchasing agent, advertising director, circulation director, production manager, promotion director, and industrial relations manager, who is in charge of highly specialized negotiations with a half-dozen trade unions.

Under the editor is the managing editor whose responsibility is the day-to-day content of the newspaper. Under him are principally the city editor charged with local news, and the wire editor or news editor, as he is variously called, who is charged with other-than-local news, the regional, national, and international stories which come in from correspondents and the wire services. There is the photo editor who both runs the paper's staff of local photographers and screens wire photos for suitability. The copy editor checks raw copy for accuracy and style, writes headlines and sets approved stories into a "page dummy" provided by the advertising department on which the day's quota of advertisements is already indicated.

One of the reasons behind journalese, the inverted pyramid style of newspaper writing which presents information in declining order of significance, is in recognition of the reality that no matter how experienced, no one can tell exactly how much space in the final form a given story will occupy. Journalese permits cutting stories from the bottom when they do not fit the allotted space without sacrificing essential content. The least significant material is eliminated first, an enormous rewriting time-saver.

The major departments outside the city room are more or less autonomous. Sports, women's, business and financial, and entertainment sections often have their own editors and staffs and are generally allocated so many pages daily to fill with their specialties. The Sunday department has charge of special Sunday sections—real estate, travel, television, home and garden, books, opinion, and the like—and generally special editors are employed for these various sections. It is in these special sections that the majority of feature stories occur. The editorial pages have their own staff who answer to the editor or publisher or both.

Within all these departments are specialists, sometimes called editors, in science, medicine, youth, education, religion, the environment, military, farming, senior citizens, politics, and the like. Generally, they are not allocated specific space, but are required through their expertise to keep up with the developments in their fields and present timely articles.

At the lower level of the hierarchy are the reporters and correspondents who actually unearth and write the news, who have most of the personal, on-the-scene contact. Reporters can be general assignment, delegated to stories at the direction of the city editor, covering fires, murders, accidents, and Rotary Club luncheons, often taking a photographer with them. Special-assignment people stay on location at city hall, the state, federal, and county beats, the courthouse, or police headquarters. They, too, are specialists, assigned to the principal sources of the news, those locales where news is made.

THE NATURE OF NEWS

Walter Lippman noted long ago the nature of the news: "Something definite must occur," he said, "that has unmistakable form." This is what happens at city hall and the courthouse: form and a tangible frame are given to human interactions which permit them to be isolated and written about—reported. These are the events that comprise the news, identifiable from the mass. Thus, while news is certainly the clearest expression of the information function, it is an artificially contrived form of information, leaving much unsaid, unreported, and unprinted.

> "All I know is just what I read in the papers."
>
> Will Rogers

There are hundreds of reporters and correspondents and specialists on a metropolitan newspaper; they are supervised by dozens of editors. There are batteries of two or three dozen teletypes spewing out reams of copy and miles of punched tape daily, and all of this must be condensed by personnel into a relatively few pages, the number of which is determined fiscally by the volume of advertising committed for a given day. In addition, there are scores of features on all conceivable topics, mail and phone calls from bureaus overseas, in Washington, New York, and the state capital. There are stringers and correspondents in outlying communities. There are also scores of press agents advocating their clients' causes in numerous fields.

All of these personnel funnel their output into the newsroom, where a half-dozen or so harrassed senior editors sift through it to

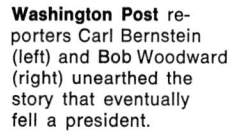

Washington Post reporters Carl Bernstein (left) and Bob Woodward (right) unearthed the story that eventually fell a president.

Newspapers

decide what to print. They are the gatekeepers of a newspaper; on their judgments rest what visions of reality the public shall see, what events, in essence, take place. A rule of thumb is that only about one tenth of the available news gets into print, leaving a remaining 90 percent, an overpowering figure, that does not get printed.

Fortunately, because of the variety and pervasity of competing media all along the spectrum, the chances of running into a news item, if it is significant at all, are pretty good. But this does not detract in any way from the responsibility and, in a sense, the power of the gatekeepers or editors or, for that matter, the reporters who write according to their own perceptions and views of the world.

THE MOSAIC OF NEWS

In the end, a newspaper is a relative hodgepodge, a potpourri, a smorgasbord, a mosaic of unrelated items thrown together more or less indiscriminately under extreme time pressure, lacking the resources for full treatment. Only about a quarter of the stories in a newspaper—generally the front page and sports section—achieve as much as 30 percent readership. Only 4 percent of the readers read another quarter of all items. Thus, half the editorial content of a newspaper falls somewhere between these two fractions, a minimum of 4 percent and a maximum of 30 percent. Not everybody reads the same thing, and a kind of balance is achieved by a smorgasbord presentation as the metropolitan paper seeks to be all things to all people within a small geographic segment of the nation. Even the *Los Angeles Times'* one million circulation is less than 0.5 percent of the nation's population, and its area of influence is restricted to the southwest corner of the southwesternmost of the forty-eight contiguous states.

A newspaper mirrors its community far more than it influences it. It must reflect the community in that it must reflect the goods, services, and entertainment available there, if only through its advertisements; a newspaper is a measure of public taste. It serves a basic economic purpose. If a paper does not ideologically pattern itself after the general mores of its community, readership will drop; this is the beginning of the end. Waiting in the wings are other media and other newspapers anxious to borrow or steal readers and the additional revenue they represent, not only in subscriptions but, much more significantly, in an added advertising volume and higher advertising rates.

SUMMARY

The newspaper, as it has developed, is a uniquely American phenomenon. It is not a mass medium in the sense that other media are, but is rather restricted to serving certain geographical areas.

The American newspaper, with its interwoven, technological, commercial, and social forces, represents the most unique contribution of print technology.

Newspapers are supported by advertising to the extent that

about three-fourths of their revenue is so derived. Advertising volume and rates are determined by audience size, so a circular effect takes place in which newspapers constantly seek additional audience to attract more advertisers to show more profit to attract more audience.

The history of newspapers in the United States can be roughly separated into eight eras: (1) the Colonial press; (2) the Revolutionary press; (3) the kept press; (4) the penny press; (5) the era of the personal editors; (6) the era of yellow journalism; (7) the era of jazz journalism; and (8) the era of maturity and consolidation. This last, contemporary era, is marked by television's impact, and is characterized by the decline of metropolitan papers and the growth of more flexible community dailies; it is also marked by the newspaper adaptation of revolutionary printing and computer techniques. As a result of economic forces, there has been a decline in competing newspapers; however, while there are more single-newspaper cities, there are also more cities with daily newspapers.

An enormous affluence on the part of the public is necessary to support the number of newspapers found today, both metropolitan and community, in addition to other media, as well as to buy the products advertised and therefore keep the cash registers ringing and the presses rolling.

The rationale for the growth of community newspapers on the periphery and suburbs of metropolitan areas has been that the metropolitan paper cannot adequately cover the intensely personal news of a dozen or a score of local communities; neither can the local merchant afford to pay for the enormous exposure that a metropolitan paper affords when he needs only a tiny fraction of it.

Advertising volume determines the size of a paper, on a proportionate 60–40 basis. Only about one-tenth of the available news and features on any given day sees print, in contrast to 100 percent of the advertising, which illustrates the essentially commercial base of American mass media. This fractional content imposes great responsibility on the gatekeepers who determine what news the public will see. Other media may supplement this percentage, thus providing a balance.

Advertising can be divided into display and classified; display can further be broken down into retail and national.

Deadlines are established by the time necessary to deliver a newspaper to its farthest customer. Newspapers often seek to widen their areas of penetration by publishing a series of editions, and by developing branch plants.

Weekly newspapers compose the bulk of America's press; generally, they are small, provincial operations, providing a service and showcase to isolated communities which otherwise would have none.

Newspapers vary as widely as the communities that they serve, for they mirror more than they lead, and what they reflect is the spirit of the community.

11 MAGAZINES

**FLUX
AND
CHANGE**

Nowhere is a medium's ability to survive and to thrive after it has been superceded on the continuum by a more efficient form in terms of speed and numbers of audience better illustrated than in the magazine. Nor is the remarkable diversity of American life better demonstrated than among the extraordinary variety of magazines.

Just a list of the general headings of such magazines alone is staggering. There are men's and women's magazines; shelter, travel, fashion, sports, opinion, and news magazines; pulps or confession magazines; comics, how-to-do-it magazines (of a wondrous variety themselves); consumer magazines; religious, farm, and trade publications; scholarly journals; science fiction, sex, and financial magazines; corporate annual reports, and also an increasing number of catalogs that are read as magazines—to name but a few categories of nearly twenty thousand magazines. There are magazines that look like newspapers and others that look like books. Magazines are sold by subscription or on racks in over a hundred thousand retail outlets, and some, called "controlled circulation," are given away.

Magazines are published by magazine groups, by individual publishers, by newspapers, by small esoteric societies, by giant corporations, by trade associations and churches, by varying levels of government, and by all political parties. The roster of publishers is almost as varied as the titles themselves. Magazines are issued daily, weekly, semimonthly, and monthly for the most part, some bimonthly and quarterly, and a few annually. They can be as general as the *Reader's Digest* or as specific as the *Gun Collector*.

Magazines all have these things in common, however; they are published regularly; they appeal specifically to some

Reprinted from PSYCHOLOGY TODAY Magazine.
Copyright © Ziff-Davis Publishing Company.

OCT. 1971 ONE DOLLAR

psychology today

Sport:
If You Want to Build Character Try Something Else
Women Sit in the Back of the Bus

Deviants:
Society's Side Show

The Campus:
Coming of Age at College
Toward Elitist Education

Black Diaspora?

Curiosity & Animals

Behavior Mod: Punishment

A magazine success. An appeal to an audience with affluence, education, and leisure in turn appeals to advertisers.

SAN DIEGO MAGAZINE

DECEMBER 1973 / ONE DOLLAR

CHICANO ART   CALIFORNIA WINE   RUSSIA   25 YEARS ON CAMERA

The city magazine, recent phenomenon in the media continuum

fractional segment of the body politic; and they appeal in terms of interest. In general, their breadth and diversity gives a pretty clear picture of contemporary society—the kinds of things people are interested in collectively and, through circulation figures, to what extent. Some future social anthropologist privy to the magazines of today could draw fairly accurate conclusions about the culture and the people of this society.

Nowhere among the various mass media is there greater evidence of flux and change than in the magazine field. The reasons for this apparently lie in the fact that magazines are a sort of hybrid medium, falling on the continuum somewhere in between televison's "massest" mass audience and instantaneousness on the one hand and the leisurely book's self-selectivity on the other. Magazines reflect this middle ground in other respects also. They cost more than television, but a lot less than a book. They lack television's demanding ubiquity, but are more readily accessible than books. They are more enduring than evanescent television programs, which die aborning, but lack the book's solid permanence. They occupy a respectable middle distance of perspective between the frantic mosaic of television's programming and the detailed specificity of books. Consequently, they are pressured at both ends of the continuum. The large, general-interest national magazines, have been forced to yield their audiences to television, often for some surprising reasons, even while the developing paperback phenomenon eats away at their more specific sales from the other end. Pressured at both ends, magazines, more than any other contemporary medium, are in an experimental state of flux as they seek to survive. It is in their throes of change that one can dimly perceive the kind of specific appeal by media that provides at least one of the options to the future course of mass communications.

A HISTORICAL HYBRID

Historically, the magazine developed as a hybrid form of print. It filled the audience gap left between newspapers and the more intellectually pinpointed book. It provided some entertainment and some culture in discrete doses, verging neither to the populist nor philosophical extremes which seemed to characterize the press and book-publishing businesses during most of the nineteenth century and before. Magazines, too, for a time and to a limited extent seemed to provide the only national medium in that they did cross the geographically circumscribed boundaries that newspapers carved out for themselves.

Magazines discovered rather early publics other than geographical ones, and began to appeal by interest to specific groups: farmers, women, businessmen. They also discovered advertising and began to develop a specialized form of advertising as pinpointed to their specific publics as was their content.

MAGAZINES IN AMERICA

The history of magazines is a confusing one because print technology and accompanying literacy had to become fairly well developed before clear lines of demarcation could be drawn between newspapers and magazines. Were the early courantos, for example, newspapers in their emphasis on news or were they early magazines in their foreign concentration of interest? Generally, the first magazines are credited as being the *Tatler* and *Spectator*, published in England in the first quarter of the eighteenth century, to which Joseph Addison and Richard Steele contributed so much in the way of topical essays and satirical material. Their formats were more opinion and entertainment than news.

The first magazines on American shores clearly defined as such were the *General Magazine* and the *American Magazine*, both originating in Philadelphia in 1741. Both folded; America wasn't yet ready for magazines. By the turn of the nineteenth century this had changed; *Port Folio*, followed by *North American Review* in 1815 and the venerable *Saturday Evening Post* in 1821 (which Benjamin Franklin did not found) all emerged. The *Post*'s format of fiction, poems, and essays was typical of most of that century. There were a

The **Saturday Evening Post,** piece of America.

THE BETTMANN ARCHIVE

Print Media
180

hundred or so magazines being published in the United States by 1830, proving the need for the new medium. Also, 1830 marked the founding of *Godey's Lady's Book*, the first magazine to cater specifically to women and, more significantly, the first medium to attempt to pinpoint an audience for its own.

There were additional entries into the field by mid-century, and literature, graphics, science, and travel were added to the bill of fare. *Harper's New Monthly Magazine*, the *Atlantic Monthly*, *Gleason's Pictorial*, and *Harper's Weekly* were typical of the titles that filled this newly created interest vacuum between newspapers and books. The little *Nation*, which made its appearance at the close of the Civil War in 1865, is significant because in over one hundred years of continuous publication, it has consistently lost money—every year.[1]

1. Sandman et al., *Media* (Englewood Cliffs, N. J.: Prentice-Hall, 1972).

ENTER ADVERTISING

Advertising in the 1880s provided a new impetus for newspapers and magazines alike. The newspaper profited principally from advertising by department stores, which were really a sort of local warehousing for national products, as well as from direct national advertising by the manufacturers. Magazines profited from the large volume of advertising aimed at women, which in turn spawned a flurry of women's magazines: *Ladies' Home Journal, Women's Home Companion, McCall's*. Others sought to compete for the increasing amount of advertising by national manufacturers: *McClure's, Munsey's, Cosmopolitan, Collier's*, and *American* to name a few. Several of these, *Cosmopolitan*, for example, were "insurance publications" of the newspaper barons—William Randolph Hearst in this instance—aimed at establishing publishing empires.

THE LAST FIFTY YEARS

Magazine publishing received a shot in the arm in the decade following World War I, and included were such giants as *Reader's Digest* (1922), Henry Luce's *Time* (1923) and the *New Yorker*, 1925, as well as H. L. Mencken's spritely *American Mercury* and the recently changed *Saturday Review of Literature*. The mid-thirties saw the great photojournalism efforts of *Life* and *Look*, both defunct now, as well as the first of the slick men's fashion-cum-sex magazines, *Esquire*.

For twenty years, until the mid-fifties, magazine publishing flourished in the United States and national circulations grew as the magazines provided a specialized visual quality that national network radio lacked. Then, beginning in 1956 under the impact of network television (which provided its own pictures), the days of reckoning came. *Collier's* was the first to go in that year, to be followed in time by *Coronet, American, Look, Saturday Evening Post*, and, finally, at the end of 1972, by *Life*.

However, the *New York Times* concluded in 1969 that "magazines were thriving despite a few dramatic failures." An examination of both sides of that statement is in order. The case histories of the

Magazines

spectacular failures are examined in subsequent material, together with attempts to fend them off; a couple of the modern magazine success stories are also offered to see what trends they indicate for the future.

COVER GIRLS AND CHEESECAKE

Magazines were caught on a treadmill of circulation increases first established by their cousins, the newspapers. This trend was continued as radio came into its prime. The mass media, it seems, were committed to a "numbers game."

Some of the more familiar characteristics of magazines are attributable to this trend. The cover girl is probably the best known of these phenomena. Brilliant color photography of slim, suggestive, young, and beautiful models adorned the front covers of American magazines in an effort to dress up the magazine's competitive appearance on the racks of a hundred thousand public outlets. This was the genesis of the "cheesecake syndrome," the attempt to use sometimes scantily clad but always alluring young females as bait for both men and women, men for the sensual lure, women for comparison's sake.

With scores of national magazines competing for attention on the newsracks of the nation, cover girls became big business indeed. At least two major modeling agencies—Powers and Conover—thrived on the aspirations of thousands of girls from every state who yearned for the recognition and prestige that being a cover girl or a Powers' model would bring. It was a strange time, the depression years of the mid-1930s, a time of dance marathons, crooners and swooners, gangster movies, cover girls, and magazine fiction.

Magazine marketing also became a reality as distributors fought for preferential position on the retail racks, making concessions and deals to outlets to place their magazines at top center of the display racks and to bury their competitors' magazines. Magazines also outdid one another in seeking surefire material for public appeal. This generally took the form of the memoirs of famous men. Intense bidding among the national general-interest magazines in the post-World War II period resulted in the magazine rights for Admiral William Halsey's memoirs going for $60,000, while General Eisenhower's, long before he became president, sold for an amount unheard of at that time, $175,000. A consortium of *Life* magazine, the *New York Times*, and a book publisher paid Winston Churchill $1,000,000 for his story, while *Life* by itself ventured $600,000 for the magazine rights to Harry Truman's autobiography.

In point of fact, many of America's magazines, with their alluring covers, their headlined feature stories and their deals for position, were becoming their own point of purchase promotions. Other magazines took a different tack, seeking the familiarity of a standard format. Among these were *Time*, the very familiar *Reader's Digest*, and *TV Guide*.

TELEVISION AND ADVERTISING

No other media form has been so drastically affected by television as has the magazine form. Failures of magazines have not been entirely due to the fact that most of the major national magazines were essentially entertainment-oriented and that television performs this function unsurpassingly better. Although unquestionably this has played a role, the basic reasons for magazine failures are economic. A case in point involves the two graphic giants, *Look* and *Life*. Both folded with extremely healthy circulations, numbering in each instance more than six million even while they were losing money. The paradox is that there are several magazines of the new genre with circulations of only around a half-million—less than 10 percent of those of *Life* and *Look*—that are extremely healthy financially.

What has all this to do with television? Advertising is the answer. In the past the custom has been to equate circulation size with advertising revenue because that is the way the mass media have developed. Actually they are two different aspects of the mass media's economic foundation which do not always coincide. It is not so much the "how many" that counts as the "who."

With huge national circulations of six, eight, or ten million at their peak, the big magazines grew fat off national advertising revenues. It should be remembered that, as with newspapers, only a fraction of the cost of a magazine is born by its subscription rate or sales price. The largest portion of its cost and all of its profit is carried by advertising.

When television appeared, it gradually acquired huge national audiences in previously unimagined numbers. The circulations of six million or so of the national magazines began to pall alongside the twenty million homes or thirty-five million individuals, more or less, that a television network could deliver on any weekday evening in prime time. Moreover, the advertising costs were comparable with those of television. A full-page advertisement in *Life* sold for around $60,000, color and production costs excluded. A network prime-time minute generally went for the same figure, production costs again excluded. Not only were the audiences larger, but the presentation was dynamic on television, with action, color, and complete control of sound and video—television advertising had real impact. A magazine display could offer only a static presentation. Television was the more effective sales tool for a soap, a beer, a floor wax, a detergent, or an analgesic. National manufacturers and their agencies began to use television heavily, and the sales results supported their choice.

Nor could the magazines reduce the costs of their advertising. Their production costs were up, squeezing printing and paper and editorial budgets. They were caught in a vise of rising costs and declining revenues which even six million subscribers couldn't offset, and the effects of this dilemma were spiralling. As advertising fell off, gradually at first, magazines sought to economize. They spent less on production and on research; the quality of the product suffered and this, in turn, had its effect on circulation as subscribers disappointed in the "new look" began to cancel subscriptions. Further, since the size of a general-circulation magazine, like that of a newspaper, is predicated on the volume of advertising committed (generally on a 60–40 basis of advertising to editorial content), the magazines grew thinner as advertising fell off. Customers began to feel that they weren't getting as much for their money; this, too, had a depressing effect on circulation. Thus, as circulation dwindled, national advertisers began to see that they were getting even less for their advertising dollar in a medium that wasn't pragmatically competitive anyway.

THE CIRCULATION WARS

The battle for street sales or point of purchase sales was only half of the circulation war. When television's impact was first noticed, many of the nation's most popular magazines were engaged in a ruinous subscription war which lasted from the early fifties to the late sixties. Again caught up in competitive struggle, they contracted to deliver eighteen, twenty-four, thirty, and even thirty-six monthly issues to new subscribers for a fraction of the listed cost, often offering thirty-six months for less than the original subscription price for a single year. That this was bound to arouse antagonism among the earlier subscribers was evident. What was less apparent was that these cheap contracts would return to haunt the magazines later, often making it more expensive to go out of business than to continue publishing at a loss. Hundreds of thousands of three-year contracts representing little initial revenue were to become prohibitively expensive to buy up if a magazine wished to suspend publication. Since these subscriptions were indeed contracts to deliver, they were enforceable in court; hundreds of thousands of lawsuits would have been a ruinous undertaking.

The purpose of both the street sales and subscription promotions, of course, was to build circulation. No matter how that circulation was achieved, it represented solid figures in the ABC's annual audit. It was on the basis of these audited figures that advertising agencies made their selection of magazines. Furthermore, advertising rates were directly pegged to circulation size.

The insanity of this particular course—sacrificing sales revenue in an era of rapidly mounting costs to try to attract additional advertising in a declining market—became apparent after the fact. It is little wonder that so many of the giants folded willingly after a struggle that was bound to kill them all.

PRUNING TECHNIQUES

The next step undertaken by the large general-interest magazines in their struggle for survival was exactly the reverse of the circulation war. An effort was made to curtail circulation, first, as a cost-saving device, and second, as an attempt to more specifically pinpoint audiences in terms of interest. This latter point became im-

Print Media

portant as national magazines began to discover demographics, or the computer-assisted ability to break down audiences or subscribers in terms of where they lived, their relative affluence, age, sex, and the like. These characteristics of their audiences, the magazines reasoned with some cause, could indicate a certain level of persons to which an advertiser could beam a specific sales pitch which television, in its massive generality, could not. There was an additional reason to trying to curtail magazines' audiences; such a step would remove a lot of the dead wood, those subscribers of only marginal interest who had bought long-term subscriptions at a fractional cost. If such subscribers could be voluntarily removed from the circulation rolls, it would greatly assist in any subsequent cessation of publication.

Across America in the late fifties and early sixties, the public was confronted with the unlikely circumstance of magazines writing to subscribers who only a year or so earlier had been actively solicited, telling them that they fell outside the parameters of the kind of people desired as subscribers. This was a technique scarcely calculated to win friends at a time when they were needed desperately.

The pruning technique was not successful to any great degree. At best it was a desperation measure. It did not sufficiently pinpoint audiences demographically to be of any major appeal to specific advertisers, although it did reduce publication costs to the degree that it curtailed circulation and, to that extent, made subsequent liquidations less costly.

REGIONAL EDITIONS

There were other attempts to use demographics to forestall the inevitable. Computer technology, for a while, seemed to be coming to the assistance of the national magazines. Computers permitted magazines to break down their circulation geographically, a lesson learned from the *Wall Street Journal*, which had, since the early fifties, been published in four regional editions as well as nationally. The news and comment—the content—was identical in each edition, but it did permit regional advertisers an opportunity to reach their spheres of interest at much less cost than if they were forced to buy for the entire national circulation of the *Wall Street Journal*. This was an advertising development technique specifically designed for utilities, banks, and other financial institutions that were basically organized on a regional basis and comprised the natural interest market of the *Wall Street Journal*.

For example, when adopted by *Life* this technique permitted the magazine to substitute purely local advertising for some of the national advertising that it had lost to television. Further, it permitted a Chattanooga utility or a Seattle Bank the prestige of advertising in *Life*. At the peak of this experiment, *Look* was running seventy-five regional editions at fantastic cost. *Life*, more conservative, published in seven regions and eleven metropolitan areas. Cost differentials are apparent. To buy *Life*'s full run peak of eight million or so would have cost an advertiser $65,000, but he could buy *Life*'s 150,000 subscribers in Minnesota for a mere $2,500, and still have *Life*'s prestige. The theory behind regional editions was that through an active sales effort the volume of advertising in each of the magazine's regions or districts would balance out. By and large it did, but meanwhile sales costs had considerably increased, constituting an additional drain on already dwindling reserves. At best, the use of multiple editions was a stopgap for the general-interest magazines.

However, such regional breakdowns in more specifically oriented magazines, such as the *Wall Street Journal* with its financial emphasis, and *Time* and *Newsweek* with their high news orientation, proved eminently successful. Regional editions in this instance permit advertisers and manufacturers to reach financially oriented potential customers or others whose demonstrated interest in news also demonstrates an interest in the world, a relatively high educational level, and a degree of presumed affluence. These are valuable qualities to many advertisers.

In another way the computers assisted briefly. They were also capable of breaking down magazine subscribers by relative affluence. Such affluence was established by the census tract on the theory that those who lived in wealthier neighborhoods were wealthier, and that those in middle-income areas were less so. Thus, reasoned the magazines in their death throes, they could approach such national manufacturers as the Ford Motor Company with the suggestion that the company could reach the most affluent circulation of *Life*, for example, with advertisements for Lincoln Continentals; they could advertise Pintos in the less affluent areas, with Fairlane models and the like filling in the middle ground. This was ingenious thinking, offering an element of product differentiation that television could not, but it did not work at the time.

COSMOPOLITAN

Television seems to have done away with fiction to a large degree in all the print media. Few magazines publish any fiction anymore at all, and the present ratio of nonfiction to fiction, about three to one, was almost exactly reversed forty years ago. Television does fantasy and fiction, its cousin, superbly, while print does other things better in its less time-pressured fashion. This was to have an effect on the magazine industry.

At this point, there is a success story which more than anything else seems to point the way toward specialization of magazines. This story concerns *Cosmopolitan*, one of the magazines published by the Hearst group (which includes *Good Housekeeping, Harper's Bazaar, Popular Mechanics, Sports Afield* and *House Beautiful*). (The Hearst group represents a considerable spread of consumer interests.) In the early sixties *Cosmopolitan* found itself a poor competitor in the national general-interest field, suffering dwindling advertising revenues and a dwindling readership as public taste departed from the essentially fiction format it had so successfully utilized.

Cosmopolitan felt the winds of change and decided to leave the general-interest magazine business and to seek a specific audience, chosen not by demographics but by interest. Casting about for an audience not efficiently served by any medium, it hit upon that of the unmarried working girl. This was a happy choice in that it was a market designed to grow as more women entered the work force; it was also a market designed to replenish itself. Nor was any other magazine catering to the interests of this group—to their tastes, habits, life-style. To accomplish its purpose, *Cosmopolitan* hired Helen Gurley Brown (author of *Sex and the Single Girl*) as editor and began to offer a diet of pseudopornography and man-snaring techniques which hit its mark immediately.

When *Cosmopolitan* did these things, it did something else too. It forced every manufacturer of scented douches, uplift brassieres, cosmetics, and eye shadow to advertise in *Cosmopolitan*. Television was too broad a market for the relatively few women these products needed to find. Although the magazine's circulation became far smaller, its advertising revenues were assured and grew as it continually expanded its subscription lists. It was healthy, thriving, and its costs, always a factor, were vastly reduced. There existed a close correlation between three factors: the interest level of *Cosmopolitan*'s editorial content, the makeup of its audience, and the kinds of products advertised. It was the first of several such magazines.

PSYCHOLOGY TODAY

There is also a magazine success story of a different sort—that of *Psychology Today*. *Psychology Today*, published in Del Mar, California by CRM Publications, is an indication of the media infiltration into corporate conglomerates that is beginning to characterize an era of overall corporate and perhaps social integration. *Psychology Today* was the $10,000 brainchild of Nicholas Charney, who sold it after five years to Boise-Cascade for $20 million and moved on to reform Norman Cousin's *Saturday Review*. (Boise-Cascade subsequently sold *Psychology Today* to Random House.) Charney represented dynamic change; he reasoned that there was sufficient interest in human behavior to justify a popular magazine, rather than a scholarly journal, on the subject. He was right.

Psychology Today was born at a time when the postwar emphasis on education, stimulated by the GI Bill and by an accelerating public affluence, had begun to come together. Not only was there more affluence, but this itself was translated into more education, less need to join the work force early, and more leisure, nonproductive time in quantities unthinkable only a generation earlier. With less time required to produce the necessities of life, Americans turned inward, in a sort of mass introspection manifest in many ways: in social concern and criticism and consumerism; in an interest in the environment; and in plain curiosity about behavior and that which motivates man. *Psychology Today* was an instant success, attaining a circulation of six hundred thousand within four years, with advertising revenues to match.

It is the profile of *Psychology Today*'s subscribers that substantiates the causative qualifications of affluence and leisure. Less than 10 percent of the subscribers are professionals in the sense of being either teachers or practicing psychologists. Subscribers are relatively young, with a median age of twenty-seven; they are educated in that 80 percent are college graduates, and a high percentage hold advanced degrees; their numbers are split evenly between men and women; they are affluent. What kind of advertiser seeks this sort of "new generation" marketing mix? It is not the manufacturer of rat mazes, psychiatrists' couches, Rorschach tests, or the more esoteric psychological paraphernalia. It is the manufacturer of sports cars, modern clothing, modern furniture, liquor, or the other amenities of fine living. Thus, *Psychology Today* differs from the *Cosmopolitan* approach in that its interest focus is not specific to its advertisers' products, but rather productive of a real demographic mix. It is important to note that this demographic mix is achieved naturally through self-selection on the subscribers' part and not artificially by the computer. There is a certain arrogance to demographically predetermining readership affluence by census tract, and then arbitrarily directing advertisements for sleek or sleazy product lines accordingly. However, an audience may preselect itself along these same lines.

MARKETING AUDIENCE INTEREST

In *Psychology Today* and other Charney publications, the audience is far more than a source of subscriber revenue and a target for advertising. The audience is a self-identified market for a variety of goods and services made available by CRM, including posters, games and a whole series of books: *Anthropology Today, Psychology Today, Developmental Psychology Today*. In 1970 CRM revenues were $20 million, of which only a quarter came from the magazine. Such marketing services demonstrate a new trend in magazine publishing which further emphasizes the intensely commercial nature of mass media. The magazine, in essence, provides the means of establishing a credible roster of potential customers for certain kinds of products. Charney says, "The magazine is simply a tool to identify an audience with a particular interest...and that special list of subscribers is a prime target for a whole range of other services."[2]

2. Lynne Williams, *Medium or Message?* (Woodbury, N.Y.: Barron's Educational Series Inc., 24 May 1971).

Other publications have followed suit. *Family Health*, a relatively new magazine, had little over a million subscribers in 1971 and immediately moved into the business of marketing medical encyclopedia sets with resultant sales of over forty thousand sets. *Southern Living* uses its subscribers as a potential for sales of quality Southern cookbooks, while even *New York* magazine envisages its readership as a base for selling a how-to-do-it series on survival in New York.

Nor do complementary services stop with the magazines themselves. It did not take them long, for instance, to realize that such a painstakingly developed self-identified list of potential customers was in itself a valuable asset. Some magazines have taken to selling—or, rather, renting—all or portions of their subscription list to other organizations as sales tools. A manufacturer can buy 10 or 15 percent of their list randomly selected by the computer as a test. A mailing then determines if there is sufficient interest to market the item, whatever it be: book, game, poster, home furnishings, whatever. If the test is satisfactory, the manufacturer can then buy the entire list at so much per thousand names. This is an intriguing concept in which the audience is lured into becoming its own bait. Magazines also make a healthy profit selling their subscription lists to other magazines.

Since magazines are sold both by subscription and on a retail basis, they generally have an emphasis either toward subscription or toward street sales, although most utilize both methods of distribution. Subscription provides considerable security once established, but the time lag in slowly building appreciable subscribers and the costs of acquiring the lists of others can be prohibitive. Charney folded a second magazine venture, *Careers Today,* because buying subscription lists proved too expensive—this despite the fact that his new venture was already showing more than $100,000 worth of advertising per issue. Other magazines have chosen the newsstand for launching publications, hoping thereby to develop sufficient interest and acquire subscribers. The latter method demands considerable advertising for the magazine in other media to promote newsstand sales, and this too can prove expensive. There is actually no fail-safe method of starting a new magazine.

CONTROLLED CIRCULATION vs. NONADVERTISING SUPPORT

The emphasis on audience interest as a determining factor has led recently to a new phenomenon in magazine publishing—the controlled circulation magazine. Controlled circulation generally is a euphemism for a free or marketing-directed magazine aimed at certain classes of people in terms of their presumed interests. Credit card companies were first in this field by using magazines as vehicles for advertisers of luxury goods who were interested in the established credit ratings that card holders had demonstrated. The facility of purchase was also appealing to the advertisers—readers were urged to "put it on your credit card."

Although the *Reader's Digest,* because of its huge circulation, is generally regarded as the one remaining national, general circulation magazine, it too is specialized toward an aging, conservative, Protestant-ethic audience of astonishing numbers. It publishes 28 million copies monthly, of which 11 million are sold outside the United States. A part of the reason for its continuing success may lie in the fact that it is less reliant on advertising than other magazines. Originally supported by its subscription price alone, it began to take advertising in limited quantities late in its career. While this advertising is important to the magazine today, it is far from its principal means of support. The *Reader's Digest* also goes to some pains to keep current with popular taste, running a random monthly sample of its readers to determine their continuing interests. Thus, to a degree, it has borrowed television's rating technique to ascertain the relative popularity of its offerings and to access its gatekeepers' judgment.

As magazines continue to cast about for survival formulae, another branch of the business takes an opposite tack from the controlled circulation approach. They eschew advertising completely and base their entire financial operation on sales price alone. In this they copy the formula under which the *Reader's Digest* was originally founded. In this also they come close to the book-publishing business; some are even in hardcover, such as *American Heritage*. They seek to marry the security of a subscription list with the relative freedom from advertising pressure that the book enjoys. They are a hybrid form of a hybrid form, becoming in reality regularly published books of mosaic content and pinpointed audience appeal. The new *Saturday Evening Post* is an experiment along these lines, seeking to capitalize on America's nostalgia as well as the 6 million subscribers it owned before it went bankrupt. Issued regularly at $1.50 per copy, it too is an index of increasing affluence. The price per copy covers publication costs and profit; if any advertising should eventually develop, it will represent additional profits.

READERSHIP SURVEYS

Readership surveys are not uncommon in the magazine field. Most magazines subscribe to some rating service such as the Starch Report. These reports fall short of their purpose, however, as they are principally concerned with advertising readership, the purely commercial aspect of the business, and less with content analysis, which is the principal audience bait on which all advertising hinges.

Magazine circulation is deceptive. There is an exposure factor which is not reflected in raw circulation figures. That is to say, far more people read or are at least exposed to magazines than buy or subscribe to them (as happens, for example, in doctors' offices). This exposure factor will vary widely, of course, with the nature of the magazine, running as high as six times circulation for national general-interest magazines, to little more than single exposure for some of the smaller, more esoteric business or scholarly publications. In any event, this exposure factor is far higher for magazines in general than for either newspapers or books among the print media or for all the broadcast media, for that matter, where, due to its evanescent nature, the exposure factor can never be more nor less than one. Magazine advertising, while sold on a circulation basis, is calculated on estimated exposure. This is to say, there is a kind of double standard whereby an advertiser purchases space off the rate card, which is a reflection of audited circulation, but calculates his cost per thousand on presumed exposure as indicated by the Starch Report.

ADVERTISING AS CONTENT

One of the things evident in this discussion of magazines has been the close interrelationship of this field with advertising. In many magazines advertising contributes far more than economic support, important as that is. Advertising sometimes becomes a very real part of the editorial content itself, not merely an adjunct to it, but one of the prime reasons for reading the magazine. Evidence of this fact stems from World War II when editions of national magazines with the advertising deleted were sent to troops overseas on the naive theory that soldiers were interested in the reading material only, and that they were in no position to purchase the goods advertised. This engendered immediate complaints from the troops, who felt that they were being shortchanged. They missed the ads and the memories of home that they evoked. A part of the pleasure that the troops had lay in contemplating the things to which they could return. This speaks much for the commercial base of American society, lingering even in a foxhole. It also demonstrates the integrated nature of mass communications, which acts as a carrier of culture while reflecting quite accurately the life-style of a society; advertising and editorial content are melded together.

In fact, in many slick magazines advertising has developed into an art form of colorful, aesthetic, and sensuous appeal to which, in some instances, the editorial matter plays either a secondary or supporting role. John Hohenberg, in *The News Media: A Journalist Looks at His Profession*, makes the observation that in many of the specialized slick magazines dealing with fashion, travel, or the like that the editorial matter is purely supportive of the advertising, with substantial editorial preference and even "trade-out" material awarded to major advertisers. Trade-out material is that editorial matter promised to an advertiser in exchange for a certain substantial volume of advertising. Some magazines match advertising and editorial content for major advertisers on a page-for-page basis.

Another side of the same coin concerns magazines in which the ads are clearly superior to the editorial matter: displays of colorful, attractive, interesting people doing interesting things in interesting places, superbly illustrated or photographed in what Roland Wolseley describes as "word, camera, and brush pictures of new products." The smashing illustrations of *Vogue* or *Harper's Bazaar* come to mind immediately.

THE MAGAZINE SUBNETWORK

Advertising and other pertinent data concerning America's magazines are contained in the *Consumer Magazine* and *Farm Publication* editions of *Standard Rate and Data Service (SRDS)*, published monthly. The *SRDS* lists nearly ten thousand magazines of general circulation in the United States, including their circulation size, areas of influence, general subject matter, and advertising rates. Not covered are at least an additional nine thousand magazines, or more, which are regularly issued publications of organizations and corporations aimed at their membership, employees, or stockholders. These latter rarely include advertising since they are basically informative or persuasive in content, and their cost is born as a business expense by the organization or corporation involved. Yet they do comprise an integral part of mass communications, providing those members, employees, or stockholders with data pertinent to their interests, jobs, or investments information, which is obtainable in no other way. To this extent they have a real effect on the lives of these individuals. The spectrum of such corporate publications is too broad to be covered here; a note is made of their existence and the significant role they play in providing esoteric data which, despite its limited appeal, has real meaning.

Ordinarily, there is little room for this genre of material in the mass media of general circulation due to the competition for attention and the surplus of available material from many sources. These organizational publications, therefore, comprise a sort of media sub-network serving ever smaller groups along the audience continuum in terms of significant interests. Further, they often provide grist for the mills of the larger general media. A corporate financial report, for example, may lead to extended articles in the financial press; a technological development reported in an employee bulletin may spark an expanded piece in one of the trade magazines.

THE MAGAZINE MIX

Magazines can generally be broken down functionally into three categories corresponding closely to the functions of communication. These are: (1) entertainment/escape; (2) news/information; and (3) advocacy/opinion. Within these categories fall some rather obvious examples. Comic books, confessions, and science-fiction all fall within entertainment/escape. In the news/information category there are the well-known news weeklies of *Time* and *Newsweek*, as well as a host of trade, professional, and scholarly publications, each specializing toward some facet of the culture. The category of advocacy/opinion magazines oriented toward persuasion includes not only those of the underground press but also most of the vast array of organizational or corporate publications. Most magazines represent some combination of these communication functions, with specific appeal being determined by the magazine's basic thrust or orientation.

It might be useful to examine some specific magazines for their peculiarities as representatives of trends within the publishing business. *TV Guide,* with a circulation of fifteen million, exceeded only by the phenomenal *Reader's Digest,* is the direct result of television's effect on the magazine field. It is a classic example of one medium catering to another in terms of both interest and complementary functions. Television's ubiquitous popularity demands a ready reference in more tangible form than its own evanescent promotions can offer. A weekly magazine gathers together in one handy place all programming data for the week. This is its basic function, an index, and illustrates a curious admixture of communication functions: information on entertainment. In this it supplements the daily newspapers which also publish a television log as a reader service. Apart from its huge circulation and reference function, *TV Guide* is noteworthy from a technical standpoint, being forced to publish in a near infinity of geographical editions to accommodate the various FCC channel allocations on the band.

THE NEWS-MAGAZINES

Another combination of characteristics is represented by the weekly newsmagazines, of which *Time*, with a circulation of around four million, is the largest. It is interesting that *Time*'s circulation, despite the magazine's popularity, is about half that of some of the major magazines which have gone under in the last half-dozen years, including its stablemate, *Life*. This is fairly conclusive evidence that circulation alone is not the answer to success or failure; the homogeneity of that circulation is of prime importance. Further, *Time*'s circulation is only about a quarter of that of the magazine leaders, *TV Guide* and *Reader's Digest*. Thus, its influence and that of the weekly newsmagazines in general seems to be far out of proportion to the numbers of people who read it. This can only be attributed to the significance of the information function in communication, and the particular integrity that *Time* brings to its editorial coverage. This information factor has, however, been traditionally overemphasized, because for all their influence, the newsmagazines represent only a tiny fraction of magazine publishing in terms of both number and audience. Often overlooked is the fact that the newsmagazine publishes weekly, or four times more often than most magazines, a factor which both provides additional exposure and establishes firm habit patterns in its readership.

The matter of weekly publication also makes the newsmagazine a cross between a monthly magazine and daily newspaper, filling an information void by providing a limited perspective on current events. Newsmagazines have a little more time than a newspaper to digest the significance of contemporary developments. Also, their space limitations are acute in proportion to the scope of events demanding interpretation, and they must be highly selective in what is presented. Another of their problems involves that of writing around a time lag in order to make the quasi-historical appear contemporary—last week's news must seem current. This is a technique at which their team-writing staff has become particularly adept.

Time is significant also in that more than any other magazine it has profitably perfected geographical zone distribution, both for printing facility and as an additional source of advertising revenue.

OTHER GAPS TO BE FILLED

A relatively new phenomenon in the magazine field is the so-called city magazine, such as *San Diego Magazine, San Francisco Magazine, The Washingtonian Magazine*. Here again is an example of the media covering each other's lapses.

Interestingly, the famous *New Yorker,* first published in 1923, was the first and for decades the isolated example of this kind of magazine. However, as the *New Yorker* more and more became a national magazine catering to the sophisticated across the nation, it left a void in New York City, which in the late sixties began to be filled by *New York,* published by the staff of the defunct *New York Herald-Tribune. New York* concentrates on life in the city and the problems of New Yorkers, but ironically these are of such magnitude that in their enormity they are capturing a certain national audience, and *New York* is well on its way toward becoming another *New Yorker.*

Another unique contribution to the magazine field is the little *Ford Times.* In a sense, founded in 1907, it was the first of the controlled circulation magazines, distributed to a specific list of persons, Ford owners. Unlike the more recent controlled circulation magazines, the *Ford Times* accepts no advertising. It advertises one product only—Ford motorcars. The rationale for the magazine holds that over the relatively long life of a car—three to four years—it constitutes a constant monthly reminder to owners, providing them with a series of excellently written and illustrated travel articles and constantly updating its readers on new Ford products against the day when they will inevitably make another auto purchase.

PRACTICAL CONSIDERATIONS

From a production standpoint magazines again fall somewhere between their print cousins, books and newspapers. They are not on the relentless daily schedule that the newspaper is, nor do they have the painstaking leisure that books do. Most magazines work further ahead of schedule than one might believe. The average monthly slick is prepared four to six months in advance of publication. This is to say that staff will start "dummying up" a July issue in January, committing some articles and commissioning others with the thought that, for all intents and purposes, the issue will be closed by April except for some minor loose ends of material.

Newspapers are almost entirely staff-written, and books are almost entirely written by outside authors. Magazines fall between these poles. Some are completely staff-written, others completely contracted. Most employ some balance of the two techniques, with an edge toward staff writing because, by and large, it is less expensive and more reliable than that of outside authors. Good authors are hard to come by, and those who have successfully published and have thus established some reputation can command considerable fees for their material. For some, their names also constitute an additional drawing card for the magazine. All this notwithstanding, there are surprisingly few full-time free-lance authors in the United States. There are probably less than three hundred free-lancers who support themselves entirely from their writing, and less than one hundred of them who earn as much as $10,000 a year. Under these conditions, it is reasonable to ask where magazine articles come from. For the most part, they come from experts in a given field who already hold jobs in the field and who write as a sideline. For example, *Psychology Today,* which is about half staff- and half contract-written, commissions its outside articles from practicing psychologists, university professors, and the like. A considerable number of newspapermen augment their earnings with outside articles and feature material, as do book authors. The latter, of course, bring considerable "name attraction" to a magazine.

As in book publishing, magazine editors have either a stable of acceptable authors whose work and expertise they know, or they rely on literary agents whom they trust. Agents and authors also are constantly suggesting story ideas to the magazines in the form of queries or outlines in hope of a contract. Each magazine editor zealously tries to maintain a constant tone or flavor to his publication, a proven format of exactly the right material mix, both written and graphic, which will continue to appeal to his specific readership. His is a peculiar gatekeeping function dictated less by the surplus of material than by the rigid requirements of his particular audience. He must ruthlessly prune everything, regardless of intrinsic merit, which does not exactly fit both the overall format of the magazine and the particular mix of a given issue. His is, in part, a balancing act in which judgmental factors enter more sensitively than in either the case of newspaper editors, whose principle concern is with news, or book publishers, who are concerned only with appeal in a singular sense.

SUMMARY

Magazines have developed historically to occupy a middle position between the time-consuming and self-selective book and the hurried, geographically circumscribed newspaper. The role of the magazine is essentially an appeal to audiences by interest rather than by geographical coincidence. It fills the gap between books and newspapers from the point of view of availability, cost, permanence, specificity of subject matter, and perspective.

Because the actual role of magazines has never been clearly defined functionally, it has been more subject to flux and change under social pressures than either of the other forms of print. Perhaps more than any other medium, the magazine illustrates a medium's power to survive as new and more efficient forms of communication develop. It has admirably accomplished this under the pressure of television by specializing increasingly toward ever more specific audiences that television cannot hope to reach with its ubiquitous appeal. This has led to one of the great paradoxes in contemporary communications: the spectacle of major, time-honored national magazines going out of business, and the birth of an increasing number of more specialized publications of smaller circulation in better financial shape. The big magazines failed not because of a lack of readers, but lack of advertising. Major national manufacturers, the principal support of the national magazines, found that television offered a better buy for their advertising dollar.

Alternately, those magazines which specialized toward specific interest or demographic audiences discovered that they could command the advertising for luxury or speciality items whose potential purchasers represented only a fraction of television's vast audience, and for whom, therefore, television was not an economic advertising purchase.

Following a series of ruinous circulation wars, national magazines sought unsuccessfully to prune their circulations, or to strive for geographic and even demographic distribution in which they were assisted by the computer. Costs of these techniques doomed them, by and large, to failure also.

Because magazines represent such a broad sweep between books and newspapers on the spectrum, they can be found in all sizes and descriptions, from huge national magazines, such as *Reader's Digest,* to an esoteric publication reaching only several hundred. They also include a vast and, to date, undetermined roster of religious, labor, eleemosynary, underground, corporate, and other organizational publications, including annual reports. Such publications comprise the magazine subnetwork.

While a considerable portion of magazines' revenue has traditionally come from advertising, some surprising trends have been noted. One is the advent of the so-called controlled circulation magazine which is sent to a preselected list of readers without charge. It serves simply as bait for advertisers wishing to reach that particular audience mix. The other trend is diametrically opposed to controlled circulation: some magazines publish without any advertising at all, letting the magazine's price bear the entire cost of publication and profit.

Traditionally, some magazines have existed predominantly on newsstand sales, whereas others have relied exclusively on subscriptions. Most, however, of the national magazines exist in some combination of the two.

Reader's Digest, with its combined domestic and foreign circulation of twenty-eight million, dominates the field in circulation size. *TV Guide* comes in second place with fifteen million, a perfect example of a medium's medium, totally specialized. The newsmagazines, with *Time*'s four million in the fore, have an influence beyond their numbers, probably due to the opinion leadership status of their limited readership. A relative newcomer is the so-called city magazine, seeking a broader perspective on area affairs than newspapers can give and, incidentally, offering a quality showcase to local advertisers.

In general, a magazine's readership exceeds its circulation. Magazines pass from hand to hand readily and have a life of up to a month ordinarily. Sometimes this readership factor is as much as six times the circulation, a figure that the Starch Report attempts to establish for advertisers.

In flux now, magazines will continue to change as the contemporary communication picture continues to change and, caught in the middle of the continuum, magazines must respond more readily than the more stable book or newspaper.

Part V

ELECTROMEDIA

To be considered in the following four chapters are the media which form the components of the communications or electronic revolution, the technological successor to the industrial revolution.

Today the effects of this revolution are only just beginning to be felt even as it accelerates. However, the genesis of the electric age occurred more than a century and a quarter ago when, in 1844, Samuel Morse perfected the telegraph. The instantaneousness of information transmission burst upon the world—originally between Washington and Baltimore.

The significance of electricity in communication was its difference in both kind and degree. From the point of view of rapidity, electricity foresaw the ultimate in society's struggle for ever greater speed. It achieved the speed of light, thus leapfrogging other forms of information transmission and radically altering them as it did so. Qualitatively, it introduced a new factor into the information business. It removed the necessity of production of a separate unit: a newspaper, book, or magazine for every consumer. In a sense the effects of the electronic revolution were the antitheses of those of the industrial revolution with the latter's emphasis on infinite repeatability of product. A single product now served everyone.

Discussion in the following chapters concerns film first, radio next, and finally television. This order has the advantage of tracing a chronology in the development of the electric media, showing how they evolved out of and affected one another.

A student once described film as a kind of electric book. The parallel is striking in its reference to the media continuum. The cinema does show many of the characteristics noted in books. Not only was it the earliest form of electromedia, but it is essentially self-selective in nature. It does not foist itself upon a specific audience, but rather must await an audience visit as individuals. Cinema is comparatively expensive in relation to its electric companions, and requires effort to attend. In reference to radio and television, cinema is by far the most permanent, and it tends toward unity and specificity of subject matter in contrast to a fragmentary and mosaic approach. Finally, like the book, film pays its own way with no assistance from advertising, which, of course, dominates radio and television.

Viewed in this light, it is as if the print and electric media comprised separate although parallel subcontinua of the media continuum, each developing along a similar pattern although in widely separated time frames. This is a useful viewpoint for purposes of understanding, provided recognition is given to the fact that they coexist and are integrated into a single whole by contemporary society, which they serve together.

If film is a sort of an electric book, radio has developed into a sort of electric magazine. No longer a national medium, radio has fragmented to serve specific publics, often in terms of interest. Radio is the electric application of the principle of specialization by which mass media traditionally have survived.

Both radio and television represent a departure from earlier mass communications because, for the first time, they demand that the audience provide the reception hardware at its own expense. Both require a considerable capital investment, and one that depreciates rapidly. Thus, the claim that they are free is a slight misrepresentation, a gross oversight, or both.

Radio provided the framework for television. It provided the conditioned audience, the basis of programming, the networks, the affiliate structure, the commission control, and above all, it had fought, won, and solidified the battle of commercial or advertising support. Television inherited a ready-made game plan.

Bête noire or éminence gris of the electric media, or of all media for that matter, is television. In terms of its massive audiences and its total effect, only now visible on the first generation of television babies, it is a factor more speculated about than understood. Politically, socially, and economically, its ramifications are enormous. More particularly, it has radically affected all other media, driving some magazines out of business, encouraging others, altering the role of the newspaper, and forcing the extra off the streets. It has reduced radio to a supplemental medium while marrying it to the record industry. On the one hand, television has offered movies freedom from the tyranny of the masses; on the other, it has taken this freedom away as it offers movies vaster audiences in a single night than the average film could expect in its lifetime.

Television is constantly changing. Viewing decreases, and significant competitors arise to threaten networking. Today, CATV is an unknown quantity fraught with multi-channel capacity, built-in feedback, and demographic control. Satellite broadcasting brings the world into the home directly, bypassing the networks. The Public Broadcasting System is a sickly infant that refuses to die. The full communication potential of laser and holography are not yet known, but they wait impatiently in the wings.

One further note should be made. The ogre of acceleration continues to grow. An individual can fly to Europe in less time than it took hid grandfather to go to town and back. The third generation of sophisticated computers within a decade has arrived, and man continues to develop new technologies before perfecting the hardware to handle the old. Such progress, if it be such, has been predicated on society's willingness to devote huge sums of money to research and development. Affluent products are themselves the product of an affluent society. Such has been the theme of Alvin Toffler's *Future Shock*, among others. Were society to reorder its priorities, to opt for less progress, then the money-well would dry and technology with it. Charles Reich sees such a reorientation of goals in *The Greening of America* (see "Suggested Readings," p. 457).

Such lapses of progress are not unknown in communications history. The most obvious example is that of the cloistering of the Dark Ages, a silent and illiterate time following the relative sophistication of Rome. As in all things, for all its braggadocio, communications follows society's command.

12 FILM

MOVIES: MASS OR WHAT?

Movies, motion pictures, film, and cinema all refer to essentially the same thing; all have slightly different connotations ranging from the plebian to the aesthetic. This in itself gives clue to the diversity of film, which shall be used as the generic term.

Film is counted as a major mass medium in the same sense that drama and the other antic arts are included in terms of effect upon large masses of people over a relatively long period of time. In all its variations—the art film, the cartoon, the popular extravaganza, the industrial showcase, the educational teaching aid, the social documentary, and the new genre of television "quickie"—it has unquestionably had a massive effect upon society. Few people have never seen a movie. In this sense, as a carrier of the culture, a changing mirror of changing times, film is unexcelled.

However, in another sense it is scarcely a mass medium, although at one time it bid fair for that status. Films are not regularly issued. In its commercial forms, film aims at no particular audience sector; rather, it catches its consumers as it can. This is the same thing as saying that today, at least, gatekeeping is more a matter of social and aesthetic judgment, highly experimental, than of time-tested formulae ruthlessly applied. Film constitutes a single unit, and while it does not foist itself upon its consumers daily, it has an advantage shared by no other medium. It commands attention, playing generally to captive audiences in a format over which the producer has complete control in emphasis, order of presentation, continuity, dramatic effect, and timing. These characteristics have made it over the years a superb medium for persuasion. A good half of filmmaking is not commercial in the usual sense, but is devoted to sales, training, information, education, and other public relations purposes of corporations, governmental agencies, trade associations, unions, political parties, and almost any other sector of society with a persuasive message.

It is this half of filmmaking, the persuasive portion, which is ordinarily overlooked in favor of the more dramatic and prevalent entertainment function. Yet, even from this cursory overview it is evident that films have taken at least two tracks in their development. In the introduction to this section, the similarity of films among the electric media to books in the print media was noted. The similarities are striking. Principally, both are long-term undertakings; both are nonadvertising-supported; both are relatively expensive and hard to acquire; both embrace a certain unity and specificity of subject matter. An additional parallel can be seen in comparing the commercial film and its desired box-office appeal with the trade book, and its aspirations for making the best-seller list. The counterpart of this comparison is equating the noncommercial film, privately produced and containing high informational-educational-persuasive content, with the textbook. The analogies are not exact, but indicate a similarity of function between the two media. Also, the commercial film must make its way at the box office within the first year or so, which is essentially the time frame of a best-seller, whereas the noncommercial film has a longer life dictated essentially by its purpose, just as a textbook does. Truly, a film is an electric book.

Another factor of comparison to be noted is that, like the book, film has a long and honorable history, stretching back into antiquity in the form of the drama. Film is, in effect, the mass production of drama for the same entertainment, instructional, and persuasive purposes that the dramas of ancient Greece were originally performed.

GENESIS OF FILM

Film has several origins. Along the media continuum, of course, it is an obvious extension of graphics, relying heavily on the development of photography. It is also a communications application of electricity; another is the telegraph, which led to radio. These two paths merged to create television.

The psychological principle on which film as a medium is based—that the eye retains an image fleetingly after it is gone—was discovered in 1824. A half-century later, in 1877, the principle was tested when twenty-four cameras synchronized in sequence were used to photograph a horse race. The viewing of these photographs in rapid succession led to the illusion of motion. Two years after that, Edison's invention of the electric light provided a source of illumination which made projection and, hence, mass viewing possible. Within a decade, two other essential technical ingredients of the film were developed: roll film and its sprocket feed.

By 1895 the first movies had come into being in several nations. The United States, however, took the lead in filmmaking, largely as a result of the huge waves of immigrants who passed through New

York's Ellis Island around the turn of the century. For these people, mostly illiterate and unfamiliar with English, the silent movies provided a rare entertainment. They flocked to the storefront theaters in droves and created a demand for more and more one-reel thrillers. Many of the earliest films concentrated on special effects, shots of onrushing locomotives and the like, although nearly all the familiar formats of today (such as news and social commentary) were present from the beginning. *The Great Train Robbery* in 1903 is generally credited with being the first film with a story line, setting a precedent for the future.

The earliest theaters were storefronts where half-hour showings ran continuously. In 1905 the first true theater, the Nickelodeon, made its appearance in Pittsburgh. Soon this specially designed pleasure-house spread across the nation. The period from 1903 to 1908 was the time during which the basic foundations of the film industry were laid, and the principles of wide or mass appeal, of audience turnover, formula production, and character stereotyping were firmly established. The years from 1908 to 1914 were a period of struggle for the economic control of the new medium. From this battle emerged some of the significant economic factors of the industry.

Initially and somewhat naively, the struggle for control centered around the hardware of the industry. The Motion Pictures Patents Co., a consortium of patent holders on projection equipment, sought also to control production and to tie exhibitors' film releases to contracts on their equipment rental at $2.00 per week, with no purchase possible. If nothing else, this struggle identified three major factors of the film industry: production, exhibition, and distribution.

ECONOMIC FACTORS

The moviegoing public was willing to pay more for longer films. This provided an incentive to producers which ran up production costs considerably. At the same time the longer films began to attract a more educated and sophisticated audience and to compete effectively with the theater as an evening's entertainment. Film, as it developed, radically altered the nature of the legitimate theater, effectively removing it from the national scene, more or less restricting it to a purely provincial New York medium and, incidentally, using it as a proving ground for film musicals.

Finally, the longer films reduced audience turnover and so required larger theaters, thus substituting the ornate movie palaces of the twenties and thirties for the nickelodeons. The turning point in this chain of events can be marked by the 1915 production of *The Birth of a Nation*, a long epic film which is still regarded as one of the major film classics.

The larger theaters had a voracious appetite. They had to be kept supplied with films, and films of a certain kind. Since there was no demographic identification to the potential audience once film had become popular with the middle class, films had to appeal to everyone, young and old alike. They could not be controversial, but they had to be good entertainment, that is, exciting, spectacular, sensational—nor could they depart too far from a proven mode. In this they tended to foreshadow television's later offerings in blandness, tentative sensationalism, and formula emphasis.

After the failure of the Motion Pictures Patent Company's attempt at control, the way was cleared for the establishment of the large vertical film empires and Hollywood was born. Warner Brothers and Metro-Goldwyn-Mayer (MGM) integrated production, distribution, and exhibition through their own movie houses. Distribution was the key to success, and block booking was the means used. Under block booking, exhibitors were required to contract for a number of pictures, many of them unproduced. The security of an assured film supply was offset by the fact that exhibitors had to accept a considerable number of "B" pictures, or genuine potboilers, in order to get any major productions. Often, since pictures were being booked sight unseen, they were sold on the basis of proven factors, such as actors, actresses, plots or story lines, authors, directors, and sometimes even production costs.

HOLLYWOOD

As block booking became prevalent, the star system evolved into a type of insurance. The public became acquainted with the names and faces of performers and demanded to see more of certain favorites. Cost controls became less important than the production budget, the size of which constituted another guarantee of success. There were numerous ways to spend money: on the stars who commanded fabulous salaries, on authors of best-selling novels for the film rights, on other proven writers to provide the screenplay, on well-known directors, on an array of increasingly sophisticated technical innovations, and on promotion.

Film, by its nature, demanded promotion to call attention to its wares in the marketplace. It was far more a consumer product than a medium in the historical sense. In part, the success of the fledgling public relations profession can be attributed to Hollywood's demand for press agentry for both film and star promotion.

As film became more and more organized as a major industry, it was inevitable that the artistic considerations of the medium would be subordinated to the practical. There was no room for experimentation, no room for art, and no room for departure from the proven formulae. As production costs rose, Hollywood had to turn to Wall Street more frequently to finance its ventures. This move compounded the formula situation, for the bankers were far more apt to lend speculative money on a proven project than on an unknown quantity. In turn, the demand for best-selling authors was accelerated, for expensive sets, for name stars, for proven formulae in the scripts, and for huge advertising and promotional budgets.

Left to right: Tom Mix (The Bettmann Archive); Rudolph Valentino, **The Shiek** (UPI); Clara Bow, the "It" girl (UPI); Douglas Fairbanks (The Bettmann Archive); Edward G. Robinson, **Smart Money,** 1931 (UPI); the Barrymores, in a scene from **Rasputin,** 1932: Lionel, Ethel, and John (The Bettmann Archive).

Left to right: Charlie Chaplin and Jackie Coogan in **The Kid** (The Bettmann Archive); Theda Bara (UPI); Vivian Leigh and Clark Gable in **Gone With the Wind** (UPI); Mary Pickford and Douglas Fairbanks (The Bettmann Archive); Wallace Beery in a scene from **The Old Soak** (The Bettmann Archive); Mary Pickford, America's darling (The Bettmann Archive).

SOUND AND THE DEPRESSION

When sound came to the film, it rocked the industry. The first sound film was *Don Juan*, produced by Warner Brothers in 1926, followed quickly by Al Jolson in *The Jazz Singer* in 1927. Sound disturbed Hollywood because many of the carefully built stars of the silent era couldn't make it in the "talkies." Theda Bara and Valentino, on whom millions in promotions had been spent, were lost assets, and new, talking stars had to be created from scratch. Furthermore, the nature of sound changed the vehicles, and story lines appropriate to the silent days yielded to more dramatic scripts. New formulae were required, and the dimensions of sound itself required new and infinitely more expensive technology.

Sound had barely come on stage before the Great Depression entered, injecting new social factors into moviemaking. Radio was a relatively new and a "free" medium. It provided home entertainment in the lean depression years when even the price of a fifty-cent movie was sometimes prohibitive. The excitement of sound delayed the full economic effect for several years, but the depression years for Hollywood, like the rest of the nation, were thin. Color technology, which had been held back by Hollywood lest the industry be disturbed again, made its appearance in 1935 as a counterdepression measure to offer something so vividly and dramatically new that America would spend money to see it.

While westerns, mysteries, and situation comedies were more or less stock fair, there was a certain faddishness to Hollywood productions in the thirties and forties. A series of gangster movies in the early thirties was followed by a rash of Busby Berkeley musical extravaganzas, of which *Flying Down to Rio*, with the chorus line on the wings of an airliner, may have been the all-time high. These extravaganzas were followed by a religious revival, and finally a blaze of spy and war films. Once a plot achieved any kind of box office success, every other studio rushed variations on that theme into production in order to capitalize on the trend.

A companion trend developed as the syndicated Hollywood columnist lent a new romantic gloss to the scene, filling the nation's newspapers with gossip and sex and the doings and misdoings of the movie colony. Several dozen magazines vied to outdo one another in dramatizing the scandals of "tinsel town," and both on and off screen, Hollywood provided a kind of vicarious romance for a nation in the throes of depression.

During World War II, the film industry also provided an additional form of escape and even a form of patriotism as it reached its full impact in the late forties immediately after the war. The industry reached its peak in 1949; 90 million admissions were sold that year. The major studios—MGM, Twentieth Century Fox, Paramount, Columbia, RKO, and Warner Brothers—cranked out over four hundred celluloid fantasies.

Electromedia

BURST BUBBLES

The bubble of the film industry burst, primarily due to the consent decree of 1946. Sued by the Department of Justice for being in constraint of trade, the film industry agreed under a consent decree to divest itself of its chains of movie houses. In essence, the empires were to be broken up and exhibition separated from production and distribution. By the early fifties the full impact of the consent decree was being felt; the studios lacked outlets for their potboilers. Independent exhibitors demanded a higher quality of movie.

Other factors also entered in the industry decline, one of which was the formation of separate production companies by some artists. Actors, actresses, and directors banded together to produce films. Often they relied on the major studios for distribution of the final product, and sometimes for bankrolling. Increasing numbers of films were produced abroad, primarily as a result of tax advantages to the participating stars, and also because of cheaper foreign labor. Inevitably, some of the new independent producers came under the influence of the experimental and artistic techniques of the foreign filmmakers.

Then there was television. Television took audiences out of the movie palaces and placed them back in the home. Hollywood could not compete with television on its own terms by providing an evening's entertainment. The film industry was forced to offer radically different techniques unavailable to the home viewer. Wide-screen, stereophonic sound and three-dimensional films were a part of the answer; so were the superspectaculars and the so-called first-runs playing at premium prices in selected movie houses. Another tack taken was the exploration of previously taboo subject matter: drugs, sex, homosexuality, and nudity.

The impact of television on film is best seen in the figures. From a high of 90 million admissions in 1949, the film industry declined to around a little more than 20 million admissions than twenty years later, in 1968. As the market declined, so did the need for the big movie palaces; they were the first casualties.

TELEVISION'S ADVANTAGES

Television wasn't entirely bad for the film industry; there were some hidden benefits. First, television freed the film industry from a slavish devotion to the lowest common denominator. It also freed it from a reliance on the pseudoguarantees of success: the star system, formula plots, huge promotion budgets, and the like. The breakdown of these accoutrements of a major industry further encouraged independent production as a new breed of artistic directors began to take control. Film was and is a corporate art form demanding the talents of writer, director, and actors. Where previously the economics of filmmaking emphasized the stars, the newer trend placed emphasis on the director in whose production actors were more or less incidental. This, too, was a carry-over from the foreign film influence, and the reputation of such impresario-directors as Federico Fellini.

The other big assist that television ironically offered the film industry was television itself. When television first began to make inroads on film's audiences, Hollywood fought television by prohibiting its productions from television. But beginning in 1955, the film industry discovered that television provided a brand-new market and source of revenue for old movies which were fully depreciated and had no other future potential use. Hollywood began selling old movies to television, often for as much as $500,000 a showing.

The next step in this particular chain was the use of studio facilities, first for making television serials, and later for making television films. The major studios had the technical hardware, the personnel, and the know-how to crank out television programs. More complex, however, was the television movie. Not all the contemporary films, exploring more permissive themes of sex and violence, were appropriate to television's family audience, especially since television's mores are audited by the FCC. A new type of film was required—one made for television—which would have its initial showing over the air, and later would be exported for foreign exhibition. Not only did the television movie provide an opportunity to tailor subject matter to the limits of family viewing, but it could also produce films to meet television's exact specifications as to running time and commercials, something that the Hollywood film, produced for other purposes, could never do. It was possible to interrupt the action on television movies at the exact time that a commercial would run without disturbing continuity. Further, television films, which were designed to run ninety minutes, less commercials, would not require the extensive editing that often removed significant action from the Hollywood product adapted to television.

TWO KINDS OF FILMS

1. Marshall McLuhan, *Understanding Media* (New York: Signet Books, 1966).

Thus, under the impact of television, filmmaking forked again. One branch of the industry made the smaller-budget, more socially meaningful, and artistic product that marks, in part, the current commercial trend. It is these films that led Marshall McLuhan to note that television had made film an art form.[1] To a degree he was correct, but he overlooked the other branch of filmmaking, the one which grinds out television movies, and which, if anything, is more rigidly controlled by the economics of the lcd, mass appeal, and the ever-watchful eye of the FCC than Hollywood ever was.

With film's smaller audiences came a demography of its own, and certain practical requirements that would alter the nature of commercial filmgoing. The smaller audiences were younger, with a mean age of twenty-five. They were no longer spread across the entire age spectrum of the United States. Younger audiences dictated different themes of social justice, incipient violence, and sexual freedom. They also demanded different techniques of photography and emphasis. By and large, the audience was also more educated, and one which

Electromedia

had grown up with video from childhood, more sophisticated and aware and more appreciative of graphic technique.

The smaller audiences and the smaller budgets for films rendered the big palaces obsolete. They couldn't be filled, and the cost of upkeep was too great. The new movie houses were small, even tiny affairs, located in shopping centers where parking and other services were available, or they were drive-ins where the customer brought his own seats. Today, these minitheaters often are multiple, and a single operator can manage three or four minitheaters simultaneously from a central projection room by staggering the showing hours, thus offering a diversity of product to the filmgoer. No longer is the filmgoer slave to whatever the exhibitor is showing that week. He has three or four choices, and may be cajoled into attending three or four times during the same week. Theater locations in shopping centers and their small size seems to cast a reflective eye back to the storefront theaters of the turn of the century, where the movies were born; progress has come full circle.

Actually, there are around 15,000 movie theaters in the nation, about one-third of which are drive-ins. Most of the new theaters being built are of the mini variety, reflecting minimal construction costs and maintenance, located in suburban shopping centers close to the affluent population, and having multiple auditoriums.

FILM: FIRST MASS COMMUNICATIONS EXPORT

One of the peculiarities of film, noticeable from the beginning, is that the language barrier is minimal. The immigrants at the turn of the century who first populated the storefront theaters were aware of this. Film has lent itself to cross-cultural transfer in a sense that no other medium has. Print demands language familiarity by its nature. The broadcast media, even television, is so heavily laden with verbal overtones that it hinders foreign comprehension, but film, like drama, its ancient ancestor, is universal. Film is also far more transportable than drama, and from its earliest history became an export product with significant international effects.

From the beginning of filmmaking, the United States has dominated the industry. With its superior technology born of increasing affluence, and its larger audiences, which even around the turn of the century could find sufficient leisure to support film, this industry had the early incentive to produce an ever-increasing number of films commercially. Inevitably, these films found their way overseas to fill foreign movie houses with a United States product in the absence of a sufficient quantity of local films. Thus, film became the first communications export of the United States. Americans were visible on the world's movie screens in a degree that no number of emissaries or even tourists could ever achieve. But theirs was an unrealistic presence composed of fantasy and dreams. Exposed to the nations of the world were societal stereotypes and quaint moralities, a love of violence, and a sort of synthetic history, both past and present. An incredible wealth ran through all the pictures as celluloid strived mightily to portray the good life, a wealth bound to contrast unfavorably with the surrounding facts of life in the rest of the world. An unbelievable technology spread itself across the screen, generating a sense of awe. The nations of the world thought that they were seeing America.

FANTASY vs. REALITY ABROAD

Unaware of the American experience and lacking native perspective, other nations accepted American fantasies for fact. They could not distinguish dreams from reality and accepted American stereotypes for people, and worst of all, stereotypes for Americans; thus an American stereotype was created out of the composite stereotypes of movies. American films were produced in America for the entertainment of Americans. They were accepted by Americans in this perspective, not treated as reality, but rather as an escape from reality. Abroad they were something else—dramatic pictures of a foreign land for which there was no reason not to accept them as truth. This appears to be a pitfall of mass communications transfer, and it is quite possible that what originated in Hollywood as innocuous entertainment following a proven formula emerged in Europe or in Asia or in Latin America as a social document engendering awe, envy, and resentment.

It was not so much the treatment of American films, their improbable plots, their worship of sex symbols, and their cowboys and Indians which caused this effect. It was the sheer overpowering volume of American export films, hammering away a single theme day after day, until in the absence of other exposure, the films became America. Further, the more technically perfect the films became, the greater this delusion.

Moreover, it was less the big-budget extravaganzas, often treating historical themes, which offered this false view of America as the hundreds and thousands of "B" potboilers. The very factors which characterized the old Hollywood—a large volume of production, the sacrifice of quality and technical perfection—were the same factors which betrayed the American image abroad. Far from distorting the values of other lands, American films have distorted the foreign view of America, subtly and perhaps irreparably.

FOREIGN INFLUENCES HERE

The transportability of film works two ways, and foreign films were not without influence in the United States. As more and more independent producers went abroad to take advantage of lower costs, they became exposed to some of the postwar techniques of the foreign filmmakers. Simultaneously, foreign films were acquiring a certain limited popularity in the United States amongst the avant-garde. Playing small "art" houses, they gained a currency of modishness. Principal among the foreign influences on contemporary film in America was the neorealism of the postwar Italian producers, such as Rossellini and DeSica. Theirs were films which, far from merchandizing a dream, dealt with the nitty-gritty and hopelessness of life.

Electromedia

French directors brought their "New Wave" of films which soon yielded to existentialism. Their contribution was a form of cinéma vérité, which explored—often with hand-held cameras—the actions and events of the lives of their characters—events which were often meaningless. France's contribution was also one of technique, freeing producers from studios and taking them into the open, which even at the sacrifice of technical perfection brought a greater realism to the screen. English producers, meanwhile, discovered England's lower classes and their accents. In a sense they presaged the English revolution, which would eventually erupt in the Teddy Boys and Carnaby Street, bra-less youth, "birds," and the Beatles. Indeed, a good deal of the American youth cult had its origin in English cinema.

Swedish films were and still are dominated by the genius of Ingmar Bergman who, more successfully than anyone else, introduced metaphor in film, raising cinema to an art form and exploring in the ancient Greek traditions the timeless themes of life and death, truth, and the like.

From the Far East in Japan came incredibly beautiful films, whose technical artistry and use of light, color, space, and misty camera techniques were entirely captivating. They brought the understated beauty of Japanese art to the screen. All these forces found a refocus in the United States as its film industry underwent the throes of reorganization.

Foreign films, after a slow, campy beginning, became increasingly popular as the volume of production in the United States slacked off and was diverted to television. American audiences began to look beyond an escape into more complex themes. As this happened, American independent producers began to incorporate a foreign style into their own productions by paying greater attention to the integrity and artistic merit of their work. Film began to undergo a renaissance.

The extravaganza did not die completely. There were still studios who focused on tried-and-true techniques and used lavish promotional budgets to sell their wares. However, they began to fade, and the film became more and more like its lineal ancestor the book in its independence of production.

FILM AS FANTASY

Cinéma vérité, or the technique of simply shooting footage at random to record the passage of events without a plan or viewpoint, is a kind of film surrealism, the equivalent of the literary stream of consciousness style. Cinéma vérité is actually a contradiction in terms in that film by its nature is unrealistic. It is based on an optical illusion, wherein the still frame of individual photographs are mechanically speeded up and synthetically projected until they blend into one another, creating the illusion of motion. This technique can even be applied in cartoon form to create the illusion of motion where none ever existed. Since the camera must be operated by an individual and pointed by him at something of his choice, the notion that it is possible to make a film without a viewpoint is tenuous at best. Film is a mental fraud, in a sense, which requires a suspension of disbelief in order to obtain meaning. No matter how realistically it attempts to portray a scene, through selective camera work and editing, a film will still reflect the producer's viewpoint. When scripting and dramatic effect are added, film becomes an intensely personal medium, conveying the persuasive, social, or artistic messages of its producers in unsurpassed form. It is unreal, as a painting is unreal, reflecting always the artist's viewpoint, if only in choice of subject.

These qualities make film an unrivaled propaganda or persuasive medium, and consequently, lead many contemporary producers and directors to feel that the unabashed use of camera technique and editing to paint a picture or create a mood is perhaps a more honest and realistic use of the medium than an attempt at natural portrayal. The controversial Andy Warhol, whose put-on of the media is expensively serious, perhaps made the only realistic film in history, an eight-hour shot of the Empire State Building during which a seagull flew across the screen once; the only action was supplied by the passage of the sun. Even here, his choice of the Empire State Building rather than the Chrysler or Woolworth buildings indicates a level of selectivity which removes the film from the purely happenstance or real cinéma vérité. Film is man-made; it is not natural.

FILM CONTROLS

Film was the first of the mass media to catch the public's attention in moral terms. The lax lives of the major stars in Hollywood's heyday, heavily fanned by publicity, kept focusing attention on licentiousness. During the thirties, Hollywood's constant pressing against the outer boundaries of nudity and sexual themes aroused PTAs, clergymen, and parents across the nation. For their own protection, the Motion Pictures Producers and Distributors of America, an industry association, was formed. It drew up its own loose production code, the principal purpose of which was to try to assure that evil met its just desserts, and Will H. Hays was appointed czar over the industry. Only pictures in which good triumphed could receive the association's seal of approval, which theoretically permitted them to be shown in the nation's movie houses.

The system did not work well. The code was too loose, inviting experimentation. Many theaters did not abide by the code, particularly drive-ins, and these naturally attracted more than their share of the curious. As time wore on, some producers purposefully flaunted the code, counting on prurient interest to attract audiences.

However, the code was generally adequate for films of the thirties and forties; it broke down completely after smaller, independent producers began exploring new themes and a considerable number of foreign films began to attract their own following. These films were made to different specifications from those of Hollywood, and the admonitions of the code did not apply. Often evil triumphed.

Electromedia

Recently, therefore, a new rating system was adopted, that of G, PG, R, and X. This system places the burden more on the theater owner than anyone else, many of whom are reluctant to enforce the provisions because of their obvious effect on the box office; in the case of the drive-ins, it is almost impossible to enforce anyway. Finally, many producers deliberately seek an X rating because of its patent appeal; people love sex and violence and will seek them out on the screen.

All the moral indignation that has recently been unleashed on television was at one time directed at the movies. Now that television has become the preeminent mass medium, less concern is expressed about the cinema. The smaller, younger, more sophisticated audiences do not generate the kind of moral concern that the filmgoers of yesteryear did.

USE OF OTHER MEDIA

Like the book, film, as a self-selective medium on the part of individuals, has had to rely heavily on other media to call attention to itself, utilizing a variety of promotional techniques to publicize specific motion pictures. Lacking the means of public exposure until the goods are bought, both film and books have had to rely on more obstrusive media to reach the public in advance.

Both media take maximum advantage of magazines and newspapers, which devote a certain amount of space to them. In the magazine world there are dozens of publications devoted to film. Newspapers generally have entertainment sections which lean heavily toward the movies, quite naturally since a good deal of their revenue comes from theaters advertising current showings.

CRITICS

Another phenomenon that film shares with books is the role of the critic. The critic is the public's surrogate. He attempts to keep up with film, devoting his life to it, and thus developing both a familiarity and expertise that audiences could never hope to achieve. The public's time is too limited; there is too much competition for it. The critic is a kind of intermedia gatekeeper who uses his opinion in attempting to separate the wheat from the chaff for others and to save them from exposure to the useless and meaningless. Like other media experts, critics have different goals. The critics in the *New Yorker* and *New York* magazine, the *New York Times* and *Los Angeles Times,* and those of many other metropolitan newspapers, make honest efforts to evaluate the social and artistic merits of the various films to which they are exposed. Too often, however, as John Hohenberg points out, film criticism becomes merely an adjunct to the entertainment pages and a boost to advertising.[2] Some critics on smaller papers write reviews in addition to other reporting jobs, and are entirely too prone to accept the publicity handouts and photos flowing from theatrical press agents.

One should not overlook the Academy Awards in a discussion of film evaluation and promotion. One night each year two hours of

2. John Hohenberg, *The News Media: A Journalist Looks at His Profession* (New York: Holt, Rinehart and Winston, 1968).

television prime time is devoted to one of the most universally watched and extravagantly produced spectaculars on TV. The cost of the cast of this extravaganza alone would be prohibitive (if they did not appear gratis) when one considers the name stars, directors, composers, authors, and artists who are gathered by the hundreds to participate. While the Academy Awards may have begun as an effort to honor the artistic performances of the movie colony, with the advent of television it has become a promotional tool for old movies. It is an attempt to use television and the massive audiences it commands to publicize films which, by and large, have run their life course during the last year and to inject new life into them. An Academy Award in a major category or even significant nominations for the award can start a film back on the circuits again at first-run prices, often playing to far larger audiences than it did the first time around. The 1973 Best Picture Award went to *Cabaret,* which played to two and three times its original audiences on its "academy circuit." An Academy Award is not a guarantee of second-time success, but exposure of the film industry to 50 or 60 million people is almost bound to have some salutary effect on its wares. "The Academy Awards" is a two-hour commercial whose purpose has become so distorted from the original that it is now considered camp not to be present for an award, or even not to accept it if given.

OTHER FILM TYPES

Attention thus far has been concentrated on commercial film-making, which is the entertaining and glamorous side of the medium. However, as in all media, there is a wide range to film. There are cartoons, the ultimate in fantasy, which are often used as fillers but occasionally developed to full-length movies, particularly by Walt Disney, who saw the childhood nostalgia of America's adults. There are also hard-core pornographic films, produced and marketed through an underground circuit, but these are the fringes of the film entertainment function.

Not to be forgotten are the informational and persuasive functions of film. Typically, films of these functions will play to smaller audiences than the entertainment films, but in the aggregate they far outnumber commercial films. There are about 15,000 informational and persuasive films produced each year for governmental, industrial, religious, charitable, political, labor, agricultural, educational, cultural, fund-raising, and community organizations such as chambers of commerce and visitor's bureaus. Together these films comprise well over a billion-dollar-a-year industry. In recent years many of these productions have used highly imaginative multi-media, wide-screen, and stereophonic effects to highlight their purpose and lend drama to the prosaic business of selling. Combinations of slides and film and still photos in rapid flashes, the use of colored lights, and multiple projectors have almost created a new industrial art form.

By and large, most such promotional films are shot in

16-millimeter, which is far cheaper and more portable than the 35-millimeter used in commercial theaters. They are generally shot in color with narration dubbed over, which is less expensive than "sound-on-film." A rule of thumb for budgeting such promotional films is a minimum of $1,500 per running minute, with a great many running to $100,000 and some as much as $500,000.

PROPAGANDA AND EDUCATION

Recognizing the universal quality of film, the United States Information Agency (USIA) has made a number of films interpreting American life and values for showing abroad. The USIA's efforts have been hampered somewhat by the fact that these films run in competition with and are far outnumbered by Hollywood movies which show a different side of America. Thus, a credibility gap is established in the same medium. Nor do the USIA films, no matter how well intentioned, operate in a vacuum. Other exposures—to American tourists of the Ugly American type, and to United States advertising and products, such as worldwide Coca-Cola—create a confusion of American values difficult to understand.

The USIA is essentially a propaganda agency in the broadest sense of the term, and is restricted by Congress from domestic distribution of its materials, including film. One film, *Years of Lightning, Day of Drums,* a masterfully produced history of the thousand-day administration of John F. Kennedy to be shown to his worldwide admirers, required an act of Congress to permit United States exhibition.

An increasing number of educational films are being made for use in the classroom, and new educational techniques are being developed making heavier use of video materials, including both film and television. This is an interesting innovation that may considerably modify the educational system, but it is still too early to make any substantive judgments. The use of video materials may be one way to keep up with the acceleration of technological change, and with the visual orientation of the young. As this happens, of course, print will be de-emphasized and the entire structure of education will change.

The foregoing uses of film, instructional, persuasive, and educational, are all based on its unparalleled advantages as a medium. Complete control over emphasis, continuity, and effect—the use of special effects for dramatic purpose, the genius of editing, the ability to incorporate sound and music—are all designed for maximum purposeful impact on the audience. They tell a special story vividly, commanding attention. Further, they play to a captive audience, and generally under ideal conditions. Theaters are designed to minimize outside interference—channel noise—and to concentrate all attention on the screen. Films have a pleasurable connotation; instructional or not, they are regarded as play.[3] Add to this the element of suspension of disbelief, and audiences become preconditioned to accept whatever message the screen offers them.

3. William Stephenson, *The Play Theory of Mass Communications* (Chicago: University of Chicago Press, 1967).

A good many of these noncommercial films, particularly those produced by industry and government, are of a public-service nature and are provided to schools and colleges throughout the nation free of charge for use in classroom instruction. The automotive industry has been a leader in the production of films on driving safety, and the petroleum industry has furnished a considerable number of historical site films for education. The Bell System in some areas provides complete instruction in communications with appropriate films. There are about 2,500 film libraries in the nation where such noncommercial films may be rented, and the H. W. Wilson Educational Film Guide lists 20,000 films which can be borrowed.

NEWSREELS

The information function in films started early with the filming of President McKinley's inauguration in 1897. As the film industry grew, newsreels became standard fare in the nation's movie houses. Produced weekly by such specialists as Pathé News, they were really a sort of minimagazine on celluloid, concentrating as much on features as they did on hard news. Along with animated cartoons and live organ music, they provided a varied bill of fare in the movie houses of the twenties and early thirties. Like the picture magazines, they also added a visual ingredient to the oral world of radio, the nation's principal mass medium. In many of the larger cities, minitheaters exclusively showing newsreels found a ready market. Television did away with newsreels; coverage was easier and better done on the evening and late news and could be handled daily instead of being almost a week old.

Related to the newsreel is the documentary, a film feature exploring in depth some aspect of society or of the natural world. *Nanook of the North,* a natural history of an Eskimo family, was one such documentary produced back in the silent film days. Since then documentaries have consistently improved, focusing dramatic attention on some of the major areas of American life. But they, too, yielded to television, or rather were absorbed by it, and such recent classics as CBS' "The Selling of the Pentagon," and "Poverty in America" are the direct lineal descendants of the film documentary.

Despite the impact of television, or perhaps because of it, there is a current renaissance of interest in film. More and more colleges and universities are offering courses in filmmaking, and many are establishing departments. As a mode of expression, film is unequalled and this seems a part of the current interest trend spearheaded by youth. Further, the current emphasis on artistic merit, as opposed to commercial considerations, particularly lends filmmaking to exploration. It is a freer medium now, more personal and less controlled by purely economic dictates.

SUMMARY

Through its antecedents, graphics and the drama, film stretches back along the media continuum to prehistory. It represents the first of the electric mass media which are revolutionizing mass communications and placing new emphasis on the audiovisual. Early in its ca-

Electromedia

reer, film took two paths: one concentrating on the informational and persuasive, the other on the commercial path of entertainment.

Following the technological development of the electric light, roll film and sprocket feed, the stage was set for the first halting one-reelers around the turn of the century. The first theaters were storefronts in the major East Coast cities, where droves of immigrants, uneducated and illiterate, flocked for their only available entertainment in an alien land. Thus film's ability to transcend language barriers was effectively noted early in its development. The storefronts yielded to the nickelodeons, which in turn yielded to the big movie palaces of the 1920s and 1930s. Hollywood turned its hand toward keeping a steady supply of films flowing to the big theaters. In this period the film industry was organized vertically, including the production, distribution, and exhibition of films. Major studios owned their own theaters, and distribution was the key to the industry. Block booking was a device wherein independent theaters were required to accept numerous "B" movies in order to get the big pictures. Often films were ordered sight unseen on the basis of story line, stars, director, and budget.

During this period the industry did everything in its power to treat film as a truly mass medium, catering to the lowest common denominator of appeal, sacrificing all artistic considerations to economic discipline. Hollywood was characterized by the star system, lavish promotion and publicity, and huge budgets for formula pictures; all were attempts to minimize the risk inherent in filmmaking. Films dealt in fantasies and dreams and technical perfection. Sound came to the silent screen in 1927 and color in 1935. The wide screen, stereophonic sound, and three-dimensional viewing were postwar innovations designed to compete with television.

Although television was the principal villain in bursting Hollywood's bubble, the movie city was already in trouble as a result of the 1946 consent decree wherein the industry agreed to divest itself of its theaters. This put the finishing touches on block booking and made the independent exhibitors far more selective in the films they ordered.

Within a decade television cut film's audiences in half. After initially fighting television, the film industry joined it, selling old movies to television at a considerable profit, and later lending their facilities to the production of television serials. Finally came the television movie specially designed for the medium in terms of emphasis and timing for commercials. Another branch of the film industry attempted to compete with television by exploring permissive themes that television's family audiences wouldn't tolerate. Independent producers took to making lower cost films abroad, and came under the influence of some of the foreign directors who had been experimenting with new, imaginative uses of the medium.

On the one hand television freed film from its reliance on the lcd; on the other hand, television further imprisoned another branch of filmmaking in requiring it to crank out formula episodes in huge numbers to satisfy the prime-time craving of massive audiences. More people could see a television film in a single night than would see it in its lifetime without television.

The new, smaller film audiences were younger, better educated, more sophisticated, and more demanding than their forebears. Smaller audiences required smaller theaters, and the big palaces disappeared, except for Radio City Music Hall in New York, an anachronistic memoir of the golden age of Hollywood. New theaters are concentrated today in shopping centers, close to the affluent suburbs that supply the majority of their patrons. Minitheaters often have multiple auditoriums where a single operator can keep three or four different films showing simultaneously, offering thereby a far greater diversity than the week-long run in a downtown house.

Film is a tangible, a consumer product. As such, it became the first communications export, vastly extending America's influence abroad—for better or for worse. The United States' concentration on production flooded the world market, and a good deal of the impression of America that foreign persons have come from the fantasy of Hollywood films.

Film traveled both ways across the oceans. Italy's neorealism, France's existentialist influence, Sweden's dramatic metaphor, and Japan's incredible technical artistry all found their way into American theaters, exposing audiences to a far greater range of film offerings than they had previously enjoyed.

Film is an unreal medium based on an optical illusion. It requires a suspension of disbelief in the acceptance of its material; this phenomenon has, of course, lent itself particularly to the use of fantasy. It has also made film an unsurpassed propaganda medium since the producer has complete control over selection of material, continuity, and emphasis, as well as dramatic effect.

A considerable portion of the film industry is devoted to concentrating on the informational and persuasive functions of media. During the twenties and thirties newsreels supplied a visual quality to the events of the world and ran as a regular part of every theater's programming. There were even newsreel speciality theaters.

The documentary is another aspect of informational films. The USIA, a federal propaganda agency dedicated to selling America abroad, deals extensively in documentaries on American life and values. The USIA, however, does not operate in a vacuum, and abroad its documentaries run in direct competition to the Hollywood product, creating a certain confusion among those who view both.

At least 15,000 private films are made annually by industrial, educational, governmental, religious, agricultural, labor, and commercial interests for specific audiences and purposes. There is actually no inventory of these films; their total number is unknown, but their net effect is enormous.

Such private films may be regarded as the textbook division of film, while commercial films are analogous to trade books. The similarities of film and the book are indeed striking. Both being self-selective mass media, they rely heavily on the other, more obtrusive media to call attention to themselves. Promotion and advertising are a part of their makeup. So is the role of the critic, a public surrogate who acts as gatekeeper of their offerings for the public, recommending items off the vast menu of both for audience consumption.

13 RADIO AND RECORDINGS

**RADIO:
CONSTANT
COMPANION**

Nearly 6,500 radio stations exist in the United States today, including both AM and FM. There are over 300 million radio sets in homes, cars, pockets, and purses—three sets for every two people, men, women, and children. Obviously, such a medium is big business; today it is bigger than ever in terms of programs, listeners, and dollars. But strangely enough, radio is a supplemental medium in one of the peculiar paradoxes of mass communications; furthermore, it is a necessary adjunct to the record industry.

It wasn't always thus. There was a time during the 1930s and 1940s when radio was America's prime mass medium; it was a time when most people got a good deal of their news and most of their entertainment from radio. Ironically, there were fewer stations and fewer sets and fewer listeners then than there are now. Although fewer in number, they were all concentrated; radio was a national medium. Today, by and large, radio is a specialized or local medium, or both.

It was radio which set the stage for the television behemoth. Radio developed over-the-air advertising, and fought the successful battle for the commercial base of broadcasting. Radio discovered networking, and established major networks to serve local stations with a quality of programming that none could afford by itself. Radio begat the Federal Communications Commission and the various doctrines of fairness and public interest, convenience, and necessity. Radio developed the audience and discovered prime time. Radio pioneered ratings as a feedback device. Radio adopted the star system from the movies and developed its own personalities. Radio discovered the formula of 90 percent entertainment and commercials and 10 percent information that has carried over into all of United States broadcasting.

On nearly every front, radio paved the way for television and then, in its moment of glory, turned broadcasting over to television and stepped back into the crowd. Radio was hard-hit for a while under television's more dynamic impact, but recovered and went on to a healthier life in the aggregate than it had ever known as the nation's prime mass medium.

Radio developed new prime times in the driving hours; it became portable—a constant companion; it served specialist interests. It developed a demography of its own and began to discover automation and cheaper ways of broadcasting, even as television grew more expensive. And radio became the right arm of the record industry, the aural means of marketing aural products—records, then albums, then tapes.

THE GENESIS OF RADIO

Samuel Morse in 1844 opened the door for a communications revolution with the successful operation of the telegraph, opening up the nation to a rapid exchange of information of all kinds. In 1866 the first transatlantic cable further opened up the world. Ten years later, Alexander Graham Bell invented the telephone, which not only further accelerated information exchange, but also laid the groundwork for a wired nation. Bell's invention further proved the possibility of voice transmission, and so opened the door for radio.

In 1895 Guglielmo Marconi perfected wireless, over-the-air transmission of telegraph code for a mile, and then in 1901 was successful in transmitting across the Atlantic, freeing information exchange from the physical dependence on wires. Five years later a Bell system engineer, Lee De Forest, invented the vacuum tube, which made voice transmission possible and, married to Marconi's wireless, was to form the genesis of radio. The potential for radio as an entertainment medium was apparent four years later when De Forest triumphantly broadcast the voice of the immortal Enrico Caruso from the stage of the Metropolitan Opera House in New York.

Radio was slow in coming, however, and it was not until 1916 that the first broadcast took place. Under the sponsorship of the New York *American* newspaper, De Forest broadcast the results of the tight Wilson-Hughes election in 1916. Ironically, radio's first newscast was in error: "Charles Evans Hughes will be the next president of the United States."

Broadcasting was delayed by World War I, much as television was to be delayed later by the second world war; it was not until 1919 that radio got off the ground.

America's organizational genius applied itself readily to radio. Profit was the principal motive, and in 1919 the only commercial profit that radio could show was in the sale of radio sets. In that year General Electric, Westinghouse, and American Telephone and Telegraph pooled their various patent rights for both broadcasting equipment and receiving hardware and formed the Radio Corporation of America (RCA). David Sarnoff was its first president, as well as president of its subsequent broadcasting subsidiary, the National Broadcasting Company (NBC). The philosophy of the time was to develop programming as an attraction to promote the sale of radio sets. The early radio tycoons apparently took a chapter from the story of film, for the purposes of NBC were originally similar to those of the Motion Picture Patents Company, which sought to control the hardware rather than the software of the industry. In 1919 radio was visualized as an entertainment and information medium; advertising had not yet been thought of.

NEWS AND RADIO ADVERTISING

By 1920, following the earlier lead of the New York *American,* the *Detroit News* began the first regular newscasts. A year later its station, WWJ, became the first commercial station. Radio's superiority as a news medium is indicated by the fact that only seven years later (1927) nearly fifty newspapers owned radio stations, and nearly one hundred others were offering newscasts over commercial stations. By that time the press had discovered that not only did radio stimulate the sales of newspapers by piquing the public interest in current events, but that radio advertising revenues were a natural adjunct to their own advertising lineage. The ability to offer advertising in two media was commercially attractive to both the newspapers and the advertisers. There was apparently a supplementary character to radio even in 1927.

Lee De Forest made radio history again by broadcasting the 1920 election returns of the Harding-Cox presidential race over his Pittsburgh station, KDKA. The impact of his broadcast was so great that the public flocked to buy primitive crystal receivers, and applicants for broadcasting licenses under the Radio Act of 1912 reached epidemic proportions. There were over five hundred radio stations broadcasting by 1924, and over 3 million receivers in operation. It is estimated that a record 10 million people heard the returns of Calvin Coolidge's election in 1924.

Department stores were also among the first owners of radio stations. They recognized the advertising advantage of radio, and the fact that they could promote their goods to a growing public at considerably less cost than by relying on newspapers. Thus, the commercial flavor of broadcasting was introduced early.

Advertising and networking are inseparable. Eveready Batteries sponsored the "Eveready Hour" in 1924 over a network of twelve stations linked together by telephone lines. This leasing of phone lines was the principal interest of AT&T in the RCA consortium. A year later, by 1925, AT&T had linked together twenty-six stations stretching as far west as Kansas City from its own master station, WEAF, in New York. The thought of reaching an ever-growing number of listeners in population centers across the nation proved irresistible to national advertisers, and the character of radio became no longer experimental but highly organized. Catchy jingles were developed as an audio device to retain product acquaintance. Radio began to develop its own stars and its own drama; names and serials were guaranteed to attract listeners night after night, week after week.

THE NETWORKS BEGIN

Also in 1925 RCA (now including only Westinghouse and General Electric) set up its own flagship station, WJZ, in New York.

The concept of networking was perfected in the following year, 1926, when AT&T sold WEAF to RCA for $1 million, an unheard of sum in the twenties. AT&T was getting out of the broadcasting business (it had never been in the hardware business), and saw its future in leasing lines to the broadcasters for network purposes. RCA then established WJZ as flagship of NBC's Blue network, and set up the newly acquired WEAF as the key station in the Red network.

A year later, the Columbia Broadcasting System (CBS) was established by the Columbia Phonograph Record Company, indicating even then the close relationship between radio, the music industry, and the record business. In that year also NBC established the first coast-to-coast programming. At this time there were over seven hundred radio stations in the country.

So many stations operating more or less on their own meant a good deal of conflict among a limited number of broadcasting frequencies on the band. Some stations found it necessary to jump all over the band to find a temporarily unoccupied frequency on which to broadcast. The fact that in the large cities, where the greatest audience was located, no one could receive any station clearly because of mutual interference, and the additional fact that audiences could not rely on receiving the same station on the same frequency all the time, meant a certain instability to radio as a mass medium. As a result of this, the radio industry itself petitioned the federal government for regulation.

CONTROLS NEEDED

Thus, under duress, the Radio Act of 1927 took shape, creating the Federal Radio Commission, which was the precursor to the Federal Communications Commission (FCC). A public controversy raged over radio in 1927. Some, including then Secretary of Commerce Herbert Hoover, held that the airwaves belonged to the people, that they were a public property and should not be turned over to private interests for exploitation. This was the public policy pattern for radio followed in most of the rest of the world.

Others, including broadcasters, their advertisers, and many of the newspapers that owned stations, maintained that radio was, in fact, a part of the press, and that under the First Amendment its freedom was guaranteed. This precluded government control, they pointed out. They also noted that private enterprise could supply superior programming at no cost to the consumer, whereas government ownership or control meant additional taxes in one form or another. Further, the precedent of free enterprise and advertising support of the mass media was already firmly established through the press. Thus, under the Radio Act of 1927, the commercial nature of radio and of all subsequent broadcasting was assured.

However, the right to regulate includes the right to determine who will do business, and for every license granted to a broadcaster, another was denied. The criteria of the Federal Radio Commission for the granting of licenses were: (a) fiscal responsibility on the part of the applicant; (b) experience; (c) good character and community stature; and (d) operation in the public interest, convenience, and necessity. This latter was a sop to the advocates of public broadcasting, whereby the FRC assured that the public nature of broadcasting was to be maintained. Penalty for not operating in the public interest, convenience, and necessity was a fine or revocation of license. However, the FRC primarily viewed radio as a local medium, and desired that stations succeed in that a succession of station failures and license turnovers was not in the public interest.

It is strange that with three networks already formed, one of them reaching from coast to coast, that the Radio Act of 1927 did not take networking into consideration. The FRC's only control was over the individual local stations. It had no authority, except indirectly, over the networks, which even then controlled the majority of programming and advertising. As a matter of fact, the FRC strengthened networking. First, it eliminated one hundred stations, leaving a total of six hundred. Second, it established fifty "clear channel" stations with sufficient power to reach into the rural areas that had no stations of their own. Rather quickly these clear channel stations fell into network hands.

NETWORKING

The principle of networking has carried over to television; so has FCC regulation. Networks own few stations outright. Presently, the number of these stations is limited by the FCC, and generally they are located in major population centers.

A large number of stations were affiliated with the networks, meaning that they carried network programming in return for a fee from the network. This benefited the individual affiliates, as they were provided programming, stars, and newscasts that they couldn't possibly afford on their own. These assets attracted large local audiences, which in turn permitted stations to charge more for their purely local advertising. A license and network affiliation were a lucrative opportunity. By 1934 CBS had ninety-seven affiliates, NBC Red had sixty-five, and NBC Blue had sixty-two. About 40 percent of the stations broadcasting were network affiliates; the rest were independents. The role of an independent competing against the superior programming of the network affiliates was a difficult one. Generally, independents concentrated on the local scene, attracting local advertisers on the basis of lower rates, and offering healthy doses of pure-

Electromedia

ly local news, which the network affiliates, with their national orientation, could not handle. In a sense it was the independents that best carried out the admonition of the FCC to operate in the public interest, convenience, and necessity in their own communities.

THE DEPRESSION

Radio reached maturity by 1929, just in time for the depression. This in itself was a fortuitous act of fate. Had radio been any weaker as a mass medium, it surely would have succumbed to newspaper pressure. As it was, the depression fostered radio's growth. Radio was cheap entertainment, advertising-supported, during a period in which disposable income in the United States was at an all-time low.

As early as 1922 the newspaper-dominated Associated Press wire service refused to serve radio stations with news. Radio stations threatened to turn to the United Press (UP) and International News Service (INS). As many of the station owners were newspapers that already subscribed to Associated Press, this argument had some weight.

However, when the depression came, competition between radio stations and newspapers grew more intense. Newspaper advertising lineage was dwindling, and radio was absorbing most of it. Furthermore, radio had gone heavily into the news business. These were two areas of direct competition that newspapers in duress could not tolerate. In 1930 KMPC in Los Angeles, an independent, had ten reporters on the newsbeat.

The battle reached a climax with the 1932 election results. The contest between incumbent Republican Herbert Hoover—the depression president—and Democrat Franklin Delano Roosevelt attracted wide attention, and a good part of America learned of the results over the air. The American Newspaper Publishers Association (ANPA) had had enough, and all news services stopped furnishing news to radio in 1933. Of course, this simply spurred the networks to organize their own news bureaus, which they did extensively, with regional bureaus and overseas correspondents. Ironically, this strengthened the networks' position in a news-hungry America and probably would not have come about were it not for the ANPA's ill-advised pressure. Further, the loss of revenue to the wire services, particularly in the depression, was damaging. In 1934 a compromise organized the Press-Radio Bureau, which presented two five-minute daily broadcasts of wire service news on the radio networks. It further provided bulletins on significant events. However, this system was inadequate for everyone involved, and in 1935 both UP and INS began selling full service to the radios again, while the more reactionary and press-controlled AP held out until 1940.

FIRESIDE CHATS

The first extensive use of radio for political purposes took place in 1928, when Herbert Hoover and Alfred E. Smith spent a million dollars in radio advertising, demonstrating the effectiveness of broadcast advertising. The campaign of 1932 followed suit.

Radio and Recordings

Franklin Roosevelt was first to clearly see the potential of broadcast. He took to the airwaves with his fireside chats throughout his four administrations to sooth America in troubled times. He explained the New Deal, advocated administration policies, and reassured the voters. He recognized that government was voiceless, that it was reliant upon the press to interpret its actions. Through radio he could take his case directly to the American people, quietly entering their homes as a guest in the evening, when the atmosphere was relaxed. His was an unbeatable technique, and one that he parlayed into an unprecedented four terms in office.

President Franklin D. Roosevelt in a fireside chat.

UPI

That radio was a news and music medium had been established at the outset; the first two broadcasts had been the Metropolitan Opera and the Wilson-Hughes returns. To these characteristics in the thirties and forties, partially under depression pressure, were added broadcasting's capacity as a persuasive and entertainment medium.

WHAT THE THIRTIES WERE LIKE

Prime time, the evening hours when America is generally at home, developed under radio. This is the most expensive commercial time, reaching the largest audiences. A pattern of general prime-time entertainment appeal catering to the lcd developed in the thirties with a packet of comedy shows, thrillers, westerns, situation comedies, and music. The 1930s was a musical era, the time of the big

Electromedia

bands: Benny Goodman, the Dorsey Brothers, and Guy Lombardo. All of these bands appeared periodically on radio specials; their records were daytime stock. One of the most popular of the prime-time programs of the thirties was "Fred Waring and His Pennsylvanians," a weekly musical potpourri program that included baseball scores in season. "The Bell Telephone Hour" brought symphonic music into America's homes; the networks and some of the major stations had their own house orchestras where musicians of considerable stature played (Ferde Grofe, composer of the Grand Canyon Suite, was one). Together, radio stations offered a spectrum of classical, pop, and "swing" for America.

Amos 'n' Andy, a blackface comedy team, perpetuated the Negro stereotype in the early evening. Jack Benny and Rochester for Lucky Strike and Fred Allen with "Allen's Alley" on Sunday evenings were the comedy stars of the era. Benny was among the first to inject humor into advertising. The "Richfield Reporter" brought up-to-date news of the day into American homes nightly in the late news. Burns and Allen had the first continuing situation comedy series. "The Whistler" was the first of the Gothic thrillers to send terror up and down spines in darkened rooms each Sunday evening.

Then there were game shows—Major Bowes' weekly questionnaire, and the "$64 Dollar Question," where the maximum a contestant could win was $64, arrived at in a geometric progression (a sign of depression values and subsequent inflation). There were westerns, of which "The Lone Ranger" was the model, with his superhorse Silver and his Indian sidekick, Tonto.

During the daytime hours, radio discovered that there was a demography present, that the audiences were no longer mass and inclusive, but at different hours were composed of different kinds of people. The late afternoon was kiddie time, served with a variety of breakfast food sponsors. The early mornings were news times for arising breadwinners, upstaging the morning newspaper. The bulk of the day radio found itself appealing to a largely female audience of housewives, and the soap opera was born—so named because it was almost universally sponsored by soap manufacturers such as Lever Brothers, Proctor and Gamble, Colgate, and Palmolive-Peet. Soap operas were escape, pure escape, offering either poignant sorrow that Mrs. America could sob over, or a kind of saccharine wisdom of sweetness-and-light, or both. Of this genre, "One Man's Family" was the all-time leader.

COMMERCIAL STRUCTURE OF RADIO

The networks vied with one another in competing time slots, each trying to match a popular program with something more competitively attractive. Recognizing the demography and differing size of audiences, time classifications were developed: AA for prime time, 7:00-11:00 P.M.; A time for the hours adjacent to prime; B for most of the rest of the day; and C for the wee, small hours, as there were some stations that broadcast all night for insomniacs and swingers.

Left to right: Jim Jordan and Marian Jordan (UPI); Lum 'n' Abner, 1942 (Chester Lauck and Norris Goff) (The Bettmann Archive); Fred Allen with Stoopnagle and Budd, 1938 (The Bettmann Archive); Amos 'n' Andy (The Bettmann Archive); Dennis Day and Jack Benny (UPI); Fibber McGee and Molly (The Bettmann Archive); Veronica Mimosa and Major Bowes (UPI); Freeman F. Gosden and Charles J. Correll, Amos 'n' Andy (UPI); Mary Livingstone, Jack Benny, Fred Allen, and Portland Hoffa (UPI).

Of course, AA time cost the most for sponsorship and commercials, and C was the least expensive. These classifications were based on presumed audience size, and a rate card developed based on costs per thousand (cpm)—that is, cost to the advertiser per thousand listeners. A measuring device was needed to accurately determine, and prove, this presumed audience size, so an embryonic form of rating was developed based largely on telephone polls. Public opinion polling was in its infancy and the yardstick was crude, but telephone polling was the first form of feedback, born of commercial necessity and father to the ratings.

Originally, advertising on radio had taken the form of sponsorships wherein a national commercial advertiser would sponsor and often pay for a program which would carry his name—"The Eveready Hour," for example—and which would permit him to insert commercials during the body of the program. As hour-long time slots became more expensive, half-hour sponsorships developed. Subsequently, some of the independent stations discovered that their survival lay in catering to the local community, and that while few local merchants could afford a sponsorship, they could afford a minute or two, the price of which, added up, netted the same amount, if not more, of advertising revenue. Network affiliates followed suit, selling advertising during their station breaks, or the minute or so they were permitted to identify themselves each hour. Thus, the commercial came into being, which, by and large, has supplanted sponsorship.

THE DEVELOPMENT OF RADIO NEWS

While entertainment and commercial functions were perfecting themselves, the news or information function was slow in developing. Throughout the thirties and later, Walter Winchell bridged the news-entertainment gap with a breezy, nightly report of gossip, opinion, and innuendo plus a smattering of headlines to become the first radio columnist. Under the impetus of the wire services' radio ban, the networks began their own news-gathering facilities at home and abroad. At home their affiliated stations provided a natural national network of sources akin to the wire service bureaus and member papers. Abroad, where no such facility existed, they were more or less on their own. The forceful impact of dramatic international events on radio was demonstrated by Edward VIII's poignant worldwide radio announcement abdicating the throne of England for Wallis Simpson, a divorced American commoner. In 1937 CBS sent H. V. Kaltenborn, Edward R. Murrow, and William L. Shirer overseas. Meanwhile, the Spanish Civil War provided a testing ground not only for Nazi weapons, but also for radio reporting techniques against the inevitably approaching holocaust of World War II. Kaltenborn broadcast live from battlefields in Spain.

Hitler marched into Austria and Czechoslovakia in 1938, providing the opportunity for the first multiple remote broadcast in history as CBS correspondents in Vienna, Berlin, London, Paris, and Rome gave their views of the anschluss. Later that year, during the three-week Munich Crisis which culminated in Neville Chamberlain's misbegotten "peace in our time," as many as fourteen radio reporters aired their views live over CBS to anxious audiences in America, while H. V. Kaltenborn in New York sought to coordinate and interpret their reports, becoming history's first anchorman.

The impact of World War II on radio news was enormous. The war itself engendered interest far beyond the usual human curiosity. Here was real drama written on an international stage with real actors and real stakes, rendered the more piquant because survival was at stake. Radio brought the war home, and responding to public demand, upped its coverage. For example, NBC broadcasted a bare half-hour or so of news each day in 1937; by the war's end in 1945, a quarter of its daily broadcast was news. Radio provided an international forum for the unmatched rhetoric of Winston Churchill, whose immortal speeches held a badly battered Britain together by the sheer power of words. He also consolidated the Allied cause in a time of doubt. With radio reporters America witnessed the invasion of Poland, the surrender of France. Edward R. Murrow broadcast the battle of Britain from London rooftops amid falling bombs, which provided a realistic backdrop for his remarks. He was later to ride a bomber over Berlin, where the antiaircraft flak performed the same function. Front-line radio reporters accompanied the troops. Most of the world learned of Pearl Harbor in December 1941 by radio, and a record audience a day later listened soberly to Franklin Roosevelt's measured words to Congress for a declared war on the Axis powers. News developed its own star system, and the commentator became a major figure, interpreting the events of the world into bite-sized pieces for America to consume.

BROADCAST'S EFFECT ON THE PRESS

Unquestionably, radio's instant ability to bring major events in dramatic form directly into the home had an effect on newspapers. Gradually, although they still placed a high premium on the scoop, newspapers recognized that they could not compete with radio's speed. The result was an ever-so-slow movement toward interpretive journalism. Reporters found that the additional production time that had penalized them in their ability to be first with the news was also a blessing in disguise in that it permitted them to develop stories in greater detail than was possible with radio, and to place events in a perspective to which the public could relate. Slowly, they moved away from their almost slavish dedication to complete objectivity, regardless of meaning, and paid more attention to the background of events. More space was devoted to opinion, and columnists, not unknown in the past, became more prevalent and often represented differing points of view. More attention was also devoted to feature material, an area in which radio could not compete. Newspapers began to abandon the fragmentary bulletin style for more complete and rounded writing; the extra became a has-been.

Electromedia

Meanwhile, by the eve of World War II, even the newspaper-dominated Associated Press began to provide news wires to the radio networks and individual stations. In fact, all wire services began an exclusive radio wire for their broadcast clients that was written in radio style, permitting newscasters and announcers to rip the wires directly off the teletypes and read them on the air. Journalese and radio news styles differed considerably. Radio language was, and is, punchy, brief, and "now," with emphasis on immediacy. The fact that radio newscasters no longer had to rewrite newspaper copy for the air further increased immediacy; the order of "rip 'n' read" was established, whereby announcers would simply rip a couple of yards of bulletins off the wire on their way to the microphone and read it on the air sight unseen.

COSTS OF BROADCASTING

As radio grew it became increasingly expensive. Studio staffs on major stations included news bureaus with up to a dozen reporters, a full orchestra and musical director, program people, and a corps of engineers to balance sound and splice in both network programming and commercials, as well as people to tend the transmitters. Advertising sales forces and continuity folk to develop the daily log added to costs. Radio's hardware was far from cheap as transmitters became ever more powerful, reaching hundreds of miles, and remote facilities traveled to on-site broadcasts. Top announcers and star commentators drew huge salaries, and subscription to the radio wires added to costs. All this had to be paid for by commercials, and consequently split-second timing was the earmark of radio's peak when it was the preeminent mass communications network in America. As its technology improved and it reached ever-larger audiences, its commercial rates went up and up until none but the wealthiest advertisers could afford network exposure. This limited radio's potential to national advertisers of basic consumer goods, as they were the only ones who could use such large, undifferentiated audiences. More local advertisers increasingly found the newspaper their best buy, reaching out into entire communities and metropolitan areas, and more specialized products sought advertising in an increasing number of specialized magazines.

FEDERAL COMMUNICATIONS COMMISSION

The FCC had succeeded the FRC under the Communications Act of 1933. Essentially the guidelines were the same, but a larger staff and budget under a reform Democratic president (FDR) permitted the agency to begin to take a closer look at the broadcasting it was supposed to regulate. The necessity of government regulation to allocate frequencies was a departure from the traditional American principle of press freedom, stretching a tightrope for the commission to walk. On the one hand, it was enjoined by Congress from any control over programming or any censorship, except that pertaining to obscenity and profanity. It was, on the other hand, admonished to enforce the principle of operation in the public interest, convenience, and necessity. The device it chose was relicensing, whereby every three years, when a station's license expired, the station must apply to the FCC for another three-year extension and justify this application. The FCC scrutinized each station's log to ascertain if it had, in fact, devoted the proper amount of time to community, charitable, educational, and religious matters, as well as to a proper proportion of news, and that it further had not devoted a disproportionate amount of time to commercials, and none at all to matters profane, obscene, immoral, or seditious. These guidelines were ill-defined, left purposely vague by the FCC, which elected to judge violations only after the fact. Additional safeguards were provided by the fact that any citizen could file a complaint against a station for alleged violations; the station would then have to defend itself.

As there was no FCC requirement concerning in what time slots public service programming took place, the largest proportion was allocated to C time, which included the least audience and thus was least valuable from a commercial standpoint. Consequently, the fewest people were exposed to public service announcements and programming.

NATIONAL ASSOCIATION OF BROADCASTERS

Because of the vagueness of FCC guidelines, networks and individual stations organized the National Association of Broadcasters (NAB) as a self-policing agency to draw up a broadcasting code that, it was hoped, would satisfy FCC requirements. This code specified the number of commercial minutes that could be offered in various time slots, interpreted the kinds of programming and how much would satisfy the public interest admonition, and precluded certain kinds of advertising and programming, including that of liquor. It was a loose code, and there were no enforcement provisions beyond expulsion from the NAB. In essence, the NAB became the spokesman and lobbyist for the industry to match the beefed-up FCC.

Also in the late thirties another association was formed for economic purposes. The American Society of Composers, Artists and Producers (ASCAP) was organized to protect composers and musicians against the pirating of their material during an intensely musical era, and to assure that they would receive royalties from the continued playing of their works over the air.

Eyeing network success, two large independents, WOR in New York and the *Chicago Tribune*'s WGN, organized their own network in 1934, the Mutual Broadcasting System (MBS), but found themselves unable to compete with the solidly entrenched CBS and NBC Red and Blue networks. Subsequently, MBS filed a complaint with the FCC against the networks for restraint of trade. Adjudication of the suit brought about the sale of NBC's Blue network in 1943, which became the American Broadcasting Company in 1945. The suit filed by MBS did not particularly help that fourth-place network, a loose affiliation of weaker stations. Additionally, ABC, divorced from NBC's experience and in direct competition with its parent, also found the sledding tough.

Paramount Pictures later bought ABC in 1953 after the consent decree of the motion-picture industry had forced it to divest itself of its theaters. It was a wise move to diversify interests while still remaining in the mass communications business, and to further exploit the threat of television, which, in 1953, was beginning to make serious inroads into the motion-picture industry's box office. But Paramount's management was oriented toward motion pictures and Hollywood rather than toward broadcasting, and for nearly two decades ABC remained a distinctly third-place network, never really gaining on CBS and NBC, the win and place networks of the television sweepstakes.

ENTER TELEVISION

By the end of World War II, radio had set the stage for television, and America grew accustomed to listening. The principle of public interest had been established and its parameters defined. A strong national trade association had also been established. Advertiser and agency loyalties were developing, and the methods of doing business understood. A rating system had been pioneered. Radio turned over a perfect package to television.

It took television a while to catch up with radio. That it did was largely the result of network influence. The broadcast system was inherited ready-made: major networks rapidly acquired wholly owned stations in major cities across the country, and they found it relatively simple to make affiliate agreements with other licensees. With their wealth and experience, the nets were able to develop national programming far superior to anything a local independent could afford, just as they had in radio. This expansion happened at the expense of their radio interests, which, as far as the networks were concerned, gradually became supplemental and downgraded, often supported out of increasing television profits.

The radio industry was scared; it viewed television as radio with pictures, and the death of radio was predicted. Throughout most of the 1950s this was the prevalent industry attitude.

While radio was inferior to television in dramatic presentation, it had certain inherent strengths. It demanded less attention than television. It could be perceived almost unconsciously while the listener went about other things. It was also far superior to television as a music medium; it offered less distraction. Finally, the radio band of frequencies was much broader than the television band of channels, permitting far greater diversification. This potential was never fully explored while radio was under the domination of a limited number of networks, and while the costs of radio production remained high.

NEW PRIME TIME AND TECHNIQUES

As television gradually took over the evening prime-time hours, radio discovered that it had large audiences all to itself in the early morning as a news-hungry America woke up and dressed. Radio was further assisted in this crucial period (the decade of the fifties) by a number of technological improvements. Miniaturization of parts and certain technical innovations made car radios practical and cheap. Radio found it could extend its prime time to driving hours when America went to work and returned again in the evening. Radio concentrated on a new split prime time from roughly 6:00–9:00 A.M. and again from 3:30–6:00 P.M. In fact, it increased its prime time from four to five and a half hours.

Radio: a new prime time in driving hours.

UPI
Electromedia

Miniaturization was helped by the development of the transistor, which did away with the unwieldy and perishable vacuum tubes, and by printed circuits that reduced both the bulk and assembly expense of complicated wiring. The addition of miniature batteries freed radio from the necessity of a power source and made it fully portable. Radio could take its instantaneousness anywhere that people could go. It became a constant companion and, as its parts became simpler and assembly less complex, it became cheap—almost disposable. It was possible for everyone to have a radio, perhaps several.

Such portability assured that there was an audience regardless of time of day. Radio could be where the people were; it no longer had to wait for them to gather around it. That was television's problem now. Radio became a personal rather than a family medium, which naturally extended both its sales and reach.

Radio received another boost in the final development of FM, or frequency modulation. The FM radio had two characteristics different from AM radio. Its signal, like television's, was a line-of-sight signal, which meant it had a relatively short range because of the earth's curvature. It also had remarkable clarity of tone, which meant that it was ideal for music broadcast. This characteristic was further enhanced by the fact that FM could be adapted to stereophonic sound, adding an orchestral dimension to the previously crude single-source sound of traditional radio.

FM AND MUSIC

The FM radio had been developed originally in 1933 and had begun to broadcast experimentally in 1939. However, it had been delayed by both the depression and the war in its development, and finally was downgraded by the FCC, which sought to encourage VHF television broadcasting. Necessity, they say, is the mother of invention, and under the duress of radio's competition with television, FM perfection rapidly followed.

Not only did FM encourage musical broadcasting, but its short range proved an asset for local community services. Miniaturization simplicity had been paralleled in broadcasting hardware as well as receiver sets. As large antennae and powerful wattage were not needed for local use, broadcasters discovered that they could build and operate FM stations for purely local consumption with minimal investment. FM stations began to pop up in isolated or suburban communities by the early 1960s. They served the same function in broadcast that the weekly or peripheral daily newspaper did in the press. They made it possible to carry a quotient of purely local news that the larger metropolitan stations had neither the time nor the resources to cover. They further permitted the local advertiser an outlet to a purely local audience at a price that he could afford.

Thus, portability, availability to audiences, developing musical clarity, and local emphasis began to develop a new kind of radio based on economical specialization in either music or local news or

Radio and Recordings

both. Radio broadcasters discovered there was a certain demography to musical taste, that youth wanted the new sounds of rock 'n' roll, while their parents provided a market for "pops." Other segments of the population in varying numbers sought opera, classical, country, and folk sounds. In the 1950s a new star appeared on radio—the disc jockey or DJ—who intermixed records with patter and developed a frenetic style of his own.

RECORDS

It was at this point that radio began to become an arm of the recording industry. Record manufacturers found that the new radio provided ready-made exposure for their wares. They found that only after such exposure could they expect to sell records to the music-hungry new generation. They undertook to provide the nation's DJs with records at no cost, reducing the expenses of broadcasting. In many instances they paid popular disc jockeys to air their wares. "Payola" became a household word as many disc jockey stars earned more from their record payments than they did from their broadcasting salaries. There was a pyramiding quality to all this as the record and radio industries grew closer. Weekly surveys revealed the "Top 40" records, which disc jockeys clamored to play because of their assured popularity, and the more they were played, the more likely these records were to make the "Top 40," as exposure led to sales. The "Top 40" in a real sense became musical radio's ratings.

Musical taste changed as Elvis Presley gave way to the Beatles, who in turn yielded to Mick Jagger. Rock 'n' roll became hard rock, and the plaintive sounds of Nashville caught America by surprise as country and western music became very big. A nostalgia boom recaptured some of the big band sounds of the 1930s. Meanwhile, the brittle 78s had yielded to the plastic 45s, which still only played a single tune. These in turn gave way to the 33s or long-playing records (LPs) which, besides offering a certain convenience in playing, represented far greater profit to the record industry. In time the LPs gave way to the group albums, which, of course, represented a much greater profit yet. Thereafter, records were supplemented by magnetic tape in the form of cassettes, and the superiority of magnetic tape became apparent. It provided even greater clarity; there was no needle noise and its grooves did not wear out because it had none. Largely as a result of miniaturization, FM and the recording emphasis, stereophonic high-fidelity equipment became popular, providing another source of advertising revenue to the radio industry.

AUTOMATION

Magnetic tape had another virtue on the broadcasting end of radio in that it obviated the need for a disc jockey to change the platters. Wedded to automated equipment, it greatly reduced the operating cost of broadcasting. An automated station could play all day long, requiring the services only of a single engineer on standby. As FM stations required proportionately little capital and could be operated at minimal expense, the number of stations multiplied rapidly.

Electromedia

The FCC began to pay attention to FM during the 1960s, authorizing stations to broadcast stereo and requiring that FM stations originate broadcasting at least half the time rather than merely carrying the AM programming where both kinds of stations were under single ownership. By 1970 there were over 6,500 radio stations, AM and FM, in the nation. This was well over three times the number of stations broadcasting two decades previously, in 1950, before the impact of television began to be felt.

Music stations began to offer their own "sound" and found their own followings. They fed on the musical revival of the 1960s, the proliferation of groups, the light show phenomenon, and the youth beat. Music became a language of its own, expressing the confusion and frustration of the turbulent sixties, of alienation and the generation gap, of the hippie movement and drug culture. Radio was the medium of a new language whose beat crossed oceans to find converts abroad. Like film, music is international. It requires no language proficiency but speaks with meaning of its own directly to the heart.

SPECIALIZATION

Meanwhile, radio branched out. Not all radio programming was musical. There were purely local community news stations. Network news and major independents continued to serve the least populated areas of the country that newspapers reached only by mail, and where it was not economically feasible for television to reach. (Montana and Idaho still feature the state and national news at 10:00 A.M. just as they did in the thirties.) Some operators found it profitable to broadcast pure news on a thirty- or forty-minute cycle. Others concentrated on sports. Radio offered a menu of audible diversity matched only by the variety of magazines. Under the pressure of television, just as with magazines, radio specialized to smaller, more loyal audiences and in commanding them, commanded advertisers who needed to reach them. Local stations tended to be supported by local merchants. The regional stations carried a great deal of department store and shopping center advertisements. The classical stations advertised hi-fi components, pop stations sold vacation homes, travel tours, and annuities, and country and western stations carried consumer products, while the various rock stations had a high percentage of complexion ointment commercials for the adolescent. Such still holds true today. In a very real sense, under television pressure, radio has become an electric magazine as film emerged as an electric book.

The proof of this specialization seems to lie in ABC radio's successful experiment. In the sixties ABC trailed the other two networks, NBC and CBS, always seeming to come in a poor third. While the two major networks could afford to operate their radio networks out of television profits, profitability at ABC was not that high. Consequently, ABC was forced to reconsider its entire radio network operation. Whereas previously it had affiliation agreements with a single radio station in most of the nation's major markets, it decided to scrap this arrangement in the mid-sixties and go to multiple affiliates. The truth was that ABC's affiliates in almost every instance, as well as those of NBC and CBS, were rated well behind the major independents in market after market. The independents had found the new sound, or they had moved to the tnt format (time, news, and temperature), or to a variety of other highly specialized forms of programming.

Instead of offering a single station in a major market a potpourri of national programming, ABC organized four subnetworks specializing only in news, in sports, or in two kinds of music. It then made affiliation agreements with the principal independents for each of these specialties—in effect, there were four ABC affiliate opportunities instead of one. This plan was a profitable one all around. ABC had outlets for a wide range of national advertising centering around specific audiences, making an easier and more economical package for advertisers of hi-fi equipment, for example, or after-shave. Such a system provided the independents with a broad range of services, concentrated programming, and access to national talent. It increased the size of their audiences and further reduced the costs of their own programming as much of it, if not all, came from ABC. These were smaller audiences, but they were no longer undiversified; they had a character of their own, a measurable demography. The story of the magazines was rewritten for radio.

NEW FORMATS

Radio's search for audiences in recent years has led to new innovations. One of these has been the talk show where a radio personality talks constantly over the telephone to listeners. There's a bit of the "voyeur" in all this, as people expose their inner lives and opinions to listeners, and others call in to the station to disagree and contradict. In an increasingly impersonal world, radio talk shows are an opportunity to reach into someone else's life, if ever so briefly. The success of the talk shows lies in the ability for the public to air an opinion, which is irresistible. There are parameters to this format which are forever being stretched. In New York City one radio station caters to homosexuals; in Long Beach, California, another host has developed a large following by discussing their intimate sex lives with his female callers. There seems to be emerging a pattern of underground radio, and the radio band is broad enough to accommodate it in an era of increasing permissiveness.

Nor should "minority" radio be overlooked. In areas with large ethnic populations, a number of stations do very well broadcasting in foreign languages. Spanish-speaking stations cater to the large Puerto Rican population in New York City; others serve the Mexican populations throughout the great Southwest. In Louisiana some stations still broadcast in French for the Cajuns who have clung to their patois since Evangeline's time; in parts of New Mexico, stations broadcast in Navajo.

Black radio is a relatively new addition. These stations attempt to serve the black areas of most major cities in ethnic terms. Some have met with considerable success and, in so doing, have attracted advertisers anxious to reach blacks, either to sell goods or demonstrate racial concern in a public relations sense.

SUMMARY

In the last quarter century, radio has moved from its preeminent position as America's prime mass medium to a purely supplemental medium in league to a large degree with the record industry. It has done this under the impact of television, for which it pioneered the scope, format, regulations, and techniques of broadcasting and turned them over. In adapting to a changing environment, radio has grown to three times its previous size in the number of stations on the air, to perhaps four times its size in the number of sets in operation, and in the aggregate it has vastly increased its profitability.

In appealing to audience interests, radio has followed the principle of specialization, or fragmentation, demonstrated on the media continuum. It is in a real sense a sort of an electric magazine as film is an electric book.

The genesis of radio began in 1844 with Samuel Morse' telegraph. Marconi's wireless in 1895 freed transmission from lines, and Lee De Forest's vacuum tube in 1906 made voice transmission over the airwaves a reality.

Radio development was delayed by World War I, but by 1920 the new medium had taken hold and was growing. Newspapers and department stores were among the first owners of radio stations, pointing up its information and commercial significance. Advertising sponsorship came in 1924 when "The Eveready Hour" linked twelve stations and established the principle of networking to achieve truly mass audiences from a local medium. Early radio was visualized as a means of selling the hardware, radio sets, and a consortium of General Electric, Westinghouse, and AT&T formed the Radio Corporation of America to develop programming in order to sell more sets. In 1925 AT&T had organized a network of twenty-six stations, while RCA organized another net as NBC. That year, also, AT&T sold out to RCA, and its network became NBC's Blue network. CBS was organized the following year.

By 1927 chaos existed in radio as stations scrambled for frequencies on which to broadcast, jammed one another's signals, and scurried across the band unpredictably. The industry itself sought regulation from the federal government, and the Federal Radio Commission was set up in 1927 to assign frequencies. A controversy at the time raged as to whether radio should be commercially sponsored or publicly owned. A compromise charged the FRC with seeing that radio stations operated in the public interest, convenience, and necessity. The FCC, successor to the FRC, was established by Congress in 1934 and has regulated all broadcasting since. Despite the significance of networks, FCC controls are aimed directly at the individual local station, or licensee; radio and subsequently television were regarded as local rather than national media.

Newspaper ownership of radio stations in the beginning was based on the thought that a smattering of broadcast news whetted America's appetite for more complete versions in the newspapers. However, the onslaught of the Great Depression in 1929 increased competition, and the major wire services dominated by newspapers refused to sell news to radio stations any longer. This forced the networks and some major independents to organize their own news staffs.

The depression fostered radio as a cheap form of entertainment, and the influence of the networks grew. During the thirties the general format of network broadcasting was perfected. The concept of prime time, the evening hours when the largest audiences were at home, was developed. An array of stars headed their own programs; situation comedies, thrillers, news shows, and westerns became a part of American life. On the news scene, the commentator developed as a personality, and gradually spot announcements replaced sponsorship as a more economical and equally effective commercial device.

The wire services had, by this time, restored service to radio, and radio news came of age during World War II. Following World War II, television began to take its toll of radio.

The development of miniaturization in the transistor and the printed circuit, and of battery packs that freed radio from dependence on a power source and made it portable were to have an effect of their own. New prime times during rising and driving hours were developed. When FM came on the scene, its shorter range and higher fidelity made it a natural for purely local stations in smaller communities and for music. At this point, radio began to be an adjunct to the record industry, which discovered it could market its wares over the air. The disc jockey became the new radio hero.

Magnetic tape and automation permitted FM stations to be operated at a minimal cost. The number of radio stations grew to more than 6,500.

Radio began to specialize, to find new audiences for different kinds of music in highly fragmented sections of society; each station became specialized in a "sound," in news or sports, in ethnic minorities or in talk shows. ABC developed a scheme of multiple affiliates in each market, thus taking advantage of this specialization.

14 NETWORK TELEVISION

TV: A WAY OF LIFE

Television has become a way of life for American people. No other society is so technologically advanced, hence so television-dominated. The overwhelming impact of television stems not so much from its numbers as from its exposure. There are well over three times as many radio sets as there are television receivers. There are nearly nine times as many radio broadcasters as television stations. There are three times as many daily newspapers as television broadcasters, and at least six times as many magazines. However, the number of newspaper readers and television viewers daily is approximately equal. Television's massive effect on the nation stems from its concentration and its prolonged exposure.

With about 98 percent of American homes receiving television, TV's penetration approaches total saturation. As the average family watches television some four and a half hours daily and the average watcher spends two and a half hours in front of the tube, the net effect of this medium is massive. Compared to these long periods of exposure, any other medium, or all other media in concert, occupy only a fraction of the daily time spent with television. Such indulgence has to come at the expense of other activities, for human beings, like television itself, are severely time-limited. Further, such massive exposure to essentially entertainment and commercial messages has a companion effect in accelerating the already highly commercial and entertainment-oriented trends of contemporary society. Currently television as the nation's preeminent mass medium reflects the course of a hedonistic and acquisitive society and, in so doing, like the central nervous system it is, confirms the course of that society.

Another factor of exposure is television's concentration. Most television programming, including news and commercials, comes from the three major networks who directly, or indirectly through affiliates, dominate 95 percent of the country's commercial stations. Essentially, Americans have the choice of three programs at any given moment in the broadcasting day. Since the networks are in intense competition and cater to the lowest common denominator as dictated by ratings, this choice is more illusionary than real.

Massive television exposure has had massive effects on its audience during its meteoric rise. It has also had drastic effects upon other media. These other media have their own effect on society; the total picture of cultural change is not entirely a result of television, but is partially generated by the other media as they change course to meet the electronic breeze. Television too, because of its mass, reach, and impact, has inspired the FCC to delve deeper into the regulation of broadcasting with often surprising and sometimes conflicting results.

TELEVISION'S DEVELOPMENT

Television has been around a lot longer than most people would suspect. Vladmir Zworykin perfected the iconoscope in 1923, the basic ingredient of television, permitting over-the-air transmission of pictures. In 1928 an experimental television station broadcast from Schenectady, New York. The first coaxial cable linked New York and Philadelphia in 1935, laying the groundwork for television networks. Coaxial cable was required for long-distance hookups because television's line-of-sight signal rushed off into space as the earth curved, and ordinary telephone lines were inadequate. By 1937 there were seventeen experimental television stations operating.

The FCC granted the first ten commercial television licenses in 1941, and television was off and running. That was also the year of the Mayflower Decision, a milestone in FCC history because for the first time it assumed jurisdiction over program content instead of merely the technical aspects of broadcasting. The Mayflower Decision held that a broadcaster could not be an advocate and outlawed broadcast editorials.

In 1942 a wartime freeze was placed on television. In 1945, following the war, the FCC allocated thirteen "very high frequency" channels (VHF) to commercial broadcasting, reserving one of them. This move was a boon to NBC, which had been urging its radio affiliates to seek television licenses, and a setback for CBS, which had gambled on FM development. This FCC action would delay FM radio for a decade or more.

FAIRNESS DOCTRINE

In 1946 the FCC promulgated a blue book which, among other things, required television stations to carry a certain amount of public affairs programming. This was both an extension of "public interest, convenience, and necessity" and a further intrusion into the regulation of programming. Nineteen forty-nine saw further incursions into programming as the FCC reversed the Mayflower Decision

Electromedia
244

and urged broadcasters to editorialize. This, of course, was the logical extension of the public affairs requirement, in recognition of the fact that a broadcaster must be able to express opinion on community affairs if he is to adequately serve his community. Permission to editorialize was the first of several occasions in which the FCC has found it necessary to reverse itself, a commentary both on the complexity of communications regulation and of the inherent confusion which marked the early FCC. The FCC soon realized, however, that editorializing over the airwaves which belong to the people is different than editorializing in a newspaper, which is private property, and the fairness doctrine resulted. Most simply, the fairness doctrine states that a broadcaster who editorializes must make air time available for opposing viewpoints, a reasonable enough precept, but one which would have increasingly complex ramifications as time went on.

The rush for new licenses and two competing schemes for color television from CBS and RCA caused the FCC to put a second freeze on television development in 1948 to give the commission a chance to think certain problems through. The freeze was extended by the Korean War until 1952. However, television was already well under way. There were one million sets in 1948 listening to 108 television stations. Early viewers saw such things as the first "Milton Berle Show," a radio performer having turned to television, and in the same year (1948) the first "Ed Sullivan Show," which restored vaudeville to the American scene for a full, incredible twenty-five years. By 1952 there were 15 million homes with television.

In 1953 the FCC decided in favor of RCA's color system, which, while inferior to that of CBS in some respects, did permit the black-and-white reception of color programming. This was the first of a number of technical decisions which would dictate the course of communications for the foreseeable future. In this respect 1953 was a landmark year, for the adoption of one system automatically made all others useless. The FCC is constantly and increasingly in the position of having to balance pragmatic present considerations against the possibility of future discovery and benefit.

THE NETWORKS

The three major networks—CBS, NBC, and ABC—dominate commercial television. They do not do so equally. In fact, CBS is considered the leader with 5 wholly owned stations and 200 affiliates, while NBC is next with a total of 187 stations. The difference in their total number of stations is eighteen. All these "extra" stations of CBS are located where large populations are concentrated, which means that in coming out, CBS has a distinct lead in the ratings. More people at any given time will be watching CBS because it has more affiliates. The ABC network comes in a poor third with only 127 stations allied to it, meaning that regardless of its program quality, it will still be penalized in overall ratings and never quite be able to catch up, unless a considerable number of otherwise affiliated stations are willing to change allegiance. It is the affiliated stations, each of which is in-

Network Television

dividually licensed by the FCC, that carry the networks into the nooks and crannies of America. The networks are reliant upon their affiliates.

An affiliation agreement between a station and a network is an exclusive franchise to that station to carry that network's programming in its license area. Individual stations are not required to carry the net, but generally do so because the programming is superior to and cheaper than anything they could produce. The net is their guarantee of audience. Some stations carry more network programming than others. All have the right to preempt network programming to carry other material. A "good affiliate" carries around 90 percent of the net; a "poor one" around 80 percent. Affiliated stations are reimbursed by the networks for carrying network programming at between 8 and 12 percent of their own commercial rates for the time. They also have the opportunity to sell station breaks locally and "adjacencies" or spot announcements before and after network programming.

Originally, the networks required their affiliates to carry a certain high percentage of network programming, and specified programs which could not be preempted. This provided the networks with a guarantee to their advertisers of a certain audience size. The FCC, however, outlawed these requirements, and stations now may choose not to carry the net whenever they wish. They may also pick up a rival network's programming if its affiliate in that area does not choose to use it. Affiliation agreements are a lot looser now than they used to be, and the networks' respective positions are less secure.

GROUPS AND AFFILIATES

The network situation is further complicated by the development of a number of station groups; that is, a number of stations (five only by FCC ruling) under single ownership. Such powerful groups exert considerable influence with the networks because they always represent five major outlets in five large population centers, speaking in a single voice. Westinghouse's Group W has affiliation agreements with all three networks for its five stations (two CBS, two NBC, and one ABC). This places Group W in a strong bargaining position with the networks since it can threaten to abandon affiliation with one and affiliate with another.

While the networks and the individual affiliates need each other, theirs is not an entirely happy relationship. The affiliates are concerned over the development of each year's schedule since what the network offers will affect audience size and, hence, profitability in their own areas. There are regional differences and some kinds of programming acceptable in the more liberal Northeast are less so in the South and Midwest. These interests must somehow be balanced by the networks, for whenever an affiliate does not carry the net, network ratings are affected.

Animosities arise also because affiliates sell against the network, in competition with the net. From a major advertiser's standpoint, it is much simpler to buy the net. However, it is sometimes more scientific and economical to purchase time from individual stations in specific markets to carry out a certain marketing plan. Aware of this, the individual stations, through their national representatives (reps), are constantly trying to lure advertisers away from the networks to buy time from the station individually at considerably more profit to the station and no more cost to the advertiser. One of the problems with national advertisers buying local rather than network commercial time has been the difficulty of proving whether or not the spot was actually run. The process of digisonics has come to the assistance of those locals selling nationally. It provides an inaudible "beep" on the commercial videotape which is picked up and recorded by an ultrasonic listening device, tapes from which are then sent to the advertiser as proof.

Another irritation for the networks arises when they watch the stock performance of the major groups on Wall Street. A major group's stock will rise largely as a result of network affiliation and programming, whereas network stock does not hold the same attraction to the investor because of the huge costs and gambles in program development.[1]

1. Les Brown, *Television: The Business Behind the Box* (New York: Harcourt Brace Jovanovich, Inc., 1972).

THE RATINGS

In the commercial cycle, there is a manufacturer and a product, a distributor and a consumer, and, generally, a financier. In television, the networks are the manufacturers, and programming is their product, which is distributed to audience-consumers via affiliates, while advertising provides the financing. Into this picture further the ratings are injected as a form of pseudofeedback with which to gauge the effectiveness of product consumption by the audience. Waiting for the cash registers to ring in the fast-moving and costly game of network television takes too long—it is too big a gamble when the stakes are in the billions of dollars. The FCC's figure for television's annual gross in 1972 was well over 3 billion dollars.

The ratings had their genesis in the days of radio when the then huge costs of radio production demanded an early warning system for measuring audience acceptance. Since the coming of television, technological improvements in computers and the perfection of public opinion polling techniques have developed the ratings into a near science. Actually, the ratings are less than perfect. Consider for a moment that the program tastes of 200 million Americans are measured by twelve hundred households. The sample is tiny, and there are those who argue that it is inadequate, that not all regions, the Rocky Mountain states for example, are represented in the ratings. But granting the validity of the sample, there are other questions involved. The Neilsen ratings are most generally accepted. Neilsen uses an audimeter, an electronic device hooked onto the samples' television sets which records what channels are viewed when. The tapes are sent to Nielsen every two weeks for evaluation. While the tapes reveal what channels were tuned in, they do not record how many people were watching, or if indeed anyone was watching at all. Further, they do not measure audience reaction. The audimeters are supplemented by a diary system, whereby families are asked to record for a two-week period what programs specifically were watched. There is some evidence that people tend to upgrade their program taste, marking, for instance, that they were watching a documentary whereas in reality they were glued to a situation comedy. Another example of diary error is the housewife who spends the afternoon watching old movies instead of doing housework, but is reluctant to make such an entry where her husband will see it. The Neilsen people claim they can compensate for these errors, however.

The ratings, while far from exact, do offer a yardstick to audience size. It is a crude yardstick but it is the only one available and its acceptance is due to consensus. Networks, affiliates, independents, as well as the advertisers and their agencies, have all agreed to accept the ratings whatever their shortcomings. In view of this universal acceptance within the trade, the ratings become not only a crude measurement but *the* measurement.

The ratings measure audience size—the total number of households tuned in at any given moment. This size is then broken down into audience "share," or that percentage of the total audience listening to each of the three major networks. With three networks, each should ideally develop a share of 33 percent. But, remembering that CBS has a few more affiliates than NBC and considerably more than ABC, its share should be proportionately larger. The smaller nets must run harder to keep even.

Recently, ratings have gone to demographics as well, measuring their audiences by age, sex, education, socioeconomic status (ses) and numbers of children. This data is valuable to advertisers who are enchanted with the young and relatively affluent, and with women, who comprise the majority of the viewing audience at all times during the day, drawing only approximately even to men during the late news. The young and affluent have spending money for advertised goods, and they will be consuming for a longer time. Older people, for the most part, have fixed incomes—thus, less disposable income. Their buying patterns are set and their longevity is limited. Women do the vast majority of purchasing and nearly all the supermarket buying.

There are what is known as "black weeks" in the rating system. Black weeks are periods in the year when no ratings are conducted by network agreement. Recognizing their obligation to provide a certain amount of public affairs programming under FCC dictum and recognizing further that such cultural programming loses large chunks of audience, black weeks are a device whereby the networks can satisfy the public interest, convenience, and necessity requirements for their affiliates (and wholly owned stations) in one fell swoop. Black weeks are filled with documentaries and cultural and public affairs programming that the networks can offer with impunity because there are no ratings with which to be concerned.

PRIME TIME

Television programming is a highly competitive and enormously expensive gamble conducted always with one eye on ratings. Prime-time programming is concerned not so much with the thought of developing an enormously popular program, although this helps, as with providing an evening's continuity across the prime-time hours and slotting shows to compete with offerings on the other two networks. One of the most closely guarded secrets of the networks is a forthcoming season's schedule. Prior knowledge of one network's schedule would permit the others to slot competing attractions against its most appealing offerings.

The continuity of programming is significant also. A weak show will lose an audience which may not return to the network that evening. A weak show, therefore, can be presumed to lose audience not only for that particular time slot, but for the entire evening. This is disastrous in ratings and, hence, in advertising revenue.

The preoccupation with ratings, of course, means that each network must attract not only as much audience as it possibly can, but if possible outdraw the other two networks proportionately. Appeal to the largest possible mass dictates a noncontroversial type of programming designed to appeal to the lowest common denominator. There is a good deal of the star system as television develops its own personalities of proven appeal. There is also a good deal of formula programming and plagiarizing. Whenever one network develops a successful format, be it western, police beat, hospital, private eye, situation comedy, or quasi-musical, the others are sure to follow suit. A case in point was the rash of handicapped detectives who came in wheelchairs, or were blind, obese, obsequious, or senile, but always got their man. Even in the daytime hours, networks copy one another's game and quiz shows. Such repetitive programming is bound to offer a striking sameness to network programs.

Television watching appears to be habit-forming. This has led some to propose the theory of the "least objectionable program" (lop). The theory of lop contends that programming does not have to be good, that it merely has to be less objectionable to most people than anything else on TV at that moment. Thus, it is possible for inferior shows to develop high ratings in prime time, provided the alternative offerings by competing networks are worse. In view of the costs of television production, this is a key point. There is no need for a network to spend exorbitant sums to develop an expensive program for competition against a weak one when a cheaper product will suffice.

When a show fails in the ratings, it is necessary to kill it. It is preferable to gamble with another program than it is to continue a proven loser regardless of its popularity, for one weak show affects an entire evening. Some shows are killed outright; more often they are moved into different slots. This placates the hard-core fans of the show, but at the same time destroys certain viewing patterns. Moved into a different time slot on a different night, a program is almost bound to lose some audience and go down further in ratings. This failure, in turn, is used as an excuse to kill the show. Furthermore, the continuance of the show in a different time slot permits the network to recoup a portion of its investment in the program and to satisfy the contracts it may have with performers, even though the program is already doomed to extinction.

NEXT SEASON'S SCHEDULE

Typically, as the program director for a network gets his season schedule together, he decides which programs of the previous year he will retain and which will not be continued. He is then faced with placing his shows in the most appropriately competitive time slots, shooting largely in the dark. He is also faced with the problem of what new programs to put into the schedule, relying on proven formats and star availabilities. He then entertains a number of suggestions for new programming, new serials, new approaches to old problems, new and old movies, specials, etc.

In the case of new programming, the program director generally commissions a pilot program for several of the most promising ideas. Pilots are expensive to make. They are actually full-length films or videotapes of one sequence of a new serial with character introduction, theme, and the treatment which will be followed through the entire schedule. On the basis of the pilots, the program director makes up his mind which of the new programs to run and where they will be slotted on the board. The remaining pilots will be discarded; the investment—often running into hundreds of thousands of dollars—wasted.

A network board shows every prime-time slot for all seven days of the week; the program director slots similar boards for the other two networks according to what he thinks they may do and what commercial espionage reveals they are doing.

Prime time, with its mass audience and lowest common denominator, is one situation in which television must find the way to appeal simultaneously to the sixteen-year-old Puerto Rican girl in New York City and the eighty-year-old North Dakota farmer and everybody in between.

OTHER TIME SLOTS

The daytime audience is overwhelmingly female: the housewives of America, the purchasers of America. Daytime television is an incredible potpourri of quiz shows, game shows, soap operas, old movies, and reruns. There is also a daytime audience of the elderly and the ailing, but they are not considered by programmers, for they have no purchasing power. Daytime television also tends to be inexpensive programming, as the networks conserve their dollars against the competitive prime-time hours. Much of daytime programming consists of packages made by independent producers, and as often as not contributed to heavily by advertisers. One producer is responsible for at least four game shows of varying taste; the prizes are contributed by manufacturers in return for product mention. Costs to the net are relatively small, and the drawing power of these programs is immense.

Saturday morning offers another specialty, kiddie cartoon time. Breakfast food manufacturers, toy makers, and others hawk their wares to tiny tots. The little people have no purchasing power of themselves, but they have enormous influence over susceptible parents.

Sunday morning is the "cultural ghetto" of television, when viewing is minimal. Religious programs are quite naturally slotted into this period, as well as a considerable number of public affairs and quasi-cultural programs to build up the public interest, convenience, and necessity portion of the weekly log. Often this public affairs programming (such as "Face the Nation" and "Meet the Press") carries over into Sunday afternoon unless a major sports event preempts the time.

Sports is another facet of television programming that is guaranteed to develop enormous audiences. Traditionally audiences are male, and advertising tends to center around "man" things, such as razor blades, shaving soaps, after-shaves, male deodorants, shampoos, and hair creams, with an occasional auto tire or gasoline commercial thrown in.

COSTS

Television programming costs are enormous. A quarter of a million dollars is a fair price for an hour-long segment of a prime-time serial. Many specials will far exceed this. Remote filming costs for major sporting events also are astronomical. High-priced talent, standby time, rehearsals, camera crews, sets, and dozens of union agreements all add up and annually increase.

Unlike a film, which could be expected to tour the nation's theaters for a year or more and then move to overseas sales, a television production has a very limited life. Until rather recently a television show was a one-shot affair costing $250 thousand an hour. It had some residual value in sales to independent stations for reruns, but this market was limited. It had some additional value for overseas sales, but this amounted to only about $100 million a year overall, which was minimal considering that three networks were involved and that their programming costs easily exceeded a million dollars a day each. Further, $30 million of international sales was offset by foreign programming imports for United States consumption.

As television programming costs skyrocket, more and more attention has been given to repeats in an attempt to spread the cost over two time slots instead of one. As long as this has been done by all three networks, it has worked out well. However, repeats have scarcely been a service to the long-suffering television viewer accustomed to original productions night after night. As it stands now, original programming runs from mid-September through the new year, after which repeats are encountered more often than not in the prime-time slots until the end of the television year in June. Statistics and the lop seem to indicate that audiences will watch repeats in the same sort of stupor that they watched the originals, and that many people either missed the original or forgot it quickly. There is, however, reason to believe that the increasing use of repeats is driving away some of television's audience to other media and other activities.

The summer months, June, July, and August, are vacation times when America spends a lot of its prime-time hours out-of-doors or away. This is a recuperative time for the networks. It is a period of low-budget productions, of trying out new shows and pilots, of experimentation, of a considerable amount of typically less costly public affairs and cultural programming, of reruns and repeats, while the networks get ready for their annual fall ratings battle.

THE DIMINISHING AUDIENCE

The network program directors are the principal gatekeepers of the television medium. Theirs is a different style of gatekeeping from that of newspaper or magazine editors, or even book publishers and film producers. Their style differs because they are concerned not only with audience appeal—specific or mass—as are all the others, but also with what their rivals are doing. They program as much against the other networks' offerings as they do for the audience. Thus, gatekeeping has a competitive, three-dimensional quality, and a new sophistication that is peculiar to television.

The preponderance of appeal to the lcd reflected in much of the blandness and sameness that appears on television: the high incidence of screeching auto chases, of gun fights, fisticuffs, and sickroom pathos. It may easily be that the theory of the lcd is in error. Theory holds that programming aimed at the so-called thirteen-year-old mentality will automatically reach everyone above that level: they will be capable of understanding it, and if the concept of the least objectionable program is correct, they will watch it. Those beneath this arbitrary level lack the competence and, more importantly, the purchasing power to be of concern.

There seems to be some evidence that Americans are smarter than they are given credit for being. Martin Mayer and Les Brown point out that television viewing is diminishing even as audiences watch.[2] America's exposure to television apparently peaked in 1966 and has been on a slow decline ever since. For evidence, the prime-time audience in 1966 was considered to be 40 million homes on the average. In 1972 it was still at 40 million homes, which does not reflect a population increase considered to have been in the neighborhood of 20 percent over those six years. This represents a net loss in numbers of viewers; television is not keeping up. At the same time,

2. Martin Mayer, *About Television* (New York: Harper & Row, Publishers, 1972).

Electromedia

the number of daily hours of television watching has declined about 25 percent. In 1966 the average family watched television six hours a day. That does not mean that all family members sat constantly watching for six whole hours, but rather that the television was turned on and was being watched by someone for six hours. In 1972 this average had declined to four and a half hours daily.

The networks are aware of this loss of viewers and are seeking to compensate for it. They are diversifying their interests, getting into other kinds of business. Some have acquired publishing interests; others are buying into wholly different endeavors. They are hedging their bets.

The real question, of course, lies in why Americans are becoming ever-so-slightly disenchanted with television. Part of the answer undoubtedly lies in the sameness of television. What was once enthralling has become a bore. Ironically, a part of the media specialization and fragmentation that television has forced upon books, newspapers, magazines, radio, and film, is beginning to take its toll of television. People are turning to other things more suited to their individual interests than television's commonality. In so doing, they must forsake television. It may easily be that television's massiveness is bringing about its own demise. To use an analogy, the total media menu is becoming so diverse under television's impact that there is no reason America need be satisfied with a TV dinner any longer. The younger generation, raised by "the electronic babysitter," has turned aside from the tube. Sated in their youth, they are discovering other things; they are becoming highly selective in their watching. Nor do the increasing incidence of repeats and reruns help television's overall image.

TELEVISION ADVERTISING: CPM

In the United States advertising pays the media bills, and more so in television than anywhere else. In 1968 television was taking nearly 50 percent of the national advertising dollar, with the biggest portion of this going to the three networks who were uniquely equipped to offer national service. Other media in advertising had been relegated to a complementary status, filling in the local and functionally specialized audience gaps on the continua.

National advertising uses television primarily because of its massive "reach." Television saturation, however, is probably no greater than that achieved earlier by newspapers or radio. But television offers new dynamic dimensions to advertising: drama and humor, dramatic effects, motion and color, lighting effects and music, and, more subtly, the full scope of nonverbal gesture and expression that human beings use to convey wordless meaning to one another. The ability to create mood, excitement, and drama in connection with commercial products is a real asset; combined with vast audiences, it is overpowering. Advertising agencies have proven adept at conveying impressions, at probing the inner recesses of the mind, of developing ingenious appeals to the point where many of the commercials on network television are superior from production and entertainment standpoints than the supporting programming, and this may not be entirely without design.

The costs of making a network commercial are astronomical. The commercial, after all, is the reason for the entire medium. It is not an incidental thing, but painstaking and time-consuming, utilizing all an agency's expertise and genius and all the production talent of studio professionals. It often takes weeks of writing, directing, shooting, and editing. It is not entirely unusual for television commercials to cost more than $250 thousand per minute in order to get the message exactly right, to convey the perfect impression, to be "with it" and sell. Advertisers expect to recoup a part of this investment by amortizing the cost over as long a period as possible. The more often a spot is run, the lower the unit cost on each run.

So important is advertising to television that there was a time when the advertising agencies produced their own programs as well as commercials. The networks were little more than distribution channels for the agencies, who simply bought time for their clients and filled it as they wished. However, the quiz show scandals of 1959 brought an end to this practice, and the networks reassumed responsibility for programming.

Advertisers buy television exposure on a cost-per-thousand (cpm) basis. Generally, this works out to about eight dollars per thousand homes (not viewers) for a one-minute spot commercial. ("Homes" is the basic sales unit of television for it is only homes that the ratings can measure.) Thus, $65 thousand for a sixty-second commercial on an average show entering around 16 million homes is equivalent to $85 thousand for a program in the top ten reaching more than 21 million homes. A show at the very peak of the ratings will command as much as $140 thousand per minute for a commercial, and costs are rising. Television advertising rates on the networks roughly doubled in the three years from 1970 to 1973; costs per thousand rose from four to eight dollars following the law of supply and demand. There were simply more national advertisers and products seeking massive exposure than there were commercial minutes on the air.

Ratings are as important to advertisers and their agencies as they are to the networks, and for the same reasons. It is on the basis of the ratings that commercial purchases are made in order to reach the largest audience possible, or the most appropriately demographic audience available.

Minutes have become the favored commercial medium, replacing sponsorships long ago. Minutes permit both reach and frequency, a combination impossible in print media, and far less satisfactorily attained in radio. Minutes are sold by the networks on both an "up front" and "opportunity" basis. Up-front purchases are generally made by the advertisers six months or more in advance of the season. Up-front advertising requires enormous advance commitment, but provides a certain assurance that the spots will be aired at a certain time. There is a gamble in up-fronts in the sense of buying a product, a new serial for example, sight unseen. The opportunity market, on the other hand, provides greater flexibility without the assurance of being aired, and permits advertisers to observe the progress of a new season's program offerings on the various nets before investing.

Advertisers buy across the board, sometimes seeking the top-rated shows on all three nets and sometimes concentrating on one network in order to trade on its loyalty. Sometimes agencies buy both prime-time spots and daytime television, sometimes they concentrate on movies, and yet at other times they may concentrate on various specials that creep into a season's programming. Some buy "names"; others buy format. The factors which enter into an advertiser's program choice are not determined by ratings alone, although ratings always have a bearing. The kind of audience is a factor; personal predispositions are another, as are public relations concerns, such as when the cigarette companies would not buy any time before 9:00 P.M. on the presumption that children would not be in bed until then.

All commercials are not sold at the same price. There may be as much as a 25 percent variation in the cost of spots across a ninety-minute prime-time program, depending on whether the advertiser bought up-front or opportunity spots, how frequently he buys, or the sorts of packages or deals he has made. Television advertising, while it is based on a rate card which in turn is based on the ratings, is still negotiable. Networks, however, do their utmost to protect their cpm, and at least one network has given public service announcement spots (PSAs) to the Boy Scouts rather than cut the price on Sunday afternoon professional football commercial time.

Since it is the network affiliates that do the actual reaching to the audience and since there is some selling against the networks on the part of their affiliates and the independents, the prime concern of a television station is to be considered in a major market. The advertising agencies of Madison Avenue define a major market as 100,000 homes. This is the magical breaking point below which a station will not ordinarily figure in a national advertising campaign. It was for this reason that in North Dakota the tallest man-made structure on earth rises 2,000 feet above the plains. It is a television broadcasting antenna designed to fan out over the northern flatlands to reach 100,000 homes before its signal disappears over the edge of the earth.[3]

TELEVISION NEWS?

The effectiveness of television advertising for consumer products has carried over into other fields where its appropriateness is questionable. Joe McGinniss' *The Selling of the President, 1968* is the recount of Nixon's 1968 campaign, which was based largely on McLuhan's theories.[4] The strategy was to package the candidate as one would a bar of soap and to merchandize him to the American

---

3. Ibid.

4. Joe McGinniss, *The Selling of the President, 1968* (New York: Trident Press, 1969).

The electromedia broadcast unseen, silent shockwaves that can rivet a nation's attention.

UPI

people. The public, however, is capable of recognizing that a presidential election is a matter of substance, and that consumer products are less so; people can make the distinction between substance and trivia. Nixon's television campaign can be judged a failure for, far from supporting his early lead in the polls, his lead disappeared to the point where he won by only a fraction of a percentage point to become a "minority" president. While there were other factors involved, there are many who feel that had the campaign gone on another few days, television and all, that Hubert H. Humphrey would

Electromedia
256

have been elected. Soap and presidential candidates are different products—television notwithstanding.

Some of television's drama carries over into the news. Television is basically an entertainment medium, and it cannot seem to escape from this notion even in its performance of the information function in news coverage or documentaries. It is interesting to note here that while most people indicate that they get the majority of their news from television and find it more credible than other media, the audience for news and documentaries, according to the ratings, is less educated and less affluent than the average television audience in prime time.[5] Ratings drop whenever the news comes on or a documentary is scheduled. In light of the lcd to which television appeals, this smaller audience skims the dregs rather than the cream, contrary to popular notion. A part of the answer may lie in the fact that the more educated and, hence, affluent prefer to get their news and information from more authoritative sources and in a more comprehensive format than the sensational headline form that television offers.

5. Les Brown, *Television: The Business Behind the Box* (New York: Harcourt Brace Jovanovich, 1972).

...ADD DRAMA

Television is visual, a characteristic which carries over into everything it does. When covering the news, presentation must generally be visual. Television's association with entertainment, with violence, and with the sensational adds to the dramatic effect. Most

Walter Cronkite and staff prepare for the "CBS Evening News."

CBS NEWS PHOTO

Network Television

other news media also tend to emphasize the sensational, but they have a greater depth and fewer associations with drama in which to maneuver.

The distortion incident at the Oakland induction station was noted earlier. Instances of fabricated news were documented at the 1968 Democratic National Convention in Chicago, where network camera crews bandaged a young couple and photographed them moaning about police brutality; streakers interrupted the coverage of the 1974 Academy Awards.

The national political conventions have remade their image to become television stages for dramatic action. They are produced as high drama, too often by amateurs who lose sight of audience effect in their concentration on a politically perfect script.

Televised moonshots fell flat in audience appeal. Living, factual documentation of one of man's major technical accomplishments failed to appeal to viewers. It simply was not good theater; "Star Trek" did better.

LATER REGULATION

Beginning in the mid-sixties the FCC began to intrude more and more into broadcasting. First came the unforeseen decision that the fairness doctrine applied to advertising as well as editorials in connection with cigarette commercials. Remembering that the key word in the fairness doctrine was controversy, the FCC held that since the surgeon general's findings determined that cigarette smoking was harmful, that cigarette commercials were controversial. Thus, antismoking interests were entitled to reply, and at no cost. Such action by the FCC verged closely on programming control. The cigarette ad ban by Congress removed the FCC from its role as advertising arbitrator, but the precedent of commercial controversy remains to haunt network and advertiser alike.

In the 1970s the FCC looked askance at the increasing concentration of broadcasting in the hands of a relatively few operators, the networks and proliferating groups. It promulgated the rule of seven, which provided that no single owner could hold more than seven licenses among the broadcast media, that is, seven AM radio, seven FM radio, and seven television, of which no more than five could be VHF. This action substantially reduced the acquisitions of aggressive groups.

Its next action, which took effect in the fall of 1971, was aimed at the networks. It prohibited local licensees, the network affiliates, from carrying more than three hours of network programming in prime time, that is, between the hours of 7:00 and 11:00 P.M., news excepted. As nearly all the affiliates elected to carry network news in this period, this meant that the locals were required to find additional programming for an extra half-hour in prime time. The purpose of the ruling was to encourage local programming of a civic or public affairs nature when the audience was maximal. The ruling has worked

Electromedia

out somewhat differently, since few stations were inclined to spend the money for costly local production. Instead, the ruling has proved a boom to program packagers who put together an assortment of travel, wildlife, quiz, and game shows and sell them individually to local television outlets. The result has been a reduction of prime time by one hour, a substantial loss of audience, and the extension of daytime television into prime-time hours for no particular public benefit. The networks, at first leery of the ruling, later welcomed it as they were relieved of the enormous costs of one hour's competitive prime-time production.

Other actions of the FCC have been less formal, but decisions reached on various relicensing applications provide a pattern for the future. The FCC will not permit concentration by any owner in a single market, even within the rule of seven. It is discouraging other media operators, newspapers particularly, from acquiring broadcast outlets in their own territory, although not necessarily elsewhere. It seeks to assure that groups will be geographically diversified and, in at least one instance, in Boston, has denied a newspaper's relicensing application for its radio station in that area. Further, the future of broadcasting, as both CATV and UHF become more prevalent, is clouded not only by the FCC but by the Department of Justice in a series of antitrust suits.

Meanwhile, the executive branch of the federal government, in seeking to curb the power of the networks, particularly in the area of news and documentaries, has proposed "carrot and stick" guidelines to the television industry. For some time the individual licensees have held that the three-year franchise granted by the FCC is not long enough to permit adequate capital investment. They have sought either an extended license period or indefinite renewals in the absence of a challenge for cause. Clay Whitehead, White House coordinator for telecommunication, proposed early in 1973 that local stations be given a five-year franchise in return for strict accountability for everything they broadcast. This included network news, which meant that when the nets implied an antiadministration attitude, the local stations had the choice of either not carrying that program or of providing time in accord with the fairness doctrine for administration spokesmen. As previewing network news prior to broadcast is technically impractical, little choice would have been given the stations.

This proposal hit the networks where they live—in their affiliates. The temptation for local stations, already at odds with the nets, to opt for extended license periods would be almost irresistible. Actually, while the proposal may never come to action, its purpose may have been achieved anyway in forcing the networks to adhere to a strictly noncontroversial treatment of news and documentaries to forestall the proposal. The key to this proposal is the fact that the FCC has no authority over the networks, only over the individual licensees.

TELEVISION CRITICISM

An increasingly concerned society about matters of the environment, minorities, and consumer rights has been partly responsible for a more aggressive FCC. A number of complaints and license challenges have been filed with the commission alleging unequal treatment of racial minorities, lack of access to the broadcast media, inadequate public service programming, and the like. These are all manifestations of the kind of criticism that television has engendered since it became the overwhelming mass medium.

As early as 1960 FCC chairman Newton Minow foresaw the shape of the future in his "vast wasteland" speech to the NAB, alleging that television programming was a vast wasteland and that television provided less of what people wanted than it did of what was

> "When television is bad, nothing is worse. I invite you to sit down in front of your television set when your station goes on the air and stay there without [anything] to distract you—and keep your eyes glued to that set until the station signs off. I can assure you that you will observe a vast wasteland."
>
> Newton Minow, 1961

commercially profitable and convenient. He said that the ratings, far from proving that Americans liked what television offered, indicated only what they could watch painlessly. When the only restaurant in town serves hamburger, it has no way of knowing whether its customers like steak.

Other criticism has centered around television's preoccupation with violence and its effect on youth. The best research seems to indicate that television's violence has little effect on normal children who recognize it as fantasy, but may detrimentally affect the pathologically inclined.

There have been those who criticized television's blandness, its lack of substantial fare. Much has been made of television's potential as a cultural medium, and elitists have dreamed of a national diet of opera and ballet, of Shakespeare and de Maupassant, of concerts and of tours of the Louvre and the Sistine Chapel. However, whenever anything approaching cultural uplift is aired, audience disappears. England's experience with the British Broadcasting Company (BBC) seems to bear this out. The BBC is government operated, and noncommercial, engaging in cultural uplift and developing audiences. Then England licensed a commercial network which operated similarly to those of the U.S. and offered popular fare, much of it old United States television programs. What happened? Englishmen deserted the BBC in vast numbers to watch the "shoot 'em ups."

Some have criticized television's use of stereotypes: racial, ethnic, sexist, etc. Yet in such a time-limited medium, it is difficult not to use a shortcut to character development. Television must use what

Walter Lippmann called "the little pictures in our heads" to tell its story.[6]

Significantly, all the criticism leveled against television had been earlier raised against the movie when it was America's darling. Cries of sex and violence, stereotyping, vacuousness, and racism have all been heard before. Criticism is a part of the penalty of such massive public exposure.

For all the criticism of television's blandness, sameness, presumed effect and lack of elevating concern, one fact remains. Television provides inexpensive relaxation, even comfort, to the ailing and companionship for the lonely as well as an instant summary of world events such as no medium before it. It is perhaps a necessary reprise against the pressures of contemporary life.

Herein may lie its greatest area for criticism. Television is so easily ingested and so time-consuming that it removes great blocks of time from society—time which conceivably could have been spent in more productive endeavor. There are 350 million man-hours spent daily viewing television in prime time only, day after day, week after week, year after year. The social cost for the past two decades is overwhelming, unknown, and unknowable.

6. Walter Lippman, *Public Opinion* (New York: The Free Press, 1963).

PERSONAL AND SOCIETAL EFFECTS

7. "Mirror of Opinion: Insidious Sitter," *Christian Science Monitor*, 23 November 1971.

Nor is this the entire effect of television. By the time a child goes to kindergarten, he will have spent more hours in front of the television than he will spend in the classroom, including four years of college.[7] By the time he is fourteen, he will have seen 18,000 people killed on the tube and watched 350,000 television commercials—which alone, the *Christian Science Monitor* points out, is cruel and unusual punishment.

Even though the data indicate that television violence has no particular effect on the normal viewer, this is not to say that television has no effect on young and old. Three hundred fifty thousand commercials cannot help but reinforce the commercial nature of society. Some youth turn away—tune out—alienated.

Television brings a world into the home—a fantasy world to be sure—but a world nonetheless, a situation that has led to an incredible sophistication among the young. They've seen it all—or think they have—at a tender age. But theirs is a surface sophistication in that hours spent at the tube are hours taken from other, real world activities, from play and from reading. Certainly, reading skills and literacy have been affected. A surface sophistication has been accomplished at the expense of depth.

Medical science has increased the life span by approximately ten years over the past quarter century. In view of television viewing habits, how ironic that medical science should have provided the time spent before television in a lifetime. Is this the best use that can be made of these extra years? Maybe—maybe not; judgment belongs to society.

Network Television

Also, as youth and others watch television, they find complex problems and social situations, all of which are brought to a satisfactory conclusion (NAB code) within thirty, sixty, or ninety minutes. How frustrating it must be then to emerge into a real political, social, and economic world to discover that there are problems which cannot be solved in mini time spans, problems which may take years before reaching any conclusion at all, and that there are some problems, in fact, that are incapable of solution. Youth may experience impatience first and later frustration as the fantasy world of television dissolves into the larger world outside.

Television, as Marshall McLuhan points out, is a mosaic. Within a single evening nearly 100 million Americans—half the population—will see an incredible potpourri of comedians, headline news, song and dance acts, private eyes, hospital tragedy, and travelogues. The program list is endless and regularly interspersed with soft and hard sell commercials for deodorants, floor waxes, bread, soft drinks, pain killers, and real estate—the accoutrements of the good life. The amount of mental gear-shifting is great as viewers' minds are forced to piece bits together for continuity. Television is an impressionistic medium taken in its entirety night after night. It lacks the concentration of a book or even of film, the undisrupted time for continuing a thought pattern. This may affect thought process patterns in time, but it is as yet too early to tell.

There are other disruptions originating from television. The level of channel noise is high indeed. Television occurs in the intimacy of family homes, surrounded by an individual's familiar things—the spotted rug, the torn lampshade, the chipped piece of plaster. It does not occur in the lofty silence of a movie palace where one's sole, uninterrupted attention is directed to the screen. Television viewing is subject to an almost constant interruption of telephones and doorbells and conversation, of family things—all of which, added to its impressionistic quality, force a kind of "city room" attention upon one. It might not be all that relaxing after all, and it may be boring. Television could be tense, intimate boredom—maybe; this is merely speculation.

Familiarity breeds contempt, and audiences may have grown contemptuous of the tube. The intimacy of surroundings, the predictable fantasy, and the lack of artistry subtracts from its net effect. Added to this is its diminutive size. A television is a tiny thing really, even a large color screen. Television is dominated by surroundings and people; thus, it is difficult to take seriously the action portrayed there, far more difficult, for example, than to seriously consider the heroic-sized, uninterrupted action which takes place on an enveloping theater screen. Television is much different from film in a number of intangible, unexplored ways.

Television is young; it is in its infancy yet. The first generation of television children, cared for by an electronic babysitter, are still in their youth. Inadequate research on television is at hand; there are no long-term studies. For the most part, studies of the effects of television have been defensive, commercial, and almost of a happenstance nature. The industry often uses research in attempts to answer charges of violence; note Joseph Klapper's *The Effects of Mass Communications*.[8]

8. Joseph Klapper, *Effects of Mass Communications* (New York: The Free Press, 1960).

Television has not come of age. The serious attention accorded it is inadequate considering its enormity. It was not too long ago that the collective brainpower of the entire television industry gave audiences hours of wrestlers—Argentine Roca and Gorgeous George—and hefty queens on roller skates as the ultimate in television programming. The public has come a way since then—but how far? Is what is offered today the ultimate of television's contribution to society?

Marshall McLuhan has noted the phenomenon of television's capacity for involving its audience. Remembering that communication is always an individual process, this amounts to personal involvement. Causative factors for this involvement may have to do with television's diminutive size, its simplistic treatment of complex topics, or its ubiquity in daily life; the fact remains that television is involving. The popularity of professional football, for example, has coincided with the rise of television. As home audiences watched Sunday mayhem, they became attracted and flocked to the stadia to see it live, despite the fact that they could see the action far better on television; the live game offers no slow-motion cameras, no instant replays, and most game watchers wouldn't know what to look for nearly as well as the cameramen and directors.

Skiing and golf both became extremely popular participant sports as television brought Sunday professionals on tour and winter games into the home. It looked so ridiculously simple: the easy swing to hit the little ball way down the fairway, or the curve and swoop down the slalom course executed with the grace and ease of Jean Claude Killy. Americans had to go try it themselves, and once they did they were hooked. Travel, too, has been promoted by television, as faraway scenes appear close at hand. Even books have become popular via television. When an author appears on a talk show one evening, libraries and bookstores clear out the title the next day.

Looking back to the continua, it may be that the eons of seeking ever greater speed and ever greater numbers in mass communications are at an end, and that there will follow a period in which individuals sift and sort mass communications media to the point where there will no longer be a preeminent mass medium commanding the attention of the entire audience capable of receiving, but that each medium will fall into its own particularly suited slot from which the public can choose what mode is needed most and at what time.

But television has other surprises in store. A fragmentation of the medium itself appears to be happening ever so slowly, as something close to the continuum ultimate in speed and audience has been reached. These fragments are electronic embryos conceived in television's adolescence, a medium whose growing pains must be faced even while it struggles to maturity.

SUMMARY

Television has become part of the American way of life. More than any other medium it has usurped its audience, no longer supplemental to their lives, but an intimate part of them. From the continua standpoint, it has fulfilled the twin goals of mass communications in reaching the ultimate in speed—by its instantaneous—and in an almost total saturation of around 98 percent of American homes. It is enormously time-consuming, occupying on the average around four and a half hours daily. Its commercial and entertainment emphasis both reflect and affect the hedonistic and acquisitive nature of contemporary American society.

As long ago as 1923 television became possible with the invention of the iconoscope, which made over-the-air visual transmission possible. By 1939 the FCC had licensed the first ten commercial channels.

Television development was interrupted by World War II. A postwar frenzy in license applications caused the FCC to freeze further development until 1952, when it allocated twelve VHF channels for commercial use. Television was dominated from the beginning by the three major networks: CBS, NBC, and ABC, in that order.

Television posed new problems for the FCC, which found itself increasingly involved not only with the technical aspects of broadcasting, but more and more with programming decisions such as with the fairness doctrine, in which fairness hinged on controversy. An unexpected interpretation of this doctrine in the mid-sixties held that cigarette smoking was controversial, and thus required television to provide antismoking commercials free. It should be noted that this FCC authority applies directly to the individual licensees and only indirectly to the nets through them.

Ratings are important to television. They measure audience size and the share of that size that each network receives in any given time slot, both of which are important to advertisers. Recently ratings have also delved into demography as more and more advertiser attention is devoted to the young and affluent. Women, too, who control most purchasing and who comprise at least half of all audiences, are also important to advertisers.

Programming is dictated by ratings as the programmers at the major networks jockey for position in the various time slots across the prime-time board. Selections are made for a presumed lcd of taste. But the assumptions of the lcd may be in error, since television viewing has diminished in two ways: today it is proportionately smaller in terms of viewing population, and the average number of daily hours watched has declined by 25 percent.

The least objectionable program (lop) concept contends that television is habit-forming and that people will watch regardless of what is presented, choosing only the least objectionable of what is on at any given time. Consequently, the gatekeepers of television have a complex task: they must second-guess their publics while at the same time programming against what they think the other networks are doing in the same time slots.

Production costs of an average prime-time hour run to more than $250 thousand. Costs keep rising, and the networks more and more frequently are attempting to extend the lives of their investments by running repeats.

Advertising is the dominant factor in television. Advertisers deal in minutes and homes. Minutes have far greater potential for both frequency and reach into homes than do sponsorships. Advertising is sold on the basis of cost per minute (cpm), which averages out to around eight dollars per thousand homes reached.

The networks exist through their affiliates, the individual stations with whom they make franchise agreements. Affiliates are not required to carry the network programs but do so because they are reimbursed by between 8 and 12 percent of their own rate card, and because the programming is of far better quality and cheaper than anything they could produce. Networks and affiliates are presently in a very real competition with each other for advertising revenues, often from the same source. Also to be considered is the emergence of powerful groups of stations under single ownership, which gives these stations considerable leverage with the networks.

The FCC has sought to encourage local programming by restricting network prime time. The result has been the development of individual packagers who sell program packages, including old movies and repeats, to individual stations. The FCC has also sought to diversify television and avoid concentration by its rule of seven and by a series of decisions in relicensing proceedings which have tended to drive other media owners out of the field.

The criticisms leveled at television are that it is bland, innocuous, vapid, preoccupied with violence, and that it caters to the lcd and avoids cultural uplift, never realizing its full potential as a social instrument. These were criticisms leveled at film in a previous era. Evidence seems to point out that television violence has little effect on viewers and is accepted largely as the fantasy it is.

Television's actual effects are little known, perhaps unknowable. It is an intimate medium occurring in the familiarity of an individual's home, subject to distractions and an incredible amount of channel noise. It is diminuitive, dominated by its viewers, making its offerings simplistic, easy. This may be the reason for its involving aspects, as it seems to drive people to professional football, to the golf links and ski slopes, and abroad to travel. Television even sells books.

The television medium is impressionistic in nature, forcing viewers constantly to change mental gears between a wide variety of different programs, intervening commercials, and casual interruptions of the home. The social costs of television's effects are as yet unknown.

There has been inadequate study and research into the television medium. Most of what has been done is defensive and suspect, commercial and reinforcing, and very fractional.

15 TV'S PROGENY

THE TELEVISION MIX

Television's progeny are many and varied. Some, referred to as local or independent stations, have closely followed the pattern of their radio ancestor, competing in an over-the-air market with the networks. Others have branched out on an extended spectrum of the broadcast band. These are the Ultra High Frequency stations (UHF), which may be roughly compared to FM radio in their reach and content. Evolving from National Educational Television (NET) is a "fourth network," a sort of nonnetwork, the Public Broadcasting System (PBS). Of all television's children at present, it is the most undeveloped, living in the shadow of its powerful parent. In addition, closed-circuit television, a very private system of mininetworks, serves a variety of purposes—from that of electronic private eye surveillance to corporate annual reporting. Community Antenna Television, or cable (CATV), is the most versatile of television's progeny. Beginning as an extension of over-the-air television, CATV has made some surprising alliances in the technical and economic realms to extend its reach into far-flung communities or to boost the signal where reception is poor. With the aid of the computer particularly, it has progressed to the point where it begins to threaten the parent it was designed to serve. Closely allied to CATV is another departure from the traditional upbringing of broadcast—pay TV, which is, of course, no longer free. Just how free television is in its purest form is another subject. Finally, in the reaches of outer space is yet another progeny, satellite television, which extends television from a national to an international medium. In so doing, it may render obsolete the elaborate broadcasting system that has been developed over the past half century or so.

Following the principle of specialization established on the media continuum, it would appear that television is fragmenting even as audiences watch. In fact, television appears to be diversifying even before its basic form is perfected. This poses large interrelated problems in the technological, social, economic, educational, and political realms, not the least of which is that encountered by the FCC in attempting to regulate all of television's bawling and conflicting children before it has mastered the fundamentals of broadcast regulation. A part of the problem may lie in the traditional American concept of the local nature of communications. The regulatory apparatus has proven unwieldy even for national broadcast, let alone international satellite broadcast. The problem is further compounded by the injection of strictly local jurisdictions as a result of the multiple municipal franchising of CATV in the days before the FCC took national jurisdiction. Furthermore, the principle of acceleration plays a role; technology exceeds adaptation, and new communications forms are constantly confronted before the old have been mastered. Economically, the investments required to install and perfect new systems are massive and may even lie beyond the grasp of an affluent society. Psychologically, the din of conflicting media only vaguely understood is enervating, which, combined with the increasing competition for attention, seems already to be taking a social toll. Politically, the injection of new forces of instantaneous public opinion formation and transformation appears to outstrip the time-consuming order of due process.

THE INDEPENDENTS

An FCC television license presents a lucrative financial opportunity. Certainly, this has been true of the network affiliates with their superior programming and huge audiences in every market. It is also true of the local independent stations, but where the network affiliates reap large profits, the independents are forced to settle for less. Indeed, independents only exist in the largest markets where the overall population is great enough to provide a sufficient number of network malcontents to justify additional programming. Further, since independents have no net to carry, their program costs are proportionately higher for an inferior product. By their nature, they are forced to specialize. Geographically, most specialization is directed to the local area, and demographically to the elderly or to women, giving time to local events that the networks, with their national preoccupation, are unable to do. Independents have one advantage, however, in that they provide a showcase for the local advertiser who needs only to reach his own community and who cannot afford the huge cpm of a network affiliate. Independents also tend to develop their own personalities and followings. George Putnam, former reactionary commentator for KTLA-TV in Los Angeles, was one of the highest paid of commentators, catering to a sizable conservative audience that hung on his every word five nights a week and delighted in his radical-baiting on the talk-back portion of his newscast.

Not only can local advertisers not afford network programming, but the networks have no time for them. Television is a time-limited medium that can accommodate only a restricted number of programs, and advertising. The independents provide a needed outlet. In the largest markets, there are ethnic stations catering to the black and brown communities, even as there is ethnic radio in New York, Los Angeles, Louisiana, and Texas.

Generally, the independents are forced to subsist on marginal pickings, since the number of advertisers is limited. Independents are precluded by their nature from lucrative national advertising, and local affiliates skim off the cream of local advertising. The audience profile of stations is illustrative. There are eleven stations, eight of them independent, in Los Angeles. The three network affiliates skim off 75 percent of the audience, leaving 25 percent to be divided among the eight independents, which average about 3 percent each. In New York City the situation is somewhat better. There, three network stations cater to 80 percent of the audience, leaving 20 percent for the remaining five, or around 4 percent each—if audiences were divided equally, which they are not.

Since independents have to provide all of their own programming, they naturally seek those programs that are the least expensive. Many utilize old movies which have worn out their welcome on network television. A number of reruns of network programs from the fifties makes independent television a good place to review television's past. Programming at minimum cost means sharply reduced program quality which, in turn, provides little incentive for viewing.

News programs vary widely on independent stations. Some make a genuine and expensive effort to cover local news adequately. However, remote operations are expensive, as is the equipment, vehicles, and aircraft necessary for proper coverage. Most, therefore, settle for whatever comes easily, what they can plan for in advance with minimal difficulty, and shoot on film. Independent television, as a result, has become a press agent's garden, where public relations people are able to provide inexpensive takes, or videotapes and film, at no cost—all of which carry their own persuasive messages, disguised, sometimes only thinly, as news.

There are a number of VHF independents, and they fare significantly better than other independents. Their signals are easier to pick up on home receivers, and so their audiences are proportionately greater. They reap the most from local television advertising. Furthermore, most are establishing a local following in the hope of attracting network affiliation as the larger affiliates in their area alienate the network. Some VHF independents are owned by powerful groups whose national sales ability is an asset and whose influence with both the networks and the FCC is considerable. Because so much of their concentration is local, VHFs have a favored position in the public interest, convenience, and necessity review at relicensing time.

COSTS OF FREE TV

A good deal has been made of the broadcast media's freeness—the absence of cost to the consumer. This premise is worth examining. Broadcast, beginning with radio, required the consumer to make an investment of his own in the means of receiving. This investment is not small, considering the price of a television set, plus a 20-40 percent additional outlay for an antenna. To this must be added depreciation at the rate of about 20 percent per year, plus whatever maintenance costs are involved, which can be significant at the rates charged for television repair. Broadcast media operate on electricity; consequently, the monthly utility bill will increase in proportion to the number of sets and the amount they are used. Finally, as Harry Skornia points out in *Television and Society,* there is a hidden cost related to television advertising.[1] The costs of television advertising represent an increment in the cost of the products advertised, an increment that the consumer pays as he buys them. Since these are almost universally the most widely used products, the hidden increment across the nation during a year is huge. In fairness it should be noted that television advertising may permit these goods to be sold in such massive quantities that the cost is reduced through mass production, and that the extra sales cost is offset by the lower production cost, an element that is also passed on to the consumer in a competitive economy. Regardless, the cost of television to the consumer in hardware investment, depreciation, finance charges, and utilities is considerable. Television may actually be costing more per family than any other medium that is purchased.

Harry Skornia, in *Television and Society,* estimates the cost of television to a family with a single color set, including utilities and depreciation, at about $200 per year. To this must be added the advertising increment on major products—approximately another $50—for a total of around $250 per family per year. A newspaper subscription is around $40.00 per year by comparison. In other media $250 will buy: 125 movies tickets, 40 concert admissions, 25 magazine subscriptions, or 2 books a month for a year. The money could be used to purchase a newspaper, a best-seller a month, subscriptions to *Newsweek, National Geographic, Sports Illustrated, Town and Country,* and *Harper's,* plus 20 movies or 6 concerts, more or less. Free television is pretty expensive.

1. Harry Skornia, *Television and Society* (New York: McGraw-Hill, 1965).

SUBSEQUENT DEVELOPMENT

The first CATV operation was begun in Lansford, Pennsylvania in 1950. It was an effort to extend the reach of VHF stations in the mountainous Allegheny terrain. In concept CATV is deceptively simple. It consists of a master receiving antenna to which homes are wired directly by cable. Thus, an antenna on a mountain top can distribute the signal into the valley beneath where television's line-of-sight signal cannot reach. Furthermore, since the antenna reaches high into the relatively clear atmosphere and since the signal is distributed by cable, there is minimal distortion, blurring, and fuzz. It is an extremely efficient means of reducing channel noise. Since CATV originally was conceived for this purpose only, and since it operated within the confines of a single community, the FCC did not regulate it in the beginning. The FCC felt that its responsibility was to broadcast only and that this media was wired, and further that CATV was purely local in nature and did not pertain to interstate commerce. Consequently, responsibility for CATV licensing fell to local communities, city councils, boards of aldermen, and the like, hundreds of them all over the country, each with different ground rules. In some places in the East a single apartment house becomes one CATV operation, and the one next door another. Thus, a misconception of CATVs' real nature and potential from the outset seriously confused its future. Further, it wasn't until 1966—sixteen years later—that the FCC finally took jurisdiction over CATV. By this time local precedents had been established. Also, CATV operators had become embroiled in deep controversy with the broadcasters, misunderstandings arose over royalty payments, and the basis had been laid for a form of subscription television.

Experimental pay TV was begun in 1950. Pay TV broadcasts a scrambled signal; an unscrambler on the subscriber's set translates the signal and automatically records the time watched, for which the subscriber is subsequently billed.

MULTIPLE CHANNELS

The FCC authorized seventy-two UHF channels across the nation in 1952, reserving many of them for nonprofit and/or educational use. While this action theoretically sextupled the number of channels available, there were many complications, not the least of which was the fact that it wasn't until 1962 that the FCC required television set manufacturers to include UHF receivers on all sets. Thus, for ten years UHF was virtually on its own, requiring special equipment not only to broadcast but to receive—and this was long enough to establish a tradition of nonwatching. Even after 1962, a production lag in new sets extended UHF's marginal nature, and the fact that tuning to a UHF station was comparatively difficult—more so than the snap-on VHF channels,—kept audiences away. Meanwhile, UHF had acquired a reputation, not entirely undeserved, for mediocre programming. As it developed, UHF assumed the stamp of an informal educational, cultural, and experimental network, a pattern which was partially formalized in the early seventies with the establishment of PBS, and one which proved no magnet for audiences.

Commercial UHF channels presently just hang on economically. In some instances they are supported by the profits of other stations within a group, contributing certain tax advantages to the group while protecting their license. Some wait for the cable to make reception easier and for the long-shot hope that they might pick up a network affiliation, as channel 39 did in San Diego, California, in 1973. At that time ABC was forced to abandon its VHF Mexican affiliation, XETV, across the border in Tijuana.

In 1962 Telstar was launched—an experimental communications satellite capable of relaying television signals over vast distances, including the oceans—making international television possible. Millions across the world watched the Kennedy funeral in 1963, and millions in America watched the Churchill funeral in 1964. The principle of Telstar is simple: television's line-of-sight signal bounces off the orbiting satellite and is reflected back to earth.

In 1966 the FCC belatedly assumed jurisdiction over CATV, adding another entity to the already confusing maze of state and local controls, and in the same year began to encourage UHF broadcasting. The potential marriage of these two television offshoots—UHF and cable—is a matter of much speculation yet. Cable can accommodate the entire broadcast band and, thus, theoretically makes possible the clear reception of twelve VHF and seventy UHF broadcast channels on the home receiver. Some of these channels will be reserved for emergency use—police and fire shortwave, Armed Forces requirements, and radio-controlled equipment (including taxis, buses, and the like)—but the potential for over-the-air reception via cable is enormously increased. The broadcast band is a single spectrum including AM, FM, and shortwave radio, as well as both VHF and UHF TV. Crowding of so many varied uses (information, warning, entertainment, and education) onto a single band causes problems. In Maryland, for instance, a sophisticated Air Force experimental transmitter opens all the electronic garage doors in a neighboring community whenever it operates; it is an eerie sight as the garage doors go up and down mysteriously in unison. Crowding of the band, of course, is what led to the formation of the FCC in the beginning, and is apparently a problem only partially solved after nearly half a century.

In 1968, after several years of experimentation, the FCC authorized commercial pay TV, which relies on a CATV operator originating his own programming. This in turn was one of the unsuspected dividends that cable brought—the ability to produce programming to be carried over the cable, as well as importing over-the-air signals. Thus, a new dimension was added to CATV; through pay TV it was no longer an extension of broadcast but a competitor as well.

By 1970 the FCC further compounded media problems by requiring that cable operators in the one hundred largest markets originate their own programming, thus forcing cable operators into competition with broadcasters. The networks, despite their running battle with the cable operators, were least affected by this move. They had the experience, the financial resources, and proven programming with its mass audiences behind them. Most affected were marginal UHF stations, still struggling and incapable of bringing a concise tunable signal into the home, where cable excelled. Furthermore, cable competed with UHF directly in the local rather than the national market, and had the additional advantage of being able to import network programming.

ETV AND NET

There were 287 UHF stations on the air by 1970, of which 182 were noncommercial, educational stations whose licenses had been granted to school districts, colleges, universities, and the like. Educational television's (ETV) growth has been slow. These 182 stations are all that are operating out of a total of 329 reserved for educational use by the FCC.

All of the complexity that plagues commercial broadcasting is multiplied in the noncommercial area. This area lacks the unifying theme of profit to keep it on course and, consequently, has been characterized by goal confusion and ideological chaos. Problems began during the 1948–52 FCC freeze when educators made strong presentations to the FCC concerning the potential of the new medium. As a result, the FCC initially set aside twenty-five channels for ETV, and the first of these educational stations went on the air in Houston, Texas in 1953. Very gradually, ETV grew, and in due course National Educational Television (NET) began to provide programming and distribution to the loose chain of educational stations.

Despite the educators' enthusiasm, ETV did not fulfill its promise. It was hampered principally by a lack of funds. Cut off from advertising revenues, it existed on a meager basis, receiving spasmodic contributions from municipalities, school districts, states, various agencies of the federal government, and from large foundations—but never quite enough and never on an assured basis that would permit anything more than a minimum subsistence. Furthermore, NET funds were lacking for either coaxial cable or microwave relay of programming, and ETV programs were bicycled from one station to another by mail, which scarcely led to any degree of timeliness. Under Fred Friendly, formerly of CBS, NET distinguished itself by a certain arrogance and the production of highly controversial material that many of the ETV's found unsuitable, if not offensive.[2] Operating under a Ford Foundation grant, NET's purpose, was to produce news, documentaries, and public affairs programming of a meaningful nature, free of commercial domination. Friendly set out through the Public Broadcasting Laboratory (PBL), also funded through the Ford Foundation, to rival the network's news programming, slotting a two-hour segment on Sunday evenings for this magazine of the air. The PBL lasted an inauspicious two years, but actually died on opening night, as Martin Mayer points out in *About Television*.[3] However, PBL did perform two useful functions. By comparison, it demonstrated how extremely well the networks did their news and documentaries and, ironically, PBL blazed the trail for the networks to get into the magazine-of-the-air format. Both CBS's "60 Minutes" and NBC's "First Tuesday" are successors to the aborted PBL.

2. Les Brown, *Television: The Business Behind the Box* (New York: Harcourt Brace Jovanovich, 1972).

3. Martin Mayer, *About Television* (New York: Harper & Row, Publishers, 1972).

PBS

Into this picture in 1967 came the Carnegie Commission Report to President Johnson recommending the establishment of a public broadcasting system (PBS) as distinct from ETV. The distinction between the two is not entirely clear, particularly since PBS makes use of the ETV stations in a so-called fourth network. One thing the Carnegie Commission Report would have provided was assured financing for PBS through a manufacturer's excise tax on television receivers sold. Although Congress implemented the report and established the Corporation for Public Broadcasting (CPB), it still failed to provide the funding. Currently PBS is still existing on a shoestring, its largest appropriation by Congress being $30 million out of a minimal $60 million recommended by the commission.

Essentially, PBS provides only distribution, programming, and services formerly performed by the controversial NET to its ETV affiliates who are under no obligation whatever to carry the network. It programs for three hours during prime time on weekdays, since most noncommercial stations "go dark" on weekends. The stations may use the material or not, as they wish, or they may tape it for later use. The balance of the broadcasting day is local and filler material and home classroom subjects. To date, PBS's major accomplishments have been the English-imported "Civilisation" series, which it acquired only after all three networks had turned it down (it was a gift from the Xerox Corporation) and "Sesame Street," produced by the Childrens' Television Workshop (CTW), itself originally foundation-supported.

Although PBS was supposed to be free of the tyranny of the ratings in its operation, it succumbed to an inevitable curiosity for evaluation. The results were not encouraging. There is no PBS audience at all by television standards. Nielsen gave it a rating of 0.4 percent of all viewing. A part of the problem is PBS's poor financing, resulting in available money being spread too thinly; hence, a lack of professionalism. Another part of the problem may lie in local control and the fact that local ETV station managers are on the board of PBS, which does not mitigate toward national orientation. In the final analysis the biggest part of the problem is the fact that PBS is broadcast over the same air at the same time as CBS, NBC, and ABC, and it has been the networks' business for over a quarter century to find out what America wants to watch; they have done so and they do it well, and anything else simply cannot compete. A person can subscribe to both *Reader's Digest* and *American Heritage* and read them both, but he cannot watch CBS and PBS simultaneously.

CLOSED-CIRCUIT AND VIDEOPHONE

There are two aspects of the television embroglio that have probably been given inadequate attention in considering television's total impact on society. One is closed-circuit television, and the other is the Bell System's projected videophone. Closed-circuit television has been widely used for a variety of purposes. Essentially it is a means, as the name suggests, of restricting audiences. It is used by banks, supermarkets, and other commercial establishments as a watchman, constantly scanning the premises in search of thieves and shoplifters. It has a considerable cost advantage over the human watchman and cannot be bribed. In essence, it provides automated security. Closed-circuit television is used also in hospitals to scan patients and, combined with other electronic monitoring equipment, probably does a more efficient, if impersonal, job than the nurse on duty—with less human error. It can also be used to monitor various gauges and recording devices, reducing the supervisory manpower necessary. Today, such use of closed-circuit television has been restricted to very limited audiences for very specific purposes. However, the entire question of electronic surveillance is one which was raised both in George Orwell's *1984* and in the film *Fahrenheit 425*. It is simply, unobtrusive, silent.

For a decade or more closed-circuit television has been used by business as a means of conducting sales meetings for far-flung sales representatives, by the automobile manufacturers as a means of introducing new models to their scattered dealerships, by industry to bring a video annual report to stockholders on a regional basis, and by politicians to address rallies at long distance in different parts of their constituency. It is this use of the closed-circuit that best approaches the limited-audience concept of the controlled circulation magazine.

Finally, closed-circuit television has been used as a theater adjunct. Many sporting events have been presented over closed circuits in theaters throughout the nation purely and simply because their one-shot nature generates a greater return of the box office than would selling the event to commercial television. Here again, particularly in prizefighting, the natural appeal of the event homes on a limited, though dedicated audience. Women, who comprise at least half of network television's audience, tend to be turned off by prizefighting. Such a one-shot special would have to preempt network time already profitably sold, and this would be of little benefit to the network, either in profit or ratings. This kind of "theater" closed circuit is a form of pay TV which increasingly bodes to become a familiar part of television's spectrum: witness Evel Knievel's jump of the Snake River in the fall of 1974.

Meanwhile, AT&T, never far from the broadcast picture, has been developing its much heralded and debated videophone, a telephone with pictures. This, of course, is the ultimate in audience selectivity, a one-to-one television relationship. Many claim that the videophone, in adding expression, grimace, and gesture to the already intimate telephone, will demand whole new telephone techniques or manners. Others say it will require a switch on the instrument so that either party can have the option of communicating audio or video; anything else would permit unwarranted prying. At present videophones are largely experimental and very expensive. Nor will they soon be widespread for the simple reason that circuits for a videophone demand twelve times the capacity of ordinary voice transmission. At present levels of technology, this would require rewiring the nation at a prohibitive cost. However, future technology may provide circuitry to accommodate the videophone within the existing system. When and if this happens, the Bell System will be operating its own, privately selective, television network.

PAY TV: CULTURE OR WHAT?

Pay TV is a concept which eyes the lcd programming of the networks and proposes to offer other fare—culture, travel, nostalgia, the esoteric, self-improvement—for a price to those who want it. The consumers of pay TV would be paying for it directly out of their own pocketbooks instead of the advertisers footing the bill. It is a magazine approach to broadcasting. Put thus, it seems eminently reasonable. However, pay TV carries some inherent threats. For example, if only 2 million homes were willing to pay fifty cents to follow a prime-time serial weekly, subscription would generate a million dollars per week. This is more than enough to buy the serial and take it off commercial television. One could project that the net result of pay TV might be less the presentation of elite culture and self-improvement for those who wanted it as it would be the same old thing now on commercial network television.

Already there have been examples of selected sporting events reserved for pay TV. This battle was fought in 1964 in California when Subscription TV (STV), a consortium of varied interests headed by Pat Weaver (formerly president of NBC), sought to offer three pay channels. The battleground was a state initiative to outlaw pay TV that was sponsored by theater owners and others who feared the encroachment on their terrain. Eventually, STV was killed by popular vote, although a year later the State Supreme Court found the initiative to be unconstitutional. Despite the arguments pro and con, there is undoubtedly future room for some sort of pay television for the small and discriminating audiences that wish it. Following a decade of experimentation in various parts of the country, notably Bartlesville, Oklahoma and Hartford, Connecticut, the FCC authorized pay TV in 1968. However, its dependence on CATV and the uncertain direction that CATV may take, and doubt as to the size and composition of cable audiences, is enough to make pay TV enthusiasts demure for the time being.

CABLE OR CATV?

"Televison of the future"..."the wired nation"—these optimistic terms have been used to describe CATV, or cable. They portend the almost science fiction potential of the medium, but to date cable's performance has not kept pace. Cable's potentials stem from the fact that it can both boost and import existing over-the-air broadcast as well as originate its own programming. Because it is wired like a telephone, it can be both as individually selective as a telephone, and utilize telephone's two-way capacity. These obvious assets, when married to the computer, impart a Buck Rogers aspect to the future

Electromedia

of cable. Furthermore, because it is video, it holds the potential for facsimile reproduction, which means it can duplicate materials in written form in the home, including newspapers, specialized reports, and the like. The computer capacity lends itself to information retrieval from memory banks that could either be flashed on the screen or reproduced in facsimile for the record. To date in man's history cable television represents the ultimate vision of communications' perfection. Permanence and instantaneousness, selectivity and flexibility, one-way and two-way capacity, and mass and individual communications characteristics are welded into one.

However, costs, human nature, FCC regulation, competition, and economics have deterred cable's progress. Ironically, one of its greatest strengths has proven its stumbling block: it is so versatile that it may easily be in competition with itself.

Consider, for example, that there are nearly 3,000 cable systems in the United States. Each of these is a little network and, in the aggregate, rather than developing a mass audience, they splinter it to the point where none can develop an effective mass. When the audience numbers are not there, neither is the programming. Consider further that the majority of these new systems are not located in major population centers where the largest audiences are found. Rather, they are located in peripheral and even rural communities where cable's ability to boost broadcast is an asset. Alternately, they may be located in smaller cities with only two network affiliates (for example, CBS and NBC). In these cities cable's primary use would be to provide interconnection with the nearest ABC channel.

Cable has not proved particularly successful in the largest cities for two very good reasons. First, the FCC prohibited CATV from operating in the largest markets for five years, beginning in 1966. The rationale was to give UHF an opportunity to develop, which it did not. In view of UHF's erratic performance and under considerable pressure, the FCC in 1971 did permit cable operators to wire the largest markets. In these markets, however, broadcast competition is intense. Most large cities have little difficulty in television reception and already have an abundance of broadcast channels to choose from. For instance, New York has a total of eight channels; Los Angeles has eleven. What can cable offer these cities? Perhaps additional programming. But what can cash-short cable systems possibly produce of major appeal that isn't being offered on one of eight broadcast channels? They could get into a bidding situation with the networks for first-run movies, talent, and the like, but where are cable's funds, and where is its audience? Once again the economic cycle of mass communications and media becomes apparent.

PROBLEMS

The approximate 3,000 CATV systems serve a total of around 6 million homes. Divided equally, that isn't many. Nor is audience growth likely to be rapid. Why should a city dweller pay $5.00 per month to receive channels he receives already, and what can cable offer that isn't already available? Further, when a broadcaster builds a transmitter everybody within range immediately receives. Not so with cable. The cable operator must wire a pattern of homes up and down streets, paying the municipality a substantial franchise fee for doing so. Then, at considerable sales expense, he must convince the homes on this grid to rent his service at $5.00 plus a month, and he must service the network. Costs are high. Profits may be considerable if there are sufficient subscribers, but they are generally not high enough to underwrite the mammoth investment required of television programming on a regular basis unless pay TV is included as part of the package. But pay TV demands the existence of the cable initially, and the size of audiences does not dictate much advertising potential at present.

One of cable's biggest problems with the broadcasters has been over the matter of copyright. As the networks incur considerable expense in program production, they have taken a dim view of cable operators importing their signals into distant markets without paying for the privilege. They have felt as if they were paying the production costs for a competitive system. Some cable operators, because cable can originate its own programming and commercials, were deleting network advertising and substituting their own, which they sold locally. Such a situation might be likened to a form of electronic piracy.

In a strange decision in 1958, the United States Supreme Court held that CATV was an extension of the home receiver rather than a part of broadcasting. As a part of a receiver, it was not subject to the copyright law of 1909. Cable operators were, therefore, empowered to import network programming without payment of royalties on the condition that they import the entire program, commercials and all, and not substitute their own. This Supreme Court decision still muddies the waters as CATV gets more and more into program origination. Recent FCC rulings have permitted cable operators to import distant signals into certain rural markets, provided they do not leapfrog over stations located closer to the areas they serve.

Since 1970, when the FCC reversed itself again, cable operators have been permitted to develop in the 100 largest markets in the nation, provided they originate a certain amount of programming and set aside certain channels for local government and for public access—a sort of electronic soapbox available to anyone on a first-come, first-served basis.

It should be noted that a considerable number of CATV franchises had been granted in the major markets before the 1966 freeze when the FCC assumed cable jurisdiction. These had been granted by the individual municipalities, which, ignoring any planned development, saw a revenue opportunity that they heavily exploited. Many granted multiple franchises to competing operators for different parts of the city, thus effectively fragmenting audiences at the outset and hamstringing any coordinated, community-wide development of the medium. As a part of its decision, the FCC forbade any program interference on the part of the cable operator with public access programming. The result has been some very strange programming, pressing, in many instances, against the boundaries of both credibility and taste. This does little for the cable's public image and scarcely constitutes a sales tool for potential subscribers.

DIVERSI-FICATION

In the largest markets the FCC has authorized cable operators to carry forty channels, including those of the local government, public access, network and independent, PBS, UHF, CATV, pay TV, and the like. Just what these forty channels will be used for is difficult to determine at present. However, these are forty over-the-air channels. It must be remembered that CATV is wired and, in addition, can offer an almost unlimited number of wired channels.

There are those who visualize that magazines, already specialized, may get into the CATV business, interconnecting a number of channels in large markets and offering "magazines of the air." *Sports Illustrated, Cosmopolitan,* or *Playboy* would be naturals for selective CATV networks or groups. Operating in other than prime time, they have an already developed loyal audience receptive to their kind of material. It is but a short step to convert their material into programming, and there are proven advertising revenues to be tapped. This is one of the future options for the media. Other possibilities are CATV nets operated by advertising agencies or public relations firms as a service to such clients as the political parties, major manufacturers, or department stores and market chains. Possibilities for CATV lurk on the horizon, presently only dimly perceived.

However, this concept may not be as farfetched as it seems. Among the first enterprises interested in CATV were newspaper publishers. In attempting to acquire cable franchises in their communities, they reasoned that the newspaper of the future could be easily delivered by facsimile reproduction over television. Technically, such utilization is relatively simple, comparable to a Xerox machine hooked up to the cable, delivering the newspaper page by page. Format and editing procedures would have to change radically, but the concept is reasonable. Carrier boys are, after all, a remarkably inefficient means of delivery, an anachronism from a knee-britches past. Perhaps a smattering of headlines could be offered visually, with a retrieval system hooked to a home console to deliver stock market quotations, or market advertising, or racing results by flashing them on the screen. If the subscriber wanted to read a specific item, all he would have to do would be push the facsimile print button to "freeze the frame" and record it.

Such capacity lends itself not only to the current day's news but, linked to the computer, to all that is past. The *New York Times* has already embarked on a program of cataloging and recording all of its previous issues on memory banks for the day when such a system may be feasible. It is possible now.

In addition, the development of inexpensive videotape hardware opens up a number of other doors. Even as phonograph recordings can be taped and radio programs recorded on magnetic tape in the listener's absence, so can television programs, whether network or cable, be recorded on videotape for permanent record or later playback. Inexpensive videotape equipment is already in use in the production of public access programming in New York, and many amateurs are making their own programs experimentally for broadcast over program-hungry CATV channels seeking to comply with the FCC regulation to originate programming. This is not much, but it is a beginning and it does offer people both an opinion forum and a creative outlet previously lacking. What the eventual dimensions of this capacity will be is, of course, unknown.

VIDEOTAPE

Videotape also opens up the question of video cassettes and cassette television. Video cassettes are at present available in limited form. They require an adapting device, much like a tape deck for a hi-fi system, in order to be shown over the tube. Cassette enthusiasts visualize the day when movies, opera, ballet, museum tours, travelogues, symphony concerts, immortal drama, and the like will be available in full color, professionally produced on video cassettes. These cassettes would be available for home use by rental or purchase through stores and libraries. Thus, anyone interested can more or less replay at will great performances, visit the Kasbah, or see *Gone With the Wind* again.

Videotape may have a salutory effect on the increasingly expensive performing arts, such as Broadway and off-Broadway theater, ballet, opera, and symphony. The full cost of artistic productions has skyrocketed to the point where they can no longer make their way. Appeal of these arts has generally been restricted to around 4 percent of the population. This audience is not enough to justify network television coverage to pay the bills. Performing arts, in general, have never paid their own way, but now the astronomical losses are driving away even their affluent patrons. Video cassettes offer a potential whereby performances can be recorded and the tapes sold to afficionados for home consumption with the producer receiving a royalty on sales. Another possibility, if it ever comes of age, is pay TV, with cultural channels on the cable and sponsorship as in the old days of radio from advertisers wanting to reach the affluent elite. Canned art is better than no art.

Videotape cassettes are of essentially two types. One is the professionally produced cassette available for rent or purchase. Essentially, it bears a relationship to stereo recordings and/or eight-track tapes on which masterful performances are preserved for reenjoyment at leisure. It is this type of video cassette that lends itself also to magazines and other uses, either as a magazine supplement—"Fly Fishing in the High Sierras," a July bonus from *The Fly Fisherman,* or "America's Cup," the September feature from *Yachting*—or as a supplemental sales tool—"Introducing the 1984 Cadillac" from the General Motors Corporation to its most affluent customers. The use of professional videotape cassettes intermarries the recording magazine, direct mail, and book-of-the-month club businesses in fascinating combinations, the full scope of which can only be speculated.

The second kind of videotape is the product of inexpensive tape equipment. This type may be compared to home movies, although some are being used at present for CATV free access productions. Videotape also makes possible a sort of electronic "cinéma vérité." It can tape not only television programs in the home during the viewer's absence for playback, but has the potential of filming vacation trips, children's antics, treasured moments, and do-it-yourself pornography. Videotape has the additional characteristic, unlike film, of being erasable and reusable and having no development lag or expense, thus minimizing costs and being instantly available.

HOME COMMUNICATIONS CENTER

Such fanciful use of videotape introduces the subject of the home communications center, with shades of *Fahrenheit 425.* An entire wall-size screen, perhaps in a separate room, could accommodate the networks, meetings of the city council, professional football or golf, the local newspaper, or, hooked to a videophone, relay intimate conversations with loved ones or business conferences from far away; Sir George Solti and the Chicago Orchestra could perform from the cassette, or at the flip of the console switch shopping at the supermarket or touring the shopping center could be done—all without leaving one's easy chair.

Actually, in the home communications center concept, videotape cassettes are merely a stopgap except for collectors since, with computer capacity, immortal performances, old movies, historical documents, and foreign tours can be recalled via the console from a central memory bank. Shopping over the home communications center, the consumer could freeze the frame on an item he liked, examine it, request full data over cable's two-way capacity, and press the purchase switch, which would automatically debit his bank balance, credit the store's account with the purchase price and the state with the sales tax, and start the item on its way from the warehouse to the consumer's home.

Way ahead of its time Telemart in San Diego, California, attempted such a system. The problem was that it tried over-the-air broadcast in competition with the networks on a limited number of channels rather than the selective shopping service that cable and the computer can offer.

The computer and home communications center (HomComCen) offer other potentials too. A console at the CATV studio hooked to a computer can establish certain demographics among the subscribers to the system. Thus, within the same programming, advertisements for Cadillacs could be beamed to the more affluent while minicar ads go to those further down the economic ladder. This is the kind of computer selectivity that the magazines have been using. "Back to school" advertisements would go only to those homes on the grid with school-age children. Sunday services could be offered simultaneously to Catholic, Episcopal, Lutheran, or Baptist homes. Political campaigning in Democratic primaries would enter only Democratic households, while Republicans would hear from the Republican contenders. Carried to its logical conclusion, such computerized selectivity could be utilized in much the same fashion as computerized direct mail is now used—a political candidate or furniture salesman might present an individual, taped message for each viewer. If, as the NAB says, television is a guest in the home, CATV is "the man who came to dinner."

TELEVISION AND THE FUTURE

Some media scholars see the future development of communications as taking place in three stages. The first exists at present: an overwhelming mass medium supported by an intriguing variety of complementary, supplemental, and specialized media. Next, characterized by CATV's diversity, is the "open channels" stage, in which specialization of media and fragmentation of audiences continues, with something for everyone on television or in the mailbox. This stage is marked by multiple networks interconnecting all aspects and levels of society. Finally there is the "information retrieval" stage, assisted by the computer, in which all knowledge, information, entertainment, and persuasion is stored in memory banks to be called up by individuals at the flick of a console switch. This stage effectively does away with the mass and makes the past instantly present; it is the ultimate in individual selectivity. These stages can be accommodated readily on the media and audience continua, and may easily be the shape of the future if the splintering pattern of former masses continues.

Since CATV is two-way, it also opens the door for instantaneous public opinion polling and immediate political feedback. It raises the question of government by popular whim instead of representative judgment. Nor do potential miracles stop here. In the wings lurks the three-dimensional capacity of holography. Holography, created by the splitting of a laser beam, is able to reproduce three-dimensional images in space. A screen is not required; the figures, color, movement, and action all take place in space before a viewer's eyes. Thus, the HomComCen might become a separate room where ghostly three-dimensional communications occur.

These fancies are all a part of the Pandora's box that CATV has opened up. Truly, not only the television of the future, cable bids fair to being all things to all people. The only requirement to make these things happen is economic incentive, which seems at present to be lacking. Also, there is the question of priorities—society's priorities—and whether this kind of investment in the future, requiring enormous risk capital, is where Americans wish to spend their money; money, like time, is limited, and what is spent for this fantastic system of full-color, stereophonic, two-way, three-D, multiple-channel, computer-controlled, ultimately flexible, and completely selective information system must come from something else. The economic aspects of CATV have been investigated, but its educational, social, psychological, and political ramifications at present remain a mystery.

While much of the foregoing is speculative, it is all possible at the moment. Experimentally and, in some instances, commercially, the various systems have been proven. The questions of cost and commitment, however, remain. The science fiction possibilities are discussed because they will require society's judgment in the near future. The Sloan Commission studying CATV foresees a wired nation by 1980. The kinds of judgments made this year and next, and the year after that, may prove irrevocable in terms of commitment to a path or a system.

SATELLITES

Of television's progeny, satellite television remains. The experimental 1962 SYNCOM (Synchronous Orbit Communication) established the optimum height of a communications satellite to be 22,000 miles orbiting over the earth. Originally, communications satellites had the shortcoming of passing out of television range in relaying their signals back to earth. This was corrected by placing a number of satellites in fixed orbit, that is, orbiting at the speed at which the earth revolves so that they might always be directly above a given point. Thus, at least one satellite is always within range of any point on earth for reception, and the signal can be relayed from satellite to satellite to reach any other point on earth. Satellite fixed orbit coverage is total.

The Communications Satellite Corporation (COMSAT), a quasi-public corporation, was established by Congress in 1962. With its enormous stake in the communications business, AT&T was the largest stockholder. Communications satellites, it should be remembered, do a lot more than relay television signals. They transmit all kinds of other data, including computer information and telephone conversations.

Satellites are no longer national—American; they are not bounded by oceans. They are international in nature, and it was inevitable that COMSAT would yield to INTELSAT, a consortium of sixty-five nations engaged in international satellite communications. The future of COMSAT is unclear. It may become a domestic satellite communications network carrying data with greater capacity and efficiency than either land lines or earthbound signals on the radio band, including shortwave, AM, FM, VHF, UHF, and microwave relay. Future use of satellites envisions three different kinds. First is the relay satellite, of which both COMSAT and INTELSAT are examples. With relay, earth-to-satellite-to-earth communication can take place only between a few fixed points. Distribution satellites are a refinement of the relay system, considerably augmenting the number of earth receiving terminals and redistributing the material over conventional systems. The ultimate is the broadcast satellite, with which messages can be picked up directly from the satellite by home receivers, obviating the need for television stations, FCC licenses, and even the networks. When satellites are added to CATV the dimensions of communications and its accompanying problems expand considerably.

SUMMARY

The forms of television other than national network television are many and varied. The television field, however, is so dominated by the networks that few of the other forms, despite their potential, have had an opportunity to realize even a fraction of that potential. Nor has the situation been helped by confusing and often contradictory FCC policy and rulings.

The other forms of video communications include local independent stations, both VHF and UHF, and the Public Broadcasting System (PBS) comprised mostly of UHF stations whose licenses are held by educational institutions and who are precluded from commercial advertising. There is CATV in its mind-boggling diversity. Such related forms as pay TV, closed-circuit, videophone, and satellite broadcasting bid fair to obviate the system of local stations or affiliates to which the public has become so accustomed. Finally, there is the versatility of videotape, video cassettes, and light, inexpensive television hardware.

The local independents are the poor cousins of network television. Ordinarily, they exist only in the largest markets, where population size permits a sufficient audience interest to support some sort of specialized programming. Generally they subsist on purely local coverage, providing an inexpensive showcase to purely local advertisers, or catering to highly specialized and sometimes ethnic audiences. Their existence is marginal.

The costs of free television bear examination. Television requires considerable investment in a receiving set, antennae, carrying costs, depreciation, and a continuing utility charge. Free television represents a considerable annual outlay, more in fact than any other medium. There is also a hidden increment represented by the increased price of advertised products.

The so-called fourth network, PBS, is not much of a network at all. Its programming has been substandard and its audiences miniscule. The PBS lacks funds, existing on unpredictable congressional appropriations (always inadequate), foundation grants, and occasional contributions from the private sector.

Cable, or CATV, began as a means of bringing over-the-air broadcasting to isolated communities. This is still its principle function. The FCC did not enter the CATV picture until 1966, when it assumed jurisdiction and placed a five-year freeze on CATV in the nation's largest markets. Prior to 1966 CATV had been franchised by local communities, resulting in a plethora of stations, none of which had a sufficient total audience to fulfill any commercial promise. At present there is a lack of incentive for CATV to enter large markets; it can offer little that is not there already. In 1970 the FCC began to require CATV stations in the largest markets to originate programming and to provide both local government and public access channels.

Closed-circuit television, pay TV, and the videophone are all esoteric forms of cable. Closed-circuit television has been used for a variety of private purposes, including surveillance, political rallies, sales meetings, and annual reports. Closed-circuit television has been hooked to theaters to provide a form of pay TV for such sports spectaculars as heavyweight championships. It can come into the home over the cable offering a wide range of specialized programming for those willing to pay for it.

The Bell System's videophone is the ultimate in cable's selectivity, permitting one-to-one television. Costs have hampered its development, as existing phone lines are inadequate.

The potential of CATV is enormous. Some of the original investors were newspapers who visualized the possibility of a newspaper being delivered directly to the home through a facsimile technique. As the FCC has authorized up to forty channels on CATV operations, the potential diversity lends itself to possible use by magazines and other specialized interests, including advertisers. Forty-channel capacity, when and if fully developed, is bound to have a splintering effect on the lcd programming now offered by the networks.

Other factors loom on the horizon. The two-way capacity of CATV lends itself to instant feedback, whether of a public opinion polling or automated home shopping nature. Linked to a computer, cable's selectivity would permit the simultaneous delivery of different demographic messages to every home on the grid. The spectre of holography may eventually mean three-dimensional television—images created in space.

Videotape and video cassettes offer the availability of immortal performances for sale or rental, and thus may inject new commercial infusion into the increasingly expensive arts. Video cassette supplements by specialized magazines to an already proven audience are also a distinct possibility.

Satellite development began in 1962 with Telstar. Congress set up COMSAT as a quasi-public corporation to develop satellite relay.

This has in due course evolved into today's sixty-five nation consortium, INTELSAT. At present, satellites relay information from a transmitter to a receiver that rebroadcasts it by conventional means. However, satellites are quite capable of broadcasting directly to the home on multiple channels, and when this happens, they too will be in competition with cable's diversity, and will also obviate the need for traditional broadcasting.

Part VI

INDIRECT MEDIA

The indirect media are service media. They have no audiences of their own in the sense that the mass media do, composed of individual viewers, customers, listeners, readers, and subscribers. Indirect media are the highly organized products of a complex and corporate communications system, where their direct audiences are other corporate entities through which they filter to people only indirectly. Basically, they have to do with the substance of the media, its informational, persuasive, and commercial content. These correspond closely to the functions of the media. These indirect media are the packagers of content, of information and entertainment, and of persuasion.

The packagers of information are principally the wire services, AP and UPI, supplemented by a wide assortment of feature services of various kinds. The packagers of entertainment are the independent film, serial, and show producers who serve television, the ranks of which are rapidly growing as the FCC requires more and more program origination of both over-the-air broadcasting and CATV. Entertainment packagers also include a number of the feature syndicates who specialize in comics and other addenda of the information industry that can scarcely be classified as news.

The packagers of persuasion are the advertising and public relations industries. Between these two it is necessary to make a distinction. Advertising deals in paid time and space. Advertising provides the economic incentive for most of the mass media, so that in addition to persuasion, it provides the grease that makes the mass communications wheels go round. Public relations, on the other hand, is a charming parasite. Its persuasion is often disguised as news; it sometimes conceals its purpose. It is also true that public relations is a necessary adjunct to the information business. The mass media rely on it far more than they like to admit for legitimate news of events and organizations that they themselves lack the resources, human and economic, to cover.

Thus, it seems that functions are intermixed in the indirect media as much as they are in the mass media. The press associations deal in information, entertainment, and, through public relations, in persuasion. Advertising also deals in persuasion and information. Further, one of the basic jobs of advertising agencies is to inject entertainment into persuasion to make it palatable. Public relations is by nature both informational and persuasive, and possibly entertaining. It is ulterior communications. All indirect media, of course, represent pipelines of the culture in reflecting contemporary values and mores to both posterity and to man today.

While considering the mass media packagers, their relationship to the sources of information, persuasion, and entertainment should also be considered, for they are by themselves merely distributors. The sources of information on any kind of a regular basis are all levels of government, major sports, the business and financial world, and society itself, which includes such things as environmental and racial concerns, and the doings of the great, near great, and notorious. (War, of course, is considered a governmental concern.) It should be noted that these sources of information conform closely to the major divisions of a metropolitan newspaper.

To a lesser extent and of considerably less timely concern are a number of other subjects from which information springs. These concern homemaking, fashion, travel, human behavior, science, and opinion. These, too, are divisions in major newspapers, but because speed is not crucial, they are the subjects of different feature syndicates that can mail their materials at much less cost than the wire services can deliver theirs.

The pervasity of these indirect media, their influence upon the media they serve, and, indirectly, their effect upon the various audiences, publics, and each individual, is the subject of the next three chapters.

16

NEWS SERVICES AND SOURCES

THE INFORMATION PACKAGERS

The press associations, or wire services, as they are better known, have a respectable history as packagers of information or news. Their existence came out of the costly business of news gathering that, as it became more competitive, also became prohibitively expensive for any single newspaper to bear. Essentially, wire services are a pooling of costs and effort—joint ventures.

From the beginning the press in America served a dual purpose. It was isolated and local; it was also the principal public communications link to the old world. Even in Colonial times, therefore, newspapers in the scattered population centers were eager to receive news from England and France as rapidly as possible, and through transatlantic shipping they had far better and more regular contact with Europe than they did with their sister colonies. It became common for publishers to send sloops out to meet incoming vessels and to return with the news from abroad, sometimes days before the slower oceangoing ships could beat their way into harbor and dock. Curiosity and economic advantage put a premium on such news. In due course, as the populations increased and newspapers became more competitive, relays of horse couriers sped foreign notices, the news of the world, first from the tip of Long Island and later from as far away as Nova Scotia, to the waiting presses in New York. The costs of riders, horses, boatmen, and relay stations were great, and rivalry between the competing couriers was intense.

In 1844 Samuel Morse invented the telegraph, the dim beginning of the electric age and communications revolution. Newspapers were quick to see the advantages of telegraph, which meant that they could import distant national news from Washington and elsewhere. However, telegraph costs were high—involving stringing lines and hiring operators—and it soon became apparent that there was little use in having six operators telegraph six stories about the same presidential message to be received by six editors more or less at the same time.

DEVELOPMENT

The Associated Press was formed in 1848 as a cooperative endeavor between six New York newspapers. Costs were drastically reduced, and each of the papers was assured that it would receive the same news at the same time. The Associated Press was, and still is, a membership organization, governed by a board of directors elected from amongst its client-members. Gradually, it expanded and took in new members in different geographical areas on an exclusive basis. Thus, AP membership was an extremely valuable asset to any publisher, for it meant that he alone in his territory had access to outside news. Journalism history is replete with examples of faltering newspapers selling for high prices solely because of their AP membership.

However, as other newspapers were added to the AP membership roster, they reflected a wide variety of differing political and social viewpoints. Northern newspapers tended to be abolitionist; Southern newspapers were proslavery. Partisan differences at that time were even stronger than they are today, and the AP discovered the necessity of objective reporting of the news—reporting the facts alone, without color or opinion. As a considerable portion of the news content of each newspaper gradually became wire service copy, the newspapers themselves began to adhere to the cult of objectivity on which journalism was founded.

JOURNALESE: A WAR BABY

By the time of the Civil War, the wire services were fairly well established, and the eastern portion of the nation at least, where most of the action took place, was "wired." Apart from being the first modern war in the sense of its use of long-range weapons and massive firepower that de-emphasized individual combat, the Civil War acutely demonstrated the attraction of war as a news source. The major newspapers across the nation sent correspondents to the battlefields. Most of this news flowed to the nation's editors, North and South, over the wires. However, telegraphic performance in the din of battle was uncertain. Lines could be cut by artillery barrages or sappers could snip them purposely; therefore, correspondents developed the technique of sending the most significant news first, in bulletin form, and following up with the details. Thus was journalese born in the heat of battle: the lead to a story—who, what, when, where, why, and how—was sent first, and the balance of the story followed in order of decreasing significance until the wires went out. The journalistic principles of objectivity and the "inverted pyramid" style of writing were the historical contributions of the wire services.

In the years following the Civil War, the years of laissez-faire and "survival of the fittest," America devoted herself to rebuilding and to expansion—the winning of the West. Technological innovations mounted one upon the other, and the field of communications

Indirect Media

was no exception. More and more people flocked to new cities and the older cities grew. New population centers sprang up along the railheads across the continent, and all demanded newspapers to serve them. The railroad and the industrial revolution, serving one another cooperatively, made national distribution possible, which led both to advertising and to national magazines. The transatlantic cable, which sped world news to the waiting presses, was completed in 1866, and international coverage became a part of the Associated Press' budget.

FEATURE MATERIAL

In the 1880s Samuel McClure, who published *McClure's Magazine*, decided to capitalize on his investment in "nonnews." He recognized that the growing newspapers had a need for "untimely" material of a human interest or feature nature. Material that made interesting reading, but which didn't have to make the next edition could be held against a slow news day. McClure put out 50,000 words a week to newspaper subscribers on such topics as fashion, homemaking, manners, and literature. Feature services were born—packagers of the untimely. Newspaper publishers did not have the money to produce this kind of material themselves, but when it could be purchased for a fraction of its cost on an exclusive basis in their territory, it was a filler bargain—they could save some reportorial salaries.

The growth of telegraph led to the formation of the great newspaper empires of Scripps, Hearst, and Pulitzer. It permitted them a centralized control over basic editorial policy. It assured that the treatment of international and national news would be similar in all their papers, and it made possible national advertising on a local basis.

Scripps was the first to break loose from the AP's domination of the news industry, as several of his papers were denied world news by the AP's exclusive agreements. He founded the United Press (UP) in 1907 primarily to serve his own newspapers, but he sold the service to other papers that wished it, thus defraying a part of its cost. Such a system was logical in that a part of the copy generated by the UP was local copy for his own newspapers and fed onto the wires when appropriate. Hearst followed suit in 1909 with the International News Service (INS), characterized from the beginning by the sensational Hearst style. Neither the UP nor INS ever really rivaled the AP in coverage. They were stopgaps for major papers offering different viewpoints on world and national events. They made possible outside coverage to many newspapers and communities locked out by the AP's exclusive franchises.

WIRE SERVICES TODAY

In 1958 the UP and INS merged into United Press International (UPI), which, as a merger, is large enough to rival the AP. Today AP has 8,500 members and UPI has 6,000; roughly two-thirds of each are domestic accounts, which means that they are truly international news carriers, packagers, and distributors. Their fees are based on circulation and may run from as little as $50 a week for a small weekly taking only the basic wire part of the day, to $6,000 a week for a metropolitan daily subscribing to full twenty-four-hour service. Membership in AP can be cancelled on two years notice; UPI contracts run for five. About half of the United States dailies take AP only, about a quarter take UPI alone, and another quarter subscribe to both.

There are differences between AP and UPI. Generally, AP does a better job on national and international news. On the other hand, UPI excels in covering the presidency, the Soviet Union, and Latin America; it also places a premium on writing style. In any event, the two provide two points of view, and offer a metropolitan editor with some choice. He can take whatever story comes first; he can take the story that appears (to him) to best reflect the event; he can take the one whose style he prefers; or he can assign a rewrite man to combine them.

The two major wire services are in intense competition. Probably nowhere in the mass communications business, including the television networks, is competition so intense to be first with the news. Remembering that among the nation's 1,750 dailies there is a deadline every minute, a minute's delay in flashing a wire service story may make the difference in whether a paper carries an AP or UPI story. The economics of the matter is simple. If an editor, looking back over a year's national and international coverage in his newspaper, discovers that he has used one of the wire services predominantly, he may easily decide to discard the other one and save $6,000 a week, or around $350,000 a year. Because the cost of news gathering increases with inflation and because the intense competition is driving the sales price down, all is not well with the major wire services. Currently, UPI is losing money and AP is hard pressed to keep its head above water. The future of the two major wire services, which supply America with the overwhelming majority of national and international news, is unclear.

OTHER POOLING EFFORTS

In the newspaper field, following the precedent established long ago by Scripps and Hearst, many groups are finding it advantageous to organize smaller wire and feature services principally to serve their own newspapers. Material written for one newspaper can, in many instances, be used in others in the group, thereby achieving some savings and lowering the unit cost. Alternately, some newspapers have syndicated their materials for mutual use, as, for example, the *Los Angeles Times–Washington Post* syndicate. Both papers profit from unparalleled coverage of the nation's capital and of the southern California nexus at no additional cost. Once this pooling occurs, whether on a group or independent syndicate basis, the next logical step is to offer the material for sale to other newspapers, defraying a portion of the original investment in the material.

Individual newspapers also get into the act. The *New York Times*, the nation's newspaper of record, offers outstanding comprehensive material and unsurpassed coverage of the nation's financial capital to anyone who cares to buy. Both the *Chicago Daily News* and the *Chicago Sun-Times* offer material pertinent to the country's heartland; the *Toronto Telegram Services* covers Canada. In each instance, the service represents extra income from an investment already made. In this respect groups and private services have an advantage over the wire services in that they utilize pooled information directly and derive income through subscriptions besides, while the wire services' revenue must come from media sales alone. Newsmagazines also have gotten into the packaging business, getting more revenue mileage out of their basic coverage. *Newsweek* is notable among these.

Many of these services also tend to specialize their coverage. The Women's News Service speaks for itself. The Copley News Service (CNS), serving 12 Copley papers in California and 4 in Illinois, has about 150 additional clients. The CNS has proven excellent in travel, military, and Latin American areas, with less concentration on spot news than on "think pieces" and features.

Since jet travel, it has become possible for major metropolitan newspapers to put their own reporters on a distant battleground or at the scene of a major event as easily as can the wire services. These reporters can write specially tailored news for the paper's own readership, keeping the paper's own slant and deadlines constantly in mind. An additional advantage is offered the newspaper by being able to sell the stories to other, smaller papers through its news service or syndication. In such instances the wire services are reduced to an early warning or alarm clock role, simply calling attention to an international happening. The facility of transportation has reduced the significance of wire service copy to the nation's major newspapers, newspaper groups, television networks, and broadcast groups. It is almost as if the concept of pooling, which led to the wire services in the beginning, were reversing itself as smaller consortiums get into the business of information packaging and the advancement of technology that led to pooling makes it feasible not to pool. Certainly, this diversity of packaging leads to a diversity of opinion and expression, and makes a more varied menu of news than the sometimes monotonous sameness of wire service copy.

However, with CATV operators and independent stations crying for coverage, there may be room for the wire services to branch out in an attempt to rival the networks in the preparation of daily news film or videotape for independents and CATVs—a whole new market. At present UPI operates a limited news film service, but the incentive to expand it has not yet been forthcoming.

High distribution costs also plague the wire services. Presently AP and UPI lease nearly a half-million miles of wire in the United States alone; the charges are enormous. With the coming of the satellite, it may be that the same messages can be beamed into outer space and back at considerable savings, and this may solve a part of the financial problems of wire services.

HOW IT WORKS

The wire services operate a remarkably efficient two-way, dovetailed system of both news gathering and distribution. In the distribution link, most wire service copy originates in New York for domestic consumption. It travels over trunk lines to the wire services' major metropolitan subscribers. As it travels, from New York to the *Los Angeles Times,* for example, it passes through a number of intermediate relay points where its contents are scanned by "wire filers" who take appropriate items, major stories, and material of a particular regional or local interest and forward them onto the state and regional circuits for use by smaller clients. This system can be compared to a transcontinental freight train being broken up in Kansas City, with some cars continuing on to the coast and others being sidetracked to Omaha or Dallas.

News gathering works in reverse of distribution. Most wire service bureaus are one-man affairs located in local newspaper offices. The bureau chief scans the daily stories from the local paper and files those that he feels are significant on the wire. As the material moves in reverse, the wire filers must decide whether to kill the item or pass it along to New York for national distribution. In the event of a major newsbreak in an out-of-the-way place, the wire services will send reporters from either New York or the regional bureaus to cover it. In smaller communities where they do not maintain bureaus, the wire services hire stringers, generally reporters for the local papers who moonlight for the wire services and are paid on the basis of material used. In the smallest towns services use housewives and high schoolers, paying a flat rate of five dollars an item. Both wire services have only about one hundred bureaus each in the United States, relying on part-time help for remaining coverage.

At the end of the pipeline, in the newspaper office, the wire service copy comes chattering out on a battery of teletype machines, the number of which varies depending on how many of the services the newspaper subscribes to. In recent years and on the largest papers, the teletypes print "justified" copy ready to run, together with perforated tape on the teletypesetter (TTS) ready to be fed into the typesetting machines. This has considerably reduced composing room time and permits the services to operate a little closer to the deadline than previously.

The speed of transmission has markedly increased. A good operator in the early days of Morse code transmission could transcribe 35 words per minute; with the teletype, the number of words transcribed increased to 60 per minute. Teletype also did away with the operator at some savings. Recent computerized equipment is capable of 1,000 words per minute, and the *Los Angeles Times* and AP exper-

A typical breakdown map of wire service news gathering and distribution. This one is based on the Associated Press' regional wirephoto network.

imentally have shown the way to the future with facilities capable of 50,000 words per minute.

THE NEWS BUDGET

Each of the wire services operates a number of wires: the "A" wire for major news, the "B" wire for secondary news and major features, a sports wire, a business wire that includes stock market quotations, and a racing wire. Major metropolitan newspapers most often carry all wires from both services twenty-four hours a day; a small daily will get along on eight hours of "A" wire.

The wire service day is divided up into cycles of news. Twice daily the wire services draw up a budget of news, the ten or twelve stories of the day that, in their estimate, are most important. The services wire a summary of this budget so editors across the country will know what to expect and plan for in making up their papers. Then the cycle begins, and the service runs through the major stories, interrupting the cycle with bulletins of other major events and continual "updates" on the running budget stories. Updates and new leads are so cunningly contrived that they can be fitted directly into what has been received before with a minimum amount of disturbance of material already set in type. When the cycle is completed, it begins again. On a fast-moving story there may be as many as a half-dozen updates and new leads within a cycle. Other news is relegated to the "B" wire and feature services. Because of the two-way nature of the gathering-distribution system, a client can query the wire service for data of special local interest—such as how the local congressman voted on a certain bill. In this example, the query would be relayed to the Washington bureau, where one of the one hundred or so staffers would ask the congressman's office or their Capitol Hill reporter, and flash the private answer back to the client.

International news funnels into and is dispatched out of New York and San Francisco to relay points and clients abroad. News for Europe is received in London and dispatched to the nations involved. It is translated into the native tongue in each nation, generally in the capital, which serves as a bureau; it is then placed on the national wire for distribution. The radio teletype is incredibly fast, taking only a few seconds from a filing in the Balkans through relays in Rome, London, New York, and San Francisco until the teletypes are chattering in Tokyo—taking far less time than is necessary to say the names of the cities involved in the relay. Reuters, the British news service, and Tass, the state agency of the Soviet Union, are also widely used in the United States by major papers and the television nets—Reuters for its reliability in foreign news and Tass for its insights into the secretive USSR.

OTHER SERVICES

Both AP and UPI operate separate radio and television wires. After the broadcast ban was lifted by UP in 1935, radio stations received the same wires as newspapers. This required rewriting for the less formal, more immediate audio style of the air. When AP began serving broadcast in 1940, there was a competitive incentive for both AP and UP to develop radio wires written in the audio style so that newscasters could take the wire service copy directly from the teletype and read it on the air—"rip 'n' read." The radio/television writing style is punchy, immediate, and pays less attention to grammar than does newspaper style. In addition, today UPI maintains a daily radio pickup service for its clients whereby they can tune into UPI and carry a national news budget directly onto the air or tape it for future use. Second-place UPI, the more innovative of the wire services, also provides news film for television, while AP uses color slides.

Both services deal in news photos, wiring out nearly a hundred daily to their major clients. Smaller papers receive a selection of glossy black-and-whites by mail from which they may choose what they feel is appropriate, or photomats, if they wish, which can simply be slipped into the paper without going through the expensive photoengraving process.

Related to the wire services are the various city news services. These are local, private services which follow the press association principle. The city news services maintain reporters at the major beats within a city—city hall, courts, police stations, and the like—gathering news for the small dailies, the weeklies, and the radio stations within their area. They sell this data to local media, relieving them of the expense of maintaining reportorial staff, and yet enabling them to keep current on local happenings. The more enterprising city news services also operate a radio pickup wire for local stations, sometimes on a telephone "beeper," and a few shoot film for television.

These services in the larger cities are generally supplemented by the so-called business wires. Business wires are really public relations wires, and they operate in reverse of the other wires. Instead of charging the media, they maintain teletypes in the newspaper, radio, and television outlets, and charge their sources for carrying the material. The service assures rapid and complete distribution of public relations material. The more enterprising public relations people reinforce their story with a phone call advising the editor that the copy is coming over the business wire.

CANNED CONTENT

[1]. Sandman et al., *Media* (Englewood Cliffs, N.J.: Prentice-Hall, Inc., 1972).

The proportion of wire service news in the average newspaper is high. Sandman and others estimate it to be 15 percent of all content.[1] Considering that 60 percent of the newspaper is advertising, this makes the wire service contribution greater than any other single source. Another 10 percent each goes for various syndicated features and the specialized departments such as women's, business and finance, sports, and the like, leaving only around 5 percent for local news. These percentages are a guideline showing how much of the average paper is "canned."

THE NATION'S GATEKEEPERS

The ubiquity of the two major press associations—very nearly all the nation's nearly 1,800 daily newspapers subscribe to one or both—and their limited number occasion a similarity to the news that is striking. It is quite possible, for example, to breakfast in New York reading the *New York Times* and to fly to Los Angeles for lunch to read the same story verbatim in the *Los Angeles Times.* Anyone who has driven across the country has also been exposed to the same radio wire material, differing only in the accents of the announcers, through a progression of individual local stations scattered along his route. This sameness is heightened by the similarity of both AP's and UPI's approach to the news and their objective style, which allows little leeway for individuality of treatment.

This situation places awesome responsibility and power in the hands of the relatively few editors and wire filers of the press associations who are, in fact, the gatekeepers of the nation's news. Also, only a dozen or so major stories are included on the daily budget cycle. It is these stories, by and large, that will be carried on the country's front pages. Even newspaper editors who are not particularly enchanted with a story are under great pressure to carry it, if only because the wire service did. Radio news commentators are perhaps in a more restricted position yet, using the radio wire material because there is no other available. One cannot help but speculate that as the financial pressure becomes greater on the wire services they may be forced to curtail their coverage, thereby reducing their budgets, and that the availability of information will become even more limited as a result.

Four factors operate to balance the potential threat of wire services' power. The first is the wire services' historical dedication to news, their determination to uncover it, their long-term success in doing so, and their sharply honed news judgment. Second is the intense competition between associations, who are constantly watchdogging each other. In such a competitive situation the opportunity for purposeful bias is minimized. Third is the increase in the number of correspondents and stringers employed by or representing the various newspaper and radio groups, the television networks, the several syndicates, and the larger metropolitan newspapers. They enhance the competitition as well as providing a greater variety of both news stories and treatment. Finally, there is the fact that more and more interpretive reporting is finding its way into the wire services. This is in response to the demand of their clients, who discovered that the old mode of total objectivity—itself a form of bias—was no longer adequate for their better educated and more sophisticated audiences. The mainstay of the wire services is still objective reporting, but this is larded now with an increasing number of interpretive, background, and even opinion pieces.

SOURCES OF NEWS

The news gathering or information packaging function is about the same at whatever level it occurs. News originates in basically four ways. It comes from certain permanent sources that can be consistently relied upon to provide a factual record of the transactions among people, something such as a police blotter or the Congressional Record that can be used as an unimpeachable basis of news. These sources are the institutionalized focal points of a complex society in which, from among the many diverse undercurrents of human affairs, the flotsam and jetsam surface to be scrutinized and recorded: robbery and murder, birth and death, accident and disaster, marriage and divorce, permits and bankruptcies, suits and judgments, fraud, scandal, and deviance, intermixed with a little humor and considerable rhetoric—the raw material of news. There are also a number of regularly scheduled events that provide the kind of controversy and competition that lends itself to news stories. Also, there are unexpected events that suddenly materialize. These are generally of a sensational nature—natural disasters, scandals, accidents, deaths, and the like—which, because of their pathos, make good reading; these items have been characterized by Schramn and others as being of a quasi-entertainment content appealing to the morbid side of man's nature. Finally, there are the continuing stories that may grow out of any other sources that provide the fodder for the day's news quota, day after day, until their course is run.

Nor are the sources single and discrete; often they act in combination. A permanent source will often lead to a scheduled story (as with regard to elections and the like), which, in turn, may become a continuing story. Scheduled stories may often lead to the unexpected. The 1968 Democratic National Convention, a scheduled event, led to unexpected confrontations. The 1972 convention led to the blaze of the Eagleton affair and its aftermath, both unexpected and continuing. On the sports pages, the scheduled Kentucky Derby, Preakness, and Belmont in 1973 led to a continuing story as Secretariat swept the Triple Crown of racing for the first time in twenty-five years, shattering track records along the way. Hank Aaron's assault on Babe Ruth's home-run record provided a continuing fillip of competition and suspense in the midst of the 1973 baseball schedule, carrying over into 1974. Watergate stands as an outstanding example of a continuing story arising from such regular sources as the presidency, the executive branch, Congress, and the courts.

On the local level, the city editor covers these four source areas pretty thoroughly. He maintains beat reporters at city hall, the courthouse, the central police station, the county building, and state and federal buildings where they exist. He probably has a man in the state capital. These beat reporters keep the city editor in constant touch with regular and proven sources of news. The beats provide an automatic screening device for news. To keep up with scheduled events the city editor keeps a "tickler file" to remind him when regularly scheduled events that demand coverage are likely to take place: the municipal elections, the county fair, the local football team's spring training, school opening, and graduation. For the unexpected the city editor relies on his beat reporters, on a far-flung network of stringers, on other media, and on unsolicited and often anonymous tips, as well as police and fire shortwave. As continuing stories arise from any of these sources, he makes plans and provides staffing to cover them as long as they remain news. Often routine coverage of daily events will suffer as reportorial manpower is diverted to a continuing event.

WIRE SERVICE BEATS

The wire services are no different in their news gathering operations; they simply function on a larger scale. They, too, maintain beats—with the presidency, at Capitol Hill, in the major executive departments, the Pentagon, in the major state capitals, and on Wall Street. Internationally, they have major bureaus staffed in the leading capitals of the world: London, Paris, Rome, Berlin, Moscow, Tel Aviv, Cairo, Tokyo, and Buenos Aires. Several of the major bureaus have a regional responsibility—Tokyo carries not only Japanese coverage, but most of the Far East, and Buenos Aires is the focal point for Latin American news.

The press associations also have their versions of the tickler file, noting the World Series, the Super Bowl, the Indy 500, the national political conventions, the winter and summer Olympics, the Grand Prix, and so forth. Events of such significance, news of which is in great demand by their clients and awaited breathlessly by tens of millions of Americans, produce huge logistical problems of moving dozens of personnel around, shifting assignments, and temporarily leaving the more routine beats minimally covered to concentrate on the big event that, experience has shown, will often develop an unexpected turn, or demand a continuing effort. For the unexpected, press associations also rely on their far-flung network of a hundred or so bureaus, the news gathering facilities of AP's 8,500 and UPI's 6,000 clients, and their countless stringers.

The major areas in which the wire services concentrate correspond closely to the major departments of the daily newspapers. Concentration is on government and politics, on sports, on business and finance, and on women's news.

GOVERNMENT AND POLITICS

Government's qualification as a major news source stems from two bases. First is the press' traditional role in a democracy as the watchdog of government. Related to this is the fact that stories of scandal, malfeasance in office, bribery, untoward influence, coverups, and corruption are guaranteed attention-getters, bound to become a part of the daily budget cycle. To counter this, government has employed corps of information specialists whose function is to call the press' attention to the good that government does. Out of the joint activities of government and the press arises the kind of imperfect balance that the adversary relationship represents.

Government's other qualification as a news source comes from the fact that it is here that actions taken affect the lives and welfare of citizens. Even minor actions by minor agencies of the federal government can be translated into hundreds of thousands of dollars by the enterprising; major actions may affect the pocketbooks of all Americans. The draft law of Congress and several administrations' commitment to the war in Viet Nam meant anguish to parents, time subtracted from the lifetimes of an entire generation, and, for some citizens, it meant their lives. Government is big news indeed, affecting lives, welfare, income, and opportunities. What could be of more consuming interest?

The press associations' Washington bureaus are staffed by more than one hundred people covering every aspect of government on a more or less regular basis. Even so, they are sadly understaffed considering the enormity of the federal bureaucracy and its hundreds of agencies. Consequently, a considerable portion of the wire service's Washington press corps is devoted to watching the other media: the television networks, the bureaus of the big dailies, the press and broadcast groups, the major syndicated material, the national columnists, the foreign press associations, as well as the big lobbies and news magazines. All these are potential subsources of governmental material in addition to tips from the interested, both in government and out. This is a good deal like the city editor of an afternoon paper scanning the A.M. coverage to be sure he isn't missing anything.

Politics is great copy because it represents the raw material of controversy. On the national level it becomes the epic struggle of two titans playing for real prizes—power, prestige, opportunity, and position. Political campaigns are gladiatorial in nature. Their ability to generate long-range emotion makes them indispensable to the American scene, and money in the bank for all the news packagers.

Sports shares with politics some of the elements of competition. Here again giants are seen struggling for supremacy. Everyone picks his favorites and experiences a vicarious thrill in watching them vie. In a nation increasingly sedentary and white-collar, increasingly removed from physical contact, from direct thrill and danger, athletes are surrogates—performing skills for contemporary man and doing his exercising. Sports to the American male has a kind of machismo; an interest in sports is proof of his manhood. Furthermore, in an increasingly cynical world, it is in sports that the good guys always win.[2] Victory on the athletic field goes to the better prepared, the better skilled, and the more coordinated. This is one of the reasons why scandals and payoffs in sports are particularly abhorrent to Americans, while expected of politicians. Could it be that sports is serious,

2. A. M. Watkins, "The Secret Reasons Why Men Watch Football on TV," *Family Circle*, January, 1971.

politics a game? There may also be a Walter Mitty aspect to watching sports. It is easy to identify with a hero, and sports provides heroes and antiheroes in the new mode, such as Mark Spitz and Joe Namath.

SOCIETY'S DESIRE

Another factor pertaining to sports, government, and politics as news sources is the status of their participants. In a nation of more than 200 million persons, only a tiny fraction of them can be in the news. Some of them rise to the surface at society's officially prescribed gathering points—the various news beats. Others—athletes, politicians, and officials—occupy positions that are, almost by their nature, news. Society itself, in one way or another, has chosen such persons for preferred treatment, and in response to society's demand the news packagers heavily treat their affairs, both public and private, as society's curiosity is ravenous. This formal and informal selection of individuals by society also constitutes a sort of self-screening device of news. The circularity of the communications process is seen again. News is what society says it is, and that is what the wire services will relay to the newspapers and broadcasters for replay to society.

The effect of television on the wire services is yet another media interrelationship, stemming from their contrasting roles. It is television's entertainment emphasis, combined with the massiveness of its audience, that has radically altered the concept of news. Television has appropriated its own star system from film. Its news commentators are stars in their own right with their own charisma and demonstrated appeal, often of longer duration than officeholders. The Walter Cronkites and the David Brinkleys have their own huge followings. Television news has become a major production, and many accuse it of being at least half show business, in competition for ratings. The salient point is that what 50 or 60 million Americans watch on television news is what becomes the news to them. The wire services, therefore, have little choice but to include a good part of this television emphasis in their own news treatments, particularly as nearly all the country's commercial television stations are their clients.

A 1968 Roper survey indicated that nearly 60 percent of the population got their news from television, whereas only about 50 percent mentioned newspapers (multiple answers add up to more than 100 percent). When considering news credibility, the pattern is even clearer: 44 percent found television news more credible; only 21 percent found newspapers credible. Quite apparently, television is where the news is. In the competitive and commercialized mass communications business, the newspapers themselves must keep pace with their electronic competitors. They can explain television news; they can provide a more meaningful framework for it; they can elaborate on it, but they cannot ignore it except at their own peril, and consequently neither can the wire services.

Indirect Media

NEWS AS "SHOW BIZ"

Because television is so dynamic and has such a massive appeal, it has even changed the character of the news. The quadrennial party conventions, for example, have taken on a carnival atmosphere. Rather than being political conventions, they have become huge and expensive stages for the television cameras where the respective parties parade their wares—platforms, candidates, and minority concern—much in the manner of a four-day television special. Senator Sam Ervin's Watergate hearings in 1973 became the nation's most popular soap opera with their plot of wrongdoing in high places, villains and heroes, high resolve and light banter, an underlying theme of suspense, and an unexcelled cast of characters all playing to the cameras—accused and accuser alike.

Political campaigns have become pure show biz. Joe McGinniss documents in his book, *The Selling of the President, 1968,* how candidate Nixon's entire campaign was television-oriented.[3] There is an important campaign factor that candidates today must remember. They are no longer merely in competition with their opponent. For so long as they rely on television to afford them mass coverage, they are less in competition with their opponent than they are with TV's personalities for audience attention. Thus, the style of government and politics changes as the participants cater to the video cameras.

A television commercial for a candidate is not merely competing with his opponent's commercial. It is competing always for audience attention and credibility with professional and entertaining commercial spots. Television's audiences are going to judge political commercials in contrast to others largely on the basis of entertainment merit. Thus, political campaigning seems to move further and further from the matters of issue and record, and closer and closer to matters of charisma and appeal, which are the very matters the news gatherers are increasingly confronted with and must report.

The pattern in sports differs little; the cult of the star adds an extra fillip of excitement. Far more people went to see Joe Namath than the New York Jets, which is why the other ball clubs in the AFL contributed their fair share to his whopping annual salary: it was good business both in the stadium and more particularly on camera, where Broadway Joe made his hit. The rules of baseball have been changed to speed play up for television, and this also has affected sports reporting. Monday night football was introduced to capitalize on prime-time television audiences, and night games were introduced into the World Series for the same reason. The summer and winter Olympic games are produced more as spectacles for satellite viewing than as amateur athletic contests. Like the political convention halls, the amphitheaters are designed for maximum television facilities, and the major events (the most visual and exciting) are slotted into prime time to the virtual exclusion of the rest. As television effects the worlds of politics and sports, so it also alters the objective, on-the-spot press association coverage of these events. The news packagers have little choice but to chronicle the antics of

3. Joe McGinnis, *The Selling of the President 1968* (New York: Trident Press, 1969).

the television-oriented news sources. The wire service daily budgets perforce include the new television stars and events, thereby playing to the cameras rather than to the press as in days of yore. This pattern change isn't the wire service's doing, nor even television's; it is society's.

TELEVISION NETWORK NEWS

If 60 percent of the people claim they get their news from television and more than twice as many find television news more credible than newspapers, then a good subject for study is network news, which is only partially fed by the wire services but which, in a real sense is indirect media feeding its product to its affiliates for distribution. The big difference is that the local affiliate, unlike the local newspaper, cannot edit network news. Its only choice is to carry all or none, which isn't much of a choice at all in that if it doesn't carry the network news, it is confronted with the problem of originating something else.

Network news has been a bone of contention between the networks and their affiliates. In November 1969, when Spiro Agnew startled the nation with his unprecedented criticism of network news' antiadministration bias, 60 percent of the networks' affiliated stations agreed with him. More significantly, so did 51 percent of the viewers, with only 33 percent disagreeing.[4] The figures in combination seem to say that people watch television news perhaps out of habit; while they may find it more credible, they still don't agree with it much.

Maybe Av Weston, ABC executive producer, best summed up television news: "I think television news is an illustrated headline service which can function best when it is regarded by its viewers as an important yet fast adjunct to the newspapers. When I read the statistics that show 60 percent of Americans get all or most of their news from television, I shudder. I know what we have to leave out."[5] Weston's remarks crucially point up the gatekeeping role of the television networks' news programs, a role that, combined with their statistical impact, is frightening.

Whereas Ben Bagdikian points out that only about 10 percent of the available news gets into a newspaper in any given day, only about 2 percent of the available news gets onto television via the networks, and this is where 60 percent of the people get their information.[6] To illustrate, CBS once had the entire content of its half-hour evening news with Walter Cronkite set in *New York Times* type and measured against the newspaper. The entire evening news ran less than half the front page.

To produce these ambivalent video headlines, all three nets invest large sums of money in essentially a losing proposition. The news budget of CBS runs about $50 million a year; NBC's runs a bit more because the "Today Show" is included; ABC's a bit less. All

4. Les Brown, *Television: The Business Behind the Box* (New York: Harcourt Brace Jovanovich, 1972); Martin Mayer, *About Television* (New York: Harper & Row, Publishers, 1972).

5. Ibid.

6. Ben H. Bagdikian, *The Information Machines* (New York: Harper & Row, Publishers, 1971).

maintain around twenty bureaus throughout the world—a fraction of the press associations' coverage to be sure—but CBS has approximately fifty full-time correspondents who are available for troop movements, and the network shifts these correspondents constantly to focal points of interest around the globe.

Costs are not matched by revenues. News and documentary ratings do not keep pace with the serials and specials, which is why, of course, that news is slotted out of prime time. Further, to a demographically conscious advertising industry, the news audiences are less affluent and less educated than television's lcd average. Why then do the networks continue to pour significant money, which they cannot recoup, into their news operations? There are two reasons. One is that they are generating for their wholly owned and affiliate stations a significant amount of "public interest, convenience, and necessity" time, which accrues FCC "brownie points" useful for relicensing. Second, there is a journalism status to network news, and the networks compete vigorously for their share of the reduced audiences for the professional prestige that being number one carries.

Documentaries are likewise products of television network news. They play to even more miniscule audiences than does the news and are often slotted into the year's four "black weeks" when no ratings are taken.

News operations at the networks are separate subsidiary corporations because they serve both the television and radio interests of the networks. However, television receives the largest portion of the news budget. The networks are highly reliant upon the availability of news film or videotape—action. Videotape has permitted the instantaneous relaying of visual material, a convenience lacking in the old days when the networks were at the mercy of hand-delivered film couriered by jet and motorcycle. Furthermore, their base of coverage is vastly expanded with the development of the anchorman concept. A television star in his own right, the anchorman's personality and following permits him to use material for which there is no video action. His charisma carries the more static material—provided it is interspersed with good, lively footage.

THE FEATURE SYNDICATES

As the wire services are basically packagers of the information content for newspapers, the feature services are the packagers of entertainment content, both graphic and verbal, for the newspapers. About 10 percent of the average newspaper's editorial content is composed of this canned entertainment. It includes the advice to the lovelorn columns, comics and cartoons, daily horoscopes, crossword puzzles and word games, coin and stamp collecting columns, chess features, a wide range of how-to-do-it pieces, fashion, interior decorating, cooking, dressmaking, and nostalgia. The *San Diego Evening Tribune* even has a nostalgic cooking column, so specialized has man's entertainment become. Book, art, drama, and film criticism, and a variety of humor, gossip, financial, and political columns are also included.

Newspaper editors try to achieve some sort of balance of features depending on their evaluation of the mix of their particular readership. The larger newspapers try to achieve political balance in their national columnists, offering both liberal and conservative viewpoints. While ostensibly these are presented to permit the reader to make up his own mind between two divergent viewpoints, they are actually a surefire audience formula in that a reader will read the one because he agrees with it and will read the other to get mad, which is just as "entertaining" an emotional reaction.

Most of America's features are supplied either by the wire services, both of which operate their own features services (AP Newsfeatures and United Feature Service), or by a dozen or so major syndicated services. The largest of these is King Features, a residual of the old Hearst empire, and it has income of around $100 million annually. Each service runs between twenty-five and one hundred different features available to editors. Features, like the wire services, are sold on a circulation basis with the larger papers paying proportionately more. Features are generally sold on a "tf" basis (till forbid), which means that they run continually until cancelled with from one to three months' notice.

Added to these majors are a large number of specialized feature services and the material available from the various newspaper groups, making in all a large and appealing menu. Of course, the greater the feature ratio, the smaller the news hole will be, since newspaper size is economically predetermined by the advertising volume. Feature copy comes in on the feature wires, by mail, or on the TTS' perforated tape. Some of it comes preprepared in either camera-ready columns for offset newspapers or in matrix form for letterpress.

If one recalls the quasi-literate time in the last century, it was the objectivity of the wire services that assured them of patronage among the nation's newspapers. An avoidance of opinion satisfied the relatively small range of opinion differences represented by their clients. A century or so later, increasing affluence, a much higher educational level, a diversity of interests and proliferating media to serve them required a higher degree of diversification from the wire services than previously. Objective news is not enough anymore; reflective news is demanded.

The feature services in one form or another have proliferated to serve a diversity of public tastes and the multiplying departments that the daily newspaper evidences. The features bring magazine content to the press. Society has again demanded fragmentation and specialization from even such monolithic enterprises as the two major wire services.

Like the mass media that they serve, wire services have become ponderous corporate institutions, deeply ingrained and highly resistant to change. They have not had the flexibility to adjust to increasing demands for more diverse material. Thus, it appears that their very bigness has encouraged the development of smaller and more tractable services, some of which originated from the very newspapers served by wire services. The wire services have not had the opportunity to really keep pace with change, and this may be their undoing.

SUMMARY

The press associations, AP and UPI, are packagers of information in probably its purest form. They are the result of newspapers pooling their resources to offset the increasing costs of gathering news. The AP was founded in 1848, after the invention of the telegraph, by six New York newspapers to share wire costs. It was a membership organization, which soon admitted other newspapers on an exclusive basis in their respective areas. An AP membership became a very valuable asset. Early, AP developed the technique of reportorial objectivity in an attempt to answer the differing social and political viewpoints of its many members. Later, during the Civil War, the concept of journalese and the "lead" was born to get the most important information out first against the possibility of telegraph failure.

The telegraph also made possible the introduction of national advertising into newspapers and assisted in the centralized control necessary for the establishment of the great newspaper empires of Hearst, Scripps, and Pulitzer. Scripps ended the AP's nearly sixty-year monopoly on national and international news by founding the United Press in 1907. Two years later Hearst started the International News Service for the same purpose. Both organizations found it profitable to sell their services to other newspapers in order to defray costs. Neither was an effective competitor for AP until they merged in 1958. Today, AP has 8,500 members internationally, and UPI has 6,000. They are in constant, intense competition to bring the news first to their clients in that there is a deadline every minute of the day, and to run second means to be left out of the paper and risk subsequent contract cancellation.

Today, an increasing number of smaller newspaper and broadcast groups have organized news services to serve their own papers in addition to making these services available to others. Also, some of the nation's major papers, alone or in concert, have made material available on a syndicated basis, which increases the diversity of news available in the marketplace. Both AP and UPI are at present losing money.

The wire services operate telephone trunk lines from New York to their major clients. From these trunk lines, regional and state wires break off at specified points, where wire filers determine which of the mass of information coming across is appropriate for their particular areas and clients. This system works in reverse as a news gathering facility: the wire services' bureaus are located in the offices of a major area newspaper, reliant on that newspaper's reporters for local material filed by wire for redistribution nationally and internationally.

International bureaus around the world concentrate their news in London and Tokyo for relay to the United States. Bureaus in the major capitals are supplemented by regional bureaus, roving correspondents, and stringers, who are part-timers, paid on a piece basis.

Both services issue daily budgets of the dozen or so top stories. A budget cycle contains continual updates on these major stories, plus bulletins of late-breaking major news. Once a cycle is complete, it is repeated and updated. In addition to these "A" wires, there are "B" wires carrying other news, and some feature, financial, sports, and racing wires.

Another association service is the radio wire. Also, UPI provides news film for television stations; AP provides color slides. Both operate a news photo service. Both also have their own feature services.

City news services condense municipal news for the smaller dailies and weeklies. The so-called business wires are used for public relations purposes where the source pays for inclusion and the newspaper receives it free.

The wire services are little different than the local newspapers in their news coverage. Both have fixed beats where the undercurrents of human affairs surface for observation and chronicling. Both maintain their own version of tickler files for certain scheduled events destined to be news. Both also hope that they will get adequate early warning of the unforeseen events forever cropping up.

Government, politics, and sports comprise good sources of wire service news on a regular or scheduled basis, while their far-flung networks of clients and correspondents provide some sort of assurance against the unexpected.

Governmental affairs, both at city hall and the national capital, are prime sources of news copy. Elected officials are the people's chosen, while sports figures are their national heroes who are voted for in a more informal fashion. Coverage of the activities of such surrogates is mandatory for both newspaper and wire service.

About 15 percent of all newspaper matter is wire copy. It is more than theoretically possible to read the same story verbatim in the newspapers on both coasts. Wire copy does much to contribute to the sameness of a good deal of the news.

Whereas the wire services were set up to serve the newspapers, the majority of American people seem to get their news from television, and nearly twice as many find it more believable than that of the newspaper.

The television networks are also major packagers of news, generally with a show-biz flavor. Network news loses money; it appears on the fringes of prime time in order to accommodate affiliates in program scheduling. The nets maintain their very competitive news divisions for both journalistic prestige and for FCC credits for their affiliates. Only about 2 percent of the available news gets on the air, and that only in headline form. Television anchormen have become personalities in their own right.

As television has become the chief funnel for information, the news picture has changed. Baseball has been speeded up to make a livelier television sport. Government officials and politicians eye television and tailor their remarks and events to its demands and schedule. This, too, affects the nature of news even as the wire services receive it.

Feature services started in the 1880s with Samuel McClure, who sold 50,000 words weekly to newspapers. Today there are about a dozen major feature services supplying the bulk of comics, cartoons, advice columns, political opinion, financial analysis, crossword puzzles, horoscopes, do-it-yourself items, cooking, fashion, etc. King Features is the largest. Like the wire services, the features charge on a circulation basis, so clients with larger audiences pay proportionately more.

17 ADVERTISING

ADVERTISING PAYS THE BILLS

A peculiarity of the American mass communications system is that advertising pays very nearly all the bills. This has both advantages and disadvantages. On the plus side is the fact that the American people get an incredible variety of information, entertainment, and culture at minimal cost. A disadvantage is that nearly all of America's mass communications is heavily overladen with commercial or persuasive messages. The two go together. It is commercial persuasion that permeates American mass communications, as opposed to the political persuasion evident in most of the totalitarian countries. It seems that the persuasion is always present, the question being how it is directed. Furthermore, the private sector, seeking profits, has been able to come up with the overwhelming investment necessary to develop America's ubiquitous, diversified, and sophisticated mass communications networks (note the plural); other nations (wherein mass communications is an integral part of government) have had to balance communications expenditures with many other kinds of national interests.

That advertising is a necessary adjunct to mass production is well established. Advertising is, in fact, mass sales: it is an automated salesman playing the law of averages that grows out of the correlation between degree of exposure and subsequent sales. It is on this correlation that ratings are based. The ratings do not measure a product's sales; that comes later at the cash register. The ratings do measure audience size, and subsequent sales confirm the relationship. (We should remember that most of our mass media are in the business of renting audiences to advertisers.) However, most advertising people believe that exposure is not enough. The principal role of the advertising agency today is to combine exposure (media buyers) with appeal (the creative group).

Advertising's history is one of the long, slow curve and the short, fast break. Following millenia of usage, it began only slowly to grow after the development of print technology, and matured only within the last century under the pressure of the industrial revolution.

Advertising is both informational and persuasive. The classifieds in the daily newspaper, for example, are commercial information, but information nonetheless. So are the movie ads. Both indicate the availability of a product at a place, and sometimes at a time and price. They differ little from the stock market quotations or television logs, which are pure commercial information.

THE LARGER WINESKIN

In the beginning, ads were informational. In the illiterate times of bygone centuries, advertising was graphic. The wineshop or the sandalmaker advertised his wares by hanging out a wineskin or a pair of sandals. To native and traveler alike, these signs told where wine and sandals were sold. This was pure information, the availability of a product. However, man's ingenuity never sleeps, and an enterprising wine seller one day hung out a larger wineskin. Not only was the bigger wineskin visible at a greater distance, thus automatically expanding his audience, but its size itself psychologically said that his was a bigger and better wineshop. In the course of events more people came to the wineshop with the bigger wineskin. The sandalmaker followed suit. He made a pair of giant sandals and discovered that they became a conversation piece, and that folks came to his shop out of curiosity. Orders increased, and the principle of exposure and sales was established.

An artist's rendition of early "bigger is better" advertising.

Advertising
311

The point is that the ordinary wineskin or pair of sandals was pure information. However, once man built a bigger wineskin, an element of persuasion was injected—bigger is better. Then, as now, advertising represented varying combinations of information and persuasion, plus an important extra—something to catch the audience's attention—the bigger wineskin or the enormous sandals, both a big plus in the competition for attention.

The invention of movable type, as noted, led to increasing literacy, and it was natural that advertising, while retaining its graphic elements, should also take advantage of the new medium. Most of the early printers were also booksellers, and took quite naturally to advertising available or forthcoming titles in tracts and flyers. Literacy was required to read a book, and only the literate could read a flyer. There was no overkill, as only the potential customer could decipher the advertisement. This was an early example of advertising selectivity, and a form that has achieved extraordinary sophistication in the past couple of decades.

LOCAL AND NATIONAL DIFFERENCE

Note that early advertising, like early mass media, was entirely local, serving local merchants and a local audience. This was changed by the industrial revolution. The industrial revolution brought about the mass production of products requiring mass purchases far in excess of what the local community could support. The technology of the industrial revolution spawned the railroads that affected the national distribution of goods, leading to national advertising. Further, in a competitive, free enterprise economy, the success of one new product immediately led to the development of almost identical products by competing manufacturers seeking their share of a proven market. Advertising's job became one of distinguishing between more or less identical products. More often than not, any distinction lay in the advertisements rather than in the products.

The new emphasis on advertising began to take hold in the 1840s with the establishment of a number of advertising agencies—a euphemistic term. These early agencies were in actuality little more than publishers' representatives or space brokers. Often they would contract with a publisher for a certain amount of space in a newspaper, and then sell this space to advertisers for whatever the traffic would bear. There were no published rate cards in those days and no certified circulation figures. National advertising was on a catch-as-catch-can basis, removed from the local familiarity that exercised a certain degree of control between a publisher and a merchant operating in the same town or city.

It was not until 1869 that some semblance of order came to the growing advertising scene. Rowell's *American Newspaper Directory* was published giving the approximate circulations of the nation's press. Inevitably, such a publication resulted in the establishment of published rates based on circulation size. In the same year America's oldest advertising agency was formed, N.W. Ayer & Son, which represented clients and worked on their behalf with the newspapers. It was about this time also that the commission system originated whereby accredited advertising agencies discounted their payments to the media by 15 percent in return for preparing and placing the advertisement. Publishers found the commission system an incentive to agencies to do a part of their selling while still leaving the publisher free to sell other advertisements directly. Recently, the commission system has come under considerable fire.

In the 1880s and 1890s, the competition for attention among almost identical and competing national products became intense. Department stores became the local warehouses of national products and competed with each other in the largest markets. Advertisers discovered that informational advertisements were no longer sufficient and that considerable doses of persuasion in one form or another had to be injected if their products were to move in a competitive economy. This was the period, too, when print and graphics began to come together, graphics illustrating a product or a situation and print glowingly describing it. Graphics provided an attention-getter; then, as now, a picture was worth a thousand words.

The competitive market situation also led to the embryonic beginnings of different forms of cooperative advertising. In one form, still extant, the national manufacturer maintained a national program, generally trying to establish the superior nature of his product, while the local dealer or distributor advertised locally, giving the where, when, and price. Newspapers recognized then, as they do today, the difference between these two essentially different forms of advertising; local advertising (sometimes called "retail") generally carries a lower rate than does national as an incentive to local merchants. In broadcast, in most cases, national advertising is carried by the networks while local is sold by affiliates and independents. A variation on this theme is co-op advertising, wherein the national manufacturer shares a part of the cost of local advertising with the distributor or dealer.

PEARS SOAP

In any event, by the time the Gay Nineties rolled around, it was quite clear that most consumer products were nearly identical, and any distinction would have to be created by advertising. The first attempt to do this was through the establishment of a brand name. Through positive reinforcement on a more or less continual basis, an effort was made to establish the brand name as synonymous with either the product or with quality. Coca Cola, Kleenex, and Xerox are contemporary examples, to the point that "Kleenex" means facial tissue, and "Xerox" describes photo duplication. Pears soap in England in the 1890s was the subject of the first mammoth attempt to identify a name with a product. "Pears Soap" appeared in English magazines and newspapers, on busses, light posts, board fences, and vacant walls until Pears meant soap, and the English asked not for soap but for Pears with which to wash.

While brand name usage was effective as an advertising technique, something more was required to really overcome the competition for attention. From the realm of political campaigning, advertisers borrowed the slogan. The slogan was a catchy capsule summary of the product, and as early as the 1890s Eastman Kodak came up with the first really distinctive slogan—"You Push the Button, We Do the Rest"—a masterpiece of simplicity describing simplicity. Meanwhile, Pears updated its campaign, introducing a slogan that would become a standard British greeting for at least half a century: "Good Morning, Have You Used Pears' Soap Today?" Throughout the length and breadth of the Empire, the British so greeted one another, to the utter delight of the Pears Company.

Brand names and their accompanying slogans (use of the latter requires the former) have carried on into the present. It is a mark of the techniques of persuasion, like the media themselves, that they continue to be successfully used even after more sophisticated techniques have been developed. Often they are used in combination, pyramided on each other for maximum effect. Jingles are a variation of the slogan theme, utilizing verse as a catchy memory device to get the message across; "Winston Tastes Good Like a Cigarette Should" is an unforgettable and ungrammatical example.

HALF-CENTURY HIATUS

There was little change in advertising techniques from the turn of the century until after World War II. Gradually, the industry expanded. Radio in the 1920s brought an aural emphasis superimposed upon the print techniques; it facilitated the use of jingles, and set them to music for added impact. During the 1930s, public opinion polling was quickly adopted by advertising agencies as a device for measuring audience size and program popularity in radio, which, unlike newspapers and magazines, provided no circulation figures. The clearly observable fact that women listened to radio more during the daytime, while men were at work, and that entire families listened in the evening, led to the concept of prime time and an early form of demographic appeal represented by the radio soap operas. The concept of the lcd was also born during this period. Sponsorships gave way to spot announcements as a more profitable means of selling radio advertising.

Advertising agencies grew and prospered. The advent of radio introduced a new element into mass persuasion, and increasing complexities demanded expertise that few product organizations possessed. Creativity and advertisement testing became part of the agencies' stock-in-trade. Techniques for measuring the readership of magazine advertisements were superimposed on magazine circulation figures. These are still extant in the form of the Starch Reports, which give a clue to the exposure and drawing power of a print ad-

Indirect Media

vertisement, taking into consideration such things as appeal of the artwork, layout, copy readability, and the like.

The method of advertisement testing in the beginning was remarkably simple, and variations upon it are still in use. Two different ads on the same subject were placed in a "split run" in a newspaper, that is, half the edition carried one ad, the other half carried the other ad. The ads asked readers to return a coupon for a product at a reduced price, and the relative appeal of the two ads was gauged on the basis of how many people responded to one rather than the other.

Despite growth and refinements in the advertising business, nothing really new was developed for almost a half century. Following World War II a new spirit invaded advertising. Interest in psychological warfare and propaganda had injected heavy doses of the social sciences, particularly psychology, sociology, and later the hyphenated social-psychology, into the persuasion field. Computers, which had their practical genesis during the war, greatly facilitated public opinion measurement, polling, and testing, giving birth to more accurate ratings. Further, the hiatus on civilian production during the war years had created a vacuum in consumer goods, and as America's corporations turned their enormous capacity to peacetime manufacture, they generated enormous pressure to move the goods. Advertising had a renaissance generated by new techniques, new products, and new audiences; returning servicemen, reunited families, and a baby boom created an unparalleled demand for almost everything. Also, the genesis of television in 1948, only three years after the war, added new dimensions to advertising like everything else.

THE MAN IN THE GREY FLANNEL SUIT

1. Sloan Wilson, *The Man in the Gray Flannel Suit* (New York: Pocket Books Inc., 1967); Vance Packard, *The Hidden Persuaders* (New York: Pocket Books Inc., 1968).

Advertising agencies themselves both moved to the forefront into the public spotlight and also became increasingly competitive. The 1950s were the years when Madison Avenue became a household street, and *The Man in the Grey Flannel Suit* became a national stereotype on the kind of public manipulation attributed to advertising.[1] A rash of books appeared on advertising, among them Vance Packard's *The Hidden Persuaders,* and Martin Mayer's *Madison Avenue, U.S.A.* Both were popularizations born of public fascination with the manipulative techniques of applied social-psychology.

First of these techniques to capture public attention was the unique selling proposition (usp) originated by the agency of Ted Bates & Company. The usp took as its starting point the fact that there was no real product differentiation among the various mass-produced products of competing manufacturers. In essence it said that within a relatively narrow range all soap is alike, all beer is alike, all toothpaste is alike, and that advertising must itself establish whatever difference there is to make the public buy one instead of the other. The unique selling proposition was based upon a characteristic of the product that could be dramatized, exploited, and made synonymous with the product on behalf of the manufacturer, *even though all other products shared the same characteristic.* This nonexistent difference was exploited by advertising and through the sheer power of public exposure made to appear unique. For example, Bates originated the slogan "Cleans Your Breath While It Cleans Your Teeth" for Colgate toothpaste. This was usp, and Bates built an entire campaign out of it. The slogan was a natural selling device, implying a better toothpaste. However, even a cursory examination of the proposition suggests that all toothpastes clean the breath while they clean one's teeth. There was nothing really unique about Colgate, except that Bates had hit upon the slogan and by exploiting it had effectively prevented any other toothpaste manufacturer from utilizing it. Any attempt on the part of another manufacturer's agency to utilize a similar slogan would actually be reinforcing Bates' claim for Colgate. The usp is central to the advertisement.

Another Bates' usp, for Schlitz, was that their bottles were "washed with live steam." This had a peculiar appeal in the 1950s when sanitary America was concerned about the hygiene of reusable glass beer bottles. Actually, the slogan was a redundancy (is there anything other than live steam?), and all brewers washed their bottles with steam, but Bates, by exploiting this point, had usurped it for Schlitz.

Next in the techniques of pseudoscience applied to advertising was David Ogilvie's brand image. The brand image concept also recognized that there was no essential product differentiation. However, it sought to establish a distinction on a basis of snob appeal, to create an image for products which placed them a little above the average. The thought was that people would transfer the brand image to themselves and by using the product consider themselves a little better than their neighbors. Ogilvie developed the brand image of Hathaway shirts by employing Baron George Wrangel, a Russian nobleman who wore a suggestively romantic eye patch and exuded "class." Fondling an exquisite antique ship model or a fantastically expensive, silver-chased, over-and-under shotgun, the Baron always wore a Hathaway shirt. Brand image advertising reasoned that male America transferred this "class" to itself in hopes that if it wore Hathaways, it too would magically assume some of the Baron's breeding, taste, and distinction. Brand image's snobbery was a shortcut to the aristocracy. As Ogilvie said himself, "It pays to give your product a first-class ticket throughout life."[2] Commander Edward Whitehead's bearded British accent dripped culture as he acclaimed Schweppes' "schweppervescence" for "only pennies more." The Commander was also an Ogilvie creation.

The most extreme form of advertising's romance with the social sciences was Ernest Dichter's motivational research (mr). Highly Freudian in its approach, mr maintains that people buy things for

2. J.A.C. Brown, *Techniques of Persuasion* (Baltimore, Md.: Penguin Books Inc., 1963).

SEX AND SUBLIMATION

Indirect Media

hidden reasons unknown even to themselves, and that these hidden reasons are more often than not sexual in origin. Through depth interviews mr sought to explore peoples' hidden motivations as to why they buy, and then, utilizing this data, to build an advertising campaign. The classic example of mr in action was Dichter's campaign for Ronson lighters. He built his campaign on huge color reproductions in magazines and billboards of the lighter's flame, which, in his view, was an enormous phallic symbol appealing to men and women alike: men through wishful thinking, women from lust. Dichter went on to construct a television campaign for Ajax cleanser that utilized a white knight on a white charger, carrying a great lance and galloping down the streets of Hometown, U.S.A., with no apparent attention to the traffic laws. The point is, pardon the pun, that the lance was a large phallic symbol designed to stimulate housewives in Hometown, America.

The late fifties was also a time of considerable public consternation about subliminal advertising. Subliminal advertising was the development of Jim Vicary, an advertising researcher who inserted a few single frames of "Coca Cola" or "Eat popcorn" into movies at different intervals. A single frame would pass so quickly as a movie was viewed that the mind would not be aware of having seen it although the eyes would pick it up and register it subconsciously. Using a theater in New Jersey across the Hudson from New York's Madison Avenue, Vicary discovered that when "sublimated" movies were shown, Coca Cola sales rose 6 percent and popcorn sales went up nearly 50 percent over when "straight" movies were projected. Obviously, such a technique represented a threat to the integrity of the human mind and it was quickly outlawed, considering, no doubt, the awesome political effects that subliminal advertising might engender if turned loose on television's growing massiveness.

Rationally, however, despite the stir, research evidence seems to indicate that the power of mass media and of advertising is far less than generally supposed. Vicary himself did not believe that subliminal advertising was capable of altering attitudes, only of triggering an existing predisposition toward Coca Cola or popcorn among hungry and thirsty movie audiences, who are pretty well predisposed toward the concessionaires anyway.

IS ADVERTISING OVERRATED?

It is necessary, as far as advertising is concerned, to separate inconsequentials from matters of substance. The inconsequentials are such items as beer and toothpaste, even motor cars, a whole range of consumer goods that the general public tends to recognize by and large as being alike, and recognizes further that it will make no appreciable difference whichever product is chosen. Matters of consequence, however, involve beliefs and attitudes ingrained in the person. These do not readily change and advertising is relatively impotent against them. Advertising, for example, has not proven particularly successful in political campaigning, which is perceived by the

Advertising

public as being a matter of substance, affecting the welfare and future livelihood of each individual. Martin Mayer has summed the case well: Advertising is of little use in combating a trend against a kind of product—brewers spend more than $100 million a year to advertise their beer, backing the ads with a full panoply of motivational research, but per capita beer consumption goes steadily down because advertising cannot add values great enough to overcome primary factors which lead consumers to find less and less satisfaction in using a product. Here, as on the political scene, advertising is the wind on the surface, sweeping all before it when it blows with the tide (of public opinion) but powerless to prevent a shifting of greater forces.[3]

While there have been some very well-financed political campaigns that have resulted in victory, one does not hear so much of perhaps an equal number of expensive campaigns that ended in failure (Goldwater's bid for the presidency in 1964 or Norton Simon's bid for a California Senate seat in 1970, to name only a couple). The results of political campaigns seem to hinge on factors other than advertising, and the best that can be said for political advertising is that usually it does no harm. Even so, this generality should be treated delicately.

Related to the consideration of inconsequentials and matters of substance in advertising is the fact that advertising is unsurpassed as a device for exposure—to call attention to, to make aware of, to introduce a product, concept, idea, or candidate. Once exposure is achieved, the purchase, acceptance, or election are in other, undetermined hands hidden in the vagueries of public opinion formation and change. Advertising is essential for product introduction or candidate introduction. Once introduced, some will buy and some will vote, out of curiosity, but success depends on the product or candidate. Is it good or is it perceived as good? The two are subtly different.

John Wannamaker of Wannamaker's Department Store in New York City gave perhaps the most succinct description of what is known about advertising effectiveness: "We know that half our advertising is wasted, but we don't know which half."

3. Martin Mayer, *Madison Avenue, U.S.A.* (New York: Pocket Books Inc., 1967).

POSTWAR GROWTH

The size and growth of the advertising business, which, by and large, has been concentrated on the mass media in the years since World War II, is dramatically seen in the figures. Advertising was a $4 billion industry in 1947; in 1970 it reached $20 billion and still growing, with another billion dollars spent advertising American products overseas. Nor do these figures include another $15 billion spent for packaging of products, which is difficult if not impossible to separate from point-of-sale advertising. Continued growth of advertising's dollar volume since 1970 was seen in the near doubling of television rates from then to 1973. Over a half-million people are employed in the various facets of advertising in the United States: in agencies, in the internal advertising departments of both industry and retail establishments, and by the media. Nearly 100,000 people are employed in 5,000 agencies, running from local one-man shops employing a principal and secretary in smaller communities, to the creative boutiques of Madison Avenue employing way-out people specializing in way-out effects, to the largest, highly organized, even institutionalized, agencies.

J. Walter Thompson Company is the world's largest agency, billing well over a billion dollars annually. Also among the top half-dozen or so agencies are McCann-Erickson; Young & Rubicam; Ted Bates & Company; Batten, Barton, Durstine & Osborn, Inc. (BBDO); Grey Advertising; and Doyle, Dane and Bernbach.

A controversy in the advertising world rages over whether a client is better off with a small boutique where he can receive the creative attention of the firm's principals, or with the highly organized superagency whose wealth commands superior talent, and whose depth of services and personnel provide across-the-board coverage. While the controversy is still unresolved, the following anecdote sheds some light on the matter. When Osborn first joined BBDO as the new business partner, he was competing for a major account against a smaller agency. The boutique man pointed out to the prospect that his agency would always provide one of the firm's creative principals to work directly with the client, that in case of trouble the client could go directly to the top, and that the firm's top management was always no further away than the telephone.

"And what do you say to that, Mr. Osborn?" the prospect asked.

"Only this," Osborn replied, "No agency is small by choice...."

MEDIA BREAKDOWN

Advertising that serves the media, like the media, is broken down into local and national. The major agencies tend to concentrate where the money is—on national campaigns for the nation's major clients—leaving local advertising to the smaller local agencies, or to the individual advertiser who is often served creatively by the local newspaper or broadcaster. Both newspapers and broadcasters provide ancillary services, either at a minimal fee or free, to local advertisers to help lay out ads or produce commercials.

Newspapers still take the lion's share of the national advertising dollar, about 30 percent. Television takes about 20 percent. However, it should be noted that the newspaper's share is spread among about 1,800 daily newspapers plus all the weeklies, while the television percentage is concentrated among 700 commercial stations, and most of it on the three networks. Further, newspapers tend to serve both national and local advertisers in about equal numbers, while television concentrates on national advertising. Magazines handle about 10 percent of the national advertising volume, and radio 5 percent. The remaining 35 percent of national advertising for such things as direct mail, which is very big and getting bigger all the time, and billboards, which are of decreasing significance as environmental concern focuses attention on landscape pollution.

INSTITUTIONAL ADVERTISING

Recent environmental concern points up another facet of advertising that, while it has been in existence for some time, now enjoys considerable emphasis. This is institutional advertising, sometimes called "public relations advertising." Institutional advertising does not seek to sell a product; rather it seeks to sell an idea or an institution. Many of America's major corporations, faced recently with credibility gaps and public distrust, as well as attacks from both consumer groups and the environmentalists, have taken to blowing their own horns in the mass media. Print and broadcast are filled with their protestations of good citizenship: their environmental concern, their research for a rosier future, their emphasis on equal opportunity employment, and their stress on minority rights and in-house racial integration.

The nation's utilities, operating as controlled monopolies, have been in the forefront of institutional advertising for years. The "Bell Telephone Hour" of symphonic music, both on radio and later, television, was essentially public service, institutional advertising, designed to paint AT&T as a patron of culture. Gas and electric companies today focus ironically on energy conservation, seeking to slow rather than promote growth. Their generating capacity is outdistanced by demand, resulting in shortages and brownouts with an accompanying acceleration in public dissatisfaction.

The question arises, of course, as to why a utility operating from a monopoly position needs to advertise at all. The answer is simple. Private utilities do business on public sufferance; they are reliant upon public goodwill to maintain their privileged position. There is a considerable body of sentiment, both social and legislative, that holds that utilities should be publicly owned and operated, as many municipal utilities already are. Consequently, the volume of institutional advertising from the nation's utilities has traditionally been considerable.

Two of the most innovative commercial uses of institutional advertising were developed during World War II by the Ford Motor Company and Lucky Strike cigarettes. Ford had no cars to sell; its entire productive capacity was devoted to the manufacture of tanks and airplane engines. However, it realized that at some unspecified future date the war would end, and the built-up public deprivation would result in an unprecedented demand for cars. They wanted the public to buy Fords. Throughout the war they maintained a campaign based on "There's a Ford in Your Future," always showing a crystal ball containing a Ford in a variety of imaginative settings. The thought was not to sell cars at the time, but to sell the idea "Ford," to keep it alive—and they did, getting nearly a two-year head start over General Motors when the war ended.

Indirect Media

Lucky Strike used to have a dark green package, readily identifiable with its red bull's-eye in the center. When green dye was required by the Armed Forces during the war, Luckies switched to a white package with the same red centerspot, backed by an enormous campaign—"Lucky Strike Green Has Gone to War." This capitalized on the patriotic fervor of the time, put American tobacco in the van of patriotic companies and, incidentally, engendered enormous sales that were backed up by the weekly donation of thousands of cartons of Luckies to servicemen overseas. There are cynics who say that the Armed Forces didn't need Lucky's green dye at all, and that the entire idea was the brainchild of packager Raymond Loewy, who was paid a million dollars by American Tobacco to redesign the Lucky package to appeal to women.

AN AMERICAN EXPORT

Gradually, American advertising spread around the world. Advertising is an American export, just like the products it serves. A part of advertising's expansion is due to the need of American industry to seek new markets as the domestic market becomes saturated. Also related is the gradually increasing affluence of some of the principal foreign nations: England, Japan, West Germany, France, Italy, Israel, Scandanavia, and the Benelux countries. Their rising affluence has provided not only the means to buy American products, but also a more pervasive mass communications network—newspapers, magazines, radio, and embryonic television—for advertising to use. Advertising dollars, in turn, poured into these foreign media, hasten their development, and only incidentally create an increasingly commercial flavor. J. Walter Thompson Company was early in the international field, opening its London office before the 1890s. Together with McCann-Erickson, the two control about half the foreign business. Their overseas clients number more than 1,000. They have nearly 100 offices in twenty-five countries, with employees overseas totaling nearly 10,000 (many of them foreign nationals), billing nearly a quarter of a billion dollars annually overseas alone. It is in advertising particularly that American communications influence spread abroad. However, the television nets are not far behind and film distributors count on foreign sales for a considerable part of their revenue. Foreign editions of some of the major magazines (*Time, Life,* and *Reader's Digest*) have been a stock-in-trade since the thirties.

AGENCIES—MIDDLEMEN

The advertising agency is a middleman between the advertiser, be he manufacturer or distributor, and the mass media, be they print or broadcast. To be successful, the agency must serve both interests.

It should be noted that agencies themselves have certain client preferences. Some deal in automotive accounts almost exclusively; others in food and beverages. Some specialize in electronics, others in clothing and fashion, some in travel, and others in proprietary drugs or cosmetics. Through this kind of specialization, agencies are able to become intimately acquainted with the particular facets of their clients' distinctive pricing, marketing, and manufacturing problems, all of which have a bearing on the creation and placement of ads. The specialty situation is reinforced in that an agency's success with a campaign for one client is quite likely to lead product competitors to that agency. Some agencies tend to favor print or even magazines and newspapers as their basic medium, while others concentrate in television or radio. As communications technology grows more complex, this specialization breeds a certain expertise in the medium that advertisers are likely to find attractive. Thus, the trend toward specialization that has been noted in the media has its parallel quite naturally in advertising, which serves the media.

Despite the increasing trend toward specialization, either in client type or media, all of the very big agencies are broadly based, serving a variety of clients in many lines of endeavor and maintaining the kind of in-house expertise in both product classification and media usage needed to meet any campaign. Quite obviously, only the very largest agencies can afford this kind of diversification.

However, size and institutionalization lead to a certain inertia and resistance to change. The smaller boutiques, while not nearly so wealthy, are neither so ponderous, and therefore are a lot more flexible in their ability to keep up with rapidly changing approaches to organized persuasion.

AGENCY FUNCTIONS

In any event, since they serve both client and media, all agencies embrace certain functions. They are five: client liaison, creativity, production, placement, and housekeeping. In a very large agency it is the account executive (AE), often working under an account supervisor, who maintains a constant liaison, that is, "lives with" the client. He interprets the client's problems to the agency's creative people, and in turn explains the developed campaign to the client. As large agencies generally deal with large clients, the AE usually deals with the client's advertising manager or advertising department—experts dealing with experts, both interpreting the other to their respective organization. Account executives are personality people; their forte is in getting along with others; they are the grey-flannel-suiters.

The creative group is composed of art directors and artists, copy supervisors and copywriters, layout people and graphics experts, who develop the print ads, write the copy, determine how to use illustrations or photographs, decide on black-and-white or color, and make up the storyboards for television commercials (which are static graphic depictions of what will eventually become a live, moving "minute").

Production turns the layouts or storyboards into actual commercials in matrix form or camera-ready proofs for the press, into sets of expensive colorplates for magazines, and into tape, videotape, or film for radio and television.

Indirect Media

Meanwhile, the media people select the media to be used by taking budget and audience composition into consideration, choosing between and among communications vehicles—which newspapers, magazines, and radio stations; how much television on which stations or networks, or whether to use billboards and direct mail. They consult Standard Rate and Data Service (SRDS) and talk to the various national "reps" of groups of magazines, radio stations, newspapers, or broadcasters, always keeping in mind the ratings and costs per thousand. One irony, as Martin Mayer points out in *Madison Avenue, U.S.A.*, is that the agency media buyer who spends millions of dollars of client money annually is generally a woman just out of college, the low Ms. on the agency totem, and that the people she deals with most are highly paid national reps with years of media experience behind them, backed by reams of statistical data as to why their particular group is best in cpm, in exposure, in purchasing power, or a variety of other complex demographic factors.[4] Someone once said that anything can be proven with statistics, and the national reps do it daily.

The housekeeping function of major agencies includes such things as accounting (a key function), research to develop the facts to be used in planning a campaign, personnel to take care of sometimes thousands of employees, and administration.

Some agencies, attracted by the huge commissions generated by major national automotive, food and beverage, drug, or cosmetic accounts, have tended to throw in a variety of other services in an attempt to attract and hold clients. These include public relations, public opinion sampling, market research, and promotional activities. The results of these extra services have not been spectacular. Since they are generally thrown in as an extra service, the agency tends to spend as little on them as possible; thus the job done is not generally of the highest calibre—"you get what you pay for" in advertising as elsewhere. Further, the lack of performance has tended to give many of these specialties a black eye in clients' eyes—particularly with regard to public relations.

An advertising agency is a large and complex operation. Some of the major agencies, for example, have review boards composed of major executives who play devil's advocate with any planned campaign before it goes to the client. The client liaison and creative teams are forced to defend their handiwork before a critical panel of peers. The rationale for the review board is that it is better to find the weak points of a campaign before the client or public does, millions of dollars later.

An integrated national campaign involves network television, supplemented by local television in certain markets. It involves major spreads in a dozen or so carefully chosen magazines. Also included is national newspaper coverage and supplementary radio, both in the major markets and in the very minor ones reached effectively only by radio. Billboards on highways across the country and a direct

4. Ibid.

mail campaign to certain selected demographic audiences are utilized. The problems of the traffic department are mind-boggling: those of coordination and scheduling, involving tying the media presentation together into a single theme, determining presentation priorities, coordinating with point-of-sale displays, tying in with public relations and promotional activities, and harnassing the energies of distributors and dealers and subsidiary agencies in fifty states and a number of foreign countries with language differences. However, the big three automobile makers—Ford, General Motors, and American—go through such orchestrated national campaigns every year when they introduce the new models. Most of the other manufacturers of consumer products contract similar campaigns whenever they launch a new product, which is often. About 10,000 new products are introduced annually, accounting for about 10 percent of advertising billing.

It is important to remember that whether the agency is a one-man shop, a creative boutique, or a major international agency, it must deal with both client and media in performing liaison, creative, production, placement, and housekeeping functions. A one-man agency gathers all these functions together under one hat: the owner spends his day running from a client meeting to the drawing board to a conference with television sales reps, overseeing the shooting of a commercial on the side, hiring the models and photo crew, and keeping up with the bookkeeping at night. A big agency apportions these functions amongst a platoon of overlapping experts. In either case, such activities are all performed under intensely competitive conditions. Madison Avenue is a jungle, and an ulcerous jungle at that, as agencies seek to steal each other's accounts and hire each other's personnel, and account supervisors leave to open their own boutiques, taking the agency's clients and creative people with them.

THE COMMISSION SYSTEM

The commission system began back in the 1880s as a mutual protection device for the newspaper publisher, agency, and client, assuring that each got his fair share of the advertising pie. As it has evolved, however, there seems to be ample evidence that it has outlived its usefulness.

The commission system works in the following manner. Recognized agencies are permitted by the media to discount their bills by 15 percent for advertising purchased on behalf of a client. For example, an agency buys a full-page ad costing $1,000 in a local newspaper for its client, the Gas Company. The agency bills the Gas Company for $1,000 and receives payment; in turn, the agency discounts the bill by 15 percent and remits $850 to the newspaper at the *open rate*. Theoretically, it was worth the $150 to the newspaper to have the agency act as salesman, and for this $150 the agency was expected to prepare and furnish the completed ad, minimizing the newspaper's work. However, there are a number of problems associated even with this simplified example. If this were a new ad, the $150 probably would not cover the agency's costs for research, account representation, and liaison, for the time of the creative team, for the cost of new artwork, and for preparation of camera-ready proofs. Thus, the agency may bill some of these services in addition or operate at a loss. Further, since the Gas Company is a more or less continual advertiser in the local newspaper, it probably buys its advertising on a *contract,* which means that it gets a progressively lower rate if it buys 1,000, 5,000, or 10,000 column inches of display advertising within a year. *Contract rates* are not commissionable. Consequently, the agency may add its commission to the bill. The add-on rate is 17.66 percent rather than 15 percent.

There has resulted therefore, a pyramiding of charges by advertising agencies approaching the absurd. Some agencies charge a commission (discount or add-on) plus out-of-pocket expenses—that is, any costs for entertainment, mileage, long-distance phone calls, travel, and the like—occurred on the client's behalf, plus an hourly charge to the client for personnel working on his account (AE, artists, writers, producers, researchers, and the like). In addition they may add an overhead charge representing that client's share of the agency's continuing expenses (rent, utilities, insurance, secretarial, etc.). A bill may get pretty large and, what's more, confusing, to the point where it takes teams of accountants both to prepare and interpret it. This billing confusion is another of the factors that has contributed to advertising's poor reputation in recent years.

Furthermore, the commission system may work a hardship on agency, client, or both. For example, it was noted in the case of the Gas Company that the agency probably did not recover its costs from the commission alone. It was, in effect, underpaid under the commission system. However, another agency may prepare a single ad, which will run nationally several times in 100 major newspapers, to the tune of $300,000. Its commission for preparing this single ad is $45,000. It has done essentially the same work as the Gas Company's agency and is probably being overpaid.

The commission system also places a temptation on agencies to seek the highest costs possible or to urge needless advertising in order to increase their commission. On the other hand, clients are not without fault and have been known to demand commission rebates from their agencies as a condition of keeping the account.

As a result, more and more attention is being paid to the negotiated fee as an alternative to the commission system. Under a negotiated fee, agency and client sit down to develop an approach or campaign. Once the dimensions of the approach are known, a mutually acceptable fee is agreed upon that covers the agency's services for all advertising functions plus profit, and the agency is adequately reimbursed for its planning time. There are pitfalls to this system, too, and as in most things, there is little that can be accomplished except in an atmosphere of integrity and mutual trust, which is difficult to achieve in the highly competitive advertising jungle. It is fair to say that like the mass communications system of which it is the principal support, advertising is far from perfect.

POSITIONING— A NEW APPROACH?

In recent years, the past half-dozen or so, a new concept of specialization has come to national advertising, called "positioning." Earlier advertising was based on the concept of the lcd, appealing to the lowest common denominator in the hope that differentiation in the advertising, regardless of product similarity, would attract a vague maximum response. This was really a sort of hit-or-miss approach. However, advertisers and their agencies watched as successful media specialization occurred, particularly in the radio and magazine fields where the various media pinpointed their appeal to specific audiences, and a more sophisticated advertising concept evolved. It was possible, they reasoned, to appeal to specific audiences even within the broad mass that newspapers or, more so, television represented. Positioning recognized the inherent differences in people as individuals. Thus, as the audience continuum shows, advertising itself is reaching ever closer to the individual appeal, foregoing for the moment the appeal to the lowest common denominator of taste. Positioning also recognized the inherent impossibility of any product capturing the entire potential market. It was willing to settle for a share of the market, yielding a part of the pie to its competition and ever seeking to increase the size of its own slice.

Positioning works as follows in soap, for example. Some soap users are concerned with antiseptic cleanliness. Lifebuoy goes after this market, stressing its medicinal smell, its cleansing qualities, its ability to banish the curse of body odor offensiveness. In so doing, it reaches out into the tens of millions of television viewers who are concerned, if not obsessed, with cleanliness and fear of offending; it offers a haven to the insecure. Theoretically, it locks up this slice of the market. There are others in this vast audience, however, who are less concerned with hygiene than they are with their complexions. Dove soap is for them. Emphasis is placed on its one-quarter cleansing cream content, and as the acned teenager watches the commercial, she knows Dove is for her. Likewise, for the aging matron seeking to perpetuate the peaches and cream complexion of her youth, Dove holds hope of subtracting a year or two. Positioning directs itself to the mass within the mass.

The same situation is present in advertising beer. One beer directs its appeal to the swingers: it is always being poured in a happy surrounding of youth, with people laughing, dancing, singing, always gregarious. To the party people in the audience, it is a natural; it is their beer. To the wallflowers sitting home this beer represents companionship and gaiety, and holds forth the promise of popularity by association. Another beer appeals to the manly; it is a robust beer used by active, energetic people. It's a he-man beer, and he-men should drink it; ninety-seven-pound weaklings buy it in the hope that some of this manliness will rub off on them. Positioning applies the most practical, daily use of motivational research. It seeks to segregate audiences by their very personal interests and appeal to them alone, forsaking all others. In this, of course, it is an update of the brand image, without snob appeal.

Positioning has some weaknesses. To the woman who is interested both in personal hygiene and her complexion, positioning has offered little alternative: does she choose between both soaps, or does she fall into schizophrenia and in desperation buy another brand? He who is both a would-be swinger and erstwhile he-man—what beer does he drink, or does he in desperation turn to liquor? Some of positioning's appeals are rather esoteric. Salems appealed to romance recaptured with young lovers in a bucolic setting; smoking Salems promised to bring back those sunny years. Silva Thins went after the homosexual market, while Virginia Slims appealed to feminists—"You've come a long way, Baby." Ban sought the naturalists, the environmentalists, with a wholesome, modly bespecacled girl poignantly telling her tragedy: "I wouldn't use a deodorant if I didn't have to..."

Another of the problems with positioning is that of overkill. The more specifically directed the approach is to a market, the smaller the potential market, and the greater the numbers of people reached and paid for who have no potential interest in the product approach. Positioning is a stride toward the future, but it is a dangerous game fraught with the perils of both overkill, which is expensive, and stereotyping, which places the product in a cage from which it cannot escape. Yet, the rationale of sharing of the market is hard to destroy, and the presumed cohesiveness of the mass audience on which the lcd is based is hard to maintain. Advertising innovates, as do the media, but it innovates psychologically while they innovate technologically. Increasingly, they both do it demographically.

TRUTH IN ADVERTISING

Increasingly, as a result of the consumer movement, truth in advertising has become a cause célèbre. Despite its current emphasis, it is not a new concern. Misrepresentation in advertising came under heavy fire during the muckraker movement of the early 1900s, resulting in 1911 legislation aimed particularly at patent medicine panaceas. The Better Business Bureau (BBB) was organized in 1913 as a private sector supplement policing advertising claims, a role that it has continued with varying success until the present.

In the depression years of the 1930s, during Franklin Roosevelt's New Deal, Congress passed the Wheeler-Lea Act, which created the Food and Drug Aministration (FDA) charged basically with enforcing standards of quality and safety and, incidentally, with auditing advertising claims by food packagers, drug, and cosmetic manufacturers.

Within the last decade, the Federal Trade Commission (FTC), increasingly sensitive to consumer pressure, has moved into the areas of truth in lending and truth in packaging with considerable success. Fresh from its triumphs in these related fields, it has undertaken the more complex problems of truth in advertising, noted in some detail in the chapter on controls. The FTC demands that advertisers prove their claims, which is only logical. But, further, since claims are documented, the FTC encourages advertisers to say exactly why their product is preferable to a competitor's, which, in effect, does away with brand X advertising (where claims are directed against an anonymous brand X rather than against specific competitor's product). Other FTC actions have been directed against the massiveness of some major advertisers' campaigns ($73 million, for example, spent by the cereal industry) that, it is claimed, is not needed to sell the goods, but rather tends to drive out competition.[5]

5. "Madison Avenue's Response to Its Critics," *Business Week*, 10 June 1972.

CORRECTIVE ADVERTISING

Another issue raised by the FTC is so-called corrective advertising whereby advertisers may be required to use one-quarter of their advertising budgets to correct misrepresentations, confessing their sins as it were. The industry does not regard corrective advertising as too great a threat. Only two cases thus far have been so adjudicated. One involved ITT's Continental Baking Company and its agency, Ted Bates & Company. The other suit was brought against Ocean Spray Cranberry; the company probably would have been judged innocent in court, but for economic reasons agreed to the consent decree.[6] The advertising industry presently feels that adjudication of corrective advertising cases takes years in court to enforce compliance, by which time the impetus and need for the correction will have been long gone. There is also the question as to whether the FCC would support its sister agency as far as broadcasting is concerned, and this is where, of course, the majority of the sins are committed. However, the suggestion of corrective advertising coupled with a beefed-up FTC has caused advertisers to regard the agency with new respect.

6. Ibid.

On another front, the FTC's action against Wonder Bread for spending millions making claims that any other breadmaker could have made strikes at the heart of Bates' unique selling proposition, and casts a shadow over the entire picture of advertisement differentiation rather than merely the issue of product differentiation. The great fear of the advertising industry is that commission pressure will result in a curtailment of advertising with an accompanying slowdown of sales, which, in America's interrelated economic system, could result in recession or worse.

There is some evidence that the advertising industry may be slowing down already. The industry grew at a 5 percent per annum rate during the 1960s and then slowed to 4 percent in the 1970s. However, the overall picture is spotty in that many major advertisers were increasing their advertising budgets in the same period. Proctor and Gamble, for example, moved to $190 million in 1971 from $180

[7.] Ibid.

million in 1970. General Motors went up from $42 million to $65 million in the same period; however, General Foods, Colgate-Palmolive, and Bristol-Myers all went down.[7] Advertising is in flux, and the FTC is not helping it stabilize.

There is considerable room for the FTC's complaints of advertiser deception. A razor blade manufacturer showing his product shaving sandpaper on television had soaked special sandpaper in warm detergent for several hours before shaving. A soup company put marbles in the televised bowl of soup just below the surface to create the visual impression of body.

ADVERTISING INTER-RELATIONSHIPS

The reconstituted FTC has resulted in beefed-up BBBs who, working with Advertising Councils throughout the nation, are creating local, regional, and national advertising review boards in a sort of industry self-policing action. The review boards rule on the accuracy of advertising, and any advertiser in doubt as to the propriety of his claims may submit them to the boards for adjudication. As advertising is affected by controls, so are all the media that it serves.

One of the offshoots of FTC aggressiveness has been the "no claim" ad in which the individual is left to draw his own conclusions. An example is Shell's tennis shoes: "If we can make such good tennis shoes, think about our gasoline, which is our basic business." No-claim advertising is syllogistic, implying relationships where perhaps none exist. In the example given, Shell's purpose is to point out how good their gasoline is without actually saying so and having to prove it. Syllogistically, however, it could just as easily be that the only reason they are making tennis shoes at all is because their gasoline is bad. No-claim advertising offers the advantage of reinforcement without a direct pitch, but it is still persuasive advertising.

There has been a lot of criticism of advertising over the years. Most of it has been aimed at the supposed psychological effects—namely, that it creates needs and wants and, in so doing, encourages people to "keep up with the Joneses," to live beyond their means. To the extent that these wants are left unfulfilled, it also breeds frustration; it encourages aggressiveness and perhaps crime; it emphasizes the material—and there may be some evidence to support these claims. There is little doubt that advertising is the product of a commercial and competitive society. It is the natural partner of the free enterprise system and provides the distribution extension of mass production.

Another criticism has been leveled at advertising's costs to the consumer, and these are considerable. As all advertising costs are essentially distribution costs, like transportation, they are passed on to the consumer...to the public. Consumers are placed in the position, therefore, of paying for the privilege of being persuaded, or even deceived. Combined with the previous criticism, this essentially means that the public is being urged to live beyond its means, to "keep up with the Joneses," to buy products they don't need and, in the long

Advertising

run, to be spendthrifts, acquisitive and selfish, the meanwhile paying liberally for the urging. About $100 of the cost of the average American car, for example, represents advertising costs that the consumer pays when he buys the vehicle. Without advertising, the car would be at least $100 cheaper, a sizable amount in any budget.

Particularly as far as misleading advertising is concerned, or that which employs an overdose of sociopsychological motivation, these costs are reprehensible. However, it was noted earlier that advertising is an automated salesman. The existence of advertising, coupled with a giant and diverse mass media network, which it helped to create, has made possible a greater demand for goods and services than there would be otherwise. Translated into terms of mass production, this increased demand has led to economies and savings in purchasing and on the assembly lines, and have rendered many products, including the automobile, far cheaper than they would otherwise have been—even including the extra advertising increment.

There is little doubt that advertising increases the costs of goods; there is little doubt that advertising encourages consumption, often at the expense of thrift; there is little doubt that advertising works upon the public's psyches in often devious ways. But there is also little doubt that advertising supports the largest and most diverse mass media network in the world; there is little doubt that advertising itself is a major employer and contributor to the overall economy; there is little doubt that advertising, through increased demand, reduces the overall cost of many products.

Advertising is, therefore, both a blessing and a menace, and both these roles must be recognized if the operation of mass communications in society is to be understood. As in almost everything that has been discussed pertaining to mass communications, there are tradeoffs. The bad is accepted with the good. It is not a question of either/or, it is a question of both, for under the existing system, which has had a long evolution and tradition, man cannot have one without the other, or he shall have a different system entirely.

Advertising is an integral part of the content of mass communications, and in some media it is the predominant part. As such, while it does not specifically come under First Amendment protection, it is still a part of the basic libertarian theory on which the First Amendment is based. Thus, any attempts to control advertising, particularly when it provides the economic support for most of the mass communications system, perforce controls the media it serves.

In defense of advertising, it can be said again that it is the necessary factor in the mass distribution system, that in effectively moving the goods, it is in part responsible for the high gross national product and the standard of living which it engenders. There are other assets. It makes possible the most ubiquitous and diversified mass communications system of any nation, providing unparalleled entertainment and considerable information and culture at a fraction of its true cost to the individual. Martin Mayer addresses himself to the psychological factors in advertising in his value-added theory.[8] He claims that advertising adds a vague dimension to a product: the girl who buys soap in the belief that it will improve her complexion may be more satisfied in that belief, a happier person, whether it does or not; the assurance that comes from purchasing a product of believed quality—a Hathaway shirt, for example—provides a confidence to the individual that would have been unobtainable with a cheaper shirt. In essence, Mayer states the psychological concept of confidence—that we are what we believe and that this is the added value of advertising for some of us.

8. Martin Mayer, *Madison Avenue, U.S.A.* (New York: Pocket Books Inc., 1967).

SUMMARY

It is advertising, by and large, that supports the United States' pervasive and extraordinarily diverse mass communications system. This relationship has evolved largely as the result of a competitive, free enterprise economy where the private sector has provided the investment needed to expand the mass media in return for their use in selling goods and services. Advertising serves both the media and the economy, acting as a middleman between the two.

Advertising is ancient. In historic times the wineskin identified the wineshop or tavern. Soon a bigger wineskin, visible at greater distance, conveyed an impression of a bigger (and better) wineshop, increasing trade.

Advertising is essentially of two kinds: informative and persuasive. Informational advertising merely advises the availability of a product or service; the persuasive urges its purchase.

By the mid-eighteenth century, the industrial revolution and the railroads provided the mass production of similar goods and the means to distribute them nationally, and national advertising entered the field. The similarity of products resulted in the need to differentiate among them by advertising. The oldest technique is that of the brand name. Soon slogans appeared. With the advent of radio in the 1920s, jingles came into being as a sort of orchestrated slogan. The 1930s brought advances in advertisement testing and effectiveness, plus early forms of audience measurement.

Advertising's greatest growth occurred in the years following World War II. Rapid improvement in media technology, interest in the social sciences, and a built-up backlog of consumer demand all contributed to a postwar impetus. Advertising in the United States grew from a $4 billion industry to one of more than $20 billion in the postwar period.

First of the postwar pseudopsychological techniques was Ted Bates' unique selling proposition (usp). Ogilvie's brand image technique followed shortly after, directed basically toward snob appeal, while Ernest Dichter's motivational research was highly Freudian in its emphasis on hidden reasons for purchasing. Subliminal advertising passed sales messages before viewer's eyes without their conscious knowledge and proved effective in triggering certain predispositions. Subliminal advertising was abandoned as a threat to the mind's integrity. Most recent of the advertising techniques is that of positioning, which seeks to define individuals from the mass television audience by appealing to their specific desires.

Advertising's overall effectiveness is questionable. It seems to be remarkably effective in selling consumer goods, inconsequentials that the public recognizes as trivia. It is much less effective in convincing the public in matters of substance, such as elections. It is unequalled in calling attention to a new product or candidate.

Advertising agencies progressed from space brokers in the mid-1800s to client-oriented specialists beginning in 1889. They serve both the client and the mass media and tend to specialize both in product and in media preference.

Agencies are generally reimbursed under the commission system. They are paid a 15 percent commission by the media for placing the ad. However, commissions encourage agencies to oversell and, in many instances, the agency is either underpaid or overpaid for its work. A good deal of attention is being given to the negotiated fee as an alternative.

In recent years the FTC has been pursuing truth in advertising a course that affects all media. The FTC requires advertisers to prove their claims, which encourages attacking competitors' products and eliminates the need for Brand X advertising. The FTC has recently looked toward corrective advertising as a device to counteract deceptive practices.

18 PUBLIC RELATIONS

THE VOLUME OF PR

Public relations is an enigma. It defies definition. In its broadest sense it is an umbrella that includes publicity, with which it is too often equated, propaganda, promotion, press agentry, and even advertising, plus such subspecialties as political campaigning and lobbying. Perhaps the best definition is "ulterior communication." As such, public relations makes extensive use of the mass media, contributing considerable portions of media content in contemporary society.

An annual celebration—National Public Relations Day—to commemorate contributions of the field would most dramatically demonstrate the pervasity of PR if publishers would leave blank in newspapers and magazines any story with a public relations origin; similarly, broadcasters could omit from the air any program or item that had its genesis in public relations. The sheer volume of white space and silence would drive home impressively the extent to which the mass media are dependent upon public relations and, more to the point, the extent to which society is perhaps unwittingly exposed to ulterior material.

Public relations, however, in dealing with the mass media, performs a useful service as an adjunct to its own information-gathering processes. In this sense it too is an information packager. None of the mass media have the resources, money, time, or manpower to fully cover all events. For some they are reliant upon public relations people to provide them with the news.

Successful public relations in an informational sense is dependent upon an atmosphere of mutual respect between the media gatekeepers and the public relations practitioners. The relationship is a tenuous one; both are wary of the other. Editors know that PR men represent special interests; PR people know that editors deal in the sensational, often to the disadvantage of PR clients. Most PR people have come from the media; generally, they are former newspapermen. This has considerable advantage: they are familiar with newspaper style (journalese); they know what news is and how to write it. They are aware of media problems, and they have their own contacts in the city room. The most successful PR people are the ones who know that they are performing a useful information service in providing the media with news that could, in the ordinary course of events, be obtained in no other way. While they do not go hat in hand a-begging, they are aware of the intense competition for attention. They know that they are in competition for newspaper space with a platoon of reporters, with the chattering teletype batteries from around the world and nation, with the reams of feature material, and with every other press agent in town. They have established a working rapport with the media and proven their integrity. For these pragmatic reasons, most public relations material in the mass media has a legitimate claim on news. It may be self-serving, but it is news.

PUBLIC RELATIONS AS NEWS

As ulterior communication, public relations utilizes all forms of communications, not just the mass media. It relies heavily on word-of-mouth. Public relations makes use of conventions and seminars, of group addresses, of individual contacts with opinion leaders. Nowhere in the entire realm of mass communications is Lazarsfeld's two-step theory better exemplified than in public relations. Public relations attacks the audience continuum at all points, from the "massest" mass of network television, through the various publics and groups on down to the individual himself. Public relations has developed audience identification to a fine art, and ingeniously devises sometimes imaginative means of reaching particular, discrete publics. Extensive use is made of demographics and public opinion polling. It is fair to say that both public relations and advertising, the organized forms of persuasion, are devoted to generating word-of-mouth coverage between individuals, for it is only through this means that a message perpetuates itself once it is let loose.

THE IRONY OF PUBLIC RELATIONS

One of the basic problems surrounding public relations as a practice is the inability to measure its effect. Advertising can be measured at the cash register. Public relations is a necessarily long-term intangible, so completely interrelated with everything that an organization does that it is difficult to separate the effects of public relations alone. This, in turn, has contributed considerably to the questionable reputation that public relations has. It is ironic that a field that professes to mold public opinion, to change organizational images, and to accomplish corporate and political miracles should itself have such a poor public image. There are a number of incompetents in the field calling themselves public relations practitioners. As their substandard work multiplies, the profession as a whole is libeled. There are neither standards (such as passing the bar for lawyers), nor a stipulated course study (as for doctors), nor licensing (as for architects, engineers, and accountants) for the practice of public relations. Anyone could hang out a shingle.

Recognizing this, the Public Relations Society of America (PRSA) has embarked upon a program of accreditation for its members. Beginning in 1960 on a voluntary basis, accreditation became mandatory in 1969. Members must have a minimum of five years of public relations experience. In addition, they must pass an eight-hour examination in public relations principles and techniques, and also undergo an oral examination by a panel of three accredited peers. The hope is that gradually business and government and other organizations will come to recognize that PRSA membership means that the PR person has satisfied at least the minimal qualifications of experience and knowledge, and can be expected to bring a certain amount of professionalism and expertise to any job. He is the best choice for an assignment, so that APR, just as AIA or CPA after a name, means that the individual is a competent practicioner, architect, or accountant who has satisfied professional requirements. The PRSA program has been slow; there is much to overcome. More recently, particularly as a result of excesses in political campaigning, for which public relations must share a part of the blame, there have been movements in several states toward public relations licensing. In some communities, stringent regulations of the public relations practice as it affects lobbying before public agencies and political campaigning have been placed in effect. It is quite possible that PRSA's movement toward professionalization, which is a form of self-regulation designed to forestall governmental control, may fall as being too little and too late. If widespread regulation and licensing of public relations does come about, it is inevitable that it will be another form of communications control, departing even further from the libertarian spirit. Government regulation may not be entirely undesirable, but so interwoven with the entire fabric of mass communications is public relations that control cannot help but have side effects on both the content and utilization and future development of the mass communications complex.

THE CLIPPING BOOK SYNDROME

Too often public relations is confused with publicity, identified with it in fact. Publicity is only one of the tools of public relations, an important tool to be sure, but far from the sum and substance of the profession. Publicity consists of obtaining free space or time for promotional material in the press or on the air. This material masquerades as news, but its purpose is often hidden. One of the advantages of publicity is that in a quantitative society it can be measured. The number of column inches obtained in the press can be counted. The number of air minutes can be totalled. There is a tangible record of publicity. This has led to undue reliance on the clipping book as a measure of public relations effectiveness. Public relations practitioners proudly haul their clipping books to management on a regular basis, saying, "Here's what I've done for you lately; here's how I earned my pay." Further, the number of column inches or air minutes can be applied to media rate cards and a dollar volume of publicity computed: "This coverage would have cost you $10,000 if you had not used my services," a PR man might say. These are meaningful figures to cost-conscious management, but they do not measure the effect of the publicity. Nor do they tell who, if anyone, read it or heard it nor how he reacted. It is also quite possible that the publicity repulsed the audience. In such a case, the clipping book is a liability rather than an asset. Silence might have served the corporate cause better than publicity.

Publicity is a relatively new tool of public relations, the direct result of mass media development. Public relations itself is ancient, although it has not always been called public relations. Public relations refers to two things. First, it refers to the techniques of persuasion that have come down through history, long before mass media and mass communications. This was and still is the conscious attempt to mold public opinion, using whatever techniques were at hand. It relies heavily, then as now, on word-of-mouth transmission. Second, it refers to the organized practice, the profession or subprofession, conducted in contemporary America. Public relations as an organized practice is a uniquely American development born basically on these shores, predating the Republic in whose formation it played a considerable role, and taking its bases first from political campaigning in this prototype of Western democracies; second, from theatrical press agentry as the mass media grew; and, finally, reaching fruition through business and later governmental applications, principally in this century.

DEVELOPMENT IN GREECE AND ROME

Public relations development began in ancient Greece. There the poets were the public relations people. Use of the poetic form in rhyme and meter facilitated memory, assuring that messages would be passed along in more or less the same form. Two poets, Simonides and Pindar, made a good living writing and selling odes of praise for those willing to pay. They were the first press agents. The use of poetry to manipulate public opinion became so widespread in the Greek democracy that Plato in his *Republic* advocated the prohibition of all poetry—except that written for the government. Not only was this the first example of attempted governmental control of the mass media (such as it was), but it was the first advocacy of governmental public relations, which is, of course, a big business today.

In Rome, the same techniques of poetry and praise occurred with a number of Roman refinements. The Romans refined the poetic form, adding subtlety to public relations. Virgil's *Georgics* was, on the surface, a bucolic poem extolling the virtues of country living, the pastoral scene, clean air, fresh water, and a closeness to nature. Its purpose, however, was devious. Rome was overcrowded at the time, an early version of urban sprawl. There was not enough food to feed the population. The *Georgics,* commissioned by the government, was a public relations attempt to urge people to leave the city and take up rural residence, thus at once alleviating the population pressure and providing more farmers to feed city residents. The Romans also employed "talkers" who wandered through the Roman baths and forum extolling the virtues of their clients or masters. The concept of "bread and circuses" was a public relations device of the dissolute emperors to feed and entertain the people and so keep their minds off public excesses, corruption, injustice, and the squalor in which they lived.

A master of public relations was Gaius Julius Caesar, who developed the first long-range public relations program, in both time and space, for himself and his ambition. Early in his career his talent and ambition caused jealousies, and the Senate in effect banished him to Gaul in charge of an Army, hoping that the people, with whom he was extraordinarily popular, would forget him.

Over the Roman roads which supplied the legions, Caesar sent back messengers regularly to Rome with his *Commentaries,* familiar to any beginning Latin students. The *Commentaries* were not reports to the Senate, but reports to the people on his exploits. They were read and posted in the forum for all to see. They were written in the language of the people—punchy, and alive. His famous "veni, vidi, vici" is a fine example, to the point, alliterated—"I came, I saw, I conquered"—a phraseology to feed the legend of a demagogue. The technique worked; over the long years of foreign battles, in Gaul, Spain, and Britain, he kept his legend alive until the day when he returned at the head of his victorious Army. The people hailed him and made him emperor.

Public relations in its broadest sense has always taken advantage of whatever communications forms exist. Marshall McLuhan makes the point in *Understanding Media* that Christianity, the greatest propaganda effort of all time, came about as a result of "a conspiracy of communications."[1] His thesis is that for the first time in history, during Christ's lifetime, the existence of the Roman roads and Roman order plus a universal language, Greek, made possible the worldwide dissemination of a single ethic. Had Christ lived in an earlier age, no one today would ever have known about it, but circumstances permitted Paul and the Apostles to travel the breadth of the known world spreading the word in a language that others could understand. Public relations is reliant upon the status of communications.

1. Marshall McLuhan, *Understanding Media* (New York: Signet Books, 1966).

THE DARK AGES

After the fall of Rome, the civilized world fell into decay. The Dark Ages were a constricted time of fear and superstition, of small, ingrown warring enclaves, with almost no intercommunication. The troubadours comprised about the only medium there was and, in a period of high illiteracy, they dealt in verse. It is interesting to note that as the principal medium of the long, bleak era that, as they carried information from castle to castle and town to town, they injected into verse large doses of both entertainment and persuasion to achieve a content mix roughly approximate to that of today in the mass media. Both *Le Chanson de Roland* and the Cid were products of the troubadours, panegyrics to popular heroes, building and perpetuating their legends.

In the Renaissance, Gutenberg's converted winepress and printing paved the way for mass education, mass literacy, mass communications, and mass persuasion in a sequence noted earlier. It was Henry VIII of England who first clearly saw the inherent threat that mass communications represented. Whereas word-of-mouth transmission tended to run its course like a powder train, printing made possible the simultaneous ignition of separate powder kegs all over the kingdom. Through the courts of star chamber he placed the first controls on mass communications; however, he struck not at mass communications but at the inseparable ingredient of mass persuasion that it inevitably contained.

AMERICAN GENESIS

The Revolution was not a case of the spontaneous uprising of downtrodden colonists against a tyrannical crown. It was rather a long-term public relations program masterminded by one man, Samuel Adams, with much assistance. Adams hated the English for personal reasons and, starting in 1750, began an organized effort to foster revolution and independence. He utilized the Colonial press, particularly in his native New England. He wasted no opportunity to have published instances and examples of British arrogance and oppression, only some of which were true. He made heavy use of pamphlets, one of the basic public relations tools of the time. In the period from 1750 to 1783 more than 1,500 pamphlets were published attacking the English, many of them the work of Sam Adams personally, and many of them subsequently published in the Colonial press. He painstakingly organized committees of correspondence in the thirteen colonies that kept in constant touch, exchanging information about English malfeasance. He developed the techniques of confrontation and exaggeration, of which the Boston Massacre of 1770 is an example. In reality it was a mini-massacre in which only five persons were killed. Adams' thugs goaded English sentries until they fired in an early example of the politics of confrontation. The victims became martyrs to a cause, "shot down in cold blood." Adams also invented the pseudoevent in the form of the Boston Tea Party. A pseudoevent is a contrived event whose sole purpose is to develop publicity. To protest English taxation on tea, Adams dressed his thugs as Indians and sent them down to the harbor to dump all the tea on an English ship into the water. Paul Revere made his little-known first ride to New York and Philadelphia to carry the news of the "tea party." Ad-

Advertising competes for audience attention.

"Somebody still cares about quality."

The media appearance of one advertisement requires the combined involvement of many people.

ams knew the people did not understand import duties nor particularly care about them. But a group of thugs dressed as Indians in Boston where an Indian hadn't been seen for 150 years, dumping tea in the harbor and calling it a tea party, had a certain amount of pizzazz and bore telling and retelling with a chuckle. It had drama and propaganda value in generating word-of-mouth transmission.

PAINE, FRANKLIN, AND HAMILTON

Samuel Adams' collaborators in fomenting revolution and establishing the Republic were Thomas Paine, Benjamin Franklin, and Alexander Hamilton. Paine was an inspired pamphleteer. His "Crisis Papers" provided the rationale for the revolution, and his "On a Drumhead" series, written during the actual fighting, kept alive the spirit of rebellion.

Benjamin Franklin was a great believer in self-promotion. At an early age in Philadelphia he wrote articles for the papers, and then went home to write letters of praise for his articles and had them delivered to the editors, thus creating an additional demand for his material. It was this penchant for public relations that he brought to bear on the United States' behalf when he became her first emissary to France. Franklin was the minister from a barbarous, upstart republic to the most civilized court in Europe. His native wit and the fact that he spoke fluent French served him well. He also obtained a small palace, furbished it elegantly, and gave outstanding receptions. He had a magnificent coach built and when he appeared on the streets, drawn by matched black horses and accompanied by liveried outriders, he was a sight to behold. The cumulative effect of this kind of elegance and ostentation dictated that the United States be taken seriously, for obviously a nation that could provide so cultured an ambassador who lived with such opulence was one to be reckoned with; Franklin practiced pure public relations.

Alexander Hamilton's public relations contributions were twofold. First, in the dark days of the revolution he provided a martyr—Nathan Hale. Second, he was instrumental in the adoption of the Federalist viewpoint of a strong national government as opposed to a loose confederation of separate states.

Nathan Hale was not a very good spy; he was captured by the English about fifty yards from where he started on his very first mission. It was probably Hamilton who put the famous words, "I regret that I have but one life to give for my country," into Hale's silent mouth. Hale had talked to no one since his capture. Hamilton realized that the revolution at low ebb needed a martyr, and he provided one. As the tale of Hale's heroism spread, it sparked incredible Yankee resistance at the Battle of Saratoga, where an implausible Colonial victory became the turning point of the revolution that would finally end four years later at Yorktown.

Hamilton's other contribution was "The Federalist Papers," written jointly with Madison and Jay, although Hamilton authored the

2. Alexander Hamilton et al., *Federalist Papers*, ed. Clinton Rossiter (New York: Mentor Books, 1961).

bulk of them. "The Federalist Papers" were a series of newspaper articles for the New York press, subsequently picked up by many other papers; they provided a rationale for a strong federal government. They were also admirable commentaries on the molding of public opinion, frankly propagandistic in nature. Their purpose was to sell the federalist concept to the Continental Congress, utilizing the power of public opinion upon the delegates to do so.[2] Hamilton thus became America's first political columnist.

PUBLIC RELATIONS' ORIGINS

One of the two basic sources of American public relations as an organized practice was in political campaigning. The United States, after the formation of the Republic, became the first of the Western democracies. It was the belief of the founding fathers when they set up the electoral structure that in communities throughout the land certain natural leaders would emerge and that the people would select from them leaders—those whose beliefs came closest to their own. However, as political office meant preferment, it was not long before ambitious individuals began taking steps to assure that they would be counted among the natural leaders at election time.

Some of the early political campaigns were masterpieces of pizzazz, embracing slogans, torchlight parades, brass bands, and beer busts in the effort to win votes. Andrew Jackson (Old Hickory) changed the ground rules. An Indian fighter of repute and victor of New Orleans in the War of 1812, he campaigned on a populist ticket with a slate of electors pledged to him. The election of Andrew Jackson proved the merit of populist appeal, and the business of national campaigning was born.

The other basis of public relations was theatrical press agentry, of which P. T. Barnum was the great exponent. Barnum recognized that people enjoyed being conned. He was the author of the statement, "There's a sucker born every minute," and he exploited this principle throughout his life as a showman. His buildup of General Tom Thumb, a midget masquerading as a Civil War general, was a masterpiece of promotion. Later, the production of General Tom Thumb's wedding to another midget, complete with a parade down Broadway in a tiny coach drawn by tiny horses, was another pinnacle of pizzazz. People knew that Tom Thumb was no Civil War officer, no hero of Antietam or Vicksburg, but the idea was so preposterous that they enjoyed it and were willing to pay money to hear his exploits and see him strut in his little uniform, cockaded hat, and tiny sword. It is from this origin of public relations that much of its criticism stems. The theory was that anything was valid if it generated publicity. "I don't care what you say about me as long as you spell my name right" was a summary of the substance of press agentry, not entirely calculated to win lasting confidence but still extant. While political campaigning introduced specificity of appeal, press agentry introduced the outrageous as a device in the competition for attention.

Indirect Media

"THE PUBLIC BE DAMNED"

The years following the Civil War were the years of America's expansion, the winning of the West when all was suborned to the practical business of exploiting a continent. This was the time of the robber barons and the railroads, of "survival of the fittest" (widely misinterpreted from its biological origin in Darwin to a social doctrine), and of laissez-faire, its political and economic expression. The era had its public relations counterpart in "the public be damned" attitude so succinctly expressed by William Henry Vanderbilt of the New York Central Railroad in the 1880s.

The turn of the century brought reaction in the form of the muckrakers—authors and journalists—who saw business corruption and government collusion rampant and set out to correct it, using the mass media of the time—books, magazines, and newspapers—to do so. Ida Tarbell's series, "The History of Standard Oil," Lincoln Steffen's "The Shame of the Cities," and Upton Sinclair's novel, *The Jungle*, an exposé of the meat-packing industry, are all examples of an unorganized campaign that ran a decade or so and resulted in some of the first social legislation. The muckrakers were the expression of a stirring social consciousness repulsed by the excesses of business and the timidity of government. They repudiated "survival of the fittest" as social doctrine.

Business did not take this lying down. It turned to press agents to whitewash its reputation, but the glaring discrepancies between business' whitewash and the all too visible inequities created an early instance of credibility gap. Business was in trouble. Into this picture in 1908 stepped Ivy Lee, the father of public relations. Lee had an unprecedented idea; he was a press agent who dealt in truth. He published a declaration of principles and sent it to editors with whom he dealt. It said that he dealt in news, factual information, and that the editors were free to check any of his facts independently. Furthermore, if they felt his material was better placed in their advertising columns, all they had to do was throw it away.

THE FATHER OF PR

Lee had an enormous respect for the aggregate wisdom of the people. He felt that if they were given the facts that they would make correct judgments. His basic tenet was that the public should be honestly informed of good news and bad. He proved this in the case of the Pennsylvania Railroad. The Pennsy had a wreck in which a number of lives were lost. Management's first reaction was to hush it up. Lee pointed out that a wreck could not be hushed up, with cars and engines strewn over the New Jersey landscape and bloodshed on the right-of-way, anymore than the cries of the injured could be hushed. Lee ran special trains for the press to the scene of the accident. He announced a system-wide survey of the company's roadbeds to be sure that a similar wreck would not happen; he announced the indemnification of the families of those killed, and hospitalization to the injured. In short, Lee converted a tragedy into a public relations triumph for the railroad, which was widely applauded by the press for its handling of the accident. Lee knew that it is far better to face bad news frontally than to let it linger and fester in secret until it destroys credibility, as in the case of Watergate.

The first decade of the twentieth century was a time of emerging mass media, increasing literacy, proliferating newspapers, urban growth, development of the huge newspaper chains, stepped-up wire services, national magazines, and an embryonic movie industry. This particular conspiracy of communications breathed life into public relations, and its organized practice stemmed from this decade.

WORLD WAR I AND BEYOND

By World War I public relations was sufficiently well established as a profession for President Wilson to call on it for assistance. He established the Creel Committee as an adjunct of government, so named because it was headed by George Creel, a friend and newspaperman. The committee was charged with helping to finance the war through the sale of Liberty Bonds, with convincing the American people of the war's necessity, with popularizing the draft, engendering sympathy for the Allies and hatred of the enemy—a mammoth assignment that it carried out with considerable success.

The next milestone in the development of public relations as an organized practice was engendered by Edward Bernays. Bernays had been a member of the Creel Committee, and set up practice in New York following World War I. He wrote the first book on public relations, *Crystallizing Public Opinion,* published in 1923.[3] He also taught the first course in public relations at NYU in that period. Bernays' philosophy is summed up in his phrase, "the engineering of consent."

3. Edward Bernays, *Crystallizing Public Opinion* (New York: Liveright, 1961).

In 1930, with the beginning of the Great Depression, Paul Garrett became the first public relations director of the General Motors Corporation. Asked by GM how to make a billion-dollar corporation look small (wealth was suspect in the depression), Garrett replied that he hadn't the faintest idea. Alternately, he proposed a program in which GM would use a part of its resources to provide both high school and college educations for youngsters who would otherwise go without, and in which GM would make significant contributions to schools and municipal improvements in the communities where its plants were located. These were all windfalls to public agencies in the constricted years of the depression. Garrett reasoned that GM would receive public relations credit as a benefactor, in addition to which it would be making its plant communities more efficient and would also be developing a backlog of educated executive talent against the future. Garrett's term was "enlightened self-interest," and his program was the first of the socially conscious programs of industry.

Public relations was hard-pressed during the depression to serve business, which had been cast as a villain. Furthermore, because of its intangible nature, public relations was one of the first business services to be curtailed in a time of tight money. Labor unions and government, however, forged ahead in public relations usage, and Franklin D. Roosevelt became one of the masters of its use.

FDR AND JFK

FDR's fireside chats, employing radio in the depression years to reach into America's homes to reassure a frightened people and to sell his then radical programs of monetary and social reform, were inspired. It was a technique which softened the depression.

At a later time John Fitzgerald Kennedy displayed the same inherent understanding of television that FDR did of radio. He used telvision to talk to the nation disarmingly, exploiting his personal charisma to the utmost and creating the legend of Camelot, cut too quickly short. These two examples indicate the extent to which public relations has infiltrated government and show how adroit media usage constitutes the means of projecting an image. The public relations image is not necessarily mirage; it can easily be a reality (as in the cases of FDR and JFK) that needs only the proper lens to project it where all can see. Choosing and using that lens is a part of public relations.

World War II provided additional impetus to public relations as techniques of propaganda and psychological warfare were perfected, and the term "war of nerves" came into the lexicon. President Roosevelt's Office of War Information (OWI) under Elmer Davis had charge of a full public relations and propaganda service, both domestic and international, focusing not only on American allies to strengthen and reassure them, but also on enemies to sow the seeds of doubt and despair.

PROPAGANDA

The word *propaganda* stemmed from the establishment by the Catholic Church in 1622 of the College of Propaganda, charged with propagating the faith through the means of missionaries and the like. From these innocuous beginnings, the word has taken on an unsavory connotation. One author seeks to make a distinction between "pernicious propaganda" and "honest persuasion." This is a ridiculous semantical exercise in that the only distinction between pernicious propaganda and honest persuasion is whether "they" do it or "we" do it. This also illustrates a tendency of public relations to play with words. Connotative words and phrases have a way of playing upon the emotions. Classically, this is rhetoric, another of the tools of public relations designed to sway opinion.

THE IMAGE AND THE ICEBERG

In the years following World War II, public relations grew apace. These decades saw the marriage of journalism and the social sciences into a loose union in organized practice. Public relations' lack of definition precludes a census of exactly how many practitioners there are. The problem is further compounded by public relations' image, which has meant that many people performing essentially public relations functions in government and industry and elsewhere are titled differently. The armed services lean heavily on the public information function as opposed to public relations. The terms "public affairs" and "vice-president of communications" are becoming increasingly popular, but these are actually euphemisms for public relations that, by seeking to avoid the stigma, merely emphasize it and create a credibility crisis.

In any event, there are at least 100,000 identifiable public relations practitioners in the United States, and more likely the number is two or three times that. All work in one way or another for organizations: governmental agencies, business and industry, charitable and cultural organizations, educational institutions at all levels, hospitals, labor unions, churches, professional associations, a wide, wide assortment of special interest groups, and even the mass media. All organizations have public relations whether they want it or not—some good, some bad, some indifferent—just as all individuals have personality—good, bad, or indifferent, differing with different people. Like individual personality, organizational public relations is capable of being changed by dint of hard effort over a long period. Public relations is necessarily long-term and is, in fact, a corporate personality dealing with publics rather than other individuals.

Public relations may be either of the "brushfire" type or "fire prevention." Brushfire public relations moves from crisis to crisis seeking to put the fires out; it awaits imminent disaster before taking corrective action. It is not particularly efficient. It is also widespread. Fire prevention public relations seeks to foresee crisis and avoid it. It is a continuing effort, constantly upgrading the organization, planning for the future, evaluating its own results, and utilizing this evaluation as updated research for future planning. There is a kind of "iceberg" analogy to all this. Like the iceberg, only about 10 percent of which shows above the sea, only about 10 percent of public relations is apparent to the publics: the releases and news stories, the films and promotions, the speeches and mailings, the spot an-

Ten percent of public relations.

PHOTOGRAPH BY HAROLD M. LAMBERT

Indirect Media

nouncements and television programs, and pseudoevents. The rest is meticulous grinding research and planning, painstakingly accomplished: deliberate statistical analysis, interviews, and long hours of reading. It is far from the glamorous vocation it has been painted—a misplaced stereotype of three-martini luncheons in exclusive bistros, glamorous travel, and lavish expense accounts.

CORPORATE PERSONALITY

Public relations serves organizations either internally or externally. Internally, the public relations executive is on the organization's payroll. He is a part of the company. Externally, he is a consultant retained by the company to review its public relations program, to undertake certain specific assignments, or to conduct its overall public relations program on a part-time basis. These are public relations' independent counselors.

Both the internal executive and the outside counselor each have certain inherent assets and liabilities. The internal executive knows the company intimately; in all probability he grew up with it. He knows the maze of paths to get anything done. He is aware of the personality quirks of the other executives. He is always available and he knows where any skeletons are hidden. On the other hand, his availability means that too often his time is frittered away with trivia and he has little time to think or plan. He traditionally gets all the problems that do not fit neatly into someone else's pigeonhole. His familiarity means that he is often not given the proper deference for his ideas. Further, he tends to become ingrown, lacking broad exposure, enmeshed in his own corporate world. He also may, regrettably, become deferential to management, a yes-man too often unwilling to disagree. He cannot see the forest for the trees.

The counselor, on the other hand, brings an outside viewpoint, a degree of objectivity to the organization's course; he can see the forest. He also brings a wide range of contacts and outside experience to bear on the organization's problems, and perhaps some valuable expertise in a specific field. Not even the largest organizations can afford to keep platoons of public relations specialists on the payroll against the relatively few times when their services will be needed. The counselor's disadvantages are that he is unfamiliar with the organization, and he doesn't know where the skeletons are hidden. Nor is he always available. While his opinions are listened to with respect, because he is an outsider and he is expensive, there is also a certain resentment attached to any outsider.

There is a pattern to public relations development as an organization grows. Initially in a small organization, one of the principals assumes public relations responsibility in addition to his other duties. Later, as the volume of this work increases, the organization hires a counselor on a part-time basis. As more and more of his time becomes involved with the growing organization's work, it employs a full-time public relations person at a fraction of the counselor's billing. The PR executive then grows into a department with perhaps branches in other cities, and finally a counselor is retained again for specific assignments, such as introducing a new product or lobbying the legislature or in connection with a proposed merger, or simply to bring a fresh and objective analysis of the ongoing public relations program—an outside public relations audit as it were.

A TWO-WAY STREET

Ideally, public relations is a two-way street. Not only must it use its expertise to identify the organization's various publics and interpret management policy to them, but equally and too often overlooked, it must use this expertise to interpret public opinion and anticipated reaction to management as a guide to corporate policy. Unless it does the latter and unless management is both willing to listen and willing to provide the atmosphere in which this mutual exchange can take place, public relations is not doing its whole job and management is deprived of an invaluable tool in the decision-making process.

SPECIALIZATION

In times gone by, only twenty years or so ago, the public relations practitioner was a jack-of-all-trades, a generalist counseling management, developing product promotion, handling political campaigns, writing publicity. He is a good deal like medicine's general practitioner, and like him, is rapidly becoming a thing of the past. As in medicine and the law and the other professions, public relations has become increasingly specialized.

Much of public relations counseling is conducted on a local basis. There are two reasons for this. First, a considerable portion of public relations deals with the community and community relations as a specialty, the painting of the organization as a concerned corporate citizen. Even the largest corporations have diversified their community relations into the communities where their branches and plants are located. It is a local public relations counselor who serves these individual plants. Second, and more significantly, public relations is still print-oriented in the electronic age. The emphasis on the clipping book and a tangible record is enormous; therefore, newspapers have remained the principal vehicles of public relations practice and publicity its major tool. It is, thus, the local counselor who can best contact the local newspaper that exists in a local community.

There are, of course, some major national public relations firms. These are Hill & Knowlton, Ruder & Finn, Carl Byoir & Associates, and N. W. Ayer & Son. The largest employ as many as three hundred persons and operate internationally as general public relations counselors. In addition to these are the public relations divisions of many of the major advertising agencies: J. Walter Thompson Company, Grey Advertising, etc.

Some of the other major specializations that come under the public relations umbrella are: political campaigning, financial public relations, lobbying, and fund raising. These are in addition to the

Indirect Media

broader fields of industrial, commercial, and organizational public relations, product and personality promotion, propaganda, press relations, and public affairs.

As television developed, it had a profound effect on political campaigning. The ability to reach huge masses of people simultaneously, in addition to the growth of computer-based demographics, put new and sometimes contradictory dimensions into politics. It became at once necessary to find a salient appeal to television's masses, even while constructing separate and noncontradictory appeals to smaller demographic breakdowns of the same mass. Politics is concerned with the entire audience continuum, from the TV mass down to the single individual. Whitaker and Baxter, a San Francisco-based campaign management house, was the first to specialize politically in the late thirties. Twenty years later Baus and Ross, a Los Angeles general public relations agency, gave up its roster of commercial clients to concentrate on politics in 1958.[4] Since that time, there has been a proliferation of campaign specialists across the nation as campaigning has become more sophisticated.

4. Herbert M. Baus and William B. Ross, *Politics Battle Plan* (New York: Macmillan Publishing Co., Inc., 1968).

POLITICS AND PUBLIC RELATIONS

Political campaigning differs in several important respects from organizational public relations. From the practitioner's standpoint, it is seasonal. Political campaigns occur only at certain specified intervals. The campaign specialist, therefore, is faced with a feast or famine situation, which is one of the reasons for the high costs of campaigning. Second, political campaigning is a crisis situation wherein all activity is concentrated into an always all too short a time frame. Everyone knows about the harrowing schedule of a politician on the campaign trail: the twenty-hour days, jet travel, speeches in Pittsburgh, St. Louis, and Los Angeles all in one day. The public relations people who arrange, schedule, and promote all this activity have equally appalling schedules. They worry about the press, the advertising, the crowds, the advance arrangements, the timetable, the speeches, the sources of money, the budget, the press kits, the infighting, the polls, and the candidate's blunders. Years of public relations activity are crowded into a couple of months.

Political campaigning, too, is the one form of public relations that operates within a known time frame with a known cutoff date—election day. Campaigning is also the one form of public relations that is accurately measurable—at the ballot box on election day. For this reason it seems to attract extraordinary attention, for not only does it represent controversy, but it is tangible. However, election day is too late for remediation and, like the television ratings, a device was required to measure campaign effectiveness while it is still going on. Too much is at stake in a campaign to leave campaigning to intuition alone. Furthermore, the expenditure of vast sums of money demands a spending guide for optimal results. Public opinion polls became an extremely popular tool in political campaigning with which to judge

Public Relations

Politics and public relations: the hoopla of campaign. (UPI)

Indirect Media
348

the effectiveness of a campaign, uncover weaknesses to be minimized, and indicate strengths to be capitalized.

Finally, political campaigning differs from more traditional public relations in that there are only two candidates in a general election, and only two points of view in a ballot proposition or a bond issue: candidate A or candidate B, yes or no, for or against. Thus, the entire spectrum of public opinion must be compressed into only one of two choices. In society as a whole there is a plethora of personal opinions, interests, and tastes. Not so in politics' forced dichotomy. Thus, general elections force a choice wherein neither alternative may exactly meet anyone's criteria. As often as not this choice is made on the basis of the lesser of two evils rather than on genuine conviction. This being the case, political campaigning also distinguishes itself by fighting simultaneously on two fronts. The campaign must seek to enhance the stature of its own candidate while at the same time seeking to discredit his opponent, for a vote taken away from an opponent counts as much as a vote attracted to the cause. Consequently, politics within the two-party American system is more or less forced to deal in terms of the lowest common denominator, and this accounts for the huge doses of sensationalism, rhetoric, emotional appeal, and sometimes pure entertainment that are injected into an otherwise substantive matter.

Political campaigning, with its charges and countercharges, has occasioned enormous criticism aimed at public relations, advertising, and the mass media. This is perhaps because of all forms of public relations, political campaigning is the most visible, the most clearly identified, and the most concentrated. A national presidential campaign takes on the aspect of a Roman circus. There are those who claim it provides a catharsis, an emotional safety valve every four years that permits the public to keep on a more or less even keel the remainder of the time. In defense of political campaigning, however, it should be pointed out that it represents today about as pure a form of libertarian theory as there is. It is a-no-holds-barred activity in which truth and misrepresentation are intermingled on both sides, and from whose massive exposure the public can come to a conclusion. The very scope of a national campaign assures that everyone will become aware and more or less informed. Furthermore, the polarization of candidates or issues and the defend-and-attack nature of campaigning gives some assurance that nearly all the factors, good and bad, will sooner or later be exposed. In the interests of a reasonable decision, there are few institutions in the republic that provide this kind of balance of viewpoints. Public relations with regard to political campaigning may be overdone, but it is thorough.

FINANCIAL PUBLIC RELATIONS

Financial public relations (FPR) is another specialty. It deals in the sophisticated realm of economics and finance. Actually, it makes little use of the mass media with the exception of the circumscribed financial press. Financial public relations grew out of corporate abuses and subsequent regulation of corporate finance by the federal Security and Exchange Commission (SEC) during the depression. This regulation was subsequently augmented by fifty state regulatory bodies with different rules and by the various security exchanges themselves, of which the New York Stock Exchange is the largest. Finance is a highly technical field devoted to corporate mergers, the issuance of new securities, stock splits, acquisitions, and the enhancement of the market value of corporate securities. Specialists in FPR require a talent in accounting, meticulous understanding of all the complex regulations pertaining to disclosure, inside information, registration, and the like, plus a feel for public relations. The acquisition of these particular specialized talents fairly well precludes FPR counselors from operating in any other field, just as electricians do not make good plumbers although both are specialists in the construction trades.

Corporations today are less concerned with their stockholders than they are with the "financial community." The financial community is composed of the big mutual funds, the trust departments of major banks, securities brokers, pension funds of the big unions and governmental agencies, the big insurance companies, financial counselors, and the financial press. These institutions buy and sell huge blocks of corporate stock, or they are instrumental in urging their clients and contacts to do so. Hence, corporate concern is less with the individual stockholder who buys and sells a relatively few shares as with the larger institutions who deal in tens of thousands of shares at once. Controlling the market, essentially, are the analysts, who are specialists employed by all the aforementioned and whose business it is to study corporations and securities and make recommendations for acquisition or disposal. On the analysts' recommendations ride millions of dollars worth of corporate securities. Financial public relations people are the liaison between their clients and the analysts. They deal generally on a person-to-person basis. They are both surrogates—the counselor for his client, the analyst for his institution. They deal on a basis of mutual respect. Each analyst has a portfolio of three hundred or more corporations on which he must keep a constant detailed check. Since this is difficult, he often welcomes the assistance of FPR counselors who can brief him on the plans, prospects, and prognosis of their particular clients. Such personal contact may well mean the difference between the purchase or the sale of a company's stock. Like other forms of public relations, FPR is a form of insurance, the little extra that may make the difference in a confusing and competitive society.

The financial community, for all its economic influence on society, is served by a remarkably small and specialized financial press, composed of a few specialized periodicals—*Fortune, Forbes, Barrons,* the stately *Wall Street Journal*—plus the financial sections of the metropolitan newspapers, which carry the daily market quotations, and a large number of esoteric newsletters catering to very specific interests within the financial community.

LOBBYING

Another, specialized form of public relations is lobbying. Like FPR, lobbying is essentially person-to-person contact between surrogates. It makes little use of the mass media except in specialized cases where a volume of publicity can be used to reinforce a case made personally. Lobbying, while much maligned, serves a useful corporate purpose. It is a product of a highly complex and institutionalized society, and a necessity perhaps for society's institutions to make their voices heard in a highly organized, bureaucratic, and representative government. The lobbyists are the representatives of society's institutions, as mayors and city councilmen, assemblymen, and members of Congress are representatives of the people.

An institutionalized society has found it necessary to band together for the accomplishment of certain goals. The labor unions and the major business and professional associations—National Association of Manufacturers (NAM), United States Chamber of Commerce, American Medical Association (AMA), and, for that matter, the National Association of Broadcasters (NAB), the American Newspaper Publishers Association, (ANPA) and PRSA— are all examples of institutions employing lobbyists. These trade and professional associations have found it expedient to watchdog legislation, to encourage passage of certain measures and discourage others as they affect the goals of their respective memberships. There is a certain imperfect balance to this, as the AFL/CIO rarely sees eye-to-eye with the NAM and from their conflicting arguments a certain broad exposure to all the factors involved in an issue will emerge in the legislature. From this tension occasionally comes truth.

There is a rational evolution to lobbying. It is the right of every citizen in this democracy—too little exercised—to make his wishes known to his representatives. As society became more and more institutionalized, more and more citizens banded together into groups in order to make their collective voices heard at the seats of government.

From the standpoint of government, there is a certain pragmatism to lobbying also. As a congressman or a congressional committee needs to know exactly how certain proposed legislation will affect the manufacturing industry or the labor unions, the lobbyists of the AFL/CIO and of the NAM are there to tell them, and who can provide better firsthand expertise? Each will tell a one-sided story, for they are the first of all advocates in the same sense that attorneys are, but from the two viewpoints emerges potential compromise.

Lobbying, of course, has been abused; few institutions have not. Like government itself, society tends to hear more of the sensational and scandalous aspects and less of the concrete working relationships which actually serve the public purpose and for which they were designed. There are lobbies representative of almost every facet of society: churches, labor unions, trade associations, teachers, major industries, blacks, Indians and Chicanos, retailers, veterans and, more recently, such consumer and environmental groups as Nader's Raiders and Common Cause. Actually, these latecomers to the field are a welcome addition, for they begin to provide a surrogate balance in an area which was top-heavy with corporate representation; they achieve a better balance.

Lobbying is a highly specialized form of public relations. As most corporation PR people came from the press and most FPR people came from economics or accountancy, most lobbyists come from law. It takes years for a lobbyist to establish his contacts on a basis of mutual trust in Washington, time in which he also learns the bureaucratic maze. Lobbyists are held in check by an unwritten law, an effective means of informal control. A lobbyist is expected to be an advocate, but he is also expected never to misrepresent. If he is ever found lying or withholding pertinent information, the word is passed through the legislative halls and no one will ever talk to him again; he is outcast, a pariah. Few professionals after years of apprenticeship to do their jobs effectively are willing to throw it away for a one-shot advantage.

EVENTS AND PSEUDOEVENTS

Public relations deals in events. Outside the specialties, public relations makes extensive use of the mass media, particularly the press. The press deals in news, and events become the peg on which public relations can hang its client's hat. Events at once provide the vehicle to carry a story to the press, and at the same time the rationale for an editor or news director to use it. An event may range from as simple an item as the man-of-the-year award by the local Kiwanis club to the dazzling production surrounding the dedication of London Bridge at Lake Havasu City, California, in 1972. The London Bridge dedication imported the Lord Mayor of London; a catered banquet for 1,000 was transported across the desert in a caravan from Beverly Hills; dancing on the bridge was to a name band, followed by fireworks lighting up thirty square miles of sky with a full color portrait of Elizabeth II, dissolving into crossed English and American flags. The Lord Mayor was brought to the site by Indian war canoes (for which the Indians had to attend paddling school) and the event was climaxed by thirty skydivers descending in a circle a mile in diameter as 10,000 doves rose into the desert sky.

Events and pseudoevents are related and bespeak two separate techniques. Public relations people find the means to tie their interest into a legitimate event; southern California's nursery industry capitalized on the 1970 autumn forest fires by donating seedling pine trees to reforest the devastated lands, an act which generated much favorable publicity. Pseudoevents, on the other hand, are public relations fabrications whose exclusive purpose is to generate publicity.

The London Bridge dedication at Lake Havasu City, California, 1972.

UPI

5. Hal Lancaster, "Mr. McCullough Plans a Little Celebration for a Certain Bridge," *Wall Street Journal*, 5 October 1971.

The dedication of London Bridge is a classic example of a pseudo-event used to publicize Lake Havasu City with the aim of selling real estate. It was fantastically successful, although it cost over one million dollars. It generated front-page wire service coverage on nearly every major metropolitan newspaper in the land, including the conservative *Wall Street Journal*.[5] All three networks covered it live, with follow-up. Radio and magazine coverage is uncounted. The dollar value of this publicity on television alone, at $85,000 a minute for just the single four-minute breaks on three networks, exceeds $1,000,000. Such an ostentatious pseudoevent, which by its very scope and outrageous nature demands media coverage, is known in the trade as "pizzazz." It is a device to overcome the competition for attention that plagues an accelerating society.

Publicity is far better achieved when the media cover an event themselves than if the public relations person simply provides a release. If the media invest their own time and effort in covering an event, in shooting film or videotape, they are far more likely to use the material and footage than if it is provided gratis by public relations. Thus, the most accomplished publicists spend little time writing releases and more effort in creating a situation that will demand the media's own coverage from the points of view of significance and interest. Increasingly, they become both actual adjuncts to the press, as well as more subtle and sophisticated in their operations.

PUBLICS

Another means of securing attention is by pinpointing interest. This requires first a clear definition of audience or public relations' publics. A major corporation, for example, has several discrete although interlocking publics: employees, stockholders, consumers,

Public Relations

distributors and dealers, the communities where the corporation exists, suppliers, and government at all levels. Each of these publics has a different interest in the corporation: employees in wages and fringe benefits, stockholders in dividends and appreciation of investment, etc. Yet they all share an interest in the corporation; it is their rallying point. Nor is the matter simple, for an employee may easily be a stockholder, and both are probably consumers. Yet the corporation must talk to the employees in different terms than it talks to the stockholders if it is going to hold their interest. Defining these audiences, determining how to reach them most efficiently with least overkill, and framing what to say to them is the job of public relations, as well as that of feeling the separate and collective pulses and giving the readings back to management as guidelines to policy.

TOOLS AND FUNCTIONS

The tools used by public relations to reach its various publics are many. There are the mass media, of course, but there are also specialized media—public relations films and publications, or house organs—that are used extensively to reach essentially captive audiences. Corporate annual reports are a form of public relations; so are addresses to groups and seminars and conventions, which is why speakers bureaus, often supplemented by films, are a stock-in-trade of major public relations operations. Public relations pays a good deal of attention to schools at all levels, providing educational films and, in some cases, course material. The idea is to condition the young with the thought that they will influence their parents and, when they grow up, become themselves consumers and believers. The Bell System is particularly active in communications instruction of this type.

Like advertising, public relations includes two separate although related functions: informative and persuasive. By far the easier to explain is the informational. It is this function also that comes closest to public relations as a legitimate adjunct to the news, an auxiliary news source in its own right. Information, whether offered through the press or before groups in house organs, keeps the various publics advised. It describes, delineates, and explains goods, services, events, and ideas; it seeks to break down the barriers of confusion and misunderstanding. It is this informational aspect of public relations that has proven most effective. The persuasion that exists occurs largely through reinforcement, the repetition of a theme, until the public becomes supportive.

The manipulative aspects of public relations, which has been called news management in government circles, is far more difficult. Manipulative news management is heavily bound up in the phenomena of public opinion formation and change. It can backfire easily, accomplishing the opposite of its purpose. So little is known about public opinion that manipulative public relations has to be treated with extreme caution, as politicians are increasingly aware. Manipulative public relations tends to ignore the collective wisdom of the people. Abraham Lincoln saw this and expressed it succinctly: "You may fool all of the people some of the time; you can even fool some of the people all the time; but you can't fool all of the people all the time." He was talking about public relations although the term hadn't yet been invented.

SUMMARY

Public relations, though relatively new as an organized practice, is, as persuasive or ulterior communication, as old as mankind. Its historical genesis can be seen in the poets of ancient Greece and Rome, in the Roman circuses and Caesar's *Commentaries*. With Gutenberg's invention of the printing press, mass education, mass literacy, mass communication, and mass persuasion became possible.

The American Revolution was a long-term public relations project engineered by Samuel Adams, who used all available forms of communications to foster the spirit of revolution and ideal of independence. He mastered exploitation of an event—the Boston Massacre—and developed the pseudoevent, the Boston Tea Party.

Public relations as a modern profession is essentially an American product, having its origins in political campaigning and in the theatrical press agentry that arose with P.T. Barnum.

During the post–Civil War years, American expansion and laissez-faire led to a "public be damned" attitude congruent with the social Darwinism spirit of "survival of the fittest." Reaction set in with the muckrakers at the turn of this century. Ivy Lee, in the same period, became the father of public relations, the modern practice, with his stress on honest information. In the 1920s Edward Bernays injected an element of persuasion into Lee's purely factual approach, while Paul Garrett, on the eve of the Great Depression, inaugurated industry's growing social consciousness with his concept of enlightened self-interest, originally applied for General Motors.

World Wars I and II saw an increasing amount of governmental public relations intermingled with propaganda in the form of the Creel Committee and the Office of War Information, respectively. Post–World War II has seen an enormous growth in the practice of public relations, the marriage of journalism and the social sciences. The volume of public relations to which society is exposed is staggering; it pervades all media with attempts to manipulate thoughts, votes, and dollars.

Public relations is also a legitimate adjunct to the press, providing useful information on organizations and events that the press itself lacks the manpower and resources to cover. For this reason public relations has been traditionally print-oriented, an anachronism in an electronic age. The clipping book has become the tangible record of services performed, measured in column inches, but it gives no indication whatever of the effectiveness of public relations.

The irony of public relations is that the profession itself has such a poor public image. The PRSA, through a program of accreditation, is working toward increasing professionalization in an area where there are no legal standards.

Public relations is an organizational or corporate personality. It exists, whether good, bad, or indifferent, and through the application of appropriate techniques is capable of changing for better or worse. "Brushfire" public relations meets crises as they arise; "fire prevention" public relations, through the application of research, planning, and evaluation, attempts to foresee and forestall potential trouble spots. Ideally, public relations is a two-way street in which the practitioners not only attempt to interpret organization and management policy to various publics, but also by public pulse-taking to advise management of the probable results of proposed policy.

Organizationally, public relations performs both internally and externally. Both have advantages and compensating disadvantages. The best solution, where practical, is a combination of the two, in which internal public relations takes care of the organization's day-to-day needs, and counseling performs certain specialized services plus an outside public relations audit.

Public relations is an umbrella term covering a multitude of activities: publicity (with which it is too often equated), promotion, propaganda, advertising, political campaigning, lobbying, financial public relations, etc. This profusion of activities has led to increased specialization. Political campaigning is the purest form of libertarianism extant, fighting constantly on two fronts. Unlike commercial public relations, it forces a polarization of choice, unnatural in a multiple society. Lobbying is surrogate representation in which society's institutions make their voices heard and through which a certain imperfect balance of viewpoints is achieved. Financial public relations is a specialty born of increasing governmental regulation of the securities industry.

In general, public relations is unavoidable and utilizes the mass media through exploitation of events and the creation of pseudo-events.

Public relations can be classified two ways: informative and persuasive. Informative is by far the most successful. Manipulative public relations is dangerous, backfiring easily because it is bound up with the too little understood operation of public opinion.

Part VII

INTEGRATION AND CONCLUSION

This final section is in a sense a potpourri of factors affecting mass communications in American society, yet generally excluded from examination. The mails and telephone are discussed from the viewpoint of their sheer volume of interpersonal contact, performing in a vicarious society much of the person-to-person transmission discussed by Lazarsfeld and Berelson, even while the increasing sophistication and automation of both begin to remove them as truly interpersonal vehicles. As indirect media the mails furthermore have a distinct claim as a result of the manner in which they assist many of the other mass media, particularly print, public relations, and advertising.

Computers are included in this chapter because of their service function, their roles both as storers and retrievers of information, and the manner in which they have facilitated the measurement, if not the understanding, of public opinion. Some attention is given to the potential threat computers pose to invasion of privacy of the individual on the one hand, and on the other, to their potential for freeing the individual for more creative endeavor.

Cultural transmission, the least recognized of the functions of mass communications, is examined from the viewpoint of longevity of exposure; a truly mass audience is often developed with considerable effect over a period of years, and it is into this category than many of the arts fall. Art is of course a communication process, and its net effect may easily be mass, both in the short term and the long. As language is so much a part of cultural transmission, attention is paid to the process of language change, which in turn sheds light on the mass media as both the perpetrators of the status quo on the one hand and the radical vehicles of change on the other.

The formation and change of public opinion is little understood, but of critical importance in a study of mass communications. Some insights can be gleaned from an examination of the roles of stereotypes and myths and their employment by the mass media, sometimes as useful shortcuts to understanding and other times as dangerous crutches. The various techniques for sampling public opinion are examined with their respective strengths and shortcomings. The significance of public opinion polling in television, in political campaigns, and increasingly in both advertising and media research lends new dimension to this computer-assisted tool in a discussion of mass communications.

The final chapter is a drawing together, emphasizing

the national character of mass communications. It is pointed out that media development in other lands has, as it has in the United States, closely followed the social values of each nation, and has been always directly related to both the economy and the technological status of each particular nation.

Mass communications research is explored, and some of its shortcomings noted. In the United States considerable attention has been paid to practical research and development (in which the nation has excelled), while pure research has gone off on many ill-advised tangents borrowed inappropriately from the hard sciences. The greater portion of valid mass communications research appears to have been either intuitive or accidental or both. There remains a crying need.

Some of the future options of America's mass communications network are discussed. As the central nervous system of society, mass communications will of course be drastically affected by a reordering of society's values, if this should come about, and, as the child of technology, its future course will also be determined by the state of the economy and the amounts of money available for development and leisure.

19 PERSONAL MEDIA

MAIL, PHONES, AND COMPUTERS

Due to preoccupation with the mass media in recent decades, there has been a tendency to overlook the personal media of individual communication that form a large part of the mass communications system and from which, in fact, the mass media evolved. Due to their scope (aggregate audiences, pervasiveness, and overall effect), the principal personal media are considered to be the mail service, the telephone, and, most recently, the computer. These mass media encompass a written network, on aural network, and a symbolic network.

The individual media are significant for two principal reasons. First, they are capable of reaching down along the audience continuum to the individual who composes the discrete building block of all audiences, publics, and groups, and who alone holds opinions, votes, purchases, and most importantly, reacts. Second, it was previously noted in discussion of Lazarsfeld's and Berelson's two-step theory of communication, that the principal effect of mass communications is indirect, resulting from interpersonal reaction. The personal media provide a good part of the means of this interpersonal reaction. In a complex society not all of this interpersonal reaction takes place in face-to-face encounter; a considerable part of it is remote, occurring over the great distances that mail and phone make possible.

The classification of the computer as a personal medium bears explanation. The major function of the computer in mass communications has been to pinpoint ever more closely the individual himself, and to permit the mass media to reach down with increasing selectivity to ever smaller enclaves of individuals with purposeful messages directed toward their interests. Furthermore, the computer has proven capable of selecting those single individuals from the broad mass of society who accurately represent society as a whole, making the phenomenon of public opinion polling possible.

The interaction of the computer with the personal media has enormously enhanced their efficiency, permitting them to keep pace with social acceleration. The instantaneous national service of the Bell System—permitting anyone, anywhere, at any time, day or night, to reach any other person, whether hidden in a cubbyhole in a New York skyscraper, or in the far reaches of the Idaho wilderness, or in an automobile of uncertain location speeding through the moonlit Mojave, or in a vessel storm-tossed off the Grank Banks—would be impossible without the computer.

Nor would demographics, so widely used by the mass media, by advertising and public relations, and by political campaigning, be possible without the computer. It is also this facet of computer technology that has had revolutionary effect on the mails, making possible the efficiency of computerized direct mail.

THE MAILS IN TIMES PAST

The mails are certainly the oldest form of personal media. The couriers of ancient times were, of course, the first mailmen. They carried messages, often oral, from one person to another. The twenty-six mile marathon race still celebrates the Greek messenger who ran cross-country from the Marathon battlefield to Athens to advise the city that it had been saved. The Romans, with their genius for organization, noted the duplication of effort involved in separate messengers for separate messages and organized regular courier service from the outposts of their far-flung empire to the seat of government in Rome. They introduced horse relays and built the Roman roads to speed their messengers. They also used the written message extensively to allow the couriers to carry several messages from different persons to different destinations on different topics.

The Pony Express of less than a century ago was little different from the Roman model, and today's mailman performs essentially the same functions over the city streets or rural star routes. Considering the growing volume of mail, the present system is remarkably anachronistic.

In the course of Roman administration, it became necessary to send identical orders to the various governors, proconsuls, and field commanders stretched across the face of the then known world, and the use of scribes came into being. This was an early, although limited, form of mass communication. Meanwhile, the business of individual correspondence continued. It was the basic distinction between mass mail (identical messages from a single source to several destinations) and personal mail (correspondence between just two individuals) that was recognized by the U.S. Postal Service when it established first-class and bulk rates. The significance of the mails as a distribution device for the mass media was early taken into account

Top and bottom: Then—and now. Little has changed; postal distribution is still dependent upon hand delivery.

THE BETTMANN ARCHIVE

Personal Media

when Congress adopted the second-class permit for newspapers and magazines, permitting their economical distribution.

The interplay between the mass media and the mails can be readily seen during the first half of the nineteenth century when, as the United States pushed its frontiers ever westward, many of the newspaper publishers in the new communities were also the postmasters. Postmasters enjoyed a quasi-official position that facilitated their gathering of news. They were also centrally located in their communities in that most of the population regularly visited them to post or pick up mail, thus affording a constant exposure to local events. Their modest government stipends were insulation against the chancy nature of publishing as a sole source of income. Finally, their franking privileges permitted them free delivery of their product.

MAILS DISTRIBUTE MASS MEDIA

Efficient distribution has perpetuated the mails. For all the technological advances accomplished in mass communications, insofar as the individual is concerned, personal, physical distribution of printed material is still the most efficient. A person maintains some residence; there is some discrete corner of this earth or nation that is his. His occupational address is also an identifiable physical location. It is these sites that the mails reach regularly, daily, and with remarkable reliability. The mails thus have become a major portion of the media distribution system, not only in reaching individuals but also in reaching them as demographic or interest groups. The mails furnish almost the only media contact for some groups with their memberships: churches, labor unions, cultural organizations, employees, etc. They also play the major role in the distribution of magazines. They form a part of the distribution system of newspapers, especially considering that the paperboy is nothing more than a specialized, private mail service. The mails, furthermore, are a part of book publishing, as they serve publishing's mass marketing device, the book-of-the-month club. To paraphrase Voltaire in relationship to print media, if there were no mails, it would be necessary to invent them.

DECREASING PERSONAL USE

However, the mail's original purpose of interpersonal communication as opposed to corporate or mass communications has fallen into increasing disuse. The mails take too long for a frantic society, and there is no instant feedback. Persons wishing to communicate with each other individually have more and more turned to the telephone. It is easier to make a phone call than to write a letter, find a stamp, mail the letter, and wait for a reply that may not come. The phone offers immediacy and instant feedback at relatively little expense. Emphasis on such speed seems to be a peculiarity of American society. In other parts of the world less technologically advanced and affluent, the business of writing notes continues apace.

Integration and Conclusion

The matter of letter writing is concentrated in affairs where a written record is desired and where exact phraseology is important. This means that on an interpersonal basis, the mails best serve the realms of business, government, and law—the world of contracts as it were. Even in this world of records, the mails have proven too slow for the stepped-up pace of society, and more businesses have adopted the telecopier or Telefax, which is a sort of telephone call in writing. Actually, it is an offshoot of the teletype, which, instead of typewriting over the telephone lines, reproduces in facsimile entire documents in a minute or so and transmits them by a telephoto process over phone lines. The telecopier has the advantages of both providing an authenticated record complete with authorizing signature as well as acknowledging receipt and permitting instant reply—in handwriting if desired. Even in interpersonal contact, the mass production of Christmas cards and other stylized greetings—get-well, birthday, Father's Day, and Mother's Day cards, cocktail invitations, and the like—begins to take on the vestige of mass media use of the mails.

This use of the mails is not entirely new. Caesar's scribes and the publishing of tracts and flyers by the early printers advertising their wares were early forerunners. Junk mail was not unknown at the turn of the century, but the computer has brought a new sophistication to it.

THE MEDIA'S MEDIUM

A principal use of the mails is to serve advertising and public relations, the persuasive functions of media. It has been shown that in coupon advertising techniques the mails have been used in conjunction with newspapers or magazines to pretest prospective advertisments. They are also used to prejudge audience appeal. Magazines, because of their concentration on audience interest on a national scale, sell or rent their subscription lists to a wide range of interested prospects. This sale of the lists comprises a considerable portion of magazine revenue. For example, *Psychology Today* might sell a random 15 percent of its subscription list to a potential importer of foreign sports cars; the importer then determines if there exists sufficient interest in that particular young, educated, and affluent audience mix to justify marketing the cars in the United States. If the mail response to advertising is favorable, the importer might buy the entire subscription list for a full-scale, direct mail effort, plus an integrated advertising program aimed at that particular audience. By sampling the lists of several such magazines, an advertiser can pinpoint his specific audience with incredible accuracy. *Field and Stream* might sell a portion of its mailing list to the manufacturer of a new spinning reel that he may ascertain its acceptance among sportsmen. *New York* magazine might have sampled the *New Yorker's* subscription list to find out if there were sufficient interest in another magazine devoted to Manhattan. There are several magazines, in fact, whose basic purpose is less the interest of their audience than in pinpointing it as a target for a sophisticated range of marketing programs.

COMPUTERIZED DIRECT MAIL

It is in computerized direct mail, however, that the question of audience identification becomes really complex. Public records originally provided the basis for these techniques. Registered Democrats can be expected on balance to share a different political philosophy from registered Republicans. Voter registration records are available through registrars throughout the land. Tax assessors have accurate data on home ownerships as opposed to rentals, as well as on relative affluence. Computers have facilitated the processing of this data to the point where it is economically feasible to utilize it, and have further speeded the process to the point where it can be accomplished in very short time spans. It has been noted how magazines utilize computers by circulation breakdowns on a regional basis to permit the greater access of local advertisers, and how some attempted to break down their circulations by affluence in their battle for survival.

Direct mail, of course, comes in several varieties, as does most advertising; there is schlock and there is class. "Schlock" refers to matter produced as cheaply as possible—using flimsy stock, a bulk rate, and in black-and-white only—and in which everything is sacrificed to volume. "Class" is more expensive, utilizing quality typography and color printing, frequently illustrated on good paper and sent first class. It has the advantage of more specific appeal to a higher level audience.

The computers have also proven adept at physically handling a volume of direct mail and at creating the illusion of personalizing it. A computer can sort a list demographically and insert the proper paragraphs into bulk mail (references depending upon, whether the intended recipient is rich or poor, Democrat or Republican, etc.), taking into consideration differences in religious affiliation, sex, color, age, education, and the like. It can insert not only the appropriate prewritten paragraphs, but also the recipient's name and other personal references into the body of the letter, add a facsimile signature at the conclusion, fold and insert the material into an envelope, stamp it, sort the addresses into zip codes, bundle them, and stack the bundles ready for delivery to the post office—and all these processes are untouched by human hands.

Such letters have a printed look that belies their contrived personalization. To overcome this, automatic typewriters are employed that type the letters at incredible speed and show the key marks on the paper. The volume of junk mail has grown so in recent years that many people simply throw it into the scrap basket unopened. Thus, the fourth-class permit, designed to economize on bulk mail, has fallen into disrepute; direct mail users are increasingly discovering that first-class mails stand the best chance of being read. Additionally, a number of catchy devices are employed on the envelopes to assure that the letter will be opened, such as letting shiny pennies show through, or labeling the envelope "free gift inside." All this conspires to make direct mail about the most expensive form of mass communications in terms of costs per thousand. First-class postage, computer time, an expensive stock, color printing, enclosures (that extra shiny penny), and the like run costs up. It is not possible to bring out an effective first-class direct mail piece for less than about $.16 a unit, or $160 per thousand. Compared to television's $8.00 cpm this is whopping. But first-class direct mail is also the most efficient of the mass media in minimizing overkill and pinpointing the message to an audience directly. A 4 percent return on a good direct mail piece is considered fair. No other form of advertising can match this return; translated it means that, on the average, for every thousand letters sent, forty will buy.

SINGLE AND MULTIPLE AUDIENCES

At base, computerized direct mail comes in two categories. In one the computer is used to identify a single rather discrete audience to which a single appeal is then mailed. This is the type noted in previous examples (as when a car importer or a new magazine samples a list to determine acceptance). The other use of computerized direct mail involves multiple audiences or publics, all part of a larger mass. In this instance, the computer decides demographically what particular messages will be sent to which selected subaudiences. This kind of computerized direct mail has proven increasingly popular in political campaigning, in which the basic audience is all of the voters in a constituency; this total can be demographically broken down into publics of differing interests.

For example, in the 1970 senatorial election in the state of Nevada, the incumbent decided to utilize computerized direct mail for the entire state.[1] The senator reasoned that Republicans have different interests than Democrats, that residents of Las Vegas and Reno had differing views on public improvements, and that the mining, cattle, and farming interests of the state's hinterland also saw the future differently. Accordingly, the senator's campaign staff made up two dozen appropriate paragraphs, each designed to appeal to a select group within the state's voters. The computer then was able to combine these paragraphs into letters containing about six paragraphs each, letters which were designed for maximum appeal to the recipient's geographical, demographical, and vocational interests. For instance, the senator had been instrumental in obtaining federal financing for a new airport in Reno. He wanted to make use of this fact in the Reno area but not in Las Vegas, where it might raise questions about Reno's preferment. However, in the Reno area itself, those who lived beneath the flight patterns of the new airport were constantly disturbed by jet noise, and the senator did not want to remind those particular voters that he had played a role in their discomfort. The computer proved quite capable of inserting the airport

1. Alan L. Otten, "Computing Democratic Winners in 1972," *Wall Street Journal,* 11 December 1970.

paragraph into all the Reno letters, *except to those addresses that lay beneath the flight patterns,* where it inserted instead a less offensive paragraph about tourism.

DEMOGRAPHICS

Demographics, a function that the instantaneous wizardry of the computer has infinitely facilitated, works on a sort of arithmetic progression in reverse. Whenever a demographic factor is applied to a total population the total is reduced, sometimes to nonexistence. Demographics is really a sort of "Twenty Questions" game played with computers for profit. For example, given the whole population of the United States—200 million—the qualification "male" is applied and the total is reduced to 100 million. "Catholic" is applied, leaving 30 million; "over thirty" leaves 15 million; "black" reduces the total to 1 million; "suburban resident" applied leaves 200,000; "Californian" reduces the total to 20,000; "lawyer," 200; "Kiwanian," 20; "married," 15; "veteran," 7; "native of Mississippi," 2; "graduate of Harvard Law School," 1; "golfer" may or may not leave any at all; moreover, the cutoff point may have occurred further up the progression.

While it is certainly possible to reach ever smaller groups in terms of their presumed interests through computer-aided demographics, and while it is theoretically possible to reach a single individual through the successive application of demographic factors, the present state of the technology does not guarantee that a particular demographically-identified individual exists at all. Further, as applied demography reaches smaller groups, their presumed interest becomes an increasingly questionable factor. When dealing with groups of a hundred or less, for example, cut out of an audience of millions, it can no longer be presumed that they will react like Democrats, housewives, Hoosiers, Episcopalians, Ford owners, etc. They are all individuals, and the smaller the group becomes, the more significant their own individuality is and the less significant their presumedly shared characteristics.

OTHER MAIL USES

Although most advertising and public relations agencies utilize some form of direct mail, nearly all defer to the professional mailing houses on a contractual basis rather than attempting to handle the complex and specialized process themselves.

Some direct mail houses utilize their investment in computer and mailing hardware for their own purposes. They often hammer out a series of quasi-personalized schlock catalogues with give-away come-ons for mail-order notions (household gadgets, "his 'n' her" bath towels, and imitation leopard-skin bikinis). The high markup on the goods and the fact that much of the inventory is taken on consignment make such catalogues a profitable undertaking—plus the fact that the mailings are self-screening; after awhile the computer rejects addressees from whom no orders have been received while proven customers get a stepped-up treatment.

Two additional information-related uses of the mails should not be overlooked. Some time ago the Congress of the United States granted the franking privilege to its members as a device to assist them in keeping in touch with their constituencies. This was in the nineteenth century before national communications through the wire services or even the newspapers was possible, and the mails represented about the only way a congressman in Washington could reach a remote district hundreds and even thousands of miles away from which he was absent for long periods of time. With the coming of the wire services, followed by a national press, radio, and television, this information function became less significant, and the "franks" were employed as often as not for the purpose of interim campaigning, a very effective public relations device in keeping a representative's name before the voters. Furthermore, as the press in its generic sense is preoccupied with the sensational, often an individual congressman's real accomplishments for his district are overlooked. Franking gives him the opportunity to point up his efforts of a less than sensational nature and to present his side of the story where appropriate.

The other use of mail as a media adjunct is that of letters to the editor, one of the best-read features of a newspaper or magazine. There is a craving not only for the expression of personal opinion in an impersonal world, but also for the reading and hearing of others' views. Letters to the editor also provide a feedback device to the newspaper as a guide to its editorial policy. Unlike direct mail, which represents multiple messages from a single source to many diverse recipients, letters to the editor represent multiple messages from many diverse sources to a single recipient. The variety of media usage remains astonishing.

The mails also represent the print antithesis of the book, which, as noted earlier, is essentially self-selective. An individual must go out and seek the book, seek the information it contains. The mails seek the individual with personal greetings, sales messages, and advertising pitches.

Direct mail, often computerized, is extensively used in public opinion polling also. The computer performs the several steps required of public opinion polling extremely efficiently. It can accurately determine the demographics of a public to be sampled. It can sort out the retired, the college educated, the housewives, the affluent. It can further accomplish the random sample from its memory in far more efficient fashion than persons can. Finally, it can collate returns to the original list, establishing percentages and determining how, if at all, the returns are weighted.

MAIL: MASS MEDIA

The volume of mail in the United States alone qualifies it for mass medium status. In 1972 there were 90 billion pieces delivered, and the total grows each succeeding year. That amounts to an average of 300 million pieces each working day, or 1.5 pieces of mail day

Personal Media
367

in and day out for every man, woman, and child in the United States. Successive increases in postal rates are bound to have an effect on this volume, as they are already inhibiting media distribution and discouraging mass mailing, perhaps to a greater degree than interpersonal correspondence. The rate increases also accelerate the use of Telefax, which, in large organizations with a heavy volume of mail, proves economically feasible and once installed, automatically reduces the amount of mail, thus proving its worth in a self-fulfilling fashion.

THE TELEPHONE'S VERSATILITY

Like the United States mail, the telephone plays a variety of mass communications roles quite apart from its significant contribution as a mass medium in its own right. Here again the volume of interpersonal contact conducted over the telephone is staggering. Except for face-to-face encounters in the home, on the job, in small groups of various kinds, and casually in public places, the telephone in this society is the greatest carrier of interpersonal communications. It is personal, it is individual, and whereas the mails have gradually lapsed into a more corporate role, telephone remains a basic purveyor of "gossip." Without the telephone's capacity for instantaneous long-range information exchange, the present capacity for the rapid development of public attitudes on current issues would be seriously curtailed. Society would, in a sense, regress in time to the middle of the last century. Beyond this yeoman service in interpersonal exchange, the telephone plays a number of other vital roles in the communications network.

The overnight ratings on new television shows depend on the telephone, which is, of course, a considerable instrument in public opinion polling, particularly where speed is significant. The telephone is an invaluable tool in the rapid transmission of information to newsrooms across the nation, whether press or broadcast, not only in such obvious matters as flashing an eyewitness account of a spot news event, but in such less evident logistical requirements as making assignments, scheduling camera crews, coordinating coverage on a fast-breaking story, and running down the loose ends from witnesses to a crime.

NECESSARY TO NETWORKS

In the history of broadcast development, AT&T played a major part in the original development of NBC, finally withdrawing its interest in broadcasting production to retain an exclusive franchise on land line leases. Thus, the lion's share of broadcast distribution within the United States originally belonged to the Bell System through leased lines for interstation hookup; later developments included coaxial cable, microwave relay, and finally satellite broadcast, of which, under the quasi-public COMSAT arrangement, AT&T is the major stockholder. Broadcasting is possible without the telephone company. Many independent radio and television stations get along quite well without it. However, these stations are frequently marginal operations; the big money lies in networking, which would be impossible without land lines to physically tie the affiliates to the network.

Closed-circuit television, which has been used to conduct simultaneous meetings in different parts of the country, for political reports to a constituency, or as a form of pay TV for prizefights, also requires phone lines or microwave relay.

Even CATV relies on the telephone distribution system, for in most instances it hangs its cables on telephone poles through a lease arrangement with the separate phone companies. Where underground utilities are required, cable is slow to arrive, in that digging trenches for the cable is far more expensive than leasing utility poles.

The wire services are almost totally dependent on their trunk lines to major customers, and the state and regional wires branching off these. Actually, these are all phone lines that provide the basic diet of regional, national, and international news to all the mass media. Without wire services the mass media would also regress to the middle of the last century, covering and publishing only local news and reliant on dispatches for any out-of-town information.

TALK SHOWS AND RETRIEVAL

An innovative marriage of telephones with radio and television has resulted in the phenomenon of talk-show popularity. An extremely economical form of broadcasting, talk shows make the audience a part of the cast at no cost. The audience phones in questions or opinions to a charismatic anchorman who alternately cajoles, upbraids, or ridicules them. The X-rated radio talk show in Long Beach, California, has been previously noted; an elderly roué discusses the intimacies of their sex lives with a wide variety of women callers daily—to the consternation, delight, and edification of a vast audience. The Bell System makes this and other such shows possible.

The improvements of AT&T have also been responsible for a number of imaginative retrieval devices. There are special automated telephone numbers that can be called for a variety of canned services. "Dial-a-prayer" is one example, but there are numerous others of more pragmatic if less spiritual merit. Special numbers operated by newspapers, radio, or television stations give an up-to-date taped summary of major news. Some have both national and local news numbers to call. Brokerage firms often sponsor stock market summaries on tape; a phone call reveals the daily averages plus performance on certain key issues. (It might be added here that "quotron," a semicomputer used in brokerage offices, gives up-to-the-minute trades on any given issue simply by punching the stock exchange symbols into the keyboard; it also operates on phone lines.) There are special numbers for weather summaries, for box office information at theaters and sporting events, for travel schedules, and an imaginative use for public relations radio releases in which local news media, particularly radio stations, are provided with a number. They can call and receive a taped PR news summary either for transcription or for direct release on the air, as if they were interviewing personally. This is advantageous in that it breaks up a station's news format with a different voice and adds a little variety.

As the Bell System continues to experiment with new labor-saving devices, more and more imaginative uses of these devices come into play. The range of canned messages one can receive is expanding, and as the Bell System perfects its videophone, even broader and more dramtic retrieval messages can be anticipated. The imagination could run riot with videophone possibilities of "dial-a-prayer," of box-office scheduling interspersed with scenes from the performance, or sports scores showing highlights of the game; a videophone could make for dramatic additions to that "X-rated" Long Beach talk show. Only the surface has been scratched.

BOILER SHOPS

While telephones lend themselves to automation, they do not particularly lend themselves to mass distribution. Telephoning is basically a one-to-one interchange and occupies a specific moment in time, unlike the print media, which, while time-consuming, are not riveted to an inflexible moment. However, this does not mean that people haven't tried to utilize the telephone for mass distribution of junk mail purposes, for techniques such as "boiler shops" are employed. When a prospect is called with an offer to take dancing lessons, to "win" a trip to Las Vegas, vote for Zilch, have their roof repaired, or buy insurance, the boiler shop technique is at work. Batteries of people in a room with telephones methodicly go through the phone book (either alphabetically or by number prefix, which offers a certain demography). They reach their prospects impersonally with a canned pitch. Boiler shops are a form of invasion of privacy; junk mail can be thrown away unopened, junk calls are answered like any other. As some people begin to protect themselves from the rising volume of this intrusion by getting unlisted numbers, the boiler shop operators counter by employing computer selection of numbers, which will randomly uncover both the listed and unlisted indiscriminately. At present some people counter the boiler shop technique by putting all home calls through an answering device and calling back only those desired. This takes some of the spontaneity out of telephoning and presents a risk in emergencies. But as the Bell System is working on a beeper to advise lines in use that a call awaits, so can they in due course come up with a special ring for advised emergencies. Measure meets countermeasure and interpersonal contact becomes more organized and automated.

Another of the Bell System's innovations is the punched card for frequently called numbers, which, when inserted into the instru-

Integration and Conclusion

ment, dials automatically. From here it is but a short step to a bank of punched cards demographically selected, automatically fed, and computer controlled to play the proper taped message (perhaps on videotape) to whomever answers.

THEORETICAL CONTRIBUTIONS

Telephones and the Bell System have always been in the van of technological advance. The development of coaxial cable, microwave relay, and satellite are among the physical improvements. The Bell System is also one of the principal leaders in the theoretical development of mass communications. Bell Laboratories, the system's "think tank," is devoted to an extraordinarily high degree of pure research in addition to applied research and development (R&D). Shannon and Weaver's mathematical theory of communication is an example of the latter.[2] Essentially, theirs is a study of channel capacity, with considerable attention paid to overcoming noise as a detriment not only to understanding but to capacity as well. Their theory takes into consideration the degree of language redundancy since such redundancy permits a certain leeway. (For example, how often can a scrambled paragraph in a newspaper story be pieced together by following the context?) Shannon and Weaver's theory is based on the binary concept of bits of information, a "bit" being one of two choices. It is thus the number of bits that a channel can handle that determines its capacity. Since bits in sequence and combination are the basis of the digital computer, Shannon and Weaver's theory put the Bell System smack in the middle of computer software and programming. Computers were not strangers to the Bell System in any event, for computer hardware had long been used to automate the increasing volume of phone calls as the nation grew. With a foot in the door of future computer development, the Bell System can be expected to play an ever larger role in the kinds of communications decisions that are going to determine what the twenty-first century will be like. The communications decisions made now are bound to affect the social body of the next century. As the Bell System infiltrates every aspect of the mass communications net, neither are these decisions and changes going to be restricted to the realm of interpersonal communications served by telephone calls; the entire gamut of mass communications networks—print, broadcast, and computer technology—will be affected.

It should be noted that a considerable volume of the daily phone calls placed are not interpersonal communications at all, but rather intercomputer communications as automated surrogates talk to each other in complex binary languages, making flight reservations, booking hotel rooms for conventions, balancing bank accounts, segregating the volume of securities trades, analyzing public opinion, determining television ratings, performing security checks, and checking on credit ratings.

2. Claude E. Shannon and Warren Weaver, *Mathematical Theory of Communication*, 4th ed. (Urbana, Ill.: University of Illinois Press, 1969).

SCOPE OF TELEPHONE

The scope of the telephone is even more staggering than that of the mails. There are 1.2 billion phone calls placed daily in the United States; that's an average of ten calls each for the nation's 120 million phones. More significantly, that's six calls daily for every man, woman, and child. Unlike the mails, the vast majority of these calls are interpersonal. Boiler shop calls do not account for a large volume, and the Bell System estimates that only about 50,000 of these calls are computer interlinks. There is a truly enormous amount of extended interpersonal communications carried on by phone, reinforcing some attitudes, casting doubt on others, and adding to the summary of impressions beating constantly on man's brain.

It should also be noted that the Bell System, as the nation's largest utility, has a considerable direct fiscal and persuasive effect on the communications industry through its advertising and public relations. Advertisements sponsored by the Bell System, AT&T, Western Electric (Bell's manufacturing and development arm), or any of its subsidiary telephone companies are encountered daily in almost all media: radio, television, newspapers, and magazines. It is nearly impossible to see a television program or a film without a phone appearing in it. The number of telephone company films produced for training and educational purposes alone is large and, as mentioned before, in many areas communications courses are taught in elementary and high schools by Bell System personnel.

Perhaps one of the most efficient public relations programs of any corporation is found in AT&T. What is known of the Bell System? Actually, quite a bit, far more than is known about DuPont or General Electric. How is it learned? From daily use of the product, certainly; from exposure in school, possibly; from constantly reinforced advertising and public relations reaching individuals almost daily through nearly all media and augmented by word of mouth—absolutely.

Public relations has been applied effectively by AT&T. In California's gubernatorial elections, Pacific Telephone assigns a team of communications experts to each of the gubernatorial candidates through both the primary and general elections. Each team's job is to coordinate the communications of the candidates through assigned radiophone-equipped automobiles and the like. Team members "live" with their candidate for the nine months or so of campaigning, and get to know him well. Eventually, one of these candidates will be elected governor; when that happens, Pacific Telephone, AT&T, and the Bell System will have an executive who has shared the bloodbath of campaigning, a trusted confidant with access to the governor. Nor are the efforts for the defeated candidates wasted. Each of these contenders for a governorship is a man of considerable power and prestige in his own party. He will continue to occupy, in all probability, positions of political significance, and Pacific Telephone has his ear. This is a public relations masterpiece, an adroit from of prelobbying.

Integration and Conclusion

COMPUTER GENESIS AND GENERATIONS

Necessity, it is said, is the mother of invention, and the computer was developed during World War II for antiaircraft protection against bombing attacks. A device was needed that could perform mathematical calculations more rapidly than the human brain. Given an approaching aircraft's direction, altitude, speed, and distance, a means of computing the lead to give that aircraft was needed, as a duck hunter leads an incoming duck, so that the ack-ack shell and the aircraft would meet at a predetermined point in space, as duck and shot meet where neither was before.

The first antiaircraft computers were great, bulky devices accepting data from visual tracking and stereoscopic range finders to compute a trajectory for the shell; the trajectory was then electrically transmitted to the guns, automatically aiming them at their lead point and maintaining that lead. These were analogue computers, measuring devices utilizing mechanical cams meticulously tooled to the three-dimensional curves that an infinite series of graph plottings had revealed as predictive for all known courses, speed, and directions of enemy aircraft, and all possible combinations of these.

In the postwar world the commercial application of computers became readily apparent. The mechanical cam gave way to radio vacuum tubes, permitting greater versatility than the limited function of predicting future airplane positions. The computers of the late forties and early fifties were still, for the most part, analogue in that they performed a series of continuing measurements. They were essentially slide-rule computers of considerable complexity and great speed, but they lacked memory. An almost simplistic example of an analogue computer is the gas gauge on a car, which continually reads the level of gas and converts this factor mechanically or electrically into a relative measurement shown on a dial of some sort. As gas gauges remain in automobiles, so do analogue computers remain, particularly in the engineering profession, where they are more efficient for certain limited purposes. Today, many analogue computers convert their measurements into digital data for use in the more sophisticated digital computers that began to come into being in the mid-fifties and were given a big boost by the scientific emphasis of the early sixties.

Computer development relied upon the same set of technological improvements that made transistors and miniaturization possible in radio and television. Transistors did away with bulky vacuum tubes and permitted the development of the diodes and triodes and integrated circuits and printed wiring that are at the heart of modern computers. The further development of magnetic tape, on which the computer could draw in problem solving, made a memory possible, while the incredible speed of the new computers made application of the binary theory feasible (binary theory reduces all information to bits—combinations of either/or choices).

The acceleration of computer generations has been nothing less than fantastic since these breakthroughs. Nowhere is this fact driven

Personal Media

home more dramatically than at the United States' missile tracking station at Guaymas, Mexico. Here, three huge computer rooms in succession house the devices used to track the Mercury, Gemini, and Apollo projects successively. As each project was developed, computers used for its predecessor were already obsolete, and entirely new hardware had to be built.

The incredible speed of these computers should also be noted. As a computer relays instructions to a space capsule, it demands acknowledgement—feedback from the capsule's computer. If it does not receive this confirmation within five microseconds—that's five one-millionths of a second—it begins to worry, ringing bells and flashing lights. In that tiny time period a message is relayed into space, received, translated, acted upon, confirmed, and rebroadcast to Guaymas for reception and reconfirmation.

COMPUTER MYSTIQUE

As the computer's mind-boggling speed and predictive ability under certain conditions became more generally known, a certain mystique surrounding it arose. It was credited with omniscience and even a certain supernatural quality, containing final answers. Unquestionably, computers are a great servant of mankind, but they also pose a threat to man, not necessarily to mankind in the aggregate but to man as the individual. This threat is based not on computer magic, but on their incredible infinite memory, their painstaking attention to detail, and their stupidity. Computers are not only stupid—they are amoral. They do only what man tells them to do, and they do it endlessly, right or wrong. There is a slogan in computer circles, "GIGO," that means "garbage in, garbage out." The saying illustrates two things: first, computers have two information functions—input, which includes both instructions, or programming, and data; and output, which is the end result of computations, analyses, predictions, whatever. More specifically, GIGO points out that computers, far from being infallible, are quite capable of outputting nonsense if their input is in error; they cannot distinguish quality in input. There is no such thing as computer error; there are only programming errors or errors in the interpretation of computer data, and these are human errors on the part of programmers or judgmental errors on the part of analysts.

Another portion of the computer's mystique is that they require different languages. Since at base computers are mathematical devices, it became necessary to translate verbal instructions into some symbolic system that the computer could understand and act upon. Knowledge and application of languages such as FORTRAN (although there are many others), became the essence of programming. Further, as computers became more sophisticated, new languages (with more explicit phraseology of instruction for example) were required to meet their refinements, and since these languages were

Integration and Conclusion

foreign to the general public, the computer became increasingly incomprehensible.

Another aspect of computers that many people find difficult to understand is their ability to perform a number of tasks simultaneously. People, as McLuhan points out, are linear and sequential; they do one thing at a time. The computer does not do just one thing at a time; it does thousands of things simultaneously due to "interrupt" capacities. The Guaymas computers might be adjusting orbit, monitoring and reading astronauts' heart rates and blood pressures, activating oxygen systems, and controlling temperature in the capsule all at once, in addition to hundreds of other scientific and housekeeping chores.

There are more than 50,000 major computers in the United States. They are in the hands of all levels of government and of major corporations, of hospitals, universities, the networks, law enforcement agencies, the Bureau of the Census, think tanks, and so on.

INVASION OF PRIVACY

Major computers are often linked by phone lines to terminals at remote locations from which the master computer's memory and analytical skill can be taped. American Airlines, for example, has 1,700 terminals across the nation. Each of these 1,700 terminals can request reservation information simultaneously and get it; in addition, they can ask any traveler's flight movements and, in a furious burst of activity in its anxiety to please, the computer will spew forth a complete dossier: name, flights traveled, destinations and boarding points, seat numbers, boarding times, stopovers, telephone contact (which is often a hotel), costs, and fellow travelers. All of this information is more or less innocently revealed by the traveler to American Airlines in getting a reservation. The data is innocuous by itself, but put together and memorized by a computer it begins to fit patterns that conceivably might be of interest to unscrupulous persons, or divorce lawyers, or private detectives (the latter two being the most likely categories of people to obtain this information). Furthermore, the fact that the terminals are linked to a master computer by phone lines opens the distinct possibility of "bugging" to obtain personal data that might otherwise be protected.

People already know much about an individual, often without his realization. Trash collectors know exactly how much he drinks; dry cleaners know his taste in clothing and perhaps his eating habits. The milkman who delivers knows what kind of a housekeeper the lady of the house is; the newsboy knows whether an individual is a late riser or not; the neighbors can give ample testimony to personal habits. This data is relatively easy to discover if someone really puts his mind to it; there is also data that the bank knows, the IRS, the county assessor and tax collector, the police department, the armed services and Veteran's Administration, the unified school districts, college registrars, the courts, the registrar of voters, central credit bureaus, and department stores where charge accounts are opened. If all this data exists in infinite memory in FBI, IRS, credit, banking, and college computers, it amounts to a more or less complete history of a person's every action from birth. Presently it is limited and isolated, but since it is technically possible to link all this data through phone lines between computers and to call it forth by the presentation of a single social security number, computers could happily comply, offering voluminous printouts, amounting to an entire life history, in seconds. Social security numbers are more and more becoming man's identity. The armed services are converting to social security numbers in lieu of their own; they are required on all income transactions and reported to the IRS. Soon social security numbers will be issued at birth, nine-figured symbols of a life, capable of being digested by computers wherever they are.

This is the principal reason that computers are considered among the personal media: they are capable not merely of reaching ever closer to individuals demographically, but because they can identify each person and offer reams of privy data about him, without his knowledge or consent, to anyone who presents the proper key, and, through bugging, to anyone interested in the most specious way.

REGIMENTATION OR FREEDOM?

The computer has accelerated an administrative tendency to standardize procedures that was already well under way in the early fifties. A good deal of this kind of thinking arose from World War II's "sop" (standard operating procedure) in the armed services, and from the popularity of efficiency (time and motion) studies and the like in that period. The assignment of numerical designations to people so that they could be identified for processing grew apace. With the computers came the IBM cards, punched cardboard replicas of a person, his paper soul as it were; if these were lost, he ceased to exist. Subsequently, the phrase "Do not fold, spindle, or staple" was applied to people as a travesty on how machine-controlled and regimented their lives had become. This regimentation has been fallaciously attributed to the computer. While it is frustrating to have an impersonal computer miles away take away a credit rating without recourse or to figure one's grades, the computer in the aggregate may permit a far greater diversity and individuality for mankind than was ever possible in its absence. By taking over the direction of manufacturing and making automation possible, by monitoring all kinds of equipment automatically, by performing record-keeping and accounting functions, and by extending the horizons of knowledge and assisting in instantaneous retrieval computers are providing a freedom and increased leisure for man that he never knew before. They are permitting him increased time to use his brain, employing his unique capacity on earth to reason and to create, if only he will. The computer is another step in freeing man from the tyranny of labor and the brutality of survival that has plagued him since he first emerged from the cave.

To date, the record seems to indicate that increased twentieth-century leisure is merely devoted to massive doses of entertainment represented basically by television, although there are dim signs of this phenomenon passing. Whether the twenty-first century will be radically different or whether it will represent the sullen, enervated, mindless world that Fahrenheit 451 portrayed is as yet unknown. Whether computers will bring reality to George Orwell's Big Brother of 1984 or whether they will permit a greater wisdom is something the next generation will have to decide, but each succeeding year of increasing computerization brings us closer to the fact that popular fictional portraits are becoming real options.

That computers are a part of mass communications goes without saying, and that they are the newest offshoot of the electronic revolution is axiomatic. They serve newspapers in revolutionary fashion, opening the way to automation of the "backshop" and transferring a part of its functions to the city room. Computers facilitate enormously the handling of advertising. Computers are at base responsible for today's automated radio stations, which operate themselves from rolls of tape. Not only do computers facilitate networking by instantaneously linking up the package of stations appropriate to regional broadcasts, but even such things as professional football's instant replay and slow motion are essentially computer memory operations, recalled from console. Further, since information of whatever variety is a considerable portion of the mass media, the computer's fantastic ability to store it in abundance and call any portion out instantly places computers squarely in the middle of the entire information function, including the field of education.

CYBERNETICS AND PROGNOSIS

3. Norbert Weiner, Cybernetics, 2d ed. (Cambridge, Mass.: The M.I.T. Press, 1969).

Another of the computer's remarkable functions is its self-correcting ability. Norbert Weiner, who himself played a role in the development of antiaircraft fire direction, called such self-correction "cybernetics."[3] Instant feedback combined with infinite, accurate memory has been the basis of the so-called miracles that computers can perform. Use of cybernetics in computers has led to theoretical application in terms of mass communications itself, with more and more attention being paid to self-correction on the basis of data received. The ratings of television are an admirable example of how programming is altered, sometimes radically, on the basis of the sample data that the ratings reveal. Public opinion polling is another cybernetic device whereby people's attitudes are probed as guides to future action. Extensively used in political campaigning, cybernetics has also become one of the more sophisticated public relations tools in that it not only evaluates the progress of a public relations program but, in many instances, uncovers corporate strengths and weaknesses that public relations can either capitalize on or correct.

Thus, the advent of the computer brings society ever closer to recognition of mass communications as its central nervous system. Marshall McLuhan, in fact, takes a radical view of the matter. His thesis is that all media are extensions of one of the senses, print being an extension of the eye, radio of the ear, and so forth. The computer, however, he sees as an extension of the central nervous system itself, reaching thus the ultimate in media development. Within his thesis, McLuhan sees computers as becoming the master of man rather than his servants, and far from merely providing more leisure and better data, actually ruling man's life. Man's role, as McLuhan sees it, will be as a servomechanism to his machines, keeping them clean and oiled; in time they could even do this themselves. Man would thus become only the sex organs of the computer, as they are incapable of biological reproduction. Weiner disagrees, however, seeing the possibility of computers being able to reproduce themselves through their cybernetic, self-corrective ability. These arguments are mentioned to demonstrate how radical computerization and its attendants, automation and predictability, are affecting the world of mass communications and, hence, the entire social structure.

STORAGE AND RETRIEVAL

Much has been made of the computer's informational storage and retrieval ability, from instant replays to full individual dossiers, to the location of arcane data on Tuscan etching, to the wondrously visualized CATV possibilities. These miracles are not new at all. It should be pointed out that libraries, dating back at least to the great library at Alexandria in the time of the pharaohs, are in fact information storage and retrieval devices. So too is the human mind, and the historical development of the poetic mode, apart from (or perhaps because of its aesthetics), can be easily regarded as the refinement of a mental storage and retrieval device. Similarly, with the advent of printing, books were originally regarded as storage and retrieval systems. The computer simply performs this function faster. Operating in microseconds, it can afford to waste time seeking information. It actually may be enormously inefficient in a way that no librarian would tolerate. The computer needs no Dewey decimal system to locate a volume; the author and title are sufficient. It needs no alphabetical index to find a person; his social security number is enough.

Another genius of the computer is that it can integrate data from many sources. It is not necessary to compile everything in a central location. Merely to have access to terminals that can be located anywhere in the nation, and eventually the world, is enough. In this respect, the computer's ability to integrate far-flung data is a further socially decentralizing influence, adding to the huge steps already taken by jet aircraft, closed-circuit television, and the instantaneous long-distance telephone—and videophone. These information and data transfer devices have already made their influence felt in the decentralization of industry, and undoubtedly as the future unfolds will play a role in slowing the pace of urbanization. If National Steel and Shipbuilding's automated assembly line could be computer-controlled, there would be no need for the computer to be located at the water's edge; it could be placed wherever management found it most convenient and satisfying to live. Scholars would not need to concentrate at the great universities; their videophones could bring them in instant contact with colleges while terminals tapped the most up-to-date scientific developments and historical precedents around the world. Publishers of newspaper groups would never need to visit their newspapers; Telefax could bring them every page of every edition of every newspaper—their own and their competitors'—even before they hit the streets, while they kept in constant touch through closed-circuit conference calls. (Nor is this latter particularly new; William Randolph Hearst, who was ahead of his time in many ways, ran a giant empire in the 1920s from the barren coastal wilderness of San Simeon.)

PREDICTION PROBLEMS

The computer's ability to predict accurately on the basis of samples is another of its qualities that bears examination. For example, in national presidential elections there is a three-hour time differential between the populous East and West Coasts. When the polls close in the East, the networks, utilizing their computers and some selected key precincts, have been able to predict with uncanny accuracy the outcome of the election as a whole, sometimes within fractions of a percentage point. They broadcast this information several hours before the polls close on the West Coast. There is reason to believe that this may have an effect on the voting patterns of West Coast residents who have not yet voted. Voters may either jump on the band wagon and vote for the predicted winner, or they may adopt a reverse attitude and vote for the underdog. Actually, it is believed that these two trends tend to cancel one another out. Most significantly, however, voters may stay away from the polls in undetermined numbers figuring that the outcome is already settled, and their vote counts for nothing. It is this effect that is most dangerous, for it encourages personal disenfranchisement, thus defeating the purpose of democracy. In so doing, it places a premium on East Coast voting, that is contrary to the one-man, one-vote principle, and finally, it distorts the computer's predictability, and in close elections (and several within the past decade or so have been extremely close) can easily make the difference in who is elected. It is, of course, the computer's remarkable accuracy in prediction that sets the stage for this phenomenon. If it occasionally made mistakes, people might believe their votes continued to count, and that the network computers provided only guidelines. However, its continuing accuracy leads to an infallibility factor; its prophesies in practice become self-fulfilling. In recognition of this, the networks have already agreed not to broadcast computer predictions until the West Coast polls are closed. However, the effect of such predictions poses a problem only temporarily averted, not faced and solved.

An analogous situation exists in the matter of polling. When frequent computer-directed national polling becomes feasible and major issues can be bounced off the people, there may develop a propensity on the part of politicians to follow the samples, recognizing that this is the currently popular course. However, the popular course is not necessarily the correct one. It may be born of emotional considerations that tend to dissipate on cooler reflection. Representatives at every level are elected to employ their judgment on behalf of their constituencies, not to rubber-stamp the constituency itself.

These are some of the problems generated by the computer as applied to the practical side of government, problems for which there is no constitutional answer, since these are the astonishing problems born of technology and social change unforeseen and unforeseeable by the founding fathers.

Meanwhile, computer development goes on apace. Computers are being developed that will respond to spoken instructions. Already the University of Utah computer has been able to take the scratchy recordings of Enrico Caruso's magnificent voice and, through phonetic analysis of pitch, tone, and timbre, produce high-fidelity reproductions of what he actually sounded like. So sensitive are computers to voice that a person's voice can be used as a key to activation. Understanding verbal instructions, the computer responds, although to no one except the person who vocally programmed it, or whose voice pattern is inserted as the key. Computers are being given not only ears in the form of microphones, but eyes—video cameras—thus considerably expanding their sources of input data; voices of their own and mechanical arms and legs, self-activating rollers, extend the variety of their output. Other experimentation gives logic and reasoning capacity to computers so that they can actually think—playing chess, for example, far better than the average player. However, it should be remembered that the computers are programmed successively by superior players and fed data from championship matches that, in light of with storage and retrieval facilities, can be applied to current games.

SUMMARY

The personal media are too often overlooked in man's preoccupation with the mass and with channel emphasis. The mails, telephone, and computers are mass media, striking directly at the individual, the basic building block of all audiences and the final recipient of all media. Public opinion is formed as a result of interpersonal exchange; the mails and the telephone provide two of the principal means of effecting such exchange.

The mails depend on messengers; the postman of today differs little from the ancient Roman courier. This anachronism relies on the fact that each individual requires a physical site in which to exist, and mails are still the most efficient way of physically reaching him. The mails are also the basic distribution system for magazines, although less so for newspapers.

The mails provide the means for interpersonal correspondence, although they take too long for today's hasty society and are more frequently being restricted to areas in which a record of the transaction is required.

Junk mail is a big portion of mail volume, often consisting of the solicitation of sales or votes.

Computerized direct mail takes advantage of demographics to identify and reach ever smaller publics in terms of presumed interest. Demographics as a science was immeasurably assisted by the computer. Through use of a computer, demographic audiences can become so refined that they do not actually exist. The computers are also capable of handling the physical demands of direct mail, automatically writing, addressing, folding, bundling, and stamping. A good deal of computerized direct mail is pseudopersonalized for effect and sent first class to command attention. Direct mail is the most expensive of the various forms of advertising or public relations in terms of cpm; however, it is also the most pinpointed, minimizing overkill.

The telephone carries a greater load of interpersonal contact and less commercialized appeal. However, boiler shop operations are common.

The Bell System and American Telephone and Telegraph have always been in the forefront of electronic communications. Television networks are hooked up by telephone lines, coaxial cable, or microwave relay developed by the Bell System. More recently, through COMSAT, in which it is the principal stockholder, AT&T has gotten into satellite broadcasting. Telephone lines also provide the wire services and closed-circuit television with their distribution links.

Radio talk shows as an information/entertainment device are reliant on the telephone, as are an increasing number of specialized services offering weather reports, stock market quotations, sports scores, prayers, etc. The Bell System, through their engineers Shannon and Weaver, also developed the mathematical theory of communications, a theory of binary bits applied to channel capacity that has had considerable usage in computer technology.

Computers grew out of limited World War II development of antiaircraft artillery. From the mechanical cams used then, computers have rapidly progressed through the use of vacuum tubes to transistors, diodes, triodes, and printed and integrated circuits. They have benefited from the same technology that made miniaturization of radio and television possible. They have also moved from analogue to digital computers and passed through three generations of development within a decade.

The mystique surrounding computers is irrational. Essentially they are stupid, endlessly doing only what they are told. They perform their functions very rapidly, operating in microseconds; this means that they are also remarkably inefficient in the amount of time that they can squander. Besides their incredible speed, one of their assets is their potential for interconnection through phone lines, enabling terminals located anywhere to tap the full resources of a computer.

Much has been made of the computer's impersonality. However, in freeing man from the rote and tedious, computers permit him to exploit his own unique potential for thought and creativity.

New generations of computers are becoming increasingly humanized; given ears and voices, sight, arms, and mobility, their scope of both input and output is considerably enhanced.

20 THE ARTS AND CULTURAL TRANSMISSION

PAST AND PRESENT INTERTWINED

Cultural transmission as one of the functions of mass communications is at once the most ubiquitous of its functions and the least understood. Cultural transmission is inevitable, always present, for any communication has an effect on the individual recipient. Thus, any communication becomes, if ever so slightly, a part of the individual's experience, of his knowledge and accumulated learning. Therefore, through individuals in the aggregate, communication becomes a part of the collective experience of groups, publics, audiences of all kinds and the masses of which that individual is a part. It is this collective experience reflected back through communications forms, not merely in the mass media but also the arts and sciences, that paints a picture of the culture, of an age, of a society. Heritage then is the cumulative effect of previous cultures and societies that have become a part of man's birthright and being, transmitted to him from individuals, parents, and peers: from primary and secondary groups, and from the educational process. This cultural communication is constantly modified by new experience.

Thus, cultural transmission takes place at two levels, the contemporary and the historical, unseparated and constantly interweaving. Furthermore, mass communication is a major tool in the transmission of the culture on both levels. On the contemporary level it constantly reinforces the consensus of society's values, while continually introducing the seeds of change. It is this factor that leads to the enigma surrounding mass communications of being both simultaneously the conservator of the status quo and the vehicle of change.

On the historical level mass communications transmits a birthright, the capsule summary of all previous societal experience. In this it has been subject to the cumulative judgment of previous societies in determining what shall be transmitted to posterity. This vague determination process, which has passed along the Mona Lisa and Venus De Milo, Shakespeare and Dante, has ruthlessly rejected an infinite number of other works of drama, literature, sculpture, and painting, the existence or nonexistence of which shall perforce never be known. This vague process can only be described as anonymous, historical gatekeeping.

THE ROLE OF THE ARTS

Thus far all emphasis has been on mass communications within its more traditional definition: the print and broadcast media reaching out to large numbers of people indirectly and impersonally. These media are the catalysts of thought transference indirectly experienced.

When considering cultural transmission, which of necessity leads discussion to the arts, one must view channels in a slightly different light. Rather than being impersonal and indirect mass media, they become logistical channels whose function is to bring sender and receiver together physically for personal contact. Thus dramas, concerts, ballets, professional football games, seminars, conventions,

Our historical cultural transmission extends beyond the American heritage, through the Renaissance, to the dawn of Western civilization.

UPI

Integration and Conclusion

pulpits, cocktail parties, and the entire educational complex on a more continuing basis are devices—channels—designed to bring sender and receiver, artist and audience, together in a direct experience. Similarly, museums and galleries are channels designed to permit a direct experience on the part of the audience with the singular reality of the artist.

The esoteric media are self-selective, not foisting; they await audiences who come of their own volition, interest, and curiosity. Since incentive is present on the part of the individuals that compose the audiences, the net effect can be presumed greater than the casual throw-away offerings of the mass media. It is interesting to note in an impersonal society the renaissance of the esoteric media that do provide direct living contact, not merely with the artist but with others of like interest.

The audience size of esoteric media is typically small, physically restricted to the range of vision and voice. These media are in physical plants: theaters, concert halls, galleries, museums, convention centers, public halls, and stadia. The stadia are, of course, the largest, sometimes embracing as many as 100,000 persons. However, the physical plant is not the only size criterion. There is also a repeatability factor as galleries and theaters and concert halls play to audiences night after night, achieving huge exposure over a year or a decade or more. One supposes that *Hair,* running to capacity audiences for at least two years, achieved a greater overall exposure than any but the very best-selling books, far more in the same time span than many of the smaller magazines or average movies.

IMMEDIACY VERSUS PERSPECTIVE

This introduces another factor worthy of note in the consideration of mass communications. Students of the media have traditionally been intrigued with immediacy as a factor in mass communications. Society has become so conditioned to the huge masses that television instantly reaches that it has forgotten the reality of historical exposure as a factor in mass communications. How many persons have seen the Mona Lisa, for example, since Leonardo first painted it? What kind of audiences have the centuries developed for Michelangelo's Sistine Chapel? How extensive has exposure been to the Great Pyramid over the millenia? Taken in a historical perspective rather than in relation to today's immediacy, the mass audiences of these undying works of art have been huge. The cumulative effect of these audiences and their reactions on today's society, on men as individuals, is correspondingly great, as they establish a collective standard of heritage against which to measure, judge, or equally rebel. Their long-term contributions are as great as or greater than the fly-by-night, fully incidental effect of even a top-rated television show. Similarly, while the sales of *Hamlet* or *Merchant of Venice* in any given year may be paltry alongside the current popularity of a best-seller, the bard's exposure to generations of high school and college freshman afford him status approaching an all-time best-selling author—exceeded perhaps only by Matthew, Mark, Luke, and John.

The point is that, in a broad view, mass audiences need not be immediate. They can be historically cumulative, and the media that reach them can be just as mass in terms of effect as any of today's institutionalized, impersonal, and immediate mass media.

MAN'S UNIQUENESS

Somewhere lost in the recesses of antiquity man learned to communicate with his fellows, thus establishing a societal basis for communications.

To understand the process of cultural transmission, indeed of communication itself, it is worthwhile to peer back as far as possible into prehistory.

Two things about man's communication are unique. The first is what, in his theory of general semantics from *Science and Sanity*, Alfred Korzybski called man's "time-binding" ability based in memory.[1] Man alone of all the creatures on earth has been able to consciously store his experiences and pass them along from one generation to the next so that his progress has been more or less constant. It is this ability that has led to cultural transmission as a function of the media, and to the entire institution of education, so much a part of this function. Nor should it be forgotten, particularly in today's deafening competition for attention, that only a part of this education is a formal, in-the-classroom, from-the-textbook education; an enormous amount of it is acquired willy-nilly from the mass media (most often, television) as they transmit their version of contemporary culture.

Historically man has been continually able to draw on the past and add new experience from the present to guide the future. But that is only part of the story. Not only has man been able to accumulate experience, but he has proven himself able to sort and sift amongst these memories, discarding the unneeded and ordering the rest for ease in transmission both to his fellows and to posterity. It is this process that prunes knowledge from raw experience. With other species, which lack the time-binding ability, each new generation starts more or less where its predecessor did and finishes at roughly the same state of development that all previous generations did, subject only to the ponderous process of biological evolution. This is to say that all other species are somewhat static in time, whereas man collectively and more or less consciously determines his own future. Elephants, of the twenty-first century, for all their intelligence and longevity, will be about the same as they are presently. However, it is safe to predict that man will be substantially changed—socially, politically, economically, and technologically—and that the mass communications network serving the third millenium culture as the

1. Alfred Korzybski, *Science and Sanity*, 4th ed. (Lakeville, Conn.: Institute of General Semantics, 1962).

central nervous system will be radically different both in cause and effect from that of today.

Related to all this, possibly as cause, is man's other unique distinction—his ability to deal in abstractions, to let the symbol stand for the thing, the thought, the event, the state of mind, and even for the emotion, for very complex processes indeed. For example, communication itself is an abstraction, embracing these two complicated concepts: man's time-binding capacity and his abstraction ability.

ABSTRACTIONS

To communicate man requires tools for the transfer of meaning. He employs sets of symbols, called "codes," or more simply, "languages." Chiefly, these symbols may be broken down into two categories, the verbal and nonverbal. The principal concern so far has been with verbal codes, the mainstay of current mass communications, print, and broadcast.

However, nonverbal forms of symbol codes are becoming increasingly significant. For example, the new languages of the computer are nonverbal and symbolic; the computers themselves talk in binary logarithms. Or, the language of mathematics and the new math serve to transfer meaning. Music, the mainstay of radio and recordings and all they foretell, the basic ingredient of the rock groups, the raison d'être of symphony concerts, is nonverbal language. Then there is the entire nonverbal language of body English, eye contact, mime, and expression; the lilting high-headed swing of a girl in love or the aimless shuffle of a confused old man.

GRAPHICS

Some nonverbal forms of language and the meaning they convey also stretch back into prehistory, possibly predating man's verbal efforts to communicate—graphics, for instance, symbolic representation. A part of graphics evolved into the verbal form of language, but another part remained discrete as illustration. From this latter branch of graphics came all forms of drawing and painting, leading, of course, to the serious artist desperately trying to convey his meaning on canvas, paper, or cave walls. Graphics, too, benefited from technology; invention of paper, development of canvas, the discovering of pigments and how to blend them all added dimensions to art. Graphics branched out, finding its way into fabric and weaving and sculpture, practically applied into architecture, and through decoration into the entire scope of man's artifacts. All of these artistic vehicles remain forms of communication, a transmission of the culture, and become the province of the archeologist who, piecing together the bits and pieces of these artifacts, attempts to portray a bygone era, even as content analysts try to recreate other generations through an analysis of their mass media.

Printing led to the reproduction of graphics, of line drawings and etchings, of woodcuts, and eventually it led to lithographs. Photography lent a new dimension to graphics, a clearer reality that, as it evolved, led to automated photographs, movies, color and sound film, and then finally videotape, with holography lurking in the wings. Thus, graphics has become a mainstay of contemporary mass communications to the point where there are some who feel that the verbal forms of writing and reading may be jeopardized seriously in favor of the ease and swiftness of the electronic mode.

Not only do graphics represent realistically, but they also have that inherent characteristic of a symbolic code to conjure meaning, thought, and emotion beyond what is represented. Cartoons, for example, present minimal information, a rough outline line drawing of a person or situation with perhaps a brief cutline, but the viewer gathers meaning because he draws upon his cumulative experience (culturally transmitted) to infer this meaning. Further, the cubists and surrealists and more modern linear schools do not find it necessary to even represent to convey meaning; their meaning is based on new levels of abstraction.

MATHEMATICS

Mathematics is another language, a set of symbols more abstract in its origin than graphics, but bearing a definite relationship to reality. Far beyond the relatively simple business of counting and accounting, mathematics represents a complex mode of thinking all of its own that can be translated into verbal form for facility in understanding, even as the computer that "thinks" mathematically can provide a printout of its solutions for reading. Mathematics provides the thought-core of the hard sciences. It enabled Alfred Einstein to unlock some of the secrets of the universe, i.e., $E=mc^2$, which he then translated in his theories of relativity. Today math is becoming an ever-accelerating communications code. High schools and colleges, the educational complex, are requiring a proficiency in statistics to understand new social concepts. Quite apart from the growing use of mathematics by computers and the crying need for trained technicians, analysts, and programmers, to tend the machines, the incidence and significance of ratings of various kinds, and the growing science of public opinion polling, mathematically based, demands an ever-increasing popular knowledge of the language of math. Thus, awareness of the mathematical code is becoming a necessity for twentieth-century man to keep current with information affecting his life: scientific, political, social, educational, and financial data. In this, of course, he is assisted by machines, the computers and calculators, but again, familiarity of the language of math is necessary to understand them, their product, and their operation.

MUSIC

The language of music is a language of mood capable of meaning transfer. The fact that music seems to lack rational reference to a verbal system has led some to think of it as a discrete symbolic system whose symbol sets have no reference to an outside reality what-

Integration and Conclusion

soever, but only to one another. Suzanne Langer makes this point in developing the theme that music is the ultimate abstraction whose notes refer to nothing, and that the only context of music arises from the juxtaposition of notes one with another in sets.[2] She seems to forget music's deep rhythmic stirring in the soul, long forgotten tidal rhythms, and the staccato pulse of the heart; it is to these hidden realities that music speaks and from which response is evoked. True, there is little rational information transfer, but there are deeply emotional and even practical effects to music as a communication form. For instance, a battalion of troops, dog-tired from days of battle, might straggle to the rear after being relieved. As the troops approach, the regimental band strikes up a Sousa march. Immediately and voluntarily the troops straighten up, heads high, instinctively forming into columns of four as their feet unconsciously pick up the beat, and they stride in step, erect, proud, arms swinging.

Hitler used music to perfection as a part of the pageantry of his mammoth Nuremberg spectacles. These annual rallies of the Nazi faithful were designed to inspire the audience to greater efforts as massed banners waved in unison, the strains of Wagner struck at the foundation of the German soul, and 100,000 singing voices raised in tribute to Horst Wessel fanned their martial spirit.

Music rose from antiquity. That it was one of the early forms of communication there is little doubt; whether it rose from the ritual chant of ancient tribal rites or from the idle beating of sticks upon a log in response to unfathomed internal rhythms is unimportant. Soon, Langer points out, music became inseparable from primitive religions. Among the Navajo and Hopi, it still is inseparable. Technology gradually developed new and more sophisticated instruments from the primitive drum, wind instruments, and strings.

Nonverbally music can charm, depress, excite, move, arouse, and calm. Its ability to move the listener was exploited. Industry discovered its practical application in the plant, where, played in the background, it assists in better performance and production. Music proved adaptable, as have other media, to the values of the cultures it served as a mass communications medium. In ancient Greece its rhythms in the choruses reinforced and reemphasized the themes of the drama. In the medieval years it served the Church through Gregorian chant. It attained a contrapuntal sophistication in the Age of Reason. In the United States folk music moved in a progression from spiritual to jazz, to blues, to swing, to rock, and to country and western. Music as much as anything else is reflective of a new generation; teamed with frenetic lights, it has become almost hypnotically transcendent of this world.

Through all of this, music became identified with entertainment. As a mass medium radio has as its content music for Everyman. The incidence and significance of recordings in mass communications has already been noted. In an era that increasingly seems to be leaving

2. Suzanne Langer, *Philosophy in a New Key*, 2d ed. (New York: Mentor Books, 1951).

print behind, music enjoys high popularity; McLuhan warns of the departure from print's visual rationality to a more experiential and emotional existence, which music serves and the broadcast media carry so admirably. Music suits the speedup of contemporary life, providing instant emotion without the pain of feeling.

There are some who feel that the massive orgiastic excess that Woodstock represented was the high-water mark of the counterculture, that Woodstock was not only mass entertainment for the young, but in a very real sense mass communications, conveying subconsciously in the summer sun the broad chasm that existed between the values of nature and those of the rock culture—the discrepancy between the lasting and the fleeting. From Woodstock, the philosophical pendulum swung slowly back.

Music intermingles with other communications forms. The song is the poetic form set to music. The opera is a drama whose lines are sung. The ballet takes dance rhythm, stylized body movement, mime, and expression, and sets them to music. Music is used for dramatic

The People's Republic of China has utilized the medium of the arts in mass communications for persuasive purposes.

effect and emphasis repeatedly in film and television, often becoming a shortcut to the establishment of mood when time limitations do not permit a lengthier treatment—for example, the eerie strains of faraway taps economically tells the audience that the hero has died in battle. Music is not an incidental to the verbal mass communications process, but an integral and increasing part of it.

Integration and Conclusion

MIME

Mime, gesture, and expression are other means of nonverbal communication. They are the basis of acting; they are intensely interpersonal communications modes, and it was on stage that they could first be employed as limited mass communications tools with great drama and effect. They, too, form a part of intangible charisma, the magnetism of an individual that draws others; so aptly named, mannerisms are the man. For centuries unchanged, the drama remained in its various forms the only vehicle of effective mass communications. Print changed the mode by placing emphasis on the rational and literate, subjugating emotion to logic and reason, playing down the ear and aural to the lonely visual, and led to the Age of Reason, scientific awakening, and the technologically inspired industrial revolution. Paradoxically, that industrial revolution also brought the techniques of sound, film, and later, television, which extended drama's expression, gesture, and mime first to an aggregate and later to simultaneous millions, meanwhile relegating the drama to an art form rather than as a self-conscious mass medium.

It is this quality of television, to faithfully reproduce the mannerisms of the man, that has led *charisma* to become a recent addition to the popular vocabulary and, incidentally, has led to the proliferation of thespians among politicians—for the trained actor has an edge over the amateur in using the television medium. This has caused some to speculate that the United States may require two presidents: one a charismatic TV vote-getter, the other a trained administrator to do the work. At the very least, this proposal might upgrade the role of the vice-president.

LANGUAGE

Language is a tool that man has traditionally used to communicate with his fellows and with posterity, both of which are forms of cultural transmission—the short-term and the long. Verbal language, spoken or written, (they are subtly different) is the form that is most familiar, although, as previously mentioned, there are several others. Verbal language is another symbolic system. Language exists by consensus; the symbols—words—have meaning because man has somehow agreed upon that meaning for that word. Language is a convention that society has endorsed. As society changes, so will language, and it can be seen happening. Language as a system is organized by certain rules of syntax that have also been adopted by consensus. Man agrees to these rules because they are convenient, and without them he would have chaos, and no communication whatever—what Shannon and Weaver called "total entropy."[3]

It seems apparent that in the dim past man learned to speak before he wrote. Different grunts by a prehistoric consensus came to express fear, hunger, and desire, and the basis of a language was born. But that consensus was scarcely universal; it applied only to the relatively small circumscribed area occupied by a tribe. Thus,

3. Claude E. Shannon and Warren Weaver, *Mathematical Theory of Communication*, 4th ed. (Urbana, Ill.: University of Illinois Press, 1969).

there is the distinct possibility of not one but several rudimentary languages being born more or less simultaneously in prehistory without reference to, nor even knowledge of, one another.

As time moved on, cavemen discovered that, lacking a grunt to express "sabre-toothed tiger," he could draw a reasonable facsimile of one, and graphics came into being. This proved an efficient means of communications and led to an early form of writing. However, little pictures, while reasonably realistic, were unwieldy, and with time convention was applied to them. The explicit drawings became stylized and no longer explicit. Their meanings became accepted by convention as abstractions; examples are found in both ancient hiero-

Ancient Chinese parchment scroll.

THE BETTMANN ARCHIVE

glyphics and in cuneiform writing. Both Japanese and Chinese written languages today are based on pictographs rather than on an alphabetical form. Such stylized pictographs were far easier to transmit and record than long sequential pictures similar to an ancient comic strip.

But note that the spoken and the written language were two separate and distinct things, bearing little relationship to each other. In essence, historical man had to learn two different languages, two different sets of symbols or codes—one oral, the other written. This was a lot of work, more than a people whose lifetimes focused on the plain business of survival could accomplish, and illiteracy arrived—a comparative state, to be sure. Illiteracy also tended to be self-perpetuating; the majority of people relied on word-of-mouth communication alone, lacking the ability to explore transmitted knowledge in written form and, thus, also lacking the recorded resources for self-improvement. Their time-binding capacity was inhibited and minimal. Illiteracy was also encouraged by the educated priesthood and

Integration and Conclusion

Cuneiform writing consisted of wedge-shaped symbols that transmitted abstractions through convention.

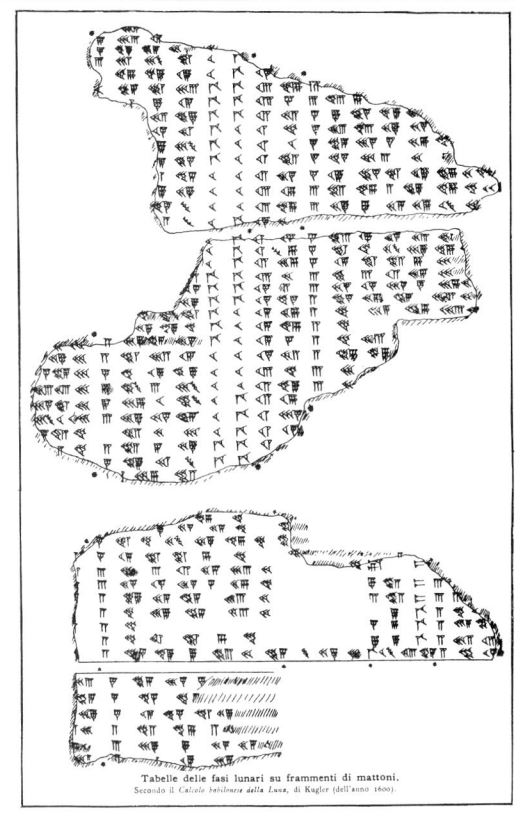

THE BETTMANN ARCHIVE

nobility, who recognized that knowledge was power and sought to conserve it unto themselves.

The development of a widespread literacy had to await a time of relative peace and leisure when all of life was not dedicated to survival alone. The requirements of peace and leisure dictated social order and economic affluence, which, in a circular process, find their roots in improved communications. Progress was slow.

THE PHONETIC ALPHABET: BREAKTHROUGH

The great breakthrough of ancient times was the development of the phonetic alphabet. With it, for the first time, came the marriage of the spoken and the written word, so complete that a reference to verbal communication means both oral and written. By assigning written symbols to certain sounds, the phonetic alphabet provided a set of symbols through whose combination anyone could compose for his neighbor, for the record, or for posterity any combinations of words and sentences his mind could conceive. It bridged an enormous gap by bringing writing and reading within reach of anyone who could speak. No longer did one have to master two different languages to communicate, nor was he forced to translate his thoughts from the spoken language into written symbols to be recorded. This breakthrough began to take popular learning away from the elite priesthoods. Subsequently, printing made the difference between tutoring and education as an organized system, vastly extending the reach of learning.

Linguistics is the study of language; two of its aspects are phonetics and syntactics. Phonetics deals with words, their origin, usage, meaning, and construction; words are the stuff of the spoken language. Syntactics, on the other hand, deals with the rules of language applied to sentences and found, for the most part, in the written form. The differences between phonetics and syntactics are evident in comparing a radio news bulletin and a newspaper story. The radio bulletin is punchy, inflective, sometimes not couched in complete sentences at all. It is the spoken language of allusion and emphasis. The newspaper story is far more formal. It is presented in complete sentences, subscribing to the rules of grammar, and furthermore, to the style of journalese. Such a simple illustration points up the basic differences between the spoken and the written language.

LANGUE AND PAROLE

4. Ferdinand De Saussure, *Course in General Linguistics,* eds. Charles Bally and Albert Sechehaye; Herman Lommel, trans. (New York: Philosophical Library, 1959).

This basic discrepancy between the spoken and the written forms of language led Ferdinand De Saussure to pose his theory of "langue and parole."[4] In essence De Saussure says that there are two languages in operation simultaneously. They are so interrelated and people so familiar with both that ordinarily no difference is noted. However, both hark back to the origins of language, to the cave grunts and the pictographs, the two basic forms that, for the Western world, were married in the phonetic alphabet, although retaining their separate identities.

Parole is the language of the people; it is street language, used in informal speaking, full of slang, idiom, and vernacular. It is here that language change occurs; new words and expressions move in, older forms move out, and the vague operation of consensus determines which will come and which will go. *Langue,* on the other hand, is more formal; it is institutionalized and transmitted, complete with rules of usage and syntax, from generation to generation, changing only ponderously, and it is most frequently associated with the written form that seeks exact expression. These distinctions are not absolute by any means, but they serve to capsulize De Saussure's theory.

An analogy would be the difference between "jurisprudence" and "the law." Both are parts of the legal system. Jurisprudence is the full body of formal law dating back to the Roman codes and English common law. It is the institution on which the American concept of justice is based. Jurisprudence corresponds to *langue.* On the other hand jurisprudence is composed of the law, the day-to-day practice of trials and verdicts and appeals and the gradual development of precedents that, in due course, find their evolutionary way into the body of jurisprudence. The law corresponds to *parole.*

De Saussure's insight is of great help in trying to reconcile the great paradox of mass communications (i.e., it is at once the conser-

Integration and Conclusion

vator of the status quo and the radical vehicle of change). The answer, as seen from language, the principal component of mass communications, is simple—it is both. As the theory of *langue* and *parole* applies to language resisting change on the one hand and encouraging it on the other, leaving convention to make the choice, so it equally applies to communication, the purpose of language, and to mass communications, its extension.

For that matter, nature itself is inherently conservative in seeking to perpetuate itself yet containing within, biologically as Darwin showed and geologically as the mountains bear testimony, the matter for change. That man as the thinking product of nature should be equally conservative by resisting change, and yet sowing its seeds, should not come as a surprise. And it follows then that man's institutions, language, and its first cousin, mass communications, must do likewise, as do jurisprudence and the law.

LANGUAGE CHANGE

A peek into some of the mechanics of language change as applied to communication might be illuminating. Complex thoughts encounter difficulty of expression for two reasons. First, their very complexity lends itself to semantic noise, resulting in differing interpretations by different receivers. Second, man is trapped in a very real sense by his own abstractions, by the limitations of his language. As any author knows, when original concepts are to be expressed there may easily be no words to express them exactly, and he is frustrated by the possession of a meaning crying for release without the verbal keys to release it. He is often forced to use inadequate alternatives.

One such alternative is to invent new words to convey meaning, hoping that consensus will adopt them. This approach is used widely in the realm of science; "cybernetics" and "videotape" are examples. Related to this is the technique of borrowing terms from other disciplines and using them where they seem to fit. The prevalent usage of the biological term "ecology" to apply environmentally or sociologically to the cultural climate is a case in point.

There is a variation on this theme in which a word from another language is borrowed in the hope that its foreign nuance will convey a new shade of meaning unavailable in the primary language. "Nuance" itself, borrowed from the French, is such an example. So its "esprit de corps," which somehow combines teamwork and pride more effectively than an English description.

Another alternative is to use new combinations of existing words, sometimes out of context, to distill new meaning from the essence of old. This is a rather poetic approach that includes the advantages of metaphor and allusion. "The sweet, small, clumsy feet of April crept into the ragged meadow of my soul" (e.e. cummings) is almost meaningless by any syntactical standards, but does indeed convey enormous feeling. It is the sort of creative use of language that a computer could not handle. In another example, "significant others" is a sociological term that, as a combination, has achieved totally new reference beyond either of the meanings inherent in its components.

Still another approach is to take an old word and give it new dimension until, having passed through a stage of duality, it takes on its new raiment completely. "Gay," in the contemporary sense of the gay liberation front, is an example of such a word in transition, meaning something entirely different than the older "gay" (as in "when our hearts were young and gay"). There exist numerous examples of words that have completed their transition, words that Suzanne Langer calls "drowned metaphors"—the fork of a road, for instance. At one time this was a brilliant metaphor whose descriptive aptness commended it to the posterity that has by now forgotten its source.

These examples give some indication of the nature of language change. Language, communication, like society and the men who created both, is a living, changing thing constantly acting, reacting, interacting, and counteracting. So too is mass communications into which language has been institutionalized. Language is a form of behavior—verbal behavior, creative behavior. Old words take on new meanings, new words are invented, others drop from sight, and increasing numbers of verbal naturalized aliens take their place in the lexicon. Yet, through all this, language remains constant, transmitting a heritage from one generation to the next, acquainting the present with the past, transacting commerce and recording all for posterity. *Langue* and *parole,* stability and change, coexist in transmission.

DIFFERENCES IN LANGUAGE

A cursory overview of language demands some attention to language differences. Languages differ not only in vocabulary but in syntax and, as any foreign traveler knows, vocabulary is not enough; a sense of things is required. Languages reflect the societies from which they arise, as they properly should. In English awkward combinations for family relationships suffice: mother-in-law, second-cousin-once-removed, a brother-in-law's wife, step-daughter. In Russian there are specific words for each of these relationships, plus dozens of others. The Eskimos, not surprisingly, have dozens of words to express "cold."

The English-speaking peoples are not concerned with gender in the language at all. The Romance languages assign masculinity and femininity to the most prosaic objects; Swahili has seven genders. These language differences reveal something about the Russians and the Swahili. They imply that exact family relationships are extremely important among the Russians, far more so than in the Anglo-Saxon world. They also imply that the Swahili cares about inanimate things; it is important to him (and his society) to distinguish something totally inanimate, such as a stone, from something that grows,

Integration and Conclusion

such as a crop, or even something that grows on animals; like wool or a toenail. The Swahili lives close to nature, and his language reflects this closeness. These illustrations briefly show how a life-style or culture or environment affects language, and they serve to introduce the matter of meaning—semantics.

Words are symbols of things, thoughts, and emotions. No symbol is exact; it is, after all, only the attempted portrayal of reality, and "the map is not the territory," as general semanticists say. Everyone knows what "flower" stands for—or do they? Since people's experiences with flowers differ, which flower does "flower" bring to mind: a rose, a violet, or daisies in the field? Man thinks in words, verbally, and words mean different things to different people. But some words are more different than others. To describe this relative difference, there is a distinction between denotative words and connotative words. Denotative words mean pretty much what they say they do. They are fairly explicit and have a general commonality in consensus with little variation in meaning from person to person. "Bookcase" is a good example; so is "blackboard."

SEMANTICS

Connotative words are less explicit; they convey, they imply. They are far more abstract, referring rarely to things but rather to thoughts and abstract concepts such as justice, patriotism, love, beauty, truth, freedom, courage. There is little commonality of acceptance in the meaning of these words. What is justice? Is it an eye for an eye or is it a more forgiving form of social adjustment? And justice for whom—the plaintiff or defendant? Beauty, it is said, is in the eye of the beholder. It must be, for an entire branch of philosophy, aesthetics, has debated since the Golden Age of Greece on what beauty is—all to no avail.

These are examples of the kinds of frustrations encountered with abstractions. Problems become particularly acute when one attempts to deal with such superabstractions via the mass media.

Connotations can be used, manipulated for advantage. Words have different meanings. Even so explicit a proper noun as "Yankee" has at least three different connotations, depending on whether it is used by an unreconstructed Southerner, a native New Englander, or a baseball buff. Equally, "soul" has three different meanings as used by blacks, Evangelists, or music buffs. While the phrase "law and order" was fairly explicit to George Wallace and his followers in 1968, it was also a code-phrase for racism in the black ghetto and among media intellectuals.

These are all problems in semantics. The choice of words is the key to the desired reaction. Knowing the predisposition of the receiver, the sender can select a word or phrase that will elicit the desired response. This is the beginning of manipulation. For example, "life insurance" is really death insurance far more appealingly named. Franklin Roosevelt coined "social security" to describe his controversial national pension program. "Accelerated amortization" is a euphemism for "fast tax write-off," while "union security" means a closed shop to management, and "right to work" means scab hiring to labor. "Soil bank" sounds less controversial than "farm subsidy." These are all examples of applied semantics.

Each person takes these vague connotative words and anchors a peculiar symbolism to himself in his head, forgetting that at best they are guides to thinking and that their meaning may be totally different to his neighbor. Further, the use of many of these abstractions (as in the emotionally charged phrase, "America...love it or leave it") is not rational, and the injection of emotion into abstraction further clouds the communications process, often by design. The extent of semantic noise that exists becomes apparent, whether accidental, purposeful, innocent, or manipulative. An earlier discussion of channel noise herein was basically concerned with its reduction or elimination in the interest of message clarity. With semantic noise stemming from a wide variety of psychosociological causes, the concern is less with its reduction in society—although this may be important—than with its application and use.

Denotative and connotative words form the basis of two approaches to communication going at least as far back as Aristotle, who pointed out the rational and the rhetorical approaches. The rational approach is a reasoned one based in fact and logic. A legal brief and a scholarly paper are examples. The tenets of journalism are founded in the rational approach of factual objectivity; the wire services use it almost exclusively. The rhetorical approach has viewpoint; it attempts to sell, to persuade, to cajole; it plays upon the emotions.

STEREOTYPE AND MYTH

Manipulation of language is the stock-in-trade of the advertising and public relations professions, and to a greater degree than would ordinarily be suspected in mass communications' information function. This manipulation is considerably assisted by the existence of stereotypes and myths that stem directly from connotative words.

In this complex society, with its mounting competition for attention, rising decibels of noise, confusion, and accelerating pace, individuals live vicariously and, for the most part, experience their world only indirectly through the mass media. Reality, in large part, is what the mass media say reality is. In this situation stereotypes and myths provide some perceptual shortcuts to understanding. They are an economic means of ordering confusion, saving both time and labor; they are a useful mental filing system permitting an individual to sort and store experience with minimal effort. When some people hear "hippies," it immediately invokes images of those who are dirty, go barefoot, and have long hair. The stereotype also works in reverse. When those people see a young person barefoot and bra-less, they automatically think "hippy," and rightly or wrongly, that individual has been tucked into a pigeonhole of understanding. People carry all sorts of stereotypes around with them pertaining to politicians, absentminded professors, hookers, bankers, ditchdiggers, and rednecks.

One of the problems with stereotypes is that they may be in error. For decades, for example, Stepin Fetchit was the stereotype in white America of the male Negro: a shiftless, subservient, comically ignorant black man of uncertain age. It was wrong, but it was convenient and it fitted well with the prevalent racial viewpoint. Thus, stereotypes, for all their usefulness and economy, must be used with great caution lest they help paint an erroneous picture of the world and inhibit rather than assist understanding.

Myths are related to stereotypes. They generally refer to beliefs and situations rather than to people. There is the myth of the power of the press, or the myth of women's superior intuition, both still prevalent. One thing noteworthy about stereotypes and myths is that generally there was a sufficient modicum of truth in them at one time to make them believable and this credibility, once established, held the stereotype over long after the original model passed away.

So much cultural transmission, both current and historical, is based on these stereotypes and myths that they are worth exploring for their role in establishing beliefs. Like language itself, stereotypes and myths, exist by consensus because a sufficiently large portion of society found them to be a convenient shortcut, and one which also suited their particular world view. Stereotypes refer to people, while myths are institutionalized stereotypes. Needless to say, myths are peopled with stereotypes and together they form a considerable portion of the content of the mass media for very good reasons of economy.

In limited time they are timesaving; in limited space they are space-saving. In a one-minute commercial, the little pictures of the good life in a viewer's head are invaluable assists in creating wants and desires. Network television is full of white hats and the black hats, good and bad personified for the audience in the quaint morality plays that compose most television series. These stereotypes remove the need for time-consuming character development.

Newsmen use stereotypes as a kind of shorthand for their readers, as they fit the fast pace and condensed style of journalism. The headline "Hippies Invade Taos" created a legend of impressions in only three words without saying much at all about what happened. Yet somehow people are deceived into thinking that they know all about it, enough at least to repeat it to a neighbor ("Say, did you see in the paper where the hippies invaded Taos?") and the stereotype passes on through cultural transmission.

Stereotypes are polarized and polarizing. They are either/or, black/white, leaving no room for the shades of middle gray where truth generally lies. Polarizations are simple, requiring little thought. They inhibit understanding and belie truth. Thus, they are dangerous.

Stereotypes are not merely shortcuts to understanding; they are also shortcuts to emotions. "America...love it or leave it" is a shorthand phrase for a highly emotional, reactionary political philosophy. All across the components of the mass media, such emotional stereotyping is common indeed. A headline of "Students Seek Curriculum Voice" and another "Radicals Demand Policy Veto" may easily describe the same event while creating totally different impressions of it. Thus, highly charged, emotional tools are put in the hands of mass communications' gatekeepers for exploitation as they will, whether to further a cause, to sell papers, to attract attention, or to appeal to the known prejudices of their particular audiences. The use of stereotypes may simply reflect the subconscious attitudes of a particular gatekeeper.

Generally, media use of stereotypes and myth is generated by their gatekeepers' views of audience orientation. There is a selectivity to an individual's perception and media consumption that leads him to pay attention to that which agrees with his viewpoints and to neglect, if not ignore, that which disagrees. Furthermore, credibility is far higher for data that reinforces an individual's psyche than for that which is opposed. There operates a process of unconscious acceptance or rejection on the basis of personal stereotypical preferences.

It is this process that leads businessmen to read *Business Week* and eschew the *New Republic* or that leads quasi-intellectuals to read *Harper's* as they eschew *Reader's Digest,* which is as chock full of the middle-American myth as *Harper's* is of liberal myth. In fact, a good case can be made for the fact that it is the degree to which the mass media fulfill the mythology of their particular audiences that determines their relative success in the marketplace.

SECURITY BLANKET

Stereotypes and myths are both useful and exploitable; they form the link between communications and interest; they are an integral part of the process of media selectivity. For the individual they comprise a mental filing system—instructions to the computer as it were—that simplifies his life and orders his decision making. In doing so they clothe him with the accoutrements of the familiar that he can bring to unfamiliar situations without feeling alienated. The late Walter Lippman pointed out:

> A pattern of stereotypes is not neutral. It is not merely a way of substituting order for a great buzzing, blooming confusion of reality. It is not merely a shortcut. It is all of these things and something more. It is a guarantee of our self-respect; it is the projection on the world of our own sense of our own value, our own position and our own rights. The stereotypes are, therefore, highly charged with the feelings that are attached to them. They are the fortress of our tradition and behind its defenses we can continue to feel ourselves safe in the position we occupy.[5]

5. Walter Lippman, *Public Opinion* (New York: The Free Press, 1963).

Integration and Conclusion

Thus, stereotypes also provide a kind of security blanket for the individual in a complicated society. Here is where a major social problem occurs. In a complex society the individual tends to rely too much on stereotypes for his view of the world. As society progresses and new knowledge becomes available and new consensuses are formed, he becomes aware of the tenuous fabric of some of his cherished myths. As he questions them and finds them wanting, he also finds himself deprived of some of the armor to his being. Myth destruction as evidenced today (note the Protestant ethic) leads to frustration and alienation, or to the fabrication of new myths (ecology) to fill the void, for, deprived of his anchors, man is cast loose on a strange and indifferent sea, drifting.

An enigma surrounds stereotypes; they are at once a major source of noise in the communications system and at the same time a baffle to that noise. They offer maximum information for minimum effort, even while they are polarizing. They highlight man's interests and reinforce his prejudices and act as barriers to full understanding while they reassure him of his own role. They are good and bad; they are actually amoral, capable of mammoth distortion for specious purposes; they are the basis for fanaticism. They are also a necessary tool for simplifying life, and an adjunct to creativity by freeing man's mind from the rote and trivial for better application.

So much of mass communications currently and historically has been filled with stereotype and myth that a good deal of cultural absorption, both in heritage and of current values, relies on these shortcuts and rhetoric. Nor is it necessary to separate the wheat from the chaff merely to be aware that they comingle, for the fantasies of stereotype and myth in their ubiquity comprise a sort of reality of their own that has been readily adopted by consensus.

HISTORICAL TRANSMISSION

A mass medium may be judged on the basis of its aggregate effect on its audience. Television, with its tens of millions of simultaneous viewers, is obviously a mass medium. The Colosseum in Rome, standing idle for two millenia, is less apparently so, yet its effect over these thousands of years has been striking. It was the scene, and remains the symbol, of Christian persecution; it was the site of the doctrine of "bread and circuses" as a political expedient. It is indicative of much of the life-style of ancient Rome. There is scarcely a schoolboy who hasn't seen its picture. It is incorporated into the heritage of Western civilization, and unquestionably has had a greater effect on Western civilization as a whole and even on contemporary society than any highly rated, Emmy-winning TV sequence. In a consideration of mass communications, one ought to take them in their entirety in terms of effect on people, as this is, after all, their purpose; their historical perspective ought not be forgotten in a fascination with both electronic technology and with the immediacy of the here and now.

It is this point of history as mass communications that Kenneth Clark makes so well in the BBC's fascinating "Civilisation" series, in which the history of the Western world is traced through its art and architecture. Not only is "Civilisation" a case study in content analysis as it describes the fears, aspirations, and values of different cultures in different eras of mutual history, but it is also an exquisite documentary on how these cumulative values have mutated into the existing one.

The historical effect of prior mass media is further heightened today as it provides content for many of the contemporary mass media. A rash of historical novels and the BBC's production of "Civilisation," subsequently extensively aired in the United States over both PBS and commercial channels are good cases in point. So are the BBC's production of "Elizabeth" and the "Six Wives of Henry VIII." When Sir John Guilgud performs "Hamlet" on television, millions are exposed to the melancholy Dane, reinforcing what they already learned in high school English, and symphony orchestras across the nation bring the musical expression of great composers centuries dead. Television is not the only medium offering examples such as these; they can be heard on radio, seen on film, watched live in concert halls or theaters, or read about in newspapers and magazines as critics evaluate such contributions.

CONTENT ANALYSIS

6. Bernard Berelson, *Content Analysis* (New York: The Free Press, 1952).

More recently, the technique of content analysis, as described by Bernard Berelson, performs for the print and audiovisual media the same function that Kenneth Clark and other critics have performed for the world of art and architecture.[6] Content analysis presumes that the perusal of the mass media of an age will exactly describe that age, its people's habits, work, leisure, relative affluence, and values of all sorts. Content analysis applied to the art and architecture of the Gothic period (its mass media) reveals the intense religious preoccupation of the age. An analysis of newspapers (those of Hearst, Scripps, and Pulitzer) in the late 1890s shows a confident America, flexing its national muscles, sure of itself and proud, ready for the Spanish-American War. Similar analysis of the press—magazines and books—through the first decade of this century reveals a growing concern with social inequality; the writings and the illustrations of the muckrakers told much of social abuse and reflected a determination to correct it.

However, Berelson points out, certainty cannot be assumed in content analysis as to whether the temper of the media reflect the ongoing values of society or whether, since the artist is prophet ahead of his time, the media reflect concerns acted upon in an age yet to come. For example, was American society from 1900 to 1910 all that concerned about social injustice or was it just the muckrakers, with society gradually following? The question is academic. The mass media carried the muckrakers' revelations and complaints, not

Integration and Conclusion

out of any particularly altruistic motive, but rather because they sold copy. There was an audience, a big and profitable audience, for these exposures, so there evidently existed a climate of growing concern. The press, as previously stated, is community; the mass media reflect their age, whether directly (through content), or indirectly (through the fact of their economic existence)—the consumer is producer.

The accelerating development of mass communications has brought an expanded dimension to content analysis. It is possible to get even clearer pictures of an age and culture now than ever before. Historical knowledge of past eras has been painstakingly developed by archeologists carefully digging and meticulously putting the pieces of a broken amphora together as though it were an ancient jigsaw puzzle. Subsequent tablets and temple writings help in giving

Archeologists reconstruct ancient civilizations from artifacts, a content analysis of art and tools.

UPI

verbal description. Later in time, manuscripts came into being and were even more valuable, but printing in this respect also performed a radical service. Considerably more of an age and its interests could be relatively quickly chronicled in books and inexpensively produced, and multiple copies meant that the chances of some surviving for posterity were greatly increased. The gradually increasing numbers and kinds of media in more recent history offer greater opportunity for content analysis to uncover ever broader pictures of an age. Graphics and film, radio and television, video and magnetic tape, and recordings all add to the potential for analysis. For example, today archeologists are not needed to uncover the artifacts of the nineteenth century. The 1897 Sears catalog offers them to all, including

Cultural Transmission

pictures, description, and price; it is a textbook of fashion, homemaking, vocational, and avocational habits of the fin de siecle. How much more so will future generations be able to tell about today's society as they draw upon presidential tapes, Pentagon papers, microfilm libraries, motion pictures, videotapes of TV serials, home movies, computer printouts, NASA records, network logs, Gallup polls, the works of Truman Capote and Harold Robbins, stock market quotations, nearly 2,000 daily newspapers, over 10,000 specialized magazines, psychiatrists tapes, and FBI investigations. For future generations the present record seems so complete that it will be as though they are reliving the last half of the twentieth century.

It is also possible to tell a great deal about an individual author or artist by analyzing his work. His choice of topic reveals his interest, as does the use of certain words and phrases. His likes and dislikes are perhaps revealed through his use of stereotypes; he can be placed on a reality-fantasy scale and the relative level of his sophistication can be determined. There is a branch of communications research dealing in values that, through a study of human institutions, found seven values to be common to all cultures in all times and thus common to man himself. The common values deal with wealth, power, skill, enlightenment, affection, respect, and rectitude. Disciples of this theory believe that the relative incidence of wealth words, power words, and the like in a person's writing or conversation reveals a character profile. Thus, a priest might be expected to use many more rectitude words than a banker, who would in turn use more wealth words than a politician, who would use power words, etc. This is an intense form of content analysis applied to the individual.

Content analysis works in reverse also. It is the individual who lies at the end of all audiences on the continuum, and communications is basically an individual process. Also, there is selectivity involved in media consumption—individuals tend to follow their interests and stereotypes. Thus, it is possible to determine within fairly accurate boundaries what kind of person an individual is if his media habits are known. Media habits include what shows he watches on television, and on which channels; whether he listens to radio and to which stations (news, rock, classical, or sports); what kinds of magazines he buys or subscribes to; what kinds of events he attends, such as concerts or professional football games or both. Though the technique of reverse demographics these media begin to pinpoint what his interests are, what he believes in, his religious affiliation, political party, sex, age, relative affluence, kinds of companions, and many more minutia that contribute to the makeup of a person. Although supposedly self-contained and private, an individual leaves records about his personal life wherever he goes, and media habits are one of the most revealing of these records in that they accurately describe his concerns, attitudes, and interests.

CONTEMPORARY TRANSMISSION

On the short-term contemporary scene, the fact that mass communications is a carrier of the culture is ominous. There is so much offered to the urban American—so much information to be assimilated, so much entertainment—that the mind begins to numb, it all begins to pall, and newer, more violent, and erotic forms of media packaging and content must be developed. The media din pounds in, constantly affecting and reinforcing or modifying the individual's experience and view of the world. Since the pace of events and the media reflecting them is quickened, nearing instantaneousness, people lack the time lag for adjustment to events that they once had. There is a new urgency created by swiftness of dissemination; it steps up the pace of living beyond what Alvin Toffler feels are the individual's psychological limits.[7] A certain faddishness develops as new thoughts and ideas are planted and take root overnight in massive audiences, where they are nurtured and fed back to the mass media, reinforcing themselves until they have run their course and disappear. The stepped-up pace, commercial emphasis, and rising excitement of media, the indolence of vicarious living, the faddishness of new thoughts too quickly seized upon—these are all a part of the cultural transmission of contemporary American media, not on posterity but on the present, the original consumers.

In addition, contemporary media offer a far higher level of information exchange on a far more specialized footing than ever before. This generation is, as a result, more aware, more sophisticated, and, in a sense, more educated than prior generations, and a good deal of this is due directly to the mass media.

There are other effects in contemporary media transmission: society is being homogenized. French is disappearing from the bayous of Louisiana, Yankee accents mellow, and Southerners drawl less. Boots and Stetsons are disappearing from the West, and even in San Francisco people wear fewer hats. This can be attributed to a continuous, long-term effect of radio and television as accents and fashions level out to meet a national mode. This factor alone has led some to condemn the mass media for reducing all to the same common level. But this is not true, for the mass media have a companion effect of fragmenting their audiences. The mass media are so universal and so diverse that now, as never before, a person can pursue his individual bent through the mass media. There is more culture, a range of events, and a variety of interests available to him; he has a choice, many choices, sometimes paralyzing him entirely.

Herein lies another of the paradoxes of mass communications: it is both homogenizing, reducing all to a common mode, and diversifying, fragmenting, offering a greater range of interests and pursuits. The continua show this as they reach simultaneously for ever greater speed and masses, and ever closer to the individual in terms of himself and his interests. It is easier to believe that the mid-nineteenth-century resident of a small midwestern single-newspaper

[7.] Alvin Toffler, *Future Shock* (New York: Random House, Inc., 1970).

town was being homogenized by his media than to feel that today's urban resident is: the contemporary city-dweller is exposed to several newspapers, a dozen radio stations, three networks and a couple of independents; he has access to the PBS, galleries, museums, concerts, opera, drama, professional baseball, football, basketball, hockey, and great libraries of knowledge stored in books and microfilm; he is personally in touch with the world by reliable mail and telephone service; he is capable of visiting any part of it in hours by jet. Of course, the nineteenth-century midwesterner had the grim reality of the physical world at his fingertips—the plow and the pitchfork—while today this is experienced vicariously through the media.

SUMMARY

Mass communication's function in transmitting the culture can be divided into two overlapping categories: historical and contemporary. Historical transmission draws upon the literature, arts, architecture, sculpture, and artifacts of bygone ages, providing a foundation for contemporary experience. The Mona Lisa, the Sistine Chapel, Venus De Milo, the Colosseum, and the Great Pyramid are all mass media of historical times in terms both of their total cumulative audience over the centuries and in their effect on contemporary culture, heritage, and experience.

Education is the mass communications institution compressing and focusing these historical media into manageable proportions and relating them to the present.

These historical instances of mass media gain considerable additional exposure as content of contemporary mass media, such as the BBC's "Civilisation" series and "Hamlet" on television, historical novels, and the like.

Basic to mass communications as a carrier of the culture is man's unique time-binding ability, whereby he can store and sort experience for transmission to future generations, thus assuring that he will progress as a species rather than simply survive. Coupled with this is his ability to deal in abstractions—codes or languages for the transmission of data and experience. The best known of these codes is verbal, both spoken and written language, but there are others: graphics, which has matured through drawing to photography; film; and television. Mathematics is language of increasing significance as a result of the computer and the doors it opens. Music is another language that deals not so much in referential reality as it does in the basic body rhythms that form a part of emotion. Mime, or body and facial expression, may have been the earliest form of communication; however, it became more refined and was translated into drama, where it added a new dimension to storytelling; it, too, has been incorporated into film and television.

Verbal language has two bases—the spoken word and the written word. Despite the fact that they have been married by the invention of the phonetic alphabet, they remain distinct to a degree. This separateness led to the theory of *langue* and *parole,* in which *parole* represents the informal language of the people, and *langue* the more codified, rigid language of writing (legal documents and the like). De Saussure's theory helps to explain how mass communications are at once the conservators of status quo and the vehicles of change. Through *langue,* the formal language resistant to change, mass communications is conservative; through *parole,* language is more readily susceptible to change, and mass communications, language-based, follows suit.

Languages reflect a culture; they reflect the culturally significant and insignificant areas of their respective societies.

In semantics there are denotative words and connotative words. The meaning of connotative words is inexact, lending them to exploitation. They are widely used in advertising and public relations to create a mood in response to the audiences' anticipated reaction.

Stereotypes rely on connotative words for part of their effect. They are the mental pictures of people that are shared by some consensus. Stereotypes and their accompanying myths are economical in that they are a shortcut to understanding, categorizing unfamiliar situations or people. But they are also polarizing, black and white, allowing no middle gray, where truth generally lies. They also may be totally in error, although at one time there was generally sufficient truth to them to lend credibility. A stereotype often lingers on as convenient shorthand after the model had passed away. Stereotypes are also emotion-charged and lend themselves admirably to exploitation and manipulation, particularly by rhetorical communication, which, as opposed to rational, deals in emotions rather than reason. Stereotypes also provide a sort of security blanket to individuals in society by assuring them of their own place and beliefs. Thus, stereotypes are both a part of the semantic noise in mass communications and a baffle to that noise.

Content analysis permits an examination of the mass media of an age in order to learn a great deal about that age. It also permits discovery of a great deal about an individual author or artist. Content analysis can work in reverse also, for by knowing a person's media habits, much is implied about that person and his interests.

Cultural transmission in contemporary mass media is almost overpowering. In one sense it is a homogenizing influence on society; regional accents and distinctive dress tend to disappear. On the other hand, the very diversity of contemporary media leads to a broader expression of individuality and interests than ever before. This is another of the paradoxes of mass communications: it can be both homogenizing and individualizing at the same time.

21 PUBLIC OPINION AND POLLS

THE PRODUCT OF COMMUNICATION

Effect is the product of communication, effect on the individual, separately and collectively. Consequently, public opinion, the aggregate affect, is the product of mass communications.

The formation and change of public opinion is the basic purpose of the persuasion function of media, toward which all advertising and public relations are bent. However, public opinion also seems to arise spontaneously, almost incidentally, in response to events reported in the news. It appears to be latent in the body politic, awaiting only the proper trigger to call it forth. America saw, for example, the massive generation of public opinion on the presidency (resulting ultimately in resignation and disgrace) triggered by Watergate and constantly reinforced by daily television hearings before Sam Ervin's Senate Select Committee. Watergate illustrates another factor in public opinion formation, the role of controversy. Controversy seems to generate public opinion, polarizing it, and, in the fashion of stereotyping, making it easier to handle. When issues are perceived as black and white it is far easier to simply choose a position than to analyze the complexities involved.

Too many scholars and professionals have been deceived by this simplistic explanation of polarized public opinion, overlooking the fact that public opinion is formed and modified not so much by the direct head-on approach provided by the mass media, but rather by interpersonal exchange, word of mouth passed from person to person. In each personal contact data is tested against the knowledge and experience of the individual and subtly modified before it is passed along.

RUMOR: THE FILTERING PROCESS

This filtering process itself, that is, data moving from person to person and constantly being tested and modified in the light of his own knowledge and experience, is further illustrated by an experiment of the U.S. Army. The Army is a closed entity, relatively self-contained, with, in many instances, not too much contact with the outside world. Rumor is important to the Army. Lacking most formal means of communications, scuttlebutt provides an informal, although effective, information source. It is, in fact, the life and breath of the troops. Rumor, which is the ongoing operation of word-of-mouth transmission, was tested in this situation. The Army introduced a number of rumors into troops, battalions, and regiments; some of them were factual, others were false. The Army was astonished to discover that after the first flurry of interest, false rumors tended to die out and were heard no more, while the factual rumors lived on and, amazingly, acquired unto themselves additional factual data that had not been a part of the original rumor. "True" rumors, when the feedback process was complete, were completely factual, considerably enhanced and almost predictive of planned events in their accuracy.

An example illustrates how such accuracy arises. A false rumor is planted that the outfit will ship out to the Aleutian Islands off Alaska. Troops repeat it with excitement. However, one man remembers that the outfit is scheduled for yellow fever shots, out of place for Alaska. Another in the motor pool, notes that the mobile equipment has not been winterized; a medic remembers seeing a large shipment of Atabrine, a malaria preventative, while a supply sergeant notes issues of khakis and mosquito netting. None of these facts indicate a cold climate. Each of these men has doubts he expresses, and the rumor dies away. Another rumor, factual, is introduced saying the division will be sent to Germany; excitement arises. Someone in divisional headquarters notes the assignment of German-speaking advisers to the staff. The supply sergeant sees a shipment of German dictionaries. A regimental clerk sees copies of orders moving the regiment to the Port of New York for staging. A soldier receives a letter from a friend serving in Germany announcing that their outfit has been reassigned stateside. All these random scraps of information embellish the original rumor; they hold up against ten thousand separate experiences. The rumor grows, persists, and it is eventually confirmed that the outfit will indeed be sent to Germany. This is the process of word-of-mouth data transfer, constantly testing and selecting until a valid public opinion is formed.

This process is also the basis of public wisdom. Essentially truth will triumph because falsehoods require compounding falsehoods to support them; in time the cumulative weight becomes intolerable, whereas truth is its own witness. Time is the necessary ingredient

Senator Sam Ervin presides over the televised Watergate hearings and confers with chief counsel Sam Dash. The hearings were both a reaction to public opinion and an instrument in its formation—stimulus and response.

for this informal testing process. Note that in each of these instances rumor was the trigger but public opinion was formed of other data.

The essentiality of time in the rational public opinion formation process has been shortchanged in part by the immediacy of much of today's mass media. Instant public opinion may not be valid since it lacks the tests of individual exchange.

However, a school of thought still persists that credits the mass media with nearly miraculous powers in the molding of public opinion. This is absurd if only because history shows that public opinion existed long before the mass media.

REVERSE EFFECTS

Residually, a naive belief in the stimulus-response (s-r) power of the press lingers on among the very professionals in politics and public relations who ought to know better. This belief maintains that the heavier the advertising—television, radio, newspapers, billboards, mailers, and the like—the better a candidate's chances of election are. Actually, this may do a disservice to the candidate. In one councilmanic election a candidate spent $40,000, a good deal of it on television advertising. He was defeated overwhelmingly by a twenty-five-year-old woman whose campaign funds permitted practically no advertising and no television at all. Actually, television probably contributed to his defeat by giving him exposure. He lisped and appeared uncertain, evidencing little of the kind of dynamic leadership his campaign proclaimed. The people did not like what they saw and

Integration and Conclusion

consequently voted for the woman who was handsome and made sense.

This illustration also points up the fact that the mass media, particularly television, are incomparable in offering broad exposure. However, exposure can be good or bad, accomplishing its intended purpose, or none at all, or the reverse of what was desired. A candidate who stutters and lisps does not benefit from a lot of exposure, and in the example cited, he should have avoided the audiovisual media, particularly in a situation where he was running against so attractive and articulate an opponent.

Another illustration emphasizes this point of reverse effect. In the early 1950s Senator Joseph McCarthy tyrannized America in his witch-hunt for Communists. For as long as he relied on the press for coverage he was on fairly safe ground in that objectivity in the press required reporting without comment any outlandish charge he made. However, his overweening ambition led him to seek television coverage of his hearings. This was his undoing, for the camera showed him as an ignorant bully; his ambition showed through the screen, and America reacted to his ugly image.

There is such a thing as overexposure. People tire and rebel, and politicians must be careful to try to attain the exact mix that keeps them before the public without boring it.

This matter of exposure that the mass media accomplish so well has considerable commercial thrust. It is invaluable in launching a new product. It makes the public aware of the new product's existence. Some will try it out of curiosity. After that the product is on its own. If it is a good product, word of mouth will sustain it; if it is a bad product, no amount of additional exposure will sell it. A certain amount of continuing advertising is required to sustain even a good product, lest consumers forget it. But this constitutes reinforcement of existing opinion and not the creation of new opinion, nor even the modification of old.

The example of the Edsel is classic in this regard. Ford's medium-priced car was launched with an advertising and public relations program involving three agencies and embracing saturation exposure in all media. Everyone heard of the Edsel and a few bought it. However, it was not perceived as a good automobile; it did not live up to the expectations advertising promised. It was regarded as overpriced, and sales slipped to the vanishing point. Ford abandoned the Edsel after a little more than a year, leaving for the record one of the greatest promotional bombs in history. J.A.C. Brown makes the point in *Techniques of Persuasion* that it is impossible through any use of mass media or persuasive manipulation to make people, either individually or collectively, act in any fashion contrary to their basic beliefs or self-interest.[1]

In trivial matters advertising has remarkable powers through the mass media. It constantly introduces and sustains a wide variety of consumer goods that by and large are almost identical. In matters of

1. J.A.C. Brown, *Techniques of Persuasion* (Baltimore, MD.: Penguin Books Inc., 1963).

substance and consequence, however—major expenditures, beliefs, politics, government—the mass media are much less effective in molding public opinion, which seems to rely on a variety of other factors. Most important of all, in order to generate or modify public opinion the substance in question has to bear some relationship to the perceived self-interest of the public. The Watergate scandals were perceived as an issue of substance since most Americans feel they have a vital stake in the presidency.

NO EFFECTS

Some years ago the colleges and universities of Michigan banded together to launch an all-out, all-media public service campaign aimed at publicizing Michigan's institutions of higher learning, their offerings, and their excellence. The campaign lasted six months and utilized newspapers, radio, magazines, direct mail, billboards, embryonic television, drop-in advertisements, specials, speakers' bureaus, and the like. At the end of six months of intensive publicity, a survey was conducted to evaluate the results. These were less than spectacular for, despite all efforts, 15 percent of the adult population of the state still could not name one single institution of higher learning within the state, including the University of Michigan itself. Higher learning at that point in time just did not interest people. There was no apparent self-interest and controversy was not invoked, so the mass media triggered nothing, no latent opinion waiting to surface. The mass media can do little if there is nothing to trigger.

In yet another example, the city of Cincinnati launched a six-month, all-media public service campaign in the late forties attempting to promote a greater awareness of the United Nations and its goals, and specifically trying to encourage a better understanding of UNESCO. In this instance, a public opinion survey was conducted in advance of the campaign as a base against which to measure its effectiveness. Further, the campaign was concentrated within a single city rather than the entire state so that the overall impact might be presumed to be greater. Following six months of intense advertising, public relations, and promotional activity, another public opinion survey was taken. This revealed no perceptible change whatever in the numbers of people aware of the UN, nor any difference in the level of their understanding of UNESCO. The people of Cincinnati were clearly not interested in UNESCO. There was nothing to spark their self-interest, and apparently the maximum level of interest possible had already been attained before the program began. An interesting note is that another public opinion survey was conducted six months after the entire program had been completed. This time some increased awareness of the UN and a slightly higher level of understanding of UNESCO was discovered—enough to be measurable.

The explanation of this phenomenon goes back to Lazarsfeld and Berelson's two-step theory, which holds that the greater portion

2. Paul F. Lazarsfeld et al., *People's Choice: How the Voter Makes up His Mind in a Presidential Election,* 3rd ed. (New York: Columbia Univeristy Press, 1969); Bernard Berelson et al., *Voting: A Study of Opinion Formation in a Presidential Campaign* (Chicago: University of Chicago Press, 1954).

of public opinion formation and modification takes place on a personal level in which the media are little more than catalysts or spark plugs.[2] Furthermore, this opinion change is generated basically by opinion leaders scattered horizontally throughout the social structure who are greater than average consumers of the media. Thus, media impact filters through opinion leaders to reach the larger audiences. In the Cincinnati case, an additional half year was required for opinion leaders to assimilate the basic information from the media and to move it along through their range of casual contacts. It is this time element (noted earlier) that is short-circuited by immediate media. Lacking real interest and drive, such a topic as UNESCO had a very low priority in topics of conversation. It was neither exciting nor controversial, nor was any audience self-interest involved; no amount of advertising know-how could raise it above the level of boredom.

These examples seem to mitigate against the power of the press, the ability of the mass media to manipulate people at will, unless the issue is perceived as insignificant, as in the case of toothpaste or beer, or unless a latent sentiment in the individual or aggregate can be unlocked.

TWO-STEP INFLUENCE

Lazarsfeld and Berelson's studies were conducted within the parameters of national presidential elections, which emphasized the polarizing effect of political campaigns—the forced dichotomy of choice. In each of these instances the lines were clearly drawn between Franklin Roosevelt (D) and Wendell Wilkie (R) in the 1940 election and between Harry Truman (D) and Thomas Dewey (R) in 1948. In each case the entire broad scope of American public opinion had to be compressed into one of two choices. Individual compromises had to be made.

The studies revealed that some people made their minds up very early concerning for whom they would vote and they did not waver from that choice. Democrat or Republican, their choice was anchored in certain psychosociological factors, including their own registration, family and peer influence, previous voting behavior, residency (urban dwellers tended to vote Democratic, rural dwellers Republican), religion (Catholics tended to vote Democratic, while Protestants tended to vote Republican), and socioeconomic status (with the more affluent voting Republican while the less privileged tended to vote Democratic).

Cross pressures were evident: a person with Republican family influences and Democratic peers might be cross-pressured. Cross-pressured people seemed to make up their minds much later and also wavered more in their decisions. Some never voted at all; they could not resolve their cross pressures. The authors also discovered that the people most interested in the election tended to make their minds up reasonably early and never wavered in their choice.

Thus, as election day approached, Lazarsfeld and Berelson found that more and more people were firmly anchored to the candidate of their choice, and that the number of undecideds was gradually decreasing. The late undecideds were also discovered to be the most cross-pressured, the least interested and least informed, the least educated with the least socioeconomic status. This means that in close elections the final decision is made by the most confused, uninterested, and uneducated elements in society, which is, in a sense, a sad commentary on the workings of the political system.

In a study after the election of what had determined the final decision of these last-minute voters Lazarsfeld and Berelson found that it was not the campaign as reflected in the mass media but often a random contact with an opinion leader. People seemed to abdicate their judgment to someone perceived as knowledgeable. These opinion leaders are not necessarily the "establishment" leaders of the community; they exist everywhere—in the classroom, on the assembly line, in the shop. Wherever people get together in groups, there are opinion leaders. One waitress in Erie County finally made up her mind because a customer, a total stranger, was overheard in conversation, and "he looked like he knew what he was talking about"—he was a perceived opinion leader.

GRADUAL CHANGE

In studying the mechanics of opinion change, Lazarsfeld and Berelson also found that it is not an abrupt process. People did not switch their votes from FDR to Wilkie immediately nor vice versa. As they wavered, they moved from the FDR pole to the vast middle undecided ground, and thence to Wilkie. There was always a gradual shift from pole to undecided to the opposite pole; if they were chronic waverers and changed back, they followed the same stepping-stone path in reverse. Thus, in any political situation or in most public opinion situations that tend to polarize, the undecideds are of importance. A candidate does not need to waste time, effort, or money on those firmly committed to him. Nor should he dissipate his resources on those firmly opposed to him, for he cannot convince them. He does far better to concentrate his resources on the middle ground of undecideds, for not only is that where the greatest potential lies, but it is far easier for them to move his way. Consequently, the candidate does well to take a position as close to the middle as he can get since here he stands the greatest chance of attracting the undecideds of differing shades of opinion (those who must reconcile their views into a single choice) without sacrificing any of the votes that are for various reasons committed to him anyway. This concept of the middle ground is well documented in Scammon and Wattenberg's *The Real Majority*.[3]

3. Richard M. Scammon and Ben J. Wattenberg, *The Real Majority: How the Silent Center of the American Electorate Chooses Its President* (New York: Coward, McCann & Geoghegan, Inc., 1970).

INNER INFLUENCES

Lazarsfeld and Berelson's concept emphasizes a factor about public opinion that is contrary to another of the current myths: that is, they contend that people do not generally exercise a free choice based on rational judgments, but rather that they tend to vote and

Integration and Conclusion

form opinions on the basis of their character and the basic stereotypes they hold. People's attitudes, which are the foundation of their opinions, are formed of heredity and environment, parental and peer influences, political stance and socioeconomic status, and perceived self-interest. All of these factors are more or less incorporated into the person and become the building blocks of his reaction to any given event or situation, whether it is a political campaign, the environmental movement, or racial prejudice. Since these inner stances are deeply anchored in the personality or psyche of the individual, not only are they not easily swayed, but they tend to generate high emotion; self-identity is involved. This is compounded by the polarized nature of controversy, which often seems to suspend reason entirely. Consequently, much rhetoric is associated with campaigns, issues, and controversy, which are at base the generators of public opinion.

Thus far public opinion has been discussed as a vague, general entity, national in scope. While there is, of course, a tidal movement to such opinion that occasionally erupts in major issues like Watergate or the quadrennial presidential elections, these instances are relatively few. The level of emotion involved is enervating. An entire people cannot sustain that peak of excitement for an extended period; neither can they return to it too often. Public opinion is generally more circumscribed, restricted to specific issues, often in regional or local areas or pertaining to specific groups.

From the audience continuum it was shown earlier that the basic subdivisions of society itself break down from the "massest" mass audience to publics of various kinds—groups, associations, and crowds—and ultimately to the individual himself, who is the basic opinion holder as he is the basic voter, purchaser, and mass media consumer.

Each of these groups, associations, and publics holds opinions of its own. The process of public opinion formation within these smaller entities is exactly the same as it is on the wider level that Lazarsfeld and Berelson studied. In fact, in Erie County, Ohio, and Elmira, New York, smaller entities were studied that represented the whole; they were microcosms of the nation. These two sites were chosen because at that time they did represent miniatures of the country as a whole.

GROUPS: MEMBERSHIP

It is convenient to examine groups in terms of their purpose and functions, structure, and reactions. Groups are generally, although not always, voluntary in nature; people join them for a purpose because they feel a need. Even when they are involuntary, as in prison, the group provides a social core to which the individual belongs. People join groups for self-interest in order to use the group's social framework for action or to avoid loneliness, to express themselves, to react with others; because they can feel significant as a part of a larger whole or they wish to give meaning to their lives, to avoid the impersonality of life through personal contact, to relax, to advance.

Public Opinions and Polls

In belonging to a group, the individual makes certain sacrifices. He is expected to conform to the mode of the group. In so doing he gives up some of his independence. He is expected to be loyal even when it is contrary to his immediate interest. It is, of course, within such groups, particularly small or primary groups such as the family, that the individual's opinion has the greatest weight. Within these smaller groups, he has the greatest chance of influencing its opinion, and the resultant group opinion is most likely to reflect some compromise with his own.

Group opinions in the aggregate contribute to the makeup of public opinion, but more particularly their collective opinion is likely to have greater weight with the larger and vaguer publics with which that group is, in one way or another, associated. The opinion expressed by a county medical society is likely to have an influence on the subsequent opinion of the American Medical Association, far more so than an opinion of Local 235 of the machinists would. There is a medical allegiance between the local society and the AMA and a commonality of interest and background. It is for these reasons that so much attention in political campaigns is paid to the solicitation of endorsements (the formal expression of opinions for a candidate or against a proposition) in the hope that these stated opinions will influence both the larger entities and, equally, the individual members of the endorsing group, reinforcing their views. Thus, group opinion works both ways: upward toward the larger affiliated publics, and downward toward the individual member.

GROUPS: STRUCTURE

The functions of groups closely parallel the functions of mass communications, which is not surprising since both play significant roles—directly and indirectly—in the formation of public opinion. Whatever the function of a group, it does reflect the interest of its members in varying degrees. Groups are interest-oriented and, as pointed out earlier, many of them participate directly in the mass media mix by publishing their own periodicals, producing their own films, and, in some instances, sponsoring their own radio and television programs.

Groups in their structure are not homogeneous nor particularly cohesive. While united to a certain degree by interest, they are still composed of individuals with widely differing motivations for joining. Furthermore, individuals of various backgrounds and experience, distinct personalities, varying degrees of forcefulness, and different convictions meld their divergent characteristics to form group opinions on a variety of subjects of concern to the group. This jelling process is influenced by the structure of the group.

Groups have a molecular structure with an inner nucleus of dedicated, interested individuals who generally comprise the leadership. These are the opinion leaders noted by Lazarsfeld and Berelson. Opinion leadership and titular leadership within the group do not al-

Integration and Conclusion

Fads are reinforced by peer group pressure and exposure by the media.

UPI

ways coincide. Outside the dedicated nucleus is a group of active participants in group affairs, the workhorses of the group, sometimes aspiring to leadership and status. Beyond them is a peripheral ring of the marginally interested who pay their dues and little more, frequently miss meetings, and sometimes wonder why they joined at all. But a group is not static; these roles change as some marginals drop away and new members join, and as other marginals perk up their activity and interest, and as leadership dwindles away and moves into the active ring. Groups are dynamic, constantly in flux. This means that opinions may also change, for they are a product of the group's interaction, and interactions of different composition will yield different results.

From a practical standpoint, those seeking to influence a group should seek out its leadership—its real and not merely titular leaders—for their endorsement is weighted as memberships defer to their status. It is a common practice in political campaigning and other forms of organized controversy to seek out opinion leaders. In asso-

Public Opinions and Polls

ciations and formal groups the opinion leaders can often, not always, be identified by their presidencies, chairmanships, executive directorships, and so forth; in informal and casual groups they are less obvious and may not be identifiable at all.

GROUPS AS FORUMS

Apart from opinions related to their purpose, groups play an important role in the dissemination process of mass communications. Lazarsfeld and Berelson have indicated the indirect effect of the mass media as it filters through the body politic. Groups provide the forum within which this interchange can take place. It is impossible to describe the kinds of personal contacts people have each day. These contacts are both formal and informal, scheduled and accidental, purposeful and trivial, but they all share the key factor of information exchange between one person and another. Some of these contacts are on a one-to-one basis; others are multiple contacts, as in a classroom or board meeting. They embrace different age levels, different sexes, different socioeconomic stati, different political views. They include the immediate family, co-workers, neighbors, and classmates. They happen in theater queues, on buses, over the department store counter, at the supermarket checkout, in the parking lot, at beauty parlors, on the beach and golf course, at the bowling league or church supper, or on the assembly line. They involve children and parents, the boss and employees, professors and students, ministers and parishioners, secretaries and clients, cashiers and bank tellers, carhops and customers, cabdrivers and garage mechanics. The list is endless, as are the situations in which person-to-person contact can take place. In each of these encounters the talk is of something purposeful or irrelevant and, often, the topic is one generated by the mass media. A person repeats it, relays it, and adds to it his own insights; repeating information is the essential substance of public opinion formation and change. Groups provide the formal or informal setting in which people can exchange their viewpoints. Much of this interchange is totally apart from the purpose of the group. An undercurrent of topical Watergate news pervaded conversations in city council meetings, classrooms, Rotary clubs, veterans' organizations, civic groups, lodge meetings, car dealers' associations, labor unions, and church services all through 1973 and most of 1974, at which time inflation rose to prime position.

THE COCKTAIL PARTY

It is in this light that the cocktail party should be viewed as a mass medium. The cocktail party serves as a channel of current information for groups that have no other reason to interchange and for whom no other medium exists. The guests are generally heterogeneous, representing many different occupations and callings. They bring divergent viewpoints into play; no consensus is generally formed, but a lot of data is exchanged. Further, the conditions, crowds, and alcohol are such as to encourage conversation, and much is said that might not have otherwise been said. Cocktail parties, far from being casual entertainment, serve an extremely useful social purpose in society. This is one of the reasons why they are so prevalent in Washington, the nation's capital. Cocktail parties provide an informal, unrecorded, and unbugged forum where officials of many different levels, political affiliations, and nations can exchange information. They are listening posts and microphones to the grapevine; they offer a flavor of public sentiment on a generally valid although thoroughly unscientific basis. The cocktail party as a medium and social institution ought to be the subject of more intensive study. It illustrates well the role that informal groups play in the dissemination of information and the jelling of public opinion.

This interpersonal exchange of information has been going on ever since man first hesitantly learned to communicate, utilizing the embryonic groups that custom and environment dictated: family, tribe, work situation, hunting party, and the like. Thus, some sort of primitive consensus was reached long before anything approaching mass communications was developed. Mass communications has merely injected greater speed and greater numbers into the public opinion process, as it has into all communication.

REINFORCEMENT

A part of the public opinion process also seems to lie in reinforcement. Little is known of how reinforcement operates, but as people repeatedly hear a viewpoint from many different sources—at home and work, at school, in the ball park, at the bowling league, etc.—they begin to accord a credence to it. Reinforcement of viewpoints appears to emerge as a consensus, and people are sometimes willing to abdicate their own judgment as a result, even if only because it is simpler to do so. In this respect, people seem willing to assign the opinion-leader role to an apparent consensus.

The process of reinforcement is greatly enhanced by the mass media with their rapid ability to repeat and remind and to hammer home. Their time limitations and condensations distort the real consensus, however, which emerges only gradually after the full effect of interpersonal exchange has had an opportunity to run its course. This is to say that the immediate first reaction of public opinion generated by the mass media may not be the eventual public opinion at all.

In a number of California ballot propositions public opinion polls have shown as much as 65 or 70 percent of the people favoring one stance, while four to six months later on election day, the final results were almost exactly reversed. In July 1968 nearly 70 percent of the voters in a statewide poll seemed to favor the Watson Initiative, a complicated and hasty tax reduction measure. In November the voters defeated it by a margin of almost two to one. The intervening period had been one of spirited campaigning on both sides in which all aspects of the issue were explored and in which the measure's numerous shortcomings had been exposed. This nearly five-month period was sufficient for the interpersonal word-of-mouth dissemination process to take place as a real consensus developed. The fact that it was a highly controversial issue, of course, both sparked interest and polarized opinion.

In another highly emotional and controversial issue in 1972, voters in a February poll seemed to favor an environmental initiative by about 65 percent. However, when the ballots were counted after the June primary election, voters had defeated it by about 65 percent as its inherent weaknesses had become apparent.

In the 1972 general election the Coastal Initiative, designed to protect California's coastline from undue commercial development, was endorsed by July voters by about 60 percent. They upheld this opinion in the November election by about 55 percent. In this instance the initial appeal of the initiative seemed to stand up against testing and retesting in the interpersonal forum of public opinion formation.

Considering the initial impact of the mass media and the time lag necessary for regular person-to-person interaction to take place, reinforcement constitutes an argument for protracted campaigning that offers an opportunity for both sides to expose all arguments, pro and con, and for the public to examine these arguments through interpersonal contact, individually and through groups. Further, the nature of political campaigning, as seen earlier, is close to the libertarian ideal that, while it has some shortcomings, is designed and almost guaranteed to expose all aspects of a controversy.

MEASURING PUBLIC OPINION

It is easier to measure public opinion than to define it or describe how it operates. But even in measuring it there are a number of pitfalls. Public opinion changes, sometimes rather rapidly. The public is fickle, swayed as by many unknown factors. Therefore, a public opinion poll is valid only for the moment when it is taken. Sometimes public opinion alters so rapidly that a poll is invalidated by the time the results are compiled and tabulated. George Gallup, in *The Sophisticated Poll Watcher's Guide*, compares a poll to a single frame in a motion picture of public opinion that rolls continuously on.[4] The computer has assisted public opinion polling through its ability to instantly compile and tabulate masses of data, shortening the time between when a poll is taken and when its results are published. As an example, several polls were taken just prior to the 1948 presidential election between Harry S. Truman and Thomas A. Dewey. All agreed that Dewey would be elected by a considerable margin. However, when the ballots were counted, Truman was victor by an almost exact reversal of the polls' percentages. The explanation lies in the fact that the polls were taken about ten days prior to the election, and required a week to compile and tabulate by hand. By the time the results were published, public opinion had changed to strongly support Truman.

4. George Gallup, *The Sophisticated Poll Watcher's Guide* (Princeton, N.J.: Princeton Opinion Press, 1972).

Integration and Conclusion

Thus, the timing of a poll is of extreme importance, and unless this information is given as a part of the poll, it is worthless. Furthermore, anyone interested in the results of a poll should be constantly aware that at best it is a guide to what the public is thinking on the basis of what it once thought. Consequently, the best use of polls is one of "trending," or taking a series of polls on the same topic at regular intervals in order to gauge the direction in which public opinion is moving and by how much.

There are two kinds of polls. There are those that measure public opinion, such as the ratings for television and political polls assessing candidates' relative strength. There are also those that attempt to describe public opinion, trying to uncover what the public thinks about an issue, or a product, or a candidate.

STEPS IN POLLING

There are basically four steps to poll taking. First is determining the questionnaire; second, choosing the sample; third, analyzing the results; and fourth, interpreting this data. A poll can be distorted during any one of these steps, which is why polls are such tricky devices and are to be regarded with extreme caution.

Polling questions are framed with great care. They must be simple and readily understood. They must be explicit, using denotative words and leaving no room for misunderstanding. There should be a limited number of them. Once framed, the questions are generally pretested; that is, they are asked of a very small sample to be certain that the answers are the kind of responses being sought and that they mean the same thing to the respondents as they do to the pollsters. Obviously, polls may be biased in the questions asked. A question such as "Don't you think our corrupt congressman is doing a terrible job?" tends to lead the respondent; whereas "How would you rate our congressman's performance: good, fair, or poor?" is more likely to elicit a reasoned response. Consequently, knowledge of the exact questions asked is important in determining a poll's accuracy.

In polling, the sample itself is one of the most difficult things to select and to understand. The sample is a microcosm of the whole, a significant fraction of the universe being studied. The size of the sample is not nearly so important as its construction. For example, if a sample is to be valid for a city it must be composed in the same demographic ratio as the city as a whole. This is to say that there must be the same percentages in the sample as there are in the city of whites, blacks, browns, reds, and yellows; of males and females; of children, youth, the mature, and elderly; of high, low, and in between socioeconomic stati; of Democrats, Republicans, and Independents; of Protestants, Catholics, Jews, agnostics, and so forth. This leads to establishment of a quota poll. In this type of poll interviewers are asked to talk to so many Jews, so many blacks, so many women under forty, so many union members, and so forth. The quota system is rarely used anymore except in cases where a polarized contrast is desirable (as in comparing the preferences of age groups, sex-

Public Opinions and Polls

es, etc.). The fallacy of quotas arises from two basic causes. First, interviewers asked to interview a number of blacks, for example, are more likely to try to find them in comfortable suburbs or central business districts rather than going into the ghettos, which could be a painful experience for them. Thus, the interviewers bias the poll's results in that the black opinion sampled is far more likely to reflect an establishment viewpoint than that encountered in the seething slums, which, in turn, is far more likely to reflect a balanced overall black opinion. Second, in establishing quotas, it is too easy to overlook a crucial demographic factor. For example, a poll on food preferences that neglected ethnic origins would omit a major factor.

A poll can be biased by the sample choice. A political poll conducted in heavily Irish-Catholic greater Boston would yield far different results than the same poll conducted in archconservative Orange County, California. Pollsters who want to obtain a given result have only to choose that element of the population likely to hold those opinions and publish the results. If, for example, a pollster wanted results showing that America was demented, he need but sample a few hundred mental patients.

THE RANDOM SAMPLE

The random sample is the preferred method used in most polling. Here, every fiftieth, every thousandth, or every ten-thousandth person in the universe population is sampled, and everyone has an equal opportunity to be chosen. Ordinarily, this is done by residency, since everyone lives somewhere. Thus, if every tenth person in every tenth precinct is selected, a broad overview of the population as a whole—by sex, color, religion, partisan preference, socioeconomic status, age, education, employment, and the like—will be included. But it must be every tenth person in every tenth precinct; if that person cannot be found, the pollster must keep trying until he or she is found. Only the randomly selected substitute can be used, not the ninth person or the eleventh person.

The bias in polling a badly chosen sample can be seen in the classic story of the *Literary Digest.* In the 1936 presidential election between incumbent Franklin Roosevelt and Alfred Landon, Republican governor of Kansas, the *Literary Digest* took a nationwide poll using a random sample of enormous size. When tabulated, the poll showed Governor Landon an easy winner and gave Republicans heart. However, FDR won that race by the greatest landslide in American history, carrying even Landon's home state of Kansas. The *Literary Digest,* anxious to find out what went wrong, discovered that it had used telephone books as the basis for its random sample. To be listed in a telephone book required a telephone, which, in the depression period of 1936, was a near luxury. Phones were far more likely to be possessed by the relatively affluent who were, in turn, far more likely to be Republican. Consequently, that choice of sample carried its own built-in bias.

The random sample technique can be applied to any population. Every twentieth name on the registrar's roster of a large university with an enrollment of 30,000 will yield a sample of 1,500, which is an exact cross section of that university's student body—with freshmen, sophomores, juniors, seniors, graduate students, males and females, diversified majors, athletes and bookworms, swingers and radicals—proportionately represented. Every hundredth name from the voter registrar's list of Democrats in a middle- to large-sized city will give a sample of Democratic opinion of all shades, balanced by age, sex, occupation, ethnic origin, socioeconomic status, religious preference, residency, education, and so forth. In surveying a metropolitan area of about one million, every twentieth person in every twentieth precinct will result in a sample of around 1,500. Precincts are used not in their voting connection but as convenient geographical subdivisions of the metropolitan area; this means that every twentieth residence—home, condominium, apartment, or duplex—is surveyed and not every twentieth registered voter. Such a technique provides a demographically valid grid of the area.

SAMPLE SIZE

This introduces the matter of sample size. A sample of 1,500 is considered adequate for most polling situations regardless of the overall size of the universe population. Television ratings are based on a sample of 1,500 homes randomly chosen throughout the nation. It is sometimes difficult to understand why the same size sample is sufficient for a town, or a county, or a state, or the city of New York, or the nation as a whole. Often people assume that the larger the universe, the larger the sample ought to be. This is not so. For instance, if a chef in a hotel has two pots of pea soup cooking, a large one and a small one, he needs only the same small spoonful from each to determine their taste. Or, if there is a small jar containing one hundred jelly beans—fifty red and fifty yellow—and there is another jar containing 10,000 jelly beans—5,000 red and 5,000 yellow—and each jar is thoroughly mixed, a single handful from either jar should yield equal numbers of red and yellow jelly beans. Once a certain size is reached, the addition of more respondents does not basically effect the validity of the poll.

However, all public opinion polls are subject to statistical error. A sample of 1,500 will give a statistical error of around a plus or minus 2.5 percent. This is accurate enough for most purposes except very close elections. A sample of six hundred gives a plus or minus 4 percent statistical error, which means a total spread of eight percentage points; this is not acceptable. However, a sample of 2,400 offers a built-in error of plus or minus 2 percent; 5,600 will give a 1.6 percent error, and over 11,000 still gives a plus or minus 1 percent statistical error. Thus, drastically increasing the size of the sample does not correspondingly reduce the statistical error. Pollsters, therefore, have to balance the economics of polling against the relevance of statistical error. As it costs in the neighborhood of twenty dollars per interview for a poll, including the wages of trained interviewers, their travel, the time spent interviewing, question construction and testing, computer time for tabulating the results, and professional time for analyzing and interpreting the printout, a 1,500 poll giving a 2.5 percent error costs $30,000. Increasing its size to 2,400 at a cost of around $50,000 reduces the statistical error by only .005. Polls of close elections (and there have been a number of them lately) are likely to be affected by this statistical error. For example, if the polls show candidate A winning by 51 percent to candidate B's 49 percent, and there is a plus or minus 2.5 percent statistical error, the data may easily be reversed with candidate A having only 48.5 percent of the vote, and candidate B winning with 51.5 percent. Thus, polls in close elections can tell little more than that the election will be close.

POLLSTERS

Public opinion polling by such reputable organizations as those of George Gallup, Louis Harris, Field Enterprises, and the California poll is fairly reliable within limitations. It is a valuable tool in advertising and public relations, almost a necessity in modern political campaigning for testing campaign effectiveness, and indispensable to television network programming. However, there are many disreputable polls capitalizing on public ignorance and fascination. Some of these are the result of pure incompetence. Some use old lists that are largely invalidated because around 15 percent of the population changes residence each year; a list that is two years old is likely to have a third of its names useless. And sometimes clients contract for polls yielding desired results. Poll slanting can be accomplished readily by the use of leading questions, biased samples, generous interpretation, and selective use of the data to be tabulated. For these reasons, the National Council on Published Polls, established in 1968, has set standards for polling that should be included in the poll itself.[5] These are: a description of the sample, the method used in reaching the sample, the size of the sample, the exact wording of the questions, the time of the interviews, and the sponsor where appropriate.

5. Ibid.

Published polls are generally commissioned by the mass media themselves because of public interest in results of election campaigns and current opinion on significant issues. Poll results are a form of news for which the media pay. George Gallup syndicates his monthly poll and releases it as feature material to newspapers, radio, and television subscribers. Other polls are commissioned by utilities, banks, industries, all levels of government, politicians, labor unions, and the like to take the public pulse on matters of sponsor interest. These privately commissioned polls are not likely to be released unless the results are favorable in some fashion to the sponsor. They are generally used as guides to action. The greatest poll of all, of course, is the U.S. Bureau of Census' decennial census, which de-

Integration and Conclusion

scribes the population of the United States. Another major pollster is the Department of Labor, which, utilizing a sample of 50,000, is able to figure the unemployment rate monthly to a fraction of plus or minus .001. Gallup publishes the *Gallup Opinion Index* each month, available in libraries, which summarizes the results of his surveys on major issues in the nation. Thus, anyone interested in learning the significant issues of times gone by and what people thought about them need only go to the reference desk.

KINDS OF POLLS

There are different methods of polling; all have some liabilities and some assets. A telephone poll is the cheapest and quickest; costs run at about $10 per interview and for many purposes this method may be adequate. However, many people resent being intruded upon and refuse to talk. There is the matter of timing in telephone polls: different kinds of people are going to be reached at different times of day. There is a problem in that telephone polls must use a very limited number of questions requiring extremely simple answers (generally "yes," "no," and "I don't know"). However, phone polls have proven useful in getting immediate data, such as the overnight ratings in New York for a new television show. Because of their lower relative cost, they are also used extensively for trending in political campaigns.

Mail polls have a problem in returns. It takes time to fill out a questionnaire, and busy people are not likely to take that time. Furthermore, there are a considerable number of people who are intimidated by forms and refuse to fill them out. Finally, returns from a mail poll are going to come from three elements of the population in disproportionate numbers: housewives and the elderly because they have the time to fill out forms, and those particularly interested. Thus, a mail poll carries its own built-in bias. If this is recognized and corrected statistically, it will not invalidate the poll. Another problem with mail polls is the huge number of questionnaires that must be mailed in order to receive back a valid sample. Allowing an average return of 2 percent, this means that at least 75,000 questionnaires must be mailed to get 1,500 back. This, too, runs into money.

The most valid means of polling is the personal interview taken from a structured questionnaire. In these polls, however, two other factors creep in. Respondents are apt to fib to the interviewer either to please him, giving the answers they think they ought, or to enhance their own self-image, saying, for instance, that they read the editorials and foreign news in the newspapers when they really read the comics and sports page. Some pollsters have found that disguising the purpose of the interview is likely to give more valid results. A respondent who thinks he is answering questions about refrigerators for General Electric is more likely to give honest answers to incidental questions about Cheverolets for General Motors.

POLLING PROBLEMS

There are two final problems to public opinion polling. First, polling itself tends to force answers. People feel embarrassed if they do not have an opinion on an issue. They are reluctant to show their ignorance to the interviewer, so they invent opinions, fabricating them on the spot. These are scarcely valid opinions, but they count equally in the computer with other opinions sincerely held, and there is no way to weigh them.

This leads to another problem. Polls deal in percentages, in numbers, in digits. Opinions are held by people and the opinions of all people are not equal. There are opinion leaders, and there are people whose dynamic personalities and personal aggressiveness lead them to have more influence in society than their fellows. Their opinions in any realistic scale should be weighted, while the opinions of those who are followers should count for proportionately less since they are easily influenced by the others. Public opinion polling cannot take this into consideration. It counts the opinion of leader and follower as equal in the sample. Since each member of the sample represents 100, 1,000, 10,000, or 10 million people in the population, this distortion is likely to affect the validity of the poll; the poll cannot tell which of its respondents was an opinion leader and, therefore, cannot reflect how that particular opinion is quite likely to have greater weight as the continuing process of public opinion formation and change goes on in society.

A pitfall to be recognized is that while polls are an extremely useful tool, facilitating commerce, communications, politics, and government, too great a reliance on them is likely to prove self-defeating. If the polls are used to discover what people want, for example, manufacturers are likely to provide them just those things, foregoing any effort at experimentation, which leads both to improvement and diversity. Since polls are an anonymous averaging, they can have a very homogenizing influence. Their use in politics and government could lead to elected officials seeking to pander to the consensus to assure reelection rather than exercising their own judgment. Carried to its logical conclusion, a total reliance on polls plus the perfection of their techniques and the development of more sophisticated computers could obviate the need for senators, congressmen, councilmen, aldermen, or assemblymen, for any issue could simply be taken directly to the people by instant polling techniques, and the elected official would become no more than an unneeded middleman.

SUMMARY

Effect is the end product of communications, and public opinion is the product of mass communications.

Public opinion existed in ancient times long before the mass media. Contemporary mass media have greatly accelerated the public opinion process to the point that they sometimes short-circuit the time-consuming process of public opinion formation as information moves from individual to individual in society in an interpersonal word-of-mouth exchange.

Public relations and advertising are greatly concerned with public opinion; it is their stock-in-trade. They seem to be most effective, however, in promoting trivial matters and introducing new products rather than in altering opinions on matters of substance.

Public opinion sometimes arises more or less spontaneously in reaction to events reported in the news, and it is the interaction of these events, like the Watergate scandals, that seems to jell public opinion. In this, public opinion is polarizing, born of controversy.

To a large degree, the power of the press to mold public opinion is nonexistent. The press can trigger latent sentiments, but public opinion depends on many factors beyond just the mass media. The mass media are, however, unexcelled in creating awareness of an issue or product and are useful in reinforcing existing opinion.

Much of what is known about public opinion comes from Lazarsfeld and Berelson's two-step theory of communications, which identified the existence of certain natural opinion leaders located horizontally through all elements of society. These opinion leaders are greater-than-average consumers of mass media, and they filter their opinions along to acquaintances who defer to their perceived leadership.

Groups play a significant role in public opinion formation. It is in the group that the individual finds his greatest influence in the opinion-making process. Group opinion reinforces and is reinforced by his own due to inherent loyalties. Also, groups have influence on the larger publics of which they are sometimes a part. More particularly, however, groups provide the forums for the process of interpersonal exchange to take place.

There is a reinforcement aspect to public opinion formation also; as a similar opinion is heard from many varying sources, it acquires a presumed consensus.

The immediacy of the mass media encourage a certain amount of faddishness in dress, custom, and life-style that, like rumor, may live awhile in a flurry of initial curiosity and excitement and then will either survive or die, depending on how public opinion views it over the long-term.

Public opinion can be measured better than it can be defined. There are, however, certain pitfalls to public opinion polling. Polls are valid only for the moment they are taken and can, in fast-moving situations, be invalid by the time they are published. The best use of polls is that of establishing trends that show the direction public opinion is moving and comparatively by how much. Polls can either measure or describe public opinion. Measurement polls are used for television ratings and political campaign standings. Description polls attempt to paint a picture of the public attitude on an issue.

There are four basic steps to polling: (1) framing the questionnaire; (2) selecting the sample; (3) tabulating the data; and (4) analyzing the results.

The sample is a microcosm of the whole; it must be exactly representative of the larger universe. This can be accomplished in two ways: through use of the demographic quota or the random sample. The quota system is tricky since it becomes unwieldy in practice, and also because it is too easy to overlook or not consider a significant demographic factor. The random sample is based on the theory that everyone within a universe population has an equal opportunity to be selected.

Sample size is not significant beyond a certain point. A sample of 1,500 is considered adequate for most situations, regardless of size of universe. Sample size does, however, affect the built-in statistical error. A sample of 1,500 holds this error to a plus or minus 2.5 percent. Larger samples are extremely costly, and do not reduce the statistical error correspondingly.

Polls can be taken by phone, which is less costly and time-consuming than other methods, but it is difficult to achieve a proper sample. Mail polls require enormous mailings to achieve an average of 2 percent for returns, yielding a necessary sample of 1,500. Also, they tend to be biased in favor of women, the elderly, and the interested. Interviewing, while slow and costly, is also the most valid polling method, although adequate results can often be obtained from other means.

Certain problems are inherent in polling. Polling tends to generate opinions where none existed, and these instant opinions are not always valid even though they are counted equally by the computer. Also, polling cannot distinguish between those whose opinions are going to have the greatest weight in the public opinion formation process.

Finally, too great a reliance on polling is likely to lead to an overly homogenized society.

22 CROSSROADS

OTHER FACTORS, OTHER PLACES, OTHER TIMES

1. Marshall McLuhan, *Understanding Media* (New York: Signet Books, 1966).

This concluding chapter will examine some factors of mass communications that have been alluded to in passing but not broken out for scrutiny. They include mass communications research, such as it is, the status and prognosis of mass communications in other nations, and finally some speculation about the future of mass communications. These factors are all interrelated for, obviously, mass communications research will have a bearing on the future. As the world shrinks through the application of improved mass communications techniques, more and more mass communications in other nations will begin to have a bearing on those in the United States. This, of course, is the "global village concept" as put forth by Marshall McLuhan.[1] Finally, it is the decisions about mass communications made in this decade that will irrevocably affect the course of mass communications for the future. An example from the past illustrates the effect of such decisions: the passage of the Stamp Act by England in the eighteenth century placed a tax on newspaper pages. Publishers were quick to adopt the largest page size possible in order to minimize the tax. Page size was restricted by the flatbed press. Despite the technological improvements in the centuries since, newspapers still adhere to that eighteenth-century page size, despite its unwieldliness, partially because of economic commitment to investments in presses of that size and the accoutrements to serve them, and partially out of tradition and habit. A decision made for timely reasons nearly three hundred years ago has affected the present beyond any usefulness. In today's highly technical and more complex society, inadvertent decisions made for expediency or profit are bound to affect future generations in many unsuspected ways. Inadequate research today will seriously limit the kinds of future options available and force lasting decisions to be made on the basis of minimal information. As America's mass communications influence extends through the rest of the world, these decisions will affect not only this society but others. Even today, the American influence carried abroad by television and film, by foreign language editions of major magazines, by exported art forms and translated books, and consistently fed by the ubiquitous wire services is having an Americanizing effect that some welcome and others bitterly resent.

The export volume of this mass communications from the United States constitutes a sort of communications imbalance of trade that does not permit nearly so significant an amount of mass communications in all its forms from the rest of the world to be imported here. Further, the competition for attention already generated by America's mass media fairly well precludes much public reception of the limited foreign quantities available, such as translations of foreign books, occasional foreign films, and a smattering of foreign magazines. Finally, a language barrier inhibits much United States consumption of foreign media except from the English-speaking countries. United States mass communications dominance extends to language also, to the extent that a good deal of the world has learned English, whereas, smug in their dominance, few Americans have bothered to become conversant in a foreign tongue.

USIA-USIS

To this barrage of mass communications export the United States Information Agency (USIA) has been added, which, through its field offices abroad in the United States Information Service (USIS), attempts to develop a greater awareness and understanding of the principles and goals of the United States. The record of the USIA since its inception in 1948 has hardly been spectacular. The reasons behind its apparent failure make a good case study and a good argument for caution in the application of contemporary American mass communications abroad.

A part of the USIA's problem has been one of goal definition. Started as a propaganda agency, it dealt in persuasion; it evolved into applied international public relations. The crux of the agency's problem arose in choosing which of two roads to follow: whether to adopt a hard-sell approach as an adjunct to United States foreign policy, or a soft-sell approach in which it simply attempted, through informational techniques, to illuminate the United States, its history, its people, its dreams. With each change of administration in the intervening years, the USIA's mission has swung between these two extremes with the net result of creating a certain amount of confusion within other nations.

Its next hurdle lay in the fact that the most underdeveloped nations (oftentimes the ones who needed some understanding of the United States most) did not reflect the relative social and economic homogeneity of the United States with its equality and large middle class. Other nations tended to have a small, wealthy aristocracy (whether called that or not) wherein all power and wealth were concentrated, and a huge, impoverished, illiterate lower class. Representatives of the USIS thus had to decide with which of these mutually exclusive factions to ally. If they allied with the establishment, they had access to whatever mass communications network the nation offered; they had the support of the necessary governmental agencies; and, finally, life was much more amenable. But their allegiance with the establishment automatically cut them off from association with the lower classes, where the greatest potential lay. This is a factor of some importance considering the unstable nature of many underdeveloped governments, and the fact that coups d'etat (overnight revolutions) change the power structure instantly. If, on the other hand, the USIS allied with the underprivileged, they could expect no assistance and considerable harassment from the power structure. They had no access to mass media; they faced deportation and were likely to be contrary to American foreign policy at the time. Basically, they were in a "damned if they do, damned if they don't" situation.

The third crucial factor confronting the agency, regardless of social allegiance, was that they were using generally sophisticated, twentieth-century public relations techniques developed on these shores, inextricably married to concepts of democracy, free enterprise, and the golden rule. These techniques, furthermore, had evolved after decades of experimentation with mass media usage and took full advantage of an accelerating technology. In essence, American representatives were making use of modern tools, developed in the United States for its own unique purposes, and trying to apply them to nations that were living 150–200 years in the past, that did not as a part of their culture believe in democracy or capitalism, and that were often non-Christian. It is small wonder then that these techniques did not work particularly well. What appeared as virtues to Americans seemed weaknesses to others, and what was odious to the American was often the accepted native way of doing things.

Finally, the greatest shortcoming of all was the fact that the USIA did not operate in a vacuum. It was only one of a number of American influences at work, and a relatively minor one at that. There was, of course, the constant import of United States films; in major cities there was television, of which the principal content was old United States movies and serials. The urban dweller was far more likely to be exposed to gangster movies and western gun fights than he was to the agrarian documentaries found in the USIS libraries. Then there were United States products—Coca Cola, for example—and their supporting advertising. American cigarettes are like currency in most countries, as are American soaps and chocolates, and the USIS had nothing similar to offer. Finally, in varying degrees there were tourists. The Ugly American syndrome arose as too

The USIS often faces a difficult public relations job in offsetting negative American exposure abroad.

often American travelers abroad painted horrid pictures of themselves and, by implication, the nation. Operating in competition with all these factors, the USIS has done a remarkable job, if only in surviving. This communications paradox is well summed up by Harry Skornia in *Television and Society*:

> The materials distributed abroad by the Voice of America are scrutinized and criticized by many congressional committees. Yet they are heard and seen by only a fraction of the people who daily view and hear programs from United States commercial broadcasters whose materials are not subject to review. The effect of the Voice of America and the rest of the United States Information Agency effort seems to be vitiated by such materials. The Voice of America shows aspects of United States life which are intended to generate respect, admiration, and emulation of our Democratic political system in other nations. For United States television networks and film companies to inundate these same nations with programs which do the opposite appears inimical to our total national objectives.[2]

2. Harry Skornia, *Television and Society* (New York: McGraw-Hill, 1965).

Integration and Conclusion

Overseas sales of old television shows and commercial movies provides a substantial revenue source to the networks, packagers, and distributors of films and programs, against whose volume the Voice of America provides but a cry in the wilderness.

ENGLAND

The British Broadcasting Company (BBC) in England was established in the early twenties as an independent governmental agency to provide radio broadcasting. The United Kingdom opted for an opposite ideal from the United States, which recognized the commercial sovereignty of broadcasting. The BBC strove for a reasonably high level of cultural programming, providing classical music, news, intellectual discussions, how-to-do-it programs, and the like. People listened because there was nothing else, fulfilling the least objectionable program concept. However, by the mid-thirties, Radio Luxemburg and a number of "pirate ships" anchored just outside England's territorial waters were providing commercial programming similar to that of the United States, complete with advertising spots and sponsorships. These programs catered to the lowest common denominator.

By 1953 the impact of television and the multiplicity of television pirate ships, plus a hard-sell public relations campaign in England conducted by J. Walter Thompson, resulted in the licensing of a commercial television channel. Today, that channel provides just about the same level of programming as the nets do here, and it attracts the major proportion of the English audience, while the stately BBC carries on with its cultural emphasis without commercials and reaps smaller ratings. However, the BBC should not be discounted entirely, for it has provided such hits for American television as "The Forsythe Saga," "Elizabeth," "The Six Wives of Henry VIII," "Civilisation," and, ironically, James Fenimore Cooper's "Drums Along the Mohawk." In fact, it is producing exactly the kind of spritely cultural programming that was visualized for PBS, and which may one day come about if adequate financing is obtained and a clear course is charted for it.

Thus, England began its broadcasting as a government monopoly financed by a surtax on the sale of radios and televisions, and has more recently developed a dual system that includes commercial broadcasting. There seems room for both in the audience mix. In the United States the opposite is true. Broadcasting began as a purely commercial operation, and has now moved to a dual system that includes the infant PBS, still suffering from growing pains.

In the United States, government is all but voiceless. It has no real mass medium of its own but is reliant upon the commercial networks and private publishers to carry its message. In broadcasting, government information is subject to the same criteria as all other offerings in a severely time-limited medium, and it usually does not make it. In print, government data is always subject to interpretation, assuming it gets by the gatekeepers (where it does not have a particularly high priority). Even when television time is preempted for the President, his remarks are subject to the instant analysis about which Spiro Agnew so eloquently complained. In an increasingly complex society, more and more governmental regulation affects more and more people; agencies exist to serve those whose existence is unknown. A public channel could serve a real need.

Japan has an extremely effective public broadcasting system, a Gift from the United States during the post–World War II occupation; it is financed by the same sort of set tax that England uses. It is ironical that the United States could devise such a needed system for another nation, and yet be incapable of developing PBS at home. The set tax may not be a particularly attractive answer to the financing problem in America, but then neither is congressional appropriation, always too little and too insecure. A better answer might easily be to finance it in part from the revenues of COMSAT or INTELSAT or, lacking that, to give pican (public interest, convenience, and necessity) credits by the FCC to commercial broadcasters for cash or kind contributions to PBS in lieu of the public service spots, they now carry in the wee, small hours. A working PBS could then carry the PSAs, which would fit far better into its format and could have a larger audience than they acquire now in the Sunday cultural ghetto or in the early morning slots.

JUSTICE AND POLITICS

There are other media differences between the United Kingdom and the United States. Earlier the conflicts between the First and Sixth Amendments and between press freedom and the right to a fair trial were noted. England has resolved this problem in favor of the fair trial. The mass media in England are precluded from any comment whatever on a trial in progress. They are permitted to note initially the arrest of a subject, his name, and the charges against him, and that is all. Commentary after the trial is permitted, but not until then. Nor do the English feel that any of their basic rights have been placed in jeopardy by this tradition.

On the political scene, the English work by different rules than Americans. General elections are held whenever the opposition party feels it has the strength to muster a "no confidence" vote; then the issue is taken to the people to resolve. A general election must also be held after a party has been in office for five years. There is no presidential election. The chief of state is the prime minister, who is elected by the majority of the members of the House of Commons from their number, and who serves until the next general election, however called. Only a three-week period lapses between the calling of an election and the election itself. Since there are no national candidates, there is no need for national elections. Campaigning is done individually in the districts of the individual members of parliament (MPs). Newspaper advertising is permitted, but no broadcast advertising whatever. The two or three major partisan leaders are permitted time on BBC for debate at no cost to themselves. Thus, the British have also answered the problem of skyrocketing campaign costs. However, this has been accomplished at the expense of the all-out, no-holds-barred kind of long-term battle, which assures that all aspects of all issues will be thoroughly investigated and aired by election time. It is useless to speculate on which system is preferable. England has her system; America has her own; both are the products of different cultures and traditions.

England has a national press; America does not. America was founded as a series of isolated pockets of colonists, and thus a local tradition was formed early, continuing to the present. England was essentially an integrated nation, or rapidly becoming one, when the Mayflower first sailed. Consequently, its press tradition is national. Its newspapers, despite their names—the *Times* of London, the *Manchester Guardian*—circulate nationally, which is not at all difficult to do on an island that measures less than six hundred miles from tip to tip and only about three hundred miles at its widest point. Because the permeation of the "telly" is not as great as in the United States—where there is greater affluence and leisure—the English are more reliant on their newspapers, as Americans used to be. Consequently, there are more newspapers in England per capita than in America reflecting differing political viewpoints; many, unlike the stately *Times,* engage in the tabloid sensationalism that characterized the American press of the Roaring Twenties.

OTHER NATIONS

In France a plenitude of political parties assures, among other things, that any government elected will be a minority government since the popular vote is split so many ways. The Gaullist years were an exception. Consequently, effective government is formed by sometimes shaky coalitions of differing parties and will survive only so long as the participants of the coalition find it expedient. This means that there is a plethora of national newspapers, each reflecting a differing view on the political spectrum, and often openly subsidized by the faction it supports. In this the French press is close to the subsidized press of the early nineteenth century in America, and reflects about the same tone of political vilification. In France a journalist is equated with a political campaigner.

France's broadcasting is also government controlled with commercials limited to certain periods. This provides a bonus to the party or coalition in power at election time—as de Gaulle demonstrated. The frequent change of governments, however, constitutes a strong argument for a diminished power of the press.

Government broadcasting in Italy restricts commercials to solid blocks of four hours on Saturday mornings. Surprisingly, this has turned out to be among the most popular programs on the air, a case of vicarious window-shopping at one's leisure. It also runs counter to the popular myth that audiences merely tolerate commercials as a necessary evil. The point has been made that many of today's commercials are superior to programming in production excellence, humor, taste, acting, camera work, imagination, and overall appeal.

It is ironical that television in most of the advanced nations—Western Europe, Japan, etc.—is technically superior to America's despite the fact that essentially she has pioneered and developed the medium and brought it to a peak of penetration unequalled to date in the rest of the world. It may be a case of others profiting by America's experience, but it is more likely that America settled for a more expedient—and cheaper—method. American television uses a coarse screen, which simply means that there are fewer little dots per square inch on the scanner. A comparison would be the coarse screen of a newspaper photograph, where often the little dots from the engraving can be seen with the naked eye, as opposed to the fine screen of color reproduction in a slick magazine, where the little dots are not visible at all, even under a glass. The standards set for television transmission by the regulatory agencies in most of the rest of the world are far more stringent than in the United States. The FCC adopted the technical standard of a coarse screen under pressure from the major manufacturers of sets and equipment, who felt it desirable because it was cheaper. Once the standard was adopted, it was self-perpetuating, and it is impossible to change now except by scrapping all television sets and all cameras in America and starting anew. This is another indication of how a hasty decision taken for expediency or without adequate research can be irrevocable. Other nations opted for the finer screen to give a better picture, figuring the higher initial cost to be a worthwhile investment. Travelers abroad have universally remarked on the high quality of the picture in foreign lands.

NO TELEVISION IN SOUTH AFRICA

In the Union of South Africa there is no television at all. Intuitively, the African government sensed the impact of commercial television on its huge black population. A repetitious drumming for sales of consumer goods, cars, furniture, and quasi-luxuries would be a constant reminder that never in their lifetimes could they afford these goods. In this, television sows the seeds of discontent. Furthermore, most commercial programming depicts an affluent, white, upper middle-class life-style, again generating hopeless aspirations. The South African government seemed to realize that commercial television programming consisting of old United States movies and programs was developed as a part of a commercial culture socially alien to their own. Better than any other nation, they recognized that mass media are a product of a society and not a generalized entity compatible to all. Not wishing to incur the investment necessary to produce African programs, they simply decided to go without the medium until such time as they could develop a suitable format and backlog of programs to suit their own purposes. Television will come to the Union of South Africa before long, but on its own terms and not as another American export.

The Union of South Africa, therefore, with some prescience has avoided the television confrontation that erupted in the Watts section of Los Angeles in 1965, and continued for several summers in the ghettos of Washington, Milwaukee, Detroit, Newark, N.J., and other major United States cities with large black populations. Does television incite to riot? Yes and no. In an underprivileged area with a high rate of unemployment, more proportionate time is spent watching television. The constant exposure to luxury goods, well-appointed homes, well-dressed men, and beautifully cared-for women is bound to be a consistently contrasting reminder of surrounding poverty—so evident even while watching television's fantasies— and of the hopelessness of ever achieving anything different. Consistent sales pitches to buy clothes, cars, and cosmetics when there is insufficient money for food are also abrasive. When the oppressive heat and stifling smog of urban summers are added the burden becomes too great; public opinion jells and erupts in violence and looting further led by mob hysteria. Television does not cause the underlying resentment; television is not responsible for the dreadful social imbalance; but television, more effectively than any medium before it, does point up these discrepancies dramatically and constantly. Again, mass media trigger latent sentiment. In the case of the long, hot summers they did so by contrasting the all too visible poverty and anguish of slum life with a supposed Nirvana—and, tragically, it wasn't a real heaven shown on the screen at all but a fantasyland contrived of dreams whose purpose was to deceive.

As television news picked up footage of the riots and looting and burning, violence had a spreading effect in other cities, where suddenly the very experience of watching a riot in person triggered a participatory impulse. This is another of what McLuhan called the "involving aspects of television." In each instance, however, it was not a question of a person watching television and suddenly getting up to loot and burn. It was a question of watching television and talking about it with family, with others in the streets, or with neighbors until an incident—a police shakedown—set off the pent-up emotion. The effects of television were less direct than they were filtered through many others in the summer heat.

MEXICO IN TRANSITION

Mexico, with the possible exception of Argentina, is the most advanced of the United States' Latin American neighbors, which themselves are considerably ahead of most of the African and Asian nations. But even Mexico, by United States' standards, is well behind, living comparably to the time of Lincoln or before. Illiteracy is still high; there are an insufficient number of schools to meet the demand even though more are being built all the time. So critical is the education problem that Mexican children have to be placed on a lottery system to determine who goes to school. In the interior of Mexico there is no mass media as known in the United States. There are no newspapers nor magazines, and no one who can read them. There is certainly no television, and few radios, for there is little electricity. Nor does the purchasing power of the potential audience justify investment in broadcasting equipment.

However, there are signs of slow change. On mountaintops between the United States border and Mexico City, there is occasionally

Sharp contrast exists between the symbols of Old Mexico and New Mexico.

UPI

the silver glimmer of a microwave relay station bringing contact with the outside world to the Mexican capital. In Mexico City itself, with its 7 million population, there are newspapers, magazines, television, and a thriving radio network. The audience size justifies the network, and little by little it expands outward to other cities, such as Guadalajara.

Nowhere perhaps is the circular relationship between mass communications and society better illustrated than in the contrast between the United States' burgeoning mass communications network and the embryonic system taking life in the Republic of Mexico. Gradually, a better educated population will provide a bigger market for mass media, first in the population centers, at the same time acquiring the skills necessary for economic advancement. This, in turn, will provide the investment necessary to construct larger and better media facilities, and a higher gross national product to purchase the goods and services advertised. In summary, Mexico is not backward relative to the U.S. because its mass communications is underdeveloped, nor is its mass communications underdeveloped because it is backward. It is, rather, that Mexico is backward because its mass communications is underdeveloped because Mexico is backward.

Integration and Conclusion

BROADCASTING ELSEWHERE

3. Ibid.

Harry Skornia, in *Television and Society,* makes a case about the intrusion of American television interests into the underdeveloped nations.[3] He maintains with some justification that American interests are financing television development in these countries in order to provide a profitable outlet for old television fare, movies and programs, and an opportunity to sell advertising time. A good many of the purchasers of this advertising are American manufacturers operating abroad—the ubiquitous Coca Cola, for example. Thus, Skornia maintains that these nations are being Americanized on two fronts simultaneously: through the injection of the commercial media system, and through encouragement of the purchase of United States products, mostly nonessentials that then become staples through habit in the new nation. He points out that the governments of these nations are only too happy to have this American assistance, lacking the resources themselves to develop an effective television network. However, the price they pay in United States commercialism is too great, according to Skornia. He would prefer an alternate system wherein highly educational content such as agricultural techniques could be beamed to backward farmers, and where the television net could constitute a sort of classroom-of-the-air. Without faulting Professor Skornia's concepts, there are other points to keep in mind. First, United States intercession does provide a television network for the government's use as it sees fit where none existed previously. The existence of any sort of a television net does make it available for useful social purposes. Second, in the matter of audience taste, the populations of these nations seem to enjoy shoot-'em-ups and reruns, and they watch in considerable numbers. It is highly doubtful, people being what they are, that there would be much of an audience at all for how-to-do-it programming. The English experience with cultural vis-à-vis commercial networks seems to establish this. Finally, classrooms-of-the-air have not been successful even in the United States, where techniques are highly advanced and the educational level is high, so there is little empirical evidence to support the thought that it would work elsewhere under less favorable circumstances.

The cost of initial investment in broadcasting equipment is only a part of the cost of television, as has been shown. The other and greater cost is to the individual viewer in the price of the set, antennae, utilities, and the like. As seen in the case of even relatively advanced Mexico, the economic level just does not permit widespread purchase of television receivers. A great portion of the underdeveloped countries have no electricity, so audiences are necessarily limited at the outset to the relatively affluent residents of the major cities who are, of course, the more natural consumers of high entertainment content and to whom agricultural instruction would be meaningless. Skornia fears that these commercialized television patterns, once set, will remain permanently. However, experience seems to show that as greater audiences develop, they receive almost exactly what they want from television programming. What that will be at some distant date is, of course, far too early to tell.

The portability of the transistor radio and its freedom from a power source has commended it to many of the underdeveloped nations. Since it is so handy governments have, in most instances, seized upon it as a useful tool. And a powerful tool it is, too, used to fan flames of nationalism and urge greater effort. Transistors are cheap, and the cost of broadcasting, if propaganda is to be the principal content, is minimal. In the United Arab Republic, with its high illiteracy, radio loudspeakers are mounted on the minaret towers to assail the populace every waking hour. Camel drivers herd their caravans across the desert, as they did in pre–Christian times, with transistors glued to their ears. It is the reliance of many of the lesser-developed nations on radio that led to the establishment of the Voice of America. Radio is quick and efficient; it can command substantial audiences and it is private.

COMMUNIST BLOC: SOCIAL INTEGRATION

In the totalitarian nations, mass communications is completely integrated with society. It is part and parcel of government, which itself does not serve, but rather *is* society. In the USSR it is the Communist party that heads society, and the government is a tool of the party, as is the mass communications network. There is little or no commercial persuasion as Americans know it because there is no institutionalized commerce. The persuasion that exists is party or governmental. Here, as equally as in the United States, mass communications serves as the central nervous system of society. As society is oriented toward different goals, so also is the mass communications network. America's exists to serve the commercial world; theirs exists to serve the party. The information function in totalitarian nations is bent to serve propaganda objectives. There is no separate mystique to the news as an independent entity; it too serves a persuasive purpose. Obviously, under these conditions, there is no adversary relationship between the press and government; ethical questions do not arise. Nor, for that matter, does any control problem arise. Simply stated, there is no press as an independent entity. Press is government; its ethics are government (or party) ethics, and there is no need for controlling something that does not exist.

In the matter of education, also, the totalitarian nations recognize the educational system as a part of the mass communications complex, far more so than in the so-called free nations. The purpose of education is the purpose of the state. Here, again, there is no independent truth to be worshipped for its own sake; the only truth is that which serves the party line. America's educational system is divided between that portion serving the commercial institution to perpetuate democratic government and the free enterprise systems, and that portion serving independent Truth as a principle. Totalitarian education systems are integrated, aimed completely at perpetuating the values of the party, which are Truth.

In a far more realistic appraisal of the role of mass communications than America's, the party line extends to entertainment also. It is not surprising at all to note the Soviet composers and authors who have been censored for revisionary work. The totalitarian nations recognize that all mass communications is an integrated whole, and that entertainment plays a propaganda role in painting, drama, music, literature, and, in Russia's case particularly, in the ballet. Thus, the entire broad sweep of items constituting mass communications, not merely the print and broadcast media, but all of education and both the antic and static arts is welded into a single whole whose unique purpose is that of perpetuating social values—a massive program of cultural transmission in which deviant voices are stilled. The Russian consumer is no brainwashed puppet but a functioning human being who, in the aggregate, is getting what he wants from his party, his government, and his media—a trinity of elements of a single social system.

It is in the People's Republic of China, however, that the evidence of culture as mass communications is most highly developed. The high illiteracy rate of the Chinese plus the inadequate development of broadcasting over China's vast spaces has led to the intensive use of art, sculpture, plays, songs, and dances, all illustrating the central theme of work and fitness and Maoism. Performances are by visiting troups reminiscent of road shows, somewhat of a vaudeville with a purpose. They are also scripted for performance by individual groups across the nation. In the absence of any real information network, a system of oral transmission is highly developed. Here again is seen foreign recognition of the role that the arts play in mass communications in terms of their effect on people, a recognition sadly and incomprehensively lacking in American society. The extreme commercial emphasis given to American mass media has set art aside as having little practical value in the selling of goods. This viewpoint fails to recognize the heavy use made of the arts in history for purely pragmatic purposes—in Greece, in Rome, during the Renaissance, etc.

The rigid conformation that artists in totalitarian nations must reflect toward the party line has a stultifying effect, doing away with originality and creativity, downgrading the individual. It would seem to make for a less virile art just as commercial illustration, despite its intrinsic merit, has never risen to any artistic heights except, perhaps, in the case of Henri de Toulouse-Lautrec. However, in the totalitarian nations, individuality itself is not regarded as a virtue. The nature of society demands that the individual submerge himself within the social structure, and thus his art conforms to society's need, as does all mass media. In the United States, of course, it is different; the individual is still regarded as supreme, independence is a virtue, and art is an expression of the individual's achievement, which is, itself, the goal of society—or once was.

THE PRINT BYPASS

In considering mass communications in its international perspective, one should note the proliferation of radio in underdeveloped nations, and that it is usually under government control. This indicates a high degree of propaganda content. Whether these nations are totalitarian or not is not the principal concern; rather, it is that there will be a highly homogenizing influence on the peoples of these nations. They will lack the diversity of programming and viewpoint that the more or less free system, for all its shortcomings, provides. Further, as many of these people are highly illiterate, the incidence of broadcasting itself provides a more than adequate substitute for print. In short, because there is so much broadcast, they may lack the incentive to learn to read and write. As this happens, of course, the peoples of these countries will be further penalized in not being able to acquire the kind of broad and technical education necessary to upgrade them economically. Ironically, broadcasting may itself play a considerable role in holding them back. This is the second of the considerations perceived by Marshall McLuhan—that is, the simplicity, immediacy, and pervasity of broadcasting may easily short-circuit the entire print era in the underdeveloped nations.

Something of this can be seen happening even in the advanced society of the U.S. In the first of the television generations a noticeable decline in reading and writing skills can be detected. Students pay less attention to spelling, punctuation, and grammar than they used to. Some college students are only quasi-literate. Time that used to be spent with books is spent before the tube, and a great amount of incidental exposure that formerly supplemented the educational system has been diverted from print to television. The case can be made that this creeping illiteracy will be even more pronounced amongst peoples who were never literate.

There also remains the possibility that ruthless governments will encourage this broadcast dependency and purposely downgrade literacy, recognizing as did the priesthoods of old that knowledge is power. Such governments, with as powerful a tool as radio in their hands, may find it expedient to perpetuate popular ignorance for the power it brings to themselves, and to rely on the broadcast media to lull and to homogenize their peoples. This may not be so far-fetched as it sounds, for it was only a few generations ago that Adolf Hitler envisioned the same kind of overall control utilizing the then new tool of radio. His failure was in not recognizing that the German people were among the most literate on earth, with a tradition of intellectual pursuit far too great to be overcome in a single generation. The results might be different, however, if the same techniques were to be applied to an already ignorant and illiterate people.

As government controlled television gradually grows in these same nations, it might merely add another and more powerful weapon to be employed in a strategy already well under way.

Counter to this, of course, is the Americanizing influence of U.S. investments that are already creating a commercial system complete with programming and ads similar to those here. How ironic it would be if the crass commercial exploitation of these nations should prove their salvation from despotic government. Questions remain about the role of mass communications in the emerging nations.

THE GLOBAL VILLAGE

Another major factor in international mass communications is the matter of international broadcasting. Such broadcasting is already existent to a considerable degree via the wire services, and more recently as a result of satellite broadcasting. But looking down the road to the future, one can visualize the results of a multiplicity of channels that cable makes available. This, combined with the direct broadcasting features of satellites, not as yet fully exploited, means that there could easily be a separate channel for every nation on earth—that those who cared could sit and watch hours of activity direct from the Red Square in Moscow, or participate vicariously in the daily routine of a Chinese commune, or window-shop along the Champs-Elysées. Chinese peasants could participate in New Year's Eve in Times Square, New York, while Sicilians could take a vicarious pack trip through the Rockies. Regardless, such usage would make for a smaller world wherein different cultures could intermingle more or less indiscriminately, and mankind could achieve a broader knowledge and experience. This is McLuhan's meaning of "the global village": a return to a basically oral society as a result of broadcasting short-circuiting print, and a gradually increased participation in the daily lives of other nations to the point that man becomes globally familiar rather than remote. When the involving aspects of television are extended to this, it can be speculated that more and more nationals of many nations will seek answers for their curiosity by traveling and even living abroad, perhaps in several nations in a lifetime, to the point that nationality will be of decreasing significance. In the extraordinary amount of foreign travel done by Americans, particularly youth, despite serious dollar discrepancies, and in the increasing amount of American travel by foreigners, particularly the Japanese, the first hesitant steps toward this global amalgamation can be seen. There are additional signs of international communications. International expansion on an accelerating scale by American corporations is having its own effect—economic, cultural, and social—and the volume of message exchange by mail, international telephone, personal visits abroad, and computer data multiplies intercultural contacts. Similarly, although on a smaller scale, there is an increasing incidence of foreign investments in the United States:

Japanese banks—the Bank of Tokyo and the Sumimoto Bank—Volkswagen assembly plants, a whole rash of Swedish, German, Italian, French, and Japanese auto dealerships, a growing number of specialty discount houses handling exotic import merchandise, and an increased amount of imported prestige consumer goods, including foreign fashions, that are finding their way into department stores, shopping centers, and boutiques. In this kind of economic and cultural interchange, jet jumbo aircraft itself must be counted as a form of mass media by virtue both of its size and frequency, and as a form of mass communications in the amount of interpersonal exchange it makes possible between nations.

RESEARCH

Mass communications research has been spotty, due both to the relative newness of the field and its interdisciplinary nature. Mass communications as the central nervous system of society cuts across a variety of separate disciplines: journalism, sociology, psychology, and social psychology in terms of individual, group, and mass effect; political science and anthropology; speech and linguistics; the broad public relations, advertising, marketing, and propaganda fields as they relate to organized persuasion; economics in its relationship to affluence and technology; history, to a degree; and, more recently since the advent of the computer, mathematics and engineering. This list of disciplines is not inclusive, but sufficiently so to make the point that any study and application of knowledge gained in mass communications will have to take into consideration a number of disciplines that traditionally have been regarded as discrete. What is lacking is a broad understanding of the sweeping inclusiveness of the mass communications field and some sort of central focal point where pertinent data can be accumulated and reconciled. Melvin DeFleur of Washington State, a sociologist himself and one of the early investigators into the mass communications phenomena, has urged the establishment of a professional society, but to date this has not come into being. Time has simply been too short in the three decades or so since mass communications began to be recognized as a field in its own right and not merely as an offshoot of journalism or sociology for all the organization necessary to correlate or even to locate the many studies pertinent to mass communications. This lack of communication in mass communications, of course, has penalized progress in the field.

Nor is the full scope of the field apparent yet. For example, it has been only within the last quarter of the century that the role of mathematics in mass communications became apparent as a result of Shannon's research for the Bell System, and Norbert Weiner's work in cybernetics began to filter through. While the application of mathematical theory to computer data and feedback mechanisms is rather clearly seen, yet to be explored is another aspect of entropy, as identified by Shannon, that appears to associate mass communications with another field of the hard sciences, physics, in reference to the first law of thermodynamics. The integrating potential that this holds for relating mass communications to the universe is exciting.

Mass communications has been referred to as the central nervous system of society. The parallel, while not exact, is striking—so striking that it might even be useful if a trained neurologist were to undertake some mass communications research. Certainly, it would do no harm and it might shed light on a field so dimly perceived. There is some precedent for a study of neuro-communications, as more and more double-degreed attorneys and doctors are entering the field of forensic medicine, which, itself, has broadly social as opposed to individual overtones.

Mass communications research to date seems to fall into four broad categories and perhaps a few subcategories. Broadly, these categories are: technical, commercial, intuitive, and accidental. The subcategories are erroneous and trivial; these are mentioned only as potential pitfalls to be avoided, for they impede and dissipate mass communications research.

RESEARCH AND DEVELOPMENT

In technical mass communications research America has been unexcelled. In the quarter-century or so since World War II the rapid development of transistors, printed circuits, diodes and triodes, television, microwave relay, laser, color television, and now an emergent holography has been distinguished. Computerization of data, memory development, offset printing, and high-speed presses are other aspects of the same practical application of technical research, known in the trade as "research and development" (R&D). The problem has been that theoretical research and understanding have not kept pace with technology so man really does not know all that he understands about mass communications and both its individual and social effects.

In commercial research also America has forged well ahead. The extremely swift and highly sophisticated ratings developed for television are fundamental to the industry, as increasingly complex readership surveys assist newspapers and magazines in pinpointing their appeals, while computer assisted demographic studies identify their audiences. Market research plots out a new product's acceptability and discovers the segment of audience that will buy. In political campaigning, sophisticated public opinion polling increasingly forms the basis of campaign direction, and its use outside the campaign as a guide to action grows. Polling is used extensively in public relations to assess public sentiment toward a corporation or any organization.

Commercial, like technical, research has a practical value that can easily be changed into either dollars and cents or power. Research and development has always been more popular than pure research for this reason: it can be pragmatically useful whereas pure research, from which the greatest insights and understanding come, is an expensive cost item that may never pay its own way and is difficult, therefore, to justify. Business and industry have been prone to leave the pure research to the universities, where under various federal and foundation grants it also has often taken second place to research of a practical nature. Regrettably, in mass communications as in other fields, there just does not seem to be a lot of money available for anyone to poke around out of idle curiosity. Because of the expensive nature of some of the research hardware, and the massive costs of public opinion sampling and computer time, basic knowledge in mass communications lags more and more.

INTUITION AND ACCIDENT

Intuitive research may be a contradiction in terms, but a great deal of mass communications theory is based on the insights of such people as Stephenson, McLuhan, DeFleur, and Wilbur Schramm. Some of these people attack the field broadly, some narrowly within the limits of their own discipline (journalism or sociology), but all have come up with meaningful intuitions that lack only the opportunity for proof, either in a designed study or on the basis of empirical observation over long periods.

McLuhan's intuition as to the broad sweep of a medium's dominance gave birth to a developmental concept of mass communications' evolution. His concept of television's involvement aspects is vitally important, but desperately needs supporting data. As a matter of fact, anyone looking for worthwhile studies in the field of mass communications would do well to take some of McLuhan's prolific theories and test them by some means. (The concept of hot and cool media would be a good starting point.) The additional data that revealed in the course of any study would be valuable indeed.

The accidental development of the two-step theory of mass communications by Paul Lazarsfeld and Bernard Berelson occurred in connection with their massive survey on the national presidential election in Erie County, Ohio, in 1940. As a part of their study, they had undertaken to discover how significant a role certain personal attributes played in voting predisposition. They also undertook to assess media influence on changing voting patterns. In doing so, they identified a continuously decreasing minority of voters who wavered between choices and could not make up their minds. In their final interview after the election, they closely questioned these waverers. They learned that in most instances waverers had been finally influenced by other people, personal contacts. Following up on this clue, they went back and assiduously sought out and interviewed every person who was named as an influence. From these sessions, which had not been a part of the original study, they discovered that the predominant number of these personal influencers were perceived as leaders within their own circles and, in addition, were, as a group, more interested in and informed about the election than the average.

Furthermore, they read more and listened more and were greater consumers of the media. These insights then led Lazarsfeld and Berelson to tentatively formulate the two-step theory of indirect media influence.

The two-step theory then became a major factor in their next study in the 1948 election in Elmira, New York. Here it was rigorously tested and proved, and formed the basis of contemporary communications theory as modified by new developments, knowledge, and technology. Lazarsfeld and Berelson by chance stumbled onto this concept. Corollaries to the theory point out that in political campaigning, increasing time, money, and effort are spent with the mass media to influence an ever smaller portion of the voters. This seems to indicate that most political campaigning is wasted effort, and that huge economies could be affected if a means could be developed demographically or otherwise of predetermining the wavering or the influential voter.

Another result of their studies was the de-emphasize the simplistic stimulus-response, power-of-the-press theory and, by implication, to suggest the limited areas of its influence in triggering latent sentiment.

THE INFLUENCE OF CHANGE

The tragedy is that such revealing studies have not been continued. Lazersfeld and Berelson's concept cannot be accepted at face value today. Society changes mightily in a third of a century and, as society changes, so will the social theories that apply to it. Social theory is not like the laws of the physical sciences, always true under all conditions. Social theory applies to the ebb and flow of people, ever changing, while scientific law applied to the timelessness of the universe. For example, Lazersfeld and Berelson found that religious affiliation in 1940 was a major factor in voting predisposition; it was less so in 1948 although it was still significant. A limited study in 1971 revealed, however, that religious affiliation no longer played any role in voting predisposition, that there was no correlation whatever between religion and voting habits (except among Jews).[4] This same study identified a new factor based on liberal/conservative bias that can be almost predictive of voting performance. However, the study needs testing in other universes. As time goes by, more and more social change seems to render some of the present communications research obsolescent, and there are no new data to take its place.

Thus, the gap between the technological curve and the theoretical curve continues to widen. If a recognized national center for mass communications research did exist, perhaps some of these studies would not be lost, and perhaps some of their findings could be dovetailed or reconciled into others to illuminate the field. Further, such a center could indicate direction needed for research, even in such a

4. Frederick C. Whitney, "Field Study, Analysis and Prediction of Voting Behavior in a Suburban Community of High Socio-Economic Status" (Ph.D. diss., United States International University, 1971).

commonplace matter as suggesting topics for Ph.D. dissertations in needed areas rather than the happenstance manner in which often trivial and repetitive data is currently being submitted by aspiring candidates, through no fault of their own. However, a program such as this takes money and direction, and there seems to be a critical shortage of both in the field.

In another area it should be remembered that Lazarsfeld and Berelson studied dichotomous situations in which poles of opinion were clearly, if artificially, indicated in a political election. What are desperately needed are equally massive studies of opinion formation and change, and the media's effects in the rough-and-tumble world of everyday living, where the issue is not identified or the extremities delineated; studies are needed to see how a particular opinion rises to the surface, when it jells, and whom it influences.

RESEARCH CRITIQUE

Regrettably, it does not seem possible to conduct such studies in laboratory situations, for the construct of the lab itself influences the course of the study. It is simply impossible in social research to isolate an independent variable. When this is done, the results—for all the pseudoscientific rigor so slavishly borrowed from the physical sciences—are invalid. As an example (and this illustrates the kind of erroneous research mentioned earlier) a laboratory study of rumor turned out results directly opposite of the Army's subsequent findings. A roomful of people were asked to repeat a few lines of prose. What emerged after it had been repeated about thirty times, from one person to another, was unrecognizable from the original passage read to the first participant. The conclusion of this study, therefore, was that rumor is unreliable. The differences, of course, between this study and that of the Army are that in the lab situation a meaningless passage was repeated—meaningless in the sense that it had no bearing on the lives or welfare of the participants. There was no need or incentive, therefore, for an individual to test it against his knowledge or experience. It was a routine exercise rather than one fraught with the drama of reality. Furthermore, the chain of repetition was contrived rather than being the random repetition that occurs in a real life situation, where a rumor is repeated more or less at the will of the repeater, repeated or not repeated as he sees fit. Thus, while the results of the contrived laboratory test may have been reliable for the phenomenon tested, they were not valid for rumor.

Another example had to do with the effect of television violence on children. A group of six- and seven-year-olds were shown average (violent) television fare. After viewing, they were handed plastic baseball bats and put into a room full of large inflated dummies (schmoos) with predictable results. The little tikes clobbered the schmoos with the bats. Ergo, said the study, television breeds violence. Nonsense. If a little kid is handed a bat and shown a roomful of dummies, chances are he'll clobber them.

Integration and Conclusion

"THROUGH A GLASS, DARKLY..."

As far as the future of mass communications is concerned, it is the future of society. Presently, the continua show a marked fragmentation of both audiences and media, a departure from appeal to the lowest common denominator. This trend is particularly noticeable in magazine publishing and in radio. The fragmentation of audiences necessarily means increasingly smaller audiences for any given medium. In this, the process aims ever closer toward the individual himself. The trend toward increasing use of demographics, much assisted by the computer, is already reaching out toward selected individuals in computerized, personalized, direct mail. If this trend continues, it can be expected to branch out into video-cassettes for even greater personalized impact. Meanwhile, the computer itself poses grave threats to the invasion of privacy, threats which daily probe deeper into the individual's life without either his permission or knowledge, and, as controls lag for want of direction, the trend may be beyond correction by the time policy is formulated.

Substantiation of these mass communications directions can be seen on other fronts. The fragmentation of audiences is apparent in the growing departure from television. Although there are millions yet watching, they are proportionately fewer. The number of viewers is not keeping pace with population growth rates, and the number of hours of daily viewing has declined by about 25 percent since television apparently peaked in 1966. At the other end of the continua, the fragmentation of audiences shows up in increasing attendance at personal contact events. There is a marked and growing box office for drama, symphony, ballet, opera, professional sports, historic sights, restorations of all sorts, and attractions such as Disneyland and Sea World. A part of this trend, so well reflected in this branch of mass communications, seems to come from a yearning for more personal contact as an antidote to the impersonal world of IBM cards and computers. Thus, action and reaction are seen at work in the world of mass communications as growing countertrends. Meanwhile, the emphasis on television and the audiovisual world has effected a decline in literacy, not as yet critical, but growing and abetted both by the "leap-frogging" of the print era in developing nations, and by the simultaneous acceleration of international communications.

The trend toward fragmentation and individualization can reach its ultimate in CATV, whose possibilities offer a science-fiction view of the future: applied demographics, two-way capacity, and infinity of channels for every purpose (with monitoring capacity), total recall ability from the memory of national computers, and eventually a marriage to holography for ersatz, three-dimensional recreation of living scenes and people in the open space of the home communications center. However, CATV has not developed as rapidly as some envisioned, despite its remarkable potential. There have not been the audiences to justify investment to date. Mass communications development is thwarted by economic realities. For the present, CATV is a victim of its own versatility. It cannot develop its greatest services because it performs its original function of extending over-the-air signals of existing television into marginal neighborhoods so well. Further, the FCC flounders, making hesitant decisions; this is tragic in that, as technology is at the crossroads, the decisions made today affect the central nervous system of tomorrow, perhaps irrevocably.

THE ALTERNATIVES

A continued rise in the gross national product will mean increasing affluence, which will be interpreted in mass communications terms in greater diversification of media across the board, smaller audiences, and an attendant increase in the competition for attention. The volume will be staggering. Previously the advertising support for most of the mass media was noted. This will be provided in the future through an increased number of manufacturers making an increased number of products to be marketed under an increased number of brand names to be sold through an increased number of outlets, all of which will find their support in an increased number of specialized media.

This specialization by interest, further protracted, can result in enclaves of people separated from one another by their eliteness, and a gradual breakdown in communication as they develop the peculiar languages pertinent to their interests.

If, on the other hand, a slowdown in the economy results from recession, or environmental or energy considerations, then man may look for a curtailment of the rate of media expansion, a concentration into fewer forms of more generalized appeal. Recession will mean fewer people attending colleges and universities, and a retrenchment, therefore, of the broad-based interests that specialized education develops. There will be less demand for specialized media and less leisure time in which to consume it.

If this alternative materializes, it will in a sense be a regression in which much of society's broadening diversity is sacrificed to a homogeneity reflected by the lowest common denominator. Having achieved the ultimate in speed of communication and the largest possible audience, the continua under social pressure may remain more or less static for a time. They may not follow a pattern of specialization and fragmentation, which can be accomplished only at enormous cost. Future direction of the media is a question of cost and what society is willing to pay to explore new techniques of mass communications development.

For example, it takes in the neighborhood of 1,000 man-hours to produce an hour-long television segment. If the number of available channels is multiplied by forty or eighty or the hundreds that CATV makes possible, the man-hours of production and all attendant costs are also multiplied by that much to maintain the same quality. The total cost is staggering, but the audiences and, hence, the potential return, is but a fraction. Such multiplication of costs accompanied by a reduction of potential return does not argue for the rapid development of cable's potential.

Already the continually increasing costs of some forms of mass media are having an adverse effect. This is beginning to show particularly in the performing arts, where production costs are becoming prohibitive when measured against the potential box office returns. A partial answer to this, some speculate, may come about as a result of videotape, through which immortal performances could be taped and cassetted and sold, as recordings are now, to defray a portion of production costs and make profit a possibility again.

In brief, society seems to have reached a crossroads in both media and social development where the future is unclear; major forces tug for expansion while others pull for retrenchment. In either instance, the mass communications system will change to serve the new social forms. In the one case it might move toward an incredible diversity that may well prove divisive. In the other instance, it might move toward consolidation and curtailment, which, while limiting the choices available, may prove unifying. In any event, the decisions made now will determine the course of society and mass communications for the foreseeable future, and these decisions are not all media decisions by any means, but also social, economic, political, and ecological decisions that inevitably will be reflected in the kind of mass communications network the future will allow.

SUMMARY

Thus far mass communications has been considered as an American institution. However, rapidly developing international communications demands attention to mass communications in foreign lands. Development of satellite broadcasting is going to bring this country closer to the rest of the world as America increasingly influences other nations and they, in turn, increasingly influence America.

The USIA to date has been the principal formal agency for American foreign influence. It has not been marked by spectacular success because essentially it has been using sales techniques developed in the literate, sophisticated, commercial, twentieth-century United States and attempting to apply them in illiterate, primitive societies living 150 years in the technological past. Additionally, the USIA does not operate in a vacuum, and other more prominent American forces are at work, often in conflict to USIA objectives. These include commercial interests, tourists, and United States troops. Further, the USIA has continually wavered in its own objectives as administrations have changed, utilizing now a hard-sell approach in support of foreign policy and then a soft-sell approach aimed only at acquainting foreign nationals with the American way of life. Such internal policy confusion breeds confusion abroad.

American interests have assisted underdeveloped nations in setting up television, thus providing an outlet for old American programming. This at least has resulted in television facilities where none existed previously and, despite commercial overtones, provides a sort of counterbalance to the ever-present temptation to use government-owned television abroad for purely propaganda purposes.

England established the BBC in the early twenties as an independent governmental agency. Its aims, first in radio and later in television, were basically informational and cultural. Twenty years ago it also licensed a commercial network that has since usurped most of the audience. England now has two networks: a commercial one and a public one. The United States approached the situation from the other direction by establishing a commercial network first and more recently coming to a public network, which is in its infancy.

England, responding to its own social pressures, permits no political campaigning over the air, and further guards justice by permitting no coverage whatever of trials in progress.

Commercials in Italy are blocked into four-hour segments that, ironically, have proved to be one of the nation's popular programs. South Africa, to date, has not permitted television at all, recognizing that the impact of affluent white television programming would be contrary to its apartheid policy and would constitute a constant abrasive on its huge black population. South Africa foresaw the kind of continuing irritation that, in American experience, erupted in Watts and in numerous major cities in the hot summer of 1965 and continued for several years.

Ironically, the technical quality of television in other nations is superior to that in the United States. Other nations have a finer screen that offers greater clarity. The system in the United States was adopted out of expediency by the FCC and demonstrates the lasting effect of decisions hastily made.

In nations of the Communist bloc, all media serve the state; indeed, they are the state and there is no adversary relationship between the press and government. Recognition of the arts and culture as mass media and that they can be bent to the state's purpose is far more advanced in the USSR and the People's Republic of China than it is in the United States.

Mass communications research is a paradox. On the one hand, man has excelled in the pragmatic kinds of research, that is, technical and commercial. However, pure research is sadly lacking in mass communications in the development of basic concepts or theoretical approaches. Part of the blame arises from the recent nature of mass communications as an integrated field and its tardy recognition as such. Another part comes from its interdisciplinary nature, with so many fields vying for attention. To date, there is no national center where existing research can be assembled and correlated, and direction given to future studies.

Most of the theoretical research in mass communications has been intuitive or accidental, emerging as did the two-step theory from researches aimed at other objectives. Some research has been faulty, largely as a result of contrived laboratory situations; some has been merely trivial.

Technology is at a crossroads where decisions taken will perhaps irrevocably affect mass communications in the future. This is why the lack of research is so critical.

The future of mass communications holds two significant choices, which will be made on the basis of other factors—political, social, and economic. In the one instance man can continue his current trend toward ever-greater specialization and fragmentation. This, while providing incredible diversity, can be divisive. The alternative is a retrenchment where, under economic impact, there will be fewer media catering to larger audiences. This can be uniting.

Man is at the crossroads, for this is society in flux, but whatever society's decisions, the mass communications network will continue to serve it on society's terms.

Each an individual.

SELECTED READINGS

Aaker, D. A., and Day, G. S. *Consumerism: Search for the Consumer Interest.* New York: Macmillan, Inc., 1971.

Abelson, Herbert I. *Persuasion.* New York: Springer Publishing Co., Inc., 1962.

Agee, Warren. *Mass Media in a Free Society.* Wichita: University of Kansas Press, 1969.

*Bagdikian, Ben H. *The Information Machines.* New York: Harper & Row, Publishers, 1971.

Baus, Herbert M., *Public Relations at Work.* New York: Harper & Row, Publishers, 1948.

Baus, Herbert M., and Ross, William B. *Politics Battle Plan.* New York: Macmillan, Inc. 1968.

Berelson, Bernard, and Janowitz, M., eds. *Reader in Public Opinion and Communication.* 2d ed. New York: The Free Press, 1966.

Berelson, Bernard, et al. *Voting: A Study of Opinion Formation in a Presidential Campaign.* Chicago: University of Chicago Press, 1954.

*Bernays, Edward L. *The Engineering of Consent.* Norman: University of Oklahoma Press, 1955.

*Brown, J.A.C. *Techniques of Persuasion.* Baltimore, Md.: Penguin Books Inc., 1963.

*Brown, Les. *Television: The Business Behind the Box.* New York: Harcourt Brace Jovanovich, Inc., 1972.

Burdick, Eugene, and Brodbeck, Arthur J. *American Voting Behavior.* New York: The Free Press, 1959.

Casty, Alan. *Mass Media and Mass Man.* New York: Holt, Rinehart and Winston, 1968.

Christenson, R.M., and McWilliams, R.O. *Voice of the People.* 2d ed. New York: McGraw-Hill, 1967.

Cohan, Lester. *New York Graphic.* New York: Chitton Books, 1964.

Cole, Barry G. *Television.* New York: The Free Press, 1970.

*Cutlip, Scott M., and Center, Allen H. *Effective Public Relations.* 4th ed. Englewood Cliffs, N.J.: Prentice-Hall, Inc., 1971.

*DeFleur, Melvin. *Theories of Mass Communications.* New York: David McKay Co., Inc., 1966.

Della Famina, Jerry. *From Those Wonderful Folks Who Gave You Pearl Harbor.* New York: Simon & Schuster, Inc., 1970.

De Vries, Tarrance. *The Ticker-Splitter.* Grand Rapids, Mich.: Eardmans Publishing Co., 1972.

Edwards, Verne, Jr. *Journalism in a Free Society.* Dubuque, Ia.: Wm. C. Brown Company Publishers, 1970.

Effron, Edith. *The News Twisters.* Los Angeles: Nash Publishing Corporation, 1971.

Emery, Edwin. *Press and America.* Englewood Cliffs, N.J.: Prentice-Hall, Inc., 1972.

Emery, Edwin, et al. *Introduction to Mass Communications.* 3rd ed. New York: Dodd, Mead & Co., 1970.

Emery, Michael, and Smythe, Ted C. *Readings in Mass Communication.* Dubuque, Ia.: Wm. C. Brown Company Publishers, 1972.

Evry, Hal. *The Selling of a Candidate.* Los Angeles: Western Opinion Research Center, 1971.

*Gallup, George. *The Sophisticated Poll-Watcher's Guide.* Princeton, N.J.: Princeton Opinion Press, 1972.

Goffman, Erving. *Relations in Public.* New York: Basic Books, Inc., 1971.

*Hamilton, Alexander, et al. *Federalist Papers.* Edited by Clinton Rossiter. New York: Mentor Books, 1961.

Hiebert, Ray E., et al., eds. *Political Image Merchants: Strategy in New Politics.* Washington, D.C.: Acropolis Books Ltd., 1971.

Hill, John W. *Making of a Public Relations Man.* New York: David McKay Co., Inc., 1963.

Hofstadter, Richard. *Social Darwinism in American Thought.* Boston, Mass.: Beacon Press, 1955.

Hohenberg, John. *The Professional Journalist.* 2d ed. New York: Holt, Rinehart and Winston, Inc., 1960.

*_____. *The News Media: A Journalist Looks at His Profession.* New York: Holt, Rinehart and Winston, Inc., 1968.

Holmgren, Norton, eds. *Mass Media Book.* Englewood Cliffs, N.J.: Prentice-Hall, Inc., 1972.

Hovland, Carl I., et als., eds. *Communication and Persuasion.* New Haven, Conn.: Yale University Press, 1968.

*Huff, Darrell. *How to Lie with Statistics.* W.W. Norton & Company, Inc., 1954.

Klapper, Joseph T. *The Effects of Mass Communications.* New York: The Free Press, 1960.

Katz, Elihu, and Lazersfeld, Paul. *Personal Influence: The Part Played by People in the Flow of Mass Communications.* New York: The Free Press, 1964.

Kobre, Sidney. *Development of American Journalism* Dubuque, Ia.: Wm. C. Brown Company Publishers, 1969.

Langer, Suzanne. *Philosophy in a New Key.* 2d ed. New York: Mentor, 1951.

*Lazarsfeld, Paul F., and Berelson, Bernard. *People's Choice: How the Voter Makes up His Mind in a Presidential Election.* 3rd ed. New York: Columbia University Press, 1969.

Lindsay, Vachel. *The Art of the Motion Picture.* New York: Liveright, 1970.

*Lippmann, Walter. *Public Opinion.* New York: The Free Press, 1963.

Lipset, Seymour M. *Political Man: The Social Bases of Politics.* Garden City, N.Y.: Doubleday & Company, Inc., 1963.

Luttbeg, Norman, ed. *Public Opinion and Public Policy.* Homewood, Ill.: Dorsey Press, 1969.

MacDougall, Curtis. *Understanding Public Opinion.* Dubuque, Ia.: Wm. C. Brown Company Publishers, 1966.

*Mayer, Martin. *About Television.* New York: Harper & Row, Publishers, 1967.

*_____. *Madison Avenue, U.S.A.* New York: Pocket Books, 1967.

McGinniss, Joe. *The Selling of the President 1968.* New York: Trident Press, 1969.

*McLuhan, Marshall. *The Gutenberg Galaxy.* Toronto, Canada: University of Toronto Press, 1967.

*_____. *Understanding Media.* New York: Signet, 1966.

_____. *The Mechanical Bride.* Boston, Mass.: Beacon Press, 1967.

*McQuill, Dennis. *Toward a Sociology of Mass Communication.* London, England: Collier-Macmillan International, Inc., 1969.

Merrill, J.C., and Lowenstein, R.L. *Media, Messages and Men.* New York: David McKay Co., Inc., 1971.

Mills, C. Wright. *Power, Politics, and People.* Edited by Irving L. Horowitz. New York: Oxford University Press, 1969.

Minor, Dale. *The Information War.* New York: Hawthorn Books, Inc., 1970.

Monagham, Patrick. *Public Relations Careers.* New York: Fairchild Publications, Inc., 1972.

*Nimmo, Dan. *Political Persuaders.* Englewood Cliffs, N.J.: Prentice-Hall, Inc., 1970.

*Packard, Vance. *The Hidden Persuaders.* New York: Pocket Books, 1968.

Pember, Don R. *Mass Media In America.* Palo Alto, Calif.: Science Research Associates Inc., 1974.

Pimlott, J.A.R. *Public Relations and American Democracy.* Princeton, N.J.: Princeton University Press, 1951.

Reich, Charles. *The Greening of America.* New York: Randon House, Inc. 1970.

Rissover, Frederick, and Birch, David, eds. *Mass Media and the Popular Arts.* New York: McGraw-Hill, 1971.

Rivers, W.L., et al. *Mass Media and Modern Society.* 2d ed. Rinehart Editions. Holt, Rinehart and Winston, Inc., 1971.

Rivers, W.L., et al. *Backtalk.* New York: Comfield Press, 1972.

Rucker, Frank W., and Williams, Herbert L. *Newspaper Organization and Management.* 3rd ed. Ames: Iowa State University Press, 1969.

*Sandman, Peter M., et al. *Media.* Englewood Cliffs, N.J.: Prentice-Hall, Inc., 1972.

Scammon, Richard M., and Wattenberg, Ben J. *The Real Majority: How the Silent Center of the American Electorate Chooses Its President.* New York: Coward, McCann & Geoghegan, Inc., 1970.

Schiller, Herbert. *Mass Communication and American Empire.* Clifton, N.J.: Augustus M. Kelley, Publishers, 1970.

Schramm, Wilbur, and Roberts, Donald F., eds. *Process and Effects of Mass Communications.* Urbana: University of Illinois Press, 1971.

*Shannon, Claude E., and Weaver, Warren. *Mathematical Theory of Communication.* 4th ed. Urbana: University of Illinois Press, 1969.

*Siebert, Fred S., et al. *Four Theories of the Press.* Urbana: University of Illinois Press, 1963.

Skonia, Harry J. *Television and Society.* New York: McGraw-Hill, 1965.

Steinberg, Charles S. *Mass Media and Communications*. New York: Hastings House, Publishers, Inc., 1966.

———. *The Communicative Arts*. New York: Hastings House, Publishers, Inc., 1970.

*Stephenson, William. *The Play Theory of Mass Communications*. Chicago: University of Chicago Press, 1967.

St. Thomas, C.E. *How to Get Industrial and Business Publicity*. Philadelphia: Chitton, 1956.

Townsend, Robert. *Up the Organization*. New York: Alfred A. Knopf, Inc., 1970.

University of Chicago Center for Policy Study. *The Media and the Critics*. Chicago: University of Chicago Press, 1968.

*Weiner, Norbert. *Cybernetics*. 2d ed. Cambridge, Mass.: The M.I.T. Press, 1969.

White, Theodore H. *Making of the President: 1960*. New York: Atheneum Publishers, 1961.

*Particularly suggested

INDEX

Aaron, Hank, 299
About Television, 273
Acceleration, principle of, 81, 82, 268. *See also* Mass media
Adams, Samuel, 40, 338, 339
Addison, Joseph, 180
Advertising
  and affluence, 321
  agencies, 38, 312-15, 321-24
    functions, 322-23
    middlemen, 321-22
    other services, 323
  and book promotions, 147
  broadcast control, 117
  Brand X, 122, 328
  cigarette, 119, 257-58
  classified, 23, 171
  commission system, 313, 324-26
  cost per thousand (cpm), 231, 254
  criticism, 329-30
  and computerized direct mail, 364, 366
  and convergent selectivity, 64
  defense of, 330-31
  effect on youth, 261
  ethics, 133
  explanation of, 310-11, 317-21, 328-29
  export, 321
  and Fairness Doctrine, 119
  and FCC, 257, 258
  and FTC, 121-23, 327-29. *See* FTC
  and film, 205, 215, 217
  functions
    information, 23
    persuasion, 23, 24, 27, 29, 310
  history of, 311-18
  institutional, 320-21
  jingles, 225, 314
  licensing, possibility of, 133
  local or retail, 23, 171, 312-13, 319
  and magazines, 24, 25, 27, 71, 179, 181-92, 233, 314, 319
  mail, 363, 366
  and mass media continuum, 70
  and mass communications development, 36
  motivational research, 316-17
  national, 23, 28, 71, 162, 171, 312-13, 319
  and newspapers, 23, 24, 27, 38, 71, 127-28, 159, 161-62, 166, 169-72, 233, 297, 312, 319
  and politics, 410-12
  and polls, 314, 424
  positioning, 86, 326-27
  power of the press theory, 53
  public opinion, 410-12
  public relations, 44
  puffery, 127
  and radio, 27, 44, 72, 222, 224-27, 231, 233, 235, 238-40, 314, 315, 319
  remedial, 123
  repetition, 9
  review boards, 134, 329
  slogan, 314
  specialization, 322, 326
  Standard Rate and Data Service, 191, 192, 323
  Starch Report, 190, 314
  subliminal advertising, 317
  and syndicated features, 297
  and telegraph, 291
  and telephone, 372
  and television, 25, 27, 47, 74, 183-84, 247-48, 253-58, 261, 268-70, 279, 305, 315, 318, 319
  truth in, 51, 121, 122, 327-29
  unique selling proposition, 315, 316
Affluence
  of audience, 75, 94, 95
  effect on
    advertising, 321
    automobile, 80
    entertainment, 27
    film, 211
    magazines, 186-90
    mail, 362
    newspapers, 158, 168, 169
    television, 268, 280-82, 305
    television news ratings, 248, 257
    wire services, 306
  and future of mass communications, 450
  in mass communications development, 37
  role in play theory, 63, 64
Affluent Society, The, 77
Agnew, Spiro T., 136, 304, 434
Allen, Fred, 229
Allen, Gracie, 229
American Broadcasting Company (ABC)
  origin, 113, 234, 235
  radio, 239, 240
  television
    affiliates, 245, 248
    Monday night football, 120
    news, 304

PBS, 274
ratings, 245, 248
Westinghouse Group W, 246
American Newspaper Publishers Association (ANPA), 227
American Society of Composers, Artists and Producers (ASCAP), 234
American Society of Newspaper Editors, 130
Amos 'n' Andy, 229
Aristotle, 398
Arts, the, 29, 30, 384-86
Audience
 affluence, 75, 94, 95
 appeal, 14
 and the arts, 385, 386
 book, 142, 143, 150, 152, 153, 155
 communication process, 6, 7, 10, 11, 13, 15
 competition for, 72
 consumer as producer, 97
 crowd, 91-94
 definition of, 85
 education, 94, 95
 and ethics, 125, 129
 expectations, 99, 112, 127
 film, 204, 206, 210, 213, 215-17
 gatekeepers, 96, 97
 growth of, 85
 and individual, 75, 85-86, 96, 99-101
 individuality of, 6, 75
 longevity of, 94
 magazine, 179, 181, 184, 188
 mail, 363-65
 massest mass, 84-88
 mass media continuum, 96
 mobility of, 94, 95
 multiple receivers, 6
 newspapers, 159
  competition for, 162
 and play theory, 63, 64
 predictability of, 70
 preoccupation, 85
 radio, 222, 226, 228, 229, 231, 234, 236, 237, 240
  competition for, 72
 ratings, 247
 secondary, 7
 selectivity, 12-13, 30, 96, 100, 400
 size, 72, 74, 78, 248
 specialization and fragmentation, 80, 81, 94-96
 stereotypes, 400
 study of, 84, 85

television, 243-44, 246, 252-54, 255-56, 257, 260, 262, 271, 272, 277, 279, 280, 305
 cable, 277, 279
 independents, 269
 news, 503
 videotape, 280
Audience continuum. *See also* Audience
 explanation of, 84-101
 in relation to
  advertising, 326
  books, 143
  ethics, 125
  the future, 263
  media subnetwork, 192
  personal media, 359
  political campaigns, 347
  public relations, 334
  television, 263, 282
Audit Bureau of Circulation, The, 162, 184
Authoritarian theory. *See* Authoritarianism
Authoritarianism, 50

Bagdikian, Ben, 304
Bara, Theda, 208
Barnum, P. T., 340
Beatles, The, 213, 238
Bell, Alexander Graham, 42, 223
Bell Telephone Hour, 320
Bennett, James Gordon, 161
Benny, Jack, 229
Berelson, Bernard, 56-58, 100, 359, 402, 412-16, 418, 446, 478
 content analysis technique, 402
 and two-step theory of communication, 56-58, 100, 359, 412-18
Bergman, Ingmar, 213
Berkeley, Busby, 208
Berle, Milton, 245
Bernays, Edward, 342
Bible, 19, 33, 69, 94, 142, 149
 print influence, 19, 33, 69
 time, 94, 142 149
Boiler shop telephoning, 86, 370
Books
 agents, 149
 best-seller, 203
 competition for markets, 76, 77
 explanation of, 142-56
 feeding into other media, 76-77, 78, 147
 and film, 147, 203, 215

Index
460

gatekeeping, 97, 98
hardcover, 142-54
historical impact, 142
history of, 142-44, 155-56
hybrid media, 150
and institutionalization, 70
in mass media continuum, 70-71, 73, 142
and magazines, 146, 179, 189, 194
and mail, 362
paperback. *See* Paperback
serialization, 154
as social revolution, 70
and television, 73
textbooks, 142, 149, 150
trade, 142, 145, 146, 149
travelers, 145, 150
and western civilization, 155-56
Book publishing
agents, 149
book-of-the-month club, 146
business, 144-47, 155
corporate structure, 154-55
and film, 215
formula publishing, 147
history, 142
hybrid media, 76, 77
and mails, 362
myth, 148-49
paperback. *See* Paperback
promotion, 147
Boone, Pat, 122
Bowes, Major, 229
Brinkley, David, 136, 302
British Broadcasting Corporation (BBC), 45, 260, 402, 433, 434
and "cultural" TV programming, 260
and regulation, 45
Broadcast media. *See also* Radio; Television
and advertising, 313
cost, 270
entertainment function, 25, 26
history, 42, 44-47
in mass communications development, 44, 45
regulation, 45, 117-21
and telephone company, 368-69
Brown, Helen Gurley, 187
Brown, J. A. C., 64, 87, 153, 411
Brown, Les, 252
Buchwald, Art, 21
Burch, Dean, 120
Burns, George, 229

Cable. *See* Community Antenna Television
Caesar, Gaius Julius, 337, 363
Campbell, John, 160
Canons of Journalism. *See* Journalism
Capote, Truman, 154, 404
Carson, Rachel, 78
Caruso, Enrico, 223, 380
Catcher in the Rye, 143
Caveat emptor, 51, 121
Caxton, William, 159
Chamberlain, Neville, 232
Charney, Nicholas, 187-89
Churchill, Winston, 182, 232, 272
Cinema. *See* Film
Clark, Kenneth, 402
Code of Motion Picture Industry. *See* Film
Columbia Broadcasting System (CBS)
origin, 44, 245
and radio
affiliates, 226
MBS, 234
network, 235, 239-40
overseas broadcasters, 232
and television
affiliates, 245, 248
and FCC, 244-45
news, 304-5
PBS, 274
ratings, 245, 248
Westinghouse Group W, 246
Commentaries, 337
Commission on Freedom of the Press, 131
Communication process
circularity of, 4, 5
complexity of, 4
Mass communication differences, 6-16
channel as media, 6
commercial limitations, 13
competition for attention, 12
effect, 7
feedback, 7-8
and cybernetics, 5, 8
ersatz, 7
indirect, 7
gatekeepers, 13-15
multiple receivers as audience, 6, 7, 12-15
consumer as producer, 15
selectivity, 12-15
specialization, 14, 15

noise, 8-11
   channel, 8-10
   repetition as cure, 9
   semantic, 11
purposeful, 4
S/R model of communication, 3-6
   channel, 4
   effect, 3, 4
   feedback, 4, 5
   message, 4
   noise, 5, 6
      channel, 5, 6
      mass, 6
      semantic, 5, 6
   receiver, 3, 4
   sender, 3, 4
Communications Act of 1933, 233
Communications revolution
   begun by telegraph, 223
   and computers, 59
   origin of, 41, 289
Community Antenna Television (CATV)
   copyright, 278
   effect, 80
   explanation of, 270-71, 276-78
   future, 282, 283
   history, 270
   relationship to
      FCC, 120, 259, 268, 271, 272, 277-80
      magazines of the air, 279
      newspapers, 279
      pay TV, 272, 276, 277
      speech, 83
      television, 81, 113, 267
      wire services, 293
   two-way capacity, 276-77, 281, 282
   videotape programming, 280, 281
Competition for attention
   explanation of, 11, 99, 100
   relationship to
      advertising, 312-14
      book publishing, 148, 152
      education, 386
      ethics, 128
      magazines, 152, 192
      public relations, 334, 340
Computers
   explanation of, 359, 360
   information retrieval, 282
   as personal media, 373-80
      history, 373-74
      invasion of privacy, 375-76
      leisure, 376, 377
      mystique, 374, 375

      prediction problems, 379, 380
      prognosis, 377, 378
      regimentation, 376, 377
      storage and retrieval, 378, 379
   relationship to
      Bell system, 360, 370, 371
      CATV, 80, 267, 276-77, 279
      computerized direct mail, 87, 364, 367
      demographic publics, 90, 360, 365-67
      HomComCen, 281, 282
      magazine circulation, 185, 186, 189
      offset printing, 170
      public opinion measurement, 315, 360, 420
      ratings, 247, 315
   vanguard of communication revolution, 59
Consensus, 85, 86, 90. *See* Public opinion
Consumer as producer, 15, 53, 63, 97-99
Consumerism, 121, 122, 134
Content analysis, 402-4
Controls for mass communication. *See* Mass communications, functions, controls
Corantos, 159, 180
Coolidge, Calvin, 224
Cooper, James Fenimore, 163, 433
Cousins, Norman, 187
Cox, Archibald, 224
Credibility gap
   creation of, 28
   public relations, 44, 344
   U. S. films abroad, 217
Creel, George, 342
Crisis Papers, 160
Cronkite, Walter, 302, 304
Crowd, 91-94
Crystallizing Public Opinion, 342
cummings, e. e., 395
Cybernetics
   definition of, 5, 377
   relationship to
      McLuhan, 58
      mass communications, 378
      mass theory, 62
      research, 444

Dante, 384
Darwin, Charles, 53, 341, 395
Das Kapital, 142

Da Vinci, Leonardo, 385
Davis, Elmer, 343
Day, Benjamin, 160
Death of a President, 154
DeFleur, Melvin, 28, 444, 446
De Forest, Lee, 42, 44, 223, 224
De Gaulle, Charles, 435
De Saussure, Ferdinand, 394
DeSica, 212
de Maupassant, Guy, 260
Demographics
   definition of, 185
   early form of, 314
   publics, 90
   relationship to
      audience continuum, 87
      CATV, 80
      computerized direct mail, 360, 362, 365-67
      magazine circulation, 185
      public opinion polls, 423
      public relations, 334
      ratings, 248
Department stores
   and books, 152
   and distribution, 38
   early owners of radio stations, 44, 224
   as newspaper advertisers, 181
   role in advertising, 313
Dewey, Thomas, 413, 420
Dichter, Ernest, 316, 317
Disney, Walt, 216
Diurnals, 159
Documentaries. *See* Film; Television
Dorsey brothers, 229

Eagleton, Thomas, 299
Edison, Thomas, 42, 203
Education and
   books, 34, 144, 150
   mass communications, 21, 34, 39
   newspapers, 158
   social responsibility theory, 132
   transmission of culture, 386
Educational television (ETV). *See* National Educational Television
Edward VIII, 231
Effects of Mass Communications, The, 263
Einstein, Albert, 388
Eisenhower, Dwight D., 182
Electricity, 71, 163, 203
Electronic age, 41, 71

Electronic media, 59. *See also* Computers; Film; Radio; Television
Electronic revolution
   beginning, 289
   and computers, 377
   effects of, 71
   explanations of 41, 42, 47
   technological acceleration, 59
Emery, Edwin, 144, 158, 299
Enoch, Kurt, 153, 155
Ervin, Sam, 303, 408
Equal time doctrine, 118, 119
Ethics
   code of, 130-31
   definition, 126
   evolution of, 129-30
   explanation of, 125-39
   private, 125, 138, 139
   public, 125, 139
   relationship to
      advertising, 133
      damage, 137
      deception, 137
      objective of interpretive reporting, 135-38
      political campaign, 133-34
      privacy, 138, 139
      social responsibility, the, 132, 133

Fair comment doctrine, 107
Fairness Doctrine
   and advertising, 123, 257
   and cigarette controversy, 257
   explanation of, 119, 245
   Nixon administration proposal, 359
   radio begat, 222
Federal Communications Act of 1933, 118
Federal Communication Commission (FCC)
   blue book, 244
   broadcast regulation, 117-20, 233-34, 244
      equal time doctrine, 118, 119
      Fairness Doctrine, 118, 119, 222
   controls, 45, 46
   decisions affecting mass communication in other countries, 434, 436
   duopoly ruling, 113
   from Federal Radio Commission, 222, 225, 233
   licensing, 36, 121, 268
   Mayflower Decision, 244, 245
   NBC antitrust, 113

neutrality, 226
origin, 222, 225
public access, 121
radio regulation
   FM, 237, 239, 244
   networking, 226, 227
   relicensing, 234
restraint of trade, 113, 234
Rule of Seven, 113, 259
and television, 244-49, 257-60, 268, 305
   CATV, 259, 268, 271-80
   ETV, 273
   pay TV, 272, 276
   programming, 120, 210
   UHF, 259, 271, 272
   VHF, 269-72
and *TV Guide,* 192
Federalist Papers, 19, 160, 339, 340
Federal Radio Commission, 45, 117, 225, 226, 233
Federal Trade Commission (FTC)
   and advertising, 327-29
   Better Business Bureaus, 327, 329
   cases against
      ITT Continental Baking, 328
      Ocean Spray, 328
      Wonder Bread, 123, 328
   tools, 123, 328
   and truth in
      advertising, 121, 327-29
      lending, 121, 329
      packaging, 328
Fellini, Federico, 210
Film, 202-18
   Academy Awards, 215, 216
   and advertising, 215
   and affluence, 211
   audience, 204, 206, 210, 213, 215-17
   block booking, 204-5
   and books, 148, 203, 215
   cinéma vérité, 213, 214
   Code of Motion Picture Industry, 130
   commercial, 202, 203, 216
   companies, 208
   controls, 214
   critic, 215
   decline of, 209
   distribution, 204, 205, 209
   documentaries, 26, 218
   economic factors, 204, 208
   education, 217
   exhibition, 204, 205, 209
   explanation of, 202, 203, 215-16

   first mass communications export, 211, 212
   foreign effects, 211-13
   functions, 26, 27, 216-18
   gatekeeping. *See* Gatekeeping
   history, 42, 203-5, 208-13
   H. W. Wilson Educational Film Guide, 218
   Hollywood, 205
   as hybrid media, 77
   and legitimate theater, 204
   and magazine, 215
   media feeding each other, 78
   Motion Picture Patent Company, 204, 205, 224
   Motion Pictures Producers and Distributors of America, 214
   and newspaper, 215
   newsreel, 218
   press agentry, 205
   and print media, 211
   production, 204, 205, 208, 209
   promotion, 208, 210, 215, 216, 217
   purposes of, 26, 210, 216, 217
   and radio, 203, 208, 218
   ratings, 134, 215
   and sound, 208
   and television, 203, 205, 209-11, 213, 215-18, 235
   types of, 216, 218
   universal quality of, 211
   and USIA. *See* USIA
First Amendment
   conflict with Sixth Amendment, 114
   context of, 106, 107
   guarantees, 34, 35, 106, 107
   relationship to
      advertising, 330
      broadcast regulation, 117
      FCC, 117
      invasion of privacy, 139
      libertarianism, 34, 35, 50
      mass media, 106
      radio, 45, 225
Fleming, Ian, 21, 147
Four theories of the press, 50-53
Fragmentation, principle of, 33, 449. *See also* Specialization
Franklin, Benjamin, 180, 339
Friendly, Fred, 273
Future Shock, 81, 100

Galbraith, John Kenneth, 77
Gallup, George, 144, 420, 424-25
Garrett, Paul, 342

Gatekeeper
   as bridge between mass media and audience, 96
   in book publishing, 148
   broadcast, 98
   definition, 13, 14
   intermedia, 215
   magazine, 195
   newspaper, 175, 176
   relationship to
      competition for attention, 100
      consumer as producer, 97, 99
      ethics, 128
      public relations, 333
      Reader's Digest, 192
      reality, 96, 97
      stereotypes, 400
      wire services, 298
   television, 252
Gatekeeping
   analogy with film, 202
   and audience appeal, 14
   corporate, 14, 36
   as editorial policy, 14
   explanation of, 13-15
   and FDR's fireside chats, 45
   historical, 384
   test in advertising and news, 28
George, Gorgeous, 263
Georgics, 33, 337
Give-'em-what-they-want theory. *See* Profit theory
Goebbels, Dr. Joseph, 53
Goldwater, Barry, 86, 318
Gone with the Wind, 148, 280
Goodman, Benny, 229
Graham, Billy, 93
Greeley, Horace, 161
Grofe, Ferde, 229
Groups
   as audience, 84
   in audience continuum, 84, 86, 88
   associations, 91, 417
   definition, 91
   formal, 91, 418
   primary, 86, 418
   and public opinion, 415-18
   and specialization, 95
Guilgud, Sir John, 402
Gutenberg Galaxy, The, 58
Gutenberg, Johannes, 32, 33, 81, 85, 143, 159, 338
   father of mass communications, 69

Hair, 385
Hale, Nathan, 339
Halsey, Admiral William, 182
Hamilton, Alexander, 19, 160, 339, 340
Harding, Warren, 224
Harris, Louis, 424
Hawthorne, Nathaniel, 163
Hays, Will H., 214
Hearst, Randolph
   and content analysis, 402
   empire of, 71, 291, 379
   in history of press, 38, 53, 54
   insurance publications, 181
   INS wire service, 291, 292
   and King Features, 306
   and magazines, 181
   and Spanish-American War, 53, 54, 163
   and stimulus-response theory, 53, 54
   and yellow journalism, 129, 162, 163
Henry VIII, 33, 34, 41, 50, 105, 338
Hidden Persuaders, The, 315
Hitler, Adolf, 53, 54, 142, 231, 389, 442
Hohenberg, John, 24, 191, 215
Holography, 282
HomComCen (Home Communications Center), 281
Homer, 33
Hoover, Herbert, 225, 227
Hughes, Charles Evans, 223, 227
Humphrey, Hubert H., 256
Hybrid media, 76, 77

Illiad and *Odyssey,* 33
In Cold Blood, 154
Indirect media. *See* Wire services
Indirect theory of communication. *See* Two-step theory of communication
Industrial revolution, 38-41, 59, 161, 312
Interference. *See* Noise
International News Service (INS), 162
Interpersonal communication. *See also* Communication process
   mail, 362
   personal media, 359
   public opinion, 418-20
   telephones, 370
Interpretive reporting, 135, 136, 252, 298
Inverted pyramid style, 161

Jackson, Andrew, 340

Jagger, Mick, 98, 238
Jay, John, 339
Jazz journalism
   and ethical evolution, 129
   in mass communications development, 38
   in mass media continuum, 72
   in newspaper history, 164, 165
   and press responsibility, 130
John, 386
Johnson, Lyndon Baines, 274
Johnson, Nicholas, 120
Jolson, Al, 208
Journalese
   development of, 290
   different from radio news, 233
   explanation of, 174
   as new standard of journalism, 161
   and public relations, 334
Journalism
   canons of, 130, 132
   influence on mass communications functions, 20, 21
   interpretive reporting, 135, 136, 232, 298
   jazz, 38, 72, 129, 130, 164, 165
   "new," 132, 135, 136
   objective reporting, 135, 136, 232, 290, 298, 306, 411
   "old," 135
   origin as a discipline, 161
   and social sciences, 343
   yellow, 38, 72, 129, 162, 163
Jungle, The, 341

Kaltenborn, H. V., 231, 232
Kennedy, John Fitzgerald, 81, 118, 217, 272, 343
Kennedy, Robert, 81
Killy, Jean-Claude, 263
King Features, 306
Klapper, Joseph, 263
Knievel, Evel, 275
Korzybski, Alfred, 386

Laissez-faire, 42, 53, 290, 341
Landon, Alfred, 422
Langer, Suzanne, 389, 396
Language
   change, 5, 6
   computer, 374-75, 387
   differences, 6, 7
   explanation of, 88, 89, 90, 387
   history of, 91, 92, 93

langue and parole, 394-96
linguistics, 394
myth, 8, 9, 400-1
semantics, 7, 8
stereotype, 8, 9, 400-1
Langue and parole, theory of, 394-96
Lazarsfeld, Paul, 7, 56-58, 100, 334, 359, 412-18, 446-48
Least objectionable program (lop), 249
Le Chanson de Roland, 33, 338
Lee, Ivy, 44, 341, 342
Leisure. *See also* Affluence
   and computers, 376-77
   and literacy, 393
   and mass communications, 37
   and play theory, 63
   and print, 33
Libel, 107
Libertarianism, 34-36, 50-51, 107, 132
Libertarian theory, 106, 330, 335, 349
Lincoln, Abraham, 355, 437
Lippman, Walter, 174, 261, 400
Loewy, Raymond, 321
Lombardo, Guy, 228
Love Story, 147
Lowenstein, Ralph, 75, 84, 93
Lowest common denominator (lcd)
   and advertising, 326
   and books, 143, 155
   and BBC, 433
   and film, 27, 209, 210
   and mass society concept, 55
   and massest mass appeal, 87, 88
   and newspapers, 165
   and radio, 26, 228, 314
   and television, 11, 29, 74, 244, 249, 250, 252, 276, 305
Luce, Henry, 181
Ludenic theory of communication. *See* Play theory of communication
Luke, 386
Luther, Martin, 33

McCarthy, Joseph, 135, 411
McClure, Samuel, 291
McCombs, Maxwell, 80, 82
McGinnis, Joe, 147, 255-56, 303
McLuhan, Marshall
   and computers, 375, 378
   concepts
      Christianity as propaganda, 337
      global village, 81, 429, 433, 434
      medium is the message, 58, 59

television
- electronic babysitter, 59, 262
- hot and cool mediums, 60-61
- involving audience, 263, 437
- as mosaic, 262

and intuitive research, 446
and mediums, 32, 70, 76, 79, 390
and public relations, 337
and television, 210
theory, 58-61, 255
and underdeveloped countries, 442

Madison, Avenue, U.S.A., 315, 323
Madison, James, 339
Magazines
- and advertising, 179, 181, 183-86, 188-90 314, 319
- and affluence, 18, 187, 188, 190
- and books, 151, 152, 154, 155, 179
- cheesecake syndrome, 182
- circulation, 178, 180-85, 190, 194
- city, 193
- corporate publishers, 192
- cover girl, 182
- daily, 77, 159
- demographics, 188
- and ethics, 127
- explanation of, 178-95
- feeding into other media, 78, 193
- and film, 215, 218
- functions, 24, 25, 192
- and gatekeeping, 96
- general interest, 181-84
- and hippy movement, 79
- as hybrid media, 76, 77, 179, 180
- history, 24, 25, 34, 179-82, 183-86
- and mails, 362-63
- marketing services, 188, 189
- mass media continuum, 33, 34, 178, 179
- names of
  - *American Magazine*, 180, 181
  - *Cosmopolitan*, 14, 97, 181, 186-88, 279
  - *Esquire*, 89, 181
  - *Family Health*, 188
  - *Field and Stream*, 14, 25, 363
  - *Ford Times*, 194
  - *Fortune*, 89, 97, 350
  - *General Magazine*, 180
  - *Godey's Lady's Book*, 181
  - *Life*, 146, 181-83, 185, 186, 193, 321
  - *Literary Digest*, 422
  - *Look*, 154, 181, 183, 185
  - *McClure's Magazine*, 181, 291
  - *Nation*, 181
  - *New Republic*, 89, 400
  - *New York*, 188, 194, 215, 363
  - *New Yorker*, 154, 181, 194, 215, 363
  - *Newsweek*, 186, 192, 293
  - *North American Review*, 180
  - *Port Folio*, 180
  - *Psychology Today*, 25, 95, 146, 155, 187, 188, 195, 363
  - *Reader's Digest*, 116, 178, 181, 182, 189, 190, 192, 193, 274, 321, 400
  - *Saturday Evening Post*, 180, 190
  - *Southern Living*, 188
  - *Tatler* and *Spectator*, 180
  - *Time*, 181, 182, 186, 192, 193, 321
  - *TV Guide*, 165, 182, 192, 193
  - *U. S. News and World Report*, 89
  - *Wall Street Journal*, 159, 185, 186, 350, 353
  - *Women's Wear Daily*, 159
- newsmagazines, 192-93, 293
- newspapers, 114, 165
- and new generation, 188
- numbers game, 182
- production, 194
- and radio, 233, 239
- readership surveys. *See* Ratings
- specialization, 178, 185, 186, 189-91, 193, 194
- subscription lists, 189-90
- and television, 179, 183, 185, 186, 192, 279

Mail
- appeal to individual, 86
- classes of, 364
- computerized direct, 87, 364-67
- distribution of, 362
- franking, 367
- history of, 360-62
- as interpersonal communication, 362-63
- as mass medium, 367, 368
- and public opinion polling, 367

Mailer, Norman, 3
Make-a-buck theory. *See* Profit theory
Manchester, William, 154
Marconi, Guglielmo, 42, 223
Mark, 386
Marx, Karl, 142
Mass communications. *See also* Mass media
- and affluence, 27, 37, 63, 82
- alternatives, 450, 451

Index
467

and the arts, 29-30
and audience size, 69, 77
and books, 144
as central nervous system, 11, 20, 30, 58, 76, 81, 125, 130, 243, 387, 444, 445
circulation, 76, 101
controls, 34, 45, 50, 105-23, 336
corporate structure, 75-76, 106
development, 31-47
and education, 21, 33, 39
effects, 54, 56, 86, 101
export, 211
functional mix, 19, 20, 30
functions, 1-30
  and advertising, 311
  cultural transmission, 18, 27-30, 142, 179, 191, 202, 383-406
  entertainment, 18, 22, 24-30, 72, 74, 116, 153, 183, 203, 222, 224, 243, 257
  and film, 116, 203
  information, 18, 20-25, 116, 174-75, 192, 203, 218, 222, 257, 289, 333, 354
  persuasion, 18, 23-30, 72, 192, 243, 310, 334, 354, 408
and the future, 449, 450
global village concept, 443, 444
and individual, 54, 57, 81
as institution, 77, 106
interdisciplinary, 49
in other countries, 430-43
process, 105
profit motive, 19, 20, 53, 70
research, 444-48
and society, 31, 77, 82, 133, 342
and speed, 34, 69, 74
status quo, 78
theory, 49-65
and time, 37, 99
Mass media. *See also* Mass communications
and acceleration, 81, 100
and advertisers, 112
as changing society, 77, 78
codes, 130, 131
and competition for attention, 16, 99, 100, 112
corporate nature of, 77, 187
and the courts, 112
definition, 6
economics of, 82, 133
feeding each other, 76-79
and government, 107-9

merging source and channel, 15-16
and new media, 39
and reality, 96, 100
as reflection of society, 55, 77-78
saturation, 81, 100
and selectivity, 82, 100
survival, 82
and technological expansion, 81
viewpoint, 28
Mass media continuum
acceleration, 81, 82
and books, 70, 71, 73, 74, 142
corporate interrelationships, 77
ethics, 125
explanation of, 69-82, 263
and film, 71, 203
fragmentation and specialization, 80, 81
hybrid media, 76, 77
and magazines, 71, 178, 179
media feeding each other, 78, 79
and newspapers, 71, 72
and radio, 71, 72, 75
stability and change, 77, 78
and television, 71-75, 263, 282
Mass society theory, 55, 56
Mathematical theory of communication, 61-63, 371
Matthew, 386
Mayer, Martin, 252, 273, 315, 318, 323, 331
Media, 77
Media, Messages and Men, 75, 84, 93
Mein Kampf, 142
Mencken, H. L., 181
Merrill, John, 75, 84, 93
Michelangelo, 385
Mills, C. Wright, 100
Milton, John, 34
Minow, Newton, 120, 260
Mitchell, Margaret, 148
Mitty, Walter, 302
Mona Lisa, 30, 354, 385
Morse, Samuel, 41, 223, 289
Motion pictures. *See* Film
Movies. *See* Film
Murrow, Edward R., 231, 232
Muckrakers
in ethical development, 130
in mass communications development, 42
in public relations development, 341
and social responsibility theory, 51, 132
and yellow journalism, 163

Mutual Broadcasting System (MBS), 234, 235

Nader, Ralph, 78
Namath, Joe, 107, 302, 303
National Association of Broadcasters, 130, 234
National Broadcasting Company (NBC)
  Blue network, 113, 225, 226, 234
  MBS, 234
  origin, 45
  radio, 232, 235, 239, 240
  ratings, 245, 248
  RCA, 224
  Red network, 113, 225, 226, 234
  relationship to
    AT&T, 368
    FCC, 113, 244, 245
  television
    news, 304
    PBS, 274
    Westinghouse Group W, 246
National Educational Television (NET), 273, 274
News
  canned, 297
  exempt from Fairness Doctrine, 119
  functions, 21, 22, 24, 26, 28
  judgment, 136, 298
  management, 110-11, 354
  nature of, 174
  and newspapers, 158, 302
  and public relations, 44, 333-35, 354
  and radio, 231-33, 236, 240
  regulation, 258
  as show biz, 303
  and society, 302
  sources, 299-305
  spot, 165
  and television, 158, 255-57, 302-5
  and wire services, 297
News Media: A Journalist Looks at His Profession, The, 191
Newspaper
  advertising. *See* Advertising, newspaper
  and affluence, 168, 169
  bias, 28
  and books, 144, 147, 153
  circulation, 172
  community, 95, 168-70
  definition, 159
  editions, 173
  ethics, 127
  explanation of, 158-76

  extras, 165
  feature services, 291, 292, 305, 306
  and film, 215
  gatekeeper, 20, 25, 96
  history, 34, 129-30, 159-65, 289, 341
  information function, 20-23
  local nature of, 159
  and magazines, 159, 166, 180-82, 190, 193
  and mail, 362, 363
  in mass media continuum, 71, 72
  mergers, 166
  metropolitan, 167-69, 175
  as mosaic, 176
  peripheral departments of, 128
  production, 170-71
  public relations, 347
  and radio, 72, 224, 225, 227, 229, 232-34
  scoop, 166, 232
  specialization, 82
  and telegraph, 71, 159, 161, 162, 289
  and television, 114, 166, 245, 253, 279, 304
  as transmitter of culture, 29
  weeklies, 167
  and wire services, 159, 291-93, 297, 298
Nielsen, 247, 248, 274
Nineteen Eighty-Four, 275, 377
Nixon, Richard M., 118, 255, 256, 303
Noise, 5, 6

Objective reporting
  explanation of, 135, 136
  McCarthy hearings, 411
  radio, 232
  wire services, 290, 298, 306
Obscenity, 116, 117
Ogilivie, David, 316
Opinion, 57, 86. *See also* Public opinion
Opinion leaders. *See also* Two-step theory of communication
  definition of, 56, 57
  in public relations, 334
  role of, 413, 414, 416-18
Orwell, George, 275, 377
Osborn, 319
Oswald, Lee Harvey, 114

Packard, Vance, 78, 315
Paine, Thomas, 160, 339
Paperbacks, 142-43, 145, 147, 150, 153-55

marketing, 151
overlap, 152
sources for, 153, 154
vulgarization, 155
Paul, 337
Pavlov, 53
Pay TV, 271, 272, 276
Pentagon, Papers, The, 109
Personal media, 359-60. *See also* Computers; Mail; Telephone
Peterson, Theodore, 53, 132
Photography, 42, 203
Pindar, 33, 336
Plato, 336
Play theory of communication, 63-65, 87
Political campaigns
  advertising in, 133, 314, 317, 318, 349
  and computers, 377
  and direct mail, 365, 366
  door-to-door approach, 87
  as entertainment, 303
  and equal time, 118
  and ethics, 133, 134
  as news, 300, 307
  and public opinion, 410-17, 419, 420
  and public opinion polls, 424
  and public relations, 340, 347-49
  Selling of the President, 1968, The, 303
  as television drama, 303
  in two-step theory research, 57, 413-16
Pornography, 117
Portnoy's Complaint, 25
Power of the press theory, 53-55, 410
Presley, Elvis, 238
Press, the. *See also* Newspaper
  attempts to muzzle, 108
  and backgrounders, 110
  commission on freedom of, 131
  and government, 108-11
  hippies, 137, 138
  in mass communications development, 35-38, 289
  radio, as part of, 225, 232
  and secret information, 109
  and trials, 115
  watchdog of government, 133
Press agentry. *See* Public relations
Press associations. *See* Wire services
Press council, 131, 132
Press freedom
  abridgment due to public access, 121
  established, 107
  and ethics, 129
  and FCC, 233
  in mass communications development, 36
  and newspaper doctrine, 158
  and press councils, 131, 132
  and "right-to-know," 114-15
  shield laws, 115, 116
  social responsibility theory, 132, 133
  in trials, 114, 115
Prime time
  classifications, 229
  definition, 120
  and FCC, 258, 259
  and gatekeeping, 98
  and news, 305
  and radio, 75, 222, 223, 227-29
  and television, 74, 80, 236, 249-52, 255, 257, 305
Print medium
  and advertising, 312
  and antitrust controls, 113, 114
  and books, 143, 144
  and film, 211
  history, 32-40, 143
  and industrial revolution, 156
  and informational thrust, 25
  in mass media continuum, 70
  and McLuhan, 32, 58, 59
  and newspapers, 158
  and printing, 167, 170
  and speech, 82
  and speed, 70
Privacy
  and computers, 375, 376
  definition, 107
  and ethics, 138
  and telephones, 370, 375
Privilege doctrine, 107
Profit theory, 53. *See also* Mass communications, profit motive
Propaganda
  disguised as information, 20
  in early newspapers, 129
  in evolution of ethics, 129
  origin, 343
  and USIA, 217
Public Broadcasting System (PBS), 267, 271, 274
Public interest, convenience, necessity doctrine
  and black weeks, 248

established, 45, 117, 222, 235
and FCC, 121, 234, 244, 270
and independents, 225, 227
and television, 251, 305
Public opinion
   and advertising, 318
   change, 56, 57, 408, 412, 413, 418, 420
   definition, 85
   dissemination, 57, 419
   explanation of, 408-26
   formation, 56, 57, 268, 408-10, 412, 413, 415, 418
   and public relations, 334, 336, 354
   and trial by press, 115
Public opinion measurement. *See* Public opinion polling
Public opinion polling
   by advertisers, 314
   and computers, 360, 377, 380
   and direct mail, 367
   explanation of, 420-26
   feedback, 7, 8
   infancy of, 231
   by political campaigns, 347-48
   and public relations, 334
   and ratings, 247
Public relations
   and advertising, 320, 321, 354
   and business wires, 297
   explanation of, 333-35, 343-46
   and films, 203, 346, 347
   functions, 28, 44, 354
   history, 160, 336-43
   and mail, 363, 366
   in mass communications development, 44
   as news, 333-34, 352, 354
   and press agentry, 205, 215, 269, 336, 340
   publicity, 335, 336, 353
   public opinion, 410, 424
   and publics, 353, 354
   specialization, 346-51
   telephone, 370, 372
   and television, 269, 279, 347
   tools, 354
   two-way street relationship, 346
Public Relations Society of America, 134, 135, 335
Publics, 95, 353-54, 416
   as audience, 84
   in audience continuum, 84, 86
   definition, 53, 88
   demographic, 90

functional, 88, 89
Pulitzer, Joseph, 38, 53, 71, 129, 162, 163, 291, 402
Putnam, George, 268

Radio
   as adjunct to recording industry, 237-38
   advertising. *See* Advertising, radio
   affiliates, 226, 227
   codes, 130
   commercial, 231
   and computers, 377
   disc jockey (DJ), 47, 238, 239
   as electronic magazine, 239
   explanation of, 222-41
   and Fairness Doctrine, 119
   and film, 224
   FM, 47
   functions, 26
   gatekeeping, 98
   history, 44-46, 82, 223-29, 232-35
   independents, 226, 227
   and magazines, 181, 240
   in mass media continuum, 72
   and music, 237-39
   networking, 226
   news, 231-33, 236, 240
   and newspapers, 114, 224, 225, 227, 232, 233, 237
   payola, 126-27, 238
   profit motive, 223
   and RCA, 224, 225
   Radio Acts, 224, 225, 226
   ratings, 231, 238, 247
   and soap operas, 229
   specialization, 75
   and speech, 82
   star system, 222
   and television, 75, 222, 223, 225, 235, 236, 239, 267
   and wire services, 298
Ratings
   and advertising, 310
   and audience, 98, 248
   and computers, 377
   explanation of, 247
   film, 134, 215
   magazine, 190
   Nielsen, 247, 248
   origin of, 8
   radio, 231, 238, 247
   and telephone, 368
   television, 74, 244, 252-57, 274
Raymond, Henry J., 161

Real Majority, The, 414
Reclam's Universal Library, 150
Recording industry. *See* Radio
Remington, Frederick, 53
Republic, The, 336
Revere, Paul, 338
Rise and Fall of the Third Reich, 25
Robbins, Harold, 21, 147, 404
Roca, Argentine, 263
Rochester, 229
Rogers, Buck, 276
Roosevelt, Franklin D., 227, 228, 232, 233, 327, 343, 397, 413, 414, 422
Rosselini, 212
Rousseau, 142
Royalties, 146, 153, 234, 271, 278, 280
Ruby, Jack, 114
Ruth, Babe, 299

Sandman, Peter, 77, 138, 297
Sarnoff, David, 224
Scammon, Richard M., 414
Schramm, Wilbur, 53, 446
Science and Sanity, 386
Scripps, E. W., 53, 71, 129, 162, 163, 291, 292, 402
Selling of the President, 1968, The, 147, 255, 256, 303
Sex and the Single Girl, 187
Shakespeare, William, 94, 149, 260, 384
Shannon, Claude E., 61, 62, 371, 391, 444
Sheppard, Samuel, 114
Shield laws, 115, 116
Shirer, William L., 231
Siebert, Fred, 53
Silent Spring, 78
Simon, Norton, 318
Simonides of Ceos, 33, 336
Simpson, Wallis, 231
Sinclair, Upton, 341
Sixth Amendment, 114
Skornia, Harry, 270, 432, 439
Smith, Alfred E., 227
Social Darwinism, 36, 42
Social responsibility theory
   and Canons of Journalism, 130, 132
   explanation of, 51, 52, 132, 133
Solti, Sir George, 281
Sophisticated Poll Watcher's Guide, 420
Soviet-Communist theory of press, 52
Specialization. *See also* Fragmentation
   and advertising, 322

and audience, 94, 95
education and, 39
as form of gatekeeping, 33, 39
and McLuhan, 59
and magazines, 95
and mass communications future, 449, 450
principle, 75
public relations, 346, 347
of publics, 95
selectivity and, 80
survival of media, 75
and television, 268
and wire services, 306, 307
Speech, 82, 83
Spitz, Mark, 302
S/R model of communication. *See* Communication process
Standard Rate and Data Service (SRDS), 323
Starch Reports, 314
Steele, Richard, 180
Steffens, Lincoln, 341
Steinberg, Charles, 143
Steinem, Gloria, 3
Stephenson, William, 63-65, 87, 446
Stereotypes, 398-400, 415
Stimulus-response theory. *See* Power of the press theory
Sullivan, Ed, 245
Survival of the fittest, 36, 53, 290, 341
Symbols, 87-91, 387-89

Tarbell, Ida, 341
Techniques of Persuasion, 153, 411
Technology
   broadcast regulation, 117
   computerized direct mail, 87
   and computers, 373
   in film development, 203, 208, 211
   McLuhan, 59
   in mass communications development, 39, 40, 44, 46, 47
   and newspapers, 177
   radio, 233, 236, 237, 238
   research development, 445-46
   television, 244, 245
Telegraph, 41, 71, 159, 161, 162, 203, 223, 289-90
Telephone, 368-72
   boiler shop telephoning, 370, 372
   history, 368-69
   versatility, 368
Television
   and advertising. *See* Advertising, television

Index
472

affiliates, 245-47
audience. *See* Audience, television
and books, 73
CATV. *See* Community Antenna Television
carrot-and-stick legislation, 121, 259
closed circuit, 267, 274, 275
color, 245
costs, 251, 252, 267, 270
documentaries, 136, 218, 257
effects, 260-64, 442
as electronic babysitter, 59, 60, 253, 262
ethics, 125, 126, 130
explanation and history, 243-64
and film, 47, 78, 203, 205, 209, 215, 218, 251
fragmentation, 80, 81, 263, 264, 268, 282
functions, 25-27, 29, 46, 47
and gatekeeping, 96-98
hybrid media, 76
independents, 268, 269, 273, 274, 443
local programming, 120
and magazines, 47, 183-84, 186, 243
in mass media continuum, 73-75
National Association of Broadcasters, 260-62
networks, 245-47
and news, 120, 255-57, 259, 269, 302-5
newspapers, 47, 243, 253, 259
pay TV, 80, 267, 271, 272, 276, 277, 280
prime time. *See* Prime time
progeny, 267-84
programming, 249-51
and public access, 121
and public relations, 47
and radio, 47, 72, 222, 223, 226, 243, 253
ratings. *See* Ratings, television
regulation, 120, 121, 244, 245, 259-60
royalties, 271, 278
satellite, 80, 267, 268, 272, 283-85
theory of least objectional program (lop), 249, 252
UHF, 47. *See also* VHF
and videophone, 274-76, 370
and videotape, 280, 281, 305
and Viet Nam, 78, 126
violence, 60, 137, 260
and wire services, 293, 298, 302
and youth, 59, 60, 260, 261

Television and Society, 270, 432, 439
Thumb, General Tom, 340
Time-binding ability, 386-87
Toffler, Alvin, 81, 100, 405
Toulouse, Lautrec, de Henri, 441
Trial by press. *See* Press freedom
Tropic of Cancer, 116
Truman, Harry, 182, 413, 420
Truth, 107, 409
Twain, Mark, 163
Two-step theory of communication, 56-58, 100, 334, 359, 412-15, 446-47
Two-way street relationship, 58, 346

UHF, 80, 267, 270-73, 277
Underground press, 78, 192
Understanding Media, 58, 337
Unique selling proposition (USP), 315
United States Information Agency (USIA), 217, 430-33
Unsafe at Any Speed, 78

Valentino, 208
Vanderbilt, William Frederick, 42, 130, 341
Venus de Milo, 384
VHF, 80, 237, 244, 269, 270, 272
Vicary, Jim, 317
Virgil, 33, 336
Voltaire, 362

Wagner, Richard, 389
Wallace, George, 397
Wannamaker, John, 318
Warhol, Andy, 214
Waring, Fred, 229
Wattenberg, 414
Weaver, 61, 62, 371, 391
Weaver, Pat, 276
Weiner, Norbert, 5, 58, 62, 377-78, 444
Weston, Av, 304
Whitehead, Clay, 259
Whitehead, Commander Edward, 316
Who, what, when, where lead, 11, 161, 290
Wilkie, Wendall, 413-14
Wilson, Woodrow, 223, 227, 342
Winchell, Walter, 231
Wireless, 71, 223
Wire services
    Associated Press (AP), 22, 168, 227, 233, 290-97
    business wires, 297
    city news services, 297

explanation, 21, 22, 289-91, 293-94, 296-98
gatekeepers, 298-300
International News Service (INS), 162, 227, 291
and newspapers, 159, 290, 293, 297 298, 300
pooling, 292, 293
radio, 44, 227, 297-98
specialization/fragmentation, 306, 307
and telephones, 369
teletypesetter (TTS), 294, 306

and television, 302
United Press International (UPI), 22, 162, 227, 291-93, 296-97
wire filers, 294
Wolseley, Roland, 191
Wrangel, Baron George, 316

Yellow journalism, 38, 72, 129, 162, 163
Yellow kid, the, 163

Zenger, Peter, 107
Zworykin, Vladmir, 244